GO FORWARD WITH FAITH

GO FORWARD WITH FAITH

THE BIOGRAPHY OF

GORDON B. HINCKLEY

SHERI L. DEW

DESERET BOOK COMPANY, SALT LAKE CITY, UTAH

Library of Congress Cataloging-in-Publication Data

Dew, Sheri L.
Go forward with faith: the biography of Gordon B. Hinckley / Sheri L. Dew.
p. cm.
Includes bibliographical references and index.
ISBN 1-57345-165-7 (hb)
1. Hinckley, Gordon Bitner, 1910– . 2. Church of Jesus Christ of Latter-day Saints—Presidents—Biography. 3. Mormon Church—Presidents—Biography. I. Title.
BX8695.H55D48 1996
289.3'092—dc20
[B] 96-36014
CIP

Printed in the United States of America

10 9 8 7 6 5 4 3 2 1

To Steve

CONTENTS

PREFACE

It will come as no surprise to anyone who knows President Gordon B. Hinckley to learn that he was the last person who wanted to see this book written. For years he resisted the urging of colleagues and family members and dodged various publishers who tried to persuade him to have his life story committed to writing. And though he finally relented and agreed to cooperate with this project, he clearly would have preferred to let his story remain essentially untold.

There are several reasons for his reticence, one of them being that he has no taste for notoriety and absolutely no need for everyone to know what he has accomplished during six decades of Church and civic service. For another, the prospect of being the subject of a literary portrait that might paint him as more than he considers himself to be has been unappealing if not painful. "You can't get a dollar bill out of fifteen cents," he has said to me more than once. I'll never forget meeting with him after he had read the first third of the manuscript. After an uncomfortable pause, during which it seemed he was searching for the words to let me down easily, he began: "I am *sick, sick, sick* of reading about Gordon Hinckley. There is just too much about Gordon Hinckley in this manuscript." I groped for a response. "Whom did you want me to write about in *your* biography?" came to mind, but I couldn't think of a respectful way to phrase the question so I remained silent.

Then I had my first exposure to a mini-sermon he would repeat at least a dozen times during succeeding months. "Adulation is poison," he said, emphasizing each word. "Adulation has ruined many a good man and woman, and I don't want this book to portray me as something I'm not." I finally replied: "President, I can see that we have just one small problem here.

You want me to write a book that says you are just a common, ordinary man." "Well, I am," he interrupted. "I was just a normal little boy who played marbles and got in fistfights and dipped the pigtails of the girl who sat in front of me in the inkwell on my desk. I have done nothing more than try to do what has been asked of me, and I've tried to do it the best I could. I don't want you to make more out of my life than is there."

So herein lay the challenge. My subject did not want to be depicted as larger than life, yet it was clear from the outset that I was dealing with a man who was anything but ordinary. George W. Durham II, the son of Elder G. Homer Durham, whose friendship with President Hinckley dated to boyhood, summarized it best when he said to me: "I don't envy you. You've been asked to write a portrait, but you're dealing with a landscape. I can't imagine how you'll pull it off." It was a sobering statement.

"Here and there, and now and then, God places a giant among men," a poet once said. How much more remarkable when that giant doesn't see himself as such, which is the case with President Hinckley. Try as I might, and search as I have, I have found nothing to support his claim that he is a common, ordinary man. Certainly he has experienced the challenges of mortality. He has laughed and cried, endured heartache and experienced triumph, made mistakes and worked to correct them. He has also kept a feverish pace, maintained his composure under fire, tackled head-on one intimidating assignment after another, and in general followed a simple maxim that he has preached all his life—that the only way to get anything done is to get on your knees and ask for the Lord's help, and then get to your feet and go to work.

It was John Ruskin who said that "the greatest reward is not what we receive for our labor, but what we become by it." If there was ever a living example of that principle, it is President Hinckley. By the time he became President of the Church, he had labored nearly sixty years at Church headquarters, the first twenty-three of them in relative anonymity. But now, after thirty-eight years of service as a General Authority, and fifteen of those in the First Presidency, his influence in such vital areas as missionary work, temple building and temple work, Church finance, and public affairs is well documented. His second counselor,

President James E. Faust, has suggested that perhaps no man who has become President of the Church has been more extensively or better prepared for that office. Indeed, there is no hyperbole in stating that President Hinckley has influenced the onward march of the gospel kingdom in a way paralleled by few others. And in the process, he has molded a life worthy of emulation.

In short, this is a man whose story deserves to be told. President Hinckley himself once said that "the most persuasive gospel tract is the exemplary life of a Latter-day Saint." May I suggest that readers will find in this biography the story of a man whose life forms an unimpeachable gospel tract.

That is not to say that President Hinckley has proved an easy subject. He has seemed to me a study in contrasts. He is deeply spiritual, yet he doesn't wear his testimony on his sleeve. His colleagues insist that he is brilliant, but even more that he is pragmatic and savvy. His tremendous regard for the past connects him to the founders of this dispensation in an almost tangible way, yet he is bold, not hidebound by convention or even tradition, a pioneer in his own right who will venture into uncharted territory. He feels passionately about the gospel and about people, yet he isn't overly sentimental. He has a deep understanding of the scriptures and the doctrine of the Church, but he constructs his sermons such that they don't overpower or intimidate. He is tremendously articulate, but he uses language carefully and in a manner that doesn't call attention to itself. He takes what he does very seriously, but he doesn't take himself too seriously—hence his often self-deprecating wit that appeals to people of all stations. It would be hard to identify someone who has more diligently defended the office of the President of the Church, yet he is uncomfortable having undue attention focused on himself now that he holds that office. And though he has great natural ability, he has not succumbed to the mortal tendency to glory in his own strength. His faith is squarely centered in a Power much greater than his own.

For all of his reluctance at allowing this project to proceed—and herein is demonstrated yet another dichotomy as well as the immensity of his character—President Hinckley has been accessible and cooperative every step of the way. He has read various drafts of the manuscript and has offered suggestions and made corrections while allowing me the freedom to maintain the work's integrity. I am grateful for his patience, his good humor, and his example. In addition, those who work in President Hinckley's office have been extremely helpful. I am particularly indebted to Lowell R. Hardy, his personal secretary, who has responded to countless requests and in doing so has contributed enormously to this project, and to Debbie Burnett, also of the President's office, who has furnished an unending supply of documents, transcripts, and other materials.

I am extremely grateful for the participation of the Hinckley family, particularly Sister Marjorie P. Hinckley, who willingly submitted to interviews and has been supportive, gracious, and an all-around good sport. At President Hinckley's side stands a woman of like stature and strength, conviction and good humor. Every minute I spent with her was pure pleasure. The Hinckleys' children—Kathleen Barnes, Richard Hinckley, Virginia Pearce, Clark Hinckley, and Jane Dudley—could not have been more cooperative, encouraging, and patient. Each consented to interviews, supplied me with family-related materials, and in general was supportive in every way. I am grateful for their friendship. The Hinckley family is unique. Despite enduring the glare of the spotlight for years, they have remained unaffected by the exposure.

Both of President Hinckley's counselors, President Thomas S. Monson and President James E. Faust, consented to interviews, as did each member of the Quorum of the Twelve and many other General Authorities. I am grateful for their insights and assistance. In particular, I express heartfelt appreciation for Elder M. Russell Ballard, who has championed this project from the outset, and Elder Yoshihiko Kikuchi, currently serving as president of the Tokyo Temple, who arranged important interviews with Asian members of the Church whose personal ties with President Hinckley date to the early sixties.

Finally, I am indebted to my parents, JoAnn and Charles Dew, and to my brothers and sisters, who with their families make up my most enthusiastic cheering section. They, along with several close friends, have for nearly two years come to my rescue again and again, often carrying my share of the load so that I could devote every spare minute to a project that, of necessity, became all-consuming. Their support has been emotional, spiritual, and at times very practical. A simple thanks can never be enough.

Though many others have assisted me in significant and important ways, I alone am the creator of this biography and accordingly take full responsibility for this interpretation of President Hinckley's life.

My exposure to President Hinckley during this project has been multifaceted. I have read every page of his journal, which provided an unparalleled look at his activities, motives, and feelings. In some thirty interviews I have asked him questions about every phase of his life, which questions he answered candidly and thoughtfully. I have personally seen him bolster the missionaries and inspire the members in half a dozen countries, as well as preside over or conduct the dedications of two temples where he spoke without notes and suited a different message to each session. His preparation and gifts of expression have been evident as he has been interviewed by journalists from a host of countries and has described the work of the Church to nonmember, and at times non-Christian, reporters without being preachy, patronizing, or overbearing. I have heard him offer prayer in a country where none of his hosts were Christian, and do so in a way that elicited their gratitude and obvious respect. I have witnessed the tremendous affection he has for the peoples of the world, as well as the love they have for him. I have read thousands of pages of the addresses, articles, and books he has written during the past sixty years, and have noted how spiritually astute he was as a missionary writing for the *Millennial Star* in the mid-1930s as well as marveled at the range and depth of wisdom his counsel has embodied in more recent years. Drawing upon these experiences and research efforts, I have attempted to put words to President Hinckley's life.

I will undoubtedly be asked whether this biography is an objective treatment. To that question I respond unapologetically and simply, "No." First, I question if such a feat is even possible. Biographers have the unwieldy challenge of sorting through and assimilating a mountain of information and deciding which relatively few materials to include. Concurrently they are drawing conclusions about their subjects' contributions, dreams, aspirations, and even motives. In any biographical effort, such responsibility is a serious charge—but when the subject is the President of The Church of Jesus Christ of Latter-day Saints, it comprises a sacred trust. With that in mind, I acknowledge that it has been impossible for me to divorce from my writing the fundamental personal belief that, while I admire President Gordon B. Hinckley and regard him as a remarkable man, that opinion is exceeded by my conviction that he is much, much more.

Even were he to be evaluated based solely upon a list of his achievements, President Hinckley would take his place among the world's great contributors. But everything that he has done, all that he has experienced—indeed, everything about him—bears witness that he is not just another accomplished man. Instead, this is a man whom the Lord has had in His care and keeping all his life, a man whose work transcends his résumé, a man who was foreordained to great responsibility and who has been refined, prepared, and made ready to assume the position he now holds by a Divine Schoolmaster whose curriculum has been complete and all-encompassing. Very simply, President Gordon B. Hinckley is a prophet of God.

A stake Relief Society president from California once told me about a group of nonmember women with whom she walked each morning. One of her exercise partners was a thoughtful woman who felt deeply about social concerns and moral erosion. One morning, as they were huffing their way up a hill, this woman raised an issue that appeared to have no solution. Suddenly, in the middle of their discussion, she looked at the stake Relief Society president and said, "You know what this world needs? We need a prophet. You know, like they had in biblical times. We need someone who can make sense of the mess we've created down here, someone who talks with God." My friend took a deep breath and was quiet for a few moments before responding, "We do have a prophet. And he does communicate with the heavens."

For members of The Church of Jesus Christ of Latter-day Saints who believe that President Hinckley is a prophet of God, an important question remains: What difference does it make to know that a prophet walks the earth? An experience I had during the preparation of this biography seared this question, and its answer, into my soul.

I have enjoyed the blessing of a testimony of the gospel for as long as I can remember. Through the years the whisperings of the Spirit have been sweet and sustaining. Though I have known something of disappointment, loneliness, and challenge, I have never borne the burden of disbelief, and I am grateful beyond expression for the gift of testimony. I know that Joseph Smith was a prophet. I have walked through the Sacred Grove and stood in the small room on the second floor of the Carthage Jail where he sealed his testimony with his blood. In those settings and many others, I have received confirmation that the work he helped restore is that of the Master.

Never, though, have I had more gratitude for modern-day prophets than I have felt since the day, just a few months ago, when an early-morning phone call brought the shocking news that my younger brother had died suddenly of a heart attack. It had never crossed my mind that my time here with my vigorous, presumably healthy, thirty-nine-year-old brother would be so short. I had assumed we would grow old together, enjoying the banter, camaraderie, and mutual respect that characterized our relationship. But it was not to be.

My brother's passing has left an indescribable void. That's the difficult part. But it has also caused me to think deeply about the faith I have embraced my entire life, for during the quiet moments of yearning that follow such experiences you find out what you really believe—and those beliefs either anchor or betray you.

What difference does it make to know that we have a living prophet who presides over the Lord's kingdom restored to the earth? It makes all the difference. One of my first thoughts after Steve's passing was how enormously grateful I was for the Prophet Joseph Smith, through whom was restored the gospel with its full understanding of our Heavenly Father's plan. How grateful I am to know that life has purpose, that it does not end with the grave, and that sacred ordinances have been restored that reach beyond this sphere and bind families together forever. How reassuring in a world of "shifting values," as President Hinckley has repeatedly described this era's moral climate, to be anchored to rock-solid moral and theological underpinnings that don't slide with the times, the trends, or the political party in vogue. How heartening to know that the heavens are open, that God has not abandoned us, and that He communicates with those who seek Him. What a transcendent gift to know that Jesus Christ, the Creator of this world, stands at the head of this Church, and that His mission, indeed His entire reason for being, is to help us return to a holier sphere. And what a privilege it is to be led by a prophet who communicates with the heavens and whose petitions and admonitions bear not even the slightest element of self-interest, personal bias, or distortion.

As President Hinckley has said many times, if we have a prophet, we have everything. If we don't, we have nothing. My conviction is that Joseph Smith saw what he said he saw in that grove of trees in upstate New York, that he was an instrument in the hands of the Almighty in restoring the gospel to the earth. And as one who has been privileged to be often in the presence of the current President of the Church and to explore his life in great detail, I state without hesitation that he too is a prophet, that everything about his life testifies of his goodness, his foreordination, and his preparation to lead the Church in this day. Indeed, we have everything—a sure guide, a clear voice, an unbiased servant whose only motive is to lead souls to Christ.

"There isn't any doubt in my mind that the man who becomes the President of the Church is schooled and disciplined by the Lord over a long period of time for this responsibility," said President Hinckley more than ten years ago. "In that process his individuality is not blurred; rather it is sharpened. The Lord trains a man and disciplines him. He tests his heart and his substance. And in a natural process that He directs, He moves through the Quorum of the Twelve a man to become the senior apostle who on the death of the President becomes the President of the Church. There is no campaigning but only the quiet operation of a divine plan that provides inspired and tested leadership. The Lord is at the helm of this work, and the President of the Church is an instrument in His hands to carry forward this work and to strengthen His kingdom."

It is this journey, the life journey of President Gordon B. Hinckley, the most uncommon of common men, that I have endeavored to tell.

ACKNOWLEDGMENTS

Though writing a book of this nature must of necessity be done in solitude, bringing it to publication has been a team effort.

Time constraints made it impossible for me to conduct all of the primary research alone. Ariel Silver, Camille Lots, Joan Willes Peterson, and Blake Johnson each helped with important segments of this critical function. As part of my research involved traveling to other countries, I am grateful for the assistance of Peter Trebilcock in Preston, England; Hanno Luschin at the Preston Temple site; President Pak Byung Kyu in Seoul, Korea; and David Fewster in the Philippines. I am also indebted to Bruce Olsen, managing director of the Church Public Affairs Department, for helping me arrange important interviews and obtain access to press conferences.

Trusted associates read various versions or portions of the manuscript. I appreciate the constructive criticism and helpful insights I received from Eleanor Knowles, Robert L. Millet, and Richard Turley.

Finally, I am deeply grateful for the support I have received from my colleagues at Deseret Book. Ron Millett, our president, has been encouraging and reassuring from the outset. I appreciate his expressions of confidence. Fellow vice presidents Gary Swapp, Keith Hunter, and Roger Toone have been supportive and enthusiastic. And the publishing staff has come to my rescue again and again. In particular, I am indebted to Jack Lyon for his constant optimism, Suzanne Brady for her technical editorial skills, Anne Sheffield for the savvy to effectively oversee the production of this complicated project, and Elsha Ulberg for rendering ongoing assistance. Most of all, I express my deepest thanks to Emily Watts, my editor, Kent Ware, our senior art director, and Tonya Facemyer, our typographer, who entered thousands of changes and corrections. The three of them turned the manuscript into a finished product and in the process made it a much better book than it would have been otherwise. I am grateful not only for their excellent professional skills but for their patience, perseverance, and friendship.

CHAPTER ONE

CARRY ON!

At precisely 9:00 A.M. on Monday, March 13, 1995, President Gordon B. Hinckley led a procession of fourteen distinguished men out of the Nauvoo Room and into the elegant and historic lobby of the Joseph Smith Memorial Building in downtown Salt Lake City, where a large contingent of local, national, and international press was waiting. When all had been seated and President Hinckley had been introduced to the gathering, he stepped to a microphone. At his left sat Presidents Thomas S. Monson and James E. Faust; seated behind them in a semicircle were the eleven members of the Quorum of the Twelve Apostles. All were positioned against a magnificent backdrop: a heroic-sized statue of the Prophet Joseph Smith that seemed to preside over the occasion. The purpose for which all had assembled was the formal introduction of Gordon Bitner Hinckley to the press and the world as the fifteenth President of The Church of Jesus Christ of Latter-day Saints.

For nearly fourteen years President Hinckley had sat at the side of three Church Presidents, had shouldered increased responsibility as each in turn had experienced the frailties of advancing age, and had helped lead the Church forward as a counselor in the First Presidency. But with the passing of President Howard W. Hunter ten days earlier, he had become the senior apostle. And according to the pattern established by the Lord and carefully adhered to since Brigham Young had succeeded Joseph Smith a century and a half earlier, President Hinckley had been ordained and set apart as President of the Church by his Brethren in a sacred assembly in the Salt Lake Temple.

It was fitting that the press conference announcing President Hinckley's ordination be held in this place. Less than two years earlier, after a massive renovation of the aging Hotel Utah, the splendidly restored building had been renamed, dedicated, and reopened to the public. In the main, his vision of how the dilapidated hotel might best be refitted for contemporary use, combined with his steady guidance throughout the restoration, had returned this once-graceful edifice to its rightful splendor on Salt Lake City's most prestigious intersection. It was President Hinckley's decision to greet the media in this building he loved for its symbolic linking of past with present, a building that represented what happened when faith, hard work, and optimism were combined with vision—virtues embodied in the new President himself.

In a brief statement, he pledged greater determination to move the work of God forward and expressed affection for his counselors, his dear friend and longtime colleague President Howard W. Hunter, and the nine million members of the Church scattered throughout the world. He also declared that the work of the Lord would continue to grow, and, in what would become a signature of his administration, he expressed optimism for the future: "We are particularly proud of our youth. I think we have never had a stronger generation of young men and women than we have today. . . . Surrounded by the forces that would pull them down and tremendous pressures to pull them away from time-tested virtues, they are going forward with constructive lives, nurturing themselves both intellectually and spiritually. We have no fears or doubts concerning the future of this work."[1]

Following his prepared statement, President Monson and President Faust each spoke briefly. Then, and for the first time since President Spencer W. Kimball had done so in 1973, a President of the Church invited questions from the press. For thirty minutes, President Hinckley responded to a variety of inquiries that focused principally upon the condition and future of the Church. Quietly in command of the situation from the outset, he revealed his warmth, wit, and vast range of knowledge. It was quickly apparent that this was a man who thoroughly understood the large, multifaceted organization over which he now presided. One prominent reporter called the experience "exhilarating"; another described President Hinckley's "debut" as impressive.[2] Taken in concert, his responses not only underscored his faith in and devotion to the work in which he had been engaged for nearly sixty years, but also revealed the unique traits, strengths, and attitudes that he brought to his new calling.

There were predictable questions from reporters interested in seeing how the new Church President would respond to awkward issues the Church faced. One inquiry focused on former Latter-day Saints whose writings and other activities had led to their excommunication. President Hinckley's reply was compassionate: "May I say first that we love these people. We would welcome them back in every respect. We regret the course which some of them may have followed, but our arms are open to receive them, to encourage them, to help them to return, to be active and faithful and devoted members of the Church. At any season or at any time that they wish to come, they will find open arms to greet them."

To a potentially volatile question about mothers who work outside the home, he replied with clarity and an allowance for personal choice: "Do the best you can, and remember that the greatest assets you have in this world are those children whom you have brought into the world and for whose nurture and care you are responsible."

When asked to identify the greatest issue facing the Church as it neared the twenty-first century, he responded without hesitating that the most serious yet exciting challenge was that of managing growth: "But what a remarkable and wonderful challenge that is," he added. "And because of the faithfulness of our people in the payment of their tithes and offerings, the Church has had the means to provide that which is needed to accommodate this growth. We are grateful for it."

His trademark sense of humor emerged when one reporter asked if the members of the media might expect more press conferences: "I haven't given it a thought. You look so formidable out there that I wouldn't dare make a commitment today." After confirming that in his nearly eighty-five years he had spent only one night in the hospital, he added, "That doesn't mean I'm ready to run a hundred-yard dash."

In one answer after another he expressed confidence in and support of various peoples and groups. When asked if Brigham

Young would be happy with the development of both the Church and the state he helped found and colonize, President Hinckley instinctively drew on his vast knowledge of Church history: "On a dark and winter day in 1849, in the old tabernacle which stood in the block west of us, when the people were hungry and cold, he said that the day would come when this would become the great highway of the nations and people from over the earth would visit us here. We're witnessing that day and the fulfillment of that remarkable prophecy." This was also a day, he stated with emphasis, in which stronger homes were needed: "Good homes produce good people. Good homes become the foundation for the strength of any nation."

President Hinckley was comfortable with the press and handled even delicate questions with deftness and grace. In response to the religious affairs correspondent from London Radio who asked if the Church was prepared to reinterpret its position on key issues, as other major religious organizations had done, President Hinckley was respectful while reaffirming the Church's position: "Every church does what it wishes to do. They have freedom to do so. We hope that we will not be blown about by every wind of doctrine and every societal change that will come along . . . but that this Church will remain as an anchor of faith and truth in a world of shifting values. We have as our guide the scriptures, the word of the Lord, given anciently and in modern times. We believe in the principle of modern revelation. We proclaim it as a basic function of the Church under its system of operation and will rely on that as we go forward with our program at home and abroad."

When a television reporter from Salt Lake City asked if President Hinckley would champion a theme during his administration, he replied: "Carry on! Yes. Our theme will be to carry on the great work which has been furthered by our predecessors who have served so admirably, so faithfully, and so well. Building family values? Yes. Fostering education? Yes. Building a spirit of tolerance and forbearance among people everywhere? Yes. And proclaiming the gospel of Jesus Christ. It is His name which becomes the name of this Church, and whose teachings and ideals we seek to emulate and promote. [We] will continue to do so."

That President Hinckley would refer to Ruth May Fox's much loved anthem, "Carry On," in fashioning a response to this fundamental question was consistent with his life's work. "Firm as the mountains around us, / Stalwart and brave we stand / On the rock our fathers planted / For us in this goodly land," the song begins, concluding with a call to arms, "Carry on, carry on, carry on!"[3] Constancy, stability, loyalty, and conviction were virtues to be modeled. With the pen and from the pulpit, in writings and sermons rich with lessons and insights from Church history, President Hinckley had long proclaimed his belief that the past is a model for the present. It was not surprising therefore that he would, as President of the Church, first acknowledge the legacy of his predecessors and then declare that the work would continue to move forward.

His practical response harked back to a poem that had stirred him as a boy, Joaquin Miller's verse about Columbus:[4]

Behind him lay the gray Azores,
Behind the Gates of Hercules;
Before him not the ghost of shores;
Before him only shoreless seas.
The good mate said: "Now must we pray,
For lo! The very stars are gone,
Brave Adm'r'l speak! What shall I say?"
"Why, say: 'Sail on! sail on! and on!' "

. . . .

Then pale and worn, he paced his deck,
And peered through darkness. Ah, that night
Of all dark nights! And then a speck—
A light! A light! At last a light!
It grew, a starlit flag unfurled!
It grew to be Time's burst of dawn.
He gained a world; he gave that world
Its grandest lesson: "On! sail on!"

The verse embodied a message President Hinckley well understood. As a boy, he had spent his summers on the family fruit farm in the rural Salt Lake Valley. There, in the pitch dark of clear country nights, he and his brother Sherman had often slept out under the stars in the box of an old farm wagon where they lay on their backs, looked at the myriads of stars in the heavens, and took turns picking out familiar stars and tracing the Big Dipper, the handle and the cup, to find the North Star. Called by some the Polar Star, or Lodestar, it fascinated young Gordon, who was awestruck with the truth upon which mariners and other navigators had depended for centuries—that regardless of the earth's rotation, this unique star maintained its position. He recalled, "I recognized it as a constant in the midst of change. It was something that could always be counted on, something that was dependable, an anchor in what otherwise appeared to be a moving and unstable firmament."[5]

President Hinckley had long admired those who were firm in their faith and resolute in their convictions. At his first general conference as a member of the First Presidency he had said: "Great buildings were never constructed on uncertain foundations. Great causes were never brought to success by vacillating leaders. The gospel was never expounded to the convincing of others without certainty. . . . Without certitude on the part of believers, a religious cause becomes soft, without muscle, without the driving force that would broaden its influence and capture the hearts and affections of men and women. . . . Personal testimony, coupled with performance, cannot be refuted."[6]

For nearly sixty years—since the summer of 1935, when he had returned from his mission in the British Isles and accepted an appointment at Church headquarters—President Hinckley had been engaged full-time in some aspect of Church service. Often his assignments had required him to blaze trails through uncharted territory and persist in the face of discouragement and even defeat. Some of his work had been done in anonymity, acknowledged and witnessed only by the relative few with whom he worked; other service, particularly as a General Authority and ultimately a counselor in the First Presidency, had been increasingly visible and subject to public scrutiny. Through it all, as he traveled the world and encountered the challenges of a growing Church, he had shown his character as a man whose underpinnings didn't shift in unstable times; as a leader who was confident in his course and would not deviate from it, even if his position was unpopular; as a visionary who could see long-range yet who graced everything he touched with a reassuring sense of stability; and as a devout follower of God the Father and His Son Jesus Christ, in whom he had unwavering faith. Over and over again, he had demonstrated his unflagging optimism that the gospel kingdom would continue to move forward with never a backward step. "These are the best times in the history of this work," he had proclaimed on one occasion, representative of countless others. "What a wonderful privilege and great responsibility are ours to be an important part of this latter-day work of God. Do not become sidetracked by the wiles of Satan that seem so rampant in our era. . . . Rather, let us go forward with faith and with the vision of the great and marvelous future that lies ahead as this work grows in strength and gains in momentum."[7]

It was with that outlook and frame of reference that President Hinckley assumed his new responsibilities as senior apostle and President of the Church. And though he had sobering feelings of inadequacy, as he himself described them at the press conference, and had hoped this calling would never fall upon his shoulders, he accepted it with an increased resolve to build on the foundation of the past and to carry on. In that respect, this was a comfortable position in which to be, for he was the beneficiary of the enduring examples of parents, of forebears, of Church leaders through the ages—all of whom had affected his life and set examples of dedication, persistence, and faith.

Thirty-seven years earlier, on April 6, 1958, the day forty-seven-year-old Gordon B. Hinckley had been sustained as an Assistant to the Twelve, he had said: "I have been thinking about the road that led here. I know that I have not come that road alone, and I feel very grateful for the many men and women . . . who have helped me. It is the same with each of us in the Church. No man proceeds alone. . . . All of us are largely the products of the lives which touch upon our lives, and today I feel profoundly grateful for all who have touched mine."[8] He had spoken those words sincerely and with emotion that day long ago. How poignantly he felt them now, for he had not come to this time and place, to this high and holy calling, alone.

Pedigrees of Gordon Bitner and Marjorie Pay Hinckley

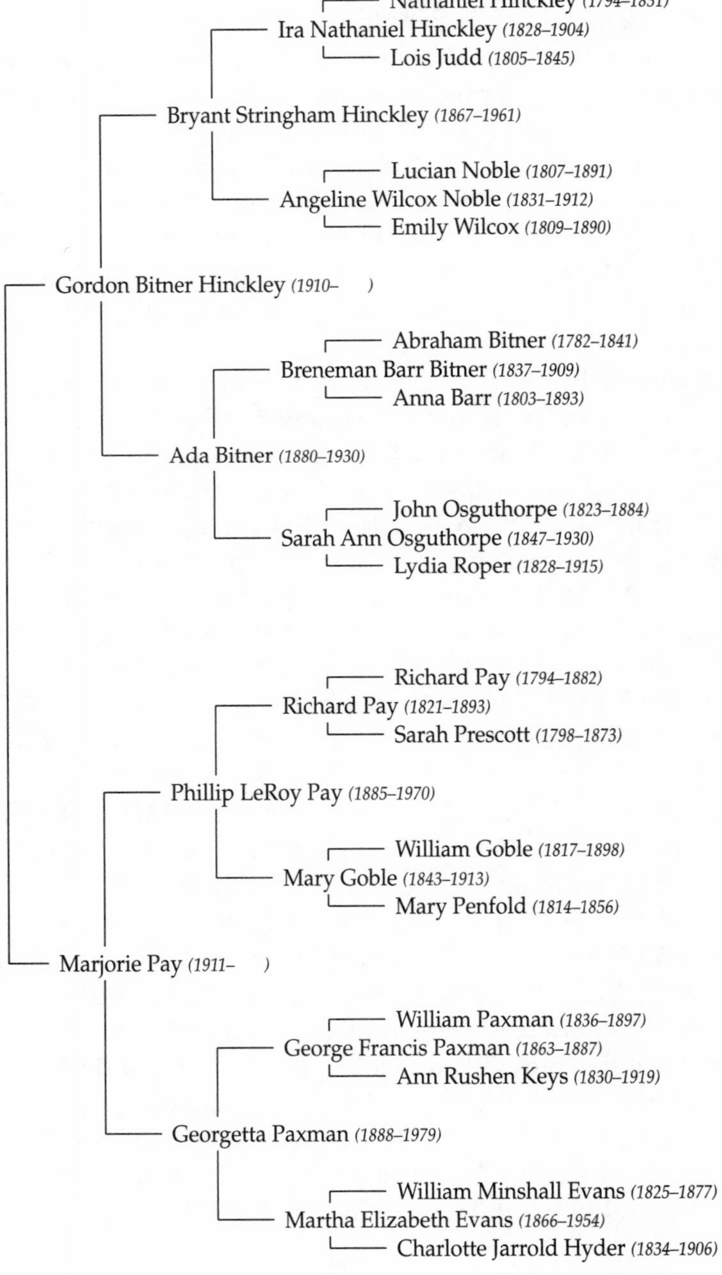

CHAPTER TWO

OF PILGRIMS AND PIONEERS

It was 1635 when the first Hinckley reportedly left his homeland and set sail for America. Samuel Hinckley, who hailed from Harrietsham in England's county of Kent, was among a small group who had severed ties with the Church of England and embraced the faith of the Puritans.[1] What may have seemed an impetuous decision to leave a home of relative serenity in search of religious liberty was not uncommon in seventeenth-century England, which witnessed a phenomenal migration of Britons to the American continent.

Bearing a surname that had survived in England for centuries, Samuel and his progeny were destined to make a significant contribution in the new world. Upon arriving in America, he proceeded to Scituate, Cape Cod, Massachusetts, and is believed to be the ancestor of most of the Hinckleys in America. His eldest son, Thomas, later distinguished himself as governor of the Plymouth Colony from 1681 to 1692.

One biographer wrote that Governor Thomas Hinckley was "a man of more than ordinary ability and influence."[2] And among his virtues was a strong devotion to his faith. Even before he became governor, a law was passed at his insistence, dubbed "Hinckley's Law," providing "that if any neglect the worship of God in the place where he lives, and set up a worship contrary to God, and the allowances of this Government, to the publick profanation of God's Holy Day, and ordinances, he shall pay 10 shillings."[3] On the whole, the record of the Hinckleys in America is "that of an alert, keen-minded, and sincere race, possessed of prudence and sound judgment, and an understanding nature."[4]

The Hinckleys intermarried with other prominent families. Governor Hinckley's great-grandson, also named Thomas, married Ruth Merrick, the great-great-granddaughter of Stephen Hopkins, who had sailed on the *Mayflower* in 1620 and, at age thirty-five, was the fourteenth signer of the Mayflower Compact.[5]

Governor Thomas Hinckley's sixth great-grandson, Ira Nathaniel Hinckley, was born in Ontario, Canada, on October 30, 1828. By the age of fourteen, he had lost both his parents.[6] And though his stepfather did not turn him out, in many respects his was the life of an orphan. The tragedies of his parents' deaths forced him to grow up quickly; after his mother died, he scoured the community of Springfield, Illinois, for odd jobs, demonstrating considerable talent with livestock and as a farmer. He also had natural mechanical skills and even as a boy became known as an efficient and talented blacksmith.

In the spring of 1843 Ira, carrying a forty-pound grip saw, walked 120 miles from Springfield to Nauvoo in just four days. Exposed to the Church as a child but not baptized, Ira was intrigued by the Mormons. In Nauvoo he frequently heard the Prophet Joseph Smith and his brother Hyrum preach in the grove west of the site where the temple was under construction. The spirit of the restored gospel began to fill and heal his soul, and on July 1, 1843, three months before his fifteenth birthday, he was baptized. In the gospel, Ira found a measure of peace and purpose his life had lacked.

Though in Nauvoo Ira found spiritual serenity, the atmosphere there was anything but tranquil. Mobbings and persecutions intensified during late 1843 and early 1844, culminating on June 27, 1844, with the brutal murders of Joseph and Hyrum Smith in the Carthage Jail. After the martyrdom, Ira and the body of Saints grieved the loss of their prophet-leader. But they soon rallied under the direction of Brigham Young and began working anew to complete the temple and to prepare for a massive migration west. As the Saints prepared to leave their beautiful homes for a wilderness refuge where they could openly practice their religion, wagons were built at a relentless pace, and Ira's skill as a blacksmith proved a precious commodity.[7]

His own journey west was delayed by financial and personal considerations. In the late summer of 1848 he married Eliza Jane Evans, and the following July their daughter, Eliza Jane, was born at Estelle Mills, Platte County, Missouri. It was not until April 1850 that Ira and Eliza accumulated enough clothing, foodstuffs, and other supplies to make the trek west themselves, and that month they joined a company of fifty-four wagons organized under the direction of Elder Orson Hyde of the Quorum of the Twelve and led by Captain David Evans, Ira's father-in-law.

The company crossed the Missouri River at Council Bluffs and traveled up the Platte to the Sweetwater, where cholera broke out in camp and Eliza became violently ill. Stunned by how quickly the disease struck, Ira watched helplessly as his young wife died. The day of her passing—June 27, 1850—he lost his half-brother Joel as well. Grief stricken, he split logs for coffins and buried his wife and brother in unmarked graves on the open prairie. Not yet twenty-two years old, he had lost both parents and was now a widower with an eleven-month-old daughter, with whom he arrived in the Salt Lake Valley on September 15, 1850.[8]

Finally in Salt Lake City, Ira built a home on the southeast corner of Seventh South and Seventh East, and on December 11, 1853, he married Adelaide C. Noble. Eighteen months later, on July 22, 1855, he entered into plural marriage with Adelaide's sister, Angeline W. Noble.[9] The companionship of first one and then a second devoted and loving wife blessed Ira with a measure of stability and contentment.

But day-to-day living in territorial Utah was unpredictable. Scores of men and women were called to colonize remote areas or to accept other assignments incident to developing the territory and building the kingdom. And so it was with Ira, who saw Brigham Young as not only a great pioneer leader but a prophet of God.

At least twice Ira left his family to make trips back over the plains to help others. One of those times was in 1862 when, at the request of Brigham Young—who had received orders from President Abraham Lincoln to equip a Utah volunteer cavalry to guard mail and telegraph lines during the Civil War—he enlisted in the United States Army. Then, in 1864, he was called to move his family to Coalville, east of Salt Lake City, and superintend the building of the first meetinghouse there.[10] But the year 1867 brought the most dramatic assignment when a courier arrived in Coalville with a letter from Brigham Young dated April 12: "We wish to get a good and suitable person to settle on and take charge of the Church Ranch at Cove Creek, Millard County. Your name has been suggested for this position. As it is some distance from any other settlement, a man of sound practical judgment and experience is needed to fill the place. Cove Creek is on the main road to our Dixie, Pahranagat, and Lower California, some 42 miles south of Fillmore and some 22 miles north of Beaver. If you think you can take this mission, you should endeavor to go south with us. We expect to start a week from next Monday. It is not wisdom for you to take your family there until the fort is built. . . . Should you conclude to go, let us know by the bearer of this letter, and when you start, come with conveyance to accompany us."[11]

President Young's invitation, actually more of an assignment, was typical of the era—life-changing and without warning. Ira sent the courier back with a simple reply: "Say to the President I will be there on the appointed day with conveyance prepared to go."[12]

Once again, life changed course instantly for Ira Hinckley and his family. The thirty-eight-year-old husband and father of twelve abandoned thoughts of a permanent home in Coalville and turned his attention to the prospects of building a fort on the lonely, windswept flats of Millard County. Just two days later he left to join Brigham Young in Salt Lake City, and together they departed for Cove Creek on April 21. As he left the green, fertile valleys of northern Utah behind and with each rotation of the wagon wheel drew closer to the hot, desolate, sagebrush-filled land of central Utah, Ira might have reflected on the cost of membership in the Lord's kingdom. There was, however, no hint of reluctance on his part.[13]

The Cove Creek area was well-known as a favorite camping place for travelers en route from the Salt Lake Valley to southern Utah. Charles Willden had built a small adobe fort there several years before, and on occasion Brigham Young had stayed overnight with the Willdens as he traveled to and from his winter home in St. George. President Young's objective in building a more solid fort in this isolated but strategic location was twofold: to protect the stagecoach, mail carriers, and telegraph operators and lines, and also to provide a safe haven against elements and Indians for travelers making their way along the "Mormon Corridor" to and from southern Utah.

What Ira found at Cove Creek was a desert with insufficient water but plenty of snakes, Indians, and loneliness born of isolation. The Black Hawk War was still on, and Cove Creek was a rendezvous point for wandering tribes of Indians. Nevertheless, he immediately launched into the formidable project.[14]

The lean, six-foot-one Ira Hinckley was known for his capacity for work, and his skills and talents were well suited to the challenge of building a fort on the open frontier. A natural mechanic with a reputation as the "best horse-shoer in the Territory," he was practical and self-disciplined.[15] Those who knew him described him as a "man of action." He was also a man of faith, which quality his children saw demonstrated repeatedly. His sons Alonzo, Frank, and Ed were partial toward a pair of high-spirited chestnut-sorrel horses that had exceptional pulling capacity. One day they used the team to haul a load of hay so heavy that the wheels cut through the sod. As the three witnessed the team's strength, Frank said to his brothers, "Don't let Father know what we think of these horses, or he will turn them in for tithing." The following week, while the boys were again working the team, Ira joined them in the field and mentioned to Frank, "Isn't that a fine span of horses?" "The best span of horses we've had," Frank replied. "Well, I want you to shine them up," his father said. "I have turned them in for tithing."[16]

That generous measure of faith combined with hard work, resourcefulness, and savvy enabled Ira and a few workers from nearby Fillmore and Beaver to build an impressive enclosure that was later described as one of the "finest structures in the territory."[17] Most other frontier forts in territorial Utah were constructed of wood, but the eighteen-foot-high walls of Cove Fort were made of black volcanic rock and dark limestone laid up in lime mortar to form a 100-foot-square enclosure. There were six rooms on each of the north and south sides, and a main gate on the east large enough for wagons to drive through and thick enough to permit a cavity between the facing boards that was filled with sand to slow bullets. Total cost of construction was approximately $25,000.[18]

During Ira's absence from home, Angeline had borne him a son—Bryant Stringham Hinckley—on July 9, 1867. But it was not until November 1867 that Ira returned to Coalville to move his family to Cove Fort, which was ready for occupancy.

Adelaide and Angeline worked full-time to bring civility to their remote outpost. They cooked and cared for their large families, bore children in the desert and then nurtured and educated them in the lonely abode, and prepared thousands of meals for the never-ending parade of hungry travelers.

In 1872 Colonel Thomas L. Kane, who had befriended the Saints in Iowa and again in the Salt Lake Valley when Johnston's Army arrived, came west with his wife and two sons. Their itinerary included a trip with Brigham Young to St. George, and en route the group slept overnight at Cove Fort. Colonel Kane's wife, Elizabeth, recorded her impressions:

> We reached Cove Creek Fort, and drove in under its archway. [Colonel Kane] soon called me outside to look at the landscape, and see how lonely a place we were in. The fort lay in a volcanic basin, geologically esteemed to be the crater of an extinct volcano. . . . Farther on the road we were to travel next day some wagons were encamped, their supper-fires already kindled. . . .
>
> I was not sorry to see a magnificent pitch-pine fire blazing on the hearth in [my room], for the . . . night air was very cold. Our room was nicely furnished, and looked very cozy as we drew our chairs around the centre-table, which had a number of well-chosen books upon it. . . .
>
> We supped in the telegraph office, where the ticking of the instrument insisted on being heard as we all knelt down for prayers.—Prayers after the patriarchal Hebrew manner; a shot-proof fort; an electric battery clicking the latest New York news; armed men; unarmed women with little children; a meal served with dainty precision in a refectory walled with rough-hewn stone: this medley of antichronisms is Mormon all over.[19]

Despite their isolated existence, Ira's children felt as though they lived in the center of the territorial universe. News of the thriving territory sped over the lines into the fort's telegraph office, and the children sat for hours watching operators tap out messages. Twice daily the Gilmore and Salisbury Stage Lines stopped by, carrying passengers to and from the West Coast and southern Utah. Prospectors, territorial officials, aristocrats with gold and currency, and Indians begging for food and supplies came through the heavy front gates.[20] For all who passed, the fort was a welcome oasis in the Utah desert.

Although all visitors were welcome at the fort, those most eagerly anticipated were Church leaders traveling to and from southern Utah. Over the course of ten years, nearly every leading Church authority sampled Cove Fort's hospitality. President Young was a frequent visitor, and the promise of his arrival inspired tremendous excitement. A long table set with a white linen cloth was laden with delicious foods, dozens of loaves of bread were baked, and the larder was filled with homemade butter and cheese. President Young's favorite room, beautifully appointed, was made ready.

Of Brigham Young's visit in April 1869 the following statement was recorded: "The company reached Cove Creek at 5:50 P.M. and were warmly cared for by Bro. Ira Hinckley and his family. Quite a contrast between the present comfortable quarters for the company and their animals and camping out without any shelter which the brethren had done in former times, when they stopped at this place overnight."[21] Young Bryant was sitting on the prophet's knee one evening when the Church President reached into his pocket and presented him with a coin. Bryant subsequently spent the money, which he later regretted.

Everyday life at the fort centered on the gospel. Bryant's brother, Ira Noble Hinckley Jr., recalled: "While at Cove Fort and associated so much with non-Mormons, we had a room on the north side of the Fort, and no matter what was going on, Father took the family there, and had family prayers."[22] Ira's faith was strong but practical. Said Bryant later: "Father was not interested in the mysteries of the Kingdom. The thing that characterized his religion was its application to everyday life. He had little use for religion that did not register in one's life, that did not manifest itself in his behavior. He never regarded religion as a cloak that could be laid off and put on at one's convenience. . . . When it came to paying tithing, helping to build a meetinghouse, assisting the poor, donating to the temple or supporting a school, he led the way. If he prayed for a thing he went to work to get what he prayed for."[23]

For ten years Ira practiced what he professed by giving succor to those in need on the desert of territorial Utah. Then on July 22, 1877, his talents were again pulled in a different direction when Elder Wilford Woodruff called him to preside over the newly organized Millard Stake—one of twenty-five stakes in the Church at that time. Of the event Elder Woodruff recorded: "This morning at Fillmore . . . a priesthood meeting was held to arrange for the organization of the stake. In the afternoon I preached and then presented the names for officers of the stake and were all received with unanimous vote. Ira N. Hinckley was ordained as President."[24] Ira felt unequal to the honor and responsibility, but he called his family together and told them that if they would support him, he would succeed, and if not, he would fail. He did, in fact, enjoy tremendous loyalty and love from his wives and children, who felt him to be the finest father in the world. On one occasion Susa Young Gates visited Cove Fort with her father, Brigham Young. While there she mentioned to Ira's daughter, Minerva, "I think it is one of the greatest honors in the world to be the daughter of Brigham Young." Minerva replied, "I would much rather be the daughter of Ira N. Hinckley."[25]

With Ira's new call, life for his family again changed drastically. Feeling that he should live closer to the center of the stake, he persuaded his brother Arza to take over operation of the fort and moved his own family to a farm five miles outside of Fillmore. Ira served as stake president for more than twenty-five years. His son Frank later said, "I think I have never seen as good a man as he was. He preached the loudest by practice and the least by noise or talk of any man I ever knew."[26] Such was the example Ira set for his immediate family as well as those who would follow in subsequent generations—that devotion to the Lord combined with hard work produces results.

Bryant Hinckley's earliest memories were of life at Cove Fort, where he and his brothers learned to ride almost as soon as they learned to walk. Many an afternoon found them atop the fort wall, their field glasses in hand, watching cowboys on fleet-footed ponies corral the wild horses and cattle that roamed the hills to the east.

Those who lived at the fort dealt with the isolation by devising their own diversions. At times their activities got out of hand. One day Bryant and his brother Edwin and a friend happened upon a six-shooter. Ed accidentally pulled the trigger and shot Bryant above the left knee. As blood ran down his leg and filled his shoe, Bryant fainted. Fortunately, Ira appeared on the scene, dispatched one of his sons to fetch a doctor in Beaver, and slowed the bleeding by applying pressure. When the doctor arrived, he probed the wound with a darning needle. Failing to locate the bullet, he finally poured St. Jacob's oil into the hole and bandaged it. How the wound ached! For nights, Ira walked the floor with his boy until he fell asleep. As long as he lived, Bryant boasted not only that he still carried a bullet in his leg, but that he was the only person ever shot at Cove Fort.

Though his first ten years at Cove Fort were filled with adventure, Bryant Hinckley came to regard Fillmore as home. As a boy, he knew every man, woman, and child in the community, and he never dreamed of living anywhere else. At age fifteen he was called as secretary of the ward Primary, and then as assistant secretary of the ward Young Men's Mutual Improvement Association. These experiences prepared him to accept other assignments—as secretary, second counselor, first counselor, and finally, at age nineteen, as superintendent of the YMMIA.[27]

In 1883, when Bryant was sixteen, Angeline moved to Provo so that Ira's five oldest sons—Alonzo, Elmer, Frank, Ed, and Bryant—could attend the Brigham Young Academy. Bryant was at an impressionable age, and the academy opened up a whole new world for the boy from rural Utah. Perhaps the most significant aspect of his stay in Provo was his association with Dr. Karl G. Maeser, the academy principal. Bryant found the German educator to be a man with a "high-powered soul," and later wrote of him, "He could stir the best that slumbers in the human heart and could transform boys into gentlemen if anyone could." Dr. Maeser was known for his oratorical skills, and Bryant, who showed promise as a communicator, consciously emulated his mentor's techniques. From his educational experience, Bryant gained more than a degree (which he received in 1890) and a familiarity with literature, history, and science; Dr. Maeser instilled within him the conviction that dedication to truth and goodness was the foundation of a successful, productive, and happy life.

Upon graduation, Bryant was offered a teaching position at the academy on the condition that he obtain further training, so he later traveled east to Poughkeepsie, New York, and attended Eastman Business College, from which he graduated in December 1892. He also completed several months of graduate work at Rochester Business University before returning home in the spring of 1893 to teach at the BY Academy and, in June 1893, to marry Christine Johnson. A year later their first son, Bryant Stanford Hinckley, was born. Eight more children followed: Josephine, Heber, Grace, Caroline, Wendell, Waldo, Venice, and Christine.

Bryant and Christine were happy in Provo, but in early 1900 an opportunity presented itself that the young educator could not dismiss. When he was offered a post as principal of the fledgling LDS Business College in Salt Lake City, he accepted the position and moved his family north. Bryant's challenges with the underfunded school were many, and he searched for ways to improve the college. At his own expense he visited some of the East's most progressive schools and returned to incorporate what he had learned. His instincts for business as well as his skill as a teacher and communicator served the college well. As a teacher he held the attention of audiences young and old, and it became difficult to get a seat in his classes of history, political science, algebra, economics, and the Old Testament. By the time he left after ten years of service, the school was considered one of the best business colleges in the country.[28]

But there were challenges and sorrows as well. One cold January day Christine went into labor with their fifth child. At the time both Heber and Grace had fevers severe enough that a nurse was attending them at home. That day, Grace suddenly took a turn for the worse, and with the nearest telephone two blocks away, Bryant was not able to summon a doctor in time. He held Grace in his arms as she died. Filled with grief, he tried to comfort his wife, who, a few hours later, gave birth to their third daughter, Caroline. "Those were tragic days," Bryant said. "We were poor and I was having a desperate struggle [at work]. . . . I could not get [the doctor], the nurse was terrified, and my poor wife was in agony with no one to help." The doctor and the undertaker arrived at the same time. The days that followed found the family occupied with a confusing mixture of emotions. How grateful they were for Caroline, but how they missed little Grace, who had been just two years old.[29]

There were other losses. Just as Bryant's career was unfolding, his father passed away, on April 10, 1904, at the age of seventy-five. It was difficult to imagine life without the man he admired as much as any other. Though it had not been Ira's style to preach to his own family, he had set an example of Church service, and Bryant was following in his father's footsteps. The same year Bryant's career took him to the business college, he was called, at age thirty-three, to serve on the YMMIA General Board, a position he held for twenty-five years. For a number of years he chaired the Junior Committee of that board, which committee in 1913 urged the Church to adopt the Boy Scout program as an integral part of its own program for young men. Bryant is also believed to have written more MIA manuals than any other man in Church history.[30]

His varied activities and high visibility put Bryant in contact with Church and civic leaders. But the relative insignificance of his accomplishments became painfully apparent when, in 1908, a series of events rocked Bryant and his children. On July 11 he and Christine set out on a routine trip to Provo; while there she suddenly became violently ill. Bryant quickly located a doctor, and Christine was rushed into emergency surgery. But it was too late: she died as quickly as she had become ill. After fifteen years of marriage, Bryant was suddenly alone, and the pain of separation was overwhelming.

Christine's death left Bryant reeling and eight children, the youngest of whom was just two months old, without a mother. Family and friends helped as they could. Carol and Christine went to live with their maternal grandparents in Provo. With the help of housekeepers and extended family, Bryant kept the other six children at home and began to work through his grief.

In time, he looked to marry again. Not only did his children need a mother, but he was lonely. Gradually he began to look differently at Ada Bitner, a beautiful and accomplished member of the business college faculty who taught English and was the first instructor of the Gregg Shorthand Method in Utah. A woman of remarkable education for that time, she was identified in various editions of the school paper, *The Gold and Blue*, as an exceptional teacher much loved by her students. J. Reuben Clark Jr., who would later serve in the First Presidency of the Church, was head of the school's shorthand department. Through the years, whenever Ada's name was mentioned in his presence, he would immediately volunteer how brilliant she was and how much he enjoyed teaching with her.[31]

Ada was a petite five feet, four inches, with large, hazel eyes and long brown hair accented with red highlights. She and the lean Bryant Hinckley cut a striking figure, and as they courted Ada "fell madly in love" with the handsome educator, who was thirteen years her senior.

On August 4, 1909, Bryant and Ada were married in the Salt Lake Temple, and from that time onward they were the central figures in each other's lives.[32] There were, however, inevitable differences: Ada had a lovely alto voice, and Bryant refused to sing; she loved to dance, and he had two left feet; he was a compelling orator, and she shied away from public speaking. Nonetheless, the two were remarkably well suited to each other. Education was important to both. Each was well schooled, interested in the arts, and something of a perfectionist. Both were avid readers and could converse for hours about their varied interests. Each was refined by nature but had a sense of humor and loved a good story. The gospel was important to both, and, like Bryant, Ada had pioneer forebears whose sacrifices for the gospel were part of family lore.[33]

When Ada married Bryant Hinckley at the age of twenty-nine, she gained not only a husband but also a house full of children who were still suffering the loss of their mother. The children needed the influence of a woman in the home, yet they had natural reservations about that woman being anyone other than their mother.

The transition was no doubt challenging for Ada herself,

whose marriage to Bryant whisked her from an orderly academic environment into a large home with immediate demands from six active children. Without the luxury of time to become adjusted to married life, she faced the responsibility of caring for the physical as well as the emotional needs of "their" children. But eight years earlier, in a patriarchal blessing, she had been promised that she would find a companion "whom she would delight to honor." She was certain that that man was Bryant Hinckley. And because she had fallen in love with him, she was willing to accept everything—and everyone—that came with him. In the same blessing she had also been told that she had a particular mission to fulfill, and that the angel assigned to watch over her at birth would direct her course and remove barriers from her way and doubts from her mind. The blessing concluded with a telling prophecy: "The eye of the Lord has been upon thee from thy birth and a decree of the Father has gone forth that thou shalt have a mission to fill, a work to do. . . . Thy name shall be perpetuated and live in the memory of the Saints."[34]

In some respects Ada was more than ready to become the mother of six. As a seasoned teacher of nearly ten years, she had a knack for relating to youth. Bright and well educated, she knew a great deal about grammar, literature, and the proper use of language, and she stepped in immediately to help the children with their homework. She was a marvelous cook, so having a large family pull up chairs to the dinner table was not intimidating to her. During her days as a single woman she had accumulated beautiful linens and Haviland china, a silver service, and tumblers made of cut crystal. The children learned the art of hostessing by watching and working with her.

Ada moved into the Hinckleys' two-story frame home in the First Ward of the Liberty Stake. The main floor consisted of a parlor (where Ada positioned her own elegant baby grand piano), a large dining room with a round oak table and chairs, and a secluded library. There was also a large, old-fashioned kitchen with a stove that heated the hot-water tank, a gas range, and a table and chairs. Upstairs were four large bedrooms and a bathroom. The front stairway with its massive banister was a tempting diversion for children who hopped aboard for a slide to the bottom.

It was into this large and well-appointed home that Ada and Bryant welcomed their first child. Bryant had been promised in a patriarchal blessing almost fifteen years earlier: "You shall not only become great yourself but your posterity will become great, from your loins shall come forth statesmen, prophets, priests and Kings to the most High God. The Priesthood will never depart from your family, no never. To your posterity there shall be no end . . . and the name of Hinckley shall be honored in every nation under heaven."[35]

The day Bryant and Ada rejoiced in the arrival of their first son, they couldn't have foreseen that he would in great measure fulfill that prophecy. Born on June 23, 1910, and given his mother's maiden name, he would be known as Gordon Bitner Hinckley.

CHAPTER THREE

BIRTH AND BOYHOOD

It was an exciting time to make one's entrance on the world stage. The twentieth century was just a decade old when Gordon arrived at the Hinckley home a few blocks from downtown Salt Lake City, and the United States was much different from the nation it would soon become, perched as it was on the brink of the modern era. In 1910, a man born in the United States, where 92 million people lived in forty-six states, could expect to live to age fifty. A can of Campbell's soup cost ten cents, a man's shirt was less than a dollar, and beef sold for thirty cents a pound in Salt Lake City.[1]

Americans were on the verge of a phenomenal transformation. Just two years earlier, Henry Ford had built his first Model T and developed the country's original assembly line. Only a few hundred miles of paved road existed in the entire nation, but that would soon change drastically. And the day Gordon was born, the front page of the *Salt Lake Tribune* lauded the inauguration of the first "regular airship passenger service" in the *Deutschland,* which had transported twenty passengers from Friederichshafen to Dusseldorf in Germany at an average speed of thirty-three miles an hour.[2] That same month the Salt Lake City council regulated "autoists" for the first time, fixing fifteen miles per hour as the maximum speed.[3] During his lifetime Gordon would be the beneficiary of advances in transportation and communication that would have boggled the early-twentieth-century mind.

In 1910 President Joseph F. Smith presided over a Church that at year's end boasted nearly 400,000 members in sixty-two stakes and twenty-one missions, with 933 missionaries serving in the field. Francis M. Lyman was the President of the Quorum of the Twelve, and all four operating temples were in Utah: St. George, Logan, Manti, and Salt Lake City. Just twenty years earlier President Wilford Woodruff had declared an end to plural marriage with the "Manifesto," and two decades would pass before the Church could celebrate the centennial of its organization. Slowly, however, it was moving from its inaugural era of persecution to one of prosperity and modest respect. The gospel kingdom was poised to surge forward after surviving eighty difficult years.

Such was the environment that greeted the young Gordon Hinckley, who, though his mother's first child, was welcomed by a ready-made family of brothers and sisters. Ada had faced head-on the challenge of establishing her own place in the Hinckley home, and she and the children were adjusting. Over the years there was no such thing as half-brothers and half-sisters, or "Christine's family" and "Ada's family." It was just one family, the Hinckleys, with care taken to make no distinction about who was born to whom.

Sixteen months later Gordon was joined by a brother, Sherman. Three sisters followed: Ruth, Ramona, and Sylvia. Although all of the Hinckley children were close, Gordon and Sherman, by virtue of their ages and gender, were nearly inseparable. Gordon was older, but Sherman was larger, faster, and stronger. A spindly, frail boy susceptible to earaches and other illnesses, Gordon was a constant worry to his mother. In the evening it was common to find Ada warming two small bags of salt, which she would hold against his aching ears. There were times when she stayed with her son through the night, applying the warm bags to give him a measure of comfort.

Gordon also suffered from allergies, asthma, and hay fever, and the living conditions of the day exacerbated his problems. Nearly everyone in Salt Lake City burned coal in stoves or furnaces, and the resultant soot hung over the city, particularly in the dead of winter, like a suffocating blanket. Freshly fallen snow was soon covered by a layer of gritty, black soot. Spring housecleaning was a major ordeal. Everything inside the home had to be thoroughly cleaned of the sooty dust that had accumulated in layers through the winter. Carpets were taken up, hung on a clothesline, and attacked with carpet beaters, and every inch of wallpaper was cleaned with a doughlike substance that removed dirt and restored some of the paper's original vibrancy.

The heavy concentration of soot and other pollutants was Gordon's nemesis. At age two he contracted a severe case of whooping cough, threatening enough that a doctor told Ada the only remedy was clear, country air. Bryant responded by purchasing a five-acre farm in the rural East Millcreek area of the Salt Lake Valley and building a small summer home. One of Gordon's earliest recollections was of visiting the farm home during its construction and watching the stonemason build the rock fireplace to Ada's design.

Constructed in 1914 for $500, the country cottage was modest. Its small kitchen had a coal stove (and later an electric hot plate), a few cupboards, and a sink. A door from the kitchen led to two small bedrooms and a bath. The roomy living room had a fireplace of native cobblestone, and a large front porch was a favorite gathering place on warm summer evenings. Thus began the Hinckley tradition of spending winters downtown and summers in East Millcreek.[4]

Rural life suited Gordon and Sherman. Though their home in the city was larger and more comfortable, their residential neighborhood didn't offer the opportunities of the country, where they were free to explore and play in the gully that ran along the south line of their five acres. They jumped off haystacks, drank warm milk fresh from the cow, played hide-and-seek in the corn patch, rode in the back of a wagon behind a horse, flew out over the big hollow in a swing, learned to "make butter" by shaking cream in a two-quart fruit bottle, and played run sheepy run, no bears are out tonight, and mumblety-peg for hours at a time, tipping the blade of a pocketknife off their noses and foreheads.

When the boys got a little older, Bryant taught them how to handle a gun, and they took their .22 rifles and went "hunting." In truth, they had more fun shooting at old bottles and other stationary targets than aiming at—or, heaven forbid, actually hitting—anything that moved. Gordon did go deer hunting once, but he got caught in a blizzard and had such a miserable experience that he never went again.

Life on the farm brought out the ingenuity in Gordon and Sherman, who even as boys were natural mechanics and applied their inventive skills to a variety of contraptions. They made all kinds of conveyances out of wheels and boards, including a horse-drawn cart, and rigged up a shower with an old water tank that used the sun to heat the water.

Over time their projects became increasingly sophisticated. And as with all inventors, at times their schemes went awry—such as the day they decided to build a carbide bomb in a can. The boys understood just enough chemistry to construct an incendiary device that exploded when they lit the match. Nothing was bruised or broken except a little of their pride and reputation as engineers. That didn't stop Sherman, however, from using dynamite to loosen up a strip of hard ground they believed couldn't be cultivated any other way. Again, the results were explosive.

Many a night the boys slept outside in the bed of a wagon underneath a sky full of stars. When it rained, they grabbed their bedding and ran for the protection of the front porch, where Ada would find them the next morning, sound asleep after the night's adventure.

The farm also presented the Hinckley children with opportunities to work. Bryant was typically up by 5:00 A.M., and he expected his family to keep an early clock. There were always plenty of chores for the boys, and each day they could plan on receiving a list of jobs to be done by noon. When the work was done, the day was theirs to do with as they pleased. But during the cooler morning hours, they had rows in the large garden to weed, several acres to irrigate, post holes to dig, fruit to pick, eggs to gather, horses to look after, and two cows to tend—a Guernsey named Polly and a high-spirited, purebred Jersey cow named Babe. The boys were to empty the water as it melted from the icebox in the cellar, but they frequently forgot and spent more time cleaning up the water that had overflowed the small pan than would have been required to take it out in the first place.

The Hinckleys grew much of what they ate. The cows gave all the milk the family could drink, and a large orchard with a variety of fruit trees—apples, peaches, cherries, pears, apricots, and plums—yielded a bounteous harvest. When Gordon and Sherman were older, their father expected them to help in the orchard and took them to pruning demonstrations put on by the agricultural college. Most Saturdays during January and February, Bryant and sons drove to the farm and pruned trees. It was not a pleasant job, but the boys' inventive natures again emerged as they built stilts of maple flooring to help them reach the higher branches. All of the pruning, year after year, yielded an important lesson that embedded itself in Gordon's subconscious: the quality of fruit picked in September is determined by the way the trees are shaped and trimmed in February.

The boys were involved in the process from beginning to end, though neither enjoyed harvesting the fruit, which was sweaty, sticky work. But the peaches had to be picked, graded, packed, and sold, and it took all hands to get the job done.[5] Indeed, the farm provided a fertile environment for any number of lessons, perhaps none of which was more pervasive than that one can reap only what he has sown. The young Hinckleys saw this lesson played out season after season as they plowed and planted in the spring, tended the crops through the summer, and experienced the reward of harvest in the fall.

If the children felt they had a lot of chores, the extra work Ada shouldered because of the lack of conveniences on the farm was enormous. But she loved their rural home and didn't seem to mind the work that came with it. Though the house was hot in the summer, and the heat of the range transformed the kitchen into its own self-contained oven, she filled hundreds of Mason quart jars with fruit and vegetables. Her sun-kissed strawberry jam was a family favorite. When Ada and Bryant invited city friends for a country breakfast, she served large bowls of fruit and cream, hot rolls, bacon and liver, and fried chicken or ham.

It was a landmark day when electrical power came to the farm. The advent of electric lights and a small stove with three coil units for cooking was like heaven for Ada. Getting water into the home proved more challenging, but Bryant eventually solved that problem as well.

As remarkable as were electricity and running water, however, there was no more dramatic sign of progress in the Hinckley home than the summer day in 1916 when Bryant *drove* up in a black Model T Ford with a shiny brass radiator. When the children saw his prize, their eyes grew wide with wonder. Although the Model T was a tremendous step forward in transportation, it was also a crude and temperamental machine. It took two men to put the car's top up and down, and the windshield was positioned such that if it rained, the water seeped into the electrical coil and made it nearly impossible to start the engine, which was an adventure in the best of circumstances. Because the auto had no self-starter, Bryant often called on the boys to turn the crank on the front of the grill—a dangerous task if not executed carefully. They learned the hard way that if they didn't retard the spark and keep their thumbs cocked back in an unnatural way, the crank could kick and break a thumb or a hand. Some days, after the boys had tugged and tugged at the crank without success, they finally resorted to coasting the unreliable machine down the hill to get it started. Because the car had no battery, electricity came from the magneto, the output of which was determined by the speed of the engine. If the engine slowed down, the lights became a pale, nearly useless yellow. A driver heading down the road at night had to keep the engine running at a steady clip. From his experience behind the wheel of a Model T, Gordon later drew an analogy: "Industry, enthusiasm, and hard work lead to enlightened progress. You have to stay on your feet and keep moving if you are going to have light in your life."[6]

Though everyone in the family loved farm life, they also enjoyed returning to their home downtown each fall. After a summer away, the children were anxious to visit favorite haunts and be reunited with neighborhood friends. An arc light on a nearby street was a neighborhood gathering point, and at night, as if by predetermined signal, the boys gathered to play kick the can or marbles, which they kept at until their knuckles were raw. In the winter they went sledding, skated on the Liberty Park pond, and played fox and geese in the snow until their hands were so chapped they bled. Their toes got so cold inside their rubber galoshes that when they got home the boys danced around the house to keep from crying.

Winter in downtown Salt Lake City called for special preparations. Because the streets weren't plowed, the Hinckleys put the Model T on blocks in the barn behind the house for the season. A man on horseback pulling a small, V-shaped plow cleared the long sidewalks on two sides of the Hinckleys' corner lot. Decades later, Gordon could still conjure up the distinctive sound of the milkman's cart creaking in the ice as he made his daily delivery. Fresh air was believed to be important to good health, so Ada insisted that the children sleep with their windows open, even in the dead of winter. By morning the rooms were frigid. Ironically, the air was pungent with smoke from coal or wood furnaces.

One advantage of returning to the city was that Bryant was closer to work. Until 1910, he directed affairs at the LDS Business College. That year, when the Church built the Deseret Gymnasium as a community recreation center, he was appointed general manager of the enterprise and charged with day-to-day operations. One notice announcing his appointment declared that "no better selection could have been made for this important office."[7] The Church spent nearly $200,000 building the gymnasium, which was one of the finest in the country.

The Deseret Gym proved to be an important community facility. An athletic club, it also became a social center. Basketball games for the University of Utah, which had no arena or fieldhouse, were played there. Students at the LDS Business College used it as their gym, and the local Boy Scouts established headquarters there. Alice Merrill Horne and other prominent artists transformed the board room into an art gallery on occasion, and men came from all over the city to play handball and basketball, take part in calisthenics, and swim. On Saturdays, Gordon and Sherman made their way to the gym to swim, exercise, and pitch baskets.

Bryant was an able businessman who kept the gym operating during even difficult financial years. His experience teaching business at BY Academy and running the LDS Business College proved invaluable. It also came in handy in the management of his personal affairs, for he gradually accumulated a respectable portfolio of real-estate holdings. In addition to his rural properties, he purchased several homes within his stake boundaries, a small farm in Millard County, and another in the western part of the Salt Lake Valley. Bryant was meticulous about taking care of what he owned, and his sons could often be found doing odd jobs at the various property sites.

Other values were also inherent in the Hinckley family culture. As a former English teacher, Ada was well-read and a purist as far as grammar was concerned. She would not tolerate sloppy language, and her children learned to speak with precision and care. To say *nothin'*, or use slang of any kind, was almost unforgivable.

Ada had been an exceptional student, and she expected the same of her children. For years Gordon treasured a small Webster's *Handy Dictionary* that carried the inscription, "Ada Bitner Reward for Excellence, 1889." Books and education were important to Bryant as well, and he had converted one of the large rooms in their home to a library that could be closed off for studying. Its bookshelves were filled with more than a thousand volumes—a complete set of Shakespeare, numerous titles by or about Abraham Lincoln, the fifty-volume *Harvard Classics* (which contained everything from the writings of Aristotle to George Washington's Farewell Address), and *The World's Best Histories*. In the center of the room stood a large, solid oak table with comfortable chairs and a set of encyclopedias, atlases, dictionaries, and other reference works. Statuettes of Joseph Smith and Abraham Lincoln graced the room with a certain dignity. No one was forced to study or read, and the children didn't spend hours poring over the pages of their parents' books, but the library was inviting. Over time, Gordon developed a familiarity with good books and came to appreciate what his parents valued—literature and history, learning and education. Years later he concurred with Emerson, who, when asked which of all the books he had read had most affected his life, said that he could no more remember the books he had read than the meals he had eaten, but that they had made him.[8] The children were all influenced to one degree or another by their parents' love of literature and, indeed, most things artistic. Each learned to recite some of Bryant and Ada's favorite poems and passages from the classics.

Ironically, for all the emphasis among the Hinckleys on literature and learning, as a young boy Gordon did not like school. At age six, when he should have started first grade, he hid from his parents on the first day of school. Because he was a small child with delicate health, Bryant and Ada decided he might do better the following year attending with Sherman.

When the first day of school arrived a year later, Gordon ran laps around the house in an attempt to avoid his mother, but Ada prevailed. Both boys entered first grade in the Hamilton School. It wasn't long before Gordon joined his age group in the second grade. Even so, when school broke for the summer recess at year's end, he could be heard chanting with his friends, "No more pencils, no more books, no more teachers' cross-eyed looks."

Weather permitting, all students assembled in front of the three-story school building each morning, pledged allegiance to the flag, and then marched into their classrooms. Boys and girls were expected to dress neatly, with shirts, ties, short trousers, and black, knee-length stockings in order for the boys. Their cotton socks tended to wear out quickly, so the boys were taught to darn—it was unthinkable to go to school with a sock that needed mending.

Despite the best efforts of parents and siblings, Gordon remained unenthusiastic about formal education throughout grade school. He was used to running barefoot all summer, and the confinement of the classroom, not to mention the formality of shirt and tie and a stiff pair of shoes, was something he resisted strenuously.

Though Gordon's early academic record was unimpressive, certain standards of behavior and achievement were nonetheless modeled and expected in the Hinckley home. Neither Bryant nor Ada was a strict disciplinarian; Bryant never raised a hand to his children. "By some quiet magic," Gordon later said, "[our father] was able to discipline his family without the use of any instrument of punishment, though on occasion [we] may have deserved it."[9] When the children misbehaved, both parents had a way of communicating disappointment and letting them know that more was expected of them. If the children didn't respond after Ada had asked them to do a certain chore, for example, she took care of the task herself, no matter how tired she was. Most of the time, that was more painful to the children than a lecture or spanking would have been.

There were, of course, times when only a lecture would do. One day Gordon, seven or eight years old, was engaged in serious conversation with friends on the front porch when he made disparaging remarks about a black family walking down the street. Ada, who overheard her eldest and was horrified by his slur, promptly marched him and his friends into the living room and gave them all a good talking-to about respect and kindness.

Though Gordon and Sherman were good friends and would have defended each other against any outside threat or insult, their closeness in age created a certain amount of rivalry that sparked occasional fights. As the stronger of the two, Sherman had the advantage physically, but his older brother was scrappy and persistent. None of their skirmishes were ever won easily. Gordon later said, "I did all right. My head was bloodied, but unbowed." Tired of such exchanges between his sons, Bryant finally brought boxing gloves home and told the two to resolve their differences once and for all. "We did, and we've been friends ever since," Gordon said.[10]

Indeed, Gordon had a feisty streak. As he prepared to enter the seventh grade, he and his friends looked forward to being the first class to occupy the new Roosevelt Junior High School. But when they reported to school, they learned that the building was already overcrowded and their class was being moved back to the elementary school for one more year. Gordon and his friends had already spent six years at Hamilton, and they felt they deserved something better than a sentence to another year with the lower grades. The following day they went "on strike" and played "hooky." When they returned to school the next day, the principal, Harold J. Stearns (whose demeanor, Gordon insisted, matched his name), greeted them at the front door and announced that they would be readmitted only after they supplied a letter of explanation from their parents. Ada was not pleased when she learned what had transpired, and her note to the principal contained a rebuke that stung her eldest son: "Dear Mr. Stearns, Please excuse Gordon's absence yesterday. His action was simply an impulse to follow the crowd." He later explained why his mother's response had cut so deeply: "It wasn't an impulse to follow the crowd. *I* was one of the instigators. But to have Mother classify me as one to do something just to follow the crowd cut me, and I made up my mind then and there that I would never do anything just to follow the crowd."[11]

On another occasion, after a particularly rough day at school, Gordon returned home, threw his books on the table as he walked through the kitchen, and let out an expletive. Ada, shocked at his language, explained that under no circumstances would those words ever come out of his mouth again and led Gordon to the bathroom, where she generously coated a clean washcloth with soap and rubbed it around his tongue and teeth. He sputtered and fumed and felt like swearing again, but resisted the urge.[12]

The Hinckleys lived in the Liberty Stake, and their home ward, the First Ward, was the center of their universe. It was not only an important spiritual center but a social one as well. Large and diverse, it was filled with strong families with youth of all ages. More than a thousand ward members fell under the care of Bishop John C. Duncan, who shepherded the congregation for a quarter of a century. Despite the unwieldy size of his ward family, he was not just their bishop but their friend and adviser as well. Bishop Duncan was present when Gordon and his brothers and sisters were given names and blessings. He later interviewed Gordon and found him worthy to be ordained a deacon, called him to his first Church assignment as a member of the deacons quorum presidency, recommended him to receive the Melchizedek Priesthood, and confirmed his worthiness to serve a mission. Gordon loved and respected his bishop, a man who was a central figure during his youth.[13]

It was to Bishop Duncan's home across the street that the Hinckleys made their annual, year-end pilgrimage for tithing settlement. A full year's tithing for Gordon might have been only twenty-five or thirty cents, but he was taught to pay it nonetheless.[14]

The ward meetinghouse itself was busy nearly every night of the week with dances, plays, speech contests, and other MIA programs, and from his earliest days Gordon participated in all that was offered that pertained to him. He was five years old when his father wrote to Ada, who was visiting on the West Coast at the time: "The little boys [Gordon and Sherman] have been to Primary today and this evening Gordon has been asking some very wise questions."[15]

At home, Bryant and Ada found ways to keep gospel principles in front of their children. Before bedtime Ada often gathered her children around the stove and read to them about Nephi, Lehi, and other Book of Mormon heroes from *Mother Stories from the Book of Mormon* by William Albert Morton, first published about 1911. Though it wasn't until later that Gordon began to read directly from the scriptures, his interest in scriptural characters and stories was first kindled during those sessions with his mother.

In 1915, when President Joseph F. Smith counseled LDS families to gather at least once a week for home night, Ada and Bryant responded, "The President of the Church has asked us to hold home night. So we're going to have home night." This pronouncement was greeted with moans from children who weren't anxious to be corralled into another meeting, but from that time forward Monday evenings were reserved for family. Bryant or Ada would give a lesson and then urge their children to perform—something that elicited smirks, guffaws, and sometimes out-and-out laughter. The children weren't natural performers, and asking one of them to sing in front of the others was, as Gordon said later, "like asking ice cream to stay hard on the kitchen stove. It took us a long time to reach the point where we could sing together without giggling. It must have been disgusting to my parents the way we giggled."[16]

But Bryant and Ada persisted. The family had regular family prayer and often listened to faith-promoting incidents from Bryant's seemingly endless reservoir of stories. Though some family home evenings were less tolerable than others, the net effect was positive. Those simple gatherings created strong bonds between parents and children, brothers and sisters—a critical element in the unification of their blended family.

Through these and other experiences, Gordon began to learn for himself that there was a lot to the Church that his parents believed in so deeply. By the time he was baptized by his father on April 28, 1919, he wanted to be a member of the organization. "We went to Church, but not under compulsion," he reflected years later. "Our parents somehow let us know what was expected of us, and we followed their lead without much argument."[17] On several occasions Bryant took Gordon to general conference in the Tabernacle. He heard President Heber J. Grant speak of the "Little White Slave," a warning against the addictive influence of cigarettes, and bear eloquent testimony of the Word of Wisdom as a divine law. The message so impressed Gordon that he silently resolved never to smoke.[18]

On another visit to the Tabernacle, when he was about fifteen, he sat high in the balcony and listened as President Grant related his experience of reading the Book of Mormon as a boy. He spoke of the influence Nephi had had on him, and then in stirring fashion quoted familiar words: "I will go and do the things which the Lord hath commanded, for I know that the Lord giveth no commandments unto the children of men, save he shall prepare a way for them that they may accomplish the thing which he commandeth them" (1 Nephi 3:7). President Grant's words bore into Gordon's soul, and at that moment he resolved that he would try to do whatever the Lord asked him to do.[19]

But one experience in particular had a profound effect on young Gordon. Not long after he was ordained a deacon, he attended his first stake priesthood meeting with his father. An awkward, freckle-faced boy in knee pants, more prone to laugh than to be serious, he felt a little out of place as he found a seat on the back row of the Tenth Ward chapel while Bryant (who was serving in the stake presidency) took his place on the stand. To open the meeting, the three or four hundred men present stood and sang William W. Phelps's triumphant anthem celebrating the life of Joseph Smith: "Praise to the man who communed with Jehovah! / Jesus anointed that Prophet and Seer. / Blessed to open the last dispensation, / Kings shall extol him, and nations revere."[20] Gordon was unprepared for what he experienced: "Something happened within me as I heard those men of faith sing. It touched my heart. It gave me a feeling that was difficult to describe. I felt a great moving power, both emotional and spiritual. I had never had it previously in terms of any Church experience. There came into my heart a conviction that the man of whom they sang was really a prophet of God. I knew then, by the power of the Holy Ghost, that Joseph Smith was indeed a prophet of God."[21]

Gordon had often heard his father speak with respect, almost reverence, about the Presidents of the Church, most of whom he had known personally. Bryant regarded the Prophet Joseph Smith as the most significant man besides the Savior ever to have lived, and he felt a personal link with Brigham Young, upon whose knee he had sat as a boy. These and the other Presidents of the Church were Bryant Hinckley's heroes. And they became Gordon's.

Bryant also spoke often of his father and other forebears who, he taught his children, deserved their esteem and respect. It meant something to be a Hinckley, and the children knew what was expected of them. Though Bryant rarely lectured his children, he often repeated favorite sayings that communicated his expectations: "Try to live up to the high-water mark of your possibilities." "Be somebody. Stand up for something." "So live that men by your good deeds may know your ancestors," he encouraged, explaining that a person best honored his parents by making honorable the name he bore.[22]

The Hinckleys enjoyed a sense of well-being and stability in their home. Many decades later Gordon recalled: "We didn't openly speak about love for one another very much in those days. We didn't have to. We felt that security, that peace, that quiet strength which comes to families who pray together, work together, and help one another."[23] The children had the assurance that their parents loved them, believed in them, and regarded them as assets rather than liabilities.

The children also felt secure about their parents' relationship. Bryant cherished his beloved Ada. When Ruth was a year old, he insisted that his wife go to California for some needed rest. His letters to her revealed how lonely he was: "It will be several days before we can in any way become reconciled to your absence. . . . But there is a comfort in the thought that you will get a long deserved rest." Always cautious about spending money, he nonetheless reassured his wife, "Spend whatever money is necessary for your comfort—we will be none the poorer for this," and concluded with a reassurance of his love: "At the evening of the first day, accept my constant and unfailing love for you. . . . It is hard to be without you but it is happy to think of you."[24]

Bryant and Ada's inherently positive outlook permeated the family atmosphere. Ada believed, and often stated, that a happy attitude and smiling countenance could boost one over almost any misfortune and that every individual was responsible for his own happiness. The children frequently heard their parents say, "Cynics do not contribute; skeptics do not create; doubters do not achieve." Despite the normal frustrations associated with rearing a large family—and Bryant and Ada had their share—the combination of optimism and personal responsibility that they exemplified created an emotionally healthy and stable home.

It helped that they both had a sense of humor that allowed them to laugh at themselves and at everyday annoyances. A good pun or joke was to be admired—and outdone. Bryant liked to tell the children that any of their faults or weaknesses—hay fever, allergies, poor eyesight—came from their mother's side, and that their desirable qualities were Hinckley traits. He enjoyed reciting the story of how Willard Done, a former president of the LDS University, had introduced him at a banquet by saying that he was not a very handsome man, but then adding, "His face grows on you, so don't be discouraged." When Bryant came to the pulpit, he replied that he was grateful for many things, one of them being the fact that Done's face had never grown on him.[25] Gordon picked up his father's wry wit and quick sense of humor—which attributes his sister Ramona claimed helped him maneuver his way out of every predicament he ever got himself into.

The Hinckleys made the most of happy occasions. Christmas, for example, was a gala affair. Spicy aromas filled the home as Ada made fruitcakes, plum puddings, and pounds of fondant. As Gordon and Sherman got older, they created elaborate decorations—a make-believe fireplace of red brick paper in the dining room, a village on the library table with a mirror as a lake and strands of sparkling lights. In anticipation of Santa, the younger children hung their Christmas stockings and the older children left a plate of goodies on the dining-room table. Early Christmas morning, the children tiptoed downstairs to the library, claimed their gifts, and ran upstairs to show their parents. Each girl usually got a special doll with at least one beautiful dress Ada had made. There were rarely fragile or expensive toys, but Gordon and Sherman were thrilled one year with a Flexible Flyer, then the Cadillac of sleds. Bryant liked to buy two or three new games each Christmas, and on holidays the family gathered around the large dining-room table and played one game after another.

There were other family celebrations. They often vacationed close to home, but one memorable excursion took them to Yellowstone National Park. Driving from Salt Lake City in the Model T over gravel roads was an adventure. They traveled long days, camped beside the road, cooked meals over an open bonfire, and got plenty of exercise pushing the car up steep hills. But once there, they enjoyed themselves immensely. Gordon and Sherman slept in the seats of the car, and one night a bear got close enough to lick Sherman's forehead. When Bryant, who was in a nearby tent, heard the animal scratching the car fenders, he lit a fire and scared the furry intruder away.

For all the happy times, however, there were periods of suffering and heartache as well. In 1918 an influenza epidemic killed more than twenty-five million people worldwide—more than half a million in the United States alone, or nearly ten times more Americans than died in World War I. While faithful Latter-day Saints were gathered for October general conference, the first signs of the outbreak in Salt Lake City were diagnosed; and within four weeks 1,500 cases and 117 deaths had been documented. A *Deseret News* headline from that month read: "Many towns are closed by order of health board; Theaters, churches and all public gatherings under ban for present; Spanish influenza rapidly spreading."[26] Utah was eventually besieged with the virus, which killed about 4 percent of the Utahns afflicted between 1918 and 1919. The winter of 1918 saw many families hit with the dreaded disease from which the weak never recovered.[27]

It wasn't long after a friend of Gordon's came home from school deathly ill that Gordon, Ruth, Venice, and Bryant contracted the vicious strain of influenza. Ada, who was carrying her fifth child, nursed them back to health. The children moved into the front bedroom, where they were confined for several weeks as they tried to overcome the illness that sapped every ounce of strength from them. Ada was relieved when Gordon pulled through, for he was still a skinny boy susceptible to illness.

As unpleasant as some of his health challenges were, no experience during Gordon's first ten years was more traumatic than receiving the news that arrived in late November 1918. A letter from Elder B. H. Roberts, a member of the First Council of the Seventy stationed in Europe as chaplain of the 145th Field Artillery, brought word that Bryant's eldest son, Stanford, who had enlisted in the army during World War I, had died of pneumonia in a hospital in Bordeaux, France. His death had come less than a month before the Armistice, and he was buried in an American military cemetery in Suresnes overlooking Paris. It was the first time Gordon and Sherman had seen their father cry, and they too wept.

Bryant and Ada were consoled by the fact that Elder Roberts had comforted their critically ill son during his last hours and had been at his side when he died. When the official letter from the War Department arrived some time later, it had with it the telltale Gold Star awarded every family who lost a loved one in World War I. Gold Stars hung in windows throughout the country and even in their own neighborhood, but the keepsake didn't lessen the pain or sense of loss. Sherman later referred to his eldest brother's death as one of the "first sad days of our existence."[28] It was a traumatic time that left a permanent mark on eight-year-old Gordon. The experience was something he would not forget.

CHAPTER FOUR

A BOY BECOMES A YOUNG MAN

Life was good for a teenage boy living in Salt Lake City in the 1920s. Though Gordon had chores and other responsibilities, both on the farm and in the big house downtown, pressures were few and opportunities plentiful.

He may have balked at going to first grade, and he had been less than enthusiastic about most of grade school and junior high, but when Gordon entered LDS High School, his attitude about education changed dramatically. There was great morale and rapport among the student body—a "tremendous spirit," as he called it—and once he began to identify his interests and talents, learning took on new appeal.

Even as a teenager Gordon had an apparent flair for language. His appetite for literature developed naturally, and it was not uncommon to find him at the large table in the library, digesting another book. Not all of his natural talents were cerebral, however, for he also had excellent mechanical instincts. He loved to tinker with almost anything. When the gramophone broke, he could always get it playing again. Asa Kienke, his high school shop teacher, instilled in him a love for sharp tools and sweet-smelling wood. When Gordon was twelve, Bryant gave him and Sherman a set of tools, and together the boys built and carved a variety of creations: doll furniture for their sisters, household items for Ada, and other "inventions." Gordon took a drafting class in junior high and found that he enjoyed sketching cars and houses, which he drew to scale with every detail in place. He worked for hours on the Model T, taking it out for road tests and then tinkering some more.

As with most teenagers, what went on outside the home became increasingly important to Gordon. The Liberty Stake First Ward provided a gathering place for neighborhood youth. Roadshows, plays, speech contests, dances, and an almost endless array of other activities provided them with opportunities to spend time together while also staying involved in the Church. The ward was *the* place to be.

Across the street from the Hinckleys lived the family of Georgetta and LeRoy Pay, whose daughter Marjorie first caught Gordon's eye when, as a girl in pigtails, she gave a reading at a ward social. He noticed her dark, naturally curly hair and big brown eyes, but he also observed how talented she was in front of an audience. Gordon's sister Ramona later said: "Marge was polished and impressive, even as a young girl, in giving readings and performances in our ward. All the other kids would just stand up and mumble through something, but Marjorie was downright professional."[1]

Many families in the ward were large and struggled to make ends meet. But most were honest, God-fearing people who owned their homes and were trying to rear responsible children. Outside distractions were few, though Gordon was fascinated when the family acquired its first crystal-set radio with earphones. The twelve-year-old enjoyed listening to the KZN Deseret News radio station, the forerunner of KSL.

Other things also captured the attention of a teenage boy. When President Warren G. Harding visited Salt Lake City in June 1923, the city turned out en masse to honor the chief executive. With hundreds of other children and youth, Gordon and his siblings lined the streets of Salt Lake City to wave flags as the president's motorcade drove by. For his part, the president was impressed with what he found in Utah: "I have found a new slogan in your wonderful country, which I am delighted to adopt, namely, the one which refers to 'Utah's best crop.' I do not know when I have seen so many happy, smiling, sturdy children in so short a period of travel. A thousand delights have come to us in getting more intimately acquainted with your wonderful country . . . but I love, above all else, the boyhood and girlhood of marvelous Utah."[2]

Perhaps no event in the 1920s was more exciting for a teenage boy, however, than Charles Lindbergh's solo New-York-to-Paris nonstop flight in his single-engine plane, *The Spirit of St. Louis*. Newsboys ran through the streets shouting "Extra!" as they peddled special editions of the paper. Lindbergh instantly became a hero larger than life, someone who had taken on the impossible and succeeded. Just a month from turning seventeen, Gordon was caught up in the exhilaration of Lindbergh's triumph and stirred by the realization that nothing in this day and age was impossible. The world was waiting to be conquered.[3]

There was always an awareness in the Hinckley home of what was going on in the world around them, but the Church came first. Ada served in various auxiliary presidencies on both ward and stake levels, and Bryant served as second counselor in the stake presidency from 1907 to 1919 and then as first counselor until 1925. That year he was named president of the Liberty Stake—the largest stake in the Church, with some fifteen thousand members living within its boundaries. He would serve in this capacity until 1936.[4]

By virtue of the fact that he led the largest stake in the Church, and one that was located only a few blocks from Church headquarters, Bryant Hinckley's influence extended beyond the boundaries of his stake. He was a prolific author and an eloquent speaker who had the reputation of giving the best two-and-a-half-minute talks in the Church; he even spoke in general conference on occasion. Bryant felt passionately about the sacrifices and contributions of his forebears, and he wrote widely on Restoration and pioneer themes and published numerous articles about Church leaders. At one time he undertook a series of short biographies of members of the Quorum of the Twelve, published in the *Improvement Era.* For many years it was more common than not to see his byline in the *Era*, the *Instructor*, and the *Millennial Star*. In several books, hundreds of pamphlets, talks, and articles, and dozens of lesson manuals for Sunday School, MIA, and priesthood courses of study, he bore testimony of the gospel of Jesus Christ.

Bryant's name became a household word in Salt Lake City, where he regularly spoke to a wide listening audience on a Church radio series broadcast over KSL. His brother Alonzo, who was later called to the Quorum of the Twelve, wrote from the West Coast while serving as a mission president: "I receive many high compliments that I do not earn at all and they should in all righteousness be sent to you. I am often given credit for having delivered the series of sermons over the radio so I shine largely by borrowed light but I try faithfully to accord the glory and honor to whom it belongs."[5]

Bryant's files bulged with letters as his voice and pen became well-known and highly respected. When he spoke, he painted with broad and often poetic strokes a vision of what could be. Part of his appeal was no doubt his practical approach to the gospel: "What Is Religion?" he posed in one article. "We like to think of religion in terms of fine living, not as doctrine in cold storage. Religion can have very little significance when removed from life. In other words, a man's religion isn't worth much and it will never save him, if it does not carry over into the details of his daily life."[6]

Bryant's themes were not lost on Gordon, who absorbed what his father had to say. Though Bryant sermonized from the pulpit, there was very little preaching around the house. But he was a storyteller and an avid reader of biography and history, and he had a knack for extracting inspiring examples from the lives of those he studied and referring to them when occasion warranted. His subjects ranged from faithful forebears and Church members to heroes and heroines through the ages whose lives were worthy of emulation. Abraham Lincoln was a hero to him, as were George Washington and others of the Founding Fathers whose personal sacrifice had brought forth a land where people were free to embrace their own convictions. Bryant believed that one should expect the best in others, that there was decency and goodness in the common man and nobility in the working class. He explained to his posterity on one occasion: "There is no royalty like the royalty of high endeavor. We do not belong to a family of geniuses. We cannot depend upon our good looks or our native brilliance of mind to carry us forward. Each of us must pay the price of hard work if we achieve. We belong to the working class—a distinction. Only workers are found among the chosen people. Honesty, industry, and common sense make a good combination."[7]

If it was somehow noble to be among the working class, in the late twenties and early thirties it was also tremendously challenging. Though Herbert Hoover told the American people, as he accepted the Republican nomination for president in 1928, that "we in America today are nearer to the final triumph over poverty than ever before in the history of any land,"[8] in reality the society built upon the veneer of post–World War I prosperity was on the verge of economic collapse. On October 24, 1929, the stock market crashed, and by year's end some fourteen billion dollars of personal wealth had vanished.

Though a relative few were directly affected by the crash itself, a severe and sustained economic slump followed the Wall Street catastrophe. By December 1929 the number of unemployed workers in the United States leaped from half a million to more than four million, and by the spring of 1933 nearly one of every three wage earners was out of work, or nearly fifteen million people. Soup kitchens, bread lines, and Hoovervilles where the homeless lived in makeshift quarters sprang up in big cities around the country; so many men sold apples on street corners that the Bureau of the Census classified them as employed. As weeks and then months rolled by without much improvement, and it became clear that the economic situation was more than a temporary downturn, the emotional and social climate suffered as well.[9]

Conditions in Salt Lake City were no different. The Depression affected everybody, and its impact was quickly felt. As a stake president, Bryant Hinckley faced the challenge of not only caring for his own family but helping those within his stewardship as well, for the crisis cut a wide swath through the spiritual, temporal, and emotional well-being of his people. Men with good jobs suddenly found themselves out of work. Blue- and white-collar workers alike went from odd job to odd job. One family in the neighborhood lost their home because they could no longer meet the payment of eight dollars a month. Decades later, Gordon recalled: "Those were tough, tough, tough days.

No one who didn't go through them knows how difficult they were."[10]

Somehow the Deseret Gym stayed open, though not without a struggle. For an extended period Bryant received only a portion of his $3,000 annual salary, dividing up the remainder among employees who needed it to live on.[11] He and Ada repaired, mended, refurbished, or simply went without. But there was always food on the table, and the family's clothing was clean and pressed, if not always fashionable. Somehow Bryant managed to pay the taxes on the property he had accumulated.

Gordon graduated from LDS High School in 1928 and enrolled in the University of Utah that fall, just a year before the onset of the Depression. His good friend, and the smallest young man in his graduating class, G. Homer Durham, wrote in his yearbook: "I'll grow one of these days. Remember, you were my size in the eighth grade." Though Gordon was never overpowering in size, there were other ways in which he comfortably exerted himself. His intellect and mental acumen were keen, and, as he intended to prepare himself to earn a respectable living, education loomed large in his future. He expected to work, and work hard—but he wanted to labor at something he enjoyed and through which he could make a contribution. He had once entertained thoughts of being an architect, but as college approached he decided to pursue a different course.

When he went to register at the University of Utah, he found to his chagrin that all sections of freshman English were filled. Then the English department added another section to accommodate the latecomers and brought in three older professors, each an accomplished educator, to rotate teaching the class. Gordon was a beneficiary of this change, for from George Marshall, regarded as the most competent grammarian in the state, he learned the intricacies of grammar. Marshall was a stickler, and Gordon took naturally to his tutoring, as it proved an extension of his mother's insistence that her children speak with precision.

Louis Zucker was another of Gordon's instructors. A bright man from the East, he was ruthless in his critiques of writing, but his classes were stimulating and motivating. Gordon progressed noticeably under his tutelage, and in return Zucker took an interest in him. Other courses were equally compelling and rigorous:

classes in Milton and Longfellow, Emerson and Carlyle, Shakespeare, and other European literature from Chaucer to modern writers. He also pursued a minor in Latin and Greek and read the *Iliad* and the *Odyssey* as well as some of the New Testament in Greek. He took courses in classical languages, anthropology, economics, sociology, and geology. His was a liberal arts education that provided a well-rounded background.

During these days of the Depression it was not easy to stay in school. Tuition for the School of Arts and Sciences was nineteen dollars a quarter,[12] a sum that was hard to come by. A bowl of boiled wheat with figs, topped with sugar and cream, could be had for a dime at the campus cafeteria, and that dish was a staple for Gordon. Textbooks were expensive, and when possible he did without, though he purchased his Shakespeare text and hung on to it throughout his life. He worked his way through college, paying all of his own tuition and fees, by handling routine maintenance at the Deseret Gym.

During his four years of study, he acquired an enviable familiarity with the great writers of English literature, and he could converse intelligently about them and quote familiar passages at will. As he progressed in his undergraduate studies, Gordon decided he would work toward studying journalism in graduate school, and he began to save money for that purpose.

Few people came through the Depression unscathed. It was a dark era, and many people became pessimistic and cynical as they struggled to survive. Traditional standards and values were questioned by even the faithful, and the political and social air reeked with insecurity and doubt. For many, life was a grim exercise in endurance.

As Gordon worked his way through the university and made the transition from dependence upon his parents to personal responsibility, he, like many of his peers, began to question assumptions about life, the world, and even the Church. His concerns were compounded by the cynicism of the times. "Only those who lived through that era could really ever understand the depth of the economic catastrophe that hit the nation," he later explained. "It was a time of terrible discouragement, and it was felt strongly on campus. I felt some of it myself. I began to question some things, including perhaps in a slight measure the faith of my parents. That is not unusual for university students, but the atmosphere was particularly acute at that time."[13]

Fortunately, he was able to discuss some of his concerns with his father, and together they explored the questions he raised: the fallibility of the Brethren, why difficult things happen to people who are living the gospel, why God allows some of His children to suffer, and so on. The environment of faith that permeated Gordon's home was vital during this period of searching, as he later explained: "My father and mother were absolutely solid in their faith. They didn't try to push the gospel down my throat or compel me to participate, but they didn't back away from expressing their feelings either. My father was wise and judicious and was not dogmatic. He had taught university students and appreciated young people along with their points of view and difficulties. He had a tolerant, understanding attitude and was willing to talk about anything I had on my mind."[14]

Underneath Gordon's questions and critical attitude lay a thread of faith that had been long in the weaving. Little by little, despite his questions and doubts, he realized that he had a testimony he could not deny. And though he began to understand that there wasn't always a clear-cut or easy answer for every difficult question, he also found that his faith in God transcended his doubts. Since that evening many years earlier when he had attended his first stake priesthood meeting, he had known that Joseph Smith was a prophet: "The testimony which had come to me as a boy remained with me and became as a bulwark to which I could cling during those very difficult years," he said.[15]

Gordon subsequently reflected on the key elements that pulled him through that confusing era: "There was for me an underlying foundation of love that came from great parents and a good family, a wonderful bishop, devoted and faithful teachers, and the scriptures to read and ponder. Although in my youth I had trouble understanding many things, there was in my heart something of a love for God and his great work that carried me above any doubts and fears. I loved the Lord and I loved good and honorable friends. From such love I drew great strength."[16]

As he was searching for truth, Gordon became well versed in the gospel, and his talent as a communicator gained him a reputation as an excellent speaker. On one occasion U.S. Senator Reed Smoot was scheduled to speak at sacrament meeting in the First Ward. When an unexpected problem took the senator away, Bishop Duncan improvised by asking Gordon and his home teaching companion, Bob Sonntag—both of whom were just twenty years old—to fill in. Gordon had to take his watering turn at the farm that afternoon but made it back to the meetinghouse in time to be on the stand with his friend as an overflow crowd gathered, expecting to hear a message from Senator Smoot. Although the audience members were no doubt initially disappointed to find the senator replaced by two young men, they apparently were not unhappy with the outcome. Said Bob Sonntag, "When Gordy Hinckley finished speaking, people had forgotten all about Senator Smoot's absence. The boy really stirred them."[17]

As troubling as his young adult years had been, there were other challenges that taxed Gordon's faith and tested his emotional stamina even further. One day Sherman was working alongside his father in the orchard when Bryant suddenly broke down and began to cry. Sherman, who wasn't quite sixteen, was unnerved. He had never seen such an outburst from his father, who was nearly always the picture of deportment and good cheer. "Your mother has cancer," Bryant finally admitted. A small lump in Ada's left breast had been diagnosed as malignant; her physician subsequently performed a radical mastectomy and pronounced her chances for survival good. For a couple of years, she got along well; though the threat of cancer lurked in the perimeter, there was reason to believe that she had beaten the disease. But it was not to be. In March 1930 Ada accompanied Bryant on a trip to the East Coast, and by the time they returned her left arm was swollen and she was in considerable pain. The doctor's diagnosis was grim: the cancer had returned.

Ada immediately began taking radium treatments, which made her violently ill. In the evenings she and Bryant would sit on a bench outside the farmhouse, and Gordon couldn't bear to watch them together. Even worse, the fear of what lay ahead was suffocating. On the one hand, he tried desperately to exercise faith in the Lord and to plead for his mother's healing; on the other, it was hard not to fear the worst. For the Hinckleys, summer and fall that year were clouded with anxiety and apprehension.

Despite Ada's rapidly declining health and the unspoken reality that she probably had but a short time to live, she insisted on accompanying her daughter-in-law Beulah on a Gold Star Pilgrimage—an all-expenses-paid expedition for the mothers and widows of servicemen who had lost their lives in World War I—to Europe to visit Stanford's grave in July. Bryant was apprehensive about letting his wife go without him, but Ada insisted; she and Beulah joined thirteen other women from Utah on the trip.[18]

Frail health notwithstanding, Ada enjoyed the experience immensely. Her letters home assured Bryant that her sense of humor and optimistic spirit hadn't been undermined by the disease that ravaged her body. From the train en route to New York City, she described the first leg of the journey: "Most of the women are much older than I, the eldest being 77, and some have never ridden on a train before. . . . I have laughed myself sick over their experiences. . . . [One] woman didn't know how to turn off her light. She pushed every hole, screw, and button but the right one and finally left the light burning all night. . . . Then her daughters had insisted on her getting a new Spirella corset. . . . This new corset reaches from her armpits down below her thighs. She went through all kinds of contortions trying to get it off and finally gave up and slept in it all night. So with the light and the corset, she feels a wreck this morning. I laughed myself sick while she was telling it. . . . But they are all wonderful women, all battle-scarred, but cheerful and philosophical and are good sports."[19]

The group sailed on the *S.S. George Washington* from Hoboken, New Jersey, and Ada took in everything her stamina would allow. She befriended missionaries on board, made new friends, and once in Europe made copious notes about what she saw—Versailles with its beautiful gardens, the Louvre and Notre Dame, and other exotic historical sites. The sweetest experiences, however, were her visits to the American Military Cemetery at Suresnes outside of Paris, where Stanford was buried. The cemetery was situated on a serene and gentle slope near the Seine on Mount Valerian, a famous French shrine. On the day of her last visit there she recorded in her journal: "Visited for the last time Suresnes cemetery. Came away with the satisfied feeling that the American dead could not be better cared for, and [a] more beautiful memorial could not be built. The government is sparing no effort in an attempt to compensate for the terrible but seemingly unavoidable loss of life in the world war."[20]

The trip would have been better only if Bryant had been with her, and she repeatedly lamented that she longed to have him there. In one letter she yearned, "How I wish and wish you were with me," and two days later from Paris she wrote, "We are in one of the best hotels in Paris and are being treated royally, but every time I go anyplace I wish you were with me."[21]

It wasn't until she had been gone nearly two weeks that Ada mentioned her health: "I'm feeling pretty well. . . . Don't forget to pray for me. I need faith and prayer more than anything else in the world. I haven't told a soul, not even Beulah, that I'm not well. I don't want any of them to know. I will get along better if they don't know, but I have to appeal to the Lord often. After all He is the only one who can help me and I'm sure He will not forsake me at this time."[22]

But when Ada stepped off the train in Salt Lake City in late August, one look told Bryant that his wife's condition had deteriorated. Ruth later recorded her memories of that time: "Immediately after [Mother's] return she started going downhill fast. She suffered such excruciating pain constantly that it was almost too pitiful to bear. But I have never witnessed such an uncomplaining little soldier. I had graduated from high school and in the fall offered to stay home and care for her, but she would have none of it."[23] Despite her mother's protests, Ruth opted to attend the university only half days and did her best to keep up the large house and care for Ada in the afternoons.

Bryant, who was desperate to find something that would cure his wife or at least delay her decline, learned of two noted physicians in Los Angeles who had developed a possible cancer cure. In early October, he sent Ada and her sister Mary to California so Ada could receive the Coffey-Humber treatment. Although the potent drugs eased her pain, they did nothing to halt the progression of the disease. In early November, Mary sent word that Bryant should come to California immediately, and he left on the next train. Perhaps in an effort to prepare his children for what appeared imminent, he wrote home after arriving: "Mama seems a little weary, otherwise not much change this morning. We are hoping for an improvement but are reconciled to what ever may come. Thus far we have done all that we could do and we seem powerless. She is in the hands of the Lord. He can spare her life and raise her and if it is his will, she will live. If not, all will be well. There is a very tranquil and sweet influence here. . . . Mama is just as calm and patient as an angel can be. Go about and do your work and do what is right and all will be well with us."[24]

To the end, Ada demonstrated the kind of faith that had characterized her life. She wanted to live but did not fear what lay beyond the veil. She was concerned for her children but was thankful that, thus far, they had been true to the gospel. Said her sister Ardella: "I did not think such courage possible. She looked out on eternity with trust and perfect faith. He who had taught her how to live surely taught her how to die."[25]

On a beautiful Sunday morning, November 9, 1930, Ada Bitner Hinckley passed away. For Gordon and his brothers and sisters, time seemed to stop. Gordon had never felt such emptiness or hurt. He and his siblings went to the train depot to greet their father as he arrived home from California, but it seemed unbelievable—inconceivable—that the hearse parked near the station was waiting to take their mother's body to the mortuary. Gordon said later, "My brokenhearted father . . . stepped off the train and greeted his grief-stricken children. We walked solemnly down the station platform to the baggage car, where the casket was unloaded and taken by the mortician. We came to know even more [than we had] about the tenderness of our father's heart. . . . I also came to know something of death—the absolute devastation of children losing their mother—but also of peace without pain, and the certainty that death cannot be the end of the soul."[26]

It was a somber, gray day, Thursday, the thirteenth of November, when Ada was laid to rest. Gordon said later: "We put on a front of bravery and fought back the tears. But inside, the wounds were deep and painful."[27] For Bryant it was beyond comprehension to be living through this nightmare again. For his children the experience was devastating: some of them had now lost two mothers. Gordon was twenty years old; his youngest sister, Sylvia, ten. Regardless of age, they mourned the loss of the woman who had made their home such a place of warmth, good cheer, and security.

With Ada's death, Bryant once again faced the ominous responsibility of rearing a large family alone and of coping with the pain of separation from a woman he loved and cherished—this time after twenty-one years together. For Gordon, the first few months after his mother's death crept by in slow motion. Adjusting to her loss was more painful than he would have ever imagined. All the world looked gray, and it was hard to conceive of ever feeling carefree again. As Ada's oldest child, he had enjoyed a close, trusting relationship with his mother. She had nursed him through one childhood illness after another, and in many ways, he had become a reflection of her—a bright, artistic young man with a love for learning and a natural tendency to be both faithful and full of faith. He wished now that he had felt less awkward about telling his mother how much he loved her, yet such open expressions hadn't been their family's way. Now he and the rest of the family bore their grief in silence.

Ada's death punctuated the already gloomy era. Coping with the Depression was challenge enough—to somehow put on a happy face and salvage the upcoming Christmas seemed impossible. Three years later, on another Christmas, Gordon wrote his father and reflected on that holiday season: "I remember well that first Christmas without mother. I was as tall as you then, and we were both awkward in wrapping and setting out presents, weren't we? You smiled a Merry Christmas; we all tried to. But I thought I saw a tear behind that smile."[28] Ruth was sixteen at the time, and she later confessed, "It was very difficult that year for anyone to take away the heartache."[29]

As hard as it was to adjust to life without their sweetheart and mother, the Hinckleys pressed forward, taking one day at a time. For as long as he could remember, Gordon had heard his father say that things might not always go the way you wished, but the challenge was to move forward and never look back. "Never looking back" was a Hinckley family trait. With his mother's absence, however, Gordon occasionally found himself reflecting on the tremendous wealth of the home in which he had been nurtured—a wealth measured not in dollars but in love, support, and caring. "There was a residual that remained with us that gave us strength and guidance and discipline," he said later. "From Mother I learned so many things, including respect for womanhood, together with an appreciation for the tremendous strength which she carried within her, including a bright and happy zest for life."[30]

As his mother's oldest child, Gordon felt responsible to help his brother and sisters adjust to their new circumstances, and he became a surrogate parent of sorts. For example, he set aside money from his graduate school savings to buy Ramona a dress for an important high school event. And when daily household chores went undone, he outlined a work schedule for his younger siblings and saw to it that the cleaning woman knew what tasks needed to be completed.[31]

Perhaps Gordon assumed that life would go on as usual, with him shouldering some of the burden at home and helping shepherd his younger brothers and sisters along. So he wasn't prepared for the day, early in 1932, when Bryant called his children together and announced that he was going to marry again. His intended was May Green, the office manager at the Salt Lake Clinic. May was a woman of great capacity, a hard worker with an infectious sense of humor. But as far as Gordon was concerned, her virtues were irrelevant. He was determined to preserve his mother's memory and upset that his father was prepared to replace her.

When Bryant announced his intentions to his children, the resulting silence was deafening. He was so nervous that he shook visibly at the encounter. "In our wildest dreams," Ramona said, "I don't think we imagined Father would remarry. We just couldn't imagine him with anyone but Mother."[32] A couple of nights later Bryant returned home late to find Gordon in the library studying for finals. Gordon was obviously still troubled, for when Bryant tried to initiate a conversation he made a remark that stirred up the issue again. Their discussion was becoming emotional when Bryant finally asked his son, "Do you want me to grow old alone? Do you want your sisters to feel responsible for taking care of me when I get to be an old man?"

He reassured Gordon that he loved Ada dearly and that his feelings for her would never fade. But he also acknowledged how lonely his existence would be if he were forced to live the rest of his life in solitude. Father and son talked into the night, and Gordon's heart softened as he saw in a new light how devastating his mother's death had been for his father.

On February 22, 1932, Bryant married May, who, as a young woman, had been promised in her patriarchal blessing that she would marry and be a mother to many children. At first there were tensions and awkward moments between the children and their new stepmother. May didn't do things the way Ada had, and it was difficult for the children to see their father show affection to anyone other than their mother. But in time Aunt May—as the children called her—won a place in their hearts. From the outset she made it clear that she had no intention of trying to replace Ada, and that she wanted only to make her own place.

May was sensitive to the fact that her husband had been happily married twice before and that Christine's and Ada's children needed the assurance that their mothers had not been forgotten. For Christmas 1933 she gathered family photos and pasted into a scrapbook those of Bryant and the home where he was born. Then she arranged photos of each of the thirteen children and, for those who were married, of their spouses and children. Finally, she asked each child to write a letter to Bryant, to be added to the scrapbook. May completed the gift with a poem of her own composing:

It mars not the passing of present hours
The recollection of fragrant flowers.
So with the sentiment of companions dear,
Who may have gone, but yet are near,
I, too, add my sentiment of you,
Expressing the love of the other two
You're a sweetheart, a lover true.
A kind and dutiful husband, too.
From the bottom of our hearts, we say:
We love you—Christine, Ada, and May.

May
Christmas 1933

In time, Gordon and his brothers and sisters grew to love the woman who so eagerly loved them. "We were not little children, but she took hold of [our] family, not in any officious way," Gordon later said. "I don't know that it was easy for her to step into our family, but she did it well. We all respected her. We all loved her."[33]

The younger girls in particular became attached to their stepmother, but May found ways to nurture the older children as well. "I remember a time when I was terribly discouraged, and I was brooding," Gordon reflected later. "I was sitting [in the library] reading, but not reading, just sympathizing with myself. She came in, and in a quiet, very understanding way talked to me. I don't know what the adversity was, but it didn't look to be much of an adversity after she had finished talking with me.

"She could pour oil on troubled waters," he continued. "There are little differences that occur in every family, in the very nature of family life, and she knew how to subdue those feelings. We're a strong-willed, outspoken family. I never heard her, in all my experience, give an unkind retort to anything that was said."[34]

Despite the emotional interruptions occasioned by his mother's death and his father's subsequent remarriage, Gordon pressed toward graduation. In June 1932 he was awarded a bachelor of arts degree, with a major in English and a minor in ancient languages, from the University of Utah. Bryant was proud of his son's persistence, but Gordon couldn't help but imagine how delighted his mother would have been. He hoped she somehow knew. His graduation was an important milestone, even in an era when prospects for the future looked dim. Unemployment was still roughly 30 percent nationwide and higher than that in Utah.

Determined to further advance his education and to better prepare himself for his life's work, Gordon intended to enroll at the Columbia University School of Journalism in New York City, then considered perhaps the finest journalism school in the country. Years later he counseled: "Whatever you choose to do, train for it. Qualify yourselves. Take advantage of the experience and learning of those who have gone before you in whatever field you choose. Education is a shortcut to proficiency. It makes it possible to leapfrog over the mistakes of the past."[35]

As it turned out, however, Gordon's preparation was to be more expansive and far different from what he had envisioned. On a Sunday afternoon not long before his twenty-third birthday, Gordon was invited to Bishop Duncan's home. The bishop got right to the point: Had he thought of serving a mission? He was shocked. In those days of depression, missionary service was the exception rather than the rule. The distressing financial picture had made the burden of supporting a missionary virtually impossible for most families; indeed, few missionaries were even being called. Nevertheless, as soon as his bishop raised the subject, he knew what his answer must be: he told Bishop Duncan he would go.

The reality of financing the mission loomed, however. Bryant assured his son they would find a way, and Sherman volunteered to help. Gordon planned to devote the modest savings he had accumulated for graduate school. Unfortunately, not long after he committed to go, the bank where he had established his savings account failed and he lost everything. But some time later the family discovered that for years Ada had nurtured a small savings account with the coins she received in change when buying groceries and had earmarked the fund for her sons' missionary service. Gordon was overwhelmed with his mother's years of quiet sacrifice and prescient foresight. Even after her death she continued to support and sustain him. More important was his mother's example of consecration, and he considered sacred the money he received from her savings.

In those days missionaries were asked where they would like to serve. French was the international diplomatic language, and with his interest in journalism in mind and some self-interest motivating his recommendation, Gordon suggested France. But it was not to be. When his call arrived, he learned that he was needed on the other side of the English Channel, in the heart of one of the most literary regions of the world. Elder Gordon B. Hinckley had been called to serve in the European Mission, headquartered in London, England.

Many years later a mature Gordon said: "Every child, with few possible exceptions, is the product of a home, be it good, bad, or indifferent. As children grow through the years, their lives, in large measure, become an extension and a reflection of family teaching."[36] He himself was the product of a home filled with love and based on a carefully defined set of values and a general sense of well-being and optimism. Though as a boy and young man he had faced illness, disappointment, doubt, and heartache, he had also developed a reservoir of faith and a sense of family heritage that together formed a steady anchor. As his father later said to his posterity: "Remember you are not ordinary people. Whenever your names are mentioned I want to hear something good about you. Inheritance can't make you great, but it can always be a source of inspiration and encouragement."[37]

It was a theme that was not lost on Gordon, who from the time of his youth had felt a responsibility and desire to live up to his heritage and to bring honor to his parents' name. Many years later, after he had become a father, grandfather, and great-grandfather himself, he reflected on his beginnings: "I have experienced my share of disappointments, of failures, of difficulties. But on balance, life has been very good. I have tried to live it with enthusiasm and appreciation. I have known much of happiness, oh, so very much. The root of it all, I believe, was planted in my childhood and nurtured in the home. . . . I cannot be grateful enough."[38]

CHAPTER FIVE

A MISSION AND BEYOND

The news that Gordon Hinckley had been called to the British Isles created quite a stir around the First Ward. Serving a mission was not even a topic of discussion in most LDS households. Missions cost money, and most families were doing well just to keep a roof over their heads. Few young men and women were both willing and able to accept a mission call. Gordon Hinckley was one of just 525 missionaries who would be sent to the thirty-one operating missions that year. To complicate matters, living in England was inordinately expensive, costing what would have been the equivalent of roughly $500 a month in 1990 dollars.[1]

As of late Gordon and Marjorie Pay, the girl across the street, whom he had begun to court, had become increasingly interested in each other. She wanted him to serve a mission, so when the call was announced she was thrilled. But as the day neared for his entrance into the mission home, she began to sense how much she would miss this young man who had become her best friend and confidant. She would be nearly twenty-four years of age when he returned. Would she still be single? And how would he feel about her? There was no way of knowing what the days ahead would bring. She was certain of one thing, though: It would be hard to have him gone, but it was right for him to go.

On Sunday, June 11, 1933, a farewell testimonial was held in the First Ward for the departing Elder Hinckley, who then reported to the Mission Home, just north of the Beehive House on State Street in Salt Lake City. During his week there, he was set apart as a full-time missionary by Elder George Albert Smith, and he went through the Salt Lake Temple for the first time. He and his missionary colleagues also received instruction from various General Authorities, among them Elder David O. McKay, who asked each elder and sister to write an essay on what it meant to be a missionary. Elder Hinckley complied, and a couple of days later he was summoned to Elder McKay's office. When he presented himself before the apostle, he found his essay lying on the desk. Elder McKay complimented Gordon on both the style and the content of his writing and added that it was the best he had seen. He wondered if Gordon would mind if he quoted from it. Gordon was both surprised and pleased.

But as Elder Hinckley prepared to board the train at the Union Pacific Depot in Salt Lake City a few days later, he was less confident and even apprehensive about what lay ahead. His father, who must have anticipated his son's concerns, handed him a card on which he had written five words, the words of the Lord to Jairus when the ruler received news of his daughter's death: "Be not afraid, only believe" (Mark 5:36). Then with a quick but warm good-bye to family and friends, including Marjorie—who had come to see off her best friend with the understanding that there was no understanding between them—he was gone. "As anxious as I was for him to serve a mission," Marjorie said later, "I will never forget the feeling of emptiness and loneliness I felt when that train pulled out of the station."[2]

Gordon and his traveling companions purchased coach seats on a train headed east to Chicago, where the 1933 World's Fair was under way. Bryant had obtained permission for his son to spend one night with an aunt living there and to accompany her to the fair, so he separated himself from the other missionaries, promising to meet them in New York City the next day.

In the meantime, he was fascinated with both Chicago, the largest city he had ever seen, and the Chicago World's Fair, which despite being held during the Depression drew more than thirty-eight million people with its upbeat theme, "A Century of Progress." The fair intrigued Elder Hinckley, who was taken with the exposition's futuristic aspects and the imaginative creations on display. He also enjoyed the Church's exhibit. The Windy City lived up to its name, though; while there he got a cinder in his eye that caused so much swelling he could barely see. The ailment was still causing him difficulty when he caught the train to New York City and with his two traveling companions—Elder Hoggan and Sister Cullimore—

boarded the SS *Manhattan* for the weeklong ocean crossing to England.

It was all a little overwhelming for Elder Hinckley, who celebrated his twenty-third birthday on the high seas. How quickly life could change! Just weeks earlier he had been focused on the Columbia School of Journalism; now here he was in the middle of the Atlantic on his way to a foreign country. There would be no language barrier, but he imagined that dealing with the British would be far different from anything he had experienced in the Liberty Stake. For a young man who thought of himself as backward, a self-impression that stemmed from his inherent shyness, the prospects of what lay ahead were intimidating. He couldn't quite imagine approaching a stranger and striking up a conversation about the gospel.

While on board ship, Elder Hinckley pulled out the patriarchal blessing he had received at age eleven from patriarch Thomas E. Callister. He couldn't remember having read it since the day the patriarch had come to the Hinckley home and pronounced blessings upon him and several of his brothers and sisters, but now he was interested in reviewing those promises made a dozen years earlier. "Thou shalt grow to the full stature of manhood and shall become a mighty and valiant leader in the midst of Israel," the patriarch had promised. "The Holy Priesthood shall be thine to enjoy and thou shalt minister in the midst of Israel as only those can who are called of God. Thou shalt ever be a messenger of peace; the nations of the earth shall hear thy voice and be brought to a knowledge of the truth by the wonderful testimony which thou shalt bear."[3] Perhaps, he thought, this mission to England would fulfill at least one part of his blessing—that he would bear testimony to the *nations* (England and the United States being a plurality) of the earth.

After nearly a week at sea, the SS *Manhattan* docked at midnight in a port at Cobh, near Cork, Ireland. As Elder Hinckley looked down from the ship's deck, he heard an Irish tenor singing a penetrating rendition of "Danny Boy," and it would forever after be one of his favorite songs. The stop in Ireland was brief, however, with the ship then sailing on to Plymouth, England, where it docked on Tuesday, June 27, 1933.[4] When no one was there to meet them, Elder Hinckley and his two traveling companions took the boat train from Plymouth to London, arriving at Paddington Station around midnight. Again, no one met them, and they found themselves alone in the middle of the night in one of the world's largest cities. With only their resourcefulness to sustain them, they secured rooms at the nearby railway hotel and stayed overnight. The next morning, with the mission address in hand—33 Tavistock Square, London WC1—they headed out. Later in his mission, after Elder Hinckley had lived in London for nearly nineteen months, he couldn't imagine how they had found their way around the intimidating English metropolis that first day alone.

Despite their inhospitable introduction to England and its capital city, the trio arrived at the mission home unscathed. Elder Hinckley had been called to serve in the European Mission, then under the direction of President John A. Widtsoe, but President Widtsoe was traveling on the Continent and he had asked British Mission President James H. Douglas to put the new elder to work. The five-foot-ten missionary who arrived in England weighing a scant 143 pounds had a brief interview with President Douglas and then headed to the Euston train station, having been assigned to labor in the Liverpool Conference, headquartered in Preston, Lancashire, some two hundred miles north. The two companions with whom he had traveled to England stayed behind in London.[5]

Elder Hinckley was on his own, and as he boarded the train for Preston and then watched from the window as London slowly faded from view, he felt terribly alone. Everything was new and unfamiliar. His brief reception at the mission home had not been encouraging or warm. It was hard not to wonder what he had gotten himself into.

Elder Hinckley had been in England less than forty-eight hours when, holding an old, grained-leather satchel in one hand and a briefcase in the other, he stepped onto the flagstone platform of Preston Station in the late afternoon of June 29 and spotted a young American waiting for him. Elder Kent S. Bramwell, a bright and enthusiastic district president from Ogden, Utah, vigorously shook his hand and then led the way to their "digs" at 15 Wadham Road.

Elder Bramwell had no intention of breaking his new companion in gradually, and as they walked home he announced that they were set to hold a street meeting that night at the marketplace in the public square. The thought of preaching to uninterested passersby was daunting, and Elder Hinckley responded immediately, "You've got the wrong man to go with you." But Elder Bramwell was undeterred, and a few hours later the two missionaries walked to the market and began to sing. Gradually a crowd gathered, and both missionaries taught and bore testimony. "I was terrified," Elder Hinckley later admitted. "I stepped up onto that little stand, looked at that crowd of people, and wondered what I was doing there. They were dreadfully poor and looked to have absolutely no interest in religion."[6]

The worldwide depression had hit Lancashire with terrible force. Men who wore no shirts because they couldn't afford them improvised by wearing small dickeys beneath any old jacket they could get their hands on. Their dress and grooming reflected the times in which they lived, and the crowd looked menacing that first night as Gordon peered into their faces. Though all spoke the same language, Gordon was a Westerner from the United States and the people of Preston spoke in a thick Lancashire brogue. In time, as he saw beneath the surface of poverty and came to understand the goodness of the English people, he learned to focus on their similarities rather than their differences. But his missionary initiation was intimidating.

In the providence of the Lord, Gordon had been sent to the area where Heber C. Kimball and his associates of the Twelve had baptized thousands of new members nearly a century earlier. That first night in the town square—or flag market, as the local people called it—Gordon had his introduction to a place laden with history. In Preston Elder Kimball and Brigham Young had first preached the doctrines of the restored gospel of Jesus Christ in the British Isles. Every President of the Church from Brigham Young to Heber J. Grant had labored in England.

In time, Gordon became intimately acquainted with the city that had proved so fertile a field for proselytizing in the nineteenth century. He and his companion often walked the street where Elder Kimball and his colleagues had, their first day in

Preston, come upon a large flag bearing the gilded motto "Truth Will Prevail," which they took as a sign that the Lord had them in his keeping. Elder Hinckley visited the lodging house on Saint Wilfred Street where Heber C. Kimball had had a terrifying experience with evil spirits, and passed frequently by the musty, old Vauxhall Chapel where by invitation the early missionaries had preached to a packed house the day after they arrived in Preston. The River Ribble with its tram bridge, where Elder Kimball performed the first baptisms in the area, the Cock Pit and Temperance Hall, and the obelisk in the marketplace all became familiar landmarks. Preston was rich in Church history, and Gordon reveled in the sense of time and place the area gave him.[7]

Nonetheless, the social and religious climate Gordon Hinckley found in Preston differed significantly from that which he had known at home. Homes were smaller than in Salt Lake City, and most were warmed by little fireplaces, sometimes four or five to a house. A common joke among missionaries was that they got warm on one side, then turned and got warm on the other. Many people were on the dole, and even those who weren't didn't have much in the way of temporal goods. The Britishers Elder Hinckley came to know, however, were a high-principled lot, a strong-minded, plainspoken, and straightforward people who knew how to use the King's English properly and who were, by and large, honest men and women.

Religion was a difficult subject to address, however. Many refused to back away from a fundamental question: If there were a God, why would he permit so much suffering? Despite being among the proverbial salt of the earth, the residents of Preston were largely uninterested in and even prejudiced against what they considered to be an upstart American religion. To complicate matters, not long before Elder Hinckley's arrival two missionaries had violated mission rules and been sent home. Their indiscretions had been noised about, giving ammunition to those who claimed that Mormons could not be trusted. It had been little more than a decade since the movie *Trapped by the Mormons*, inspired by Winnifred Graham's inflammatory book of the same title, had inspired widespread anti-Mormon rhetoric throughout the British Isles. Sentiment against the Church, initiated to some degree by the clergy and fostered by the English press, had infected the whole of Britain.

To make matters worse, Elder Hinckley was not well. The lush hillsides and meadows of Lancashire were a more vibrant shade of green than he had ever seen in Utah. Allergic to the grass pollen abundant in the area, Gordon was miserable from the moment he stepped off the train. "In England the grass pollinates and turns to seed in late June and early July, which is exactly when I arrived in Preston," he later remembered. "The day I arrived there I started crying"—tears of hay fever, not homesickness, though his stamina, energy, and frame of mind were at an all-time low. Gordon's outlook might have been brighter had his friend Homer Durham, who was also serving in the Liverpool Conference when he arrived, remained there. But on July 12 Homer was transferred to the British Mission office in London to act as president of the mission YMMIA.

After he had taken as much as he felt he could, Elder Hinckley wrote his father that he wasn't getting anywhere with missionary work, and that he couldn't see the point in wasting his time and his father's money. Responding as both father and stake president, Bryant Hinckley sent a reply that was brief and to the point: "Dear Gordon, I have your recent letter. I have only one suggestion: forget yourself and go to work."

Earlier that day he and his companion had studied the promise recorded in the Gospels: "For whosoever will save his life shall lose it; but whosoever shall lose his life for my sake and the gospel's, the same shall save it" (Mark 8:35). That scripture, combined with his father's counsel, seared his soul. With the letter in hand, he went into his upstairs bedroom at 15 Wadham Road and got on his knees. As he poured out his heart to the Lord, he promised that he would try to forget himself and lose himself in the Lord's service. Many years later he indicated the significance of that series of events: "That July day in 1933 was my day of decision. A new light came into my life and a new joy into my heart. The fog of England seemed to lift, and I saw the sunlight. Everything good that has happened to me since then I can trace back to the decision I made that day in Preston."[8]

The experience proved pivotal, for it was the beginning of a rich and wonderful, though difficult, mission. The routine of studying the gospel and bearing testimony on a regular basis, combined with the personal sacrifice inherent in missionary service, enhanced his convictions in a remarkable way. As time passed, he came to better appreciate what the Brethren who had proselytized there a century earlier had accomplished—under much more difficult circumstances than he now faced. Their mission and sense of vision evoked within him a respect that bordered on awe. Despite their extreme poverty, they had come to England and converted a large congregation of Saints who subsequently infused the blood of Britain into the weakened body of the Church. As Gordon contemplated the faith and courage of Elder Heber C. Kimball and his Brethren, his own faith and spiritual stamina increased.

It was an interesting transition for a young man from Utah to adjust to Church units that were small and sparsely staffed. The branch in Preston met in a shabby, rented hall at 96 Friargate, one flight up from a storefront. The drab brown wallpaper designed in artificial wood grain made the room feel dark. Hanging at the front of the room were dust-covered pictures of the Prophet Joseph Smith and the Savior. Two unshaded bulbs, their cords wound around nails to hold them in place, provided light. The floor was uneven, and chairs were scattered about the room. The branch president tried to keep the few local members active and involved, but with only a small number to draw from, their meetings left something to be desired.

Changing the complexion of the branch was not easy, as the missionary harvest wasn't particularly fruitful. In fall meetings of the Liverpool Conference, held October 1, 1933, in Preston's Prince's Theater (ironically, the purveyor of many anti-Mormon movies), the statistical report recorded by Elder Hinckley indicated that the district included nine branches with a total membership of 765. Since the last conference, held six months earlier, the four missionaries of the district had distributed 13,030 tracts but only nineteen copies of the Book of Mormon. There was no mention of baptisms.[9]

For the most part, the Church throughout England was composed of small, struggling branches. Local leadership was weak, and missionaries often presided over branches and districts. In a descriptive essay that he enclosed in a letter to Marjorie, Elder Hinckley lamented the spiritual malaise of the people: "Old Preston . . . how intimately I learned to know you ere I left you. Cobbled Fishergate lined with shops where the elite buy; Church street whose beginning is marked by the high steeple of the old grey parish church; . . . the old-world flavor of market day when anything from a second hand book on etiquette to a dented teething ring for the baby can be bought; the lazy Ribble that creeps along its tortuous bed to the sea; the flag market where we held our open-air meetings on the same spot from which Brigham Young and other early Saints first expounded the doctrines in England. . . . When will you put away that unwarranted pride, look at yourself for what you are, and accept a word of light that a couple of young fellows are feebly preaching?"[10]

Missionary work had benefits beyond conversions, however. Gordon's testimony and understanding of the gospel grew steadily as he and his companion studied together each morning. Favorite texts were the Book of Mormon and the Gospel of John.

In the mission field Elder Hinckley's literary gifts flourished. He had been in England just a month when his first article in the *Millennial Star* was published. "A Missionary Holiday" recounted the experience he and other missionaries had on July 4 when they visited the beautiful Lake District north of Preston and slept out on a grassy meadow that rose from Lake Windermere and Lake Grasmere. "What a picture! A smooth, glistening pearl set in the quiet of rolling green and wooded hills, the sun of a new day streaking across the waters," he wrote by way of description.[11] In the September 14, 1933, issue of the *Star*, his article expounding on the virtues of the MIA also revealed his philosophy about the effect of the gospel in a person's life: "'Mormonism' is a religion of refinement. It reasons that every man has within him God-possibilities, that salvation is essentially development. It argues that every man is potentially a great man. And through an inspired system, it offers the most extensive facilities in all the world for every man to discover himself and his possibilities, to so live that he can stand on the summit of his life and look back upon a trail of accomplishment and not a slough of wasted energies. Very few at most, and perhaps none of us will ever carve immortal names in the roll call of the great of the earth. Maybe none of us will achieve outside the narrow pale of our immediate surroundings. But this much is certain: happy will be the man or woman who has tapped some hidden resource and given it voice. To such a character will come the sweet satisfying feeling of strengthening powers, of having done something that has made life a little nobler. God has generously blessed us all with talent. . . . Catch the silent thrill of growth!"[12]

Even Gordon's letters showed his journalistic prowess. His were not typical recitations of the week's events. In one letter to Marjorie he included a short essay that described an experience he had on a bus:

> "You're a lot of infamous rats," were the final words of that fat, neatly dressed office manager as he moved toward the door of the bus, throwing the torn bits of my card out of the window without ever reading it.
>
> At the next stop three or four dirty, raggedly clothed colliers boarded the bus. One of these men sat beside me. His red lips and the white of his eyes stood ghostly against the sooty background of his face. His clothing smelled of the damp, gritty dust of the mines. His back and shoulders were muscularly round and broad, his chest hollow. He seemed to whisper as he breathed.
>
> Since small boyhood—all day in the mines, at night recuperating for another day in the mines. What did the heavens, the flowers, the gods mean to such a man? Edwin Markham's words came to my mind:
>
> "Is this the thing the Lord God made and gave
> To have dominion over sea and land;
> To trace the stars and search the heavens for power;
> To feel the passion of eternity?"
>
> I made a try at conversation. "Been a hard day today?"
>
> He turned quickly as if surprised to think that anyone should pay any attention to him. "Yes, we have to do our bit."
>
> We chatted a little about his work. Then I introduced myself and handed him a tract.
>
> "Ta," he said. "I can't read, but our Annie reads to us. Ta." The bus stopped. He nodded good-night, his tea bucket ringing as it hit the door frame. I heard his clogs clattering across the wet cobbles.
>
> For the next five miles I was alone in the bus save for the conductor who was counting his tickets. Rain was beating against the window, and quietly I thought of two men I had met that day.[13]

After having such experiences for four months in Preston, Elder Hinckley was transferred to Nelson, a mill town in Lancashire some thirty miles away. There he saw the ravages of the Depression at its worst.[14] His experience there gave him a great appreciation for "the short and simple annals of the poor," as Thomas Gray described them.[15] The people of Nelson worked hard yet had little.

In Nelson, Elder Hinckley and his companion boarded in a home at 10 Wickworth Street owned by Mr. and Mrs. Ayrton. Though not members of the Church, they were generous people who treated their tenants graciously. The missionaries soon met Robert Pickles, a young man just two years Elder Hinckley's senior whose grandmother had been one of the first individuals baptized in their village. The branch there had an average attendance of twenty or so at Sunday meetings. When Bob first met Elder Hinckley after his transfer to Nelson, he wasn't sure what to make of him: "At first he seemed so serious in nature. But I soon found out that behind his seriousness there was joviality and a good sense of humor."[16] On occasion Elder Hinckley and Bob tracted together, and in those and other experiences the Englishman came to appreciate Elder Hinckley's strengths: "His feelings about the gospel were strong, and he made an impression on me because he had a positive approach to things. Even when there weren't many who wanted to listen to the missionaries, he stayed positive."[17]

Conversions were hard to come by. Elder Hinckley identified at least one reason in a letter to Marjorie: "In walking down the streets of Nelson, England the other day it was interesting to note that with but one exception, every individual walked out into the street to avoid crossing under a ladder that reached up over the walk. . . . Our landlady studiously sets the poker against the grate so that its point is directed up the chimney. She actually believes that this makes the fire draw better. . . . A girl's portrait fell from the mantel the other morning while our landlady was dusting; this was incontrovertible proof that bad news was forthcoming concerning the girl. . . . Is it any wonder that people in Twentieth Century England ignorantly hang on to the notion that Mormons are harem keepers and that Salt Lake City is a walled fortress, a trading metropolis dealing in white slaves?"[18]

After three months in Nelson—November 1933 through January 1934—Elder Hinckley was called back to Preston. But his return to the city he had come to love for its rich tradition was short-lived, for on March 3, 1934, he was transferred to London to work in the European Mission office as assistant to Elder Joseph F. Merrill of the Twelve, who now presided over all the missions in Europe.[19] During eight months in the Liverpool Conference, Gordon had distributed 8,785 tracts and pamphlets, spent more than 400 hours with members, attended 191 meetings, had 200 gospel conversations, confirmed one person, and baptized no one.[20]

When Elder Hinckley received the letter of transfer, he couldn't have been more surprised. He had worked hard in Lancashire, and had earned the respect of members and missionaries for his optimistic nature and ability to teach the gospel with conviction, but there was nothing about his record that would have attracted the attention of the mission office.

London immediately captivated Gordon, who quickly fell in love with this jewel of the far-flung British empire. Perhaps at that time the world's greatest metropolis and capital city, it was a tremendous center for art, music, drama, and commerce. Looking out of a third-floor window at the European Mission office at 5 Gordon Square, Elder Hinckley could see black taxicabs weaving in and out of traffic, little horns mounted on the outside. Bobbies with nightsticks walked the streets. Red mailboxes on street corners symbolized a postal system whose efficiency was unrivaled anywhere in the world. London was intoxicating. The pace, the cosmopolitan nature of the population, the sophisticated culture—it was invigorating for a young man from Salt Lake City. He came to believe that no one could "live in London for long without developing a love for the place."[21] And working side by side with an apostle was a rare privilege for a young missionary; Gordon had never supposed such an opportunity would come to him.

Elder Merrill was a pragmatic, down-to-earth leader, a scientist who, before his call as a General Authority, had been dean of the school of engineering at the University of Utah. Though stern and somewhat somber, he was friendly in a professorial sort of way. Each morning he studied with his young assistant and the two others in the office staff, and they enjoyed stimulating gospel discussions.

Under Elder Merrill's direction fell administrative responsibility for the missions of Europe. In general, the Church was plodding along there and converts were hard to come by. Though Elder Hinckley didn't accompany President Merrill on trips to the Continent, they talked at length each time he returned. And through their many conversations Gordon developed a picture of the Church there as well as in the British Isles.

The European Mission office and the British Mission office were housed in the same building, so missionaries from both offices often worked together. Thus Gordon was reunited with Homer Durham, and the two ate together in the scullery in the basement. There they experimented with unique dishes and enforced an ingenious system for getting money to launder the white linen tablecloth: anyone who soiled the cloth had to cover the stain with coins. Those who served in the European Mission office with Elder and Sister Merrill (including Elder Hinckley; Richard S. Bennett, the associate editor of the *Millennial Star*; Howard Cullimore, the mission secretary; and Lucille Cullimore, Howard's wife) worked in the office during the day and did missionary work at night. Each Sunday they participated in the Southwest London Branch and then held street meetings.

Unless it was raining torrents, two missionaries each from the European and British Mission offices caught the bus from Oxford Street to Hyde Park, where they held a street meeting alongside other preachers and the vendors who had gathered there. After singing and offering prayer, they preached to the unruly crowd from their portable podiums. Occasionally the men and women in attendance were sincerely interested in religion, but more often the street meetings drew an experienced lot of hecklers who relished any opportunity to try to distract and humiliate the young missionaries. It was sport for them, an opportunity for fun. And as long as they didn't physically touch the speakers—which was cause for arrest—they could do anything they wished. Gordon came to particularly enjoy the most experienced hecklers, who held a cane by the end and waved it as close to a missionary's nose as possible without actually touching his face. At the same time they taunted the Americans with shouts of "Aye, lad. Get out of here. Go home, Yank." Elder Hinckley was intrigued with one heckler who always seemed to know when they were there. He enjoyed sparring with the detractor and his cohorts.

Many Sunday afternoons the missionaries repeated the experience at Regents Park. The exercise probably did more for the missionaries than for the masses, for if a missionary was timid, as Elder Hinckley was at the outset, he got over his fear quickly. Street meetings taught the elders to speak with confidence amid confusion and to maintain presence even before a hostile audience. Elder Wendell J. Ashton, who was transferred to the British Mission office in the spring of 1935 to serve as associate editor of the *Millennial Star* and as Gordon's companion, said: "We didn't baptize many people in London in those days, but Elder Hinckley was a knockout in those street meetings on Hyde Park corner. We learned to speak quickly on our feet, and Elder Hinckley was the best of the bunch. He gained tremendous firsthand experience defending the Church and speaking up courageously for its truths."[22]

Gordon had other opportunities to hone his speaking skills. When he was called to teach Primary in the Southwest London Branch, President Merrill told him, "Do it, Brother Hinckley. If you can learn to hold the interest of children, you'll never have difficulty holding the interest of adults."[23] On another occasion he accepted the assignment to teach a group of unruly teenagers who had scared off several instructors. Gordon determined to work on their behavior, and in time the class became one of his joys. He savored the challenge of getting through to uninterested students.

Elder Hinckley's principal teaching responsibility, of course, was missionary related. Elder Merrill was unsatisfied with what few materials existed to help missionaries proselytize. When his assistant demonstrated excellent communication skills in his assignment to oversee the mission's publicity, Elder Merrill asked him to prepare several filmstrips using black-and-white slides as teaching aids. One filmstrip portrayed the coming forth of the Book of Mormon, another highlighted important events from Church history, and a third presented a favorable image of Salt Lake City. Each proved useful in helping missionaries gain entrance to homes and then dispel some of the distasteful rumors that had persisted for years in England about the Mormons.

Elder Hinckley also continued to write, and many of his essays were published in the *Millennial Star*. His range of interest was broad, his ability to express himself enviable. But he may have had his most far-reaching influence as a writer when, in February 1935, the *London Monthly Pictorial* magazine published his article "The Early History of the Latter-day Saints." This seemed to represent a significant shift in the attitude of the London press toward the Church.[24]

Gordon's personal literary efforts may have increased his appreciation for the exposure he received in England to some of the world's finest literature. He had a profound respect for those who thought deeply and expressed themselves eloquently, and England was home to some of the most enduring essayists, poets, and novelists of all time. Consequently he spent what little free time he had feasting on English literature and culture. He and Elder Ashton often spent their preparation days visiting historic sites and attending cultural events. In an article for the *Millennial Star,* Gordon elaborated on his feelings about good books: "It is both relaxing and invigorating to occasionally set aside the worries of life, seek the company of a friendly book and mingle with the great of the earth, counsel with the wise of all time, look into the unlived days with prophets. Youth will delight in the heroic figures of Homer; or more modern, will thrill to the silent courage of Florence Nightingale on the battlefield. . . . The power of Cicero's oratory may awaken new ambitions in middle age, or the absurdity of Don Quixote riding mightily against a windmill may make your own pretentiousness seem ridiculous; if you think the world is against you, get the satisfaction of walking the streets of Athens with Diogenes, lantern in hand in broad daylight in search of an honest man. . . . From the reading of 'good books' there comes a richness of life that can be obtained in no other way. It is not enough to read newspapers. . . . But to become acquainted with real nobility as it walks the pages of history and science and literature is to strengthen character and develop life in its finer meanings."[25]

Quotations from the literature Gordon had studied became more meaningful as he lived in the land of their origin and came to appreciate how nicely some concepts meshed with the gospel. When facing certain challenges, for example, he thought of Robert Browning's statement: "A man's reach should exceed his grasp."[26] If there was any endeavor to which such a motto applied, Gordon thought, it had to be missionary service. Each day new challenges required him to reach further than he had before, to tackle something more complicated than he felt he had the talent or experience to handle.

One morning during their study session, President Merrill showed Elder Hinckley several London newspapers containing reviews on a newly published book claiming to be a history of the Mormons. The book, however, was less than flattering. "Elder Hinckley," President Merrill instructed, "I want you to go down to the publisher and protest the publication of this book." Gordon's immediate reaction was one of fear: "Why are you sending *me*? I am just a boy, and you're a distinguished man. Why don't you go yourself?" He kept his thoughts to himself, however, and agreed to go.

Although his exterior appeared calm, Gordon's stomach churned. The assignment was more than a little frightening. But he went to his room and knelt in prayer, wondering if this was how Moses felt when the Lord told him to go and see Pharaoh. Believing the Lord would help him, he caught the underground to Fleet Street and the offices of Skeffington and Son, Ltd., of England, publisher of the offending book.

With the boldness of a young missionary, Gordon presented his card to the receptionist and asked to see Mr. Skeffington. She disappeared into an inner office, then returned to tell him that the publisher was too busy to give him an audience. Elder Hinckley announced that he was there representing the Mormon church, that he had come five thousand miles, and that he would be happy to wait. During the next hour the receptionist darted back and forth to Mr. Skeffington's office. Finally she indicated that Gordon could have a few minutes with the publisher.

At that, Elder Hinckley walked into a large office and introduced himself to the man, who was puffing on a long cigar. With a look of disdain that clearly communicated, "You're bothering me," Mr. Skeffington asked what he could do for the young American. Gordon produced the book reviews that had run in the newspapers and began to talk. At first the publisher was defensive, but as Elder Hinckley reasoned with him and explained the problems with the book just published, Mr. Skeffington suddenly softened. "I am sure that a high-principled man such as yourself would not wish to do injury to a people who have already suffered so much for their religion," Elder Hinckley concluded. At that, the publisher made a remarkable concession and agreed to recall the books from the bookstores and add to each copy a disclaimer stating that the text should not be construed as a history of the Mormon people, who had a respected and courageous history, but should be regarded as fiction without any basis in fact. Elder Hinckley realized that this was an extraordinary decision for a businessman who had much to lose and nothing to gain financially for his effort.

Mr. Skeffington was true to his word. He recalled the books, and when they were returned to bookstore shelves the promised disclaimer had been added. From that time forward until he passed away, the publisher stayed in touch with Gordon by sending him an annual Christmas card. "It was a tremendous lesson to me," Elder Hinckley later said. "I came to know that if we put our faith in the Lord and go forward in trust, he will open the way. We need have no fear about defending that in which we believe. I've never forgotten it. That experience left a mark upon my life."[27]

Not everything worked out as well. There were disappointments along with the triumphs. In London, meetings were held in a rented town hall in Battersea. The congregation sat on folding chairs on a hardwood floor, and the racket from the shuffle of chairs was annoying. Even worse was the noisy socializing of the members before, after, and sometimes during meetings. One Sunday, Elder Hinckley and his companion invited an investigator family to church, and the mother and children came. Unfortunately, when they arrived, the hall was filled with the sound of members chatting and visiting. After taking in the scene before them, the mother and children quietly moved toward a row of chairs, knelt for a moment in prayer, and then sat quietly amidst the surrounding commotion. At the meeting's close they left as unobtrusively as they had come, and when the elders later stopped by their home, they spoke openly about their disappointment at the lack of reverence. Elder Hinckley was embarrassed.[28]

There were other discouraging experiences—times when it seemed no one was interested in hearing the gospel message, periods when opposition became intense, days when it would have been easier just to have gone home. At times, particularly when things seemed unusually gloomy, Elder Hinckley felt the comforting and encouraging influence of his mother. On those occasions he felt that she was nearby, doing her part to comfort and sustain him. "I tried then, as I have tried since, to so conduct my life and perform my duty as to bring honor to her name," he said. "The thought of living beneath my mother's expectations has been painful, and has afforded a discipline that otherwise might have been lacking." Even in death, Ada's influence on her son was profound.[29]

It had been difficult to shake the melancholy that settled in after his mother's passing. But gradually Gordon's natural optimism poked holes through the unhealthy cloud. Now he sought to keep her memory alive in the hearts of his brothers and sisters and to help them feel hopeful about the future. On Ruth's nineteenth birthday he wrote his sister: "You are a daughter of our Mother. No pen can write her virtues, but it is for us to feel her power in the destinies of our own lives. We have an example. We can match it."[30] In another letter home Gordon summarized, "Ramona and Sylvia seem to be doing well at school. If we can keep them at that, and keep me at this, and keep all of you as well and happy as you now are—the world will continue to be full of sunshine and the honey that makes life tasty."[31]

Elder Hinckley's pattern was to expect the best and then work to make it happen. He focused on what could be done, rather than what couldn't, looked for solutions to problems rather than resigned himself to them, and learned to be happy even when things weren't going well. His was an attitude of abundance rather than scarcity, and he often reflected on the spirit of gladness his mother had cultivated in their home. To reinforce his optimism, he and his companion shook hands each morning and said to each other, "Life is good." And truly, in contrast to his experience those first weeks in Preston, Gordon was finding that life in the service of the Lord was rewarding and sustaining in a way he had never before experienced.[32] For the rest of his life he would both preach and practice the value of positive attitude. "Generally speaking, the most miserable people I know are those who are obsessed with themselves; the happiest people I know are those who lose themselves in the service of others," he said on many occasions. "There is nothing that dulls a personality so much as a negative outlook."[33]

Gordon also felt support from home, particularly from his father and brother, whose financial aid made it possible for him to stay in the field, and from Aunt May, who was a source of encouragement and strength. In a letter to his father that first Christmas away, he wrote: "Dear Dad. This is the first time in all my life that I have not been home for Christmas. While sitting before a boarding house fire and watching the flames go up the chimney, pictures pass by in memories of other Christmas days. There is the morning when, pajama-clad, we hurried downstairs long before the rooster in the back yard was awake. Such excitement—bulging socks, games, horns, a bright sweater, candy and nuts and fruit. Then we ran back upstairs blowing harmonicas to show all those wonderful things to you and mother. You were tired out but you played with us, and kissed us before sending us back to bed before daylight. During the day you pulled us up and down the street on our new sled, and we knew you were the biggest, strongest man in all the world. . . . Last night I missed the thrill of expecting Santa Claus. You have not come around this morning. I miss you. [But] with distance between us, I begin to see in your life the spirit of Christmas beyond the magic of Santa Claus. . . . There is a deep and silent expression of the virtues of Him whose birth we honor on this day. God bless you, dad, and keep you ever wonderful to me."[34]

As absorbed as he had become in his mission, it was nonetheless natural for Gordon occasionally to look ahead to the day when he would return home. With about seven months remaining, he mentioned to Ruth, "Life goes on—we grow older. . . . And my mission draws nearer its close, which means I must work harder in the remaining months than I have in those that have gone before."[35] It wasn't as though he was anxious to leave England. In just eighteen months his opportunities, challenges, and encounters there transcended anything he had previously experienced. There were so many things that were more easily learned in the mission field, so many concepts that seemed clearer.

As Elder Hinckley's two years drew to a close, President Merrill asked if he would consider staying six more months. Gordon was more than willing—if his father and Sherman agreed to continue their support. But a few days later President Merrill approached him again, this time to ask if he would instead be willing to leave for home immediately. He had received a letter from the First Presidency with a discouraging response to his concerns about the lack of materials available to help missionaries in their proselytizing. "I haven't been able to help the First Presidency understand our concerns," President Merrill explained. "I want you to go home, meet with the First Presidency in person, and explain our needs to them. Perhaps you can describe our situation in a way I can't seem to put across in a letter." The thought of meeting with the First Presidency and counseling with them about *anything* seemed presumptuous to Elder Hinckley, but he accepted the assignment from his leader and began preparing to leave England. Gordon, Homer Durham, and Heber Boden, mission secretary in the British office, were all being released at the same time, and they wished to tour Europe briefly before sailing for the United States, as it was customary for missionaries to do in that era. President Merrill agreed that it wouldn't hurt to delay Gordon's presentation to the First Presidency another two weeks.

One of Elder Hinckley's last assignments in the mission field was to speak at the first annual British Mission MIA conference, planned by Elder Durham and held in the rug-weaving city of Kidderminster in the English Midlands. Elder Hinckley's message, "A Challenge to the Youth of Britain," was powerfully delivered, according to Elder Ashton. He concluded his address with words designed to move the youth to action: "Was there ever a time in this country when we needed to listen more keenly for the words the Master uttered on the shores of Galilee that early morning—'Feed my sheep'? . . . What a delightful world this would be if . . . burning in each young heart there was an individual, soul-satisfying testimony that God lives and that Jesus Christ is His Son, the Redeemer of the world! Out of our love for Britain, may we take hold of the challenge to prepare ourselves for wonderful opportunities. . . . May we grasp the torch, become 'yeomen of England,' go forth with courage and determination like the 2,000 stripling warriors of Helaman to build Zion today."[36] Elder Durham reported that Gordon's address received more coverage in the *Kidderminster Times* than any other speech given.[37]

Back at their small hotel room that evening, Elders Hinckley and Durham and others basking in the glow of the conference vowed to preserve the association they had enjoyed in England by forming a club, the Windsor Club, when they returned home. With that, it was time for Elder Hinckley to leave the British Isles.

Gordon's mission had been a rich experience, beginning with his labors in Preston and concluding in London, a world capital that he would ever after refer to as "my town." It was difficult to articulate how these two years in England had affected him, other than that they had literally changed his life. He knew that what he had learned, spiritually and otherwise, could not have been duplicated in any other setting—certainly not in the classrooms and ivy-covered passageways of Columbia University. The harvest of baptisms had been sparse for him as well as his associates, but he was unconcerned about his tally of converts, for he was a different person than he had been just twenty-four months before when he had written his father that he might as well come home. "What a blessing it became," he later said, "to set aside my own selfish interests to the greater interests of the work of the Lord."[38]

How Elder Hinckley admired the faithful British Saints for their strength in the face of opposition and their unflinching loyalty to the gospel! From the lush beauty of rural England, with its green hills and meadowlands, to the cultural and historical treasures of London, Britain had stamped its imprint upon his soul. Years later he reflected: "I feel thankful for . . . the call by the Prophet Joseph Smith to those early missionaries to go to Britain in declaration of a great millennial vision, in expression of a tremendous faith, in demonstration of personal courage, with a statement of everlasting truth. I am profoundly grateful that while laboring on the ground which they hallowed by their efforts, there came into my heart a great consuming love for this work of God and for His Beloved Son, the Redeemer of the world, in whose name we all serve."[39]

On June 20, 1935, Elder Wendell J. Ashton recorded in his journal, "In the morning the elders of the office trooped en masse to the railway station to bid farewell to three departing missionaries: Elder Gordon B. Hinckley, G. Homer Durham, and Heber I. Boden. Not all eyes were dry."[40] With a hundred dollars each in their pockets, the three missionaries left the Liverpool Street Station en route to the Channel ferry and Rotterdam, the first stop on their European adventure. The Channel crossing was made interesting by a group of fifteen American coeds who became violently ill during the rough voyage. "They were the sickest bunch of girls you ever saw," Gordon remembered, "hanging over the rails in a pathetic fashion. When we first started out they looked right sharp and pretty, but by the time we docked they were a stringy-haired, sad-looking lot."[41] Gordon himself spent some miserable days while touring the Continent. Homer Durham noted his friend's condition the night they traveled from Rotterdam to Berlin: "Then occurred the most magnificent case of hay fever on the part of G.B.H. I ever expect to witness: fluid apparently flowing from eyes, nose, and epidermis of the face."[42]

His bout with hay fever notwithstanding, Elder Hinckley was fascinated with what he saw on the Continent. Throughout Europe he and his friends took in the sights by day and traveled by train at night, attempting to sleep on hard seats in the third-class coaches. Their trip was marred, however, by the threat of war that hung in the air. For some time Winston Churchill had been barnstorming England, warning its people about Adolf Hitler. Many Britishers had accused Churchill of warmongering and failed to take his admonitions seriously. Elder Hinckley had found his petitions difficult to dismiss, however, and from what he could see, it looked as though Hitler was scheming to change the face of Europe forever. Germany appeared ripe for his spellbinding oratory, in which he hypnotized his countrymen with promises of glory, power, and vengeance over injustices imposed by the Treaty of Versailles. The trains in Germany were filled with Nazi troops, and Gordon was fascinated with their appearance and demeanor. They were spit and polish, their uniforms pressed and immaculate, their manner efficient and precise as they goose-stepped in unison and on command thrust their fists into the air in salute.

In Munich the threesome witnessed a company of Hitler Youth marching through the streets. Homer recorded: "It was somewhat frightening, yet stirring, to see a big troop of young men—older Scout age perhaps—march by in brown shirts, swastikas on the arms, and a motto here and there visible—*Blut und Ehre* [Blood and Honor]. They all but goose-stepped, marching in precision, arms swinging."[43] "It was incredible to contemplate," Gordon said, "that a people would take fourteen- and fifteen-year-old boys, put them in battalions, and raise up a generation of soldiers. If I hadn't seen it with my own eyes, I would not have been able to fathom the insanity of it all."[44]

The missionaries arrived in Nuremberg just three days after Hitler had staged a huge stadium rally that electrified the city. Nazi banners and flags still flew from poles around the arena. In Dresden, as they visited a memorial to an earlier war, an elderly woman approached the monument. Poorly dressed, her face wrinkled with age, she laid a bouquet of flowers at the Unknown Soldier memorial and then knelt to pray. When she arose Gordon could see that her eyes were filled with tears; at the same time, from a nearby street, the sound of drums and marching youth filled the air. "History is going to repeat itself," Gordon said to himself. "In a coming day, men and women will kneel at this monument and mourn the loss of the youths marching just a block away."[45] He left Germany with the impression that they were "sitting on a front row in the bleachers of history."[46]

All was not gloom and doom, however, for everywhere they went, the missionaries took in Europe's marvelous historical and cultural sites. In Paris they visited the Louvre and purchased inexpensive seats for a performance of the Paris Opera. Homer seemed to know where every treaty of importance had been signed, and they visited one monument and museum after another with him as their guide. But the trip's highlight for Gordon took place on a beautiful hill overlooking Paris at the American Military Cemetery in Suresnes. Homer recorded the experience: "Stretching to the gates were 1541 graves marked with white marble crosses. . . . Then GBH led us to row 11, #5, and said, 'Brethren, there's my oldest brother.' We read: 'Stanford Hinckley, Utah, October 19, 1918.' After a few moments' silence, Brother GBH spoke again—'Brethren, this grave has probably never been dedicated.' It has been now. We stood in silence while our companion, in power, prayed that this might be a hallowed spot until the day looked forward to."[47] The peace there was a poignant contrast for Gordon, as he reviewed in his mind images of the German war machine he had seen just days before, then thought of his brother whom he had lost to war, and of his mother, who had made her last pilgrimage to this hallowed place.

After tromping around Europe for two weeks, the missionaries made their way to Le Havre, France, where they boarded the SS *Manhattan*, the same ship Elder Hinckley had taken coming over, on the Fourth of July. It was a festive beginning for the final leg of their trip home. A band played patriotic songs, and the Stars and Stripes waved in the breeze. After all he had witnessed, Gordon felt a surge of pride in and gratitude for his American citizenship. He loved England and the British. But how wonderful it was to be going home!

Seven days later, on July 11, the ship docked at New York City. After his tour of Europe, Gordon's clothes were unpressed and limp. He wanted to look decent upon his arrival, because his sister Christine was planning to meet him when he came down the gangplank, but his suit was beyond immediate repair. Then he remembered the blue, double-breasted, worsted-wool suit he had purchased on Regent's Street in London. He retrieved the handsome but wrinkled apparel from his trunk. Though it was unbearably hot for New York's humid July weather, Gordon decided it looked better than anything else he had.

When the ship docked and his sister was nowhere to be found, Gordon hurried off the vessel to find a tailor's shop near the wharf where he could quickly get his suit pressed. He ducked into the first such place of business, where the cigar-smoking proprietor directed him to a back room to undress. When the tailor came to get the heavy, wool suit from Gordon and saw him standing there in what appeared to be another layer of long cotton underwear, he pulled the cigar out of his mouth just long enough to exclaim, "My hell, man, where did you just blow in from? The Arctic?" Gordon didn't even try to explain.

Before leaving New York City, Gordon took the bus to 116th Street and walked across the campus of Columbia University, just to see what he had missed and to inquire about applying for admission. The missionaries then went to Washington, D.C., and from there took the train north to Rochester, New York, and the nearby Hill Cumorah. President Heber J. Grant had arrived there to unveil and dedicate the heroic-sized, antique bronze statue of Moroni that now stood sentry atop the storied hill. Nearly two thousand guests gathered to hear President David O. McKay, second counselor in the First Presidency, deliver the dedicatory address and President Grant the dedicatory prayer. Gordon and his companions witnessed the ceremony and attended the accompanying pageant, now in its second year. It was a stirring conclusion to their two years as ambassadors of the Lord.[48]

From upstate New York the young men took the train to Detroit, where Gordon picked up a new four-door Plymouth sedan—at a cost of $741, a tidy sum during the Depression—for his father. It was a practice then permitted for missionaries. Homer also took delivery of a car for his father, and they began the long drive home. Their route took them through Illinois, where they stopped at Carthage to visit the jail where assassins' bullets had ended the lives of Joseph and Hyrum, and walked the dusty streets of Nauvoo. From there they followed as much as possible the trail of the vanguard company of pioneers. It was an opportunity Gordon relished, as he had no way of knowing if he would ever have occasion to pass that way again.

During the sixteen-hundred-mile drive from Michigan's motor capital to Salt Lake City, he had time to reflect on his experiences of the past two years and to turn his attention to what lay ahead. It occurred to Gordon that at least one promise of his patriarchal blessing had been realized. He had been told that he would raise his voice in testimony in the nations of the earth. During recent days he had borne testimony in London, Berlin, Paris, and Washington, D.C.—four great world capitals. "Well, that part of my blessing is fulfilled," he commented to himself.

But new adventures, he realized, now awaited him—not the least of which was a reunion with Marjorie. For two years their letters had sailed between Utah and England. Often Gordon's read like a journal; occasionally he had openly expressed his love for her. As much as she had meant to him when he was home, she had come to mean more during their separation. In return, Marjorie's letters were full of news, encouragement, and humor. As much as she had dared, she had let Gordon know that he was rarely out of her thoughts. Now he knew the days of simple dating were behind them, that important decisions weren't far away. During his absence, Marjorie had refused to "put all of her eggs in one basket" and had dated other young men. But no one measured up to Gordon. Both were nervous but eager to see each other again.

Elder Hinckley described the last few miles of the long journey home: "In the middle of a July night, after being absent for more than two years, we drove down through Parley's Canyon in the Wasatch Mountains. As we reached the mouth of the canyon there suddenly appeared before us an unforgettable picture. For 30 miles lights twinkled in the valley below. After two years away, it was a great sight. We were home."[49] The Hinckleys were ecstatic when Gordon walked through the front door, and they gave him a hero's welcome. He was simply relieved to be home. After two years in England and another month on the road, he was down to 126 pounds. He knew one thing for sure—he had no desire ever to travel again. So when Bryant and Aunt May decided to take the family to Yellowstone in the new car, Gordon was true to his word and stayed behind while the family vacationed.

What he *was* interested in was a little time to do with as he pleased—most notably, to spend time with Marjorie and to take care of the assignment President Merrill had given him before he had left London. As promised, a few days later he went to

Church headquarters and introduced himself to Joseph Anderson, secretary to the First Presidency. They set an appointment, and at 8:00 on the morning of Tuesday, August 20, the twenty-five-year-old returned missionary presented himself before President Heber J. Grant and his counselors, Presidents J. Reuben Clark Jr. and David O. McKay.

It might have been an intimidating experience, but Gordon was still filled with the confidence of a missionary. "Nobody scared me in those days," he remembered. "I could have marched in to see the queen just as easily."[50] When he was ushered into the stately council room the First Presidency had met in for decades, however, and shook hands with each member of the Presidency, he was suddenly overcome by the circumstances in which he found himself. President Grant took the lead, handing Gordon his card, which bore on one side his signature in the beautiful handwriting for which he had become known, and on the reverse the statement of Ralph Waldo Emerson that he had adopted as his personal motto: "That which we persist in doing becomes easier to do, not that the nature of the thing has changed but that our power to do has increased." President Grant then said: "Brother Hinckley, we'll give you fifteen minutes to tell us what Elder Merrill wants us to hear."

Gordon rehearsed the concerns he and President Merrill had discussed before he left England—that what few materials missionaries had to help them in their work were inadequate and unattractive. After Gordon had taken his fifteen minutes, the Presidency began to ask questions. One led to another, and it was an hour and fifteen minutes before the recently released missionary emerged from the room.

President Heber J. Grant noted afterward in his journal: "At 9:30 met Gordon B. Hinckley . . . who has been on a mission in Great Britain, and made suggestions regarding getting articles in the British Press. He was very successful while laboring in the British Mission in getting a great deal of fine matter in the London and other papers and magazines."[51] President Grant was apparently impressed with the young returned missionary. The next day he noted in a letter to a friend that Gordon had "made a most excellent record" while in England.[52]

From Gordon's viewpoint, he had been graciously received

and was relieved to have completed President Merrill's assignment. In his mind, his mission was now truly over, and it was time to move ahead and plan for the future. Though the economy was showing only the most preliminary signs of improvement, he wasn't overly concerned. With a graduate degree in journalism from Columbia, which he now intended to pursue, he felt he could provide for a family as well as follow a profession that would stimulate and intrigue him.

But once again his life failed to follow the course he had outlined. Two days after his meeting with the First Presidency, Gordon received a telephone call from President McKay: "Brother Hinckley, we discussed in the meeting of the Presidency and the Twelve yesterday what we talked about during your interview with us. And we have organized a committee consisting of six members of the Twelve, with Elder Stephen L Richards as chairman, to address the needs you outlined. We would like to invite you to come and work with that committee."

Gordon hadn't realized that his meeting two days earlier would turn out to be a job interview. Though he felt torn between pursuing his chosen career and responding to the First Presidency, Gordon took President McKay's invitation as a command and accepted the position. The job as executive secretary of the newly formed Church Radio, Publicity, and Mission Literature Committee (so named because it was to include every form of media the Church employed) was initially to be part-time and pay $65 a month.

Worried about supporting himself—and anyone else, should the need arise—he welcomed a call from Elder John A. Widtsoe, the Church's Commissioner of Education, who hired him to teach a seminary class at South High School for $35 a month. One hundred dollars a month was enough for the time being. So once again Gordon Hinckley put his Columbia brochures back in a drawer and detoured from his planned course. It was a direction that would change his life forever.

CHAPTER SIX

GETTING STARTED: THE CHALLENGES BEGIN

The prospect of working at Church headquarters aroused an abundance of emotions within the young returned missionary. Gordon was apprehensive yet excited about the challenge to create something where nothing currently existed. His father had enjoyed a warm relationship with many of the Brethren, and he himself had had a taste of working for and with a General Authority during his time in the European Mission office under Elder Merrill, who had been a stickler for competence, propriety, and follow-through. But it was another matter entirely to sit on a committee with half the members of the Twelve and to be charged with developing materials for missionaries Churchwide. The challenge was one of immense proportions. With characteristic aplomb, however, Gordon dived headlong into his new assignment.

Several who learned of his appointment to work on a committee chaired by Elder Stephen L Richards pulled Gordon aside and offered a gentle warning: "You'll never be able to work for him—nobody can. He's too exacting, too demanding." The grandson of Willard Richards, Elder Richards had a law degree from the University of Chicago. Before his call to the Quorum of the Twelve, he had distinguished himself as an attorney and was regarded as a man of pronounced ability and impeccable judgment. Gordon could only imagine what it would be like to take direction from a man who apparently inspired both apprehension and admiration among co-workers.

Even had he wanted to, there wasn't anyone with whom

Gordon could talk about the position in which he found himself, for he quickly learned that he was an oddity. The Depression had placed a strain on Church resources, and in 1935 the number of employees working at headquarters could be counted on two hands. Joseph Anderson and Bertha Irvine provided secretarial help to the First Presidency, along with two financial secretaries. Harold Reynolds served as mission secretary and transportation agent. Three women served as secretaries to the Twelve, the First Council of the Seventy had a secretary, and there was one switchboard operator. So hiring a "civilian"—and a young one at that—to work with the Brethren and giving him open-door access to almost any office in the building was without precedent.

It was a new experience for the General Authorities as well, who weren't accustomed to rolling out the carpet for newcomers. On Gordon's first day, Elder Richards told him he could use the empty office adjoining his. Gordon quickly found that Elder Richards meant literally what he said—the office was not merely unoccupied but completely empty. He had not been provided so much as a chair, table, lamp, or trash can. Undaunted, though puzzled at the reception, he called a missionary friend whose father owned an office supply store and with his help located an old warped table with a short leg. He hauled the table to his new office, situated a block of wood under the damaged leg, and brought his old typewriter from home. When he asked the man who parceled out supplies for a ream of paper, the employee responded with astonishment, "Do you realize how much paper is in one ream?" "Yes, five hundred sheets," Gordon replied. "What in the world are you going to do with five hundred sheets of paper?" the secretary asked, apparently having never entertained such a request. "I am going to write on it one sheet at a time," Gordon answered. He got the ream of paper.

Before 1935 the Church's public relations efforts (with the exception of Tabernacle Choir events) had been unorganized, haphazard, and largely ineffective. Other than a few tracts, no materials existed to help missionaries in their proselytizing. A few mission presidents, desperate for resources, had developed slide lectures and pamphlets to use in their own areas. But essentially nothing had been created for use on a Churchwide basis.

Elder Richards chaired the Radio, Publicity, and Mission Literature Committee, which included Elders Melvin J. Ballard, John A. Widtsoe, Charles A. Callis, Alonzo A. Hinckley (Gordon's uncle), and Albert E. Bowen. Though Gordon worked under the direction of the full committee, it was he who was expected to shoulder the day-to-day workload.

The committee's beginnings were without fanfare. Elder Richards assigned Gordon to recommend where they should begin, and he went to work, focusing initially on scripts that could be written and produced as slide presentations to help missionaries in their proselytizing. When Gordon drafted a text for a proposed slide lecture, Elder Richards called the committee together and Gordon presented the material, often reading it aloud to the group. If changes were suggested, he made modifications and subsequently coordinated the production of slides, script, and music or audio track. One project led to another. Committee meetings provided an opportunity to present new ideas and discuss potential scripts, as well as to talk openly about the various challenges missionaries faced, appropriate ways to deal with critics of the Church, and the kinds of teaching aids that would be most useful to missionaries. Gordon soaked in the discussions. Such association with members of the Twelve, in a forum where they freely discussed issues and challenges related to teaching the gospel worldwide, was the beginning of a most unusual education in Church administration and leadership.

Slowly but steadily the first materials initiated at Church headquarters—slide presentations, pamphlets, brochures, and audio presentations on subjects ranging from latter-day prophets and temples to pioneers and the Book of Mormon—began to appear. Inherent within Gordon's pioneering effort was the need to learn quickly and to commit as few errors as possible. He alluded to that challenge in a letter to President Joseph F. Merrill, who kept tabs on his former assistant and protégé: "I know, Pres. Merrill, that you have wondered why you are not getting this material more quickly. I have just come from a long talk with Brother Richards. Brother Richards kept the 'Pioneer Trails' manuscript to go over it carefully. This morning he congratulated me on the language, but expressed himself as feeling that instead of trying to tell a story . . . I simply delineate the facts for the elders to use as best they can. . . . I am having to change some of my ideas of writing, but with the help of the Lord we shall finally get something of the first order."[1]

From the outset Gordon had to first identify which subjects and projects to tackle, then determine how to execute each one in such a manner that it would be effective regardless of culture or setting. To President Merrill he described the essence of the challenge: "Here is the difficulty: This committee wants these lectures to be suitable for the missions throughout the Church. [I prepared one lecture] from the viewpoint we had discussed in London, and its sequence is perhaps not the best for conditions in America. It is this difference of viewpoints that I am trying to reconcile. . . . Of course, there will have to be a lot of rough edges rubbed off in getting this work under way. I only regret that it takes so long."[2]

In the main, however, Gordon was energized by the challenging nature of the work. Again to President Merrill, after explaining the complications on just one project, he concluded almost by way of postscript: "There is a terrific lot of work ahead, but I am not afraid of it."[3] Indeed, he found there was much more to producing filmstrips and other materials for missionaries than he had first imagined. He was responsible for not only conceptualizing and writing scripts but arranging for their production and distribution as well, and an infinite number of details had to be coordinated with mission presidents, scholars who reviewed his writing for accuracy, radio station managers who were reluctant to air Church-related programming, and companies whose services Gordon contracted.

There were, for example, exasperating problems to resolve in those days preceding color photography. Unable to find a dependable color-reproduction process, Gordon hired workers to hand tint each frame of each copy of the filmstrip—a tedious process that created a terrific bottleneck in providing enough slides for distribution. At the same time he repeatedly consulted with experts in Hollywood and Europe, looking for new films and processes. In a memo to Elder Richards, he reported, "At the present time six artists are coloring film. . . . But at best the work is slow and tedious. They are paid 5 cents per frame. This is the most expensive item in the process, but I do not think these people are over-paid, one girl having recently discontinued because of eye strain."[4]

After being disappointed by several companies who did not deliver what they promised, Gordon was elated when representatives of Technicolor in California demonstrated a new film that appeared to have the qualities he desired. He was hopeful that the days of hand coloring individual slides would soon end.[5]

Through it all he learned by trial and error. Localisms that kept a brochure or filmstrip from being applicable everywhere in the world must be avoided; critical review from scholars could prevent unforeseen problems later on; materials must have a practical application.

Early projects produced by the Radio, Publicity, and Mission Literature Committee included "Down Pioneer Trails," a slide lecture Gordon wrote and produced in 1935 that pictured and described significant locations along the pioneer trail, and "Forgotten Empires" and "Before Columbus," film lectures on the colonization of the American continent that concluded with an introduction to Moroni and a testimony of the Book of Mormon.

"Historic Highlights of Mormonism," a slide presentation released in 1942 and the first produced in Technicolor, focused on significant people, events, and places associated with the Restoration and the pioneers' journey west. The Sacred Grove and Kirtland Temple, the Susquehanna River, Chimney Rock and South Pass—these and sixty other places of consequence were identified and their significance placed in context. To prepare for this project, Gordon retraced the pioneer trail. Near Scottsbluff, Nebraska, he had an experience that reinforced his admiration for those who had endured the travail of pioneer life. He wrote afterward:

> Of the thousands of Mormon emigrants who were buried along the trail . . . the graves of only a few have been found and marked. Among the better known of these is the grave of Rebecca Winters. . . .
>
> I wanted to include this in the series of photographs along the trail, but had been unable to find anyone who knew exactly how to get there. . . . I arrived in Scottsbluff between six and seven in the

> morning, but could find no one on the streets who knew anything of the grave.
>
> The ticket agent in the Burlington station informed me that the grave was a timing station, listed as "Winters" on the time-table, and said that it was about three miles back down the line. He didn't know how to direct me to it, other than by walking the ties.
>
> Finally the section boss arrived. . . . I followed his directions, and after slogging through the mud of a wet field with a dog yipping at my heels, I climbed the fence to get to the railroad right-of-way. Down the track a short distance I could see the white posts and iron rails that enclosed the sacred spot for which I was looking.
>
> Within the enclosure was a little monument and the rusting wagon tire which still plainly bore the inscription, "Rebecca Winters, Aged 50 Years." It had been hastily chiseled while a company of Latter-day Saints sorrowfully paused to bury a Pioneer mother.[6]

The experience affected him profoundly, as he acknowledged: "It seemed a lonely place that summer morning. This sacred spot, kept green and lovely by those who appreciated its significance, was a token of the faith of men and women who sacrificed their all to reach and build Zion."[7]

His week on the trail also provided insights into the manner in which the pioneer story must be told. "As I stood on these historic spots pictures of dusty wagon trains, of weary handcart pioneers, of graves dug in the prairie while the wolves stood by, of old men dropping from exhaustion and young men winking at bonnetted girls, of a hundred voices singing 'Come, Come, Ye Saints' and Pitts brass band playing music for a dance—these and a thousand other pictures passed before my mind's eye," he wrote later. "There's a story in every mile of that trail, and as I stood there over the graves of men and women who had walked a thousand miles over all kinds of ground, I felt that their story is deserving of a better telling than we are giving it. . . . The job now before us is to make the drama as vital as the real thing was."[8] With each new historical discovery or insight, Gordon's admiration and respect for the men and women of earlier generations increased.

The theme and scope of a seemingly endless number of filmstrips, brochures, small books, recordings, radio programs, and presentations under Gordon's direction ran the gamut from doctrinal treatises to more general articles inviting a return to values or providing an accurate glimpse of the Church and its people. Each was conceived as a tool that would enable missionaries to better teach and represent the message of the restored gospel. The new materials were greeted enthusiastically by mission presidents and missionaries, the most frequent complaint being that more materials were needed faster. Elder Joseph F. Merrill's memo to Gordon of March 18, 1936, was not unusual: "We do think it is only right that the European missions shall be considered first . . . because all the missions on the American continent have the use to a great extent of the radio, of the publicity of the weekly hook-up that the [Tabernacle] choir has given."

Gordon's response was sympathetic but realistic: "Let me assure you that the European missions will be supplied first. However, all the States' mission presidents will be in this week, and in spite of the fact that they have the radio and other means they are anxious for these films and will make their demands known."[9]

A letter from President LeGrand Richards of the Southern States Mission, in which he requested additional copies of five films, was just one example that proved Gordon right: "You may feel that our wants are excessive, but our missionaries are having so much success . . . in getting into homes and opening doors for preaching the Gospel, that it seems a shame not to be able to supply their needs. Kindly do all you can for us to enable us to supply the missionaries with the necessary films at the earliest possible date."[10]

Gordon's reply was encouraging: "It is delightful to note the manner in which you have taken hold of this project, and are using it to good advantage. While it may take some little while, we shall have films . . . as per your order. Everything is going at top speed, but the demand is so great that it has simply been impossible to keep pace. If you can be patient just a little longer, we shall do our best."[11]

Demand exceeded supply at least in part because missionaries found the new materials to be highly effective. The experiences of missionaries in New England illustrated the value of one twenty-four-part series of fifteen-minute recordings that local radio stations had agreed to air as programming. One missionary reported that a station manager who had previewed the recordings was "very much impressed. He was set against long, call-to-repentance type of programs but thought that short preachments would fit into his program very well. So beginning August 18, we will be on the air."[12]

There were numerous other success stories, as indicated in a report from Gordon to Elder Richards: "The California Mission has found [the slide lectures] of such value that during the past few months they have purchased twenty [projectors], the Southern States now have 20, the East Central 15, the Northern 13, and the Central 14, and are generous in their praise concerning them."[13]

President Merrill praised three filmstrips that centered proselytizing on the Book of Mormon: "Our presidents have found that these illustrated lectures are our most fruitful means of making new contacts so we call them 'contact' lectures. They are not sermons and a lot of people will come to the lectures that would not come to a preaching meeting. But the lectures arouse their interest and then many of them, we find, want to know something about our religion." Elder Merrill, whose inspiration to have his young missionary meet with the First Presidency had resulted in these and many other projects, added: "Again may I say that we are extremely grateful for the devoted, able service you have rendered us in this cause."[14]

Gordon's "part-time" job was rewarding but all-consuming. He prepared the agendas for committee meetings, organized public relations events, conceived the ideas for and directed all production of projects, and pecked out hundreds of proposals, scripts, talks, and pamphlets on the old typewriter atop the rickety, warped desk in his office. Elder Widtsoe had dubbed Gordon "the Slave," and the nickname stuck. When yet another assignment came before the group, Elder Widtsoe would typically say, with some humor, "Let the Slave do it," and as far as Gordon could tell, the designation was on target. (Gordon jokingly referred to himself as the Slave for years, and his workhorse tendencies did little to dispel the notion.) Though he felt confident that the Brethren appreciated his efforts, their praise did not translate monetarily. For the first six months of 1936, he earned all of $450.[15]

The scope of Gordon's responsibilities went beyond the conceptualization and production of new public relations and missionary materials. On November 16, 1924, KSL had inaugurated a series of LDS programs aired on Sunday evenings under a variety of titles but typically referred to as the "Church Hour."[16] These programs now fell under the direction of the committee, and for nearly a quarter of a century Gordon planned, organized, and often wrote scripts for the weekly broadcasts, in which Church members from various walks of life were invited to speak on gospel themes.

On occasion he took part in the series himself. Back just a year from the mission field, he delivered a moving address, "Pioneer Frontiers," on the July 19, 1936, KSL program. His message revealed spiritual maturity, a gift for language, and respect for those who had laid the foundation of this dispensation: "I am of the second generation from those people of the plains. None of my age has felt the choking dust of the prairies as ox-drawn wagons in a long convoy lifted it from deep ruts to be caught by hot winds and thrown against sunburned faces. None of my friends has bowed to the tug of a handcart when splintering wheels commenced to squeak and mountain blizzards hedged in men and women with hunger and death. None of my generation has met the lash of bitter persecution that was raised against a handful of pilgrims. Those were the trying experiences of our pioneer forebears who long since earned their title to true greatness and passed on to another glory. In the words of Carlyle, they made a 'nook of God's creation more fruitful, better, worthy of God.'" He concluded with his testimony of the gospel kingdom: "I know of but one way to rid the earth of strife and contention. That is to change men's lives, to lift them to a higher plane of thought and endeavor. . . . Mormonism is a world religion with a world vision."[17]

Sixteen months later he again took to the airwaves, this time to deliver the last address in a series entitled "An Open Forum of Gospel Discussion." In doing so, he addressed a theme about which he felt passionately and to which he would return again and again throughout his life: "Mormonism has a world vision. The gospel of Jesus Christ is for everyone, and to the Church has come a divine commission to preach the glad tidings. . . . Once weak and oppressed, Zion is today strong. Strong because of its teachings; strong because of its organization; strong because of its people."[18]

In the process of arranging, producing, and often writing and participating in these radio broadcasts, Gordon became acquainted with individuals whose expertise represented a broad spectrum of interests. In turn, the name of Gordon Hinckley, like his father's before him, became familiar to those who regularly tuned to KSL. In January 1938, on a weekly KSL series, Gordon was introduced as a "prominent young Salt Lake City journalist." His name was mentioned periodically in the press as he spoke at various Church- and Utah-oriented events. Though he had assumed that his career in journalism had been permanently tabled when his plans to attend Columbia were derailed by the First Presidency's invitation to work for the Church, he now found himself at the hub of the Church's newly formed media wheel.[19]

Gordon seemed instinctively to understand the potential influence of electronic media, and he eagerly embraced the power of radio to take the Church's message to a larger audience more quickly than any other medium.[20] But radio broadcasts, brochures, filmstrips, and the like composed but one facet of the committee's activities. There were other opportunities to introduce the gospel to large numbers of people. In the late 1930s, for example, the committee decided to create an exhibit for the 1939 World's Fair at Treasure Island, near San Francisco. Predictably, the Slave was assigned to work out an idea to recommend to the committee. Gordon was suddenly grateful that his father had arranged for his brief Chicago stopover to see the World's Fair en route to England, for at least he understood something of the scope this exhibit must have. The Church's display must be highly creative, or it would pale next to the others. What ensued was a project of immense proportions that proved to be one of the fair's more distinctive exhibits.

Sensitive to the fact that much of the public had a distorted image of the Church, Gordon suggested that the exhibit capitalize on the fame of the Tabernacle Choir by creating a replica of Temple Square, including a domed-roof Tabernacle complete with organ and seating for fifty people. A high wall on one side of the building was decorated with four large photo murals, one of which provided a backdrop of the temple, helping create the illusion of actually being on Temple Square. Gordon worked on the project for months, calling on the talents of artists, photographers, builders, and other artisans who lent their professional skills to the complicated undertaking.

The effort and anxiety were well worth it, however. Few displays were more popular at the Golden Gate International Exposition than the Church's exhibit, which drew more than 1,400 persons on the opening day alone and some 320,000 over the thirteen months of the fair's operation (February 18 to December 2, 1939, and May 18 to September 29, 1940). Elder G. William Richards, a missionary serving in the area, played the organ while a slide presentation guided the exhibit guests on a tour of Temple Square and reviewed events from Church history as well as basic gospel principles. At the conclusion, missionaries from the local mission sang a verse of "Come, Come, Ye Saints" or another favorite hymn. The program was repeated forty times a day.

The location of the exhibit in the Homes and Gardens Building proved fortuitous. Amid the glamour of commercialism, the Tabernacle offered opportunity for quiet repose. It was not unusual for visitors to stay for several performances. Fair officials frequently dropped in to rest and hear the program. One woman told missionaries she had heard about the exhibit in Switzerland from another world traveler who had been to the fair. Missionaries stationed at the exhibit contacted more people in one week than they would have met in two months of tracting.[21]

As the exposition drew to a close, one missionary summarized the effects of the exhibit in a report to the First Presidency: "This has been missionary work on a grand scale, for we have received an average of 700 people a day in our little Tabernacle, where we have proclaimed in humility and sincerity the Restoration of the Gospel of Jesus Christ. We have appreciated the excellent supervision of Elders Stephen L Richards and Gordon B. Hinckley of the Church Radio Committee."[22]

With its success at the exposition, the committee eagerly accepted the opportunity to participate in another West Coast celebration nearly ten years later. Because of its unique tie to the event, the Church was invited to join in commemorating the centennial of the discovery of gold in California. Henry Bigler, a member of the Mormon Battalion who subsequently went to work for John Sutter on the American River at Coloma, California, provided the first documented evidence of gold in his journal under the date of January 24, 1848: "This day some kind of mettle was found in the tail race that looks like goald."[23]

Once again Gordon was assigned to determine what the Church's participation might be, and he recommended that they re-create the cabin in which members of the Mormon Battalion had lived in Coloma. He supervised construction of the cabin and created a presentation explaining the Church's connection to the celebration. Again public response was overwhelming. Tens of thousands of guests visited the Bigler cabin and at the same time were introduced to the gospel. (Nearly five decades later the exhibit still stood in the Gold Discovery Stake Park.)

In the late thirties another unique opportunity presented itself to the committee. A Hollywood radio promotion company, Mertens and Price Radio Feature Service, approached the Church about developing and sponsoring a series of thirty-nine half-hour radio programs. Entitled the "Fulness of Times" series, it would present dramatized episodes from Church history. Gordon subsequently supervised what proved to be a massive, trend-setting project that significantly advanced the quality and scope of Church-related programming. "What we want," he explained to G. L. Price, one of the radio company's executives, "is the story of the Church told in an engaging way that will catch the interest of our listeners and make them sit up, take notice and realize that . . . there is something challenging and fine in Mormonism."[24]

Chase Varney, a Hollywood writer, wrote the first thirteen scripts. Gordon traveled to the West Coast to represent the Church's point of view in the production of each episode. There was, for example, one cast member who stubbornly insisted on pronouncing *Moroni* as Moro-*knee* and *Nephi* as *Naph*-ee. "He was obstinate about his pronunciation," Gordon remembered, "but I was more obstinate."[25] Though the quality of music used in the programming was never up to his expectations, the actors were first-class and carried off the productions professionally.

Differences aside, Gordon was comfortable interacting with his nonmember counterparts, as indicated in a letter he received from G. L. Price: "I [am] especially glad . . . that you are a member of the script committee. We both feel that while you have all of the spiritual qualifications for an Elder, and your absolute loyalty to the Church cannot be questioned, you also have a breadth of vision, and a tolerance for the Gentile point of view, which will make you a particularly valuable co-worker for Chase and me."[26]

When circumstances developed making it impossible for Mr. Varney to continue scripting the series, and with air time scheduled and deadlines to meet, Gordon was asked to fill in temporarily and write a couple of scripts. His writing was so compelling that the producers requested that he continue. In turn, Gordon invited stiff critical review of his scripts. "Let me say again," he wrote Mertens and Price, "that while extensive editings or rewritings may entail more time in getting approval, we want you to suggest the things—all the things—that will make for an outstanding result."[27]

The results were apparently worth the effort. On occasion Mr. Price acknowledged how the programming affected him personally: "There are no reservations in my endorsement of the show we made this afternoon. . . . It made me cry, and when a show can do that to me, it must be good. Driving back to the office I had that sensation which comes only a few times in a lifetime of spiritual cleansing. . . . Again, I say you ARE a people chosen of God—perhaps you'll make a Christian of me yet."[28] After reviewing yet another script, he wrote to Gordon: "It gives me great and genuine pleasure to tell you how much I've enjoyed your script of 'The Dawning of a Brighter Day.' I say 'your' script advisedly, for I am sure I detect in it a lot of Mr. Gordon B. Hinckley. It is beautifully written, it hangs together, it tells a splendid story of a Great Church."[29]

Good scripts did not come easily. Though his writing was

praised by all who reviewed it as both articulate and poignant, Gordon agonized over the process, sometimes torturous, of putting words on paper. And that was after he had spent hours in the Church historical library searching journals and diaries for stories that could be retold effectively over the air.

Providentially, history fascinated Gordon, and he enjoyed the excuse to absorb himself in research. If these scripts had been all he was responsible for, the project would have been more delight than pressure. But they represented only a portion of the load he was carrying. He was still essentially a one-man office, expected to carry out all the assignments of the committee. The pressure to complete the "Fulness of Times" historical series, and after that to write thirty-nine additional episodes on the Book of Mormon, was intense. Deadlines loomed constantly. The workload and inherent strain had its effect: "I'm losing weight, hair and my good disposition trying to meet half a dozen deadlines, among which I rank the 'Fulness of Times' as the most important," he wrote G. L. Price. "Writing does not come easy for me. It's slow, hard labor and because I have so many other things demanding attention, I do not get things out as rapidly as I should."[30] He brought in Frank Wise, a skilled photographer with an excellent eye, to help with graphics, and he later benefitted also from the assistance of Joseph J. Cannon, former president of the British Mission and an experienced newspaperman and publisher. But even then, more of the workload fell to Gordon than to anyone else.

Despite the pressure of more to be done than time in which to do it, Gordon had a temperament that was in some respects well suited to the challenge. After a meeting with one of the "Fulness of Times" producers, he fired off a letter that revealed something about his personal style and how he managed his workload: "I too enjoyed the brief visit with you the other day. If I seemed unduly restrained I am sorry. I am one of these fellows who is by nature slow to warm up, even in the presence of old friends. Then too, I knew you were busy and since I had no particular news I did not feel justified in just talking and taking up your time. I sometimes get a little out of patience with people who come in, sit down, and while away the time when there is a stack of work staring me in the face. This has made me a bit sensitive about occupying other people's time when I know they are busy. Please do not think my attitude was a conscious coldness."[31]

Gordon's work bore fruit. Broadcast over as many as four hundred stations at one point, the "Fulness of Times" presented for the first time an accurate glimpse of significant events in the Church's history. The series, which ran for nearly five years and attracted a wide listening audience, was not without opposition, however, as he documented: "In one city in the East where [the 'Fulness of Times' episodes] were running the local ministerial society pressured the station into giving them control over all religious programs. Result: the station was compelled to drop the 'Fulness of Times.' It was in Toronto, Canada . . . that the ministers threatened the station which was running the series with a boycott of its advertisers if the programs were allowed to continue. Shades of Missouri and Nauvoo! The old spirit that tarred and feathered Joseph in Ohio; that issued the Extermination Order in Missouri; that desecrated the Temple at Nauvoo; that killed missionaries in the South and jailed them in Germany, Switzerland and Scandinavia still burns more intensely than is often apparent. On the other hand the reception given the series has been surprisingly fine. They have been run on a large number of stations in the United States—many of them small, it is true, but nonetheless effective—and they have been heard from South Africa to Sweden and from New Zealand to Canada on the portable machines which our missionaries have."[32]

Gordon produced other radio programs that also found an appreciative audience. The series "A New Witness for Christ" dramatized passages from the Book of Mormon. Aired over the Church Hour, the program made that book of scripture come to life. As Gordon explained to an associate: "I have always thought that we will do our best work when we get people interested in the Book of Mormon to the point where they will read it. It is then that the Spirit can bear witness of its divinity."[33]

Another series, "The Church's Attitude," was designed to address the Church's response to modern-day problems. "I believe that with the right participants, some good problems, and put over in such a fashion that it has spice and spontaneity," Gordon wrote to a colleague, "it can be an effective program—

much more so than a series of sermons. But it will take a lot of thoughtful, prayerful, careful consideration." He continued, lamenting the press of time under which he constantly labored: "I had hoped that once we got the Fulness of Times out of the way and the film on which we are now completing production, together with one or two other worrisome jobs that are now winding up, that there would be something of a respite and I could sorta loaf along. But whenever I get to a spot like that, something else bobs up to smash the picture. But, life's like that—and it wouldn't be very interesting if it were not."[34]

Another project was conceived when Gordon obtained permission from motion picture director Cecil B. DeMille to use approximately seventy-five frames from his black-and-white film *The King of Kings* as the basis for a Church filmstrip with the same title. Preferring a colorized version, he hired workers to hand tint the frames. His sister Ramona worked on this as well as other projects. "I never worked so hard in my life," she claimed. "Gord wanted things done just right, and I didn't want to let him down."[35]

Gordon's numerous and varied writing and producing assignments formed the foundation of an extraordinary education—self-directed though it was—in Church history. His father was well versed in history and had demonstrated respect for leaders present and past, and now Gordon's own testimony of and reverence for the past began to mature. He repeatedly found himself reconstructing in his mind scenes that had played out in earlier generations: long trains of wagons crossing inhospitable prairies; men, women, and children suffering with fever, black canker, and the plague; a grave-marked trail leading up the Platte and Sweetwater Rivers and over South Pass; weary immigrants pushing handcarts through snowstorms and riverbeds; and broken wagon wheels and handcart remains dotting the western landscape. The more he studied and wrote, the more real these images became to him. His earnest interest in the history of the Church evolved into a profound and penetrating respect, as he realized how connected he was to those who had grubbed sagebrush and buried loved ones in shallow graves as they nurtured the gospel kingdom.

Decades later Gordon articulated the practical philosophy

that governed his veneration of the past: "It is good to look to the past to gain appreciation for the present and perspective for the future. It is good to look upon the virtues of those who have gone before, to gain strength for whatever lies ahead. It is good to reflect upon the work of those who labored so hard and gained so little in this world, but out of whose dreams and early plans, so well nurtured, has come a great harvest of which we are the beneficiaries. Their tremendous example can become a compelling motivation for us all, for each of us is a pioneer in his own life, often in his own family, and many of us pioneer daily in trying to establish a gospel foothold in distant parts of the world."[36] The experiences of Joseph Smith and other early Saints had become real to him, and he was determined that the sacrifices of the past would not be for naught: "Thanks be to those who remained true while walking through those testing fires. What a price; what a terrible price they paid, of which we are the beneficiaries. We had better never forget it."[37]

As he pored over journals and diaries and then condensed his findings into useful forms of media, he began not only to understand but to *feel* the Saints' fervor and vision of a spiritual kingdom that would ultimately extend far beyond their own small, bedraggled group. And his vision of what could be—and would—motivated him far more than pressing deadlines.

This sense of vision was also nurtured by the privilege of working intimately with the Brethren and observing them as they evaluated problems, made decisions, and handled delicate situations. Gordon's was an unparalleled opportunity for a man of his age and experience. And because members of the committee quickly came to trust his instincts, motives, and judgment, they talked openly with him, answered his questions, and took him into their confidence.

With an ever-present gleam in his eye, Elder John A. Widtsoe frequently reminded Gordon that his door was always open. Gordon prized moments of one-on-one discussion with this man of great intellect, whom he found to be not only brilliant but also down-to-earth and personable. Elder Stephen L Richards, with whom he interacted almost daily, became the young writer's mentor. Although Gordon came to understand the early warnings about how exacting President Richards was and how difficult he could be to work for, the two of them got along famously. Elder Richards *was* demanding and deliberate, and those who worked with him learned to plan carefully and execute with precision. But by nature Gordon was meticulous and painstaking in his recommendations and preparations. As good as one filmstrip or slide presentation might be, he found ways to make the next one better—an approach that resonated with Elder Richards's methods. And though there were moments when Gordon wondered if he could measure up to Elder Richards's standards, his hard work and optimistic nature carried him through discouraging times. In the process he came to appreciate the fruits of rigorous preparation and attention to detail, and he developed tremendous respect and esteem for his leader. Indeed, other than his father, perhaps no individual had more influence on the young Gordon Hinckley than did Stephen L Richards.

From her vantage point, Marjorie, with whom Gordon now spent as much time as possible and in whom he confided many of his experiences, could see that Elder Richards and her beau were soul mates: "They were both quick. Elder Richards was smart, Gordon was smart. And they worked well together because of their intellect. Gordon learned a lot from him, particularly about how to deal with people. He learned that you don't quarrel with people, you compose your differences."[38]

It was an education that even the finest university couldn't have provided, though occasionally Gordon felt a touch of melancholy that his plans for advanced education appeared to have been permanently derailed. As Homer Durham neared completion of his doctorate, Gordon extended congratulations to his longtime friend: "By this late hour you are in the midst of the Herculean task of culling, scrapping, welding, pasting, clipping, annotating, arranging, assembling, getting weak-eyed over thousands of notes and paragraphs which will some day be the Durham dissertation. My good fellow, my heart envies you your progress along the ladder which leads a man to the roof of achievement. Would that I too were on a rung of the same stature. With all my heart I congratulate [you] on the splendid job you've done. Let me wring your hand in advance with a sincere compliment for the determination and faith that made of G. Homer, returned missionary . . . [a] Doctor of Philosophy who has kept the faith."[39]

He didn't regret his decision to accept the position the First Presidency had offered him, but there were times when Gordon wondered (and even worried about) what kind of future he could expect to have working for the Church. Again, in response to Homer, he acknowledged: "Your compliments on the radio programs are appreciated. We are now working on a continuation of the series. Much to do. The work of this committee with a long name is growing larger and more complicated and more interesting. . . . [R]adio, films, and literature of various kinds also serve to keep me praying, humble, busy, and at work for long hours . . . [as well as] pounding late many an evening to meet deadlines which seem to spin round as fast as my well-oiled light meter. All of which has served to make me a little more dependent upon glasses . . . a little more round-shouldered, a little more settled, and a little more full of wonder as to what this all leads to."[40]

Though it was impossible for Gordon to divine what the future might hold, one immediate and even remarkable consequence of his employment was the opportunity to be tutored in matters of the kingdom by the Lord's schoolmasters. In the process, Gordon gained a unique view of the men called to serve as General Authorities. He later said: "I got along wonderfully well with those great men, who were very kind to me. But I learned that they were human. They had weaknesses and problems, but that didn't bother me. In fact, it enhanced my estimation of them because I saw rising above their mortality an element of the divine, or at the very least an element of consecration to a tremendous cause that came first in their lives. I saw the inspiration that was at work in their lives. I had no doubt concerning their prophetic callings or of the fact that the Lord spoke and acted through them. I saw their human side, their foibles—and they all had a few. But I also saw the great overriding strength of their faith and love for the Lord, and their absolute loyalty to the work and to the trust that was placed in them."[41]

Gordon's outlook was a mirror image of his father's, for

Bryant had always nurtured a profound respect for Church leaders. And they, in turn, appreciated and admired his contributions to the kingdom. Late 1935 brought him yet another opportunity to serve when he was called to preside over the Northern States Mission, headquartered in Chicago. He and May left to assume their new responsibilities in the Midwest in January 1936, leaving Gordon to care for both the home downtown and the East Millcreek farm. Bryant's departure affected Gordon more than he might have supposed. In a letter to a friend he admitted, "Since my folks left I've had to chase a lot of things at fast speed, now having the responsibility of a house and farm, but no wife."[42]

As if that weren't enough, he was also teaching an afternoon seminary class at South High School. It was challenging to hold the attention of teenagers at the close of a long day in school, but he thoroughly enjoyed shepherding his class through the scriptures. Marjorie said: "He packed them in, *after school* no less. Those kids stayed because he was a gifted teacher. He could hold their attention, and he also became their friend."[43]

When Gordon was offered a job as a full-time seminary teacher, he was tempted to accept. But learning of the offer, Elder Richards countered, "No, we want you to work full time for *us*." Gordon accepted Elder Richards's invitation: "I decided I'd rather work for the apostles than teach seminary. I made the right choice, though it was a challenge to do everything they expected me to do."[44]

It was a pressure-filled but exciting time for Gordon. Decisions that had lifelong ramifications seemed to lurk around each corner. Though his "career," as it were, had taken an entirely unexpected course, he was having experiences he would scarcely have dreamed of even a year or two earlier, and getting a bird's-eye view of the Church and world in the process. And while he was being tutored by the Brethren and growing daily in his understanding of the fundamental tasks required to operate the growing Church, he was progressing on another important front as well.

CHAPTER SEVEN

MARJORIE AND THE ART OF HOME BUILDING

During the time since Gordon's return from England, he and Marjorie had become nearly inseparable. Any other romantic interests had long since faded as it became clear that theirs was to be a long-term relationship. But it was still "the bottom of the Depression," as Gordon referred to it then and ever after, salaries were meager, almost no job was regarded as steady, and they like most young couples were cautious about marriage. "In those days," Marjorie explained later, "you didn't get married unless you had a job and could provide. But there was no question about *whether* or not we would get married. It was just a matter of when."[1]

For all their reservations about the financial ramifications of marriage, they had no qualms about compatibility. Gordon and Marjorie were attracted to each other's sense of humor, love for the gospel, innate optimism, and love of life. Through the years Marjorie would often say that the only way to get through life was to laugh your way through it, and even as a young woman she had a buoyant, cheerful disposition that was like an elixir to Gordon. It resonated with his native tendency to see the positive and to believe there was a solution to anything. She had a light heart without being light-minded. In turn, Gordon's dry wit delighted Marjorie, who loved the fact that although her beau was practical, self-disciplined, and serious about the things that mattered to him, he didn't take himself very seriously and was often the first to poke fun at his own quirks. They enjoyed bantering back and forth. Marjorie had no difficulty holding her own with him, but she always made him feel that he was equal to any challenge. Throughout their lives, in diverse settings and circumstances, she would tell others, "Gordon is amazing. There isn't anything he can't do. *Not anything!*"

They shared other things as well. Like Gordon, Marjorie had roots in the gospel that went back several generations. She too was indebted to forebears who had accepted the gospel and laid the groundwork for the comforts she enjoyed and the beliefs she had herself embraced.

In 1855, missionaries taught the gospel to twelve-year-old Mary Goble and her family in Brighton, Sussex, England, and Mary's mother, also named Mary, was eager to join the Saints in Utah. The following spring, on May 19, 1856, she and her husband, William (Bill), and their six children—Mary, Edwin, Caroline, Harriet, James, and Fanny—boarded the ship *Horizon* in Liverpool and set sail for America.

After six weeks at sea, they landed at Boston and made their way by steam train to Iowa City, where they were outfitted for the trek across the plains. Bill purchased two yoke of oxen, though he knew nothing about driving a team. But that concern paled when compared with other challenges that quickly arose. Before the family even left Iowa City, tragedy struck. Fanny, who had contracted measles on board ship and subsequently been exposed to damp weather, died just four days before her second birthday. The family laid her to rest on what still felt like foreign soil. Realizing they would probably never return, they visited her grave one last time the morning they began their journey west. Mary wrote simply, "We felt very bad to leave our little sister there."[2]

The season was late when the pioneer company led by Dan Jones (and later John Alexander Hunt) set out, and they didn't reach Council Bluffs until late September. They hoped to reach Utah before winter, but the company was not far from Council Bluffs when it became apparent that if anything the season was changing earlier than usual. Young Mary later told of their resultant travail, including the birth of an infant sister named Edith who lived just six weeks before dying of lack of nourishment.

With no choice but to bury their child in a shallow grave on the prairie, the Gobles swallowed their grief and pressed forward.

Bill Goble was the camp hunter, and he provided his fellow Saints with food. When the wagon train came upon the Martin handcart company, Bill was assigned to stay with the handcart pioneers in case his help was needed. The family's willingness to remain behind exacted a terrible personal price. Mary wrote: "When we arrived at Devil's Gate it was bitter cold. We left lots of our things there. . . . My brother James ate a hearty supper and was as well as he ever was when he went to bed. In the morning he was dead. My feet were frozen also my brother Edwin and my sister Caroline had their feet frozen."[3]

Devil's Gate was aptly named. There pioneers of the Martin handcart company and the Hunt-Hodgett wagon trains were trapped together as unrelenting waves of snow made travel impossible. With the death tally increasing daily, it began to look as though everyone would perish on the high plains of Wyoming. What the Gobles and their companions didn't know was that word of their plight had reached Brigham Young. On Sunday morning, October 5, 1856, the prophet delivered the opening address of general conference in the Bowery on Temple Square: "Many of our brethren and sisters are on the Plains with hand-carts . . . and they must be brought here. . . . I will tell you all that your faith, religion, and profession of religion, will never save one soul of you in the celestial kingdom of our God, unless you carry out just such principles as I am now teaching you. Go and bring in those people now on the Plains."[4]

When a scout from the rescue party reached the handcart companies stalled near South Pass, Wyoming, those who were physically able sang songs and even danced. But as they crossed the final mountain before entering the valley, Mary's mother died. Wrote Mary: "We arrived in Salt Lake City nine o'clock at night the 11th of December 1856. Three out of four that were living were frozen. My mother was dead in the wagon. . . . Early the next morning Bro. Brigham Young and a doctor came. . . . When [Brigham Young] saw our condition—our feet frozen and our mother dead—tears rolled down his cheeks. The doctor amputated my toes using a saw and a butcher knife. Brigham Young promised me I would not have to have any more of my feet cut off. The sisters were dressing mother for the last time. Oh how did we stand it?"[5] Mary's family subsequently moved to Nephi, Utah.

A young man by the name of Richard Pay had also emigrated from England and endured adversity while crossing the plains. The daughter he and his wife were blessed with in Iowa died at Chimney Rock, and then Richard's wife passed away at Fort Bridger. He arrived in Salt Lake City alone, and the following spring he tied all his belongings into a handkerchief and walked to Nephi, Utah, where he later met and married Mary Goble.

In time, Richard and Mary Pay were blessed with thirteen children, their youngest, a son named Phillip LeRoy, arriving on November 14, 1885. As the last born, Roy had plenty of attention from older brothers and sisters, but his first experience with grief came early. He was just seven when his father returned from a trip to the temple one evening complaining of pain in his abdomen. Mary immediately summoned the doctor, but he arrived too late. Richard died from appendicitis on April 18, 1893, at the age of seventy-one.

Roy was crushed by the loss of his father, and Mary was forced to activate her skills as a nurse to provide for her family. Though there was never any extra money, she was able to supply the necessities for her children. As a teenager, Roy worked summers on a farm in nearby Eureka, where he learned firsthand about the law of the harvest and came to appreciate the fruits of obedience and faith. Roy was later hired to run the candy store in Nephi, during which time he first met Georgetta Paxman, a petite young woman with thick, shiny, dark hair and beautiful, deep-set, hazel eyes.[6] Over time their friendship grew, and they both sensed that theirs might be a permanent relationship. First, however, Roy would serve in the Southern States Mission.

While Roy was in the mission field, Georgetta moved with her sister, Frances, and her mother to Salt Lake City, where she and Frances continued their education. A good student, Georgetta graduated with a two-year normal degree from the University of Utah in the spring of 1908. Despite her social opportunities, however, she couldn't seem to dismiss thoughts about her modestly handsome boyfriend from Nephi. When Roy returned home from his mission in May of that year, what had been a teenage romance blossomed into much more, and on September 7, 1910, they were married in the Salt Lake Temple. Their first child, a daughter they named Marjorie, was born fourteen months later, on November 23, 1911, in Nephi. Three years later the family moved to Salt Lake City.

For nearly five years Marjorie was an only child. Then, on July 18, 1916, Roy and Georgetta were blessed with a son, Harold George. Their happiness was short-lived, however. Just a few days after Christmas that year, they awakened to find Harold suffering from convulsions. After watching their son suffer for several hours, Roy and Georgetta knelt in prayer to plead with the Lord for his life but ended their petition with "thy will, not mine, be done"—the hardest words either had ever uttered. A few minutes later, Harold died.[7]

A second son, Douglas LeRoy, was born on August 24, 1918, and only then did Marjorie know what it was like to have a sibling in the home. In time, she and Douglas were joined by four sisters—Helen, Evelyn, Dorene, and Joanne—and the five girls developed a strong bond that provided them with great support and camaraderie through the years ahead.

After Evelyn's arrival, the Pays determined to build a home large enough to accommodate their growing family in the ward they had come to love since moving to Salt Lake City—the large Liberty Stake First Ward. They secured a lot next door to Bishop John C. Duncan and across the street from Bryant and Ada Hinckley.

Those were happy years. The children found many friends in the neighborhood, and the family was thoroughly involved in the ward. Georgetta taught the Beehive girls, and Roy was president of the YMMIA. "Even before we were old enough to go to Mutual," Marjorie remembered, "we were caught up in everything our father did. We would stay up until he got home from activities and make him tell us everything that had happened. Church was *fun*, and we loved everything about it."[8] Later, as a Beehive girl, Marjorie was even more enthusiastic. All major activities in the neighborhood, it seemed, centered on the First Ward MIA, and Marjorie thought it phenomenal luck that her father was involved with the program.

Georgetta and Roy were warm, generous people who opened

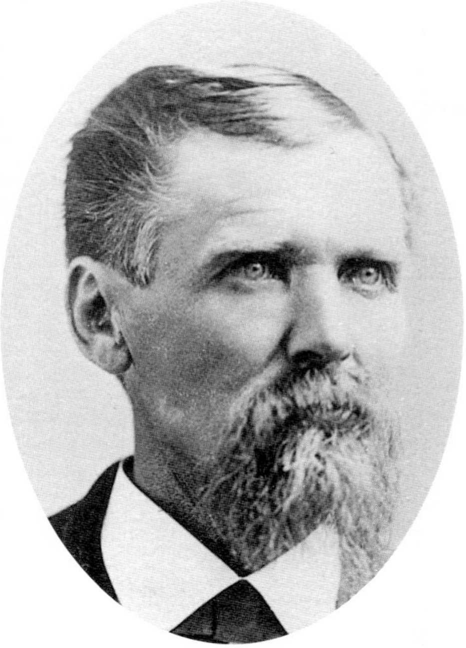

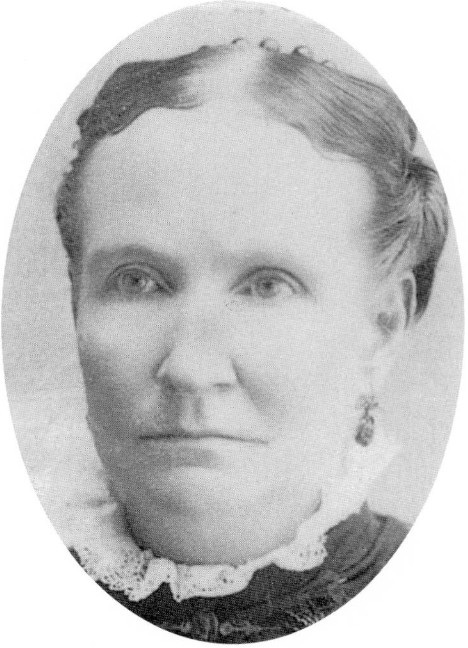

Ira Nathaniel Hinckley and Angeline Wilcox Noble, Gordon's paternal grandparents

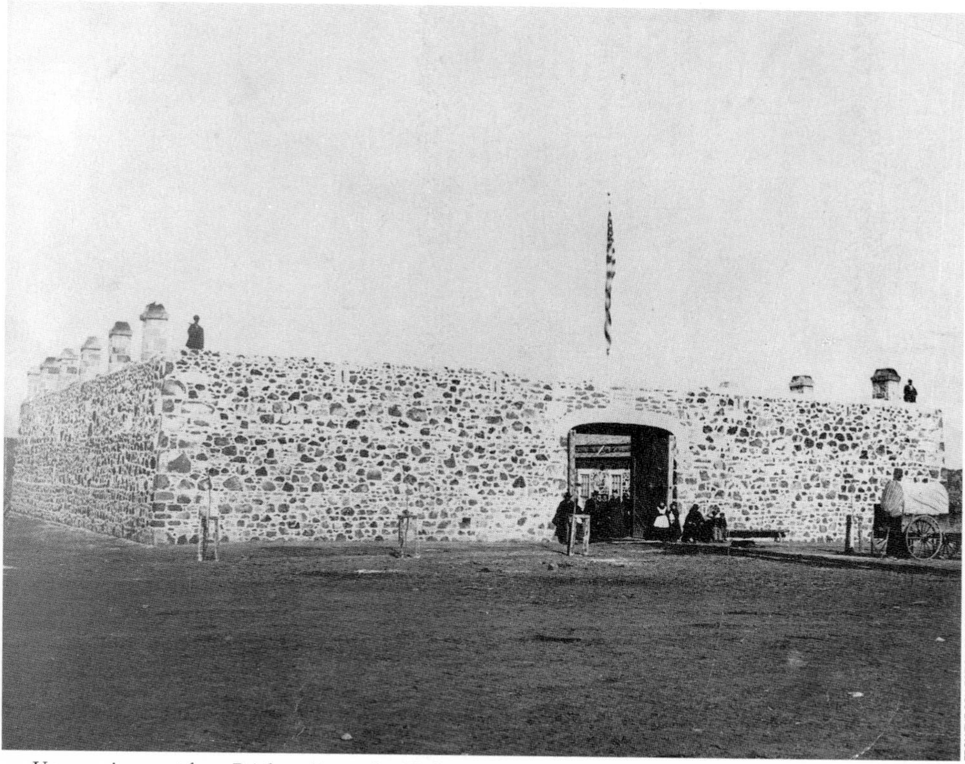

FROM THE COLLECTION OF JOSEPH AND RUTH HINCKLEY WILLES

Upon assignment from Brigham Young, Ira Nathaniel Hinckley oversaw the building of Cove Fort in 1867

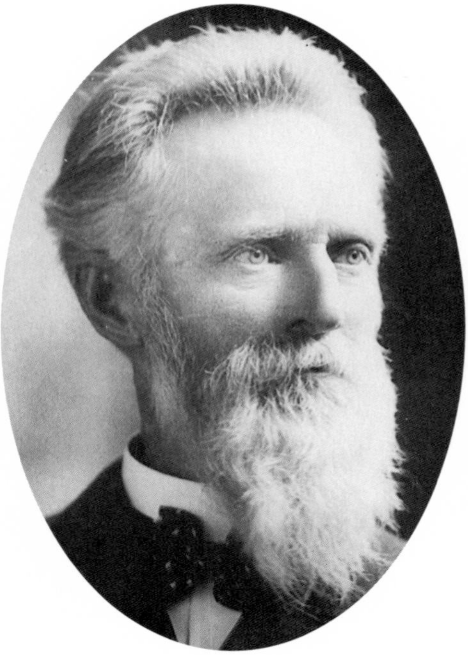

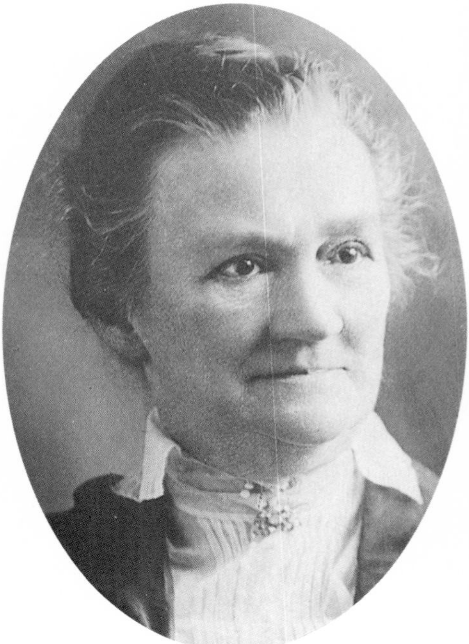

Breneman Barr Bitner and Sarah Osguthorpe Bitner, Gordon's maternal grandparents

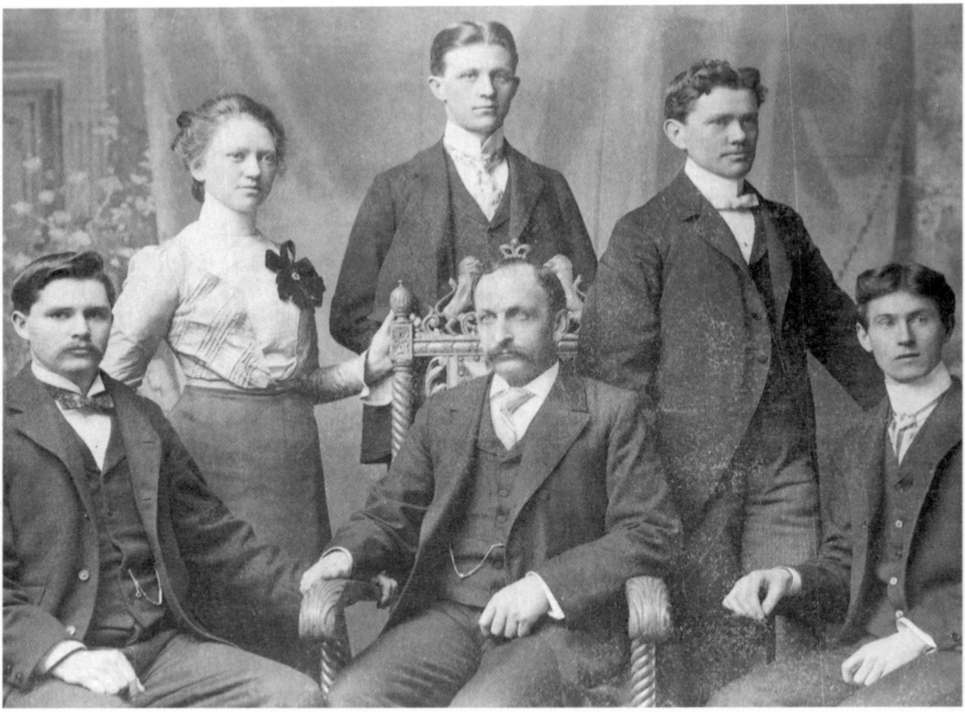

FROM THE COLLECTION OF JOSEPH AND RUTH HINCKLEY WILLES

Prior to her marriage, Ada Bitner taught at the LDS Business College, where the faculty also included (front row, left to right) J. Reuben Clark Jr., Joseph Nelson, Milton H. Ross; (back row) Walter E. Maddison, Matthew A. Miller

Bryant Stringham Hinckley and Ada Bitner were married on August 4, 1909

Bryant and Gordon in 1911

FROM THE COLLECTION OF JOSEPH AND RUTH HINCKLEY WILLES

Bryant and Ada

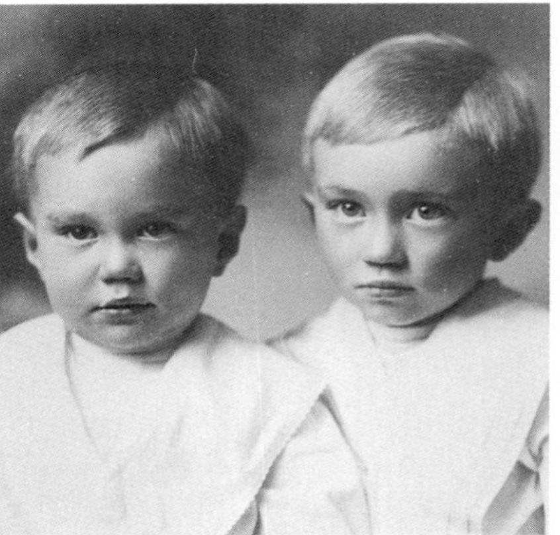

With Sherman, around 1913

FROM THE COLLECTION OF JOSEPH AND RUTH HINCKLEY WILLES

With Sherman on the farm in East Millcreek

FROM THE COLLECTION OF JOSEPH AND RUTH HINCKLEY WILLES

With Polly, one of the family cows, on the East Millcreek farm

FROM THE COLLECTION OF JOSEPH AND RUTH HINCKLEY WILLES

Bryant with Sherman and Gordon
during a family vacation to Yellowstone

At about twelve years of age

FROM THE COLLECTION OF JOSEPH AND RUTH HINCKLEY WILLES

Bryant and Ada's children (Sylvia, Gordon, Ruth, Sherman, and Ramona) in 1928

FROM THE COLLECTION OF JOSEPH AND RUTH HINCKLEY WILLES

Gordon, Bryant, and Sherman during an outing to Utah's Bryce Canyon in June 1929

FROM THE COLLECTION OF JOSEPH AND RUTH HINCKLEY WILLES

Upon his graduation from the University of Utah in 1932

The cross marking the grave of Stanford Hinckley in the American Military Cemetery in Suresnes, France

FROM THE COLLECTION OF JOSEPH AND RUTH HINCKLEY WILLES

Speaking at an open-air meeting in London's Hyde Park

FROM THE HORACE HULME FAMILY COLLECTION

Missionaries from the British and European Missions serving in London on May 6, 1935;
Elder Hinckley is second from the left on the second row

With missionary associates Angus Nicholson, Richard S. Bennett, and Ormond J. Coulam

Enjoying a visit to Oxford, England, in July 1934, during his service in the European Mission

FROM THE COLLECTION OF JOSEPH AND RUTH HINCKLEY WILLES

This photo of Bryant Hinckley is inscribed
"To my son Gordon, Christmas 1935"

On the East Millcreek farm in February 1936

Georgetta Paxman Pay with her daughter Marjorie in 1912

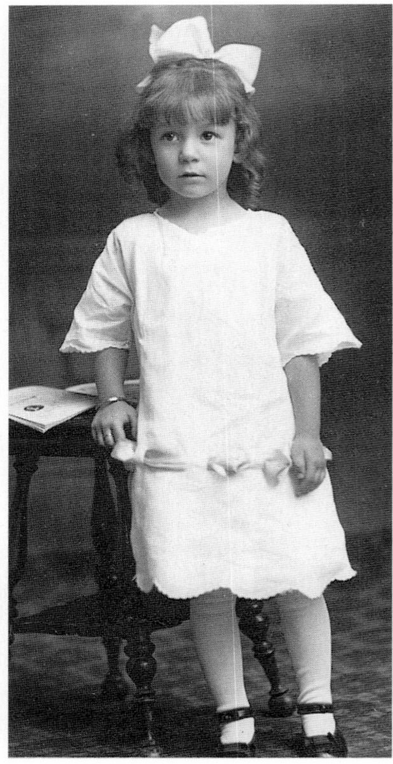

Marjorie Pay at around age five

The Pay family around 1937: (clockwise from left) Evelyn, Helen, Douglas, LeRoy, Marjorie, Dorene (seated on arm of chair), Joanne, and Georgetta

Marjorie inscribed this photograph on April 29, 1937: "To my darling, on our wedding day"

Working as executive secretary of the Church Radio, Publicity, and Mission Literature Committee in 1935

Vacationing with Virginia, Clark, Dick, and Kathy

The East Millcreek home that Gordon built

President David O. McKay visits the East Millcreek Stake, where Gordon is serving as first counselor to Lamont B. Gundersen (second from right). H. Leroy Erickson is on the far left

With Elder Richard L. Evans and President J. Reuben Clark Jr. as they prepare for a radio broadcast on January 17, 1948

Gordon conceived, wrote, and produced some of the Church's first visual materials

Gordon (third from right) supervised the construction of this exhibit at the 1939 Golden Gate International Exposition, which simulated the Tabernacle on Temple Square. Fair visitors heard brief addresses and organ music

PHOTO BY HAL RUMEL/DESERET NEWS

President David O. McKay introduces Gordon B. Hinckley as the newest Assistant to the Twelve on April 6, 1958

PHOTO COURTESY LDS VISUAL RESOURCES LIBRARY

Elder Hinckley's family at the time of his call as a General Authority: Virginia, Marjorie, Jane, Gordon, Kathy, Dick, and Clark (kneeling)

PHOTO BY J MALAN HESLOP/DESERET NEWS

With Elder Richard L. Evans, President David O. McKay, President Joseph Fielding Smith, Elder ElRay L. Christiansen, and (back row) A. Hamer Reiser, temple president Selvoy J. Boyer, and temple architect Edward O. Anderson at the dedication of the London Temple in September 1958

Making his first trip to Asia in May 1960

On April 28, 1961, Elder Hinckley convened a historic meeting at the American Military Cemetery on the outskirts of Manila during which he opened the Philippines to missionary work. (President Robert S. Taylor is at his right.) Only one Filipino member of the Church, David Lagman (photo at right), was in attendance

their home in a comfortable way that drew friends and family to them. On Sunday evenings Marjorie and her friends came home after sacrament meeting for waffles—a weekly ritual so sacred that when the waffle iron quit working, Marjorie's friends pooled their money to buy the Pays another one.

Both parents had a light touch when it came to discipline. Roy's sternest form of reproof was looking up from his paper when the children were misbehaving and saying firmly, "That will do, children." Georgetta had her own way of dealing with her children. "I don't ever remember Mother telling me I was naughty," Marjorie reflected years later. "When I was misbehaving, she would say, 'This must be Sally from the mountains in my kitchen. My little girl would never act this way.' And I would reform."[9]

In general, Marjorie was happy and good-natured. She did well in school, was eager to experience new things, and, like her parents, was unfailingly optimistic. Said Marjorie of her growing-up years: "My parents created an environment of contentment and peace. Even during the Depression we didn't feel deprived or worried about what was going to happen to us. Somehow, Mother always managed to have a dollar in her purse, and that gave us a sense of security. We didn't have a lot of money, but we made a lot of fun."[10]

There were a few modest pleasures. On Christmas morning Roy was the first to turn on the tree lights and see if Santa had come. "Well, someone has been in here and messed things up a bit," he would announce to the children. There was always a family game or two and perhaps a new jigsaw puzzle under the tree. Each summer the family went to Black Rock Beach on the shore of the Great Salt Lake so that everyone could bob in the salty water and roast hot dogs around a roaring bonfire that night. The year of the stock market crash, Roy somehow found a way to present his family with a radio for Christmas; thereafter on Sunday evenings they gathered around the marvelous device to listen to Jack Benny and others.

Georgetta loved good music, recited many poems from memory, and encouraged her children to read well and speak clearly. As a young girl, Marjorie took elocution lessons and learned to be confident in front of an audience.

From her father, she learned to be generous and flexible. Regardless of how depleted their pantry was, Roy couldn't turn anyone away hungry, and friends and relatives knew they were always welcome. It wasn't uncommon for Marjorie to come home at night and find a note pinned to the lamp explaining that someone was sleeping in her bed. Nonetheless, although there was affection in the Pay home, there weren't many open displays. "Hugging and kissing would have embarrassed us," Marjorie said, "but there was a lot of love in our home that was undeniable. It was wonderful, and it gave me a feeling of being worth something."[11]

Roy often told his family that he might not leave them much of a temporal inheritance, but that they would never lack for something of greater worth—his love and his assurance that God lives. When he was more than eighty years old he summarized his life's experience: "We haven't had a surplus of money, but we haven't starved to death either. What we have is far greater than any money we could have stacked up anywhere. . . . I don't know if there could be two people in the world who have been happier than mother and I. . . . We have a family we are proud of. . . . If we had this life to live over we couldn't ask for anything better than what we have had. If we could just all live so that in that Celestial Kingdom of Heaven we could be together it will be a marvelous, marvelous thing."[12]

Within this environment of faith, love, and optimism, Marjorie Pay grew and developed her own view of the world. In the main, her outlook on life was uncomplicated, perhaps even a little naive. Reared in the relatively protected environment of Salt Lake City, she knew little of the world. When she was sixteen, her parents allowed her to accompany a girlfriend on a week's tour to San Francisco. It was an adventure that exceeded her most glamorous expectations. When she saw the Pacific Ocean for the first time, Marjorie felt she had seen it all. But when their tour guide took them to an oceanside restaurant fabled for its seafood and announced that this was an excellent place to order a fish cocktail, Marjorie and her friend looked at each other and said, almost in unison, "*Cocktail!* We'll just sit on the bus."

From an early age, Marjorie accepted the faith of her parents, something she attributed in part to them. "My parents' love for the gospel was contagious," she said, "and mother taught us early to love Jesus Christ. We prayed about and over everything, even not burning the soup. I grew up believing my prayers would be answered, and that if I prayed for something it would happen." Hanging in the bedroom where she and her sisters slept was a large picture of the Savior. "Every morning when I woke up," she said, "the first thing I saw was the beautiful face of Jesus Christ. I was grown and long gone from home before I realized what an impact that had on me."[13]

Marjorie found it easy to believe the teachings of the gospel. "I think I was born with a testimony," she explained. "I never remember not having one." She was about seventeen when she decided to put that knowledge to the test. Her approach was straightforward and spiritually confident: "There was a time when I wanted to be sure my testimony was really *mine,* and that I wasn't leaning on anyone else's. So I took that problem to the Lord and got it solved. I have a lot of faith, and I can thank my parents for that. I somehow knew the Lord wouldn't let me down. And he didn't."[14]

Like her mother, Marjorie didn't lack for friends. She too was petite, energetic, and full of fun and life. The youth in the neighborhood didn't all attend the same high school—some, including Gordon, went to the LDS High School, which required extra tuition; others, Marjorie among them, went to East High School, the nearby public facility. But the teenagers in the Liberty Stake First Ward mingled frequently at dances, Mutual activities, and firesides. Because they attended different high schools, Gordon and Marjorie didn't cross paths socially except at church—and even then, Marjorie wasn't terribly aware of him at first. "Of course," she admitted, "it wasn't until I was a senior in high school that I realized there were two genders and began to look around. I didn't really see Gordon until then."[15]

When Marjorie was a senior, Gordon invited her to the Gold and Green Ball. "If you got a date to the Gold and Green Ball, you were set for the next year of your life," she remembered. "It was wonderful." By this time Gordon was a university man, and it was heavenly to walk into the dance on his arm. Their first date was the beginning of a friendship that eventually evolved into courtship. Early on, Marjorie told her mother that this was a young man who was going somewhere. "He was different from anyone else," she explained. "Everything he did, he did with a flair unique to him. And he had wonderful integrity. I never had to worry a minute about anything he told me."[16] Even as she watched him struggle with his feelings about the gospel during his university years, she remained unworried: "Gordon always had a testimony. But he was very bright, and he had questions about *everything*. Everybody has to come to their convictions on their own, and so did he."[17]

Marjorie graduated from East High School in June 1929. The day she went to register at the University of Utah, she returned home to find that the company where her father worked had folded. Without hesitating, she immediately found full-time work as secretary to the local manager of the Owens Illinois Glass Company, but the opportunity for formal education never presented itself again. Meanwhile, as Gordon approached his graduation from the University of Utah and looked toward doing graduate work back East, he found himself beginning to at least consider future possibilities with Marjorie. Gradually they reserved their attention almost solely for each other.

It wasn't long after Gordon received his bachelor of arts degree, however, that he left for his mission to England. Though Marjorie refused to go into hibernation during his absence, she missed him terribly. Through his letters she shared his experiences vicariously, and though separated by an ocean, she could see that he was changing. "Before he went on his mission," she said, "Gordon was still trying to sort through some of the elements of the gospel. But once he returned, there was no turning back with him in terms of what he felt was important. The gospel had become number one in his life."[18] Now that he was home and absorbed in his work for the Church, Marjorie saw the proverbial writing on the wall: "As we got closer to marriage, I felt completely confident that Gordon loved me. But I also knew somehow that I would never come first with him. I knew I was going to be second in his life and that the Lord was going to be first. And that was okay."[19]

Such a realization might well have discouraged some other

brides-to-be, but Marjorie was unruffled. "It seemed to me that if you understood the gospel and the purpose of our being here, you would want a husband who put the Lord first. I felt secure knowing he was that kind of man," she explained. She also wondered—though she kept such thoughts to herself—if Gordon's opportunity to work with the General Authorities and to shoulder heavy responsibility at such an early age might not be an omen of things to come: "I knew that Gordon was extraordinary, and I took it for granted that he would do extraordinary things," she reflected years later.[20] Indeed, she had been prepared throughout her childhood to live—and live happily—with a man whose commitment to the Lord would dominate their life together. "Mother taught us by example that the most wonderful thing in the world was to have a husband who loves the Lord. It did not occur to me that there was any other way to live."[21]

As well suited as they were to each other, Gordon and Marjorie experienced some moments of tension in their long courtship—a result, at least partially, of their self-imposed wait. In their mid-twenties, they were getting "old" by the day's standards. Many of their friends had already settled down, including Homer Durham, who in June 1936 married Eudora Widtsoe, a daughter of Elder John A. and Leah Dunford Widtsoe. But for the time being there were practical reasons for them to hold off on marriage. Among other considerations, Marjorie's salary continued to help provide her family with a steady income.

Finally the day of their wedding approached. But Gordon in particular was anxious about the economic realities of marriage. On the eve of their wedding he called Marjorie and asked her to meet him at Keeley's Cafe on Main Street. As they sat at the lunch counter he explained their problem: He had totaled up his assets, and they were less than $150. More alarming, he earned only $185 a month.

Marjorie, whose basic philosophy was that things always worked out somehow, was not concerned. A hundred and fifty dollars sounded like a fortune to her, and she replied with characteristic optimism that she had hoped for a husband and now she found out she was getting $150 too. "This will work out wonderfully," she told him. "If you've got $150, we're set."[22]

Finally, Gordon Bitner Hinckley and Marjorie Pay were married by Elder Stephen L Richards in the Salt Lake Temple on April 29, 1937. The ceremony was beautiful in its simplicity and powerful in its promise. Gordon later said of that day, "Marjorie had grown into a wonderful young woman, and I had the good sense to marry her. The wondrous aura of young womanhood was upon her. She was beautiful, and I was bewitched."[23]

With Bryant and May in Chicago, where he was serving as president of the Northern States Mission, and because there was little money to spend on traditional wedding fanfare, the newlyweds dispensed with a reception. After the temple ceremony, they headed for the solitude and privacy of southern Utah's beautiful state parks, traveling as far as Fillmore the first night. They then ventured on to Zion's National Park and other scenic areas before returning home.

The year 1937 was a momentous time to begin life together, a year of highs and lows, good news and bad. In 1937 Walt Disney released his first full-length animated feature, *Snow White and the Seven Dwarfs*; John Steinbeck published *Of Mice and Men;* and the Golden Gate Bridge spanning the entrance to San Francisco Bay opened. Unfortunately, the good news was tucked in between waves of bad. Amelia Earhart disappeared during a flight over the mid-Pacific; the German dirigible *Hindenburg* exploded in Lakehurst, New Jersey; and Hitler and Mussolini continued to solidify their alliance.

Though the world was poised on the cusp of a new era that would see the end of the Depression but the beginning of what would escalate into the most devastating war in modern times, Gordon and Marjorie's life together was, at the outset, uncomplicated. After their honeymoon to southern Utah, they moved into Bryant and May's farm home in East Millcreek, the cottage where Gordon had spent his boyhood summers. But although the home had provided Bryant's family with many delightful vacations, critical improvements were needed to transform it into a suitable year-round dwelling. It had, for instance, no kitchen cupboards or bedroom closets. More serious, there was no furnace, and heat was essential if they were to live there during the winter.

Gordon immediately ordered a furnace and began to study the complicated installation instructions. With no money to pay a serviceman to install the device, he would have to do it himself. The furnace was delivered the first of September, and he immediately set out to lay a brick flue and install the new hardware. Had he been able to afford to hire the work done, he would not have done so, as there was in his mind a certain illogic to hiring a professional when his personal motto was, "You're just as capable as the next man and probably a darn sight better." With the furnace installed and functioning, Gordon built cupboards and added other amenities. In time, the newlyweds turned the farmhouse into a cozy, comfortable home.

The farmhouse wasn't the only project that demanded Gordon's time and attention. Upon returning home from his mission, he had been called as first the assistant superintendent and later the superintendent of the Liberty Stake Sunday School, which office he held until his marriage. On November 17, 1937—at the age of twenty-seven and after being married just seven months—Gordon was called to serve as a member of the Deseret Sunday School Union General Board.[24] The general board was a large, energetic body of accomplished men and women—among them Tabernacle organist Alexander Schreiner, noted scientist Carl F. Eyring, and Adam S. Bennion and Mark E. Petersen, who were later called to the Quorum of the Twelve. As a junior member, Gordon slowly learned the range of his responsibilities. Board members wrote lesson manuals (one of Gordon's, *Leaders of the Scriptures*, which he co-authored with Marion Gibb Merkley, was published for more than twenty years in various forms, under different titles, and in numerous languages), conducted Sunday School conventions in stakes throughout the Church, published the *Instructor*, served on various committees, and generally took an active role in overseeing the Church's vast Sunday School program. For Gordon, the privilege of associating with fellow board members, many of them seasoned leaders whose lives had been filled with a diverse array of service, was an unexpected bonus.[25]

He and Wendell Ashton, who was called to the board not

long after he was, were noticeably younger than many of their colleagues. One weekend they arrived early for a stake Sunday School conference they were to conduct and went to introduce themselves and make preparations. When the stake presidency spotted them walking the halls, they assumed the two unfamiliar young men were traveling with the board members and asked, "Where are the brethren from Salt Lake City?" The stake presidency were shocked when Gordon and Wendell explained that *they were* the brethren.

Gordon's experience on the board broadened his youthful point of view. Other than his mission in England, this was his first exposure to the Church outside of Utah, and the view was eye-opening: "It gave me the insight that there was great strength in the stakes of Zion away from Salt Lake City. I began to see that the Church wasn't just a provincial, Utah-based organization," he later said. "There was strength, there was faith and testimony, there was power away from Church headquarters."[26]

While he continued to learn more about the administration of the Church, Gordon was also finding there was plenty to keep him occupied at home as he and Marjorie adjusted to living with each other. And there *were* adjustments. Shortly after they had announced their engagement, Emma Marr Petersen, Mark E. Petersen's wife, had warned Marjorie that the first ten years of marriage would be the hardest. Her comment both puzzled and shocked Marjorie, who later admitted: "I was just sure the first ten years would be bliss. But during our first year together I discovered she was *dead right!* There were a lot of adjustments. Of course, they weren't the kind of thing you ran home to mother about. But I cried into my pillow now and again. The problems were almost always related to learning to live on someone else's schedule and to do things someone else's way. We loved each other, there was no doubt about that. But we also had to get used to each other. I think *every* couple has to get used to each other."[27]

Despite such adjustments, both Gordon and Marjorie were so busy living that they had little time to philosophize about how things should be. She was still working as a secretary, and he juggled his time between Church headquarters and his assignments on the Sunday School General Board. There was an unspoken understanding about how their family would operate, a natural division of responsibilities that neither questioned or resented. Gordon would earn the living, and Marjorie would take the lead in managing the household and rearing the children. Her mother had always referred to her years with young children at home as "golden years," and Marjorie felt she would do her most important work as a mother.

In the late summer of 1938 the Hinckleys received news they had been anxious to hear: come spring, they would be parents. Not long before the life-changing event, Gordon acknowledged some of his insecurities in a letter to Homer Durham: "Marge and I have sorta shut ourselves out of the social circle these days, spending much time in spring housecleaning, planting carrots and peas, and other things which leave no time for parties, shows, or the like—all in contemplation of our firstborn within the next fortnight. Things are going nicely, but I have a case of jitters. You of course understand."[28] On March 31, 1939, nine months of anticipation were rewarded with the birth of their first child, a daughter, whom they named Kathleen.

The event transcended anything either had imagined. "It was scary to think about being responsible for another human being, but wonderful in the way it made me feel," Gordon said.[29] For Marjorie, the experience was one of "sheer excitement." "I didn't know enough to worry about what might happen," she admitted. "I didn't know that people sometimes have problems with their children. So having one of my own was even better than anything I had imagined."[30]

That Christmas in the family newsletter, Gordon summarized life as he saw it: "This is the farm hand speaking. . . . Cheerio!—and a Merry Christmas! We three go in our usual way—Marjorie P., Kathleen, and Gordon B. We go a-diggin' in the dirt on Saturday afternoons, a-scurryin' off to Church on Sunday nights and mornings, a-pilin' in the wash on Mondays, a-hoppin' to Sunday School Board meetings on Tuesdays, a-tremblin' to Radio Committee meetings on Wednesdays, a-racin' to spend all we earn on Thursdays, and a-hopin' Saturday afternoons will come on Fridays. They're great weeks we live—that are piling into rich years. The car we drive is beginning to look like the same Plymouth mentioned in the history of America—1620. The house in which we live is the same one in which we grew up. . . . And the job we do is the same one we've been doing for the last four years. But we have one thing new—She's the sweetest little gal that ever swished an eyelash."[31]

Gordon and Marjorie found that the addition of a child to the family called for adjustments to their previously well-ordered life. Though the three of them fit nicely in the one-bedroom farm home, it was apparent that they would soon need to seek larger, more permanent quarters. When in the fall of 1940 the Hinckleys learned that they were again expecting, Gordon realized he must find a solution to the problem. Furthermore, in April 1939 his father and Aunt May had returned from the mission field and were anxious to move back into the country cottage.

Bryant Hinckley offered his son a building lot on his East Millcreek property. Gordon was grateful for the ground, which was down the lane and through the orchard from the farm home. Though it had been used as a dumping ground for years, and garbage and morning-glory vines covered mounds of half-buried debris from one end of the lot to the next, Gordon owned it free and clear. And it was in an area that felt like home.

Early in his university training, Gordon had flirted with the notion of becoming an architect. Like his grandfather before him, he was a natural mechanic and could draw blueprints for and build almost anything. With these fundamental skills, he set out to build his own home. It wouldn't be *his* home unless he had his hand in it from the beginning, nor could he afford to hire the job out anyway. So with a few drafting tools left over from a junior high school course, he drew up a floor plan, made a scale model out of cardboard, and went to work on the home Marjorie would ever after refer to as "the house that Jack built."

Indeed, when Gordon and Marjorie's children would later tell friends that their father had built their home, few took them literally. From the outset of the project, however, Gordon's vision of the finished product guided every decision. He knew how he wanted things done, and he hired out those jobs that required specialty skills or that were so large he couldn't complete them fast enough working alone.

On Thanksgiving Day of 1940, Gordon and a friend, Rush

Christensen, began digging footings on the project that would consume Gordon's holidays, early mornings, evenings, Saturdays, and days off for many months. In addition to acting as the general contractor, he wired and plumbed the home and did some of the finish carpentry. He hired out the bricklaying and Sheetrocking, a technique coming into vogue. The days flew by, and though the plumbing and electricity were installed and working by the end of April, the house still wasn't habitable by May 2, 1941, the day Richard Gordon Hinckley was born. Marjorie was so elated with the arrival of their first son, however, that the condition of their living quarters caused her little concern. "I was so thrilled to have a girl and a boy. It made me feel complete," she explained. "I knew that if I was unfortunate enough not to have any more children, at least I had one of each."[32] She was worried when Dick came down with a jaundice-like condition that kept him in the hospital longer than usual, enough so that she stayed with her in-laws and later with her parents while she and Dick gained strength.

Meanwhile Gordon worked night and day to finish the home. Every spare moment found him in work clothes and tool belt overseeing subcontractors, completing the carpentry, attending to a myriad of construction details, and finally painting. The project was tiring, physically and mentally. There would be many times throughout his life when Gordon would feel exhausted, but whenever he would begin to complain about how weary he felt, he would catch himself and proclaim to his wife, "But I'm not as tired as I was the day I moved you into our new house."[33]

Their new dwelling became much more than a place to hang their hats. Not only did their East Millcreek home stand as a monument to Gordon's tenacity and skill, but it provided the backdrop for years of family memories. Compared with the tiny farm home, the two-bedroom, 1200-square-foot house with its large yard seemed palatial.

With Gordon's family settled in a home of their own, Bryant and May returned to the farm home in East Millcreek. Their years presiding over the Northern States Mission had been fulfilling ones for them both. Largely due to Bryant's efforts, the

Chicago Stake was organized and the Carthage Jail restored during his time there. Soon after their return, May Hinckley was called by the First Presidency to serve as the third general president of the Primary, and she was overwhelmed by the assignment. In issuing the call, President Grant said simply, "May, we're going to give you 102,000 children," further fulfilling the promise in her patriarchal blessing that she would be a "mother to many children."[34] Under May's direction, the Primary simplified its program, which proved essential during World War II, and introduced its seal and colors—the primary colors of red, yellow, and blue.

Marjorie had always felt a little intimidated by her in-laws, and these high-profile assignments did nothing to alleviate her apprehensions. Bryant Hinckley had been her stake president as well as a popular figure in the community. But both he and May made an effort to build rapport with their daughter-in-law. Their proximity to each other now made frequent association convenient and increasingly comfortable. Bryant broke the ice with Marjorie when he called one evening to see if she would accompany him to a university lecture. "From that time on it was wonderful," Marjorie remembered. "I hadn't really known if I was accepted by him before then. But he was a wonderful man who had absolute integrity. And he was a wonderful speaker. I told Gordon many times, 'If you keep trying you'll be as good a speaker as your father.' He gave the best two-and-a-half-minute talks I ever heard. And he treated me wonderfully."[35]

Marjorie felt less confident about her relationship with her mother-in-law. Though Aunt May was always cordial and friendly, her strong personality made Marjorie uncomfortable. But after Dick was born, the two women grew to better understand each other. It was Aunt May who insisted that Marjorie and Dick stay with them downtown after the baby's birth, and in time Marjorie came to enjoy a cherished bond with her. Although she had at first been apprehensive about living too close to her in-laws, she came to love having Gordon's parents nearby.

The Hinckleys were one of many young couples in the area trying to establish themselves. The rural community of East

Millcreek was quickly transforming itself into a suburban neighborhood. With urban development came the challenges of managing growth, and as a new homeowner Gordon was interested in having a voice in civic decisions. For a time he served as a director of the East Millcreek Irrigation Company and as president of the East Millcreek Betterment League, a volunteer chamber of commerce that looked for ways to improve living conditions in the rapidly expanding community. The latter position was time-consuming, and he found it increasingly difficult to manage everything for which he was responsible. On one occasion he described the balancing act: "I am terribly busy with a large number of things in the office, and my time away from the office is crowded with a thousand and one things—president of the civil league of the community in which I live, . . . writing a course of study for one of the auxiliary organizations of the Church, wading through some difficulties in which some property in which I am interested is involved, trying now to get my house completed and the lawn ready for planting when I have reached a point where I have to do the job myself, trying to find a few minutes to take my wife and kids for a ride and panting hard to keep up with the rising cost of keeping alive."[36] In another letter a month later, he wrote, "I don't know of a time in my life when I have had more pressing and important work than I have on my hands right now. I work here all day long and go home and pound a typewriter far into the night."[37]

While Gordon was focused on matters close to home, the war in Europe was having a serious effect on the number of missionaries serving worldwide. On August 24, 1939, the First Presidency directed all missionaries in Germany to move to neutral countries and subsequently to return home. Just eight days later, on September 1, the German army invaded Poland. Britain and France declared war on Germany two days after that, and World War II had begun. Though it would be another year before President Franklin D. Roosevelt signed the Selective Service Act, inaugurating the first peacetime military draft in U.S. history, increasing numbers of young LDS men were already enlisting.

Concerned about the unique needs of Church members

serving in the armed forces, Gordon had them in mind when he prepared in 1943 *A Brief Statement of Principles of the Gospel*. The small but dense book, 370 pages in length, included selected hymns, instructions on how to perform various priesthood ordinances and conduct funerals, and a letter from the First Presidency with sensitive words of counsel and consolation.

Indeed, a dark cloud hung over much of humanity as the war escalated and one nation after another was pulled into hostilities that now extended to the Pacific. As late as 1940 the war overseas still seemed a world away for many Americans, some of whom had not felt the impact directly. But on Sunday morning, December 7, 1941, America's remaining complacency was shattered when Japanese planes bombed the U.S. fleet at Pearl Harbor. The "day that would live in infamy" united the American people in a zeal that would sustain them during their country's involvement in a long, bloody war.

In a matter of hours, life changed for almost every American. The home of the Stars and Stripes had been thrust into the bloodiest, most intense part of the war, and the effort of almost every able-bodied person was required, in one way or another, to support the war effort. A combination of fear and patriotic fervor swept through the country. There was nothing to insulate the Hinckleys from the effects of war, which extended into the suburb of East Millcreek and reached their tentacles around the young family.

CHAPTER EIGHT

WORLD WAR II AND ITS AFTERMATH

On New Year's Eve of 1941 Gordon wrote a friend: "Here we are at the end of another year and the beginning of a new one. No year in my life has gone by so rapidly. . . . [But] the New Year opens with foreboding for all of us. It goes without saying that we shall all see great changes in our lives. There is only one course to take, and I believe our nation is doing its best in following it. Values will shift, but the eternal verities will remain. To them we must cling."[1]

In minutes, the Japanese attack on Pearl Harbor had radically changed the face of American politics and swept away any remaining resistance to U.S. involvement in the global conflict. With America's subsequent declaration of war against the Land of the Rising Sun and Germany's against the United States, most Americans found themselves in one way or another looking for ways to support the huge war machine.

Not only were individual citizens profoundly affected, but organizations also adapted in the face of shifting priorities. To accommodate the circumstances of its members, the Church made adjustments in operations. On January 17, 1942, the First Presidency instructed all general boards and auxiliary organizations to discontinue holding conferences and other stake meetings to help members meet wartime restrictions on travel as well as to reduce personal expenses in light of increased war-related taxes. The Relief Society's conference scheduled for April to commemorate its centennial anniversary was canceled, and the annual April general conference was closed to all but General

Authorities and presidencies of the 141 stakes then in existence. On April 5, 1942, the First Presidency closed the Tabernacle for the duration of the war. During that time conference sessions were held in the Assembly Hall on Temple Square and in the solemn assembly room on the fifth floor of the Salt Lake Temple.

The missionary program, however, may have taken the hardest hit. Missionaries in many countries were evacuated, some missions were closed down entirely, and the call of new missionaries all but ceased. On March 23, 1942, the First Presidency announced that for the duration of World War II only older men who had been ordained high priests and seventies would be called on full-time missions. With missionary work grinding to a standstill, Gordon's job providing effective proselytizing materials became less pressing. Realizing that his workload would be diminished for the duration of the war, and feeling a responsibility to assist somehow with the war effort, he joined a friend in responding to a newspaper notice recruiting potential naval officer candidates. He was discouraged when his friend was accepted into the program but he was not, his history of allergies and hay fever disqualifying him. "I was depressed over the rejection," he admitted later. "The war was on, and everybody was doing something to help. I felt that I should participate in some way."[2]

With the escalation of the war, it was hard for Gordon to imagine that the draft would pass him by, allergies or not. For a man with a wife and two young children, the prospects of landing squarely in the middle of the infantry seemed more threatening than did enlisting as an officer-in-training.

"With the army engulfing men by the millions, I may be bathing in a canvas tub before long," he wrote an associate in late May of 1942. "I seriously expect that perhaps by fall those in my class will be moved either into the ranks or to the assembly line." He continued, acknowledging the strain he was still under at Church headquarters: "The more I labor over writing—radio scripts and all this other stuff I have to deal with—the more I feel I was never made for such work. Maybe I feel especially that way now, with a warm spring outside and a faint odor of flowers from the garden below, while beside me on the desk is a ponderous manuscript on which I am doing some editorial work. I suppose all of us are kids who hanker after a fishin' pole and bare feet when the lazy May days come round."[3]

A month later he revealed more of his concerns to his friend G. L. Price, with whom he had worked closely on the "Fulness of Times" series, about the prospects of going to war and the introspection that possibility had motivated:

> I've just turned 33—a wife and two children, it's true—but young enough to be inducted and with enough practice and a lot of inoculations and anti-fear toxins have the makings of a soldier, though probably a very poor one.
>
> . . . I have had considerable experience in plumbing, steam-fitting, electrical work, and water filtration and chlorination. That was all years ago, but I understand they are [drafting] every man who has had background experience in these lines. So if you bump into me sometime with grease on my face and a lunch bucket in my hand, don't be surprised. I wouldn't care to go back to twisting dies and tugging on stillson wrenches, but it does run a little more to my tastes than bayonet technic.
>
> Often these days I find myself feeling that I ought to pitch in to do something to promote our war effort. I could be hardened up—though I'm disgracefully soft and short-winded now—and could make some worthwhile contribution. And I sometimes get awfully weary of swivel chair and desk work, and long for a siege of overalls and tools. . . .
>
> However, in spite of all these day-dreamings I come back to the reality that what the world needs today more than anything else is spiritual stabilization; and the eternal truth that I have tried to put into some of these scripts that men and nations can find peace only in the gospel of Christ. To win the war we need math and chemistry, bones and sinew, but to win the peace we need "a broken heart and a contrite spirit." We need the equality of the Atlantic Charter, but we more urgently need the equality that comes from a knowledge that we are all sons and daughters of God in a very literal sense and are therefore brothers and sisters. There is no gainsaying we need the bravery of Bataan, but we need also the courage of righteous conviction. Perhaps if I can use what strength and ability I have to promote these things I shall have made some small contribution to the world's good.[4]

As Americans embraced the war effort, the nation became united in an unprecedented way. Whereas there had been an almost universal sense of isolation during the Depression, the war created an intense sense of belonging and commitment to the notion that society's needs came before those of the individual. Families dug up lawns to plant victory gardens; men and women, boys and girls scoured attics and basements in a perpetual scavenger hunt for reusable metal and rubber; everyone learned to do without gas, sugar, nylon, and other scarce commodities; and American industry hummed into high gear and learned to mass-produce airplanes, ships, and other tools of war.[5]

If the military didn't deem him worthy of joining its ranks, Gordon decided, he would look for a job integral to the war effort. As it happened, Salt Lake City had been identified by the War Manpower Commission as a city where there was a critical need for more laborers. (According to the April 1940 census, 149,000 people were employed in the state of Utah; by late 1942 at least 65,000 additional workers had jobs.)[6] So finding such work shouldn't be difficult.

He was still stinging from the Navy's rejection when, feeling he must somehow become involved in the war effort, he got an introduction to a manager at the Denver and Rio Grande Railroad. In a stroke of fortuitous timing, he inquired about a job the very day an opening for an assistant stationmaster in its Salt Lake City yard became available. Though he had no experience in the transportation industry, he applied for and landed the job as assistant superintendent of the Salt Lake City Union Depot and Railroad Company, owned and operated jointly by the D&RG and Western Pacific Railroads. The year was 1943.

He had spent more than seven years in a pressure-packed job at Church headquarters, but Gordon now faced what he called the "fearsome" responsibility of keeping rail traffic moving through Salt Lake City during a time when trains were cycling in and out of the train yard like streetcars. Although he didn't know much about the railroad business, he wasn't afraid of hard work, and he attacked his responsibilities with energy, common sense, and a resolve to learn everything he could as quickly as possible. The first lesson of the rail yard was simple but imperative: Keep the trains moving, on schedule, and out of each other's way.

Though Gordon now went to work just a few blocks from Church headquarters, life at the D&RG yard seemed a galaxy away. Activity at the yard was frenzied and fast-paced, there was little room for error, and the environment was uncivilized. The contrast between his work at the Church, where even the slightest off-color remark would have been unthinkable, and his post at the railroad was vivid and startling at times. Among other irritations, many of the men he worked with had made profanity an art form. One day he handed written instructions to a switchman who, upon reading the directions, flew into a tantrum. The scene that followed disgusted Gordon: "He was a fifty-year-old man, but he acted like a spoiled child. He threw his cap on the ground and jumped on it and let forth such a string of expletives as to seem to cause the air to turn blue around him. Every third or fourth word was the name of Deity spoken in vain. I thought, how childish can a grown man be? The very idea of a man acting and speaking like that was totally repugnant. I could never again give him my full respect."[7]

As though the strain of coping with a new job and other consequences of war weren't enough, the era brought other worries and even heartaches. One day in April 1943 Gordon admitted Aunt May to the hospital for treatment of acute arthritis. On the drive there she seemed in unusually low spirits and admitted that she didn't want to go to the hospital. "I've known enough of medicine that I know that's where people go to die," she lamented.[8] May's condition hadn't seemed serious, but she contracted pneumonia in the hospital and, on May 2, one day after her sixty-second birthday, passed away. Aunt May had long since won not only her stepson's affection and admiration but his gratitude for the compassion and sense of hope she had brought into their home after his mother's death. Her death filled him with a deep sense of loss and melancholy.

At the same time, the outlook internationally was discouraging. The Germans in Europe and the Japanese in the Pacific seemed to hold the upper hand, though U.S. citizens supporting the war at home and abroad were mobilizing as never before. Meanwhile, the railroad was under pressure to operate faster, smarter, and more efficiently. The wartime economy notwithstanding, the remarkable growth of the railroad created constant demand for more and better-trained supervisors and stationmasters.[9] Accordingly, Gordon was one of those invited to attend a school sponsored by the railroad for up-and-coming management in Denver in the summer of 1944.

Though the railroad industry was a new arena for him, some of his native abilities were crucial in overseeing the D&RG yard. He was resourceful and productive, a born administrator who improved efficiency and got things done with a minimum of motion. Eager to grasp the intricacies of his new position, he asked more questions during the supervisors' seminar in Denver than all the other participants combined. "Because I hadn't grown up in the railroad business, there was much I didn't know," he said. "I was anxious to learn, and those fellows didn't scare me. I figured I had worked for better men than they would ever be, and it didn't bother me in the least to speak up."[10]

D&RG officials took note of the assistant supervisor from Salt Lake City, and two weeks later he received a call from railroad headquarters. Would he consider accepting a job as assistant manager of mail, baggage, and express for the entire D&RG system? The promotion would bring an increase in salary and opportunity but would require him to move his family to Denver. He realized that the "decision" essentially lay outside his control, for the railroad expected him to make the move. Marjorie was willing. She felt confident that they wouldn't be gone forever, so the thought of being separated from family and friends was bearable—though she was once again expecting a child, their third, due in February 1945. She saw the opportunity to live somewhere other than Utah's capital as an adventure, however. Both she and Gordon regretted leaving their comfortable new home behind, but they knew they would have no difficulty renting it during those days of acute housing shortage. Kathy and Dick were young, so moving wouldn't be hard on them. After weighing the important factors, the Hinckleys concluded there was nothing to do but relocate in Colorado.

Gordon left almost immediately for Denver to assume his new responsibilities and look for housing, and Marjorie remained behind to find a renter for their home. Housing was at a premium in Denver—even converted garages and attics were renting for top dollar—and he found it more difficult than he had expected to locate something suitable. As the weeks rolled by, Marjorie became increasingly anxious. She was eager to join her husband in Denver before her pregnancy became so advanced that it was not feasible to make the move, and she did not want to have her baby alone.

While he waited for something to open up, Gordon lived in a small hotel and worked nearly around the clock. With severe labor shortages caused by the huge number of men recruited for military service, those left behind had to pick up the slack. There was no such thing as a forty-hour work week. After putting in a long day at the railroad yard, he rode trains at night to learn the ropes. Many a night found him riding out to Grand Junction, Colorado, and back in baggage cars filled not only with luggage but with coffins and other vivid reminders of war. The setting provided many hours to contemplate the horrors of such conflict, and often his mind wandered back to the day he had learned of Stanford's death, then raced forward to consider families who were receiving similar telegrams now. What an indictment on men's inability to live in peace one with another!

Gordon and Marjorie disliked their separation from each other, which stretched to nearly six months. She began one letter to her husband: "This is a terrible life. I've been away from you enough during the last year to last me for the duration of this existence and I hope Heaven is a small place or travel is by instant atomic force."[11] Gordon alleviated the situation somewhat by using his Pullman pass to make the twelve-hour trip home on weekends, catching a train west as early Friday as he could get away and returning on a late-night express Sunday evening. The pattern wasn't convenient, but it made the separation more tolerable. By year's end, Gordon had finally located a small home in downtown Denver, and in January 1945 he moved his family to Colorado's capital city.

Marjorie was relieved to have their family living under the same roof again, though the transition to life in Denver was difficult for a young woman who had never spent more than a few days away from Salt Lake City and her extended family. "The first three days lasted for about six weeks apiece, but this week has been a little better," she wrote her parents shortly after her arrival. "Of all the mumps and measles I have had, homesickness is the worst. If you've never had it, you don't know what you've missed. . . . I'd just get my mind off it and Gordon would say, 'So you're homesick, are you?' and then he would shake with laughter while I ran for a handkerchief. . . . However, I'm doing much better now. I can listen to the radio announcers say 'This is KVOD Denver' without even batting an eye."[12] Marjorie's mood gradually improved. Not quite two weeks later she noted in a letter home, "Not doing so bad this week."[13]

Her frame of mind wasn't improved by the fact that Dick was sick with the croup and rheumatic fever almost from the moment she and the children arrived. But the neighborhood was filled with couples whose children provided playmates for Kathy, and young mothers befriended Marjorie and even brought remedies for Dick's maladies.[14] Letters from home and occasional visits from family and friends kept her going. When two members of the Sunday School General Board visited Denver on assignment, Gordon and Marjorie relished a day of reunion with their old friends.

The general board had declined to release Gordon when he left for Colorado, extending instead a leave of absence, and almost immediately he had an opportunity to practice what he had been preaching when he was called to teach Sunday School in Denver. It was the only time during their lives that any of the children would remember sitting with their father during sacrament meeting.

Though their move to Denver hadn't taken them even into a new time zone, life couldn't have been more different for the Hinckleys in the Mile-High City. The Church was small, and they found themselves living in a totally non-LDS environment. Most of their neighbors—as well as Gordon's colleagues at the railroad—knew very little about the Church. Many who had heard about the Mormons had impressions that were biased or based on inaccuracy. Daily interaction with those who did not understand the Church and its members interested Gordon, who for ten years had searched for better ways to introduce the gospel to this very group. As he interacted with his peers and new friends, he found himself making mental notes and jotting down ideas for later use. And at Elder Richards's request, he occasionally caught the train to Salt Lake for a long weekend to keep a few missionary-related projects going.

Gordon assumed that after the war he would return to his behind-the-scenes public relations work at the Church. But for now, he was doing his part to keep the railroad running. Several major railroads crossed the United States—the Northern Pacific and Southern Pacific, the Great Northern, the Union Pacific, the Santa Fe, and the Denver and Rio Grande in conjunction with the Rock Island and the Missouri Pacific on the east, and the Western Pacific on the west. Denver was a crucial hub, and the train yard bustled with activity night and day. It was not uncommon for every track in the station to be filled and other trains down the line waiting for the signal to pull in and unload. "At all cost," Gordon explained, "we had to keep the line clear and the rail traffic moving, because if anything caused traffic to stop, problems rippled throughout the entire system."[15]

One day there was a wreck on the line in a canyon some distance from Denver. Gordon was sent to troubleshoot, with instructions to resolve the problem quickly. He found five cars tipped over and the line blocked. There was only one solution, and he immediately ordered three loaded freight cars dumped into the Colorado River. That bold decision cleared the line and opened it to traffic backed up for miles. The incident impressed itself upon his mind. "I learned the importance of keeping the traffic moving, of doing whatever is necessary to keep the line open," he said.[16] The principle had many applications that embedded themselves in his subconscious.

Not every milestone in the Mile-High City was work-related. On February 8, 1945, Gordon and Marjorie welcomed the third addition to their family—Virginia, who would be called Ginny by family and friends. Kathy was nearly six, Dick almost four—both old enough to be excited about the tiny, red-headed sister who came to their home. Gordon and Marjorie were thrilled. Their infant daughter was healthy in every respect, Marjorie recovered quickly, and the miracle of birth continued to be an awe-inspiring experience for the young parents.

Marjorie's joy was obvious in a letter to her parents a few weeks later: "You mentioned Virginia's *brown* hair [but] . . . there is nothing brown about it. It gets redder every day, and *lighter*. The new hair is coming in like a crop of spring carrots. And now

I know love is blind because I've never cared for that brand of red hair, but on her—well it looks just as beautiful as if it were coal black or honey blond."[17]

Virginia's birth came at a momentous time in world history, occurring as it did on the brink of several landmark international events. Three months later, on May 7, the Germans surrendered, and the following day the welcome news was announced on what became the official VE Day. The exhilaration of victory in Europe was tempered by word of the death of President Heber J. Grant on May 14 at the age of eighty-eight. Though President Grant had been frail since suffering a stroke several years earlier, Gordon had hoped to see him again. He had tender feelings for the prophet whose compelling testimony had stirred him as a boy sitting in the Tabernacle balcony, who had received his report as a young returned missionary, and who subsequently had brought him to work for the Church. President Grant had been President of the Church since Gordon was eight, and he couldn't remember any other prophet. He wished he were in Salt Lake City where he could pay his respects to a leader who had influenced him profoundly.

Less than three months later circumstances developed that brought Gordon and Marjorie home for good. When Japan ignored an ultimatum from President Harry S. Truman, Winston Churchill, and Joseph Stalin to surrender or suffer "complete and utter destruction," the United States dropped an atomic bomb on Hiroshima the morning of August 6 and another on Nagasaki three days later. Japan subsequently surrendered, and for some 140,000,000 Americans, there could have been no sweeter news. The war was over, the troops would start coming home, and civilians who had taken jobs dependent on the wartime economy—Gordon among them—could return to normalcy. The owners of the home the Hinckleys were renting in Denver announced their intention to return immediately, so without delay Gordon submitted his resignation. By the last weekend in August, Marjorie and the children had moved back to Salt Lake City, leaving him behind to ease the transition for his replacement at the railroad.[18]

Gordon had left his employment at the Church without the promise of a job at war's end, but he presumed that something would be available. During the summer of 1945 Presiding Bishop LeGrand Richards had written him with the offer of employment in the Presiding Bishop's office, but Gordon had felt too committed to the railroad to consider it seriously.[19] And throughout the war he and Elder Stephen L Richards had stayed in close contact. As soon as Elder Richards learned that he was free to come home, he offered him his old job back. But the Denver and Rio Grande liked what they saw in the manager from Utah, and they countered by offering a promotion with a salary greater than he could ever expect to make working for the Church.

The offer was tempting. His young family was growing, and no one knew quite what to expect of the postwar economy. With Marjorie already back in Utah, Gordon wrote her about the duel between his current and former employers. She responded by return mail: "I will be glad when we are together, as this setup just does not suit me at all. Grumble, grumble. . . . I miss you and long for you." From that point, however, her reply was practical, accommodating, and to the point: "As for the job you had just better make up your mind to do the one which you enjoy the most, as you will spend quite a bit of your life working at it. As for me, I can make myself reasonably happy wherever you are, and as for the children, it is a question either way and is something we can not possibly foretell, no matter how we speculate and wonder and worry." She concluded with her only stipulation: "Let's hurry and take up life together again. I like it better that way."[20]

The railroad had been good to Gordon and appeared to offer the best potential for advancement as well as the greater challenge to his capitalistic instincts. But his heart was back at 47 East South Temple, and he felt that he belonged there—if, that is, he could modify his old job. He told Elder Richards that he would come back if he could "bake a cake without having to do the dishes all the time." When Elder Richards assured him that he could hire some help, Gordon informed railroad officials that he was returning to Salt Lake City. "Don't make a decision yet," they urged. "Take a ninety-day leave of absence, and then decide. We'll hold the position for you until then."[21] Gordon agreed and left for Utah.

The Hinckleys were thrilled to return to their home in East

Millcreek with the large yard and hollow out back. And when Gordon walked back into Church headquarters, it felt as though he had never left. It was so good to return to an environment more suited to his nature, and to concentrate on issues he felt passionate about. After thirty days, he called D&RG officials and explained that he would not be coming back. Still the railroad didn't give up; in the spring of 1947 they approached him with an even better offer. Elder Harold B. Lee noted in his journal: "Gordon B. Hinckley came to discuss with me the offer of the D&RG Railway Company at Denver, to become a department head at $510 per month."[22] Despite what would have been a generous raise, Gordon found this decision relatively easy to make. He explained to a friend: "This is the Lord's work. I feel I will make my best contribution in life by continuing to do my humble part to further the cause."[23]

Though the Denver experience had been a positive diversion, it was wonderful to be back among friends and family. In particular, the Hinckleys were anxious to spend time with Bryant. Thirteen months after Aunt May's death in May 1943, he had married Lois Anderson, a principal in the Salt Lake City school system, and they were now living in the East Millcreek farm home. Shortly after his father's fourth marriage Gordon had left for Denver, and there had been little time for him and Marjorie to become acquainted with Bryant's new wife. Now Kathy and Dick resumed their visits to Papa Hinckley, and Dick was old enough to be enthralled with his grandfather, whose stories about Indians, cowboys, and growing up at Cove Fort fascinated him. Papa Hinckley was larger than life.

The General Authorities and employees at Church headquarters seemed genuinely pleased to have Gordon back. His reputation as "the Slave" was intact, and as conditions around the world slowly began to return to normal, his talents were again sorely needed. Elder Ezra Taft Benson of the Quorum of the Twelve left for Europe in February 1946 to administer to both the physical and spiritual needs of the Saints there and to pave the way for missionaries to return to the Continent. Most European countries were just beginning to sort through the rubble in the aftermath of the war, and it would be some time before missions there were fully operational, but the number of missionaries serving in other areas of the world began to increase almost immediately.

Resuming his duties with the Radio, Publicity, and Mission Literature Committee, Gordon again began writing and producing scripts, filmstrips, and other missionary and public relations materials. As before, his writing style was clear, to the point, and unencumbered by literary excesses: every word meant something, one concept built upon another, and the writing never drew attention to itself but simply advanced the message.

His experience in Colorado had persuaded him that many people still had a distorted view of Mormons and what they believed, and it had given him a different perspective about how to introduce the gospel more effectively to nonmembers. These insights proved invaluable when President George Albert Smith asked him to write a book to be used in connection with the centennial of the pioneers' entrance into the Salt Lake Valley. The President described the need for a straightforward description of the gospel that a member could comfortably place in an investigator's hand. The result was a 230-page book organized in two sections, the latter of which outlined the history of the Church from the Restoration to the present and was later reprinted as a separate volume titled *Truth Restored*.

"Here is a question which has been earnestly asked for more than a century," Gordon wrote by way of beginning. "Over the years numerous answers have been given to it. The books alone which have been written around this query fill many feet of library shelf. It has been the theme of countless magazine articles, newspaper stories, pamphlets, and sermons. In the early days of Mormonism these writings and discourses were motivated largely by a spirit of blind prejudice, for the question was most often asked in an atmosphere of ignorance and bigotry. Fortunately, that has changed. An honest question deserves an honest answer. *What of the Mormons?* Who are they? What do they believe? What is their program? What is their organization? What is their history?"[24] For decades *Truth Restored* served as a standard reference text for hundreds of thousands of missionaries.

Gordon was comfortable handling this and countless other projects in relative anonymity, but gradually he was gaining stature and even some prominence in the LDS community, particularly in the Intermountain West, where his radio broadcasts and occasional mentions in the press brought him and his family public attention.

The nature of Gordon's work, like that of his father's, served to refine and hone his skills as a communicator. During the late forties, he contributed frequently to the *Church News* "Salt of the Earth" series, in which he heralded the contributions of ordinary men and women whose quiet goodness might otherwise have gone unnoticed.[25] As he wrote an increasing number of magazine articles and newspaper columns, turned out more slide presentations, and delivered one radio address after another, his own influence began to extend far beyond what he might have anticipated.

In the late forties Elder Henry D. Moyle of the Twelve approached Gordon about completing a biography of Elder Moyle's father, James H. Moyle. Author John Henry Evans had only begun the project prior to his death in 1947. Gordon agreed to the enormous undertaking and attempted to squeeze in his writing around his full-time job and Church assignments. A noisy family at home didn't help matters, as he tried to shoehorn the project into rare undisturbed moments. As the deadline loomed, Marjorie sensed her husband's predicament and took the children to a cabin in a nearby canyon for several days so that Gordon could have peace and quiet for his thinking and writing. The arrangement worked out nicely for everyone—the children filled their time hiking to nearby lakes, reading books, and enjoying a leisurely break from city life, and Gordon worked from dawn until dusk on the project that weighed on him.

Though the obligation to the Moyle family added pressure that he didn't particularly need or relish, Gordon was well suited to writing biography, combining as it did his love of history with heartfelt admiration for a life well lived. Later that year *James Henry Moyle: The Story of a Distinguished American and an Honored Churchman* was published.

Some of Gordon's writing enjoyed exposure beyond the LDS audience. In the spring of 1951, *Look* magazine invited him to respond to an article published in its April 24, 1951, issue entitled "The Mormons: We Are a Peculiar People," written by Lewis W. Gillenson. He was unflinching in his review of

Gillenson's interpretation of the Church: "[This article] is a disappointment after reading some of his other writings on the Protestant churches in America. . . . In general . . . it is a caricature of the Mormon people," Gordon began, identifying specific reasons for his uncomplimentary appraisal: "His lead heading reads: 'Joseph Smith's "chosen people" revel in their singularity as they prepare for the gathering of Israel in the desert.' What does he mean by this? Would he have us believe that the Mormons are a long-haired, fanatical sect, who spend their days aloof from the world, preparing some kind of asylum in the desert for scattered Israel? . . . Mr. Gillenson infers that Joseph Smith's followers were a credulous lot—'frontier disciples,' men of 'heady hopes' and 'simplicity.' The fact is that most of the early converts to Mormonism were from the New England States. They were at least as well educated as any class in the country, and as cultured." Gordon concluded, "It is unfortunate that in reviewing the history of a people who have accomplished so much in the face of staggering odds, Mr. Gillenson relied so heavily on evidently untrustworthy sources. In so doing, he has drawn the kind of picture in which the reader has difficulty in distinguishing fact from fiction."[26]

In general, as the *Look* article seemed to imply, the visibility of the Church was increasing. In 1947, one hundred years after the first company of pioneers had arrived in the Salt Lake Valley, Church membership reached one million. In October 1949, at least partly as a result of Gordon's encouragement and efforts, general conference was first telecast over KSL television. For years before that, he had arranged for the private wire hookups that transmitted general priesthood meeting to congregations around the world, and he continued to be involved in other radio programming as well.[27]

As missionary work surged forward, Gordon wished he had time to implement every idea and seize every opportunity that presented itself. There were times, however, when he felt stretched to the limit. Complicating his schedule, he and Marjorie had still been getting settled upon their return from Colorado when, on April 20, 1946, he was sustained as second counselor to Lamont B. Gundersen in the East Millcreek Stake presidency. The call had come as a surprise. Elder Stephen L

Richards later told Gordon that his appointment had been discussed by the Twelve in their temple meeting, and they had determined that in this case the call to the stake presidency should supersede his general board call. Gordon was pleased at the prospects of laboring among his own friends and neighbors, and thus began an extended period of Church service in East Millcreek. After serving for two and a half years as second counselor to President Gundersen, he was called on November 14, 1948, as first counselor, replacing Ralph S. Barney, who was released due to ill health.

The challenge of helping oversee the East Millcreek Stake, situated in one of the most rapidly growing areas in all of Utah, was invigorating. In addition, as he filled various priesthood assignments, Gordon became acquainted with priesthood leaders in nearby stakes, further increasing his circle of friends. For example, he worked with a young attorney serving as a counselor in the Cottonwood Stake presidency, James E. Faust, and with Thomas S. Monson, who was serving as a counselor in the Temple View Stake.

Gordon's activities formed an interesting juxtaposition: By day he devised ways to introduce the gospel to nonmembers, and in the evenings he sought solutions for integrating a large concentration of Saints into the programs of the Church. At the same time, he and Marjorie were attempting to rear little Saints of their own.

Life in the Hinckley home was rarely monotonous, often lighthearted, and almost always noisy. On October 30, 1947, Marjorie and Gordon were blessed with their fourth child and second son, Clark Bryant. Now the mother of two boys and two girls, Marjorie couldn't imagine being any happier with her lot in life. The demands of rearing young children seemed to energize rather than discourage her. Though she was often left to manage her brood alone while Gordon attended to his responsibilities in the stake presidency, she had always taken it for granted that he would have demanding Church responsibilities. She was comfortable with his stewardship and happy about hers.

None of the children questioned who was ultimately in charge at home, however, though Gordon was seldom involved in settling disputes or managing the numerous tasks that went hand in hand with taking care of children. Neither he nor Marjorie was heavy-handed either in disciplining or in setting rigid rules. Marjorie's parents had been gentle in their approach to child rearing, and her grandmother's statement, "You don't teach a child not to hit by hitting," filtered often through her subconscious. Gordon liked to say that his father never laid a hand on him except to bless him, and he intended to follow suit. Nor were the couple terribly demanding of each other. "Gordon always let me do my own thing," Marjorie explained. "He never insisted that I do anything his way, or *any* way, for that matter. From the very beginning he gave me space and let me fly."[28]

Despite the normal confusion associated with running a household and rearing children, an aura of well-being permeated the Hinckley home. As Gordon had in previous decades, his children loved where they lived. Their property could no longer be considered rural, but there was still plenty of room to run and play. With Papa Hinckley and Aunt Lois just up the hollow, there was constant foot traffic from one house to the other—including Gordon, who shoveled the snow, kept everything in working order at his father's home, and in general tried to make life for Bryant and Lois pleasant and worry free.

Life at Church headquarters, however, was not tranquil. Gordon had his hands full with the constant and never-ending challenge of helping steer the Church into more professional and productive public relations and communications. Wonderful opportunities loomed on the horizon. With the trauma of World War II behind them, young men who had given several years to their country were eager to put down roots, as were the young women who had remained behind. In contrast to the decade just ended, the fifties began with a feeling of goodwill. Americans in general trusted their leaders to tell them the truth, to make wise decisions, and to keep the country out of war.

That is why the crisis that struck at 4:00 A.M. on June 25, 1950, hit like a thunderbolt. When North Korean soldiers stormed across the 38th parallel into South Korea, few Americans realized how profoundly this incident halfway around the world would affect them. But by November, when U.S. aircraft were attacked by North Korean MIGs, the country found itself squarely in the middle of another international conflict. Then, as the April 1951 general conference approached, President George Albert Smith left the hospital after an extended illness. His counselors, J. Reuben Clark Jr. and David O. McKay, visited him for the last time on April 2. Two days later, after having served as President of the Church just under six years, he was gone. Both the Korean conflict and the prophet's death would have a profound and direct influence on Gordon's life.

CHAPTER NINE

ON THE FIRING LINE

With the passing of President George Albert Smith just two days before the April 1951 general conference began, David O. McKay was sustained as President of the Church in a solemn assembly held Monday, April 9. His ordination was in keeping with the established pattern of succession, but a ripple of surprise swept through the Tabernacle when the vigorous new prophet, whose stature and shock of wavy white hair accentuated his commanding presence, broke with recent tradition and named Stephen L Richards and J. Reuben Clark Jr. as his first and second counselors respectively. For eighteen years President Clark had served as first counselor in the First Presidency; during much of that time he had carried the major load.[1]

Gordon witnessed the proceedings of the solemn assembly in the Tabernacle and, like others, was caught off guard by what took place. But he eagerly sustained President McKay, whom he saw as a leader of magnificent proportions. He wondered, however, how President Richards's new assignment might affect their working relationship, and assumed that he might now have less interaction with his trusted friend.

The new First Presidency assumed leadership of a rapidly expanding Church. With 1.1 million members living in 42 missions and 191 stakes, the pace was quickening, and all who worked in and around Church headquarters sensed that the kingdom was poised to move forward in an unprecedented way.

Not long after the reorganization of the First Presidency, President Richards called Gordon to his office. There was nothing unusual about the request, as the two had conferred regularly for more than fifteen years. But Gordon was unprepared for what then unfolded. "President McKay has given me responsibility for the missionary program of the Church," President Richards began, "and I need you to help me." Gordon quickly learned that his "help" was to be on much more than a casual basis, for President Richards named him executive secretary of the General Missionary Committee and charged him with overseeing the day-to-day operations of the Missionary Department. It was a large and unwieldy responsibility. In the past, the various phases of the missionary program had been divided among four different committees at Church headquarters; now all were consolidated under one.[2]

Gordon was willing to serve wherever and however the Brethren saw fit, and he was pleased to continue his close association with President Richards, who was like a father to him. But as President Richards outlined the challenges that lay before them—including the intensified military conscription fueled by the Korean War, with its consequent effects on the missionary program—Gordon responded, "President Richards, you don't want me in this position; you want a lawyer." The reaction was firm: "I am a lawyer. I don't want to litigate this. I want to compose it."[3]

Though Gordon may have wondered why President Richards had placed such a burdensome responsibility on his shoulders, he was a logical choice for the job. Perhaps no other non–General Authority had enjoyed his unique schooling and preparation regarding the Church's mandate to acquaint the people of the world with the gospel. This new assignment gave him stewardship over the full range of missionary-related issues.

To the Missionary Department fell responsibility for essentially everything relating to missionary work: translation of all missionary materials, including the scriptures, into an increasing number of languages; the call and training of missionaries and mission presidents; the preparation and distribution of mission literature and other teaching materials; the continued development of media tools, radio broadcasts, and public relations efforts; and the obligation to respond to the never-ending problems of several thousand missionaries serving throughout the world.[4]

Had this been an era of tranquillity, the workload and pressure associated with supervising the missionary program would have been challenge enough. But the Korean War complicated matters and altered the missionary landscape drastically. Almost everyone forced to deal with what seemed a meaningless conflict was finding it to be an exercise in frustration. Dean Acheson, President Harry S. Truman's Secretary of State, put the situation in context: "If the best minds in the world had set out to find us the worst possible location in the world to fight this damnable war, politically and militarily, the unanimous choice would have been Korea."[5] It was a war that no one wanted, in a desolate, harsh land about which most Americans knew little or nothing. Korea, known anciently as *Chosun*, or Land of the Morning Calm, was anything but that.

Certainly this "police action" was wreaking unprecedented havoc with the missionary program. In short, the government wanted to draft the same young LDS men who wished to serve missions. After the enactment of the Selective Service Act of 1948, the Church and national Selective Service agents had presumably reached a working agreement whereby the missionary program and the draft could coexist amicably. On January 30, 1951, the First Presidency released a letter that provided priesthood leaders with strict instructions regarding which young men were eligible for missionary service. In general, those who were draft-liable were not to be called on missions. In a lengthy statement drafted by then-Elder Stephen L Richards, the Church reaffirmed its long-standing policy of supporting government in its military activity. "No exemption is being asked for the Church membership in general," the document clarified. "The missionaries concerned make up only a minor part of the Church and have an exact counterpart in ordained ministers or missionaries of other sects. The general membership of the Church is available for military duty and will perform it with distinction, as in the past."[6]

These conciliatory efforts notwithstanding, the conflict intensified as the military's need for soldiers increased. The law providing for the drafting of young men allowed for certain exemptions as well, one of which was a ministerial, or 4-D, classification. The Church's official position—and Gordon's primary point of advocacy—was that a missionary devoting his full time to religious service legitimately merited classification as a minister, which temporary classification only postponed rather than exempted his military service. But some draft boards did not agree. With Gordon's new assignment came responsibility for sorting through the bureaucratic chaos and representing the Church in the conflict between draft boards and missionaries.

Though Church leaders had reached what they thought to be consensus with the Selective Service, they found themselves facing uncooperative and even hostile draft boards around the country. Some local boards categorically refused to grant any ministerial classifications to missionaries, regardless of their draft status. Other boards ordered young men in their jurisdiction to leave the mission field and return home to report for active duty.[7] Ironically, draft boards in Utah and Idaho were among the most uncooperative. "I am happy to say that in the majority of draft boards outside the state of Utah we have had the fullest cooperation and good will," Gordon recorded. "In fact, many of the draft boards have urged that the Church continue calling missionaries and they would be glad to defer any number which the Church asks. . . . They could see the advantage of the fine training program of the Church."[8]

In any case, the uncertainty was unnerving to anyone with a vested interest in missionary work—particularly potential missionaries and their parents and leaders. No young man knew what his future would be or what he could plan for. Complicating matters, the Korean War was not a popular conflict in the United States, and the patriotic enthusiasm for enlisting that had prevailed during World War II had long since dissipated.

Despite everything at stake, and though the heavy workload and complex nature of the problem were overwhelming, it was not Gordon's nature to dwell on the dark side of things. He at times was worried and perplexed, but he was rarely gloomy. Neither was he inclined to surrender without a fight to mounting pressure and interference from the government, though unraveling the Selective Service's bureaucracy was a mind-boggling assignment. There were local draft boards and appeals boards at both state and federal levels. A young man who was drafted could appeal that decision to the state appeals board. The federal appeals board would hear a case only when there was a split decision by the state appeals board, or on appeal from

General Lewis B. Hershey, national director of the Selective Service.

Gordon had learned to keep his head down and stay out of the cross fire, but that approach was becoming increasingly difficult to follow as several events thrust him into the eye of the swirling controversy. A young man from Idaho was ordered by his draft board to leave the mission field and report for active duty. His case was appealed—and lost—at both the state and federal appeals boards. President McKay, President Richards, and Gordon subsequently met with the young man's parents and stake president to examine their options. After a lengthy discussion, during which they considered the precedent-setting nature of the case, President McKay suggested that perhaps the Church should devote its resources to reversing the decision. When asked for his counsel, President Richards offered a different view of the matter: "President McKay, we could fight this all the way to the Supreme Court if we chose to, but we do not appear to have a strong case. What if we lose? Would the entire missionary program be jeopardized? This young man has served for seventeen months, and though I know it is a disappointment to him and his parents, perhaps it is better for him to accept his induction order than for the Church to risk the possibility of losing the missionary program."[9]

President McKay concurred, but other disappointments followed. The draft board in a small Idaho town, for example, ordered every young man then serving a mission to report on the courthouse steps one week hence for preinduction physical examinations. President Richards and Gordon drove to Idaho to represent the missionaries before the draft board. "Stephen L Richards, who was about as persuasive a man as I've ever known, talked with that draft board, most of whom were members of the Church," Gordon remembered. "All he got out of them was a deferment on the reporting date. They were unwilling to grant any 4-D classifications." Both President Richards and Gordon left the meeting disheartened about the situation.[10]

With such decisions being made in a state heavily populated by members of the Church, where a sympathetic attitude toward missionaries might have been expected, it was clear that the Church would never make substantive headway by dealing exclusively with local boards. So President Richards and Gordon traveled to Washington, D.C., for a meeting with General Hershey that had been arranged by Senator Wallace Bennett and his assistant, Robert W. Barker. Their purpose was to clarify the intent of the missionary program and to reassure the general that the Church did not expect its young men to be excluded from military service, but simply to have their induction delayed long enough for them to serve missions.

General Hershey, reluctant to interfere with any church's program for carrying on its ministry, was sympathetic to the Church's cause. Later, on a visit to Utah, he invited Gordon to present the Church's case before the state's Selective Service boards, which he did.[11]

Between February 1951 and July 1953, the Church refrained from extending mission calls to young men who were eligible for military service. By that time, the Church's missionary force had plunged from 4,849 in 1951 to 2,189 in 1953; only 872 missionaries were set apart in 1952. New measures were called for.[12] With General Hershey's support, and after winning a number of federal appeals, Gordon worked with the Selective Service to achieve what appeared to be a reasonable compromise: a quota that allowed a restricted number of missionaries to serve at any given time. Beginning in July 1953, each ward and branch in the United States could call one young man to serve a mission that year and perhaps two the following year.

A First Presidency letter of July 10, 1953, outlined the quota's objective: "This change will not supply us with the corps of missionaries we have had in past years, but it should help to alleviate the serious impairment of the work that we are suffering by reason of the very limited force now in the field." The letter also provided instructions for implementing the quota: "Bishops and stake presidents will please see that their recommendations are spread over a period of months in such a manner as to avoid, insofar as possible, an exceptional demand on the pool of any one draft board at a particular time. We are appreciative of the fact that this program will impose on our bishops and stake presidents the burden of selecting and recommending one or two men. . . . However, the responsibility of recommending missionaries has always involved discriminative selection."[13]

The quota was not an ideal solution, but it was preferable to having the missionary program shut down altogether. Yet even with this tentative truce between the Church and the Selective Service, problems remained. The quota system was by nature divisive, and it created strain in wards where the parents of sons drafted into military service sometimes resented those whose sons managed to avoid or postpone induction by serving missions. While one boy went off to war, another was called on a mission—both out of the same ward, the same neighborhood, the same priests quorum. Gordon heard from and counseled with many of those families.

Some local and state draft boards refused to allow the Church even its quota of one boy per ward per annum. President Richards's meeting with General James A. May, head of Selective Service for Nevada, was representative of others. General May admitted being offended that he had not been consulted about the quota agreement and warned that he had no intention of adopting it: "I hope you won't start any appeals in this state because if you do you will have these boards bristling." President Richards responded that the Church hoped to work things out without the necessity of appeal but that it would always appeal "the fact that our missionaries are ministers of religion. If anyone questions that, we will take it to the last resort for decision."[14]

At times the conflict was for Gordon intensely personal. One young man living in Ogden, Utah, filed a suit against the Selective Service on the grounds that he was being inducted into the armed forces because another young man in his neighborhood, who he believed should have been drafted in his place, was serving a mission because of a 4-D classification. When President McKay was named a codefendant in the suit, Gordon was assigned to take his place throughout the lengthy proceedings. Among other things, he represented President McKay and the Church in a grueling deposition during which the government subpoenaed all of the existing missionary files. "How many trucks do you want to send?" Gordon asked when he heard their request and envisioned the enormous quantity of pertinent records. Fortunately, the war ended before the case went to trial.

▪ ▪ ▪ ▪ ▪

As far as Gordon's job description was concerned, his responsibilities as executive secretary of the Missionary Department were administrative in nature—but he found that he couldn't separate his day-to-day work from his personal interest in the missionaries themselves. Ned L. Mangelson was called in 1953 to serve in the Swiss-Austrian Mission. A promised deferment had not come by the time he entered the mission home in September. When his father spoke with the chairman of the local draft board, he was told that the board had no intention of issuing the deferment. The Mangelsons met with Gordon about the situation and outlined a strategy, but the deferment had not come by the time Elder Mangelson completed his stay at the mission home. "Brother Hinckley admonished me to have faith, to proceed to New York for embarkation, and that the release by the draft board would be waiting for me there," Ned recorded. "When I arrived at Hotel Wellington in New York City the release from the draft board had arrived by mail, which was an answer to prayer. Brother Gordon B. Hinckley was a great help to us in that crisis situation when he taught me to have faith that the Lord would open the way."[15]

Such incidents were common, for there were many days when, after doing everything humanly possible, Gordon could only exercise faith that the Lord would soften hearts and intervene as necessary. Certainly General Hershey had come to recognize the legitimacy of ministerial status for full-time missionaries. When the general retired, Gordon wrote to express his appreciation for the professional, objective way he had conducted affairs regarding the Church. The general replied that he wished all his interactions with religious groups had been as cooperative.

The signing of the peace accord ending the Korean War on July 27, 1953, reduced the urgent need for soldiers, but the draft remained intact, and for several years thereafter Gordon wrestled almost daily with conflicts between missionaries and local draft boards. He was constantly on the phone, trying on one hand to educate local draft boards about the merits of the missionary program, and on the other to calm tense missionaries and their parents.

"Gordon walked the floor a lot during those years," Marjorie said. "The pressure was very hard on him." Even Gordon, ever optimistic, conceded that it was a "terrible time. I have seen other terrible times, but those may have been the worst. Every day was a battleground. The very survival of the missionary program of the Church was at stake, and every day brought a new fight. I would never wish to go through the experiences of those years again."[16] Even years later, mention of the Korean War, the name of General Hershey, or anything else associated with the ongoing crisis evoked a flood of unsettling memories in Gordon's three oldest children, who had witnessed the pressure their father was under. It was one of the rare times his stress showed at home.

Finally, on June 28, 1955, a resolution on the floor of Congress declared that LDS missionaries were to be regarded legally as ordained ministers of the Church and therefore subject to ministerial deferment.[17] In some respects, the action was too little too late, for by this time the pressing need for servicemen had diminished to the extent that the quota was no longer needed anyway. Indeed, just two months later, in a letter to local priesthood leaders dated September 1, 1955, the First Presidency announced that the quota had been abolished and the limitations on mission calls lifted.[18]

It was hard to imagine that a war in a country half a world away had caused Gordon such grief, inspired so many sleepless nights, and led to such an endless round of meetings, negotiations, telephone calls, and deliberations. One positive outgrowth was that he continued to benefit from close association with President Richards, whose mentoring was providential. Gordon said: "To the credit of this wise and inspired man, situations that appeared impossible to handle were resolved in such a way that young men of the Church could honor their military obligations and serve missions."[19] On a personal basis, Gordon learned firsthand how to deal with bureaucracy, and he came to understand the effect of decisions from the Church's highest councils. "President Richards was thoughtful, deliberate, careful, and wise," he explained. "He never rushed into action but looked cautiously before he proceeded. I learned that you best proceed carefully in this work, because whatever decision you make has far-reaching ramifications and affects the lives of many people."[20]

In return, President Richards had high regard for his young associate. Following the end of the Korean War, he expressed his gratitude in a holiday greeting: "I cannot tell you how deeply I appreciate your association and help. I do not see how I could carry forward my assignment without the efficient service you so willingly give. I am sure the Lord will bless you for it, for you are a great contributor to his holy cause."[21]

For all of the agony associated with keeping the missionary program functional, the results were worth the effort. The number of full-time missionaries in the field gradually rose to more than six thousand by the end of the 1950s, and during that decade more people—nearly half a million—were baptized than during the Church's first ninety years, from 1830 to 1920.[22]

In the United States the fifties were a decade of religious resurgence. It was acceptable, even fashionable, to profess a belief in God. In 1954 Congress added the words "under God" to the Pledge of Allegiance. Opinion polls showed that 95 percent of all Americans considered themselves religiously inclined, and half of the adult population regularly attended some kind of worship service.[23]

Such trends and attitudes were reflected in the number of individuals being drawn into the gospel net. During the eight years (1951–59) that the Missionary Department fell under President Richards's—and Gordon's—direction, missionary work moved forward on an unprecedented scale: the 7,740 missionaries who were sent into the field, together with 28,281 men and women serving as stake missionaries, baptized more than 185,000 converts. And as the program grew, certain procedural changes were inevitable. On March 25, 1953, for example, the First Presidency announced that returning missionaries would no longer report directly to General Authorities but, rather, to their stake presidency and high council.[24]

Such increases in conversions were, at least to some extent, a direct outgrowth of the intensified pace of the Missionary

Department. Selective Service–related challenges and issues were only a part of what Gordon dealt with daily. As the department grew in scope and size, others would be brought in to assist—among them Boyd K. Packer, who would subsequently be called to the Quorum of the Twelve, D. Arthur Haycock, who would serve as personal secretary to five Presidents of the Church, and James M. Paramore, who would later be called as a General Authority. But for the time being, though he relied on the assistance of two secretaries, Gordon *was*, in effect, the Missionary Department. Consequently his phone rang at all hours of the day and night, at work and at home: "I would get to work first thing in the morning, and before I could get my hat off the phone would be ringing," he explained. "All day long, and half the night, my phone rang with calls from all over the world. When missionaries were physically sick, homesick, seasick, or lovesick, I got the call."[25]

If a missionary was injured or became seriously ill and needed hospitalization or treatment of some kind; when regulations governing passports or visas in a country changed; when a stake president or bishop needed counsel about a potential missionary's situation; if a translator trying to get the right shade of meaning in a translation of missionary materials needed clarification; or when a General Authority wished for someone to assist him in training local priesthood leaders on implementing member missionary work—in response to these and many other issues, Gordon's phone rang at what had become a vital nerve center of the Church.[26]

Each day he moved quickly through the mound of details that fell to him. He had the capacity to absorb large amounts of information and make decisions without belaboring the point or second-guessing himself afterward. He knew every mission president in the world and had helped train them before they entered the field. And for each, he was the first-line contact at Church headquarters: He was the Slave, the crank behind the wheel, as he described his role. At a later date his contribution was put in context when he was introduced to the BYU student body before an address in November 1959: "Sometimes we do not fully appreciate the man behind the scenes who sits quietly at his desk in the capacity of a secretary to a great committee, but it is in that capacity that Gordon B. Hinckley has made his weight felt around the world."[27]

As early as 1951, and prior to his appointment as executive secretary of the General Missionary Committee, Gordon had recommended to President Richards that the Missionary Department adopt a uniform curriculum for missionaries so that translators could provide study aids in various languages and the same manuals could be made available to all.[28] Three or four missions had developed plans of their own. These were all reviewed and developed into a "Systematic Program for Teaching the Gospel," the first standard approach to proselytizing ever implemented Churchwide. Though use of the plan was at first optional, by 1961 the First Presidency determined that a uniform teaching plan would be part of the mandatory curriculum for training missionaries in the mission home in Salt Lake City.[29]

After nearly two decades of full-time focus on missionary work and public relations, Gordon was constantly evaluating ways to present the gospel message more effectively. When a report confirmed his suspicion that bureaus of information at Nauvoo and Carthage weren't being utilized fully, he sent a memo to President Richards outlining his concerns: "We spend thousands of dollars on construction, appoint a director, and then give him neither direction nor facilities," he reported. "In my judgment we simply are not getting from these places the missionary possibilities that might be realized. . . . It is as important to have expert direction in telling our story as to have an architect in planning the building." For emphasis he added, "At the moment my feelings on this matter are somewhat strong . . . because I have before me the copy of a pamphlet for distribution. . . . It was written by a man who will do an excellent job of directing [one of our bureaus]. . . . But, according to his own story to me, his English teacher passed him only because the coach needed him on the varsity football team."[30]

As Gordon trained local leaders, mission presidents, and occasionally prospective missionaries in the finer points of missionary work, he typically emphasized that investigators should be truly converted *before* they were baptized. And he pushed local leaders to intensify their member missionary work.

▪ ▪ ▪ ▪ ▪

As he immersed himself in helping missionaries teach the gospel, Gordon found that his own testimony of the Book of Mormon as a key to conversion increased dramatically. The pressure to provide additional translations of the Book of Mormon steadily increased as citizens of non-English-speaking lands joined the Church and the need for new language versions of the Book of Mormon became apparent. During the 1950s new, revised, or updated translations of the Book of Mormon were published in German (1955 and 1959), Norwegian (1959), Portuguese (1951, 1952, and 1958), Spanish (1950 and 1952), Swedish (1959), French (1952 and 1959), Japanese (1957), and Finnish (1952). Gordon spent many hours working with translators who understood the terminology and nuances unique to the Church to produce precise foreign-language editions of the scriptures. All other missionary-related materials had to be translated as well, and supervision for the *Liahona*, the Church's official Spanish-language periodical, also fell on his desk.

During this period he found himself often coordinating the printing of various editions of the Book of Mormon, as well as other missionary materials, with Thomas S. Monson, who oversaw Church printing as part of his responsibilities at the Deseret News Press. The latter described their interaction: "We had in our catalog of mission literature well over one hundred items, and Brother Hinckley had the immense task of keeping a sufficient supply on hand of all of those items. We would plan what to print, how many to print, and when to reorder. The biggest job was placing orders for the Book of Mormon. Every time it was printed, regardless of the language, we would plan together how it should be handled."[31]

During this era, perhaps no one in the Church was more familiar with the missionary program and its various intricacies of operation than was Gordon B. Hinckley. Elder Bruce R. McConkie, who had been called to the First Council of the Seventy in October 1946, officially recognized that fact by presenting Gordon with a medal inscribed "Mr. Missionary." Gordon later reflected: "We did all we reasonably could to take the gospel throughout the world. We worked long and we worked hard, and we tried to use to advantage the tools and opportunities available to us. Compared with what would follow, our efforts were rather quiet and simple. But we did all we knew to do."[32]

In 1961, on the ten-year anniversary of President McKay's becoming President of the Church, Gordon paid tribute to the venerable Church leader for the tremendous growth of missionary work without so much as hinting at his own participation: "Never has the work of teaching the gospel moved so splendidly forward as it is moving today. . . . [D]uring the ten years that President McKay has stood as President of the Church, more than 24,000 full-time missionaries have gone into the field, notwithstanding the fact that many of our young men were prohibited from going because of military problems beyond their control. During this same period more than 261,000 converts have been baptized. . . . I can think of no more fitting memorial to the marvelous work of our great missionary President than the fact that in these last ten years more than a quarter of a million people have entered the waters of baptism."[33]

Many times in subsequent years and decades, Gordon would summarize his feelings about missionary work. "I wish to invite members of the Church to consider anew the great mandate given by the Lord to all who desire to be known as his disciples," he said on one occasion representative of many others. "It is a mandate we cannot dodge, and one from which we cannot shrink. That mandate is to teach the gospel to the nations and peoples of the earth. . . . Truly we are engaged in a marvelous work and a wonder. . . . The progress of the Church in our day is truly astounding. The God of heaven has brought to pass this latter-day miracle, and what we have seen is but a foretaste of greater things yet to come."[34]

This intense emphasis on missionary work spilled over into Gordon's home life. The children listened to an endless recitation of stories about missionaries who had been magnified in their labors, as well as something about the challenges missionaries faced. The family became used to phone calls at all hours of the day and night. After hearing for months about missionaries "in the field," Dick—who was used to running at will through the fields that bordered their property—asked what seemed to him a logical question: Why did the missionaries always stay out "in the field"? Why didn't they ever come inside?

Inevitably some challenges arose among the large corps of missionaries serving worldwide, and when those problems surfaced they became Gordon's as well. He had reasonable latitude in dealing with circumstances that came up and could take action personally in situations for which there was a clear-cut precedent. If there was no established criterion, he sought President Richards's counsel.

As he worked through the myriad of details, questions, requests, and predicaments that found their way to his desk, Gordon came to love the workers as well as the work, and he took a personal interest in the well-being of missionaries and mission presidents. When one young elder suffering a serious illness was forced to leave the mission field to undergo surgery in a Salt Lake City hospital, the Church secured a room nearby in which he and his mother could stay while he convalesced. Unfortunately, the room became almost unbearable during a particularly hot summer. When Gordon realized how unpleasant conditions were for the two, he loaned them the electric fan from his own office.

Faced with making decisions regarding the misconduct of missionaries, Gordon leaned when possible toward the side of compassion. When a rebuke or discipline was necessary, he seemed able to communicate that his first interest was the welfare and future of the wrongdoer, and that any action taken was based on love.

One day Gordon was present when a prominent member of the Church whose missionary-age son had been denied a call—a denial based on a moral issue—protested the decision to President Richards. After the father concluded his lengthy and demanding argument, President Richards responded: "I have some responsibility for the affairs of this Church. If you were seated where I sit, knowing the circumstances I know, you would feel exactly as I do. In your position as a member of this Church, as one who holds the priesthood, you too have a responsibility for its growth and program, and for its discipline. My heart goes out to you, for I know that what you say comes of love for your son. However, I am asking you, as a man with a responsibility for the progress of the Church, to look at the larger affairs of the kingdom. Then you make the decision in that light." After a long period of silence, the father agreed that his son should not serve.[35]

Such experiences with President Richards and other members of the First Presidency and Quorum of the Twelve provided Gordon with unusual exposure to those serving in the Church's highest councils. Repeatedly he observed their approach to delicate issues, participated in discussions where decisions with far-reaching implications were made, and was schooled in matters of Church government and administration. The Brethren in turn developed a high degree of confidence and trust in his judgment, ability, and integrity—which placed him in a position to accept an increasing range and degree of responsibility.

CHAPTER TEN

LIFE WITH FATHER

As Gordon's responsibilities at Church headquarters expanded, his family grew as well. When he and Marjorie learned that a fifth child was on the way, they were elated. Their youngest, Clark, was six years old and had started school. Virginia was nine, Dick nearly thirteen, and Kathy would soon turn fifteen. For everyone from eldest to youngest, the birth of Gordon and Marjorie's third daughter, Jane, on February 27, 1954, was cause for celebration.

Life was lively for the seven Hinckleys. Gordon was constantly juggling his workload at the office, assignments in the stake presidency, and projects around the house or yard that begged to be finished. With two teenagers, two grade-schoolers, an infant, and a home to manage, Marjorie had her hands full. And at the Hinckley home, every season seemed to have a life of its own.

It was hard to tell who looked forward most to summers—Gordon, who felt almost claustrophobic during winter months that confined him indoors; Marjorie, who loved the sound of the screen door slamming shut as children ran in from the backyard; or the children, who relished their freedom to run at will around the thirty or so adjoining acres that belonged to the extended Hinckley family. Marjorie savored the days she had her five to herself, and she went to great lengths to keep summers unstructured so her young ones would have time to lie in the gully and listen to the birds sing if they wanted to. She wept each fall when it was time to send her brood back to school; even when school was in session she looked forward to the moment each day when her children burst through the door and started scrounging for an afternoon snack. One day when Dick had to stay after school for some grade-school discipline, Marjorie marched over to his classroom and announced to his startled teacher, "You can do anything you want with this boy all day long, but after 3 P.M. *he's mine*."

As much as Gordon loved East Millcreek, where he had enjoyed the carefree days of boyhood and was now rearing his own family, and as protective as he was of the property he had groomed and the home he had built with his own hands, his threat to move the family closer to town was as predictable as the changing seasons. He blustered routinely about the distance of his commute, as though his daily eleven-mile drive were an unbearable burden. But each spring as he smelled the cherry blossoms and began to dig in the soil, and as Marjorie delighted in the huge, double-petaled lilacs that bloomed on their property, they would say, "How could we bear to leave all of this behind?"

For the children, "all of this" was sheer heaven. With the orchards and pasture and huge backyard bordering a hollow filled with trails and hiding places, they believed they lived in the best place on earth. The hollow Gordon had played in as a boy was equally enticing to Dick and Clark, who made forts in the lush undergrowth and slept overnight in the orchards to "guard" the fruit from would-be raiders. The girls went from house to house on their bikes or had "picnics" on the swing at Papa Hinckley's. Most evenings they all played until past dusk, and there was never a shortage of things for the children to do at home to keep them both entertained and occupied.

From the outset, Gordon had designed their home in such a way that it could be added upon as family needs changed. He still handled repairs and remodeling personally; consequently, he was often in the middle of one project or another. What time he could find between work and Church obligations found him elbow-deep in some task: throwing up a wall, tearing down another, adding a bathroom, and so on. For years the dining-room table was covered with rolls of blueprints.

The construction chaos unnerved Marjorie at times, for it was nearly impossible to renovate in one part of the house without creating confusion elsewhere. But because Gordon's improvements always made the home better, and because the physical labor was therapeutic for him (when pressure at the office was greatest, he would come home, change into a pair of work trousers and a worn white shirt, put on his nail apron, and begin to hammer), she indulged his projects.

As the boys got a little older, they were expected to work alongside their father, and if they weren't up by seven or eight o'clock, Gordon would come looking for them: "What are you doing still in bed? The day is half gone." Nonetheless, Dick relished Saturdays with his father, and together they repaired, remodeled, planted, and planned. Gordon got everything done he could that day, knowing he would be able to sneak in only a few hours here and there during the week. Even still, hiring a repairman or builder was not an option. He knew how he wanted things done, and though he was frugal and resourceful, the more compelling issue was one of competence. One simply did not hire done what one could do as well—or better—oneself.

"It didn't matter whether or not Dad had ever done something before," Ginny later explained. "If he decided something needed to be done, he saw it through. I don't think it ever occurred to him that he couldn't do something, and I can't think of one thing he tackled that he did not pull off."[1]

Time was the limiting factor, not skill—Gordon was resourceful and could build or repair almost anything. Whether it was the gearbox of the old Thor washing machine, a lawn-mower engine, or the car, he could solve the problem, and usually without buying replacement parts. When a repair was needed, he headed for the basement or shed and tinkered until he had fashioned a fix out of something left over from another project or reworked the device so that it bypassed the defective part. Kathy was stunned when she heard someone at a friend's home casually mention that she needed to pick up the toaster at a repair shop. "I couldn't believe it," Kathy said. "I didn't know you could take appliances somewhere to be fixed. I thought that's what fathers did—fix everything."[2]

The house was perhaps the most visible monument to Gordon's mechanical skill, long-range vision, ingenuity, and knack for creative problem solving. When he built the home, he left studs out of certain sections in the walls, assuming that as he remodeled and expanded the house he would run hallways or add doors where needed. For several years the family room boasted a hidden record player that appeared when a door was opened in a false beam. A skilled plumber, he had a furnace for melting lead to make hot lead joints in cast-iron drainpipe. Over time, he converted the original patio into a family room and the master bedroom into a kitchen, divided the garage into two bedrooms, made an entryway of the dining room, and converted a storage room into a bath, among other things. Only the original bathroom escaped Gordon's hammer and saw. Though his family chided him at times about the recurring construction upheaval, Gordon had only one motive with his constant renovation: "I felt the pressure of a growing family, and I knew the home could be made more convenient and more interesting. I did what I did because I hoped to make things better."[3]

Like the house, the yard was the product and imagination of its creator, who, according to the master plan filed in his head, envisioned what his acreage would look like when it reached maturity. Clark explained that from the outset his father "had a vision and a plan for the future. He was always thinking not only about how to improve conditions, but how to make them better years down the road."[4] For example, the original landscaping plan called for a row of fast-growing Chinese elm trees along the south lot line planted alternately with slower growing but more appealing hardwoods. The strategy was simple: once the hardwoods reached maturity, the elms would be removed, leaving a row of beautiful shade trees. Unfortunately the scheme had one flaw: the hearty elms grew so rapidly that they became a nemesis that nearly overtook the large backyard. The elms produced millions of seed pods that had to be swept continually from the asphalt driveway; worse, an alarming number of seeds took root, sprouting hundreds of tiny trees in every corner of the lot. During one summer alone, when Clark was assigned to uproot any elm not planted by design, he disposed of at least two hundred trees.

As the children grew older and one by one began to move away, maintenance of the imposing yard became increasingly difficult. In time it seemed clear that, as with the house, the sheer immensity of the master plan defied its ever being completed.

The family grew used to the continual efforts toward an end that, while never completely realized, was an invigorating goal nonetheless. Though modest even by the standards of the day, their two-bedroom, one-bath expandable wonder (which eventually boasted four bedrooms and two baths) became a source of cautious pride to the children. As Dick said many years later: "I felt as though we were part of the landed gentry. It wasn't that we had much money. But Dad took great pride in making our home as fine a place as it could be. I couldn't imagine that there was anywhere I would rather live."[5]

From the time his children were small, meetings took Gordon out of the home many nights of the week and virtually every Sunday. Only Kathy could remember—and vaguely at that—a time when he wasn't "President Hinckley." At times the boys wished their dad had more leisure time to spend with them. "We had our time together, it just wasn't hunting or boating," said Dick. "It was pounding nails and sawing. Once in a while I felt a little sorry for myself. As I got older I realized we really had spent a lot of time together."[6]

In the summertime Gordon and Dick, and later Clark, handled the irrigation turn that came early each Monday and Wednesday morning, without which it would have been impossible to maintain the large property. Dick frequently slept outside those nights so he could turn the water on at 4:00 A.M. By the time the water made it down the ditch and onto their property a half hour later, Gordon was up, and together he and his son spent the next two hours nursing water down rows that funneled the precious liquid into every corner of the yard.

In the natural course of daily life there were other occasions when the family had uninterrupted time together. Dinner each evening was sacrosanct; everyone was expected to be home. The conversation around the table typically revolved around practical matters: "Who needs the car tomorrow?" "How did you do on your test?" "The water comes at 4:00 in the morning, so we had better get to bed early."

On Sundays, Gordon was busy with stake business during the morning and evening, but the afternoon was family time. Typically he came home from meetings and loaded up everyone for a round of visiting with family and friends. It was a rare Sunday that they didn't stop for a bowl of ice cream at Papa Hinckley's, and everyone, including children, sat in the living room and talked. The children loved these Sunday excursions that made them feel part of their parents' world.

On Sunday afternoon, time seemed to stand still—a welcome change of pace for everyone. For into the remaining six days Gordon squeezed an unbelievable amount of work, Church service, and household chores. Efficiency and punctuality were Hinckley trademarks—hence his impatience with anything that infringed on his time, such as crowds and lines. On Memorial Day the family began their annual pilgrimage to decorate Grandma Bitner's and Aunt May's graves well before 7:00 A.M. to "beat the crowds." (As adults the children were shocked to find that they could drive right to their grandmother's grave at noon without getting caught in traffic.) By Gordon's definition, half a dozen cars in a given place at any time constituted a crowd.

Each summer the family did go to the drive-in movie at least once, but they literally never saw the end of a show. Before the feature was over, Gordon would head for the exit rather than risk getting penned in by a line of traffic. If a wedding reception started at 6:00 P.M., he and Marjorie arrived at 5:30 to avoid the crowd. If he scheduled a meeting to begin on the hour, those attending learned to be in their seats ten minutes early, as he was just as likely to begin then as not. On weekdays, he went to work early and was typically at his desk before 7:00 A.M., but he left the office in time to make the commute home before traffic became heavy around 5:00. On many days, he changed into his work clothes and put in an hour on his latest project before changing back into white shirt and tie and heading for the stake center.

"Dad has always been able to squeeze more into twenty-four hours than anyone I have ever known," Kathy said. "He has never had patience with a lack of discipline, and has even less patience with those who waste time, particularly his."[7] From Gordon's point of view, there was good reason for such a preoccupation with time. In his experience, those who were disciplined, had a vision of what they wanted to accomplish, and worked hard usually succeeded. "There is nothing you can't do if you want to do it and are willing to work hard enough," he repeatedly told his children. "You are as bright and capable as anybody, and if you want to do something, then do it." Though he didn't necessarily see his sons and daughters as unusually gifted or talented, he wanted them to catch the vision of their own potential.

He also told Marjorie that he hoped their children would marry in the temple, get a good education, and see the world and meet its people. He wanted them to see beyond the life they were experiencing in East Millcreek and to catch a sense of the adventure and potential that awaited them. Books and education were means to that end. Both Gordon and Marjorie were readers, and they made good literature a family staple. Like his mother before him, Gordon loved words, and the dinner table at which he presided often provided the forum for a grammar lesson as he corrected the children in the way they used language, structured sentences, and pronounced words.

In addition, the children were expected to take their schoolwork seriously and to do their best. Gordon apparently kept abreast of their progress, as indicated in a letter he sent to the elementary school principal commending one of Dick's teachers: "I was unable to get to any of the P.T.A. meetings, but saw [William Naylor's] exceptionally good work reflected in my own boy and others of his students. Certainly one of the standards by which a teacher can be judged is the motivation which he gives his pupils, and in the case of Mr. Naylor, I have seen exceptional motivation."[8]

Neither Gordon nor Marjorie lacked for motivation, for there was never a shortage of obligations to manage. While Gordon juggled the time pressures of service in the stake presidency with increasing demands at work, Marjorie managed the home and handled challenging assignments of her own. In time, she would serve as president of the ward Relief Society, YWMIA, and Primary, chair the community cancer drive, and take on many other projects that benefited from her enthusiasm and ability to rally others to a cause. For years she taught cultural refinement lessons in Relief Society, and she earned the reputation of being an outstanding instructor. The family became used to seeing books scattered around the house as she prepared for her next lesson.

Marjorie was a unique blend of support and independence,

a woman whose warmth and genuine friendliness drew people to her. With her there was no pretense, no maneuvering for power or position, no putting on airs. And she had the ability to make those with whom she interacted feel accepted and good about themselves. As Jane later explained: "Each of us has always loved being with Mother. It is impossible to spend time with her and not leave feeling as though you're the greatest person on earth. She makes everyone feel that way."[9]

Gordon's full schedule and time demands required that his wife be accommodating and flexible. But though inherently optimistic and even-tempered, she was also fiercely independent and inclined to speak her mind and to draw the line when she saw fit. If she felt strongly about something, she let Gordon know about it. And typically he responded. Just as he didn't keep a thumb on his children, neither did he try to control his wife. He wasn't interested in monitoring a woman whom he knew to be entirely capable of managing their home and taking the lead in rearing five energetic children.

"Mother's independence is an interesting thing," Clark maintained years later. "She has always been supportive of Dad, but she is also the only person who can make him back down. If she told him, 'You are *not* going to tear up the kitchen this week, and that is final,' he didn't touch the kitchen. And he has always loved that side of her."[10] Gordon later told a Churchwide audience: "Unfortunately, some women want to remake their husbands after their own designs. Some husbands regard it as their prerogative to compel their wives to fit their standard of what they think to be the ideal. It never works."[11]

What did work for the Hinckleys was mutual respect and cooperation. Whereas the amount of time Gordon spent at home decreased over the years, Marjorie was almost always there. Together they created an atmosphere of stability and love in their family, as much by how they interacted with each other as by what they expressed verbally. Because Gordon and Marjorie were content with their lives, the children had a sense that everything else was fine as well.

Which is not to say that there was never discord at home. The Hinckleys experienced the predictable irritations and annoyances that are part of typical family life. But, in general, things fell into a fairly standard routine. Family and friends knew not to call late because lights were out by 10:00. Throughout his life Gordon would claim, "If you go to bed at 10:00 and get up by 6:00 A.M., things will work out for you." And there were other formulas that he not only preached but practiced. "Get on your knees and ask for help, and then get up and go to work, and you'll be able to find your way through almost any situation" was just one rule of thumb he repeatedly emphasized with his children.

One issue over which the children prayed each summer was that nothing would come up to postpone or, worse, cancel their annual family vacation, which Gordon always promised they would take "when things got finished at the office." Marjorie and the children were never quite sure what day that would prove to be, so when he announced that tomorrow was the day, there was a flurry of activity as everyone pitched in to pack, fill the canvas water bag that hung from the car bumper, and select books to read en route. The day of the trip they arose at 4:00 A.M. but never got away until an hour later—with Gordon grumbling about the late start. The children were almost always fussing at each other before they reached the city limits, at which point he would pull the car over and announce impatiently, "We are going home *right now* if you can't get along with each other." Said Clark, "We weren't mean to each other, we were just normal. We squabbled a lot."[12] Once the vacation was really under way, everyone had a wonderful time.

Vacations took them throughout the scenic West—to Bryce Canyon, where Gordon, Kathy, and Dick hiked to the bottom of the magnificent canyon and crawled back up to the top; to Moab and Monument Valley, where Dick got carsick from the washboardlike roads and proclaimed that "when Heavenly Father created the earth, he forgot to finish this part"; and to Yellowstone National Park, where they held their noses as they tiptoed around the lava pots. By the time the children were grown they had seen, according to Marjorie, "every square inch" of Utah and had learned to love their home state, from its magnificent red sandstone formations to the peaks of the Wasatch Mountains. They also traveled to many places outside Utah.

Marjorie read to the family as they drove, and together they explored the world of literature and became absorbed in the stories that she made come to life. When she finished reading *Where the Red Fern Grows*, everyone in the car was crying. The tender last chapter coincided with their arrival at their destination, an aunt's home in Nevada. Gordon drove around the block several times so they could compose themselves before knocking on the door.

He believed vacations were wonderful educational opportunities, so he stopped at nearly every roadside historical marker and rehearsed the history memorialized by the monument. He seemed to know the dates and details about every place of historical interest. When possible, Gordon stopped at Cove Fort or Fillmore, where he repeated the stories about Ira Hinckley and other forebears.

Neither Gordon nor Marjorie was inclined to impose on the children a lengthy list of rigid rules and regulations. He insisted that he did enough preaching elsewhere—he had no desire to come home and do more. Discipline was handled much the same way. They both believed that harsh corrective measures only created resentment. "Mother and Dad taught us that there was a difference between principles and rules," Ginny explained. "There are never enough rules to tell you what to do in every situation. But they did put a few principles in place. We felt free to make decisions because we knew the fundamental principles against which everything could be measured."[13]

The Hinckleys communicated those principles—being responsible, working hard, doing what you say you'll do, getting an education, being disciplined, finishing what you start, keeping the commandments, and so forth—to their offspring through example, the ultimate textbook. Dick recalled a crucial period in his own life: "When I was going through some years of questioning and doubts as a teenager, Dad was like an anchor. I don't recall discussing many of my concerns with him. But in my heart I knew *he* knew the gospel was true, and that was terribly important to me. I knew he was a believer—not because he talked overtly or often about his feelings, but I just sensed that he knew. God was real and personal to him. Joseph Smith's experiences were real to him. There was no question in my mind that he had any doubt of their authenticity. Mother and Dad taught us more by example than by preaching. We observed them adhering to principles, and then we followed."[14]

After Kathy was married, an experience clarified what she had learned growing up in her parents' home. She attended a conference where her father was speaking, and at the conclusion of his talk he bore his testimony. "I think for the first time in my life I really heard him and realized he had a testimony that was profound and solid and secure," she said. "I had always known it without really realizing it. It wasn't that Dad was running around the house bearing his testimony. But we knew it was there. We knew it because of his commitment and dedication to the Church, and because of the way he prioritized his life. The gospel was his number-one priority. By his actions he essentially told us over and over, 'If you center your life on the gospel, you'll be okay.'"[15] Many times in later years Gordon would tell parents, "Your example will do more than anything else in impressing upon [your children's] minds a pattern of life."[16]

Gordon used stories to convey his admiration for people and character traits. As the family sat around the dinner table or worked in the yard, he told stories—about Ira Hinckley building Cove Fort, about his own boyhood or mission, about a neighbor or friend he admired, about pioneers who exhibited faith and fortitude. "We got a clear idea of what Dad appreciated by the way he spoke about others," Ginny said. "He used phrases like, 'He is a person of ability,' or 'He is a person of capacity.' He was very open about the strengths he saw operating in other people's lives, and over time we got a sense of what he valued. He valued integrity, goodness, competence, and people who do what they say they'll do."[17]

Conversely, he also occasionally referred to circumstances where bad choices had caused people trouble. "I don't know if Dad told those stories purposely to plant in our minds the fact that it's no fun to be in trouble," Dick reflected, "or whether he was just talking about what he observed from day to day. But there was never any doubt where our parents' loyalties lay in terms of the Church. They weren't pious. We didn't sit around the dinner table discussing gospel topics. But they were always totally immersed in the gospel. There was never a discussion about whether we were going to church. It was just the way we lived."[18]

There was, of course, normal jockeying between parents and children, and there were plenty of times when Gordon's children stretched his patience, though he wasn't inclined to explode or lose his temper. When the inevitable challenges of child rearing arose—traffic tickets, minor accidents, lateness coming home, and the like—Gordon had his own way of coping: he got his clippers and went outside and pruned trees. The exercise was good therapy.

Though specific curfews were rarely imposed, Gordon and Marjorie expected their teenagers to come home at a reasonable hour, the definition of which at times varied between parent and child and from event to event. Gordon would routinely ask a son or daughter when he or she had come in the night before. "Oh, I don't know. It was about 11:30," would come the answer. "It was more like a quarter after twelve," Gordon would challenge. "We knew that Dad knew when we got in," Ginny said. "We knew that when he said a quarter after twelve he really knew it was a quarter to twelve. But he made his point: that coming in late wasn't okay. We pushed a little, and he pushed back a little. But nobody ever pushed very far."[19]

Through it all, the Hinckley offspring came to understand that a certain standard was expected of them. With a code of conduct in place, Gordon and Marjorie didn't have to constantly look over their children's shoulders. They wanted their sons and daughters to establish the strength within themselves to make their own decisions and go forward. Several decades later Gordon told a Churchwide gathering of youth: "Never forget that you were chosen and brought to earth to live as a child of God for something of importance in his grand design. He expects marvelous things of you. He expects you to keep your lives clean from the sins of the world. You are the line through which will pass the qualities of your forebears to the posterity who will come after you. Did you ever see a chain with a weak link? Don't you become that weak link."[20]

Family prayer was one of the basics that Gordon and Marjorie relied on to insulate their children against the world's ills. Years later Dick had vivid memories of the effect his father's prayers had on him: "I can't remember a day when we didn't have family prayer. When it was his turn, Dad prayed very sincerely but never with a theatrical or emotional air. We learned much about the depth of his faith by listening to him pray. He addressed God with great reverence, as he would perhaps a wise and revered teacher or mentor, and he referred to the Savior with deep feeling. As a child I knew they were real persons to him—that he loved and revered them, and that he felt deeply the Savior's suffering."[21] Gordon prayed regularly for the children, for their teachers, and for those who were "downtrodden and oppressed" or "alone and afraid." Among other things, his prayers taught his family where they could always turn in times of need. One phrase he used frequently may not have had its full effect while the children were young, but it stayed with them as adults: "We pray that we may live without regret."

Said Marjorie: "I think family prayer had a great deal to do with the way our children responded to us. Even though Gordon didn't preach to them, they heard everything we wanted them to hear in family prayer."[22] Some years later Gordon endorsed the importance of praying as a family: "I know of no single practice that will have a more salutary effect upon your lives than the practice of kneeling together as you begin and close each day. Somehow the little storms that seem to afflict every marriage are dissipated when, kneeling before the Lord, you thank him for one another . . . and then together invoke his blessings upon your lives, your home, your loved ones, and your dreams. . . . [Through this practice] your children will know the security of a home wherein dwells the Spirit of the Lord."[23]

There were other family characteristics that added to a feeling of security among the Hinckley offspring. Neither Gordon nor Marjorie promoted doing things for the sake of appearance. "It was always a surprise to have other people insinuate that we needed to be perfect," said Ginny. "Mother and Dad never made us feel that we had to look good for them."[24] Gordon and Marjorie did, however, communicate their expectation that their children would act with integrity and contribute whenever they were called upon to do so. "Our parents had a way of making us feel that we were the best kids in town," Clark said. "They never led us to believe we were better than anyone else. But we thought *they* thought we were probably a little bit smarter, a little harder working than other kids."[25] Gordon often told his children that he wasn't interested in having any geniuses in the family, that the penitentiary was full of geniuses who were too smart for their own good. "But Mother and Dad gave us the feeling that even if we weren't the most gifted children in town, we were immensely satisfying to them," Ginny added.[26]

Somehow Gordon and Marjorie managed to monitor what went on in their children's lives while staying far enough in the background for them to learn to make their own decisions. As a senior in high school, Kathy learned that she was expected to purchase a pin to graduate from seminary. The pin cost $4.50, which seemed extravagant for something she would never wear again, so she and several friends elected not to purchase the jewelry. As graduation approached, however, everyone but Kathy responded to the seminary principal's urging to buy the pins, and she ultimately stood alone in her boycott. The situation was made more awkward when Gordon was invited to speak at the graduation banquet, and the principal feared embarrassment when everyone but Kathy received a pin. By now, however, the issue had become a matter of principle, and Kathy refused to change her position. One evening the phone rang. From her father's side of the conversation Kathy could tell that her principal was reciting the seminary-pin crisis. "Oh, really? Well, I guess that's her decision," Gordon said, ending the conversation. "That was the principal calling about the seminary pin," he reported to her. "I don't want to spend $4.50 on that pin," Kathy explained. "But it might be awkward for me to go to the banquet if I am the only one who won't receive one," she added. "Oh, well," her father responded, "you've heard everything I have to say."

Kathy did not purchase a pin, nor did she go to the banquet. "Neither Mother nor Dad ever said another word about it to me," she said. "I am sure they wondered why I couldn't just conform, but I had made a choice and they respected it. That incident was one of the things that taught me what was important to them—it was me, and not a seminary pin."

On another occasion Kathy's Sunday School teacher insisted that the entire class bear their testimonies the following Sunday during testimony meeting. Kathy was annoyed at the attempt to force something so personal on her, and she announced to her family that she had no intention of participating. Again, her parents declined to make an issue of the situation. "Mother and Dad operated on the principle that we were intelligent and could make our own decisions," she explained. "They didn't throw up fences, and so there was nothing to jump over. They let me test my wings and figure out things for myself, trusting that I would eventually come to the conclusions they hoped I would make in the first place."[27]

Each of Kathy's brothers and sisters had similar experiences. Ginny's attendance at MIA was less than perfect during her senior year in high school. There weren't many other girls her age in the ward, and with her heavy load at school she sometimes stayed home to study. At one point, the YWMIA presidency called on Gordon and Marjorie to explain that because of Virginia's inconsistent attendance her sixth and final Individual Award—an annual recognition based heavily on attendance—was in jeopardy. Suffering from the hypersensitivity of adolescence, Ginny was sure that the leaders were less concerned about her well-being than about how it would look to have Gordon Hinckley's daughter not receive an award. After the leaders left, neither parent said anything about the conversation to their daughter.

As a junior high student Jane casually mentioned to her mother that a friend couldn't come over to study because she was grounded. "Grounded? What in the world is that?" Marjorie questioned. Jane explained that her friend had misbehaved and was for the time being allowed out of the house only to go to school. Seeing it as an arbitrary form of punishment, Marjorie was incredulous: "That is the most ridiculous thing I have ever heard!"[28]

For Marjorie, there were certain kinds of things that didn't merit intervention, anxiety or, worse, punishment; most definitely they weren't worth creating conflict between parent and child. "I learned that I needed to trust my children," she said later, "so I tried to never say no if I could possibly say yes. When we were raising a family, it was a matter of getting through every day and having a little fun along the way. As I could see that I wasn't going to be able to make all of my children's decisions anyway, I tried not to worry about every little thing. I think that came from my parents, because they had absolute confidence in me and my siblings. As hard as it has been at times, Gordon and I tried to have the same confidence in our children."[29]

One Sunday morning as the family was getting ready for church, Ginny complained to her mother, "Do I have to go to church today?" Without hesitating, Marjorie responded calmly, "No, you don't have to go if you don't want to." After a pause, she added, as though it were simply a logical arrangement: "But if you're going to stay home, would you get dinner on for us? It would be wonderful to come home from church and have dinner ready." Ginny agreed, and Marjorie left worrying that she should have handled the situation differently. The family returned home to find the meal prepared and Ginny waiting for everyone on the front lawn. "Virginia never stayed home again," Marjorie said. "She found it was better to just go with the family than to stay behind alone. In that situation, it helped to not make a federal case out of the issue."[30]

There were instances when the teaching between parent and child was more direct. One day Kathy asked her father how it was that General Authorities could have different opinions about things, and yet Church members were supposed to follow the prophet. Gordon's answer was firm: "You keep your eye on the President of the Church, and you will never go wrong." On another occasion, Kathy and her father were walking downtown when they stopped to talk with a man he knew. Kathy found herself staring at the man, whose appearance disturbed her. As they walked on down the street she asked her father why the man looked as he did. "He has the look of a man who doesn't honor his priesthood," Gordon replied. It was a lesson Kathy never forgot. "Dad's statement had great impact on me," she said. "I drew the conclusion that one thing that made the world safe was a man who honored his priesthood."[31]

Through such experiences Kathy, along with her brothers and sisters, came to trust her parents implicitly. "Even as a young girl I recognized in Dad what I considered unusual wisdom and judgment," she later reflected. "He always seemed to know and understand things beyond the obvious. He did not dictate to us, nor did he philosophize, but he asked us questions that inevitably led to a statement that was on target. He seemed to innately be able to see the big picture. I sensed that he always knew exactly what was and was not appropriate."[32]

Gordon and Marjorie's reactions to seminary pins, awards, and the like were tempered by their unpretentious natures. "It helped," Jane said later, "that Mother and Dad could laugh at themselves and find humor in what happened. Somehow they avoided overreacting to all of our little daily crises."[33] Marjorie admitted, "We tried not to take ourselves too seriously. We learned that you get in trouble when you do that."[34] Indeed, both Gordon and Marjorie saw their own foibles and laughed at them openly. Humor became the trademark in a family where the ability to laugh at oneself was required for survival. Gordon loved to hear or tell a good story and would laugh so hard as he approached the punch line that he could hardly speak or breathe. Watching him react was almost more fun than the joke itself. Family gatherings became laugh-fests, and at times the hilarity got out of hand.

The Hinckley children often heard their mother say, "The only way to get through life is to laugh your way through it," and Marjorie Hinckley took that approach with her husband and family, refusing to take offense where none was intended and filtering daily events through an attitude of good humor. Though a "world-class worrier," as described by her children, she tried to laugh even when she wanted to cry. One day she took what she thought to be a delectable casserole out of the oven, only to have Dick ask innocently, "Mom, how come you baked the garbage?"

As parents, Gordon and Marjorie relied on their instincts, and though the result may not have been parental perfection, they nonetheless wove a strong, warm family fabric. He had never read a book on parenting, but Gordon later spoke to millions on the subject. His counsel always revolved around the basics, as in one address in which he identified four simple principles parents might consider in rearing their children: to love them, to teach them, to respect them, and to pray with and for them.[35]

CHAPTER ELEVEN

TEMPLES TO DOT THE EARTH

With the Korean War ended and the promise of a gradual return to more normal policies regarding the calling of missionaries, Gordon might have hoped for a respite from long days and relentless pressure. But it was not to be.

On August 5, 1953, President David O. McKay broke ground for and dedicated the site of a temple in Zollikofen, Switzerland. This occasion held great significance for members of the Church—both those in Europe, who would benefit directly by having a temple on the Continent, and the greater membership, who heralded this milestone as evidence that the Church was becoming an organization of international scope and import. Though Gordon didn't realize it at the time, the event would have a personal and penetrating influence on him as well.

One day in the fall of 1953 President McKay invited him to his office for a private interview, and there he outlined some of the unique challenges posed by the new European temple. "Brother Hinckley," he began, "as you know, we are building a temple in Switzerland, and it will be different from our other temples in that it must serve members who speak many languages. I want you to find a way to present the temple instruction in the various languages of Europe while using a minimum number of temple workers." President McKay indicated that President Joseph Fielding Smith of the Quorum of the Twelve and Elders Harold B. Lee and Richard L. Evans had been assigned to a committee overseeing the project, but that he would have responsibility for completing it in time for the dedication, scheduled just two years hence in the fall of 1955. And this assignment was to run concurrent with his responsibilities in the Missionary Department.

It was a charge of enormous significance. No superlative did justice to the assignment. For nearly two decades Gordon had led pioneering efforts in the Missionary Department and on the Radio, Publicity, and Mission Literature Committee, and he was well acquainted with the challenges involved in championing something that had never before been done. But the ramifications of this project were enormous, as they would extend far beyond the temple in Switzerland. This temple, which would be the ninth operating, would be but the first of many designed to serve a multilingual audience. The new commission placed upon him a responsibility laden with pressure and concerned with issues as sacred and sublime as any within the scope of the gospel.

A spacious and totally private place to work was needed. President McKay authorized use of the fifth floor of the Salt Lake Temple. This area included a smaller room where Gordon could study and ponder the direction this project should take. Known as the Talmage Room, as it was believed to be the room where Elder James E. Talmage had written *Jesus the Christ*, this sacred hideaway became a place of study, prayer, and refuge. Evenings, Saturdays, and some Sunday mornings found him poring over the language of the temple ceremony, sketching out ideas, and pleading with the Lord for guidance.

President Smith, Elder Lee, and Elder Evans were helpful and supportive, but in short order Gordon found himself working with President McKay, who often met with him on the fifth floor early on Sunday mornings. There the two shared ideas about how the wording and presentation should be adapted to fit the purposes the prophet had outlined. The pressure was intense. Only Marjorie knew the nature of her husband's project and the reason that he was suddenly gone from home even more than before.

After much study, reflection, and discussion with President McKay, Gordon made a recommendation: It appeared that the most effective way to conduct large numbers of temple patrons through the sacred service in a variety of languages and with a minimal number of temple workers was to put it on film. Such a conversion would allow temple sessions to accommodate more people in less time and space.

The challenge now was to produce a film that would not

only safeguard the temple instruction but be a fitting representation of that sacred work. Gordon gathered a group of capable, creative, and temple-worthy colleagues to help develop and produce this first-of-a-kind effort: Frank Wise, an excellent cinematographer who had assisted with missionary filmstrips and other projects; Paul Evans and Joyce (Joe) Shaw from KSL; Joe Osmond, the Church's electrician; Winnifred Bowers, an expert with costumes; Harold I. Hansen from BYU, who directed the Hill Cumorah Pageant; and Bill Demos, a set design artist.

They set to work. The ornate, three-story room in which President Wilford Woodruff had dedicated the temple in the first of thirty-one sessions seemed ideal. Gordon and his associates began by converting the large area between the stands on the east and west ends into a makeshift movie set. They hung a huge, floor-to-ceiling scrim as a backdrop for the cameras, used heavy-duty pulleys to lift various props through the room's large windows, and installed a power line capable of handling the increased voltage requirements of lights and cameras. The temple elevators inside the back door made it possible to carry smaller materials directly to the fifth floor without attracting the attention of temple workers.

From dawn until dusk on Saturdays and holidays they worked, fitting the all-consuming temple assignment in and around their regular jobs. Countless decisions had to be made. Gordon consulted regularly with President McKay, and their ongoing Sunday-morning meetings moved the project forward.

After a year of long hours and unrelenting pressure, the English-language film was completed. And though the finished product was to be improved in later versions, President McKay was pleased with the pioneering effort. With the English film in place, the sacred service was now to be produced in French, German, Dutch, Finnish, Swedish, Danish, and Norwegian, and for each film different casts and new translations were required. During subsequent months translations were also provided in Spanish, Tongan, Tahitian, Samoan, and Maori. Not until much later would one film be adapted for use in multiple language versions.[1]

When the production was finished, another sensitive problem arose. Where could the films be processed without risking disclosure of language regarded as sacred? After weighing various options, Gordon contacted an old friend, James B. Keysor, a member of the Church in California who used his Hollywood connections to arrange for a laboratory to process the film in such a way that only those authorized would ever see the frames.

Finally, the product was finished. But there was still much to do in preparation for the temple dedication, scheduled for September 11, 1955. Projection and sound equipment had to be installed in the temple, the audio and filmed segments synchronized, and any potential problems detected and corrected so that ordinance work could commence upon conclusion of the last dedicatory session. He therefore prepared to leave for Switzerland in advance of the dedication to ensure that all would be ready when President McKay arrived. Much to his delight, Marjorie had been invited to go with him.

The prospects of traveling to Europe with her husband and spending a month there were thrilling for Marjorie, who had never been farther away from home than the West Coast. But as they prepared to leave, rather than enjoying the euphoria that might have preceded such a trip, Gordon was preoccupied with the logistics of safely transporting the temple materials to Switzerland.

Consequently, elaborate precautions were taken to protect the materials that portrayed the sacred ordinance. With the reels of 16mm film packed in two small suitcases, and the audio recordings placed in two small, barrel-like drums that Gordon carried with him, he and Marjorie left for Switzerland. What a miracle this was, he thought, allowing himself the luxury of reflection as they flew high above the Atlantic in a prop-driven DC-6. Though he did not enjoy travel for travel's sake, he was eager to return to Europe.

Around noon on a Saturday they arrived in Basel, where the first serious challenge arose. When the customs agent asked what the small drums contained, Gordon responded, "Church film and lectures." "I can't let the film through customs without approval from the federal film board," the agent responded, adding that the film reels must be transferred to Bern, where they would be considered by the film board on Monday. Gordon tried to gently persuade the agent to let him take the film on through, but then he relented, feeling it was better to avoid an argument than to attract undue attention to the precious baggage. Reluctantly, but not knowing what else to do, he placed the film reels in bond and arranged for them to be transferred by Swiss Customs to Bern, where he would pick them up Monday morning.

The next day, Gordon and President William F. Perschon of the Swiss-Austrian Mission fasted and pled with the Lord to keep the sacred films out of other hands. Early Monday morning they reported to customs in Bern, where Gordon was again asked to declare the contents of his luggage. "Church film and lectures," he responded a second time. The customs agent accepted the declaration and sent the men to the federal film board office, where an officer asked a series of questions. "What is this film?" "Church lecture and music," Gordon responded. "What is its purpose?" "It will be used in the new temple we are building in Zollikofen." "What is its title?" the agent inquired. "It does not have a title," Gordon answered. "How can all of that film have no title?" the agent asked. Gordon answered carefully, "This is just a lecture, and we don't title every lecture given in our church." President Perschon later recorded that as they were explaining the nature of the materials to the officer in charge, "a friendly understanding seemed to come over him, and to an unusual degree for a Swiss tax official, he cooperated."[2] Finally the agent stamped the papers with the necessary seal and indicated the number of Swiss francs due. "I've never seen anyone reach for money faster than did President Perschon," Gordon remembered. "The duty was only twenty-seven dollars. We gathered up the reels of film, placed them back in the barrels, and took them to the temple. Nobody ever saw a frame or listened to a word of it."[3]

With the temple films safely stored inside the temple, the Hinckleys settled in at the City Hotel in Bern. Marjorie could scarcely believe that she was actually in Switzerland. The wonder of it all was almost more than she could take in. During their brief stopover in England en route she had dashed off a postcard to the children: "I hardly saw a glimpse of the Atlantic because we were above the clouds, so I did not have to look down at the scary water. Everything is simply marvelous."[4]

As thrilled as she was about her maiden journey overseas, however, Marjorie was also anxious about her first experience being away from the children for any length of time. Jane was still in a high chair, and Kathy was only sixteen. "When we arrived in Switzerland and I realized there was an ocean and a continent between the children and me," she later admitted, "I burst into tears. It was three days before I decided everything was going to be okay and I might as well enjoy the experience."[5] She adapted quickly, and to stave off moments of homesickness she wrote the children almost daily with vivid descriptions of everything she and their father were experiencing.

There was much to write about, for both Gordon and Marjorie became immediately absorbed in the flurry of events unfolding in Zollikofen. He quickly realized there was more work for him to do than time in which to do it. Early each morning he and Marjorie took the tram out to the temple, both prepared for a long day's work. Marjorie helped do everything from ironing clothing to vacuuming.

In the meantime Gordon, Paul Evans, Joe Shaw, and Hans Lütscher, the newly appointed temple engineer, began installing the projectors and audio equipment, synchronizing the film and audio segments, and reviewing each language version of the film. The deadline loomed. He noted later, "We had so much work to be done, and we couldn't even think of letting down President McKay. So we worked our heads off, night and day we worked."[6]

But the long hours and prededication frenzy were more than compensated for by the events that followed. Sunday morning, September 11, dawned bright and beautiful in Zollikofen. The temple grounds were glorious for the throng of members, missionaries, and curious townspeople who converged upon the area. When President and Sister McKay arrived, missionaries lined a pathway for them. The air was electric as President McKay entered the celestial room for the first of ten dedicatory sessions. Dressed in white, his wavy white hair accentuating his distinguished appearance, he *looked* like a prophet. For Marjorie it was an unforgettable moment: "President McKay was so beloved by the people. And he was such a handsome man who only became more so as he aged. When he entered the room that morning in Switzerland, it was as though Moses had arrived."[7] The Tabernacle Choir was on hand for the dedication, and they were seated around the perimeter of the celestial room as well as in the main assembly room.

Afterward President McKay recorded: "When the time came to welcome the hundreds who crowded the rooms at the first session, it seemed proper to express also a welcome to an unseen, but seemingly real audience, among whom were possibly former presidents and apostles of the Church, probably headed by the Prophet Joseph Smith . . . also his nephew, President Joseph F. Smith, who prophesied forty-nine years ago in the city of Bern that 'temples would be built in divers countries of the world.' . . . We all agreed that the veil between those who participated in those exercises and loved ones who had gone before seemed very thin."[8]

President McKay presided over two sessions on that and each succeeding day until Thursday, September 15. He invited Gordon to address the Norwegian and Danish session held on September 14. Speaking through a translator, he emphasized the importance of temple work by referring to an observation he had made at an earlier session: "The other morning . . . when the German Saints were coming in here, I saw a man come through the front door; his clothes were shoddy, but neat and clean. He looked the picture of poverty, but he was well scrubbed. I think he was from Austria. He carried in his hand an admittance card, and as he walked through the room downstairs to these rear doors there was a light in his eyes and a look in his face which were almost celestial. I thought, 'He won't look very much different when he walks into the Celestial Kingdom.' This was the fruition of all his dreams. This was the thing for which he had saved and prayed. And I said to myself, 'Certainly this is a foretaste of Heaven.'"[9]

It was for Gordon as well, for the entire experience—beginning with the overwhelming assignment from President McKay and culminating with his recent around-the-clock effort prior to the dedication—had been as sweet and spiritually fulfilling as anything with which he had ever been involved. "As

I saw those people gathered from ten nations to participate in the temple ordinances," he later reported, "as I saw elderly people from behind the Iron Curtain who had lost their families in the wars that had washed over them, and witnessed the expressions of joy and tears of gladness which came from their hearts as a result of the opportunities that had been given them; as I saw young husbands and wives with their families—their bright and beautiful children—and saw those families united in an eternal relationship, I knew with a certainty even beyond what I had known before that [President McKay] was inspired and directed of the Lord to bring these priceless blessings into the lives of those men and women of faith gathered from the nations of Europe."[10]

It had been determined that temple work would not commence until Monday morning, September 19, but President McKay, concerned about members from nearby countries who had to return home immediately, asked Gordon if sessions could somehow begin without delay. He and those assisting him worked most of the night following the last dedicatory session on Thursday so that two companies of German-speaking Saints could be ushered through the temple the following day. When members from the French Mission asked for early sessions in French, their request was accommodated. Similar inquiries from the Swedish and Dutch Saints followed. The result was that temple work ran continuously from 7:00 A.M. Friday until 7:00 P.M. Saturday. Gordon and the others assigned to shepherd hundreds of Saints through the temple for the first time again worked through the night.

In a letter to President Richards, Gordon described those first two days of work in the Swiss Temple: "If [my response to your questions] appears to be a muddled statement it is because I have been up all night for the second night in a row. Thursday we worked until four in the morning to get things ready for the [first] service. The first group went through at eight o'clock yesterday morning and the last group finished at six-thirty this morning with no let-up in between. I have had to handle all of the equipment used in the presentation since they have not had a local man who has been through the Temple. The local engineer went through yesterday, and I am hopeful now that he can get onto the mass of detail in a few days and that I can go home.

President McKay witnessed the first German session yesterday and expressed satisfaction with the result. We have since had another German as well as French and Swedish sessions and they have gone remarkably well in consideration of the language problems and the fact that the people have had little background to prepare them for temple work. I am satisfied that it would have been extremely difficult to present the service in the six languages, and to do so effectively, without something of the program we are using."[11] The following month at general conference President McKay acknowledged the "indefatigable efforts of Elder Gordon B. Hinckley," which made it possible for thousands of European Saints to go through the temple before returning home.[12]

For Gordon, the time in Europe had been both enriching and exhausting, and the stress had taken its toll. He was tired, sick, and wheezing from asthma by the time President McKay left Switzerland. During a stopover in London, the prophet called him to see how he was faring and suggested that he take a few days of vacation before returning to Utah. Gordon accepted President McKay's invitation and accordingly changed his and Marjorie's tickets to travel home via Italy, Spain, and Portugal.

Though he was physically and emotionally depleted when he left Switzerland, Gordon was exuberant about all that had transpired. Had it not been for the help of dedicated colleagues who had worked tirelessly for months, and for divine guidance that had steered them through the arduous process of committing the temple service to film, he knew he could not have fulfilled President McKay's charge. For him, the experience was a vivid personal confirmation that out of the weak and simple, great things come to pass, and that the Lord directs and sustains those who serve him.

The brief vacation was a welcome break for both Hinckleys, as it was their first chance in months to enjoy time together without the press of other urgent obligations. Soon, however, they were on their way home. Gordon was anxious to get back to work, and though she had enjoyed the trip immensely, Marjorie had been away from the children as long as she could tolerate. They arrived home to find all well, though circumstances were different from the way they had left them. The children had determined early in their parents' absence that they could get along nicely on weekends without the services of the live-in housekeeper whom Marjorie had hired to take care of them for the month. "The children essentially fired the baby sitter," said Marjorie. "Their excuse was that they didn't like the way she was treating Jane, but I suspect they just didn't care for her rules." Gordon had reluctantly left the car keys for Kathy in case of "extreme emergency," so she had been able to run necessary errands. It had helped that their close family friend and next-door neighbor, Bessie Osguthorpe, seemed to be constantly at her kitchen window, from where she monitored the goings-on at the Hinckley home.

From eldest to youngest, the children were thrilled to have their mother and father home after an absence of nearly a month. Their parents' first trip abroad together had a lasting effect on them, however, as Dick explained: "If Mother had written home that it was raining all day and that travel was hard, we may have had an entirely different reaction to their experience. But she made everything seem so adventurous that we never saw the world quite the same again." As a group the children later reflected on this turning point: "We had always been a family to 'dream the impossible dream,' but now we knew that impossible dreams came true. Geography became a desirable subject. . . . Our opportunities were limitless if we just dreamed big and worked hard."[13]

Back in Salt Lake City, Gordon began the tedious process of sorting through the mountain of work that had accumulated during his absence. He and President Richards had been in frequent contact during his extended stay in Switzerland, and where possible Gordon had offered help from a distance. "I hope that my prolonged stay is not adding materially to your heavy burdens, and that you will leave for me such items as can wait," he had urged in one letter to his superior.[14] Now he refocused his attention on the Missionary Department and attended to other pressing concerns.

At President McKay's request, however, he also continued his involvement with temple work. Another temple—this one in Los Angeles—was scheduled to be dedicated in just a few months, and Gordon was uniquely trained to handle many assignments connected with preparing the sacred edifice for operation. He also served as a member of the dedication committee, and in so doing he had his first experience helping administer the array of details associated with such an event—arranging for tickets, ushers, choirs, interpreters, and so forth.

President McKay invited Gordon to attend the dedication. With the West Coast just a day's drive away, he and Marjorie determined that this was the perfect opportunity to take the children to see the ocean and experience California firsthand, as well as to participate in a temple dedication.

The children marveled as they crossed the Mojave Desert and were fascinated as they drove past the homes of movie stars in Beverly Hills. They also went to the ocean, though the Hinckley version of a trip to the beach was unorthodox. "When we went to the beach, we went to look, not to play in the sand," Marjorie explained. "Five minutes after we were there, Gordon said, 'Okay, you've seen the ocean. Let's go.'"[15]

On March 11, 1956, six months to the day after he had dedicated the Swiss Temple, President McKay conducted the first of eight dedicatory sessions of the Los Angeles Temple, the first temple on the West Coast and only the third one outside Utah in the continental United States. As had been the case in Switzerland, the dedication was the setting for a marvelous spiritual outpouring. In Gordon's experience, nothing compared to the way he felt in the temple, especially as a temple was dedicated. With each new temple-related experience, he marveled at the singular opportunity that had been his to immerse himself in this sacred work.

Gordon welcomed these spiritually satisfying experiences, because many of his obligations in the Missionary Department remained demanding, complex, and administrative in nature. As the number of missionaries called to the field gradually increased following the end of the Korean War and the subsequent relaxing of Selective Service requirements, his range of responsibility within the Missionary Department expanded until he was either accountable for or directly involved with nearly every aspect of the work. On one occasion he described at least one benefit of his day-to-day labors: "I have been touched by the mission presidents with whom I have worked. As I have known their stories, the great sacrifices which they have made to go into the world, the devotion with which they labor, the manner in which they give of themselves, I have been humbled. I have been inspired by the missionaries with whom I have had association. I have seen them as they have gone out in all kinds of weather . . . doing their work and bearing testimony, often at great sacrifice, and bringing a marvelous harvest of souls into the kingdom of God."[16]

Though Gordon still carried a full load of missionary-related responsibilities, it soon became clear that his involvement with temples would continue, as President McKay expected him to duplicate in temples under construction in New Zealand and London the role he had played in the opening of the Swiss and Los Angeles Temples. Accordingly, he returned to Switzerland in November 1956 to hand deliver new reels of film and to evaluate and address problems that had arisen since the temple's opening. He reported his findings in writing to President McKay: "We were able to take the Temple material through Customs without difficulty and without exposing it to anyone. . . . I went through [one] session and I was pleased and gratified at the manner in which the session was conducted. It was inspirational and all who participated seemed to enjoy it. . . . I then went to work on the film that I took over and spent the next three or four days putting this together so that it would be ready for use. I instructed carefully the building engineer on details of how this should be done so that he should be able to take care of future shipments of film."[17]

While in Bern, Gordon had an experience that provided stark contrast to the serenity of temple worship. One morning while standing in the train station, he witnessed the Swiss people's reaction to the Soviet Union's surprise invasion of Hungary, initiated to quash widespread demonstrations against Communist rule.[18] That morning, as tanks rolled down the streets of Budapest and students were massacred by machine-gun fire, every church bell in Switzerland began to ring. "At the conclusion of that ringing every vehicle stopped—every car on the highway, every bus, every railroad train," Gordon described. "That great, cavernous station became deathly still. I looked out the door across the plaza. Men working on the hotel on the other side of the street stood on the scaffolding with bared heads. Every bicycle stopped, and every man and woman and child dismounted and stood, hatless and bowed. Then, after three minutes of reverent pause, trucks, great convoys of them, began to roll from Geneva, across Austria to the Hungarian border, laden with supplies—food, clothing, and medicine. The gates of Switzerland were thrown open to refugees. As I stood there that December morning, I could not help marveling at the miraculous contrast—the devilish oppressive power of those who were snuffing out the sparks of freedom on the streets of Budapest, in contrast with the spirit of the Christian people of Switzerland who bowed their heads in reverence and then rolled up their sleeves to provide succor and refuge."[19]

Through his assignments at Church headquarters, Gordon was cultivating a broad world view of the growing Church. Through his calling in the stake presidency, he had opportunity to work at the grassroots level, where the broad policies and procedures actually touched the people. For more than ten years he had served as a counselor to President Lamont B. Gundersen in the East Millcreek Stake presidency. Because their stake was situated in one of the most rapidly growing areas of the valley, their presidency was constantly dealing with issues related to growth and change. During the years Gordon served in the stake presidency, at least fifteen new wards were created and the stake was twice divided to become four large stakes.

One such division occurred on October 28, 1956, when Elders Harold B. Lee and George Q. Morris divided the eleven-thousand-member East Millcreek Stake into three smaller stakes and called Gordon B. Hinckley to serve as president of the East Millcreek Stake.[20] It was a call filled with historical implications, as he was the third generation of Hinckleys to be so called. His grandfather had presided over one of the twenty-five stakes then in the Church; his father had led what was then the Church's largest stake; now he assumed leadership of the 150th stake.

When Elder Lee presented Gordon Hinckley's name to the East Millcreek audience, a murmur of approval swept through the congregation. Later, in setting him apart as stake president,

Elder Lee counseled him to "listen to the whisperings of the Spirit, even in the nighttime, and neglect not the impressions which come to you."[21] Elder Lee's blessing had a profound effect on him, and many times throughout his life he reflected on the promises made by Elder Lee as he set him apart as stake president.[22]

The East Millcreek Stake over which Gordon and his two counselors—H. Leroy Erickson and O. Layton Alldredge—presided had some four thousand members living in five wards. Though he had spent a decade in the stake presidency, he learned immediately how much more demanding the calling of stake president was. Stake members now looked to him for spiritual direction and counsel. Difficult issues—many of which involved members' eternal welfare—fell to him to decide. In addition, he was immediately confronted with an unusually burdensome physical facilities challenge.

The stake division had been effected in such a way that only one building, and an old one at that, lay within the new stake boundaries. People were moving into the area so rapidly that he was faced not only with building chapels to house five wards but also with planning and preparing for the inevitable new wards. If that weren't enough, every stake was required to have its own welfare farm; the one his stake owned jointly with the Canyon Rim Stake would not suffice. Further, his stake was one of those charged with raising funds to build a seminary facility at Olympus High School. It was clear from the outset that managing the temporal affairs of the stake would be both complex and worrisome.

Almost immediately he set out under procedures then in operation to build a stake center (the stake was obligated for half the cost), raise funds for a seminary building (area stakes were to raise 100 percent), and buy a stake farm (which also was to be funded 100 percent by stake members). The immediate financial commitment was staggering. As he and his counselors considered options, they worried about placing an additional monetary burden on young families. Just before the stake's division, they had built two new ward meetinghouses. Unfortunately, neither of those buildings now lay within their stake boundaries, but

Gordon knew many members felt they had already contributed all they had to give.

One of President Hinckley's early decisions left an impression on his youngest son. "One of Dad's first official acts as stake president was to cancel our stake Lagoon day [a local amusement park] and invite members to take whatever money they would have spent there and put it into a new stake building fund," Clark remembered.[23] Such contributions were a pittance when measured against the demand, however, and the financial pressures weighed heavily upon President Hinckley. But true to Elder Lee's promise, one night he had a sudden and clear impression: "It occurred to me that this wasn't my problem alone," he explained. "This was the Lord's church, and it was the Lord's problem. I knew at that moment that He would help me determine how we should proceed." After consulting with his counselors, Gordon called a stake priesthood meeting and there outlined the financial challenges ahead of them, introducing the subject for discussion by stating: "Brethren, this is not my stake. This is the Lord's stake, and it is your stake. All of you are stockholders in this organization, and tonight we wish to talk about our needs and how we can best meet them together." He then invited comments from anyone who desired to express himself.

Things did not begin well. After a few moments a man on the front row stood and said: "All I have heard since I moved into this stake is money, money, money. I am moving." A second man arose and expressed similar sentiments, asking President Hinckley when *he* was going to stop asking for money. Yet a third man complained about the financial drain the Church had been since he moved into the area. Gordon's mind raced. How would he salvage the meeting?

Finally a man who had been sitting quietly on an aisle seat toward the back stood slowly and began to speak: "Brethren, this is the Lord's work and, as President Hinckley has said, the Lord's stake. The Church has to have facilities if it is going to operate. As you know, I am a mail carrier, and I don't earn much money. But my wife and I have a small savings account, and I know she would support me in pledging what modest amount we have to these projects."

What then occurred was marvelous to behold. One by one,

priesthood holders stood and offered their support. Some committed specific sums of money; others made suggestions about how funds could be raised. Many simply promised to do whatever was necessary to help meet the stake's obligations. It was a profoundly moving experience for Gordon, who learned a lesson that would guide him for the rest of his life: "This isn't your problem, it is the Lord's problem. And if you will listen to the whisperings of the Spirit, pay attention, and counsel with your brethren, He will tell you what to do and open the way."

With the stake's priesthood quorums behind him, President Hinckley and his associates went to work. In the following months they purchased ground for a new stake center, hired an architect and had a blueprint prepared and approved at Church headquarters, and began construction. They also purchased the Canyon Rim Stake's equity in the 250-acre welfare farm, and they helped the other stakes in the area raise funds to build the seminary. Members made personal donations, and priesthood quorums and ward auxiliaries collected dimes and dollars to purchase everything from Herefords for the farm to draperies for the stake center. "There may have been a few murmurings," President Hinckley acknowledged later, "but the faith of the people overrode all of these. They gave generously, notwithstanding the stresses of their own circumstances, and the Lord blessed them in a remarkable way."[24]

President Hinckley had faith that if the people did their best, the Lord would ultimately provide. Such commitment was a hallmark of both his administrative style and his counseling. When a man whom he knew well came for a temple recommend interview and, during their conversation, acknowledged he was not paying his tithing because his debt load was too high, Gordon told him that he would not be able to pay his debts until he paid his tithing. The man continued in his established pattern for some time before he and his wife determined to heed their stake president's counsel. Later he reported to President Hinckley: "What you told me has proved to be true. I felt I could not pay my tithing because of my debts. I discovered that no matter how hard I tried, somehow I could not manage to reduce my debt. Finally my wife and I sat down together and talked about it and concluded we would try the promise of the Lord.

We have done so. And somehow in a way we can't quite understand, the Lord has blessed us."[25] Such experiences reinforced Gordon's faith.

President Hinckley found he couldn't separate the temporal and spiritual well-being of his people. He took a stand, for example, against area stores that opened on the Sabbath. To one local grocery store he wrote: "I am advised that all other grocery stores in the area will be closed. . . . We are urging our people to observe the Christian Sabbath. If the stores remain open, then inevitably many of our people are compelled to work. If you remain open then your competitors apparently will feel that they must remain open. We earnestly solicit your cooperation in this important matter."[26]

As a stake president, he had substantial latitude and autonomy, and he directed the affairs of his stake as the Spirit prompted and as his judgment suggested. When unusual challenges or problems arose, he had the advantage of ready access to many General Authorities, who offered counsel and suggestions at his request. Further, through his assignments at Church headquarters, he had worked with countless mission and stake presidents and bishops, and in the process he had been exposed to various leadership styles. As he picked his way through the numerous issues that came before him, he drew liberally from a full reservoir of personal experience and observation.

Home was a refuge where Gordon was rejuvenated to handle the increasingly heavy load he carried, though his children weren't always aware of the obligations he was balancing. Said Clark: "Even when Dad was stake president and working in the Missionary Department and helping with the opening of new temples, I never got the sense that there was a great deal of pressure on him. He had a good sense of humor, and he would come home from the office and repeat jokes he had heard that made him laugh so hard he couldn't catch his breath."[27] Marjorie agreed, adding, "Gordon's sense of humor got us through all of the crises in our lives."[28]

Even with the heavy burdens of caring for the spiritual welfare of his people and managing the stake's burgeoning temporal affairs, Gordon held no more meetings than were absolutely essential. He became known for his efficiency, his capacity for work, his compassion, and his sense of humor. Don Sperry, stake clerk, attended many meetings conducted by President Hinckley. "He had a way of making you feel good," he said. "I never dreaded having to get up early Sunday morning for a meeting because I knew there was going to be some good activity, a lot of inspiration, and a lot of humor as well."[29] Indeed, although Gordon took his responsibilities very seriously, he was the first to poke fun at himself when the opportunity arose.

President Hinckley's meetings began and ended on time. He expected stake leaders to be well prepared and to speak their mind. When sensitive issues arose, he seemed able to grasp the essence of the matter quickly. From there, it was a matter of combining earnest prayer with hard work. In fact, he often reacted to challenges with the statement, "I don't know how to get anything done except by working, so let's get going." Once a decision was made, he didn't look back. And when things were most discouraging he typically told his counselors, "Things will work out."

It was an ethic Gordon came by honestly. In a message at a family reunion in 1955, Bryant Hinckley announced that the Hinckley family had been admitted to the exclusive Society of Mayflower Descendants. He then briefly explained the significance of their heritage: "My kinspeople, I congratulate you on your ancestry. If the time ever comes that any of you think you are nobody, and can't amount to anything, remember that you have a noble heritage that comes down to you for 300 years. There were 102 people aboard the Mayflower when she left England on the 6th of September and she reached these shores on November 9. It was a perilous journey all the way. They landed on Plymouth Rock, December 21, 1620, and every day during the long bitter winter the graveyard grew larger and the colony grew smaller. When the Mayflower was ready to return in the spring, only 49 people had survived. No one went back. This spirit is born in you fellows—the spirit of never turning back."[30]

Gordon's father had delivered such messages for as long as he could remember. Nonetheless, even Gordon didn't foresee events that would soon unfold, the nature of which would affect the course of his life dramatically, requiring him to make commitments from which he could never turn back.

CHAPTER TWELVE

ASSISTANT TO THE TWELVE

The first week of April 1958 the weather turned cool. A spring storm brought steady rain, then snow, blanketing Temple Square in white. The previous general conference had been canceled due to a flu epidemic, so twelve months had passed since the Saints had last heard from their leaders in that setting. But as much as he looked forward to conference, Gordon was preoccupied. A recent stroke had confined his father, now nearly ninety-one, to the hospital, and the prognosis was not good.

Early Saturday evening the phone rang at the Hinckleys'. Dick answered and immediately recognized President McKay's voice, though the Church President did not identify himself. Dick ran outside and called his father to the phone, then heard him say, "Yes, sir. I'll be right there." After a quick shower and change of clothes, Gordon hurried downtown. En route he wondered if the President needed him to take care of something before tomorrow's sessions of conference. But when he walked into President McKay's office, he sensed that this was not a routine summons. After greeting him cordially, President McKay got right to the point: He wished for Gordon to accept a call to serve as an Assistant to the Twelve.

President McKay's words shocked Gordon. "It was a blow, a complete surprise," he admitted. "I had worked around the Church administration building for many years, and I knew these men who were called as General Authorities very well. I knew their strengths and their weaknesses. I knew they were mortal, but I also knew the great good in them. I knew they were special people, and to join their ranks was an almost unbelievable thing. It was overwhelming to have the President of the Church issue such a call."[1]

The following day, April 6, 1958, President McKay stepped

to the pulpit during the Sunday afternoon session and asked for the sustaining vote for the forty-seven-year-old stake president from East Millcreek, Utah. As Elder Hinckley approached the imposing pulpit that looked out over the audience, he caught his breath. From this vantage point the Tabernacle in which he had attended meetings since boyhood looked cavernous. A lifetime of memories surrounding that signal podium surged through his mind. As a boy, he had sat in the balcony and listened to President Heber J. Grant. As a young man, he had witnessed his mentors—men whose work made them more than men to him—deliver inspiring and at times profound addresses from this same pulpit. He simply could not comprehend the call that had come to him.

Elder Hinckley began his remarks with a touch of the self-deprecating humor for which he would become known in subsequent decades: "I am reminded of a statement made by my first missionary companion when I received a letter of transfer to the European Mission office. After I had read it, I turned it over to him. He read it, and then said: 'Well, you must have helped an old lady across the street in the preexistence. This has not come because of anything you've done here.'" After pausing to accommodate the laughter that rippled through the audience, Elder Hinckley continued, his remarks indicating something of the shock with which he was dealing: "I am overwhelmed with a sense of inadequacy. I feel shaken."

In a spirit of reflection, he then acknowledged those whose influence he had felt most deeply throughout his life: "I have been thinking about the road that led here. I know that I have not come that road alone. . . . We grow according to the help given us by those who teach us and lead us." Among others, Gordon singled out the Brethren with whom he had worked closely for more than two decades: "I do not know why under the blessing of Providence I have had the marvelous association which I have had with President Richards. . . . For almost a quarter of a century I have worked under his direction and have been tutored by him. I have partaken of his wisdom—his great wisdom—and his kindness and graciousness. I shall ever be in his debt, and I want him to know of my love and appreciation for him." Elder Hinckley reserved a special tribute for his father: "If I feel any selfish satisfaction in this honor, it is the satisfaction that comes from the realization that one of his sons has been found worthy of the confidence of the Brethren. And if I feel any regret, it is that, unless the Lord rules to the contrary, he will not know of this in mortality because of the condition in which he lies today. [Bryant had recently suffered a stroke.] No son ever had a better father."

In conclusion, the new General Authority testified of the divinity of the work in which he had been engaged all his adult life: "I would like to bear testimony that I know that God lives, that Jesus is our Redeemer, the Only Begotten of the Father in the flesh, the Savior of mankind who gave his life to atone for our sins; that Joseph Smith was indeed a prophet of God, the prophet of this dispensation; that the Lord's work is here and is real and under his direction; and that President David O. McKay stands . . . to lead the kingdom of God, as the stone which was cut out of the mountain without hands, which should roll forth and fill the earth. God help us, you and me, to live up to the testimonies which we carry in our hearts."[2]

The next day's *Deseret News* described Elder Hinckley as "a man whose quiet and almost incredibly effective work behind the scenes of the Church administration is known to comparatively few," and added that "his faithful attention to details, as well as his ability to conceive and carry out big, imaginative plans, [has] made him as a strong right arm to the brethren."[3] Indeed, for the better part of twenty-three years, Gordon had devoted his energy and talent, in one capacity or another, to missionary work. He had survived one pressure-laden assignment after another, demonstrated his integrity and sense of propriety, and handled gracefully the stress of critical areas of responsibility. But in coming days it would become clear that everything he had done had merely laid the foundation for what was now just beginning.

Four days later, President McKay set Elder Hinckley apart as an Assistant to the Twelve. Among other things, the Church President blessed him with protection and guidance, sound judgment, and physical strength. He also referred to Elder Hinckley's prior service: "The Lord is pleased with your devotion in the past, with your willingness to lose yourself for the good of the work. You have demonstrated it, and the people appreciate your service, and the Lord accepts you." The prophet then gave Elder Hinckley his charge: "Go forth in the performance of this great labor under the inspiration and guidance of the Holy Spirit. You now are . . . representing our Lord and Savior Jesus Christ. May your testimony of Him become real—more real than it has been in the past, though you have known clearly, as we note through your service, of the reality of the great saving work pertaining to humanity on this earth. The Lord bless you abundantly that you may feel in your very soul the responsibility which is yours to declare to an unbelieving world the necessity of their obeying the principles of the Gospel of Jesus Christ." Afterward Elder Hinckley said simply, "I feel inadequate, but I pledge you my best."[4]

During the almost twenty-three years Gordon had worked at Church headquarters, he had developed a warm relationship with many General Authorities, particularly members of the Twelve and the First Presidency. To now be numbered among them seemed inconceivable. But as President Stephen L Richards told him, "You have been doing the work all of these years. You might just as well have the title."

In 1935, when Elder Hinckley had returned from his mission in the British Isles, there had been three quarters of a million Church members residing in 115 stakes. Now there were a million and a half members in 273 stakes, and he had witnessed that growth from the unique vantage point of headquarters. Once again, however, his life had taken a new and unplanned course. Though he had long immersed himself in "Church work," both professionally and ecclesiastically, it was sobering to realize that the course of the remainder of his life had effectively been taken out of his hands. For a brief time he felt almost as though he had been preempted. There would be no retirement, no opportunity to try his hand at business. Moments of relaxation would be scarce. He would travel extensively—something he endured rather than enjoyed. And his young family would have to adjust to his frequent absence. He wished he could talk through his feelings with his father, but Bryant's stroke had left him unable to communicate.

On the other hand, it was now Gordon's opportunity and responsibility to place his life in the hands of the Lord and to devote himself completely to His service. In practical terms, this new assignment felt in some respects like business as usual, for he had tried to follow that pattern throughout his adult life. And there were other matters that remained much the same. Elder Hinckley still made the same commute to the same building. Because he continued to serve as executive secretary of the Missionary Department, his office wasn't even changed. Neither were circumstances adjusted immediately in the East Millcreek Stake, where he continued to serve as stake president. He worked by day as a General Authority, held stake meetings on weekday evenings, and divided his time on weekends between his own stake and assignments to attend conferences in other areas. The first few times he participated in calling new stake presidents were a little unnerving, and he returned home feeling drained emotionally and spiritually. But he found the spiritual outpouring remarkable.

At home the family took Gordon's call in stride—largely because he and Marjorie were determined to maintain a semblance of normalcy—though the older children had strong reactions to the news. Kathy was a freshman at BYU when she received word of her father's new calling. "I didn't take Dad's call very seriously at first," she admitted latter. "It is not that we hadn't been taught to respect General Authorities. But we just couldn't imagine that they had called our father to be one. At home, he didn't make an issue of it."[5] At thirteen, Virginia was at an age where her parents looked less than perfect to her: "I was aware of the human weaknesses my parents displayed, and so Dad's call came as a little crisis of faith for me. I thought, 'How could the Lord call somebody like my dad who's so average and sometimes lacking?' At the dinner table that first afternoon while we were getting over the shock of what had happened, I said, using an expression I had heard Dad use in referring to missionaries, 'Well, I guess the Lord is just going to have to work with what he's got.' Everyone laughed, but to me that was an expression of my faith. I really believed the Lord would have to turn him into something more than my father."[6]

Some of Elder Hinckley's first responsibilities as a new General Authority put him on familiar ground. Shortly after the

April general conference, he and Sister Hinckley left for New Zealand to participate in the dedication of the temple there. Once again, they traveled in advance of President McKay so that Gordon could finalize arrangements for the dedication and the beginning of ordinance work. In contrast to their trip to Switzerland three years earlier, however, Gordon and Marjorie were anxious about leaving the country for an extended time, for Bryant Hinckley's health was failing noticeably. Fearful that he might not see his father alive again, Gordon administered to him the day before he left. During the blessing he had the impression that his father would not pass away while he was on assignment, and that Bryant would even regain a measure of strength.[7]

Marjorie was comfortable leaving the children at home, knowing that Bessie next door would keep an eye on things. "We all knew Bessie wouldn't go to bed until all of our lights were out," Dick said. "Many times when my parents were away I would think to myself, 'I'd better not be late getting home or Bessie will never get to sleep.' Once when I came in later than I should have, I turned off the headlights and the motor and coasted up the driveway. The next day Bessie said, 'You came in a little late last night.' I knew I had met my match."[8]

Despite the reassurance of help at home, it was unnerving to begin a trip of such distance. International travel was still a little overwhelming to the Hinckleys, though they both loved the exposure to new lands and peoples. Certainly New Zealand was their most exotic destination yet, and as they mingled with Pakehas and Maoris, Tongans and Tahitians, and had their first glimpse of cultures they had previously only read about, they could scarcely believe what they were experiencing. President McKay's arrival was greeted with a glorious spectacle in which various groups of Polynesian Saints in native costume entertained, sang, and danced for nearly four hours.[9] The pageantry was unlike anything the Hinckleys had ever seen.

This trip afforded them the privilege of staying with President and Sister McKay at the home of the temple president. It was Marjorie's first opportunity to associate with a Church President in an informal setting. "I got to see what President McKay was like, whether he liked cold pie or hot pie, so to speak," she said. "And it was wonderful. I would sit across the dining room table after we had eaten and just revel in the experience of being with a prophet. President McKay had an aura about him that was simply overpowering."[10]

On April 20, 1958, President McKay dedicated the temple, located in Temple View some seventy-five miles south of Auckland. Elder Hinckley was inspired by members throughout the South Pacific, some of whom had made extraordinary sacrifices to attend. He took particular note of one man from the far side of Australia who had initially determined he could not afford to make the trip but then had had a change of heart. He had looked at his wife and children, realized that he couldn't afford not to go, and then sold all that he had to obtain the necessary funds. His story was representative of many others.[11]

Elder Hinckley returned from New Zealand to find his father showing modest signs of improvement, though Bryant would never completely recover. In addition to family worries, the newest General Authority was feeling a certain degree of occupational pressure, perhaps much of it self-imposed. On June 5, as he gave BYU's baccalaureate address, he pleaded with the graduates to conform their lives to gospel standards.[12] In and of itself, the assignment was not an extraordinary one, for he had delivered hundreds of addresses to audiences equally imposing. But now he was speaking as a General Authority. Perhaps he was just imagining it, but it seemed that audiences expected more of him, that his words were given added weight. The responsibility was fearsome at times, and he found himself wondering if he was measuring up.

Another source of pressure revolved around the East Millcreek Stake. Still serving as stake president, he struggled to keep the stake going while attending to a growing list of other obligations. After a couple of months of double duty, Elder Hinckley called to the attention of President Joseph Fielding Smith the fact that he was holding down two demanding jobs and doing justice to neither. "We'll take care of that one of these days," President Smith promised. Finally, on August 17, 1958, four and a half months after being sustained as a General Authority, Elder Hinckley was assigned to assist Elder Harold B. Lee in reorganizing the stake, which experience Elder Lee detailed in his journal: "We had an unusual experience in receiving direction for this reorganization. Gordon had been sentimentally inclined to name his first counselor as his successor. In the midst of our interview with him, President H. Leroy Erickson, I was impressed that he should be ordained as the stake patriarch. . . . Gordon said that last night . . . he suddenly had the same impression, but felt it was not his place to suggest it. We named the second counselor, O. Layton Alldredge, the stake president. . . . In his conference talk Brother Erickson said that after we told him of our decision to make him the patriarch, he went home and read his patriarchal blessing . . . and to his amazement, he found that this new calling would give him a fulfillment of one part of his blessing which he had heretofore overlooked."[13]

With this change, Elder Hinckley felt better about leaving the country for another extended period, this time to England to participate in the dedication of the London Temple. How he and Marjorie had looked forward to this event!

Again, the Hinckleys traveled to England in advance of the official party so that he could coordinate final arrangements for an occasion that was to bring the largest group of General Authorities to England since 1840. The new temple, located twenty-five miles south of London on what was formerly an Elizabethan farm, generated a great deal of prededication attention. Nearly seventy-six thousand visitors sloshed through England's summer rains to tour the temple during its open house, at times jamming the road from London to the rural Surrey town of Lingfield with so many cars that the Automobile Association had to put up yellow signs marking the way. *Time* magazine predicted that the new temple was sure to draw many converts to Mormonism.[14]

Elder Hinckley was at the temple site during much of the open house, and he enjoyed the opportunity to talk with nonmember visitors. One evening a young couple approached him outside on the temple steps and asked to know more about eternal marriage, a concept that had caught their attention during the tour. Elder Hinckley immediately responded, "Do you believe that life is eternal?" The woman replied that she did. "Do you believe that love is the finest expression of life?" Again, she responded in the affirmative. He then asked if the couple had been married by the vicar. When she said that they had, Elder Hinckley asked boldly, "Did you realize that when the vicar married you, he not only solemnized your marriage but decreed your separation as well?" An energetic discussion ensued, and though Elder Hinckley never knew whether the couple joined the Church, he was certain they were both surprised by and interested in the truths he shared.[15]

Following the open house there were just three days in which to make final preparations for the dedication itself. As was typically the case, last-minute adjustments and details kept workers, among them both Hinckleys, busy up until the morning of the dedication. In a postcard home Marjorie hinted at just one unexpected challenge: "The fire department had to come and pump water out of the temple basement last night after a rain. Most of the men worked all night. I had hoped to go back to London this morning with dad but will have to stay and join the mop-up brigade."[16] Indeed, a fierce lightning and rain storm, the likes of which Elder Hinckley had never seen, had created havoc. Late that night he, temple president Selvoy Boyer, and Elder ElRay L. Christiansen, all dressed in their pajamas, stood in waist-deep water bailing out a stairway area that led into the temple basement.

The momentary crisis was resolved, however, and the first of six dedicatory sessions commenced on Sunday morning, September 7, as scheduled. President McKay, who celebrated his eighty-fifth birthday on the second day of dedicatory services, read the dedicatory prayer at each of the six sessions. Elder Hinckley spoke at afternoon sessions on Sunday and Tuesday, on each occasion reflecting on the sacrifice and contribution of the early English Saints. All in all, the dedication was a spiritual feast framed within an atmosphere of celebration.

Before leaving England, Elder and Sister Hinckley made the two-hundred-mile drive north to Preston for Marjorie's first visit to her husband's initial area of labor as a missionary. She had heard so much about various landmarks that everything seemed familiar as they visited Vauxhall Chapel, 15 Wadham Road, and the River Ribble and walked across the old flagstone market where, more than twenty years earlier, a young and timid Elder Hinckley had first preached to unsympathetic crowds.

For Gordon, the memories were so tender that he walked along in silence, at a loss to express his feelings even to Marjorie. It was impossible for him to forget the scene that had greeted him more than two decades earlier—poor men whose worn coats and scarves were their only protection against the winter chill, and women who struggled to put something on the table from sparsely stocked pantries. They were rough people who had made sport of berating young Mormon elders. But it was here that he had faced a day of decision, here that his testimony had matured. "As I looked into the faces of the people of Lancashire, I could not help feeling sorry for them," he said after returning home. "I felt sorry for the fact that the majority of their forebears had rejected the gospel 121 years ago when the first missionaries came there. And frankly, I felt sorry that they had rejected us."[17]

The Hinckleys returned home via Brussels, where they enjoyed half a day at the World's Fair, and Paris. What awaited them in France was much less pleasant than either England or Belgium had been. Elder Hinckley was assigned by President McKay to meet with a handful of missionaries who had been misled by a clever apostate. He was heartbroken by what he found, as he noted in his journal: "I talked to them at length and gave them my assurance that no good would come of their actions, and that the day would come when they would regret what they were doing. I bore them my testimony of the gospel and tried every way I knew to persuade them to reverse their course, but to no avail. At that point there was little for me to do but make sure they had a way to get home. We felt we owed that to their parents."[18] His heart was heavy as he and Marjorie boarded the plane for home.

For the most part, however, Elder Hinckley's first months as a General Authority provided opportunities to observe the positive influence of the gospel in people's lives, and in his second general conference address he spoke of the divinity of the work he had witnessed from Europe to New Zealand.[19] Despite his talent with language, however, he found preparing to speak at general conference to be one of the hardest things he had ever attempted, and he agonized over the process. (He would find through the years that it didn't get any easier with practice.)

Not all assignments were as taxing. Some—indeed many—brought sheer delight. Although Elder Hinckley was always exhausted afterward, getting out among the members at stake conferences was a spiritual high. Dedicating new buildings was also a highlight—a physical manifestation of the growth of the Church and the sacrifice of its people. He found few assignments more satisfying than the one to dedicate a new stake center in the East Millcreek Stake—the building for which he had initiated plans two years earlier. On May 17, 1959, he arrived at the stake center to find the parking lot filled with shiny automobiles. The experience illustrated a principle he never forgot. "Nobody ever missed what he gave for that building," he said, "and that has been my testimony to Saints all over this Church. You don't miss what you give to the Lord."[20]

As the 1950s drew to a close, significant national and international developments foreshadowed the clamorous decade to follow. In 1959, Alaska and Hawaii were admitted to the union, NASA selected its first seven astronauts, the Soviet Union's Nikita Khrushchev made an unprecedented tour of the United States, and Fidel Castro overthrew Juan Batista to become Cuba's head. Closer to home, the decade's benedictory year found the Hinckley family undergoing dramatic growth pains as well. In May 1959, Kathleen announced her plans to marry Alan Barnes in November, and Dick graduated from Olympus High School. A candidate for the draft, he enlisted in the U.S. Army Reserve and was ordered to Fort Ord in northern California for basic training.

Realizing that the complexion of their home life would soon change forever, Gordon and Marjorie seized the opportunity to take their family on one last vacation together. They drove to San Francisco and during the several days prior to Dick's induction rode cable cars, walked along Fisherman's Wharf, took the Bay Cruise around Alcatraz, ate in Chinatown, and saw a stage version of *My Fair Lady*. A woman who had always relished having her children nearby, Marjorie did not find the transition easy.

When they returned from California, having left Dick behind, she locked herself in the bathroom and cried.

Kathy's impending marriage prompted dramatic changes as well. All of her father's building, remodeling, and tinkering of the past paled in comparison with the major renovation he undertook when they decided to hold her wedding reception at home. Gordon's plan called for converting the master bedroom along the back of the house into a kitchen, turning the old kitchen into a bedroom, building a new master bedroom in the garage, cutting a front door into the dining room, which would then become the entrance hall, and converting the family room into a dining room. It was a bold and ambitious project, one that few men would have attempted at all, let alone just a few months before a wedding reception was scheduled to be held there. But Gordon was not to be deterred. Recalling her father's plans, Virginia explained: "It never occurred to Dad that he couldn't accomplish something. When it came to the wedding, he liked having a deadline. He was always changing something anyway, and a firm deadline gave him a concrete goal that dictated when the job had to be finished."[21]

The massive remodeling was simply good sense as far as Gordon was concerned, for the changes would make the home more convenient for his family. Therefore, all summer and into the fall Marjorie and the children awoke early each morning to the noise of hammer and saw as he put in an hour's work before leaving for the office. Major jobs, such as plumbing the kitchen or moving the front door, were reserved for holidays and the occasional Saturday when he didn't have a conference assignment out of town.

The day before the wedding there was still wallpapering and painting to be done. "I've always been up against the gun," Gordon said later. "My whole life I've been right against deadlines. When I was in the university, I turned in papers the last day I could hand them in. I have lived with pressure."[22] That evening Alan picked Kathy up from classes at the university, brought her home, changed into work clothes, and hung the wallpaper in the kitchen. "After all," Gordon told him without a hint of apology, "anyone who is marrying into this family needs to know how to work."

On the morning of November 13, 1959, Elder Hinckley performed the marriage of his eldest daughter. That night the reception was pleasant for guests and nothing short of miraculous as far as the family was concerned, as they had seen their modest home undergo a magnificent transformation.

With all the pressure to have the home ready for Kathy's reception, it was no wonder that Elder Hinckley almost overlooked an assignment to address the BYU student body just nine days before the wedding. The evening of November 3, he turned over his calendar to find a note he had scrawled on the next day's schedule—"BYU—10:00 A.M."—and immediately felt the anxiety of facing thousands of students without much time to prepare. He confessed his near faux pas as he began his remarks the following morning; then, perhaps preoccupied with Kathy's impending marriage, he spoke to the subject of building an eternal home. "The nation is no stronger than the homes of the people, and the Church is no stronger in its practical aspects and in the faith and devotion of its members than the homes of the people," he began. After a practical message on this most fundamental of topics, he concluded—again, almost certainly with his own daughter in mind: "In the philosophy of the Gospel, the girl you take to the temple is not a doll or a toy, she is not a chattel or a slave. She is a daughter of our Father in Heaven, and she is a companion and an equal, and without her you cannot achieve the highest degree of exaltation in our Father's kingdom. . . . The children who come to your home are likewise the children of our Father in Heaven, and he will hold you responsible for them. I believe that children should respect parents, but I believe also that parents should respect children."[23]

On this subject Elder Hinckley knew whereof he spoke, for he and Marjorie both nurtured a healthy respect for their children. Both had long encouraged their children's unique personalities, and now that he was a General Authority, they were determined that his visible position would not undermine their children's ability to progress and develop normally. When his weekend conference assignments were nearby, Gordon occasionally took one of the children with him, and they relished the one-on-one time with their father. "Most of my experience related to Dad's call as a General Authority was positive," Clark reflected. "I did not grow up expecting him to be home a lot, so in that respect things didn't change much. And we each had opportunities to spend time with him in unusual settings—the kind of thing that our friends didn't get to do with their fathers. There were trade-offs, but we all felt lucky to be Hinckleys."[24]

There were, of course, changes for everyone in the family, not the least for Elder Hinckley himself. Tuesday morning, May 19, 1959, he and others of the Missionary Department assembled at 7:30 in President Stephen L Richards's office for the weekly meeting in which missionary assignments were made. When President Richards was late arriving, they wondered if they should begin the meeting, but decided against doing so. Finally the phone rang, and the caller relayed sobering news: President Richards had been rushed to the hospital after suffering a heart attack. Less than an hour later, he was gone. The news stunned Elder Hinckley. He knew his mentor had had a heart condition, but there had been no warning that his passing was imminent.

Invited to speak at the funeral, he summarized his experience with President Richards: "It was a stimulating experience to work under him. . . . I have been the beneficiary of his great kindness. I have partaken of his unfailing courtesy. I have witnessed his unyielding loyalty to his honored leader and to his associates. I have marveled at his matchless wisdom, his incisive mind, his persuasive expression. His sense of justice was universal in its application. . . . His devotion to duty was undeviating. His love of God was the polar star of his life, and his desire to help his fellow men his chief ambition."[25]

President Richards's death left a void in Gordon's life. Next to his father, this man had had greater influence on him than any other. And with his father's ability to communicate limited by poor health, he felt a surge of loneliness. "It was a traumatic thing," he remembered. "President Richards was a great and good, wise and wonderful man. He was thoroughly dedicated to the Church. And I knew immediately that his death would mean a change in how things operated for me."[26]

On June 12, 1959, President McKay reorganized the First Presidency, naming J. Reuben Clark Jr. as first counselor and Henry D. Moyle as second. President Moyle now supervised the Missionary Department, so almost immediately he and Elder

Hinckley began conferring regularly on the range of matters that appeared before them. When it came to assigning prospective missionaries to their field of labor, Elder Hinckley often took the related paperwork to President Moyle's home, where, in the comfort and privacy of his library, they were free from distraction and could pray about the assignments.

In short order, Elder Hinckley came to love President Moyle. Though his leadership style was much different from that of President Richards, Elder Hinckley admired his energy and the bold manner in which he operated. "President Moyle was remarkable in many ways," he later reflected. "He was less concerned about the handbook and rules than in finding what was best for the kingdom in a given situation. I marveled not only at his energy and vision, but at his spirit of consecration. When he was called as an Apostle he closed his law office, moved his own furniture to Church headquarters, and never looked or went back. I am sure he would have given everything he had to the Church."[27]

One day in early 1960 President Moyle called Elder Hinckley to his office. Because the two met frequently, President Moyle's summons was not unusual. On this occasion, however, the item for discussion had broader ramifications than usual. Pointing to a large world map that lay on his desk, President Moyle explained that he would soon propose to the First Presidency and Quorum of the Twelve that they divide the world into areas, each to be supervised by a General Authority. "I have every area covered except one," he said, "and that is Asia. I can't bring myself to ask anyone to go to Asia." Elder Hinckley responded, "President Moyle, if you need somebody to supervise Asia, I would be happy to try." "You would? You would be willing to supervise an area halfway around the world?" President Moyle asked. With Elder Hinckley's simple "yes," the assignment was formalized.

Marjorie was not surprised that night when Gordon described the interchange in President Moyle's office. "Nobody else was jumping at the chance to take on an area so far from home where the Church was in its infancy, the languages were difficult, and there was a lot of work to be done," she said. "I immediately recognized that this would affect our routine, and that he would probably be traveling a great deal. Asia was huge, and he had tremendous territory to cover."[28]

Other assignments also occupied Elder Hinckley's time and attention. In March 1960, he was asked to sit on the General Priesthood Committee, chaired by Elder Harold B. Lee, to study Church curriculum with the object of providing for better correlation of all programs and activities. And he continued to supervise the work of the Missionary Department. At a Sunday evening "missionary session" held in connection with the April 1960 general conference, he outlined a four-point approach for preparing missionaries and then observed, "It is the hardest, toughest and roughest work . . . it is discouraging work, but it is also the most fruitful, wonderful and glorious work in all the world."[29] To the BYU student body he noted the substantial increase in conversions between 1954 and 1958 (during which time they more than doubled), and then bore testimony of the consequences of such a missionary harvest: "These converts are not peas in a pod, they are not automobiles on a production line; they are men and women, sons and daughters of our Father in Heaven, into whose hearts have come the truths of the restored gospel. . . . Nobody knows, nobody can predict the consequences of those conversions."[30]

As immersed as he had been in missionary work, Elder Hinckley would soon observe its fruits in a new and poignant way. The assignment to oversee the work in Asia would be a consuming responsibility and opportunity—one in which he would sample anew the roughest and toughest yet most glorious work in all the world.

CHAPTER THIRTEEN

WEST MEETS EAST

What Elder Hinckley knew about Asia and its peoples didn't extend much beyond what he could read in an encyclopedia. He knew that it lay halfway around the world, that it covered an immense area (approximately 30 percent of the world's land mass), that it was home to some of the world's most densely populated cities and approximately half its population, and that the various languages spoken there bore no resemblance to English.[1] He couldn't remember having ever associated closely with anyone of Oriental descent, and he had no particular feeling for the Asian peoples. If anything, the Selective Service red tape he had found so tedious and worrisome during the Korean War had left him with a certain uneasiness about, if not a distaste for, that part of the world.

Elder Hinckley did know that the Church was small and weak along the Pacific Rim. Although the gospel had been introduced by faithful LDS servicemen in Japan, Taiwan, Okinawa, and Korea, its administration in those countries was still largely dependent on the Americans (expatriates, servicemen, and missionaries) living there. Despite its overwhelming size, all of Asia was divided into just two missions—the Southern Far East and the Northern Far East—and the Church owned only two buildings in the Orient, a house being used as a mission home on Kowloon across from Hong Kong Island, and a small house on Hokkaido, the northernmost island of Japan. Tiny branches of Saints—a dozen here, twenty there—met in members' living rooms and rented halls scattered throughout the vast continent. There were no stakes.

Elder Hinckley's new assignment would be a pioneering effort in every sense of the word. He was to give direction to mission presidents, motivate missionaries, teach and tend to the needs of the Saints, and develop leaders throughout the immense and highly diverse region. But his first challenge was to become acquainted with the peoples over whom he now had stewardship. In the spring of 1960, therefore, he prepared to make his first trip to Asia for an extensive tour of both missions.[2]

Travel to the Orient was still considered exotic, reserved largely for the professional and social elite. Though Elder Hinckley didn't relish the thought of traveling halfway around the world to half a dozen countries foreign to him in every respect, he recognized the opportunity as something rare. One evening he announced at the dinner table that he was going to Japan. There was no response. Once again he remarked, trying to sound casual, that he would soon be leaving for Japan. Again, no reaction. Finally, surprised that his news hadn't inspired some reply and perhaps even a little awe, he stated with emphasis, "I said, your fa-ther is go-ing to Ja-pan." At that Dick, who was home from basic training and would turn nineteen while his father was gone, looked up from his plate and asked, "Could you get the car radio fixed before you go?"

If Marjorie was concerned that her husband was leaving on a two-month-long overseas excursion, she didn't voice the sentiment. Both she and Gordon did everything they could to keep his send-off upbeat. But later, as his plane soared high above the Pacific, he felt both eager and apprehensive about what lay ahead. He couldn't visualize what awaited him.

Elder Hinckley first set foot on Asian soil in Tokyo, where he went through customs and immigration before pushing on to Hong Kong. There President Robert S. Taylor of the Southern Far East Mission and a small group of missionaries and Church members greeted him as he stepped out into the hot, steamy climate of Southeast Asia.

The next day, his introduction to the "Pearl of the Orient," as he would refer to Hong Kong ever after, began in earnest. What a fascinating city! The streets bulged with activity—bicycles, pedicabs, and small cars wove in and out as though each knew where the others would go in a traffic system that seemed to have neither rhyme nor reason. And he had never seen so many people, a seemingly never-ending stream emerging from countless alleyways, buildings, and streetside shops. It was a wonder that this mass of humanity moved itself about without constant injury! Buildings covered almost every square inch of ground, and the unfamiliar smells were pungent and spicy. He had been to London, Brussels, Paris, and Auckland, but he had never seen anything like this. Nor were the dominant sounds common or even pleasant to his ear. Cantonese, with its short syllables and staccato tones, sounded to him like a henhouse full of chickens.

But from his first day in Hong Kong, Elder Hinckley was captivated. The city's red buses and traffic roundabouts with vehicles moving on the left-hand side of the street gave the city a British ambience, though most of its residents were dark-haired and olive-skinned. There were obvious displays of wealth in the substantial business community, yet extreme cases of poverty—the worst he had ever seen—in other quarters of the city. The Star Ferry conveyed traffic back and forth between Hong Kong and Kowloon, part of the British Crown Colony on the coast of mainland China. And in the New Territories, a rural area near Kowloon leased by the British, men and women still used water buffalo for beasts of burden as they worked the rice fields.

Almost immediately Elder Hinckley determined that the missionaries must be the primary object of his attention. The more effective they were, the faster the gospel would move forward. On his second day in Hong Kong he met with the forty-five missionaries laboring there, and after interviewing each one he noted: "They are doing good work and appear to be happy. . . . I am confident that we would not go to any mission anywhere else in the world and find a better spirit among the missionaries."[3]

Despite the positive attitudes he observed among both missionaries and local members, he also identified challenges to the work in Hong Kong, some of them formidable, which he outlined in a memo to President Moyle. The native Chinese were immature in their Church experience, he reported. Language texts were inadequate, and missionaries struggled to communicate. Cantonese was spoken in Hong Kong; Mandarin was the language of Taiwan. "Even the Chinese cannot understand the Chinese," Elder Hinckley wrote. The muggy climate was also a deterrent to energetic missionary work. "The hot, humid air is extremely enervating," he reported. "The missionaries do not go at the pace that they go in other parts of the world, and this is understandable. However they can do better than they are now doing, and . . . I can make some suggestions to help them in organizing their work and budgeting their time."[4]

Each day Elder Hinckley uncovered more problems and challenges. Interested in locating a suitable building the Church could buy, he inspected a potential site. Undesirable by U.S. standards, it listed for $200,000, a staggering sum as far as he was concerned, though he would find that land was at a premium throughout Asia. He was also concerned with the teaching plan the missionaries were using. Long and involved, it did not allow them the flexibility they needed in a city where they taught everyone from Christian Protestants to Buddhists. Elder Hinckley believed he could rework the plan to be more effective, if he only had time to do so. He was busy from dawn to dusk visiting branches, inspecting property, and holding meetings and interviews with missionaries and members. He visited one-on-one with every young man and woman serving in the area so that he could assess their well-being, kneel with them in prayer, offer counsel and encouragement, and give blessings of healing or comfort as needed.

During meetings with small groups of members, Elder Hinckley came face-to-face with the challenges of training priesthood leaders whose language was totally foreign to him. As he sketched out details and information on a chalkboard, an interpreter followed behind, translating the words into Chinese characters. It was a tedious process, but the Church would never grow without leadership from local members who understood gospel principles as well as Church administration.

After eight days in Hong Kong, though he felt he hadn't begun to address the issues that begged for his attention there, Elder Hinckley flew to Manila, where his first order of business was to begin the process of obtaining official recognition for the Church in the Philippines. He found one small branch with forty-five members, most of them U.S. servicemen. There was only one known Filipino member of the Church.

Though he would have been hard-pressed to believe it just the day before, in the Philippines he encountered a culture, people, and land even more unusual than he had found in Hong

Kong. The climate was even more sultry, and most of the people appeared to live in abject poverty. The wild traffic he had encountered in Hong Kong seemed tame compared to what he now experienced. "The roads here are narrow and the people drive like mad," he recorded. "Old trucks and old buses compete with horse-drawn carts for the highway. Caribou . . . pull farm carts with solid wooden wheels."[5] Thousands of Jeepneys, a colorful and uniquely Filipino adaptation of Jeeps left over from World War II, were packed with people who either crammed themselves inside the elongated vehicles or hung from the sides and rear like cable car passengers in San Francisco. Outside of Manila, banana trees and coconut groves stretched before him, and as he drove through the countryside he imagined it to look like Hawaii before the early missionaries arrived there.

Elder Hinckley instantly liked these Filipino people, who were warm and friendly, even gregarious—more like those of the South Sea islands he had met in New Zealand than the reserved Chinese with whom he had spent the previous week. And despite their depressed living conditions, they seemed bright and capable. It became immediately apparent, however, that the government of the Philippines was mired in red tape, and Elder Hinckley's initial impression of the country was that it held little promise for missionary work. But after holding a small meeting in Baguio, north of Manila, he began to feel differently. "This evening we have had a testimony meeting that has been an inspiration," he noted in his journal. "We have listened to 30 of our members bear their testimonies. . . . Almost without exception they spoke of the great possibilities for doing missionary work here and made pleas that this land be opened for missionary work. As I listened to them I felt strongly that missionary work should be undertaken in this land."[6]

With each day, Elder Hinckley felt increasingly optimistic about the potential in this third-world island republic. At a conference of the Luzon servicemen's group he discussed their obligation to lay a foundation for missionary work. "I expressed the view that missionary work will be done in the Philippines in the future and that it will be as fruitful as it has been in many other places in the world," he recorded afterward.[7]

Throughout the Philippines Elder Hinckley traveled, speaking to servicemen's groups, interviewing members, and meeting with national officials to seek permission for missionaries to enter the country. On his fifth evening there he attended a dance festival and found himself seated next to the consul general of the United States, a man who had served in posts throughout Europe, was familiar with the Church, and asked how the missionaries in the Philippines were doing. When Elder Hinckley explained that he was currently seeking permission to allow proselytizing, the consul general expressed surprise that such authorization had not already been given and pledged his support.[8] Elder Hinckley hadn't been enthusiastic about attending the festival, but now realized why he had.

With official recognition in the Philippines unresolved, he left for Taiwan, where the Church was small but organized. For nearly a week he toured the island with President Taylor, looking for property (the price of which continued to astound Elder Hinckley, who was beginning to realize that even modest meetinghouses that could double as missionary residences would cost the Church millions in the aggregate) and meeting each day with small groups of missionaries, members, and investigators. Only a few native Chinese were members of the Church, but they showed promise. "One sees now and again a man and a woman with real potential," he noted. "I am fully satisfied that we have local brethren and sisters here who can be trained quickly to positions of leadership if they are given the opportunity."[9] The presence of American servicemen scattered throughout the island bolstered the work significantly, and in many cases, their assignments in these isolated areas produced additional benefits. After one testimony meeting with a group of military personnel, Elder Hinckley recorded: "We have some wonderful service people in this part of the world. Some of them had done nothing at home and had they not been in the service, it is likely that they never would have done anything in the Church. However in these remote areas they have sought association with Church people and have become active. It is an inspiring thing."[10]

There were few days that Elder Hinckley didn't spend time with missionaries. In Taiwan he marveled that, though they had unique challenges learning Mandarin, they spoke more fluently after a few months than did most Americans who had lived abroad for years. "I know that it is done only because the Lord blesses them," he reflected.[11] He also looked constantly for ways to buoy them up. Occasionally there were opportunities to counsel and help young men and women in difficult circumstances. In Taiwan one missionary confided an earlier misdeed that most likely would have precluded his serving a mission. After long discussion, during which Elder Hinckley felt impressed that the missionary was genuinely repentant and had served faithfully for many months, he counseled the young man to write his bishop and stake president, as well as the General Authority who had interviewed him for his mission. "I have told him that if he receives forgiveness from these men to whom he failed to tell the truth, he will be permitted to remain and complete his mission, and I have suggested to him that he prove his repentance by the manner of his work," he concluded.[12]

Elder Hinckley focused much of his instruction to missionaries on gospel principles and ways to teach more effectively, but he was concerned also with practical matters. He was appalled, for example, at some of the missionaries' living conditions. "Their mothers would be shocked if they were to see the circumstances under which they live," he recorded in his journal. "I told them to put screens in the drains to keep the cockroaches and rats out . . . [and that] there was no consistency in brushing their teeth with boiled water and then leaving their toothbrushes out all night for the cockroaches to crawl over."[13] Such challenges notwithstanding, the missionaries' affection for the Chinese was evident, leading him to conclude, "The work has a tremendous potential here."[14]

Travel throughout Southeast Asia was often adventurous. The plane Elder Hinckley took from Taipei to Tainan was basically an old flying boxcar fitted with the most rudimentary of seats. Ground transportation wasn't much better. After touring one region of Taiwan he wrote, "We rode in a 1954 Plymouth painted red, yellow, and blue. The driver was a Taiwanese man [who] . . . honked the horn constantly. I made a count while looking at my watch and discovered that he honked the horn at least every ten seconds during a trip of approximately 135 miles."[15] Traffic may have been worse than usual during Elder Hinckley's visit, as Taipei was teeming with visitors on hand for Chiang Kai-shek's inauguration for his third term as president of the Republic of China.

Elder Hinckley was used to maintaining a rapid pace, but the unfamiliar surroundings, terrain, cuisine, jet lag, and climate were hard on him. He found himself awake before dawn morning after morning, though he had gone to bed exhausted after tramping from city to city in the sultry, steamy climate. "The heat takes the starch out of me," he admitted while in Taiwan.[16] Though he had at first been concerned about a lackadaisical work ethic on the part of some missionaries, he began to appreciate the conditions under which they labored: "They are not doing nearly as much proselyting as they should, but I think they need more rest than they do in some missions. The hot humid air is hard on them. It is very tiring for me."[17]

His tour of the Southern Far East Mission nearly complete, Elder Hinckley returned to Hong Kong to organize the voluminous notes he had made during his month-long visit and to investigate prospects for translating the Book of Mormon into Cantonese and Mandarin. It had been a difficult month, but he was already beginning to feel an affinity for the unique Oriental cultures. He didn't pretend to understand these people—but he liked them. He was drawn to the industry, tradition, and graciousness inherent within their cultures. And he felt great surges of compassion for those who lived in poverty. "There now comes to a close this interesting experience in China," he noted his last day in Hong Kong. "Between Hong Kong, the Philippines, and Taiwan, I have seen many interesting things. I have become attached to this area of the world."[18]

From Hong Kong, Elder Hinckley flew to Tokyo, where he was greeted by President Paul C. Andrus of the Northern Far East Mission, as well as by cooler weather. But the difference in temperature wasn't the only notable distinction between the two missions. The tempo throughout Japan was markedly upbeat.

Tokyo fascinated Elder Hinckley. "Taxi cabs dart around like ants," he noted. "It is a harrowing experience to ride one." He marveled at the large crowds that milled about shopping districts where everything from exquisite rugs to parasols was for sale. The unique courtesies and characteristics of the Japanese culture also intrigued and impressed him, and he enjoyed one "first" after another—bowing as a form of greeting, removing his shoes in the entryways to buildings, sleeping on a thin mattress on the floor. One experience shocked him, though. In Tokyo he inspected a beautiful Japanese home on a piece of prime property on Yoyogi Street. The location was excellent, just a ten-minute walk from the beautiful park in which the Meiji Shrine, a revered Shinto memorial, was situated. But when Elder Hinckley heard the price, he was horrified: $682,000! "It is an excellent site but the price is terrible," he noted.[19]

For days he agonized over whether or not to recommend to the First Presidency that the Church invest such a sum in one building. Yet he felt it imperative that they begin to acquire property in the Orient. Buildings not only housed branches—important in and of itself—but gave the Church increased visibility and helped members feel proud of the organization to which they belonged. The more he investigated Tokyo real estate, the more apparent it became that it would be impossible to find either an existing structure or property on which to build in a suitable area without paying a terrific price for it. In the strong economy the price of land was escalating, so there appeared to be no advantage in delaying purchase. But the burden of recommending what he knew his leaders would regard as an exorbitant asking price weighed heavily on Elder Hinckley. After petitioning the Lord for direction, he conferred by phone with President Moyle. The Church had never paid such a sum for a meetinghouse, he warned his younger colleague. "Well, if we are to get property in Japan," Elder Hinckley replied, "we'll pay that much for it. I have been to visit the resident manager of the National City Bank and had a good discussion about property values here, and this is what it will take."[20] President Moyle promised to visit with President McKay and cable a response. The next day he wired Elder Hinckley with instructions to use his best judgment and, if he felt inspired, to make the purchase. The response was not what he had hoped for—he wanted clear-cut instructions from the First Presidency.

As he pondered the situation, he could almost hear the words of his mission president, Elder Joseph F. Merrill, ringing in his ears: "I will be more careful with the Church's money than

I will with my own." He couldn't get out of his mind the fact that all such monies came from the tithes of the people, yet he also felt that the Church would grow in Japan and that it was time to face up to the price of real estate there. "It seemed unlikely that property would ever cost less, and this building was in an excellent location," Elder Hinckley explained. "After weighing all the facts, and praying earnestly about the matter, I had the strong impression that we should proceed and I committed the Church to purchase the land."[21] With mission president Paul Andrus he then worked through complicated negotiations to complete the sale and participated in a formal signing ceremony customary among the Japanese. Afterward he noted in his journal, "Following conclusion of this procedure, I felt greatly relieved and had the feeling that we had done the right thing."[22] When Elder Hinckley returned home, he found that some of his colleagues, unfamiliar with the unique challenges of the Asian real-estate market, were uneasy about his decision. But as it turned out, the site proved to be a fundamental building block of the Church in Japan. It was sold years later at more than thirty times the purchase price, becoming one of the best real-estate investments ever among many transactions Elder Hinckley made for the Church.

It was a significant step—purchasing one of the Church's first buildings in Asia—and Elder Hinckley marveled that he had been part of it. But then, each day, each country, was bringing him new experiences. On June 1, while he was still in Japan, he recorded in his journal, "This is the beginning of a new month. It is Brigham Young's birthday, and I cannot escape the thought that the Church is still pioneering. It will go on pioneering for a long time to come."

The tremendous pioneering effort needed throughout the Orient drove him to set a feverish pace. His day with the missionaries typically began around 7:30 A.M. and continued until late afternoon. Often they came fasting, and after Elder Hinckley gave several hours of instruction, he invited each to bear testimony. Then he interviewed them one by one.

In the evenings and on weekends he met with members. The branches and districts throughout Japan tended to be slightly larger than those he had found in Hong Kong, but the challenge of training a generation of Asian converts to become leaders was the same. In one meeting after another, Elder Hinckley took off his shoes, sat on the floor with the local brethren, and taught them. "I learned that there was one way to work with those people," he reflected later, "and that was to get down on the *tatami* mats with them, teach them the principles of the gospel, and let their hearts be opened to the meaning of this work."[23]

From the outset, Elder Hinckley had an affinity for the Asians. He admired the integrity, resourcefulness, and work ethic of these determined people, and he was attracted to their manner, which though somewhat formal was gracious and accommodating. Though the Church was small and struggling, he saw potential in the modest core of members. Kenji Tanaka, who later became the first stake president in Asia, attended a priesthood meeting during Elder Hinckley's first trip to Japan. "Our expectations were so great," he remembered, "and Elder Hinckley's excitement could be seen in his sparkling eyes. His first word to us was *Subarashii!* ["Wonderful!"] The atmosphere of that meeting changed from stiff and formal to friendliness and closeness to him, and a warm feeling prevailed. During that meeting he told us, 'Those who gather together here today are holding the most important power, a far greater power than the Prime Minister of Japan, for the Japanese people.' He inspired us, he motivated us to aim high with strong and clear goals. He had a core of energy that was radiating and full of love."[24]

Wherever he went, Elder Hinckley took particular note of the local youth in attendance. In Osaka he was impressed with a missionary from Tokyo who bore a strong testimony of the gospel. "If he keeps the faith, he will someday be a leader in Japan," Elder Hinckley wrote. "I feel much encouraged by some of the young people who have joined the Church here. They have great potential."[25]

Yasuhiro Matsushita, who was later called as president of the Japan Kobe Mission, attended a district conference on the island of Hokkaido. Yasuhiro and his fiancée had recently announced their engagement and were to become only the fifth couple married as Church members in Hokkaido. When Elder Hinckley learned of their upcoming marriage, he held them up as examples to their peers.[26]

▪ ▪ ▪ ▪ ▪

One overwhelming aspect of supervising the work in Asia was negotiating the huge distances involved. After six weeks of nonstop travel, during which Elder Hinckley had traveled to a new city almost every day, he had done little more than visit major metropolitan centers. He felt he was leaving much undone in Japan when he flew on to Korea, where a crowd on the air terminal's observation deck greeted him with a large sign that proclaimed, "Welcome to Korea Elder Gordon B. Hinckley."

Korea shared similarities with other countries in Asia, but there were also noticeable differences. After thirty-six years of Japanese domination, followed by the bitter civil war that had ultimately involved the United States and other world powers, South Korea had one of the world's lowest gross national products, and its economy was severely depressed. The people were poor—financially and spiritually—and few had any confidence in their ability to lead out. Elder Hinckley was sobered by the living conditions of the Korean Saints, many of whom struggled to provide even the basic necessities. His heart went out to them.

In South Korea, Elder Hinckley found some 650 Church members divided among five small branches—four in the capital city of Seoul and one in Pusan, a port at the end of the Korean peninsula. Upon his arrival in Seoul, one of his first requests was to visit Sister Pak P'il-gun, the widow of Dr. Kim Ho Jik, who had played an instrumental role in opening the way for the missionaries in 1956 and had passed away the previous fall.[27] After paying his respects to Sister Pak, Elder Hinckley instructed President Andrus to make sure that she was taken care of as far as housing and food were concerned. During subsequent years, each time he visited Korea, Elder Hinckley sought out Sister Pak to express his love and look after her welfare.[28]

Despite Korea's economic blight, the Church was making some headway there. Few couples seemed interested in the Church, but the missionaries were having some success among the youth. "If we can get fine educated young people, the Church will grow and be secure in Korea," he noted.[29] He made frequent reference in his journal to young members who demonstrated potential and noted things he could do personally to encourage them. During a district conference in Seoul he ordained a twenty-one-year-old man, Han In Sang, an elder. Said Brother Han of that experience: "My faith was small as a convert. But as he gave me the blessing, I knew the man who laid his hands upon my head was a man of God, and I made a commitment at that moment to never turn my back against the Church or against the man who was ordaining me. After that, each time I picked Elder Hinckley up at the airport when he arrived in Korea, I would shake his hand, look up at him, and say silently to myself, 'Elder Hinckley, Han In Sang still faithful.' "[30]

From one intimate gathering to another, Elder Hinckley reassured the Korean Saints that they had the ability to lead the Church in their country and that the gospel had great potential among their people. From city to city he sounded what became a familiar theme: "You are just as capable as anybody in this world. You can carry the work of the Church forward as well as people can carry it anywhere." Elder Hinckley found the Koreans to be bright and able people who did not yet understand their potential.[31] "From 1909 until the end of World War II we had been governed by someone else," Brother Han explained. "And then came the Korean War. We were confused about our own identity. But Elder Hinckley told us we were important and that we could be leaders. No one had ever said that to us before."[32]

Rhee Ho Nam, who had joined the Church in 1954, was among the handful of Korean Saints who met with Elder Hinckley in this and many subsequent visits. "He always gave us encouragement," he reflected later. "We were living a difficult life, almost a hopeless life. We didn't have many expectations. But every time Elder Hinckley came, he met with us, gave us his personal attention, and left us with a feeling of new hope." During one of those early meetings, Brother Rhee remembered, a Korean brother asked Elder Hinckley if there would ever be a temple in Korea. "Back in those days we had less than a hundred members, and here my friend was asking about a temple. I was a little embarrassed for him, and I poked him and whispered that he shouldn't have asked that question. But Elder Hinckley just smiled and in a very encouraging tone promised us that if we stayed close to the Lord and were obedient to the Church there would one day be a temple in the Land of the Morning Calm. When he spoke to us it was as though something tangible happened. At that moment I thought that maybe such an impossible dream would actually come true one day. Very simply, Elder Hinckley is the father of the Church in Korea."[33]

As he became acquainted with the few members of the Church in the country, Elder Hinckley often found himself almost overcome by emotion as he contemplated their stark circumstances. "I have shed so many tears in this land," he would say years later. "I first came to Korea in its days of poverty. I saw too many men, women, and children suffer."[34]

From Korea, Elder Hinckley pushed on to Okinawa, where more than three hundred LDS servicemen were stationed and where the Church was beginning to grow among the native Japanese. There were, of course, also challenges with which to deal. When Elder Hinckley identified a potential site for the first chapel in Okinawa, local members tried to dissuade him. The land he selected housed the famous old Buddhist shrine *Sogenji*, which was considered a national treasure and was protected by city ordinance. Complicating matters, the city was attempting to develop a children's park there and had already prepared a blueprint. Brother Toma, who accompanied Elder Hinckley on his excursion to look at real estate, told his wife, Misao, he could not understand why Elder Hinckley insisted on purchasing land that appeared impossible to buy. Elder Hinckley counseled Brother Toma and others to be patient, to abide by the laws, and to make known their desire to purchase the land. The way would open, he promised, for the Church to acquire the property. Indeed, in time, and without explanation, the site became available for sale and the Church made the purchase.[35]

Meetings in Okinawa with members and missionaries were fruitful and fulfilling. Kensei Nagamine, a convert who later served as a branch president, a district president, and the first stake president in Okinawa, described the district conference Elder Hinckley conducted: "It was so spiritual, and he left many blessings with us. He cried during the conference and expressed his love for us, the Okinawan Saints, and the servicemen. I had a strong impression that he was a kind father figure. He was so gentle and kind. I have never forgotten the warmth of his handshake."[36]

Few days passed without tender experiences of one variety or another. But after two long months away from home and family, Elder Hinckley knew he must return to the United States, realizing he had scarcely begun his ministry among the Asian people. Before leaving, he visited Hiroshima, where just fifteen years earlier tens of thousands of Japanese had fallen to the atomic bomb. The Hiroshima Peace Park was to him a grim reminder of the tragic past. "One cannot walk through this park, even for only a few minutes as we did," he noted, "without sensing something of the tragedy that occurred here and of the tragedy that might destroy the world unless men learn to live together in peace."[37]

It was remarkable for Elder Hinckley to contemplate that just a few years earlier the United States had been engaged in a bitter war with the Japanese. Now he had been asked to help bring the gospel of peace and love to this people. As he flew east over the Pacific en route home, he pondered the immense scope of the work that lay ahead of him and reflected on two hard months of effort that nonetheless seemed modest compared with the job at hand. But he had initiated his Asian ministry during this grueling tour that only twice had allowed him to sleep in the same bed two nights in a row. He summarized in his journal: "We have many problems in our missionary work in this part of the world, but I think they are essentially no different from those found in other areas. As a matter of fact, the missionaries generally are happier. This is difficult to understand in view of the circumstances under which they are living. . . . However, they are well and happy and devoted and it has been inspiring to see them at work."[38]

It was wonderful, also, to return home. He had missed his family tremendously and had been separated from Marjorie far too long. It was a relief to see her and the children again.

Gordon and Marjorie's family was growing up, and each season seemed to bring something new and even life-changing. Such was the case as 1961 dawned, for in January the Hinckleys experienced two firsts: Dick left on his mission, and Kathy presented them with their first grandchild, a granddaughter named Heather.

As an administrator in the Missionary Department and now as a General Authority, Elder Hinckley had helped send thousands of missionaries into the field; he loved both the labor and the laborer. More times than he could recall, his heart had ached for missionaries in trouble; likewise, he had exulted over their growth and success. But none of his missionary-related experiences affected him quite like having his own son enter the field. Missionary work suddenly took on a very personal dimension.

Dick's departure for Germany was a historic family event. That day Elder Hinckley came home from the office early in the afternoon. After a family dinner and the customary round of group photos, Dick walked up to Papa Hinckley's to say good-bye. Bryant had not always been alert since his stroke nearly three years earlier, but that day he spoke clearly to his grandson. When Dick kissed him good-bye, both men began to cry, perhaps sensing they would not see each other again. At the airport, as Dick's DC-7 taxied toward the runway, Marjorie's eyes filled with tears, and Gordon felt a tug at his heart. "I have participated in sending about 25,000 missionaries into the field. This is the first of my own. I am proud and sad, and I think most parents feel the same under similar circumstances," he wrote that evening.[39]

Three months later, Elder Hinckley embarked on his second extended tour of Asia. He was pleased to find the missionaries in better spirits than they had been the year before and living under much-improved conditions. After a meeting with the missionaries in Taiwan, he exulted in his journal: "I marvel at these young men and women. They are so devoted and energetic even in this land of great rain and hot, humid air. We had fasted for this meeting, and it was a marvelous spiritual experience. There is no group on earth like our missionaries."[40] He was likewise encouraged by the caliber of recent converts, some of them university graduates who appeared to be fast learners and potential leaders.

But the trip's most memorable event occurred in the Philippines. In spite of red tape that still posed serious barriers to obtaining official recognition for the Church and visas for missionaries, Elder Hinckley arrived in Manila with authorization from the First Presidency to initiate missionary work there. Because the Church owned no buildings in the Philippines, he obtained permission from the American Embassy to hold a meeting on the beautifully manicured grounds of the American Military Cemetery on the outskirts of Manila—the place he regarded as the most hallowed spot in the Filipino capital city. On the morning of April 28, 1961, he arose early and went to the cemetery well in advance of the sunrise service. "This cemetery is the most beautiful place I have seen in the Philippines, also one of the most tragic," he noted in his journal. "Here are buried 17,168 war dead and on the walls are inscribed the names of an additional 36,230 who are missing. Here is told in beautiful stone and sweeping lawns the tragedy of World War II."[41]

As he walked along the quiet memorial at the predawn hour, looking across the rolling lawns filled with white marble crosses and Stars of David arranged in perfectly symmetrical rows, he noticed the name of a boy who had grown up in his neighborhood, whose plane had last been seen spiraling toward the Pacific. Gordon thought of the young soldier's mother, who had grieved over the loss of her son, and there came into his mind the words: "Thou shalt live together in love, insomuch that thou shalt weep for the loss of them that die. . . . [but] those that die in me shall not taste of death, for it shall be sweet unto them."[42] He photographed the name engraved on the marble wall for the young man's mother.

By dawn a group of nearly one hundred Saints, most of them servicemen from Clark Air Force Base and the naval base at Subic Bay, had gathered in the early morning mist in front of the memorial's small chapel. At this hour, with the sun rising over the mountains and the sea to the east adorned by golden clouds that hung in the sky, the setting was spectacular. Seated in the small audience was Maxine Grimm, a Utah woman who had served with the Red Cross in World War II's Pacific campaign and who, with her American army officer husband, now lived in Manila. She had pleaded that missionaries be sent to the island nation, and her husband had initiated legal work to make it possible for them to enter. This morning Sister Grimm brought the portable organ she had carried throughout the Pacific so that the congregation could begin their meeting by singing songs of the Restoration.

From the moment Elder Hinckley convened the meeting, the Spirit descended in a powerful manner. Among those who spoke was David Lagman, the only known Filipino member of the Church and the first to be ordained an elder, who recited the story of his conversion. As a child he had found a *Reader's Digest* that contained an article relating the history of the Mormons. The word *prophet*, as used to describe Joseph Smith, had caught his attention. Years passed, during which the tragedies of Corregidor and Bataan occurred and his homeland endured enemy occupation. After the Philippines was liberated, he learned that an American officer for whom he worked at Clark Air Force Base was a Mormon, and he summoned the courage to ask the officer if a prophet really guided his church. When the officer bore his testimony to that fact, the young Filipino's heart was stirred, and he subsequently joined the Church.

Elder Hinckley concluded the meeting with brief remarks, during which he explained that the Philippines had been dedicated by President Joseph Fielding Smith on August 21, 1955, and that the purpose of this meeting was to inaugurate missionary work. "What we begin here will affect the lives of thousands and thousands of people in this island republic, and its effects will go from generation to generation for great and everlasting good," he promised those assembled. It was fitting, he added, that they were met in a place hallowed by the sacrifices of many who had died so that others would have the freedom to worship God as they chose.

After bearing his testimony, Elder Hinckley offered a prayer in which he invoked the blessings of the Lord upon missionary work throughout the Philippines and blessed the native people with receptive minds, understanding hearts, faith to receive the gospel message, and courage to live correct principles. The service was brief but beautiful and filled with power and emotion. He noted in his journal, simply, "It was an inspirational meeting, and one that I shall never forget."[43]

As glorious as was the early-morning service, the glow of that event was soon replaced with frustration. Later that day

Elder Hinckley learned that the commissioner of immigration had determined that Latter-day Saint missionaries should not be granted visas. Elder Hinckley immediately borrowed a typewriter from the hotel and drafted a response, afterward noting, "We must now pray and wait. However it is in the hands of the Lord. We shall do our best and await the outcome. If we cannot get what we need through one channel we shall try every other until we secure the proper entry documents. The foundation has been laid. I am confident that somehow it will go forward. This is the Lord's work and while it may be delayed, it will not be stopped."[44]

Elder Hinckley's next destination was Japan, where he was encouraged to find an increased number of native brethren serving in branch presidencies. Again, however, some missionaries were discouraged and not working with the intensity he had hoped to find. After spending a day with elders in the Tokyo-Yokohama area, he noted: "Some missionaries are working very hard and accomplishing great results. Others are coasting."[45] He wasn't one to coast, and he was unimpressed with those who did. After three days in Japan he recorded: "We have been on the go as fast as we could move with missionary meetings each morning and traveling to a different city at night. Thus far we are none the worse for wear."[46]

From Japan, Elder Hinckley flew to Seoul, and he was pleased to find progress in Korea. The missionaries there were the most productive of any in the Far East, averaging fourteen baptisms each per year, and there was an impressive core of young adults joining the Church. He delighted in setting apart the first two native Koreans called as branch presidents.

The more he interacted with and served the Asian Saints, the more attached he became to them. Though he experienced only modest success learning a little Korean, Japanese, Mandarin, and Cantonese, he picked up enough words to make the people feel he was trying. And he conveyed his feelings in other ways. Said Han In Sang, "No other Church leaders visiting Korea wept as Elder Hinckley did. When he met with the members, he wept. When he met with the missionaries, he wept. And he remembered all of our names. When he came back the second time, he could remember who we were. He told us that he loved us, and that is what bonded us to him."[47] Years later Elder Hinckley reflected, "One reason I loved those people so much was that they lived under such adverse conditions. I couldn't help but reach out to them in a spirit of love. And they reciprocated. If you love people, they'll love you also."[48]

For all his optimism, he was learning that these lands posed unusual challenges and that life there could be volatile. Three LDS servicemen escorted him to Panmunjom in the Demilitarized Zone, where the armistice ending the Korean War had been signed on July 27, 1953. Armed camps were poised on both sides of the DMZ, and the threat of open conflict was unnerving.

Eerie though it was, however, the DMZ proved peaceful compared to what Elder Hinckley experienced in Seoul three days later. At 4:30 A.M., he awakened to a loud crackling noise outside his hotel window. His first thought, "What a terrible time for a Chinese wedding!" quickly vanished when what he had assumed were firecrackers didn't stop. Without considering the ramifications, he poked his head out the window, only to find a sky filled with gray smoke. A deafening noise that sounded like thunder continued, and suddenly he realized that the hotel was caught in the crossfire of heavy artillery. In minutes President Andrus of the Northern Far East Mission, who was traveling with him, was at his door reporting that he had seen tracer bullets outside his window. In the confusion of hotel patrons running up and down the hallways, it took a few minutes before they learned that a revolution was under way. As Elder Hinckley quickly dressed, he rehearsed his options. If the North Koreans moved in, he could personally be in danger. He deliberated on what to wear and then selected his black rather than his brown shoes, believing them to be the more comfortable pair, and a wrinkled Dacron shirt over a freshly laundered broadcloth, as it would be easier to wash and hang-dry if necessary. Then there was nothing to do but wait.

At daybreak, he and President Andrus found that they were not permitted to leave the hotel: The military had rebelled against the government and a full-blown coup had taken place. Marines in battle dress filled the streets. Many windows of their hotel had been shattered, and the exterior walls were pitted from machine-gun fire. Throughout the day "condition green" was in effect, and no Americans were to be on the streets. Banks, airports, and seaports were closed and curfews imposed. Traffic essentially ceased in a city where thousands of taxis, bicycles, and pedestrians normally created ongoing street chaos. With time to do so, Elder Hinckley wrote a story about the situation and wired it to the *Deseret News* in Salt Lake City, who thereby received word of the coup even before the Associated Press.

Though he was comfortable, Elder Hinckley found it frustrating to be confined to the hotel. By evening things had quieted enough that he and President Andrus took a short walk and discovered that the Ministry of Home Affairs, just across the street, had been shelled. "The windows are shattered," he noted in his journal. "It is evident that the battle took place right by my window although I could not see it because of a low building which stands in the way."[49] As night approached and the curfew went into effect, the city's deathly quiet was punctuated occasionally by the sound of shell fire. The following day tensions eased somewhat, and on the third day the airport opened and Elder Hinckley caught a flight to Japan. It was a relief to feel free again, and the temporary restrictions with which he had dealt only increased his empathy for a people who had suffered domination for decades.

When he headed for home after his month in the Orient, Elder Hinckley noted that he had given fifty-two talks, interviewed 240 missionaries, borne testimony through interpreters in English, Cantonese, Mandarin, Korean, and Japanese, and survived one coup d'état. He wrote: "This has been a fast and busy month. I hope that it has been profitable for all whose lives I may have touched. It has been a humbling and encouraging experience to go about with our devoted mission presidents, to meet our wonderful missionaries, and to feel of the spirit of the faithful Saints. But we have many who have come into the Church and then left it. Far too many. Something must be done to increase the activity of the membership in the branches so that their faith and testimonies will grow."[50]

In all of Elder Hinckley's travels, there was one constant: He kept close to the missionaries. From the fog of London to the oppressive humidity of the Orient, he had comforted them in their discouragement, counseled them in difficult situations, rejoiced at their accomplishments, and spent hours on his knees with those in distress.

Frequently he seized the opportunity to do some proselytizing of his own. On one occasion an airline official at the San Francisco airport inquired about Elder Hinckley's business in Asia. "I represent the Mormon Church. Do you know anything about the Mormon Church?" he asked in return. "Oh, I know a little," the man responded. "My wife is a Mormon. But she is rather backward in talking about it." "Where does your wife come from?" Elder Hinckley asked. When the gentleman supplied the information, Elder Hinckley, who coincidentally was acquainted with the family, replied with enthusiasm: "Your wife comes from wonderful people, great stock, pioneer stock. Wouldn't you like to know something about the faith of your wife's people?" When the man said that he would, Elder Hinckley called the local mission president with the referral. Eight weeks later the airline official joined the Church.[51]

On one Atlantic crossing he found himself seated across the aisle from a couple traveling from England. When he learned that their son wished to study forestry in an American university, he recommended Utah State as an excellent institution of higher learning. The young man later came to attend the northern Utah school, and the Hinckleys picked him up, drove him to Logan, and helped him get situated. That young man and his brothers subsequently joined the Church, married in the temple, and reared faithful, active families.[52]

Over the years Elder Hinckley had gradually refined the way he taught and represented the gospel, and he was comfortable telling almost anyone about the Church. He was articulate without being pompous or preachy, and fearless when it came to bearing his testimony of Jesus Christ, Joseph Smith, and the Book of Mormon. In his address at the April 1960 general conference, he spoke about the process of conversion: "When we started emphasizing in our missionary program the truth about God as a basic and fundamental and primary principle, and began to encourage those who were willing to listen to get on their knees and ask him . . . concerning the truth of that teaching, we began to get converts in such numbers as we had not had in many, many years."[53]

In June 1961, Elder Hinckley and others of the General Authorities presented the first-ever seminar for all mission presidents and, for the first time, introduced a standardized plan of six lessons to be adopted by every mission. They also encouraged the leaders throughout the Church to emphasize President McKay's slogan "Every member a missionary." At this seminar the missions of the world were divided into nine areas, with General Authorities called to administer each.

Elder Hinckley still handled many of the day-to-day affairs of the Missionary Department. He was the person, for example, whom nineteen-year-old Jeffrey Holland was told to visit in the summer of 1960 to see if he might gain permission to leave on his mission prior to turning twenty years of age: "Here I was, an unknown boy from St. George who showed up without an appointment at Elder Hinckley's office," he remembered years later. "It was obvious that he was busy. There were stacks of paper everywhere. But he treated me as though I were as important as the General Authorities down the hall. I made a short and simple appeal to be able to leave on my mission a few months before turning twenty, which was the standard age then. He told me that the process was complicated but that he was grateful I wanted to serve a mission and that I should watch the mail. I wasn't sure what that meant, but ten days later I got a letter calling me to the British Mission. I am sure that special permission was granted because of the intervention of Gordon B. Hinckley."[54]

With extended trips away from home and heavy assignments to occupy his attention when he was in town, Elder Hinckley was finding that life as a General Authority was rigorous and demanding. If Marjorie hadn't had a "business-as-usual" approach to home management, his responsibilities might have had greater impact on their family. She traveled with him when Church policy permitted, but with grade-school and teenage children still at home, she also felt a responsibility to provide a sense of stability and routine for them.

When he left for assignments away from home, rather than moan about his absence, Marjorie might say to the children, "Oh, good, your father's gone. Let's order pizza"—something they rarely indulged in otherwise. Or she took the girls shopping—again, an activity reserved for times when they were home alone. "Mother put no pressure on Dad," Ginny remembered. "He was free to do what had been asked of him, without worrying that she was secretly resenting his time away. Mother made us feel it was a privilege for our father to do what he did."[55]

Other factors, however, accentuated the drawbacks of Elder Hinckley's lifestyle. He had been home from a trip to Asia only two weeks when, on June 5, 1961, his father passed away. One editorial summarized Bryant Hinckley's long and distinguished life: "Of some men who have risen to renown, it might be said that they won high esteem among their fellows, but little affection; of others it might be said that they were loved far more than they were esteemed; but of Bryant S. Hinckley . . . it must be said that he won both esteem and love in equal and overflowing measure. . . . [He] wanted goodness in the world, brought so much of it with him, and left it for our benefit and blessing."[56]

With his father's death, Gordon found himself deeply absorbed in memories of their experiences together. He remembered the way his father had cared for their large family during the Depression and pondered the faith he had seen him demonstrate time and again. He reflected on the way they had laughed together, on the times he had sat spellbound as his father spoke, and on his father's perpetual optimism. Bryant's passing filled Gordon with a deep sense of loss and a renewed determination: "My great desire was to so conduct my life that it would reflect only good upon my father and my mother," he said. "Having them both gone renewed within me that desire. I only hoped that one day I might measure up to my heritage."[57]

CHAPTER FOURTEEN

QUORUM OF THE TWELVE

At 7:00 A.M. on Saturday, September 30, 1961, the phone rang in the white frame house in East Millcreek. Marjorie answered to find President McKay on the other end of the line. Might he speak to Gordon? "Have I interrupted anything?" President McKay asked when Gordon answered the phone. "Only my morning prayers," he responded. "Could you come to my office as soon as possible?" Gordon indicated that he would hurry downtown.

Less than an hour later the two men sat knee to knee and President McKay explained the reason for this early visit prior to that morning's session of general conference: "I have felt to nominate you to fill the vacancy in the Quorum of the Twelve Apostles," he told Elder Hinckley simply, "and we would like to sustain you today in conference." The words took Gordon's breath away, and he searched without success for a response. How could it be, that such a call would come to him? He had known, of course, of the vacancy in the Quorum. But never for a moment had he—or would he have—thought he would be called to fill it.

President McKay continued: "Your grandfather was worthy of this, as was your father. And so are you." With these words, Elder Hinckley's composure crumbled, for there was no compliment the prophet could have paid him that would have meant more. "Tears began to fill my eyes as President McKay looked at me with those piercing eyes of his and spoke to me of my forebears," he remembered. "My father was a better man than I have ever been, but he didn't have the opportunities I have had. The Lord has blessed me with tremendous opportunities."

Later that day Elder Hinckley was sustained as the newest member of the Quorum of the Twelve, filling the vacancy created in June when President Hugh B. Brown had been called to serve as a third counselor in the First Presidency. The following afternoon he spoke briefly during the concluding session of conference. He began: "Sister [Marion G.] Romney told me yesterday afternoon that she knew that I was the one to be sustained because of the appearance of my eyes when she talked with me yesterday morning. I confess that I have wept and prayed." He then admitted an overwhelming sense of inadequacy: "I am subdued by the confidence of the Lord's Prophet, and by the expressed love of these, my brethren, beside whom I feel like a pygmy. I pray for strength; I pray for help; and I pray for the faith and the will to be obedient."

He concluded with his testimony of the divinity of the work in which he would be engaged for the rest of his life: "I would like to say that this cause is either true or false. Either this is the kingdom of God, or it is a sham and a delusion. Either Joseph talked with the Father and the Son, or he did not. If he did not, we are engaged in a blasphemy. If he did, we have a duty from which none of us can shrink—to declare to the world the living reality of the God of the universe, the Father of us all; and his Son, the Lord Jesus Christ. . . . I give you my testimony that this is true."[1]

The impact of what had happened was just beginning to register. As the seventy-fifth man in this dispensation called to serve as a member of the Quorum of the Twelve headed home, he tried to sort through the range of emotions swirling within him. "It was a sobering thing," he later recalled. "Such a call brings with it a tremendous sense of responsibility and duty to bear witness of the Lord."[2]

Such singular life experiences invite reflection, and Elder Hinckley found himself pondering what he had witnessed during his lifetime. The Church now had 1.8 million members living in 345 stakes, or nearly five times the number there had been the year he was born. More missionaries were serving in the field (more than nine thousand) than there had been convert baptisms the year he left for his mission (around seven thousand). He was two generations removed from his grandfather, who had helped colonize Utah, yet he had engaged in some pioneering of his own, particularly with respect to temple work and public relations. Now it was impossible to imagine what lay ahead.

In a letter he pecked out on his own Underwood manual typewriter, he wrote his missionary son serving in Duisburg, Germany. "I thought I would let you know that I have been called to the Quorum of the Twelve Apostles," he told Dick. "I don't know why I have been called to such a position. I have done nothing extraordinary but have tried only to do the best I could with the tasks I've been given without worrying about who got the credit." Dick said later, "I could tell from the letter that Dad was overwhelmed with it all. I myself was surprised with the news. The thought had never crossed my mind that he might be called into the Twelve. I was quite overcome as I thought about what had happened back home."[3]

Public response to Elder Hinckley's call was immediate and favorable. Telegrams, letters, and phone calls poured into his office. G. Homer Durham, then president of Arizona State University, said of his longtime friend: "Gordon has magnificent gifts of written and oral expression. His judgment stands up in every situation. His insight into human character and situations is rich and meaningful. He knows when silence is better than utterance. He has a sense of humor that endears him to all."[4] Thomas S. Monson, who was serving as president of the Canadian Mission and with whom Elder Hinckley had worked on the printing of missionary materials, nearly cheered out loud when he heard the news announced during the radio broadcast of priesthood meeting that night.

On October 5, assisted by his Brethren of the First Presidency and Quorum of the Twelve, President David O. McKay ordained Gordon B. Hinckley an apostle and set him apart as a member of that quorum. The experience was at once overwhelming and tender. As he entered the room on the fourth floor of the Salt Lake Temple where the Twelve regularly met, he was overcome with feelings of awe and inadequacy. The fifteen chairs surrounding the table had been filled by men who had been his heroes and whom he had sustained and upheld. Heber J. Grant, David O. McKay, Stephen L Richards—each had, at one time or another, occupied the twelfth chair. The responsibility to bear witness of the Lord Jesus Christ was both glorious and burdensome. He wondered if he would ever be able to fulfill this mandate to the full satisfaction of the Lord.

The days that followed were filled with introspection, pondering, prayer, and many tears. Above all else Gordon desired to be worthy of this calling, but he felt acutely aware of his personal failings. For a time it was as though he was experiencing his own dark night and in the process coming face-to-face with his inadequacies. He found himself pleading with the Lord to make him equal to the mantle he now bore. Perhaps the intensity of the loneliness, the realization that he of himself wasn't equal to the call, was for a reason—so that he would never forget whose errand he was on and who would make him capable of filling this overwhelming assignment.

It was an emotional time, made all the more so the day after Elder Hinckley's ordination when his longtime friend and mentor President J. Reuben Clark Jr. passed away at the age of ninety. President Clark had been solicitous of Gordon during his formative years at Church headquarters, and over the years the two had spent many hours together. Elder Hinckley admired President Clark for his keen judgment and masterful oratory. He concurred completely with President McKay's funeral tribute that "a truly great man [had] gone back to his creator."[5]

Two days after President Clark's funeral, President McKay reorganized the First Presidency, naming Henry D. Moyle as first counselor and Hugh B. Brown as second. New assignments, leaders, and opportunities were a given. But for the time being, Elder Hinckley continued to be deeply involved with missionary work, though he now relied heavily upon others for assistance. During the recent conference, Elder Boyd K. Packer had been sustained as an Assistant to the Twelve, and one of his first assignments was to assist Elder Hinckley in the Missionary Department, which itself was undergoing continual evolution as the needs of missionaries and members changed and expanded. In November 1961, a Language Training Institute was established at Brigham Young University for missionaries called to non-English-speaking countries. The Institute, later renamed the Language Training Mission (LTM), was an attempt to better prepare missionaries for service. And just four months later, the age at which young men could be called on missions was lowered from twenty to nineteen.

Elder Hinckley's feelings about missionary work had only intensified, if that was possible, since he had sent his own son into the mission field. Seeing firsthand what young men and women all over the Orient were accomplishing, often in difficult circumstances, also affected him. He was anxious to return to Asia, and his next trip, in February 1962, promised to be different, for Marjorie was going with him. He had not enjoyed their long separations during previous journeys but had been reluctant to subject her to the rigors of travel in areas where conditions and accommodations were often inhospitable. And she had been concerned about leaving the children for such an extended period—particularly Jane, who was only eight and missed her parents terribly when they were gone. Nonetheless, he had vowed after his last trip: "Next time you're coming with me. The Saints in Asia are starting to wonder if I have a wife."[6]

For Marjorie, the thought of such an adventure conjured up "pure excitement," though her ties to home were perhaps greater than ever, for now she also had a granddaughter she would be leaving behind for several weeks. Marjorie felt a constant tug between her responsibilities there and her desire to be with her husband. On the other hand, she was intrigued by different cultures and she loved meeting people. "Travel gets old fast," she explained. "But when you get where you're going and meet the people, it's wonderful because *they* are wonderful!" She had a comfortable way of putting others at ease and making friends easily.

In early February the Hinckleys left for Asia, with Manila their first stop. Elder Hinckley was pleased to find that missionaries who had arrived a few months earlier had already baptized thirteen Filipinos. Marjorie would never forget one meeting they attended where twelve people gathered in the living room of the missionaries' apartment. In the midst of bearing her testimony, an eighteen-year-old convert explained that her friends had deserted her because of her decision to join the Church. "But I don't care," she proclaimed, "because I love the Church." Marjorie later said: "That girl did something for me. She had joined the Church in sacrifice, and I realized how little I had

Elder Hinckley listens as his name is read announcing his call as the newest member of the Quorum of the Twelve on September 30, 1961; immediately following the conference session he is congratulated by his General Authority colleagues

PHOTO BY J MALAN HESLOP/DESERET NEWS

With members of the Deseret News Publishing Company board, pictured here on December 6, 1961: (clockwise) O. Preston Robinson, Ernest L. Wilkinson, Elder Mark E. Petersen, George L. Nelson, Henry R. Pearson, Mark B. Garff, D. Arthur Haycock, Elder Sterling W. Sill, and Frank M. Browning

With Marjorie in Tokyo, November 1962

Speaking with the aid of interpreter Goro Yamada at the Tokyo West Branch

PHOTO COURTESY LDS CHURCH ARCHIVES

With Elder Marion D. Hanks in the Orient

PHOTO COURTESY SPENCER J. PALMER

Han In Sang translates for Sister Hinckley during a visit to Korea

PHOTO COURTESY LDS CHURCH ARCHIVES

The Quorum of the Twelve Apostles in 1963: (seated) Ezra Taft Benson, President Joseph Fielding Smith, and LeGrand Richards; (standing) Gordon B. Hinckley, Delbert L. Stapley, Mark E. Petersen, Thomas S. Monson, Spencer W. Kimball, Harold B. Lee, Marion G. Romney, Richard L. Evans, and Howard W. Hunter

The Hinckleys, approximately 1965: (standing) James Pearce, Virginia, Richard, Clark, Jane, Kathy, Alan Barnes; (seated) Marjorie, Gordon, and grandchildren Angela and Heather

PHOTO BY J MALAN HESLOP/DESERET NEWS

Presenting President McKay with the first copy of the
Chinese translation of the Book of Mormon on January 19, 1966

PHOTO COURTESY ALLEN C. ROZSA

Visiting South Vietnam with Elder Marion D. Hanks (fourth from right) in October 1966. Elder Hinckley is standing between mission president Keith Garner and Major Allen C. Rozsa

PHOTO COURTESY ALLEN C. ROZSA

Greeting an LDS serviceman on the tenth floor of the Caravelle Hotel on October 30, 1966, after having dedicated Vietnam for the preaching of the gospel

PHOTO COURTESY LDS CHURCH ARCHIVES

Arriving in Okinawa with President Hugh B. Brown to a greeting from President Adney Y. Komatsu

Visiting with Chilean Saints on his first trip to South America in May 1967

While supervising the work in South America, Elder Hinckley made numerous visits to that continent

With Marjorie, Kathy, and Alan and their family (Celia in her father's arms, Angela and Heather standing) at the Polynesian Cultural Center in Laie, Hawaii, in February 1968

PHOTO BY GRAPHIC PICTURES HAWAII

Inspecting damage with President Allen E Litster of the Andes Mission following a devastating earthquake that hit Peru on May 31, 1970

With Elder Hanks and Lt. Nguyen Cao Minh, the first elder ordained in South Vietnam

Elder and Sister Hinckley and Elder Spencer W. and Sister Camilla Kimball pose next to the River Ribble in Preston, England, in August 1971

During Harold B. Lee's tenure as President of the Church, Elder and Sister Hinckley accompanied him and Sister Freda Joan Lee on two trips to Europe

On Mars Hill in Athens with President Harold B. Lee

Greeting President Lee at the October 1972 general conference

Meeting the press on August 1, 1975, with President Kimball

Addressing a small audience in the Sacred Grove outside Palmyra, New York, in 1975

Elder Hinckley and Elder David B. Haight effect the reorganization of six London-area stakes and the creation of three new ones on May 28, 1978, in Royal Albert Hall

Inspecting a Church building project

Elder Hinckley receives an enthusiastic welcome from President Rhee Ho Nam and Saints from the Korea Pusan Mission when he arrives to organize the first stake there in 1979

Elder Hinckley first visited mainland China in May 1980

Reading a proclamation from the First Presidency and the Quorum of the Twelve from the Peter Whitmer farm home in Fayette, New York, during a session of the April 1980 general conference

Gordon and Marjorie atop the Great Wall of China during their May 1980 trip

On July 23, 1981, President Gordon B. Hinckley was named and set apart as a counselor to President Spencer W. Kimball in the First Presidency, and Elder Neal A. Maxwell was called to the Quorum of the Twelve

PHOTO BY O. WALLACE KASTELER/DESERET NEWS

The First Presidency attend the first dedicatory session of the Jordan River (Utah) Temple on November 16, 1981

PHOTO BY O. WALLACE KASTELER/DESERET NEWS

Hosting President Ronald Reagan at a visit to the Church cannery in Ogden, Utah, in September 1982

OFFICIAL WHITE HOUSE PHOTOGRAPH

Meeting in the Church Administration Building with President Ronald Reagan in 1984

sacrificed for the gospel, which was handed to me as on a silver platter. I vowed to do more and be better."[7]

The work was also progressing in Hong Kong, where some 350 individuals had joined the Church the year before, raising the membership there to 1,763. The need for property on which to build a meetinghouse was becoming urgent. During this stay, Elder Hinckley formally organized the Church corporation in Hong Kong.

The next stop was Taiwan, where the missionaries continued to live in conditions that in some instances were shocking. The elders seemed happy, however, and the previous year 304 Chinese had joined the Church, increasing native membership to more than 800. At a testimony meeting in Taipei, held in a cold, concrete block of a room, Elder Hinckley was touched by the words of a handsome elder, measured by breath so cold that it could be seen. The young man made a simple statement that became a classic with Elder Hinckley: "I thank the Lord for eyes to see, and mouth to speak, and feet to carry me from door to door, to teach the gospel of Jesus Christ to the wonderful people of China."[8] It was through such devotion that the work continued to go forward.

From Taiwan, the Hinckleys flew to Fukuoka on the south island of Japan and worked their way north through the island nation. Teaching the gospel to the Japanese wasn't easy. "It was difficult, even discouraging at times," Elder Hinckley said years later. "The Japanese young people were under tremendous pressure for schooling. They felt they didn't have time to be involved in a lot of Church activities. The missionaries were wonderful young men and women, but they got discouraged. Gradually, however, one family was converted, and then another. And we began to strengthen the work."[9]

In Hokkaido one missionary was so ill that he had gone to the hospital to get a shot just so he wouldn't miss the conference with Elder Hinckley. "I could have cried every time I looked at him," Marjorie wrote home. "Even Dad felt depressed. When we got on the plane to return to Tokyo he said he felt like we were running off and leaving those young people to the wolves. It's rough up there."[10]

In Osaka, a "little town of 5 million people," as Marjorie

described it, she went tracting for the first time. "What an experience!" she wrote the family. "At the first couple of houses I wanted to run and hide, but after that it got quite interesting. We were in a good neighborhood where all the homes had walls around them. The biggest problem was opening the gates. When you get through the gates and past the dogs you don't bother with such formalities as knocking—you just open the doors and walk into the entrance hall and call to see if anyone is home. Either the maid or the lady of the house comes and drops on her knees and remains kneeling during the entire conversation. The first few gave us the 'too busy' brush off. . . . Between houses the Elders made me hand out tracts to all the passers-by and repeat a Japanese phrase which says 'Please read this, please.' I just about choked on it the first time. . . . They got an appointment to go back to one place. . . . I would surely like to have been there to go back with them."[11]

Everywhere Elder Hinckley went, he engaged in the recurring ritual of looking for suitable property. Marjorie joined him for an eye-opening tour of Seoul as he inspected potential building sites. She wrote home: "For a place to see [Korea] is a clock stopper. And I guess we looked as curious to them as they did to us. Every time we would stop a dozen children and old folks would gather around to stare, so everyone was staring at everyone. Their native dress is so different—everything from white blouse pants like the Egyptians to beautiful satin brocade coats worn by the women over six or seven layers of long johns and sweaters and other clothing. Women walking down the streets with big jars of water balancing on their heads, oxen drawing big loads of bricks, men carrying huge pieces of furniture on A-frames on their backs. The whole thing was a sight to behold."[12]

Elder Hinckley continued to lament the conditions endured by the Korean Saints. During some meetings they wrapped in blankets and put their feet on hot bricks to keep warm. The hall where he presided over a district conference in Seoul was bitter cold. Oil barrels burning in the corners provided some heat, but the temperature never rose above twenty-six degrees Fahrenheit during the entire meeting. He was amazed by a group of children who sat uncomplaining in front of the pulpit on blankets.

Said one American who lived in Korea for a number of years: "I can still see Elder Hinckley seated in some dark, unheated, partially lighted meeting hall where people were crouched in discomfort. But he always had a peaceful, happy look on his face. He would express his faith and inspire the people to think that this was paradise if they could have the Spirit of the Lord in their lives."[13]

Rhee Ho Nam remembered one meeting held in the Chung Woon Dong area on a cold winter day. A large pipe connected to the stove that heated the room came loose, throwing black soot all over Elder Hinckley and everyone else. He just smiled and continued to speak.[14]

For her part, Marjorie couldn't get over her first experience in the Land of the Morning Calm. Every turn of the road introduced a strange sight. "The smell of garlic and pickled cabbage and fresh ginger everywhere, and poverty the likes of which would put you into a state of shock," she wrote to her children. In Taegu, she and Elder Hinckley walked up one street and down another looking for property where the elders could live and hold meetings. They often went all day without eating (as it was risky to do so outside of a recommended hotel), traveled in vehicles of ancient vintage, and stayed in run-down hotels.

After one meeting, a young couple confided in Marjorie that Elder Hinckley's message the previous year had so inspired them that they had decided to get married. "We were just delighted, as this will be one more strong family here," Marjorie wrote home. Indeed, the progress in Korea was encouraging. The previous year, missionaries had averaged eighteen baptisms each, most of them university students and the majority males. Elder Hinckley later recommended in his report to the Twelve that a mission be established there as soon as a Korean-speaking mission president could be located.[15]

Marjorie was always hungry for news from home, and she read and reread every letter that caught up with them as they dashed from city to city. Her frequent letters filled with detailed descriptions of people and places helped the children feel a part of their experiences. She was thrilled when a couple of letters found them during a thirty-minute airport stopover in Tokyo, and she promptly responded to the one from Kathy: "I sat right down in the middle of 10,000 people and laughed and laughed. As soon as we got settled back on the plane I handed your letter to Dad and when he began to read about Heather . . . I thot he was going to burst his safety belt. It really struck him funny." Her parting comment revealed her longing to stay in touch: "Send us another letter as soon as you can. . . . What I wouldn't give to get hold of [Heather] for just 5 minutes!"[16]

Though each country was different, Elder Hinckley followed a similar pattern wherever they went. One of Sister Hinckley's letters home described a typical schedule: "Sunday was a full day. We started with a Servicemen's Conference at 8 A.M. Then a conference with all the Chinese members at 10 A.M. Said good-bye to Taiwan and all our friends, many of whom came to the plane. Flew to Okinawa and got there 30 minutes late for a meeting with the Japanese members at 7:30 P.M. and then rushed across the island for a Servicemen's Conference at 8:30 P.M. Monday morning we started the routine all over again."[17]

Marjorie could now better appreciate the long trips her husband had made to the Orient. To Kathy she wrote: "There is surely a lot of work that needs to be done here to strengthen the church. . . . Dad could spend his full time here to advantage, just going from mission to mission and district to district, but I'm not about to mention it."[18] There was plenty of opportunity for her to participate as well. "I've never done so much preaching in my life," she wrote home. "The English gatherings aren't too hard but the ones with translators are beastly. . . . Dad does a wonderful job—especially with the missionaries. He has been sharp with the wit and they really enjoy him. It is amazing how he can remember their names and faces."[19]

Marjorie fell in love with Asia and its people as easily as had her husband. "All last week we were in Taiwan and I loved every minute of it. . . . I went to a Chinese Relief Society in Taipei. It was cold and had a concrete floor, no drapes, and was about as cheerful as a prison cell, but those sweet service wives were there even tho they couldn't understand a word."[20]

During seminars and meetings where her presence wasn't required, or while Elder Hinckley interviewed missionaries for hours on end, Marjorie took a closer look at the local culture. One afternoon in Tokyo she lunched at a fine department store, which proved an adventure. "They were serving about 1000 people at once, and there was no such thing as getting a fork or spoon, so I had to manage with the chopsticks. I made it to the bitter end, but found I had an audience. But I am getting used to that now."[21]

Throughout the Orient the shopping was extraordinary. Rugs, clothing, lacquerware, bolts of silk, and whale meat—everything was exotic and, often, inexpensive: "My idea of a good time," Marjorie wrote her daughter, "would be to have a purse full of money and go shopping in this part of the world with you. . . . Dressmakers about 3 to a block who will make a dress to order for $1.25 to $2.50. No patterns required. . . . I paid 60 cents for a shampoo and set at the hotel in Taipei, and [thought] that was good, but the servicemen's wives say they can get the same on the outskirts for 25 cents."[22] In Hong Kong she tracted with the sister missionaries in the resettlement flats, where she was astounded to find one bathroom for seventy-five people. They walked along the balconies, looking through open doors to find people to teach. When they finally located a family who invited them in, they sat on packing boxes during their discussion. Marjorie couldn't take her eyes off a small vase of artificial flowers positioned on a high shelf. "No matter what conditions women find themselves in," she said later, "they find a way to bring beauty into their lives."[23]

All in all, this first experience in the Orient more than lived up to Marjorie's expectations. When they left Asia for Hawaii, Elder Hinckley was also satisfied. There was progress. The missionaries were working hard, and native members were slowly joining the Church and gaining experience and understanding.[24]

Still, Marjorie was relieved when they touched down in Honolulu. "It was like landing in the Garden of Eden," she wrote. "Everything so green and lush and prosperous."[25] By now, however, the strain of six weeks of rigorous travel was beginning to tell, and Marjorie worried that her husband wouldn't be sharp for a stake conference that weekend in Laie. "Dad was so tired by this time that I wondered how he would ever make it," she confided to the family. "We had lost a night's sleep in the time change and he looked gray. But that morning he gave one of the best talks I have ever heard him give. He told of some of the experiences we had during the past 5 weeks and everyone was weeping. I have seldom heard him bear such testimony as he did that morning."[26] The pace didn't let up. "The next three days were very hard, because we were all but exhausted. Dad was so far gone that voices were beginning to sound far away and he had to sit down occasionally during the workshop sessions to keep from falling. We were really on the countdown. But notwithstanding it was still a wonderful three days."[27]

As exotic as Asia and Hawaii had been, Marjorie was relieved when she walked into her own home. She had loved spending the previous month and a half with her husband, but it had been hard to be away from her children so long. There had been days, in fact, when she had indulged herself in a good cry over the fact that the huge Pacific separated her from the family.

Elder Hinckley also enjoyed returning home, though he was beginning to take these jaunts halfway around the world in stride. Perhaps to no one's surprise, he took as a text for his April 1962 general conference address the work in Asia. "I wish you might have been with us recently in a conference in Hong Kong to hear our young Chinese brethren and sisters sing the songs of Zion in their native Cantonese and bear witness of the truth of this work to congregations numbering more than eight hundred," he said. "I wish you might have been with us in Taiwan to hear a handsome and brilliant young man discuss the gospel in his native Mandarin. He was a local missionary, a young man whose forebears for generations before him had been Buddhists. . . . How I wish you might have been with us in the upstairs room in Tsim Sha Tsui in Kowloon, where for thirteen hours the elders and sisters bore testimony of their love for the Chinese people."

Though he had championed the cause of missionaries for nearly thirty years, Elder Hinckley's experience in Asia was expanding his vision of the work. He concluded with a plea to all Saints: "The work is becoming very much enlarged. It does require a commensurate accumulation of men and means. It requires an expansion of mind and energy, ability and perseverance. Let us prepare ourselves more diligently for the great assignment which God has laid upon us to carry this work to the children of the earth."[28]

Not long after Elder Hinckley returned from Asia, President Moyle asked him to outline what he did on these extended tours—and particularly what he did with the missionaries. After hearing his report, President Moyle invited him to join him in California to hold seminars with the missionaries there. That trip was followed by a similar one to Chicago, after which President Moyle continued on to Europe while Elder Hinckley was joined in the Midwest by Marjorie, Virginia, Clark, and Jane, who came to help him drive home a new car he had purchased. The brief vacation during which the Hinckleys drove home from Detroit was a welcome break, and the family enjoyed having Gordon to themselves for several uninterrupted days. They told stories, read books aloud to each other, and stopped at historical markers along the way as they drove to Salt Lake City. Some patterns, regardless of the children's ages, never changed.

They had just pulled into their driveway and walked into the house when the phone rang. It was President McKay, who asked Elder Hinckley if he had heard from President Moyle. When Gordon explained that he and his family had just returned home, President McKay indicated that President Moyle would soon be calling from Europe. About an hour later the phone rang again. "Gordon," President Moyle began, "I've scheduled a seminar for tomorrow night in London with the missionaries, and I want you here." A few hours later Elder Hinckley was on his way to England, where he and President Moyle began a twenty-three-day canvassing of all twenty-one missions in the British Isles and Europe. Each day they conducted a seminar in a different city. "I took the morning hours until noon, and President Moyle took the afternoon hours," Elder Hinckley explained. "Then we packed up and flew to the next city. It was the most tiring thing I've ever done." In less than a month, however, they got a first-hand look at missionary work throughout Europe—including Germany, where Elder Hinckley spent a few hours with Dick.

At the end of their tour, President Moyle presented his colleague with a pair of binoculars as a memento of their experience together. Elder Hinckley treasured the keepsake as a "reminder of a great and good man who magnified his priesthood."[29] President Moyle returned home by ship, hoping to rest in the process, and invited Elder Hinckley to join him. But Gordon preferred to fly so he could enjoy a few days off with his family. The experience with President Moyle, however, was one he would never forget. He later said: "He was a champion, a crusader, a clear-thinking, unequivocating exponent of any cause he espoused, unrelenting in his advocacy. . . . I [witnessed] his unrelenting drive, his untarnished devotion to this great work, his unforgetting love for the young men and women who are in the world as ambassadors of the Lord."[30]

During the general conference that followed two months later, General Authorities serving in Europe described the effect of President Moyle's and Elder Hinckley's visit. Elder Theodore M. Burton said: "Usually in summer we have quite a drop in converts during the time the Europeans take their summer holidays. . . . This year, just as the holidays were beginning, we had a wonderful visit from President Moyle and Elder Hinckley. These two wonderful men, devoting themselves to the work of the Lord, came over to help us. . . . As a result of their visit our August conversions were twenty-eight percent above our conversions for July. Our September conversions were thirty-seven percent above our August conversions."[31] Elder N. Eldon Tanner, who as an Assistant to the Twelve was serving as president of the Western European Mission, added: "These two men, I believe, had fourteen consecutive meetings in fourteen consecutive days, in fourteen different towns in four or five countries. I do not see how they stood it, but if anybody ever forgot himself or lost himself in the service, this is an example of it."[32]

About this series of mission conferences, Elder Boyd K. Packer later said: "They seemed to have a tremendous effect on the missions of the Church. It was an energizing movement that helped give missionary work worldwide a significant boost."[33] President McKay subsequently reorganized the Missionary Executive Committee with President Joseph Fielding Smith as chairman and Elders Harold B. Lee, Marion G. Romney, Gordon B. Hinckley, and Boyd K. Packer as committee members.

Elder Hinckley's appointment to the Missionary Executive Committee was only one of many assignments. One of his first as a member of the Twelve had come immediately after the October 1961 general conference, when Elder Harold B. Lee had organized the All-Church Coordinating Council, with correlation committees for three groups—adults, youth, and children—to be headed by Elders Marion G. Romney, Richard L. Evans, and Gordon B. Hinckley, respectively. As the forerunner of what became the Correlation Committee, this council functioned as the screening process responsible for coordinating the teaching programs of the Church.[34]

Elder Hinckley's numerous and varied assignments required him to switch gears constantly. But regardless of the setting or obligation, he was immersed in his work. He concluded a stirring address to the BYU student body with a challenge: "What a tremendous thing it is to be a part of a Church that has a great heritage, . . . that speaks of faith and courage and sacrifice and giving. If we ever lose it, we had better close up shop. Without sacrifice there is no true worship. . . . As you go forward with your ambitious programs, forget yourselves now and again. Lay aside your selfishness; lose yourself in the service of others and in some great cause."[35]

The great cause in which Elder Hinckley had lost himself was the gospel of Jesus Christ, and for the time being, he was focused intently on that cause as it related to the Orient. In late November 1962, he and Sister Hinckley returned to Asia, where both had learned to expect the unexpected and to enjoy the region's unique intrigue. Though Asia was halfway around the world in distance and even further in culture, with each trip Elder Hinckley's attachment to and affection for the Oriental Saints increased. He felt strangely at home with these olive-skinned people whose resilience had been tested through untold hardships.

Elder Ray Goodson was serving in Hong Kong during Elder Hinckley's early visits, and was one of four missionaries transferred into the Philippines to open the work there. "Elder Hinckley was the first General Authority to come to Asia who wasn't convinced he was going to die before he got back to Salt Lake," he said, "though it took him a while to understand the people. On his first visit to Hong Kong he talked about the Boy Scout program, and the Chinese sat there puzzled. But by his next visit he was more comfortable, his talks were appropriate, and the Asians started to warm up to him. He wasn't afraid to shake their hands, ride their public transportation, walk their streets, or eat their food."[36] One notable exception was the Koreans' *kimchee*, a pungent side dish made of oriental cabbage, radish, and cucumber pickled in garlic and red pepper. Elder Hinckley could not stomach either the taste or the smell of the Korean staple. In return, his Korean friends teased that nothing could be as bad as American blue cheese dressing.

He may not have always enjoyed all of their cuisine, but Elder Hinckley loved these people. At another general conference he said before beginning his prepared text, "My heart skipped a beat this morning when I looked into this group and saw a man from Korea, one of my beloved brethren."[37]

The affection was reciprocated, and despite the reserve and formality inherent in most Asian cultures, soon each group of Orientals—the Japanese, Koreans, Filipinos, and Chinese—adopted him and Sister Hinckley as their own. Elder Hinckley was the first General Authority to make repeated trips to Asia and to venture into outlying areas. And he was perhaps the first to instill in the Asian Saints a confidence that he understood them. As a result, they responded to both his testimony and the manner in which he expressed his love for and confidence in them. The Koreans teased him that after he died, he would be resurrected a Korean.

Seiji Katanuma, who later served as president of the Sapporo Japan Stake and as a Regional Representative, said, "Elder Hinckley made me feel like a brother who lived next door. He gave us counsel as an Apostle of the Lord and talked and listened to us as if he were an Oriental. I have never forgotten his words, 'Your generation is the pioneer of the Church in Japan.' This made me visualize myself as I would like to be in the Church."[38]

When the Hinckleys arrived in Japan for the first time after President Dwayne Andersen assumed leadership of the Northern Far Eastern Mission, Sister Andersen described the occasion: "We never stopped to catch our breath. They arrived and we left immediately for a serviceman's retreat in Hakone, Japan. Afterwards they spent much time shaking hands with these lonely servicemen. I wrote in my journal: 'Oh, how Apostle Hinckley loves these servicemen, and they know it, for he truly shows it!'" After two days of nonstop meetings with servicemen, missionaries, and members in Tokyo, Sister Andersen again recorded her impressions: "As we sat in front of hundreds of Saints, I glanced at Elder Hinckley. He was weary, and he turned to my husband and asked what he should talk about, that he had drawn a blank. Dwayne gave him a suggestion, and Elder Hinckley stood up and spoke almost completely to the subject suggested. He delivered a marvelous message, so sincere and meaningful, and the Saints' faces radiated. They seemed to understand his English even before the interpreter started each thought pattern. It was obvious that he loved those Japanese people every bit as much as he did the servicemen! He could make anyone feel loved."[39]

Sister Hinckley also related well to the Asians, who had won her admiration and respect. She told one interviewer: "I always find spiritual refreshment among the Oriental people, who have the gifts of humility and sincerity. They are receptive to the message that assures them of a personal God and a Savior. Their many talents . . . seem to unfold as they apply the gospel in their lives. For example, one discouraged woman in Hong Kong was working in a dingy food establishment when the missionaries found her. Five years later she is managing a prosperous export-import business, has a fine family of children, and is an officer in the Relief Society."[40]

Augusto Lim, an early Filipino convert, described Sister Hinckley's interaction with his people: "Sister Hinckley would go out of her way to shake our hands and embrace us, and she always kissed my wife. She was so easy to be with, so caring and loving and concerned about our mutual friends as well as our own welfare. In those early days she spent a lot of time among the people, and that is what impressed us."[41] During the Hinckleys' early trips to the Orient, accommodations weren't always favorable. "We didn't have any decent hotels in Korea," Han In Sang explained, "so it was a tremendous sacrifice for them to come. Sometimes they would sleep at the mission home. We didn't have a boiler system, so we would heat water on a big kettle for them to use. Sister Hinckley never complained. In fact, she made us feel as though what we had to offer was a palace. In return, she always brought several pounds of chocolates to give to the missionaries and members."[42]

Perhaps without their realizing it, the manner in which Elder and Sister Hinckley interacted with each other appealed to many Asians. "Elder Hinckley was always looking after his wife, taking care of her and protecting her," Han In Sang continued, "but almost as though he were her big brother. It was easy to see that he loved her, but he did it in a way that impressed the Oriental people. Another leader from Salt Lake City told us we should tell our wife we love her every day. We love our wives but we don't say it that way. Elder Hinckley told us, 'Just express it in your own way.' He understood us."[43]

With each trip to the Orient, the Hinckleys better understood their new friends. Their visit in late November and early December 1962 was much like their earlier trip in the spring. In July the Korean Mission had been created, and Elder Hinckley spent time with the new mission president, Gail C. Carr, as well as Presidents Jay A. Quealy and Dwayne N. Andersen of the Southern Far East and Northern Far East missions, in a president's seminar in Tokyo.

Although there were always concerns in the Far East missions for Elder Hinckley to address, he remained optimistic about Asia. In Hong Kong he and Sister Hinckley attended a dance festival with more than five hundred Chinese youth in the Kam Tong Hall. "I could see in their presence a vision of the future of our work here," Elder Hinckley recorded afterward. "If we can just hold these young people and keep them busy and active and set up situations under which they will marry honorably in the Church, the future of the Church in this part of the world will be assured. Many of them are fine-looking, intelligent people. I am sure that all of the brethren would have been tremendously impressed had they witnessed this."[44]

The following morning Elder Hinckley presided over a district conference in Hong Kong attended by nearly nine hundred members, and he thrilled at what he witnessed there: "The Sunday morning session was like a stake conference. In fact, it looked better than many stake conference congregations I have seen. It was a thrilling sight to see all these wonderful Chinese people. . . . It was a sight to make us weep."[45]

There were many experiences that evoked great emotion. On November 20, 1962, in the Fukuoka Branch on the island of

Kyushu, Elder Hinckley and President Andersen convened an all-day zone conference that, for the benefit of the largely American audience, was conducted in English. Elder Yoshihiko Kikuchi, the lone Japanese missionary, understood only that which his companion translated for him.

As part of the conference, Elder Hinckley invited each missionary to bear testimony. One by one the elders did so, until only Elder Kikuchi had not spoken. Finally Elder Hinckley arose and, pointing to Elder Kikuchi, invited him to come forward. His companion quickly translated Elder Hinckley's request, and Elder Kikuchi asked if he could bear his testimony in Japanese. "*Hai, hai,*" yes, Elder Hinckley responded. At that, Elder Kikuchi walked to the pulpit. Almost immediately a powerful spirit fell upon him and he began to speak in English. "It must have been very simple English," he remembered years later, "but it was as though I was lifted by the Spirit and my tongue was loosed and my ears could easily comprehend the other language. The sweetness and the celestial glow that I felt was unforgettable. I was moved by the Holy Spirit. I was touched by the sweetness of how the Holy Ghost can work with people. I felt the shadow of my mind fade away, and I caught a glimpse of the great light of the gospel."[46] As he spoke, Elder Hinckley wept, as did most in the room.

As soon as he said "Amen," Elder Kikuchi's mind closed to English, and his companion had to translate what happened next. Elder Hinckley walked to the pulpit and, in a voice filled with emotion, said, "I do not usually bless people from the pulpit, but I feel impressed to pronounce a blessing upon this young Japanese man. Brother Kikuchi, this missionary system is a great blessing to your life. If you are faithful and humble always, and keep the commandments of the Lord continually, the Lord will prepare you to establish the Lord's kingdom in this part of the vineyard. The Lord is preparing you to serve him in a greater way."[47] It was the beginning of a strong bond between the seasoned Church leader and the Japanese elder, who was later called as a General Authority.

Not all encounters were as joyful. Local leaders looked to Elder Hinckley to solve difficult problems that arose in the lives of Church members. He grieved, for example, over a young man who had served with distinction as a local missionary but had subsequently fathered a child out of wedlock. After counseling with the young man and outlining the steps of repentance, he wrote: "Notwithstanding the gravity of his offense, I feel disposed to help him in every way possible, and to encourage him so that he may get his education. He is a most capable young man who has slipped, and it would be tragic if his entire life was blighted because of this."[48]

Despite such episodes, there was much to be encouraged about throughout Asia. The Church was clearly moving forward there.

Though he spent an enormous amount of time during the early 1960s in the Orient, Elder Hinckley's assignments weren't limited to that part of the world. In May 1963, for example, he traveled to the Windward Islands in the heart of French Polynesia, where he found himself charmed by the exuberance of the peoples of the South Seas. Among other obligations, he was to dedicate a chapel for the Haapu Branch on the island of Huahine. Several hundred members of the Church from neighboring islands chartered small trading boats to attend the dedication and hear Elder Hinckley speak, and afterward the atmosphere was festive as the Polynesian Saints celebrated the landmark event in their own unique and colorful style.

At the end of the day, some fifty members and friends from the nearby island of Maupiti boarded an old boat, the *Manuia*, to begin their overnight voyage home. Many of the islanders' livelihoods revolved around the sea, and this excursion was no different from hundreds of others they had made. Their journey proceeded normally until the ship passed between the islands of Raiatea and Tahaa, where the ocean was suddenly filled with sudsy bubbles that experienced seagoers recognized as a sign of rough water ahead. By the time the boat reached Maupiti, where the channel through the coral reef into the calm waters of the lagoon was one of the most dangerous in all of the South Pacific, the seas had become very rough. As the captain attempted to maneuver the vessel through the narrow opening, he lost control of the ship and it hit the reef, rolled three times in the pounding waves, and broke apart. Fifteen of the fifty aboard drowned, including all but two of the Relief Society sisters of the Maupiti Branch.

It was the following morning before Elder Hinckley, who had returned to Papeete, Tahiti, with mission president Kendall W. Young, received word of the tragedy. Heartsick at the news, he immediately canceled his return flight to Salt Lake City. By late afternoon he and President Young had located a seaman who agreed to sail them to their destination some 160 miles away on his old World War II PT boat. At dusk Elder Hinckley and President Young set sail for Maupiti. Elder Hinckley tried to sleep out on the deck, but he spent most of the night worrying about those whose lives had been irreversibly altered by the tragedy.

About noon the next day, as their boat wended its way through the reef and they caught sight of the mangled *Manuia*, the horror of the tragedy became apparent. Elder Hinckley wept as he stepped onto the pier and greeted the grief-stricken people. "I picked up the little children who had lost their mothers and struggled to hold my emotions," he recalled. "It was heartbreaking to see those motherless children and the men who had lost their wives. To see that stark hull ravaged on the coral reef was one of the most difficult moments I have ever had."[49]

Elder Hinckley conducted a memorial service that afternoon and did what he could to extend comfort and sympathy. That evening his party left by boat for Bora Bora. Some of the survivors accompanied them to Tahiti for medical attention, among them Claire Teriitehau, a nonmember nurse who had attended the dedication at Huahine. During the voyage she consented to receive a blessing from Elder Hinckley, who told her that she would join the Church and explained that she was needed by the Lord. A short time later she was baptized.[50]

Elder Hinckley was deeply affected by what he had witnessed, and he found that he couldn't erase from his mind the image of those small, motherless children, many of them clinging to their fathers. His heart was heavy as he began the trip home.

Other experiences were sobering as well. Early in the morning of September 18, 1963, President Henry D. Moyle passed away unexpectedly. The news shocked Elder Hinckley, who grieved the loss of the counselor and friend with whom he had toured many missions of the world. Theirs had become a warm and collegial relationship, beginning in earnest when Gordon had written James H. Moyle's biography and continuing with their association in the Missionary Department. He was highly complimented, and a little overwhelmed, by invitations to write a memorial about President Moyle for the *Improvement Era* and to speak at his funeral. In his eulogy he honored President McKay's counselor as a man of unwavering devotion under whom missionary work had gone forward in an unprecedented way. During the three and a half years President Moyle had chaired the Missionary Committee, the number of missions increased from forty-seven to seventy-one and 267,669 converts joined the Church, Elder Hinckley explained. "Perhaps of comparable significance," he continued, "is the miracle wrought in the lives of thousands of young men and women who, under the influence of his pleading, his logic, his challenges, went into the world as ambassadors of the Lord. . . . Within a period of three years the number of missionaries more than doubled as he pleaded over the Church for workers in this dedicated service."[51]

Once again, there would be changes in the First Presidency. On October 4, 1963, at general conference, Presidents Hugh B. Brown and N. Eldon Tanner were sustained as first and second counselors to President McKay, and the vacancy in the Quorum of the Twelve was filled by the thirty-six-year-old returned president of the Canadian Mission, Thomas S. Monson. On the Sunday morning of conference Elder Hinckley was invited to deliver the address broadcast nationwide on CBS Radio's "Church of the Air" program. Drawing his subject from the words of the psalmist, "Except the Lord build the house, they labor in vain that build it," he developed a theme that gave him increasing concern—the quality and stability of family and home life. With his characteristic blend of optimism and stark honesty he began: "I am not one to believe that all was good in the long ago, and that all is bad today. I think that this is the greatest age the world has known. But I am also confident that there is trouble in the land." He then declared that no nation is stronger than its homes and that, as simple as it might sound, "a return to the old pattern of . . . family prayer in the homes of the people, is one of the simple medicines that would check the dread disease that is eroding the fiber of our character. We could not expect a miracle in a day, but in a generation we would have a miracle."[52]

The talk apparently struck a chord, for notes and telegrams of appreciation flooded his office. It was a message Elder Hinckley believed in passionately, a practice he and Sister Hinckley had cultivated at home. Family prayer had been and was the central stabilizing force in their own family.

The year 1963 brought with it difficult moments, but there were joyful occasions as well. After thirty months in Germany, Dick returned from his mission. As pleased as Elder Hinckley had been to see his son enter the mission field, it was more wonderful to welcome him home. Where had the time gone? His children were growing up so quickly and one by one leaving home. Kathy had a daughter of her own, Virginia had graduated from high school, Clark would graduate in just two years and leave soon thereafter on his mission, and Jane was nearly ten. It was sobering to realize that even his youngest child, who had been a source of unusual delight to him, would spend only a few more years under his roof.

In the fall of 1963, as Elder and Sister Hinckley prepared for another trip to the Orient, they decided to take Jane with them. A third grader, she had little idea what her parents did when they left for weeks at a time; she knew only that she disliked being left behind with her older sisters or an aunt. As the youngest child, Jane perhaps bore the brunt of her father's high profile and frequent absence. Elder Hinckley's rationale for taking Jane with them was simple: "At her age we can take her for half price, and we feel that we would rather put some money into this kind of investment than spend so much on new cars and such things." On Saturday, October 19, the day they left for Honolulu, he noted, "Jane was so excited she could hardly contain herself."[53]

The three Hinckleys arrived in Hawaii around midnight, and after a hot, muggy night they arose for a Sunday during which Elder Hinckley dedicated two buildings and toured the new Polynesian Cultural Center, which had been dedicated a week earlier by President Hugh B. Brown. The next morning they were off to Tokyo, where he inspected the renovation under way on the mission home and, as always, was fascinated with the process. "I am amazed at the construction required by the Japanese government," he noted in his journal. "Piles had to be driven in the ground for a distance of thirty feet and then heavy concrete piers are placed on these. It looks like construction for a ten-story building, rather than a two."[54] The builder in Elder Hinckley never failed to notice the architecture in everything from the hotels he patronized to new skyscrapers under construction.

This visit to the Philippines provided an unusual experience for two sister missionaries who greeted the Hinckleys at the airport. His arrival in Manila coincided with an elaborate gathering of several international leaders who had come to attend a summit conference, and the atmosphere was one of pomp and circumstance. Jets flew in formation, military attachés and diplomats lined red carpets, and cheering crowds greeted arriving dignitaries, who were then whisked away in black Cadillacs. After the leaders had all arrived, the red carpet was rolled up, the jets circling overhead disappeared, and the military officers walked back into the terminal. Shortly thereafter, Elder Hinckley's plane landed. Sister Mary Ellen Edmunds, one of the missionaries, observed in her journal: "And then down the ramp came an Apostle of Jesus Christ. A man chosen of God. The most beautiful person who walked down the ramp that day. Elder Gordon B. Hinckley. No earthly fanfare greeted him, except the loud beating of my heart and a feeling of great happiness just to be close to him. More authority in this one servant of God than all the leaders assembled for the summit conference could muster together—even with all their material wealth and titles."[55] Later, Elder Hinckley teased an audience of members and missionaries that he hoped they weren't disappointed to find that he was short, losing his hair, and not terribly good-looking. Wrote Sister Edmunds: "The members weren't disappointed, and neither were we. We were filled beyond our greatest need and expectation. How he lifted our spirits and renewed our dedication to God's holy work!"[56]

One of the tour's most memorable experiences occurred

during a Sunday worship service in Seoul with sixty LDS servicemen. After many of them bore testimony, Elder Hinckley recorded:

> It was one of the most moving experiences of my life to listen to them. Here were strong military men who wept as they thanked the Lord for the Gospel, for their families, and one another. . . . Colonel Hogan, who is executive officer of the Air Force installation at Taegu, wept as he spoke. . . . He told of how he had been ordered to Korea, and of how he had concluded that he would resign rather than leave his family behind him. There appeared no way that he could take his dependents. But the way suddenly opened, and he brought his six children with him. Then the Falconer boy stood up. He said that he knew why the Hogans had come to Taegu. He said the Falconer family . . . had prayed that another LDS family might be sent there so that they could organize a branch. . . .
>
> A veteran artillery captain told of how he was drifting downhill following his transfer to Korea. . . . Then Colonel Plant, who had been the servicemen's district president until recently, visited him and got on his knees [and prayed] with him. He had changed the course of his life. . . . And so it went for the better part of three hours to become an unforgettable spiritual experience.

Elder Hinckley concluded: "I have never seen a group of men anywhere in the world who evidenced such love for the Church. What an experience to have had this morning. There is something about Korea that gets me. It is the grayest, saddest land I know. Perhaps this is the reason I feel the spirit of the Lord so strongly each time I come here. It is the great gratitude which both the missionaries and our servicemen have for the gospel. The contrast is so great and so apparent."[57]

Elder Hinckley's faith was always strengthened by the testimonies of those wearing olive drab, and whenever he spoke with servicemen, Elder Hinckley promised them that those who lived the gospel were indeed missionaries.

Such experiences were not lost on Jane, who saw her father with new eyes as they met with the Saints. "I remember thinking that Dad loved what he was doing," she later said. "And I saw the mantle of his calling rest on his shoulders. Even as a young girl I could feel something when he bore his testimony of the Savior and his great love for the Prophet Joseph Smith."[58]

This was the first of several international trips for Jane, and Marjorie rejoiced that they were able to share their experiences with their youngest daughter. She often told her husband that her only regret about their trips to the Orient was that she longed to have the family with them. "I want to walk the streets of Hong Kong with my children," she said again and again.

The following spring Elder Hinckley wrote a series of articles on the Church in Asia for the *Improvement Era*. Identified as president of the "Hawaiian-Oriental Missions," he had become the most visible and enthusiastic supporter of the Asian people and the missionaries who served them. He concluded his message with a vision of what would come: "To date, our labors have been relatively small among so many, but they have been tremendously significant. We have not touched the millions of the Chinese mainland. . . . We have not as yet taught other millions in other areas, but it is apparent that the Spirit of the Lord is brooding in the hearts of men in this part of the earth, and that doors now locked will some day open."[59]

It was clear to Elder Hinckley that the responsibility to move the work forward in Asia lay heavily on his shoulders. Church headquarters was half a world away, and some of the traditional methods of missionary work were not effective among the distinctive Asian cultures. All he could do was seek the direction of the Lord, then roll up his sleeves and go to work.

His willingness to blaze trails was evident in other areas as well. Since the mid-1930s, when he had first become responsible for helping produce the Church's Sunday evening programming aired on KSL, he had been involved with developing Church-oriented material for broadcast. He was fascinated by the power and the reach of electronic media and had been since boyhood, when he had built a crystal radio set and then marveled over being able to pull sound out of the air through a steel wire on a crystal.

In 1957 his link to KSL had grown even stronger when President McKay named him first to the board of directors of the Radio Service Corporation of Utah (or KSL) and subsequently as a member of its executive committee. With others, he had been involved in making broadcasts of general conference available to the public; the first nationwide broadcast took place in April 1962.[60] In early 1964, after lengthy negotiations, the Church purchased KIRO-TV and KIRO-AM/FM in Seattle, and he was elected a director of that company.[61] He had also been involved two years earlier with the purchase of a New York shortwave station, WRUL (later WNYW), acquired to facilitate broadcast capabilities to Europe and South America.

In 1964, when it appeared that the Church would continue to acquire media properties, Bonneville International Corporation (BIC) was created to supervise the management of all broadcasting entities. A signatory for the incorporation of that company, Elder Hinckley was named a vice president, a member of its board of directors, and a member of the executive committee.[62] Decisions at Bonneville ran the gamut, and as he and other principals looked for ways to appropriately extend the Church's broadcasting influence, it became increasingly clear that new technologies would open up the world in ways never before imagined.

Elder Hinckley was anxious to use technology more creatively in spreading the gospel. If anything, he believed, the Church needed to expand its use of media. His experience in Asia alone suggested that the time and number of missionaries required to make personal contact with every soul rendered such an approach impractical.

In early November 1964, he set out on a trip that would take him around the world and in the process give him even greater appreciation for the vast regions as yet untouched by the gospel message. He and Marjorie would miss Thanksgiving with their children, and the idea of being separated from the family on such a holiday pained Sister Hinckley. But this trip was unusual in that they were to visit countries Elder Hinckley had never before seen, and he wanted her with him.

At times it seemed almost incredible to him that the progress of the Church rested largely in the hands of young missionaries—hence the countless hours he spent teaching, interviewing, encouraging, and blessing them. He had found it necessary on a previous trip to deliver a stern message to missionaries serving in Japan. Afterward President Dwayne Andersen of the

Northern Far East Mission had worked to increase the spirituality of his missionaries so that the next time Elder Hinckley visited they could lighten his load rather than add to his burden.

One evidence of progress occurred on this trip. The morning of November 26, 1964, Elder Hinckley and President Andersen arrived at the Tokyo Central Branch building to find eighty missionaries singing "Come, Listen to a Prophet's Voice." Elder Hinckley entered the back door, removed his shoes, and then suddenly stopped. After a few moments, he proceeded up the middle aisle to the front of the room. Tears filled his eyes as he admitted that he had come fasting and had expected to speak sternly with them. "But I felt your spirit when I came in, and I can see that things have changed here." He then asked if there were any sick among them. President Andersen remembered: "We had three missionaries with serious health problems. I anointed them and Elder Hinckley sealed the anointings and gave each of them a very special blessing. The Spirit was so strong that there was not a dry eye in the room. Over the years I have had many missionaries recall this sacred occasion as one of the choicest spiritual experiences they had ever had."[63]

Elder Hinckley seemed to have the ability to encourage members and missionaries to greater works. "Everywhere he and Sister Hinckley went," Sister Andersen explained, "the Saints thronged to hear them, shake their hands, and feel of their genuine love. When missionaries were discouraged, Elder Hinckley could lift them with just a few words of comfort and counsel. Sometimes he shared discouraging times in his own life, and that changed their spirits."[64]

After visiting the cities that they typically included on their itinerary, Elder and Sister Hinckley headed west, to countries where the Church was still limited to small groups of scattered members. With President and Sister Jay Quealy they traveled to Bangkok, where they met with a few expatriate Latter-day Saints. On the one hand, it was exciting to find Saints in such faraway places; on the other, the visit to Bangkok was sobering. "When we come to this part of this world," Elder Hinckley noted in his journal, "we are almost overwhelmed by a realization of the immensity of our task in preaching the Restored Gospel."[65]

From Bangkok the Hinckleys and the Quealys flew to Saigon

(later named Ho Chi Minh City), where nearly sixty Saints awaited them in a hot and steamy room in an American school. A horde of bugs crawled over Elder Hinckley as he attempted to address an audience composed largely of servicemen, though two Vietnamese converts participated in the meeting. The Hinckleys' brief experience in Saigon was eerie. "One would never think South Vietnam is at war," he noted. "The people seem to go about their business with an indifferent attitude. This appears to be the chief problem in the conflict. The people are not involved in it. . . . At home we read the newspapers and think that Saigon is a strife-torn city. It certainly does not appear that way."[66]

The quartet flew on to Singapore and then to India, which proved to be a singular experience. Their dilapidated hotel room on the outskirts of Madras was inhabited by ants nearly an inch long. In Coimbatore they witnessed a degree of poverty that stunned them. "Some of the people are dressed only in rags. Many were naked from the waist up. Squalor and filth and poverty and hunger are evident on all sides," Elder Hinckley recorded.[67] There they also met Paul Thirithuvodoss, a man who had written to the Church requesting baptism. At his invitation they drove to Medukerai to tour his school for underprivileged children and attend religious services for several hundred of his associates. Some were beating drums and playing an organ, all of which reminded Elder Hinckley of a Salvation Army gathering. To these "poor of the earth," as Elder Hinckley described them, Paul delivered a Pentecostal-type sermon. Despite his repeated request that he and others be baptized, Elder Hinckley was concerned: "My thoughts are greatly troubled over what I have seen. I do not know what we should do. These are earnest people, but they have been schooled in the Pentecostal ways which are not our ways. . . . We certainly need the inspiration of the Lord in whatever action we take here."[68]

Both alone and with President Quealy, Elder Hinckley pleaded with the Lord for direction. He ultimately declined to perform the ordinance, recommending instead that missionaries be sent to teach Paul and others. It was not an easy decision: "We said goodbye to him and his group with real affection in our hearts, particularly for him. . . . I go to sleep somewhat troubled in my mind over not performing the ordinance in his behalf, but fully satisfied that good has been accomplished by our coming here and that the end results will be very much . . . in harmony with the Lord's will."[69] Paul was later baptized.

From India the Hinckleys bid the Quealys farewell and flew on to the Near East, stopping in Beirut to meet with a small group of members and then continuing on to Jerusalem. This was their first trip to the Holy Land, and everything they saw aroused emotions of one kind or another. Their route from Jerusalem to Bethlehem, which crossed a no-man's-land with Arab soldiers stationed on one side and Jewish guards on the other, reminded Elder Hinckley of Korea's DMZ and of the Berlin Wall. Most poignantly, it served as a stark reminder that peace would not come to the world until men accepted the teachings of the Master.

Despite such impressions, he and Sister Hinckley marveled as they walked in the footsteps of history at Golgotha, the Mount of Olives, and other sites central to the Savior's life and ministry. Elder Hinckley felt strongly the presence of Him who had lived and died there. "There may be some uncertainty about the specific site but there is no uncertainty about the fact that this is the area in which the Savior of the world was born, lived and taught, and gave His life as a sacrifice for all men. It is a sobering and wonderful experience to be here," he wrote.[70]

Their last night in Israel, Elder Hinckley became violently ill; by morning he was so weak that he could scarcely hold his head up. Against Marjorie's protests, they left for Athens as scheduled. The smell of food on the plane only aggravated his condition, and he feared he would pass out during the flight. Once in Athens, they had scarcely arrived at their hotel when the phone rang. The leader of the small group of Saints there was calling to request a meeting. After inviting the man's family to the hotel for dinner and agreeing to meet with any who could be gathered together, Elder Hinckley fell into bed. "When it came dinner time, I was extremely ungracious," he recorded. "I asked them if they would feel all right about eating in the coffee shop where I could get two boiled eggs and some soda water. . . . I was so tired and weak I could not hold my eyes open. I was ashamed of myself."[71]

By morning his illness had passed, and he and Marjorie enjoyed some quick sightseeing around the Greek capital before leaving for Frankfurt. Elder Hinckley was eager to stand on Mars Hill, where the Apostle Paul had preached his famous sermon on the unknown God. "It was a sobering experience to stand where Paul had stood to declare the true nature of God our Eternal Father, and His Son, the Lord Jesus Christ. It gave me a sobering sense of the high and holy calling which has come to me," he recorded.[72]

Just six days before Christmas, the Hinckleys arrived in Frankfurt to a welcome surprise. Though Elder Hinckley had expected to meet there with Elder Ezra Taft Benson, who was serving as president of the European Mission, he and Sister Hinckley had not expected the Bensons to greet them at the airport and invite them to stay at the mission home. They were delighted to accept the Bensons' invitation. "Their home is beautifully decorated for Christmas and it is a wonderful thing to be . . . with these good people," Elder Hinckley recorded afterward. "The spirit here is so different from that in hotel rooms."[73] By the following evening the Hinckleys had flown on to Brussels. Their brief stopover in Germany, however, had revived them, as Sister Hinckley explained in a thank-you note to Sister Benson: "After going through the Orient and across Asia, where there was so little evidence of Christmas, and then to suddenly find ourselves in your beautiful home with the Christmas tree and the lights, and music and the red-ribboned staircase, and . . . most of all, the sweet spirit and peace of a Latter-day Saint home, was something that will always remain with us. After weeks in hotels and strange cities, you could not possibly know how we felt when we saw you at the airport."[74]

From Brussels the Hinckleys flew to London, which always rejuvenated Elder Hinckley. This brief stopover was particularly delightful, as for the first time this holiday season they had a few moments to enjoy the bustle of shoppers and a rare evening of entertainment, during which they indulged in a roast beef and Yorkshire pudding dinner and tickets to Noel Coward's *Light Spirits* (known as *Blithe Spirit* in America). It had been a long and tedious trip. Before leaving for the airport, Elder Hinckley dictated a few benedictory thoughts about their around-the-world tour: "We will have circled the globe when we arrive in Salt Lake City tonight. . . . I am grateful to say that notwithstanding a bout of illness I feel stronger and more rested than I did three weeks ago. For one thing, the cool weather has done much to revive us. . . . [But] it has been an inspirational experience. I have interviewed 479 missionaries [and] have met with many of the Saints. . . . I have listened to their testimonies and felt of their spirit and my own faith has been strengthened and my testimony bolstered. Surely God lives and Jesus is the Christ. Surely this is Their work, and it is good to be engaged in it."[75]

When the Hinckleys finally touched down in Salt Lake City, it was just two days before Christmas Eve. Ten-year-old Jane, who had been panicked that her parents wouldn't make it home for the holidays, was thrilled when they walked through the door. For their part, as much as Elder and Sister Hinckley enjoyed the far reaches of the world, there was nowhere they were more comfortable or content than home.

CHAPTER FIFTEEN

GROWING IN ASIA

In the United States, the sixties were a volatile decade, a dizzying era of highs and lows, triumph and tragedy. The president was assassinated on November 22, 1963; hot spots in the cold war between East and West threatened to ignite; and angry college students, feminists, and blacks bent on challenging the status quo demanded the nation's attention. But despite the proliferation of special-interest groups opposed to anything that represented a traditional institution or way of life, the Church continued to grow at home and abroad. During 1963 Church membership crossed the two-million mark, and some of that growth was occurring in the Far East and Pacific Rim.

In July 1965 Elder Hinckley flew to Hawaii to participate in a historic event. In a seven-thousand-mile journey believed to be among the longest temple excursions in Church history, 131 adults and 29 children from Japan flew to Hawaii to attend the temple. For the first time ever, all of the work of the temple was available in Japanese.

Elder Hinckley's reunion with Japanese friends in Hawaii was joyous. For several days he performed sealings, participated in temple instruction, posed for pictures with happy families, and saw in the faces of good friends the delight of being linked eternally to their loved ones. While in Hawaii, he also attended a testimonial for the newly called president of the Northern Far East Mission, Adney Y. Komatsu, a Hawaiian-born Japanese man who was the first of his race called as a mission president.[1]

Such happy occasions were the fruits of missionary work, and though Elder Hinckley had been relieved of handling the day-to-day affairs in the department, he served as managing director of the Priesthood Missionary Committee. Accordingly, it fell to him to deal with the difficult administrative problems that affected the expanding program. Late 1965, for example, found him preparing budgets for the operation of the Missionary Department, travel of missionaries, and other related items for all missions throughout the world. The process was tedious and demanded precision, and he never began the annual ritual without reflecting on the first budget he had prepared in 1938 at the request of President J. Reuben Clark Jr. That year he had budgeted $85,000 for the Missionary Department, and President Clark had taken him to task for being too imaginative and extravagant in the projects he proposed. Now the department's annual budget ran to millions of dollars.[2] Of course, during the intervening years the number of missions had more than doubled (from thirty-six to seventy-six), and there were now more than 12,000 missionaries in the field, a number that would have been unfathomable twenty-seven years earlier, when only 1,146 new missionaries were set apart all year.[3]

When the First Presidency, Quorum of the Twelve, and Presiding Bishopric assembled as the Council on the Disposition of the Tithes, where the Church's budget for the following year was reviewed, modified, and finally ratified, he was relieved that the Brethren approved the missionary budget without changing so much as a dollar. He had worried about how they would respond to his proposals, particularly a substantial expenditure for automobiles. "This is a meeting," he recorded, "in which there are frequently differences of opinion but also a meeting in which the inspiration of the Lord is felt when the President of the Church finally announces the decision on various matters."[4]

Other challenges confronting the missionary program weren't addressed as readily. Escalation of the conflict in Vietnam (the number of U.S. troops there increased from 11,200 at the end of 1962 to nearly 200,000 by the end of 1965) had fueled the government's need for draft-eligible young men. Once again Elder Hinckley found himself negotiating with Selective Service officials regarding LDS men who were eligible both to serve missions and to be called up in the draft. As before, there were no easy answers. And this time, the steady hand and voice of Stephen L Richards were not available. Numerous meetings with Selective Service officials, including General Lewis B. Hershey, who was still national director, and others with whom

Elder Hinckley had worked closely during the Korean crisis, led finally to a First Presidency letter, dated September 22, 1965, in which a new missionary quota was announced: one missionary per ward each six months was allowable, with ward and branch quotas transferrable within stakes and districts.

At the priesthood session of the October general conference Elder Hinckley devoted his remarks to this arrangement. "I suppose, brethren," he began, "that not in a long while have we had a communication which has brought greater disappointment than did the First Presidency's letter . . . placing restrictions on the number of young men who may be recommended for missions. No one feels more concerned than I over the thought that possibly some of our young men who have counted on and dreamed of missions may not be able to go." He concluded with an expression of faith: "Several bishops have been in during the last few days and have said that our young men have been saving money for years to go on missions. What shall they do? I say keep saving and praying. . . . I feel satisfied that God will hear our prayers and that most of those young men who want to go on missions will have the opportunity to go on missions."[5]

Decisions about young men torn between the armed forces and the mission field were never easy ones, and as the demand for troops in Vietnam increased, tensions intensified with the Selective Service. After a meeting with Utah Selective Service officials, who asked the Church to further reduce its number of missionaries, Elder Hinckley recorded in his journal: "This is a matter that greatly worries me. My phone rings constantly both day and night asking for some liberalization of quotas so that more young men may go on missions. At the same time I am under pressure from [the] military incident to the war in Vietnam. I pray night and morning that somehow our Father in His power will bring to pass a cessation of hostilities there so that our young men may go without restriction into the world and teach the gospel of peace."[6]

Problems relative to the draft only increased throughout the duration of the Vietnam War. It was an emotional issue, with an eerie sense of déjà vu in the efforts to create a delicate balance between the requirements of government and those of the Church. On occasion this conflict left Elder Hinckley feeling isolated and even misunderstood. In response to a memorandum from Elder Harold B. Lee to the Missionary Executive Committee outlining complaints regarding the quota system, he presented a detailed review of the problem to the Twelve. "I was greatly concerned," he confided in his journal. "I felt as though I were presenting a case to an unsympathetic jury. I covered the subject in every aspect and tried to anticipate every question. The Lord blessed me. When I had finished there was no criticism and much appreciation. Marion G. Romney was especially complimentary and said, 'As I heard you I thought you had been trained as a lawyer.'"[7]

Despite such frustrations, Elder Hinckley was absorbed in his work and grateful to be so engaged. On Christmas Day of 1965 he recorded: "We have received many gifts but best of all our good health, testimonies of the truth, love one for another, and the friendship of marvelous people. Furthermore, it is a privilege and a great trust to be engaged in the Lord's work."[8] Three days later he received a gift more precious than anything he had unwrapped on Christmas morning when four copies of the new Chinese translation of the Book of Mormon arrived at his office. He immediately took a copy to President McKay, and the ninety-two-year-old Church president was delighted with the gift. When a formal presentation was later made, the prophet's copy carried an inscription that read in part: "The Book of Mormon is now available in the language which is the mother tongue of more people than any other on earth. May it go forth among them as a witness of the Son of God, the Savior of the World. With sincere respect and deep affection. Gordon B. Hinckley."[9] President McKay took his associate's hand in his and said warmly, "You have done a great work in this part of the world. The Lord has blessed you and He will continue to bless you."[10]

When he had received the assignment to supervise Asia nearly six years before, two of Elder Hinckley's priorities had been publication of the Book of Mormon in Chinese and in Korean. With the first off the press and the latter nearing completion, he was grateful for the translators who had completed those difficult assignments.

▪ ▪ ▪ ▪ ▪

Though Elder Hinckley was frequently inundated with the administrative aspects of his calling, his responsibility to bear testimony of the divinity of the Savior's life and mission weighed foremost on his mind. The more he traveled the world and saw the diversity of its ills, the greater was his testimony that only in the Savior lay the power and strength to overcome the pitfalls and heartaches of mortality. In the April 1966 general conference he denounced those who sought to undermine Jesus Christ: "Modern theologians strip [the Savior] of his divinity, then wonder why men do not worship him. These clever scholars have taken from Jesus the mantle of godhood and have left only a man. They have tried to accommodate him to their own narrow thinking. They have robbed him of his divine sonship, and taken from the world its rightful King." To those who hungered for "a faith that would satisfy," he promised: "If you will read the word of the Lord, if you will serve his cause, if in prayer you will talk with him, your doubts will leave, and shining through all of the confusion of philosophy, so-called higher criticism, and negative theology will come the witness of the Holy Spirit that Jesus is in very deed the Son of God, born in the flesh, the Redeemer of the world. . . . It is your opportunity so to know. It is your obligation so to find out."[11]

Three years later at conference, he spoke on "The Wonder of Jesus," again declaring that through Christ lay solutions to societal maladies: "One of the complaints of the young pot smokers and drug takers who are seeking escape from reality is that the world has become intolerably impersonal. If this be the problem, the answer is not the kind of escape in which they waste their lives. The solution lies in implementing the transcendent teachings of the Son of God, who more than any other walked the earth [and] gave dignity and worth to the individual. He declared us each to be a child of the living God, endowed with a divine birthright, capable of eternal achievement. Who, I ask, possessed of such conviction, would seek relief in the euphoria of debilitating drugs? . . . Is there relevancy in Jesus for our time? The world never needed more urgently the power of his example; the world never needed more desperately the vitality of his teachings."[12] Following this address, even the modest Elder Hinckley allowed in his journal, "I spoke on the relevance of Jesus to the lives of people in our time and bore witness of his living reality. I think this to be one of the most satisfying talks I have ever given. I was in harmony with my calling as a special witness of the name of Christ in all the world."[13]

Perhaps he would always wonder if there were more he could and should be doing to magnify his calling. That feeling, coupled with his numerous community-oriented assignments—he was serving on the boards of Beneficial Life Insurance Company, Zion's Bank, Bonneville International, KIRO in Seattle, and the Deseret News Publishing Company—allowed him precious few opportunities to relax. Perhaps nothing cleared his head or revived him more than doing physical labor outside. And occasionally he actually took a short vacation. In July 1966 he, Marjorie, Clark, and Jane drove up Provo Canyon to the Aspen Grove family camp, situated nearly seven thousand feet above sea level behind the commanding Mount Timpanogos. There they hiked, read, and relaxed. On July 24, the Hinckleys spoke in the camp's sacrament meeting, with Jane and Clark joining their father on the program. Their "Pioneer Heritage" theme was a Hinckley favorite. Kathy and Virginia and their families joined their parents for dinner in the mountains one evening, and the Hinckleys persuaded Kathy to leave five-year-old Heather—"a pixie," her grandfather called her—with them for the remainder of their stay. The relaxation was just what Marjorie had hoped for on her husband's behalf. Nevertheless, after four days he was restless and anxious to get back to work, so two days earlier than planned he drove home, leaving the rest of the family behind to enjoy the remainder of their week.[14]

Marjorie considered any break her husband took as a triumph, however, for she saw him bearing an ever-increasing burden as well as maintaining an ambitious travel schedule. In October 1966, they left on another trip to Southeast Asia and were greeted in Tokyo by an enthusiastic entourage of Saints who had stretched a huge "Welcome LDS Church Leader" banner across the balcony. Though Elder Hinckley grumbled quietly to his wife about such conspicuous attention, he wrote afterward in his journal: "We belong to the greatest society of friends on earth. . . . No matter where you meet them, no matter the language they speak, no matter whether they are round-eyed or almond-eyed, they are the same."[15]

One aspect of his call to the Twelve that bothered him at times was the attention paid him at every turn. It was embarrassing and sometimes distracting, not to mention dangerous. "Adulation is poison," he often said, and he meant it. He had been known to tell individuals assigned to introduce him, "I'd appreciate it if you'd just delete all the fancy talk and let us get on with the battle."[16]

Enduring any related attention on this trip was worth it, however, for while in Korea he dedicated the chapel of the East Seoul Branch, the first such building constructed on mainland Asia. It was an emotional experience for him to look into the faces of more than four hundred Korean Saints who had gathered for the historic event. "It was a big affair, with a capacity audience and city and government officials," Marjorie described in a letter home. "I thought surely Dad would let me off speaking, but he did not. . . . It was by far the best Korean audience I have ever seen. They were well dressed and well groomed. Every man had on a white shirt and tie and they were very sharp looking people. The reverence was something to behold." That the Korean Saints were delighted to have the Hinckleys with them was obvious. "These people are just great," she reported in the same letter. "They are so friendly and they make us feel like they are genuinely glad to see us. They came up to me by the dozens and said, 'I love you. Thank you for coming to Korea.'" The feeling was mutual. She wrote, "I feel sad in leaving Korea. Dad seems so sure that he is not coming back."[17]

In Naha, Okinawa, more than 350 members crowded into a new chapel that stood in the shadow of the Shuri line, where 21,000 American soldiers had died during one of the bloodiest campaigns of World War II. Kensei Nagamine, who later became the first stake president on Okinawa, remembered that meeting: "When Elder Hinckley dedicated our chapel he wept as he said, 'I love the people of Okinawa and the American people who are living in Okinawa.' As I was looking at Elder Hinckley and his weeping countenance, in him I saw the Savior represented and heard the Savior saying to me, 'Behold, my bowels are filled with compassion towards you.' This was seen not only by me, but also by many other people. We shall never forget the message of the Savior's love that he expressed to us who are here, scattered on these isles of the sea."[18]

This particular trip, marked by a series of chapel dedications, was evidence that Elder Hinckley's efforts to provide the Saints with facilities were bearing fruit. In Taipei he dedicated the first building erected by the Church in China, and in Manila nearly a thousand members crowded into the dedicatory services of the small Luzon District chapel.[19] It had been only five years since Elder Hinckley had inaugurated missionary work in the Philippines, and the growth there was astonishing. Sister Hinckley described the meeting in a letter to the family: "The dedication was a thrill. There were 1,000 there and they could all speak English. What a relief! . . . When I stood up I didn't know what in the world I was going to say, but we had the Spirit with us all through the meeting and we came out just walking on air. Dad has never done better. We shook hands with the entire congregation, which was very tiring but also very thrilling. The Filipinos are so affectionate and loving and warm. . . . The Church is simply going wild here."[20]

The chapel dedications throughout Asia filled Elder Hinckley's heart almost to bursting. Although the growth of the Church in Asia was infinitesimal when compared with the number of people yet to be reached, there had been progress during the six years he had been coming to the Orient. Everywhere he went, Elder Hinckley thanked the people for their faithfulness and hard work.

In Hong Kong mail from home caught up with the Hinckleys, and Marjorie expressed her delight in a quick reply. "Thank you, thank you, thank you for your letters," she wrote. "After three weeks I was getting to the point where I was dreaming about all of you every night . . . so it was wonderful to be reassured that all is well. I just wish I could enjoy this without wishing so much that you were here. . . . Let's all plan to come together sometime. I love every street in this crazy city." Her parting words were filled with characteristic enthusiasm and promise: "Be good children and work hard, so you can . . . see this gorgeous, wonderful world and meet all these wonderful people. It is the greatest thing in the world to be a Latter-day Saint."[21]

In Hong Kong, Elder Hinckley and Elder Marion D. Hanks of the First Council of the Seventy, who with his wife, Maxine, had joined the Hinckleys, met with the missionaries, after which Elder Hinckley recorded: "My spirits have been revived and my testimony enriched. . . . How marvelous to feel the spirit of these young men and women who dedicate their lives to the work of the Lord. As they were speaking, I looked over to a corner of the room and saw in my mind's eye a sailor who had dropped in on such a meeting some years ago while his ship was anchored in Hong Kong harbor. He was touched by the spirit of that meeting and out of the impressions of that day came his conversion. I met him in the eastern part of the United States the other day as a member of a branch presidency. Tomorrow we go to Vietnam. . . . I wonder how many of the good young men with whom I have talked today will . . . find themselves in the hot jungles of that sad land as soldiers of war."[22]

The next day, as Elders Hinckley and Hanks and President Keith Garner of the Southern Far East Mission soared over the delta country of the Mekong River en route to Saigon, Elder Hinckley observed how beautiful the land appeared—a stark contrast to the bloody conflict being played out on the terrain below. It was steamy hot as the three Church officials landed at Tan San Nhut Airport in Saigon. Elder Hinckley bounded off the aircraft first and greeted Major Allen C. Rozsa, the president of the South Vietnam Zone of the Church, with the words: "Your father sends his love. He is proud of you. I saw him not long ago in California." Major Rozsa said later: "Being in a combat situation, it was wonderful to hear something from home. Though I had never met him before, it was as though I had known Elder Hinckley all my life. He made us feel as though he really wanted to spend time with us."[23] After their initial interchange, Major Rozsa asked Elder Hinckley for his signature on a waiver absolving the U.S. military from liability while he was in Vietnam. It was an eerie beginning.

As an advisor to South Vietnam's Air Force Photographic Reconnaissance Squadron, Major Rozsa had arranged for a Vietnamese Air Force C-47 (with an American flight crew) to transport the Church leaders around Vietnam. They all climbed aboard the "Gooney Bird" and strapped themselves into uncomfortable basket-type seats along the sides of the cargo hold. Once the plane was airborne, Elder Hinckley noticed the camouflage coveralls and survival gear on a rack at the rear, though he doubted he would know what to do with them if it came to that. When he asked Major Rozsa if they were flying along a safe corridor, the major responded, "We're safe as long as we stay out of the range of enemy fire." Elder Hinckley was calm until the port motor began to lag and sputter. "Strange thoughts fill your mind under such circumstances," he admitted. "Our spirits lifted when the engine caught hold again."[24] As they approached Da Nang, Major Rozsa warned Elder Hinckley that if they were going to get shot, it would happen as they landed. Once safely on the ground, Elder Hinckley better understood the gravity of the situation as he watched an admiral's plane land with a five-helicopter escort.

In Da Nang the Church leaders were greeted by the base commander and then driven to a Quonset hut chapel to meet with more than a hundred LDS servicemen. What he experienced would etch itself indelibly in Elder Hinckley's mind. "I shall never forget that picture or that meeting," he wrote. "What a sight they were! What a wonderful group, these young brethren of ours. We loved them the minute we looked into their eyes."[25]

Dressed in battle fatigues, with mud caked on their boots, the soldiers had come down from the Rock Pile and Marble Mountain along the DMZ, where the fighting had been vicious and the smell of cordite and death hung in the air. As they entered the chapel, they stacked their M-16 automatic rifles along the two back rows and sat down, most of them with pistols on their right hips and knives on their left.

Three LDS men had died the previous week, and Elder Hinckley began the meeting with a memorial service and concluded by inviting anyone who so desired to bear his testimony. During his own remarks, Elder Hinckley offered to call the loved ones of anyone who asked, and almost every soldier listed a telephone number on an improvised sign-up sheet. "Elder Hinckley made us feel that we weren't forgotten," said Major Rozsa. "His visit boosted our morale in a phenomenal way. He made us feel that we were good, honest men, and that what we were doing was honorable."[26]

At six o'clock, the Air Force mess hall staff served dinner under the eaves of the Quonset hut. When a small group of Jewish servicemen approached the makeshift chapel for their scheduled Saturday evening meeting and saw the large contingent of LDS men, they invited them to use the building for the remainder of the evening—so Elder Hinckley convened another meeting with the soldiers. He lamented in his journal: "It was an experience both wonderful and depressing to be so close to these good young men, men who hold and honor the priesthood, men who are valiantly doing their duty as citizens of this country, but who would rather be doing something else. I thought as I talked with them that they ought to be in school . . . rather than walking fearsome patrols in the dark of the Asian jungle where death comes so quickly and quietly and definitely. These are the kids who ran and laughed and played ball back home, who drove the highways in old jalopies, who danced with lovely girls at the Gold and Green balls, who administered the sacrament on Sunday. These are boys who come from good homes where the linen is clean and showers are hot, who now sweat night and day in this troubled land, who are shot at and who shoot back, who have seen gaping wounds in a buddy's chest and who have killed those who would have killed them. I thought of the terrible inequality of sacrifice involved in the cause of human liberty."[27]

That night, with no guest quarters available, the Church leaders were loaded into a field ambulance and bounced along a rutted road until they came to an unfinished hospital where beds with clean sheets awaited them. Every few minutes throughout the night an F-4 Phantom jet roared overhead, traveling north at lightning speed. With each one Elder Hinckley wondered, "Will it come back?"

The next day Elder Hinckley and his group climbed aboard the Gooney Bird and lifted into the sky as dawn made its appearance across the South China Sea. Their first stop was Nha Trang, where they convened a meeting much like the one they'd held the night before, and then they returned to Saigon. Elders

Hinckley and Hanks had arrived in Southeast Asia with authorization from President McKay to dedicate South Vietnam for the preaching of the gospel if they felt impressed to do so. After their experiences of the past thirty-six hours, they believed such an action was in harmony with the Lord's will, so with the sound of mortar and cannon fire in the distance, they convened a meeting of 205 Church members and friends on the roof of Saigon's Caravelle Hotel. After the opening prayer, offered by Brother Nguyen Cao Minh, the first Vietnamese man ordained an elder in South Vietnam, President Garner and Elder Hanks gave inspirational messages. Elder Hinckley then spoke and offered a dedicatory prayer, in which he acknowledged the role that soldier–priesthood holders had played in introducing the gospel to native Vietnamese and pleaded with the Lord to touch the hearts of leaders and settle the conflict: "We have seen in other parts of Asia the manner in which thou hast turned the hand and the work of the adversary to the good and the blessing of many of thy children. And now we call upon thee at this time that thou wilt similarly pour out thy spirit upon this land."[28]

That evening Elder Hinckley presided over a final meeting in Saigon. Again, artillery fire crackled in the distance as those present bore testimony to each other. "Soldiers who know they may never return home have a unique perspective of life," said Major Rozsa, "and their testimonies were filled with great emotion and conviction. It was a profoundly moving meeting. I will never forget how we felt when Elder Hinckley told us he had stood at his brother's grave in France and thanked the Lord for the sacrifice of those who died protecting our freedom, and then told us there were no better LDS men on earth than those in uniform doing their duty as holders of the priesthood of God."[29]

The next morning Elder Hinckley and company took their leave of Major Rozsa, but as they lifted off and watched Saigon fade into the distance, Elder Hinckley's mind was filled with the haunting images of those with whom he had worshipped over the past forty-eight hours. He thought of the young man from a quiet country town who had seen sixty-eight of his company of seventy killed, and about soldiers who had contributed their combat pay differential—more than $3,000 by the men of the Saigon Branch on a single Sunday—to a fund for chapels they would never see or use. The horrors of war exceeded anything a peace-loving and God-fearing person could imagine or tolerate. But he believed the Lord would use these events for His good, as he expressed in a subsequent general conference: "I make no defense of the war from this pulpit. . . . I seek only to call your attention to that silver thread, small but radiant with hope, shining through the dark tapestry of war—namely, the establishment of a bridgehead, small and frail now; but which somehow, under the mysterious ways of God, will be strengthened, and from which someday shall spring forth a great work affecting for good the lives of large numbers of our Father's children who live in that part of the world. Of that I have a certain faith."[30]

The three priesthood leaders were reunited with their wives in Bangkok, where, on November 2, 1966, at 6:30 A.M., in Lupini Park, Elder Hinckley dedicated Thailand for the preaching of the gospel. Later that day he and his associates met with the minister of education and religion, who, after energetic discussion, agreed to open the way for missionaries to enter the country, though on a severely restricted basis. From Thailand, the Hinckleys, Hankses, and Garners flew to Calcutta, and after being thwarted in an attempt to stop in Madras went on to Bombay. The morning after their arrival there, they understood why their efforts to reach Madras had been blocked. A violent storm with hundred-mile-per-hour winds had struck the city, and ten thousand people were left homeless, rail traffic had ceased, and the airport was closed. From India the Hinckleys took leave of the Hankses and flew to the Holy Land before returning home.

As they flew westward, leaving behind them the Far and Near East, Elder Hinckley reflected on all he had experienced over the past five weeks. Testimonies borne in the midst of war, countries opened to the preaching of the gospel, the faithfulness of members separated from the body of Saints—there was much that bolstered his own faith. Likewise, he was encouraged by the growth of the work in Asia. Local leaders were emerging, and he had already identified several men who he felt would have tremendous influence in their respective countries. A number of new buildings had been dedicated or were being built, and by early next year the Korean edition of the Book of Mormon would be available.[31] He found himself thinking about the winter in

1839 when most of the Saints had been dispossessed of all they had and had fled across the bottomlands of the Mississippi to find asylum in Illinois, leaving Joseph Smith incarcerated in the Liberty jail. Under those circumstances, the word of the Lord had come to the Prophet: "The ends of the earth shall inquire after thy name, and fools shall have thee in derision, and hell shall rage against thee; while the pure in heart, and the wise, and the noble, and the virtuous, shall seek counsel, and authority, and blessings constantly from under thy hand." (D&C 122:1–2.) Elder Hinckley was witnessing, he believed, the fulfillment of prophecy.[32]

Marjorie and Gordon were also witnessing the fruits of their labors at home, for they had reached the stage of life where their family was scattering. Though it was satisfying to see their children mature and make sound choices, it was also difficult to watch their home empty. Dick had returned from his mission, graduated from the University of Utah, entered graduate school at Stanford University, and announced his intentions to marry Jane Freed; Clark had graduated from high school and was preparing for his mission; and Jane was soon to be a teenager.

In September 1965 Virginia had married James Pearce, which event had again ignited a flurry of remodeling as the Hinckleys prepared to host a second daughter's wedding reception in their backyard. They added a patio, improved the landscaping, and remodeled the kitchen slightly. Things went reasonably well until a few days before the wedding, when a stray horse helped itself to the new front lawn and left it looking as though a tractor had cultivated the ground for planting. The problem was solved by ingenuity, hard work, and some sod. Elder Hinckley officiated at Virginia and Jim's temple sealing, and that night the home and yard looked beautiful.

The evolving nature of his family's life was on Elder Hinckley's mind when he noted that New Year's Day in 1967 dawned as a "day of gladness and a day of sadness": "The largest measure of our joy comes from the fact that all of our children are with us, and our sorrow comes from the fact that it will be a good while, even years, before it will happen again." It was a happy table around which the large contingent of Hinckleys gathered for a holiday dinner. "All of this served to remind us that our family is leaving the nest," Elder Hinckley concluded in his journal entry. "Clark and Dick bade one another goodbye. It will be at least two years before they see one another again."[33]

Two months later Clark entered the LTM, bound for the North Argentine Mission. Not long after that the telltale signs of spring appeared at the Hinckley home, the most predictable of which was Gordon's annual "let's-sell-this-place-and-move-closer-to-town" refrain. Though it might have been more convenient to live closer to Church headquarters, neither Marjorie nor the children took seriously his routine complaints about the amount of work around "the place," or his threatened move. The home and lot had become permanently intertwined with his life, and everyone in the family knew it.

As Dick's wedding approached in July 1967, Marjorie took solace in the fact that this time the festivities would not call for a major overhaul of the yard or house, as the reception was being arranged for by the bride's parents. Her comfort was short-lived, however. When she and Gordon decided to host the wedding breakfast in their own home, and they determined that the dining room might not accommodate the crowd, he hit upon a logical solution. He would enclose the patio, add a fireplace for atmosphere, and then remove the wall between the dining room and patio so tables could be extended the full length of what would then be one large room. He would rebuild the wall after the wedding was over. As always, the last coat of paint was applied the night before the event.

The fuss didn't seem at all unusual to Dick, who took his father's unorthodox scheme in stride. It amazed his new wife, though, who had been at first apprehensive about dating an apostle's son and then relieved to find that Dick's family was a lot like hers—they laughed, chattered, teased, and generally enjoyed each other.[34] When she arrived at the Hinckley home for the wedding breakfast, however, she was astonished. "Dad and I didn't knock the wall and bay window out until the day before the wedding," Dick explained, "so Jane hadn't seen our renovation, and she couldn't believe her eyes. I suppose it was out of the ordinary. But we just did those sorts of things. Our house was relatively small, but Dad made up for it with ingenious improvisations."[35]

Despite going to great lengths for certain events, Elder Hinckley didn't encourage a great deal of socializing at home. He was a private man who found refuge there from his demanding schedule. A notable exception was the Hinckleys' annual hosting of the Windsor Club, which had met monthly for decades. Preparing to entertain some of their oldest friends was nothing short of an ordeal. The house and yard had to be perfect, so everyone in the family was recruited to prune, trim, dust, and deep-clean. Inevitably the event prompted some new project—pouring concrete, redoing flower boxes, painting entryways.

The Hinckley home had also become a gathering place for their Asian friends who traveled to Salt Lake City for general conferences. As Marjorie told her daughters, "I think the Orientals think that dinner at the Hinckleys after the Sunday afternoon session is a regular part of the conference program." Nevertheless, they loved feting their friends. At first the dinners were small affairs, but as the number of Asian visitors to Utah increased, so did the festivities at the Hinckleys', and the home was sometimes filled wall-to-wall with people.

Gordon and Marjorie also enjoyed their extended families. Marjorie in particular maintained close ties with her sisters. They enjoyed each other, confided in one another, were the first to come to each other's aid, and even took occasional trips together. Marjorie's attachment to her younger sisters made it even more difficult when in January 1967 her sister Helen was killed in an automobile accident, leaving her husband seriously injured and eight children without a mother.

As devastated as Marjorie was personally with her sister's death, it was more heartbreaking to see her niece and seven nephews mourning the loss of their mother. She couldn't help but think of the tens of thousands of miles she had traveled, in unfavorable weather and circumstances, and of the weeks she had been separated from her children. Yet her sister had died in an accident a few miles from home. Such a tragedy would be unbearable, she reflected, were it not for the hope of an eternal family. That knowledge had never been so poignant or appreciated.

▪ ▪ ▪ ▪ ▪

Three months later, on April 11, 1967, when Elder Hinckley left again for the Orient, Marjorie did not accompany him. He had mentioned to President McKay that no member of the First Presidency had ever been to mainland Asia, and asked if such an assignment might be considered. The prophet subsequently asked President Hugh B. Brown to make a tour of the Orient, and Elder Hinckley was accompanying him. Because he knew his attention and energy would be focused on President Brown, he felt it best that Marjorie remain at home. But it was with some reservation that he left her behind. "It was a little difficult to say good-bye to Marge and to leave for the Orient without her," he confided in his journal. "It is always so much better when she goes along."[36] After he had arrived in Hong Kong, he mentioned old friends with whom he had been reunited and added, "The only thing missing was my wife Marjorie."[37]

This trip took President Brown and Elder Hinckley to the Orient's primary metropolitan centers, with Elder Hinckley taking pains to make President McKay's eighty-three-year-old first counselor as comfortable as possible, even securing first-class accommodations rather than the economy seats with which he generally made do. Everywhere, large numbers of members and missionaries gathered to meet with the two Church leaders.

In more than one setting, President Brown prophesied about events to come. At a meeting of the Abeno Branch in Japan, a particularly unforgettable experience occurred. Elder Hinckley felt prompted to say there would someday be stakes in Japan, but that this depended upon the faithfulness of the youth. President Brown was visibly moved during the meeting, and he subsequently prophesied that some who were in the audience would live to see the day when a Japanese man would sit in the leading councils of the Church. "I do not know when that will happen," he said. "I will not live to see it, but some of you young people will. And I feel to make this prediction in the name of the Lord." He then added that they would also live to see the coming forth of further records, that the gospel would be preached to the Russians in their own country, and that Japanese missionaries would go to the people of kindred nations. It was, as Elder

Hinckley described it, an impressive pronouncement that those present would never forget. That evening Elder Hinckley discussed the day's events with his file leader. "I told President Brown that while I felt reluctant to say this, I had a feeling tonight that he would not live to see the fulfillment of that which he had said, but that I would, and that the Lord had sent me here to become acquainted with these people that I might be prepared when the day of fulfillment comes," he recorded.[38]

Nearly a hundred Saints gathered at the airport in Tokyo to bid farewell to the visiting Church authorities. Many carried flashlights, two of which they gave President Brown and Elder Hinckley so that they could signal to the crowd after they boarded the plane. "I have a great love in my heart for these good people of Japan," Elder Hinckley wrote, "and for all of our Saints throughout the Far East. It is always hard to leave them."[39]

There was, however, nothing quite like getting one's feet back on home soil, and Elder Hinckley was happy to be home. The day after his return he and Marjorie celebrated their thirtieth wedding anniversary. It hardly seemed possible—three decades together! He presented his wife with a diamond he had purchased in Hong Kong, and though it was larger and more vibrant than the one she had worn for three decades, she still preferred the original. "It has been a rich and wonderful experience," he reflected, "although when I look back upon our early years I shudder to think we had to get by on so little. This is probably a blessing, but it is almost frightening to realize how little we did manage with and at the same time build a house and have a family. I suppose that out of such experiences come the real joys of living."[40]

Elder Hinckley had been home less than two weeks from his Asian tour with President Brown when he left on another international trip, this time to South America. Despite having traveled hundreds of thousands of miles, he had never before set foot on South American soil. His first sighting of Rio de Janeiro from the air took his breath away; the ultramodern city flanked by two great arcs of oceanfront was stunning.

Though he met with mission presidents, missionaries, and gatherings of Saints during his ten days in Brazil, Argentina, Chile, Peru, and Mexico, the primary purpose for this trip was connected to Bonneville's ownership of WNYW, a shortwave station in New York City that had been purchased with the intention of improving communication with the Saints in Europe and South America. The station had never been profitable, however, and Elder Hinckley wanted an on-site appraisal of its potential in reaching the Latin American members.

His ten days in South America proved to be grueling. But when he returned to Salt Lake City, he possessed the information he had been seeking: WNYW was not effective and probably never would be; he subsequently recommended that Bonneville sell the property. Time would unveil other and better ways of communicating with Saints around the world.

Other problems had no easy resolution. For one, as the war in Vietnam dragged on, problems with the Selective Service continued to dog Elder Hinckley, and it seemed that one meeting after another, often charged with emotion, was required in order to keep the missionary program functioning. And then there was the semiannual dilemma of what to speak on in general conference. Though Elder Hinckley was regarded among his colleagues as an articulate man who spoke well even on a moment's notice, pulling together his address was nearly always an ordeal. Often he was still fussing with his message just days before conference. One spring he noted: "I am concerned about my General Conference talk. . . . Anyone not faced with this responsibility would have difficulty in appreciating the weight of the burden."[41] One fall he still did not have his talk prepared five days before conference was to begin, and he was "much worried." Two days later he noted, "I have been working on a conference talk, a constant recurring problem every six months. I worry much and pray much, and confidently hope that I will have something acceptable to the Lord and inspirational to those who listen."[42]

His struggle was rewarded on that occasion with an address he titled "Feed the Spirit—Nourish the Soul," in which he proclaimed that the forces against which honorable men and women labored were tremendous and that they must rely on more than their own strength. The October 1967 general conference was also memorable in that sixty-nine men were called to serve as Regional Representatives of the Twelve—evidence that the Church was moving forward.

With general conference behind him, Elder Hinckley was scheduled for another tour of Asia, and fortunately Marjorie was able to accompany him this time. That did not guarantee a perfect trip, however, and this one seemed jinxed from the outset. Typhoons played havoc with their itinerary, and then Elder Marion D. Hanks, who joined him in the Philippines, received word that his mother had passed away, necessitating his immediate return to the United States. With such setbacks, Elder Hinckley was unable alone to accomplish everything he had hoped. Following a meeting with the missionaries in Tokyo he admitted: "We had a good meeting, but I feel a deep regret over leaving here without having held with them a testimony meeting and interviewing them individually. I feel that I am not doing nearly as much good when I come on these visits now as I did years ago when I took the time to permit every missionary to bear his testimony and then had an individual interview with each missionary. However, there simply is not enough time."[43]

While in Osaka, Elder Hinckley met with officials of the World's Fair to be held there in 1970 and discussed possible locations for the Church's exhibit; in Kobe, he scouted sites for a new mission office, looking toward the division of the Northern Far East Mission. And once again, accompanied by President Keith Garner, he traveled to Saigon. The three thousand LDS servicemen scattered throughout the country were actively proselytizing among the Vietnamese, and there were now almost fifty native members of the Church.[44]

Despite a testimony meeting in Saigon in which servicemen had shared tender feelings about the gospel, after twenty-four hours in Vietnam, Elder Hinckley left for Bangkok feeling discouraged about the war. "I become angry when I think of the terrible bloodshed, the deaths and wounds of many good young Americans who ought to be going to school instead of fighting in these jungles, of the tens of thousands of orphan children, of the displaced refugees, . . . of thousands of illegitimate children born of American soldier fathers, of the corruption evident in the luxury one sees in Saigon made possible by the American presence with the expenditure of billions of dollars," he recorded.[45]

He thought of a poignant scene he had witnessed just a few days before leaving for Asia. In the Salt Lake Temple, he had performed a sealing for an Air Force fighter pilot assigned to Vietnam and his wife and three children. After the ordinance had been performed, the young husband and father had taken his family in his arms and wept at the knowledge that, regardless of the future, they were his forever now. Hours later, the pilot was on his way to Southeast Asia. How grateful Elder Hinckley was for the gospel, but how he wished there were no war to tear families apart.[46]

Despite his feelings of anguish for the LDS men stationed in Vietnam, he measured his words carefully. The last thing they needed was an apostle giving voice to the sentiment that they shouldn't be there in the first place. It wasn't always easy to hold his tongue. He was heartsick after visiting an American military hospital near Yokohama in an effort to locate Church members who had been evacuated from Vietnam. One young man's chest had been blown nearly away. Others had lost limbs or had been so tragically wounded or traumatized that they would never regain their faculties. He gave blessings to those who desired them and left feeling haunted about what he had seen.

His concerns about Vietnam were in stark contrast to what he experienced a few days later when he and Sister Hinckley checked in at the General Walker Hotel in Berchtesgaden, Germany, for a conference with nearly fifteen hundred LDS servicemen from as far away as Spain and the Azores. The hotel, which had served as a Nazi headquarters during World War II, sat high atop a hill overlooking a valley in the midst of the Bavarian Alps, which the season had painted an exquisite blend of green and gold.

During one meeting Elder Hinckley took as his text Doctrine and Covenants 50:23–24: "And that which doth not edify is not of God, and is darkness. That which is of God is light; and he that receiveth light, and continueth in God, receiveth more light; and that light groweth brighter and brighter until the perfect day." There, possibly in the same hall where a quarter century ago evil men had plotted the conquest of millions, the Saints bore testimony of Jesus Christ and contrasted those who walk in darkness with those who walk in light. That night Elder Hinckley recorded: "As I walk up and down the corridors of this old hotel I see in my mind's eye Nazi storm trooper sentries. . . . I am fascinated and intrigued with the sweetness of peace, equity, and justice in contrast with the terrible evils of war, a desire for conquest, and a terrible thirst for power."[47]

Repeatedly he reassured LDS servicemen that they could make a difference, often citing an experience he had had in Korea at a servicemen's retreat:

> I have been in many inspirational meetings in my life . . . but I think I have never been in a more inspirational meeting than one I attended in Korea. . . . The bread of the sacrament was administered that morning by a tall captain of infantry on whose chest were many campaign ribbons. He had been ordained a priest only that morning. . . . As he knelt at the sacrament table, he gave, with a quiver in his voice, that solemn and beautiful and simple prayer. Somehow the Spirit of the Lord went through that old Quonset-hut chapel in a marvelous and touching manner. When I opened my eyes, every man in that hall was weeping. . . . I was weeping too. After that, as each of the sixty-one men present bore his testimony, there was an outpouring of the Spirit of the Lord that was marvelous to experience.[48]

That meeting continued with another memorable experience:

> Then the water was administered to us by a sergeant who in his testimony afterwards said, "I grew up on the banks of the Susquehanna River and I almost inherited a hatred for the Mormons. I discovered when I was in the barracks in Korea that the man who was in the bunk next to mine was reading the Book of Mormon and I went over and started ribbing him. . . . I was mean and I was nasty. One night he got up out of his bed when I was saying something . . . and I have never seen a man stand so tall in all my life. And he held out the book and he said, "Have you ever read it?" I said, "No, of course not." And he said, "Here it is! Now you read it and you keep your mouth shut until you are through reading it and then we will talk about it." I didn't know what else to do—and I took it. And I began to read it, and as I read it, the Spirit of the Lord bore witness to me that it was true. And now I know why I was sent to Korea."[49]

These men who, in the midst of war, taught the gospel by example and precept had Elder Hinckley's deepest respect.

It was difficult to believe that Elder Hinckley had supervised the work in Asia for the better part of a decade. In 1960 it would have been impossible to know how profoundly the peoples of that vast continent would influence and affect him. Neither could he have predicted either the heartaches and frustrations or the joy and enlargement of soul and spirit that had come from his service there. From the jungles of Vietnam and the squalor of Calcutta to the quiet peace and symmetry of an American cemetery in Manila, his experiences had ranged from the heartbreaking to the sublime. And through it all, his own testimony of and conviction about the work had been magnified.

In turn, his influence upon the fledgling Church in Asia was equally great. He had traveled from branch to branch and taught men and women—at first in such small numbers that the future might have appeared dim—the fundamentals of gospel doctrine and administration. "In those early days the Church was an American Church," Han In Sang explained. "Missionaries would baptize and then hand us regulation books. Until Elder Hinckley started coming to Korea we weren't trained to be leaders. At times I was discouraged. In Oriental countries seniority is important, and I was younger than some of the others. One time Elder Hinckley said to me, 'Brother Han, I am lonely in this world and many times I have challenges, but the work is true. I'll bet you're lonely, aren't you?' Knowing he understood made it easier, and he gave that same kind of attention to many others."[50]

Through word and deed Elder Hinckley communicated his optimism for what was happening in Asia. After monsoon rains sent a wall of water cascading down a canyon near the mission home in Seoul, destroying both property and spirit, President Spencer J. Palmer's report to Elder Hinckley had the ring of a disheartened attitude. By return mail Elder Hinckley responded: "We have your letter of July 22, 1966, with reference to the flood, which engulfed the mission home property. Needless to say this was a frightening experience and doubtless a costly one. You may be interested to know that the night before the London Temple was dedicated we had a flood of serious proportions there. I stood in water to my waist with others bailing it out. This went on for hours. I only want to suggest that your experience is not peculiar to Korea. Noah had a worse time. Sincerely, your brother."[51]

"He expected us to take challenges on the chin," President Palmer explained. "He would bounce off the airplane ready to go to work, and his practical and sometimes humorous disposition in the face of difficulty was like a balm of Gilead. It was an ointment for all of us who sometimes felt that the challenges were just too great. His approach and personality were well suited to the peoples of Asia and the challenges there."[52]

Adney Y. Komatsu had similar experiences: "One of the things I appreciated about Elder Hinckley was that never once in my three years [as mission president] did he criticize me, despite all my weaknesses. . . . And that spurred me on. Every time he came . . . I thought, 'I'm going to get it right between the eyes this time. I didn't turn in this report properly or I didn't follow this program right.' But every time he came off the plane he would grab my hand like he was pumping water out of a well with great enthusiasm. 'Well, President Komatsu, how are you getting along? . . . You're doing great work.' He encouraged me like that . . . and when he left I felt I should give 105 percent, not just 100 percent. . . . He didn't come into my area and tell me all about the weaknesses that I already knew about."[53]

Elder Hinckley's frequent trips to and throughout the Orient gave him a familiarity with and working knowledge of the continent rare for an American in those days. When dignitaries, leaders, or experts connected with Asia called on Church headquarters, their visit almost always included a meeting with him. Dr. Ray C. Hillam, a professor of political science at BYU, recorded one such encounter: "During the late sixties . . . I accompanied Professor Robert Scalapino, a Harvard trained and UC Berkeley professor, to Elder Hinckley's office. Dr. Scalapino had just given a lecture on Asia at BYU and was at the time perhaps our country's leading scholar on the subject. It was a cordial visit. Elder Hinckley listened to him, asked questions and made several comments. We visited for almost an hour. Walking down the front steps of the building Scalapino turned to me and said: 'Who was that guy? He has historical perspective. He has read the literature on Asia. . . . Are all of your Church leaders that well informed?' "[54]

That the influence of Asia had penetrated Elder Hinckley's being was evident not only from his public statements on the subject but also from how frequently he referred to experiences there. After his trip in the fall of 1966 to dedicate Vietnam and meet with

LDS servicemen, he devoted an entire BYU devotional address to the subject, drawing almost exclusively upon the diary entries he had made throughout the trip. He began with characteristic light humor, telling his audience how they could react if they didn't care for the tone or text of his remarks: "Do what you do in some of your dull classes. Close your eyes and quietly dream of the girl who is sitting next to somebody else." Then he conceded that he had a "miserably difficult time" keeping a journal and that his entries were sporadic at best, added that he hoped no one would feel he was trying to inflate his own image, and then explained that he wished to share some of his experiences because of the effect they had had in building his testimony.[55]

At the next general conference, April 1967, he took the war in Vietnam as his text, praising LDS soldiers for their accomplishments in a hostile environment.[56] And a year later, at the April 1968 general conference, his address followed a similar theme: "I see the finger of the Lord plucking some good from the evil designs of the adversary. I see coming out of this conflict . . . an enlargement of the Lord's program." The growing membership in Okinawa, Japan, Korea, and the Philippines, he maintained, was the "sweet fruit of seed once planted in dark years of war and in the troubled days immediately following," when worthy priesthood bearers laid the foundation of the work to come.[57]

In addition to his frequent trips to Asia, Elder Hinckley continued to juggle numerous other responsibilities, many of them weighty. In November 1967, for example, he met with the First Presidency to present a new temple film, a project to which he had given general supervision for months. He was pleased when President McKay authorized him to proceed.

He also remained heavily involved with the missionary program. During one twenty-four-hour period, for example, he dealt both with a missionary who was excommunicated in the field for moral transgression and with the family of another who was killed in a tragic automobile accident. He noted in his journal that the excommunication depressed him for a good part of the day; the death broke his heart.[58] That same day he found himself the senior General Authority in the meeting of the Missionary Committee, which left with him the obligation of assigning new missionaries to their fields of labor. "This is a task from which I shrink because of the enormity of the responsibility," he wrote. "I have lived so long and so intimately with this missionary program that I think I have a very sensitive feeling about the importance of a missionary's assignment, not only in the area to which he is assigned but more particularly in the leadership under which he will work. Each time I have had this task I have pleaded with the Lord for direction and I have tried to listen for the whisperings of the Holy Spirit in making assignments. I know that many prayers are offered by missionary candidates, their parents and loved ones, and it is sometimes a frightening thing to recognize that I am the instrument through which the Lord will make manifest an answer to those prayers."[59]

With no more long trips scheduled before the end of 1967, Elder Hinckley was relieved to find a day here and there to spend in the yard. It was as much a relief to put on his old work clothes after being in suit and tie week after week as it was to do physical labor in the cool, crisp air of late autumn. With each new season, however, he was seriously beginning to wonder how long he, Marjorie, and Jane could stay in East Millcreek. Two days before Christmas he spent the day shining things up outside and shoveling snow from the walks. "I know I am growing older," he admitted, "because of my distaste for this kind of work. I don't know how I can keep up with the old place. In the wintertime I feel as if I am ready to move into an apartment."[60]

There were other indications that time was marching on. At year's end he reflected on life as he saw it: "Marge and I have the feeling that we are growing old. We have four grandchildren and streaks of gray hair. It is a melancholy feeling, and yet there is something pleasant and satisfying as we see our children grow to maturity and continue to walk in faith. . . . For us it has been a great year, and we look forward with anticipation to an even greater year in 1968."[61]

Perhaps he sensed that the days ahead promised to deliver an entirely new set of opportunities and challenges.

CHAPTER SIXTEEN

NEW CONTINENTS, NEW CHALLENGES

While Elder Hinckley enjoyed influence in faraway places, he also left his mark closer to home. Since Utah's earliest days as a territory, the Church had weathered attacks over social and moral issues from non-Mormons or disaffected members living there. In the spring of 1968 there was a dramatic resurgence of anti-Church sentiment, particularly in Salt Lake City, when a group of prominent citizens launched an intense and articulate campaign to legalize liquor-by-the-drink. The well-organized proponents of this measure, Utah Citizens for Legal Control of Alcoholic Beverages, quickly succeeded in convincing a large number of Utahns that the state's liquor laws restricted tourism, branded Utah as provincial, and encouraged the illegal sale of alcohol. Within a few weeks, more than forty thousand people had signed a petition to add the referendum to the ballot, and an early poll indicated that two-thirds of all eligible voters favored the measure.

Church leaders were deeply concerned about the issue, which they felt was laden with moral implications. Based on the precedent established in other states where liquor-by-the-drink had been legalized, they believed that easy access to alcohol would lead to an increase in welfare costs, crime, and accidents. After discussing the matter at length, the First Presidency and Quorum of the Twelve decided to actively oppose the measure, and they appointed Elders Marion G. Romney, Howard W. Hunter, and Gordon B. Hinckley to spearhead the Church's effort.[1]

Because one of his current committee assignments was with public affairs, Elder Hinckley was assigned to take the lead in orchestrating the Church's opposition to the issue. He immediately contacted longtime friend and advertising executive Wendell J. Ashton to help plan a strategy to oppose the referendum. They determined that because the issue affected the community at large it would be impossible to defeat the measure without ecumenical support; accordingly, they approached prominent Utahns and ministers of various faiths to make their campaign a multilateral affair. Respected non-LDS community leaders, including B. Z. Kastler Jr. and Richard Van Winkle, joined the Utahns Against Liquor-by-the-Drink committee. James E. Faust, a local attorney and president of the Cottonwood Stake, also participated. Though Elder Hinckley was himself not a member of the committee, he was instrumental in its organization and held initial strategy meetings in his office.

In early May, Elder Hinckley recommended that President McKay issue a statement in the *Deseret News* to help crystallize in the minds of members the attitude of Church leaders about the issue, which President McKay did. Then, on the afternoon of Sunday, May 12, under President N. Eldon Tanner's direction, Elder Hinckley convened a meeting of Regional Representatives and assigned them to encourage local priesthood and Relief Society leaders to spread the word about liquor-by-the-drink and to identify citizens who would speak out against the bill in local clubs and community groups. "We are headed for a real fight, and if we get licked it won't be because we did not try. We are going to give this all we can to win," Elder Hinckley told the assembled leaders. "We feel the Lord is on our side in this thing and it is time we stood up to be counted. I have heard the prophet speak on this matter, and that's all I need."[2]

Response to the Church's involvement in the issue was swift and emotional, and the community quickly divided over one of the most volatile topics to surface in Utah in years. Three days later Elder Hinckley noted in his journal: "The fat is in the fire. Sentiment is boiling up and down the state over this issue. We are being accused of trying to stop the democratic process."[3] Both major Salt Lake City newspapers published fiery editorials proclaiming either their advocacy of or opposition to the measure, and radio programs were monopolized by hot debate. On Sunday evening, June 23, Elder Hinckley outlined the Church's position in a KSL radio address. "The Church is not without experience in dealing with social problems," he explained. "With a worldwide membership, it knows something of the tragedies that result from broken homes, crime sprees, automobile fatalities, breadwinners who cannot qualify for employment, and the host of other evils . . . aggravated by alcohol." He concluded with an invitation for all citizens to join the fight against liquor-by-the-drink: "We hope that we can honestly differ with our friends who are promoting this enlargement of liquor availability. We hope we can do so without animosity or bitterness. Our disagreements are honest. Our convictions are firm."[4]

Throughout the summer and early fall, liquor-by-the-drink rhetoric became increasingly vitriolic. And although Elder Hinckley would have preferred to stay in the background, he had become identified as the Church's point man and therefore was the target of critics who resented the Church's interference in a "political" issue. His telephones at home and the office rang constantly as proponents took their frustration out on him directly and made their attacks and insults personal. Some went so far as to threaten him if he and the Church didn't back down.

Elder Hinckley referred to the debate in his October general conference address and, at the request of the General Authorities, went on the air the night before the election to make a final plea to those still vacillating on the issue. He was weary from the stress of the campaign and did not welcome the assignment, but again he reviewed the Church's rationale for its involvement: "[Critics] have singled out the Church as the culprit who has frustrated their well-laid plans. Of course the voice of the Church has been raised. The Church has spoken its opposition openly and frankly. It had a duty to do so. We did not raise this issue. But once it was raised, the Church would have been remiss in its obligation had it remained silent. This is a moral issue."[5]

Reactions to Elder Hinckley's appeal were immediate and disparate. "Elder Harold B. Lee called me as I walked in the house," he recorded in his journal. "He was very complimentary. . . . [But] as soon as Brother Lee hung up, a man called me and began swearing at me and the Church. Then a young man called who said that he was a returned missionary and thought it was none of the Church's business to speak out on this. . . . I went to bed feeling greatly depressed by the thought that I had accomplished no good and stirred up much antagonism."[6]

The next day voters defeated liquor-by-the-drink almost two to one.

Elder Hinckley's assignment with the campaign, though exasperating at times, was tailor-made for him. Through the years he had proven articulate and unflappable under fire. He projected and inspired confidence without appearing arrogant, and he was adept at relating with the non-LDS community. Hence, those who presided over him had developed confidence in his ability to represent the Church regarding delicate issues. His instincts for walking the fragile line between Church and state, responding to critics, and addressing volatile topics were finely honed. Elder Thomas S. Monson explained: "Brother Hinckley had done much creative designing of how to best present the Church's message. He rather enjoyed difficult assignments and was not shy when it came to dealing with foes of the Church. When anyone attacked the Church, Brother Hinckley stood ready to respond."[7]

Indeed, Elder Hinckley often inherited responsibility for shaping the Church's official position on challenging issues. In the late sixties Neal A. Maxwell, then University of Utah executive vice president, observed Elder Hinckley in action: "He was able and gifted as a communicator, but in addition to his prowess with language, he had a unique combination of candor and wisdom. His judgment in knowing how to handle delicate matters was impeccable, and it was obvious that the Brethren relied upon him heavily."[8]

The sixties had ushered in an era of widespread racial unrest. In 1963 Dr. Martin Luther King Jr. delivered his landmark "I have a dream" address on the steps of the Lincoln Memorial in Washington, D.C., and protests erupted throughout the country. The Church, whose doctrine restricted those of black descent from holding the priesthood, became an obvious target for charges of discrimination. Both nonmembers and members pressed Church leaders to at least clarify the Church's position if not revoke the restriction. On March 7, 1965, three hundred protestors marched on the Church Administration Building and demanded that the Church speak out in favor of civil rights. The situation became serious enough that, at times, uniformed guards were posted at the entrances to Church headquarters—a sorry and regrettable commentary, Elder Hinckley noted.

The athletic program at BYU came increasingly under fire as a visible symbol of the conflict. During 1968 and 1969, athletes from one school after another refused to compete against the Y and protestors marched outside stadiums and arenas where BYU had come to play ball. At Colorado State University, BYU's basketball squad was met by protestors carrying "Bigot Young University" signs and throwing flaming Molotov cocktails. *Sports Illustrated* reported that BYU was no longer certain whether an opponent would throw "a man-to-man defense, a zone, or a grenade."[9] As a member of the executive committee of BYU's board of trustees, Elder Hinckley was well aware of the controversy and the resultant unrest among BYU students. In May 1969 President Tanner asked him to address the sophomore class on the subject of brotherhood, acknowledging that the question of the blacks was foremost in the students' minds. To prepare for the assignment, Elder Hinckley immersed himself in everything he could find on the issue, and he found it to be broader and deeper than he had realized.

Late in October 1969, Elder Harold B. Lee determined that it was time for the Church to release a policy statement on the issue, and he committed his own feelings on the subject to writing and invited prominent educators Neal A. Maxwell and G. Homer Durham to do likewise. He then took all three position papers to Elder Hinckley and asked him to formulate from their combined thinking a statement on race and equal rights. The project was delicate and mentally exhausting, but Elder Hinckley produced a document that ultimately was released to priesthood leaders as an official Church statement.

Signed by Presidents Hugh B. Brown and N. Eldon Tanner, the December 15, 1969, statement reaffirmed the Church's conviction that all Americans deserved the rights guaranteed by the Constitution, but that religious practice was another matter. In a Church founded and dependent upon revelation, the question of who should hold the priesthood was the prerogative of God: "From the beginning of this dispensation, Joseph Smith and all succeeding presidents of the Church have taught that Negroes, while spirit children of a common Father, and the progeny of our earthly parents Adam and Eve, were not yet to receive the priesthood, for reasons which we believe are known to God, but which He has not made fully known to man. . . . Were we the leaders of an enterprise created by ourselves and operated only according to our own earthly wisdom, it would be a simple thing to act according to popular will. But we believe that this work is directed by God and that the conferring of the priesthood must await His revelation. To do otherwise would be to deny the very premise on which the Church is established."[10]

Despite its careful construction, the statement did not put an end to racial criticism directed toward the Church. This was only one of many assignments that forced Elder Hinckley to consider carefully issues related to the integration of all members into the mainstream of the Church. At the First Presidency's request, he and Elders Thomas S. Monson and Boyd K. Packer carefully studied the situation of blacks in the Church; their work led to the formation, on October 19, 1971, of the Genesis Group of the Liberty Stake. Under this program, black members of the Church remained members of their own wards but joined with other LDS blacks for auxiliary meetings and activities.

Elder Hinckley appreciated assignments that allowed him to become better acquainted with the unique challenges faced by all kinds of people. Certainly that had been the case in Asia. During the past eight years he had made more than twenty trips to the Orient and had spent an equivalent of two full years traveling there. It was a schedule that had left him exhausted from crossing the international date line again and again. Travel was an unforgiving taskmaster. Delays and turbulence from inclement weather, the constant change in time zones, packing and unpacking the same clothes in the same suitcase, missed connections—all were part of his routine.

One day after one more layover in one more airport, Elder Hinckley described the tedium: "I came in at Gate K-1 and walked down the concourse to the TV screen to see that flight 315 would depart from H-1. I went to H-1, only to be told that I could not check in for another twenty minutes. I found a chair. It was molded plastic, strictly utilitarian, and sat where ten thousand before me had sat only briefly in an odyssey taking them from Podunk to Megalopolis or from Megalopolis to Podunk."[11]

Being a General Authority was synonymous with fatigue, and jet lag was something Elder Hinckley learned to live with. Whether returning from an extended journey or a weekend trip to preside at a stake conference, he was tired. The pressure of being spiritually in tune so that inspiration would flow through him to a congregation was invigorating while it was happening—but he paid the price afterward. And he usually returned to a desk piled with work.

The best remedy for the pressure, workload, and travel was pounding nails, planting trees, or puttering about the yard. After spending a Veteran's Day holiday at home, he noted: "It has been like medicine to be out in the air. I need a certain amount of this to keep my balance, both physically and mentally. . . . Man was made to plant his feet on the soft earth once in a while. . . . This place of ours is a burden, but it is nice to be able to walk around among the trees on the lawn without bumping elbows with anybody."[12] Ironically, that same day he and Marjorie took Jane house hunting to explore the possibility of moving closer to downtown.

There was little time, however, to look seriously for property. His premonition during a spring trip to Asia that it might be his last for some time proved well founded, for on June 1, 1968, Elder Hinckley was released from his supervisory role over the Orient and assigned to oversee the work in South America. Clark was serving in Argentina, so Elder and Sister Hinckley regularly heard their son's reports about the work there, but he had visited that continent only once. He knew there was one stake each in São Paulo, Brazil; Buenos Aires, Argentina; and Montevideo, Uruguay.[13] Beyond that, he knew little about the huge continent that stretched from Caracas in the north to Cape Horn at its southernmost tip.

Elder Hinckley accepted the assignment with mixed emotions. He was eager to become acquainted with a new part of the world, but he had come to feel at home in Asia. On his first trip there he had struggled even to distinguish the Oriental Saints one from another. But over the years they had become his cherished friends. He had borne testimony to groups large and small, in makeshift chapels and in Quonset huts with the sound of gunfire punctuating the night air. He had endured the sweltering heat of Manila, the monsoon rains of Korea, and the bitter cold of northern Japan. Nonetheless, it was difficult to realize that it might be some time before he flew west over the Pacific again.

But for now, he turned his attention to South America. His brief experience there suggested that though the Church was still small, this continent held the promise of a fruitful missionary harvest.[14] In late November 1968, Elder and Sister Hinckley left for their first tour of South America, arriving in São Paulo on Marjorie's birthday. "I told [Marge] long ago I would take her somewhere on her birthday," Elder Hinckley quipped in his journal. "South America is quite somewhere."[15]

They stepped off the plane to find a beautiful day with flowers in bloom all around. While Salt Lake City was moving toward the deep night of winter, Brazil was basking in spring. Elder Hinckley immediately attended to his first order of business—dividing the one São Paulo stake into two. It became quickly apparent that a young bishop, Helio da Rocha Camargo, was to be the stake president, but Elder Hinckley was concerned about some unique challenges in organizing this particular stake. After hours of interviews he returned to the hotel and, joining a large number of mosquitoes that had taken up residence there, put his head on the pillow and fell asleep. His slumber was fitful, however, and by 2:00 A.M. he was wide awake and agonizing over the reorganization. "The problem was the most complex of any I have ever faced in the creation of a new stake," he wrote. "But out of these thoughts in the middle of the night came some rather clear ideas as to how it should be handled."[16] The next day, nearly 1700 Saints crowded into the stake center as Elder Hinckley created the São Paulo East Stake. This meeting was believed to be the largest congregation of Latter-day Saints ever assembled up to that time in South America.[17]

From São Paulo the Hinckleys flew to Rio de Janeiro, where he spent the better part of two days, from early morning until past ten o'clock at night, in meetings with the ten mission presidents from South America. After the third day in Rio, the pace and exhaustion caught up with him: "I have picked up something. My resistance seems so low. I got up wheezing and asthmatic this morning. I felt so weak I could scarcely get to our meetings." Later that day a doctor detected the beginnings of pneumonia and prescribed medication that left him feeling "as dopey as an old owl."[18]

Nonetheless, he and Sister Hinckley pressed on to Cordoba, Argentina. They arrived on Thanksgiving Day and were delighted to be reunited with their son Clark, who was serving in the North Argentine Mission under President Richard G. Scott. Though Clark was anxious to see his parents, the situation was awkward for him, as Elder Hinckley recorded: "He was placed in a difficult position because we were greeted with fanfare, and I think he felt a little embarrassed. When we got to the mission office we visited with him for a little while, and he loosened up to his own good happy self again."[19] From Clark's point of view it was "spectacular to have a General Authority come to Argentina, and it was a bonus to have him be my father. I had never been in a missionary setting with Dad, and I soon found that I was in for a real experience."[20]

Elder Hinckley quickly learned that travel in Argentina would also be quite an experience. Domestic flights were "about as dependable as the weather in Chicago," as he described it. Consequently, the Hinckleys frequently ended up driving with President Scott all night on rough, winding roads. One morning they were to have flown to Tucuman in northern Argentina, but the flight was suddenly canceled, so they began the 700-kilometer drive around noon and arrived eight hours later to find a chapel full of Saints waiting for Elder Hinckley to dedicate their building. After the meeting he shook hands and signed his autograph hundreds of times—a practice he did not relish. He recognized, however, that the gesture made an important statement to those who requested it. When the local leaders asked if he would then hold a fireside for the youth, Elder Hinckley felt the hour was too late. But he changed his mind after being assured that this was customary in Argentina, where early-afternoon siestas encouraged people to stay up late. He found that this pattern was typical, and often he didn't conclude meetings, firesides, and even interviews with local television stations until nearly midnight.

On several occasions Clark was pressed into service translating for his mother. "Mother started telling pioneer stories and I couldn't think of the words for *covered wagons*," he remembered later. "But it was quite an experience to translate for her as she bore her testimony to the missionaries and members who were my friends."[21] And he, along with his fellow missionaries, was interviewed personally by Elder Hinckley, who found the mission under President Scott to have excellent leadership. For his part, President Scott relished his time with Elder Hinckley. "As we drove from city to city, he used the time to teach me," he related. "I learned about doctrine, about how to interview missionaries when they had specific problems, about Church government and what counsel to give in various situations. He built me and made me feel that I had the capacity to do what was required of me."[22]

After five days in Argentina, the Hinckleys rode to the airport with President Scott and Clark. Marjorie became tearful as she said good-bye to her younger son, but Elder Hinckley was more pragmatic: "I felt all right about leaving him there and had practically no pangs of emotion. He seemed to be happy, and I think he was a little glad to get us out of the way so that he could do his part without feeling some embarrassment. I am sure that we cramped his style a little while we have been here."[23] Marjorie now understood why it was unwise for parents to visit children serving in the field.

At the conclusion of their visit, Elder Hinckley recorded: "It has been a quick tour, two weeks in length, which is just about right. I can handle this sort of thing; but when it stretches out to a month or two months, as I have taken in the Orient, I come back much too tired. I know that I am getting older because of the weariness that I feel while traveling and interviewing hundreds of missionaries."[24]

How different South America was from the Orient! But the people, despite vast cultural differences, were similar in their response to the message of Jesus Christ and in their desire to do good. Elder Hinckley was optimistic about the progress of the

Church in South America, which appeared to be poised on the brink of explosive growth. He also felt that the future of the Church globally had never been better. In a subsequent general conference address he stated with confidence: "I stand here today as an optimist concerning the work of the Lord. I cannot believe that God has established his work in the earth to have it fail. I cannot believe that it is getting weaker. I know that it is getting stronger. I realize, of course, that we are beset with many tragic problems. . . . I have seen a good deal of this earth. I have seen its rot and smelled its filth. I have been in areas where war rages and hate smolders in the hearts of people. . . . I have watched with alarm the crumbling morals of our society. And yet I am an optimist. I have a simple and solemn faith that right will triumph and that truth will prevail."[25]

Part of Elder Hinckley's optimism lay in his confidence in youth, and he repeatedly praised them for their integrity and proclaimed them to be the best generation who had ever lived.[26] In his own family, Elder Hinckley saw the strength of the children he and Sister Hinckley had lived with for many years. As they matured and began to rear families of their own, he was impressed with the power of their convictions. During one meeting of the Twelve in the temple, he found himself pondering the things for which he was most grateful. "I thought of the blessings of a choice companion, a woman of great faith and ability, a remarkable mother who is loved by her children. For the blessing of those children I have felt a deep gratitude this day. They are all good and able children. The three older ones are all happily married in the temple. . . . Each is prospering under the hand of the Lord. . . . A week or so ago Clark said in a letter, 'There is no place in the world I would rather be now than where I am at this time.' What a wonderful thing to have a son with that attitude. Our youngest is Jane, now 14. What a joy to have her still at home—a bright and beautiful child. . . . It is a delight to hear her pray."[27]

He relished also his opportunities to worship and work with the Brethren in his quorum, where there was a unity unlike anything he had before experienced. Absent from their discussions was the grandstanding, posturing, or politicizing that could be found in the governing bodies of most institutions. Instead, as they petitioned the Lord for guidance, the Spirit often attended them in such abundance that words failed him in describing what he experienced or felt.

"There is a tremendous brotherhood in the quorum," Elder Hinckley later explained. "I was free to speak on any issue, despite the fact that I was a junior member. Here was a body of twelve men—fifteen when the First Presidency joined us—all of whom came from different backgrounds, who represented different points of view, and whose Church experiences varied widely. Obviously there were differences of viewpoint or opinion on many subjects. Yet we were each expected to speak forthrightly. That's why we were there." At times, their deliberations were both long and energetic. "There was never animosity in the council, however, which made us able to discuss the most sensitive of subjects," he continued. "As a discussion developed, a synthesizing took place, a melding of opinions. And when all was said and done, and the President of the Church spoke, everyone agreed. Whatever a man's conviction might have been earlier, the new opinion became his own. There was complete unanimity, else no action was taken."[28]

Often as Elder Hinckley sat in their council room on the fourth floor of the Salt Lake Temple, he thought of the men who had preceded him there: the brilliant John A. Widtsoe; Stephen L Richards, his mentor and friend; Melvin J. Ballard, the great missionary apostle; and others. "As I sat in the meeting of the Twelve this morning," he wrote on one occasion, "I wondered how I could be where they had been. I felt subdued and humbled and grateful for the blessings of the Lord."[29] Always in the recesses of his mind was an awareness of the mantle he bore: "The responsibility of standing as a special witness for the Lord weighs on you constantly, and it is a very sobering thing. But there is something wonderful about such a call, in that it puts one in a position to help those in need."[30]

The longer Elder Hinckley functioned as a member of the quorum, the better he understood Elder Widtsoe's response to someone who had asked, "How long has it been since we last had revelation?" "Oh, about last Thursday," he replied. Elder Hinckley had often seen earnest prayer and sincere discussion of weighty matters open the way for the Lord to direct His church.

At times he worried that the General Authorities weren't doing enough to help members understand the vast revelatory and spiritual powers available to all who sought and lived worthy of such direction. After previewing a film the Brethren were to use in forthcoming stake conferences, he recorded his concern: "I fear that we are going out as film jockeys, rather than as servants of the Lord and prophets to the people to teach the doctrines of salvation which are so much needed. While it is true that these films help as teaching aids, I feel strongly that we need to give more inspiration from the Lord to the people of the stakes. Anyone can show a film, but not everyone can speak as General Authorities of the Church. The people hunger for spiritual nourishment, and I feel it is our place to give this."[31]

This theme was frequently on his mind, enough so that he directed one general conference address to the topic, admonishing members to awaken to the powers of God available to them. "The forces against which we labor are tremendous," he taught. "We need more than our own strength to cope with them. To all who hold positions of leadership, to the vast corps of teachers and missionaries, to heads of families, I should like to make a plea: In all you do, feed the spirit—nourish the soul. . . . I am satisfied that the world is starved for spiritual food."[32] On another occasion he challenged BYU's faculty and staff to "try a little harder to breathe a little more of the spirit of testimony into all that you teach. Teach faith in God, the Father of us all, the Creator of the universe, a living, personal Being to whom we may go in prayer with full expectation that our prayers will be heard and answered according to His will and wisdom."[33]

Some aspects of his calling as an apostle were satisfying and yet caused inordinate strain—among them, handling the volume of administrative assignments while not letting them overshadow his ministry. Elder Hinckley routinely lamented that he needed more time to think, ponder, and study, and only on rare weekends home could he indulge in such reflection. For the most part, however, he raced from one assignment, appointment, committee, or board meeting to another. There were days—perhaps more the rule than the exception—when he did little more than endure one round of meetings after another. Thus time passed, as he described it, "like lightning."[34] In September 1966 he and Presidents Hugh B. Brown and N. Eldon Tanner signed as incorporators of Deseret Management Corporation (DMC), which consolidated under one corporation all Church-owned businesses. With his responsibilities now as chairman of the executive committees of both DMC and Bonneville International, as a member of KIRO's board and executive committee, and as a member of the Beneficial Life Insurance and Deseret News boards, it was a wonder that he accepted the invitation of Zion's Bank president Roy Simmons to join the board of that institution in January 1968.

Later, on June 29, 1971, he was named president and chairman of the executive committee of the Deseret News Publishing Company at the same time Elder Thomas S. Monson was named vice president and vice chairman. The paper faced a declining circulation and profitability, and the assignment was not an easy one. The following year he accepted an appointment to the Utah Power and Light board of directors, though he wondered how he would work one more assignment into his schedule. The invitation was a compliment, however: The last General Authority to sit on this board had been Stephen L Richards. He did enjoy affiliating with businessmen of talent and influence and was eager to be tutored in the art of industry.

In his deliberations on boards of directors and as a member of the Twelve, Elder Hinckley distinguished himself as a financial conservative who deplored debt and waste. He admired thrift and often made note in his journal of those he met who, despite prosperity, lived prudently. Though he appreciated staying in comfortable hotels, he shunned anything lavish. He was concerned with operations that weren't profitable, and skeptical about business proposals that did not dot every *i*, cross every *t*, and all but guarantee a bottom-line return. He was, however, willing to support unprofitable ventures if it appeared that by sound business practices they could be turned around. He seemed able to distinguish between foolish financial profligacy and the need on occasion to make important investments—whether they be in people, buildings, or companies.

At Church headquarters, Elder Hinckley's assignments included the Missionary Executive, Correlation, Servicemen's,

Church Information, and Military Relations Committees, the Church Board of Education, and the "Heartbreak Committee" (which considered the cases of those who had been excommunicated). The latter assignment weighed on him heavily, as he indicated after one meeting: "More heartaches and more heartbreaks occur over sin than one can imagine. Oh, if only our people could see the tragedy of infidelity before it happens, they would discipline themselves more so that it would not happen."[35]

Since 1961 he had chaired the Children's Correlation Committee, and in 1970 he was appointed the advisor to the Sunday School and Primary.[36] With these assignments occupying his time and attention, he often took the subject of rearing and teaching children as a theme. In one conference address he told of a thornless honey locust tree he had planted that was so supple he could have tied it in a knot. Then he had forgotten all about it. Some years later he noticed that the tree leaned far to one side, and with a block and tackle he tried without success to reshape the tree that was now more than a foot in diameter. With no other options, he cut off a large limb. The tree subsequently straightened somewhat, though it developed a scar where it had been cut. He summarized: "Once it could have been kept straight with a string for an anchor. Now neither block and tackle nor pruning saw can make up for the neglect of its younger years. It is so with people. It takes only a string, as it were, to help children grow strong and straight in the Church."[37]

For years Elder Hinckley had shaped missionaries and mission presidents, and as a member of the Missionary Executive Committee he continued to be involved with nearly every facet of the missionary program. On one occasion, after meeting with a young man whose lifestyle had disqualified him for missionary service, he wrote: "It became necessary to tell him that he would not be permitted to go on his mission and to call his father, a member of the stake presidency, and give this news to him. These circumstances are always heartbreaking. I could have wept for the young man and also for his father."[38]

Signs of progress made worthwhile the pressures and demands of his calling. For several years some language training had been provided for missionaries learning Spanish, German, and Portuguese; in January 1969, a two-month program of language training was implemented for all missionaries called to foreign-language missions. In June of that year the first missionaries were sent to Spain, a move that not only represented a significant step forward in Europe but was of personal interest to the Hinckleys when Clark was asked to extend his mission and help open the work there. At the general conference in April 1970, Elder Hinckley summarized: "I express thanks and wonder for the marvelous growth of the Church. . . . The days of which our forebears spoke are upon us. These are days of prophecy fulfilled; and I, with you, am grateful to be alive and a part of this vibrant, marvelous work."[39]

Elder Hinckley continued to look after the portion of the vineyard assigned to his care, and after general conference in April 1969 he left once again for South America. With Virginia due to deliver twins, Marjorie stayed behind, feeling that her responsibility lay with her daughter. "With a little difficulty and real disappointment we bade each other goodbye," he wrote after their parting at the airport. He headed first for Omaha, where he gave Ginny a father's blessing, and then on to Peru, Chile, Argentina, Bolivia, Ecuador, Colombia, and Venezuela.[40] From country to country, and in one audience after another, he spoke of the need to strengthen families and homes, often repeating what he had stated at a recent general conference: "Fathers and mothers are needed who will rise and stand upon their feet to make of their homes sanctuaries in which children will grow in a spirit of obedience, industry, and fidelity to tested standards of conduct. If our society is coming apart at the seams, it is because the tailor and the seamstress in the home are not producing the kind of stitching that will hold under stress."[41] He also taught priesthood leaders that the full-time elders and sisters were missionaries to the nonmembers, that home teachers were missionaries to the members, and that the Church could not succeed unless both functioned effectively.[42]

Elder Hinckley's stop in Bolivia was his first visit there, and he quickly learned that arriving in La Paz in the central Andes was an experience like no other: "You feel all right at first," he wrote after landing at the highest commercial airport in the world, "but if you start to move around quickly, you begin to feel a little lightheaded." He was equally intrigued with the appearance of the native Indian people: "They are living for the most part in conditions bordering on the verge of desperation. Their poverty is so terrible. As we rode among them down into the city, I could not help reflecting on the glory that was once the sons of Lehi and of their terrible downfall. . . . My heart ached for the [people]. They deserve better."[43] Despite conditions, he found the missionaries in excellent spirits and devoted to their work. "This is one of the amazing and wonderful things of the Church," Elder Hinckley noted, "to see the young people, who live under difficult circumstances and who have come out of such comfortable homes, express such tremendous love for the land and the people with which they labor."[44]

In Venezuela, a cable from Pan Am caught up with Elder Hinckley, informing him that "the señoritas had arrived safely and all is well with Mrs. Pearce"—Ginny's twins had been born. On his return home, he detoured to Omaha for a reunion with Marjorie and a visit with his daughter and new grandchildren, whom he called a "forecast of much work." After the overnight stop, he once again bade farewell to his wife, "a thing I do too frequently, it seems to me," he wrote in his journal. "Yesterday was our wedding anniversary. We have been married for thirty-two years. I think our love is stronger than it was when we were married."[45]

Elder Hinckley was grateful that Marjorie was able to join him on his next trip to South America four months later, this time with stops in Brazil, Argentina, and Uruguay. He occasionally wondered if the constant travel was justified, but circumstances he encountered in one country convinced him that regular visits from General Authorities were necessary or there would soon be "a thousand splinter groups who would be pursuing rainbows only remotely related to the true program of the Church."[46] But there were also signs of progress. At a meeting of the São Paulo East Stake, there were nearly as many members present as there had been the year previous when he had divided the stake—an illustration, Elder Hinckley noted, that divisions promote growth and activity.

It was satisfying to note such improvement, for the extensive travel did not come without personal sacrifice. He and Marjorie were in Brazil when Clark arrived home from his mission. Elder

Hinckley was more pragmatic about the situation than was his wife. "Marge is homesick and somewhat depressed over not being at home when he arrives," he wrote. "However, our children and we are coming and going so much that these matters don't seem to bother us. We will arrive home to find him very busy with his own affairs, and this will be the case probably from here on out."[47] These were the times when Sister Hinckley dreamed of a more traditional life. Everyone in the family, however, had learned to cope with, if not always appreciate, their father's unusual regimen. Whereas in earlier years Jane had refused to go along when her mother took her father to the airport, for fear of bursting into tears, she now gave him a peck on the cheek as though he would be home from the office that evening.

In addition to ongoing family adjustments and challenges, other difficult circumstances lay just ahead. Early Sunday morning, January 18, 1970, Elder Hinckley was presiding over a stake conference in Idaho when he received word that President David O. McKay had passed away. Though the ninety-six-year-old prophet had been in poor health for some time, the news was nevertheless jolting. Throughout the day Elder Hinckley could not stop thinking about President McKay, the gracious and commanding figure with whom he had enjoyed a marvelous personal association. His mind raced back to that day in 1935 when President McKay had invited him to work for the Church, and to the many Sunday mornings the two of them had spent on the fifth floor of the Salt Lake Temple. "The 18th of January 1970 will go down as an historic day in the history of the Church," he noted that night in his journal, "for today we have lost one of the truly great men of this dispensation."[48] When he and Marjorie paid their respects to the McKay family at a private viewing, he thought the Church President looked at least twenty years younger than his age. He had been a striking man in life, and he was a handsome figure in death.

On January 22, a capacity Tabernacle audience heard President McKay eulogized as a dynamic Church President and prophet of God. The following day, Elder Hinckley joined the other apostles in the upper room of the Salt Lake Temple to reorganize the First Presidency. It was his first opportunity to participate in the solemn and sacred process of ordaining a new President of the Church, and the experience was profound in its simplicity and magnitude.

After each member of the Twelve had opportunity to express his feelings and all agreed that the reorganization should proceed without delay, President Joseph Fielding Smith was ordained President of the Church. He in turn named Elders Harold B. Lee and N. Eldon Tanner as counselors. Because President Lee would be serving in the First Presidency, Elder Spencer W. Kimball was named Acting President of the Quorum of the Twelve.

Elder Hinckley had no hesitation about the divinity of President Smith's call. "Joseph Fielding Smith had the reputation of being stern," he remembered. "But he was a gentle, gracious, fair man. If I were in trouble, I would rather have him sit in judgment of me than almost any other man. He was a very kind man."[49]

A few days after President McKay's death, Elder Hinckley faced a loss more personal. For some time his youngest sister, Sylvia Wadsworth, had suffered from cancer in a roller-coaster ordeal all too reminiscent of their mother's battle with the dread disease. After his Thursday temple meeting on January 29, he learned that she had taken a turn for the worse; he dashed to the airport and was soon airborne for Cedar City, Utah, where she was hospitalized. Gordon was shocked when he saw his sister, just forty-nine, who was obviously failing. Though he was impressed to promise her in a blessing that she would not go immediately, he felt that she would soon be called home. When she waved as he left the room, Gordon smiled while reining in his emotions. He knew he would not see her alive again.

Four days later Sylvia died. She had asked to be buried in Panaca, Nevada, where she and her husband had lived most of their lives, so Gordon, Marjorie, and Jane drove to Nevada for the funeral, and Dick and his wife, Jane, joined them from Los Angeles. A few miles out of Panaca, Gordon came up behind the hearse carrying his sister's body. "We followed it all the way into town," he recorded, "and somehow there was a small measure of comfort in this—that I was with her and in a sense watching over her on this last earthly ride."

Before the funeral, Gordon asked his nephew Bryant to take him to the cemetery where she would be buried. They drove up a dusty road to a fenced field on the edge of town. Just inside the gate was the open grave, freshly dug in soft, sandy soil. "It was too much for me," he wrote. "I cried in that lonely, quiet place, and cried as no grown man should cry. Here was to be the burial place of my youngest sister. . . . Now as I walked quietly about the little cemetery a certain bitterness struck me—that she of such great promise should come to so dismal an end. I cried, and then a peace came into my heart. . . . I thought of her ten children who had grown from the soil of this community. This is where she had been most loved, and one ought to lie where one is loved. I felt at peace."[50]

There were other tender and inspiring moments soon to come. On a trip to South America in February and March of 1970, during which Elder Hinckley organized the Lima Peru Stake, he and Marjorie visited Machu Picchu, where they spent three hours wandering up and down the terraces amid what had once been magnificent courts and temples. The next day, on a train ride through the Andes en route to Bolivia via Lake Titicaca, they got a close-up look at the people and culture. "We are hounded by boys selling chocolate and chicle, by girls selling bananas and oranges, by women selling bread, and by men selling trinkets," Elder Hinckley wrote of the experience. "They board at one station, get off at the next, and are replaced by another group just as persistent and noisy. . . . As we move along Marge reads Prescott's monumental 'Conquest of Peru.' It is a story of cruelty and oppression, and its tragic fruits are the Indians we see about us. We finally reach the top of the pass. At the side of the track the sign says La Raya. . . . 14,712 feet. We are really up in the air, and the atmosphere is thin, dry, and cold. . . . Following the long descent, we travel a great distance across the altiplano of Peru. This is the high, flat table land found here and in Bolivia. This part of the world looks like the Sweetwater area of Wyoming."[51]

As they pulled into Juliaca in southern Peru, Elder Hinckley suggested that Marjorie be on the lookout for missionaries. She laughed at the thought that anyone would be waiting for them in such a remote way station. "Maybe they get lonely and watch the trains coming in," he countered, at which precise moment Marjorie screamed, for there stood a pair of elders scanning the cars as they rolled by, hoping to spot Elder and Sister Hinckley, whom they had heard *might* be passing through. The two young men whisked the Hinckleys off to a gathering of members in nearby Puno, their first visit ever from a General Authority.

After the brief meeting, Elder and Sister Hinckley boarded a steamship for an overnight trip across Lake Titicaca. He hadn't been in a less comfortable bed since a fathers-and-sons outing with Clark when he'd slept on a rock all night, which ever after became the standard against which to measure a poor night's rest. Nevertheless, meeting the Saints in this lonely outpost compensated for the inconvenience.

With each trip to South America, Elder Hinckley's admiration and affection for the Saints increased. Many of them struggled to scratch out a living, but from one country and congregation to another he marvelled at the faithfulness of men and women who seemed endowed with an unusual degree of spiritual strength and sensitivity.

He also often contemplated the unique heritage that was theirs. During one zone conference in Quito, Ecuador, in which the Spirit was penetrating, he told the missionaries, "I am impressed that today we have been in the presence of some of the prophets of the Book of Mormon, and I think that they are concerned about what you are doing to see that their children are taught the gospel."[52] On another occasion he marvelled at a large turnout for a conference in La Paz: "A chorus sang in the Aymara language. They were mostly Indians, and as I listened to them there kept going through my mind the prophecies of the Book of Mormon that in the latter days the 'shackles of darkness would fall from the eyes' of the descendants of father Lehi. . . . We had several native speakers, and they all did well. All were of Lamanite stock. This has been one of the most thrilling experiences I have had, to witness these people coming into the Church."[53]

The Hinckleys scarcely had time to unpack from their latest South American trip before they left for the Orient, where he was to assist Elder Ezra Taft Benson, who currently had responsibility for the work there, in creating the Tokyo Stake, the first organized in Asia. The Hinckleys' return proved to be a joyful reunion with treasured friends. As he participated in the long process of interviewing priesthood brethren, Elder Hinckley knew nearly everyone with whom he and Elder Benson spoke. He was impressed that, among the entire roster of brethren interviewed, every one was a full tithe payer and all but one had been to the temple, despite having to travel to Hawaii to do so. "I regard this as a most remarkable thing," he wrote. "I have never seen anything like it in my previous experience."[54] On March 15, 1970, the Tokyo Stake was created with Kenji Tanaka as president. President Tanaka's first counselor, Yoshihiko Kikuchi, at age twenty-nine, was the youngest officer in the new stake.

Elder Benson asked Elder Hinckley to train the new stake leaders, and he began his instruction by asking questions that tested their familiarity with the *General Handbook*. To his first question one man responded with the answer, including the page on which it could be found in the handbook. Another man responded similarly to the second question. Elder Hinckley's third question elicited the same kind of informed response. "How is it that you are so well versed in the handbook?" Elder Hinckley finally asked. He learned that the year before, these priesthood leaders and their families had vacationed together. Each day the men spent time studying the handbook, and by week's end they knew how a stake should be administered. Elder Hinckley was humbled by the preparation of these men to whom he felt such personal attachment.

While in Japan, the Hinckleys and Bensons also participated in the dedication of the Church pavilion at Expo '70 in Osaka. An otherwise fruitful trip was marred, however, when, just after midnight on the morning of Tuesday, March 17, the phone rang in the Hinckleys' hotel room. Elder Hinckley's secretary was calling with good and bad news. One announcement had been eagerly anticipated: Dick and Jane were the parents of an infant daughter. The news that followed, however, crushed Marjorie: Her father had just passed away. She had agreed to come to Asia only after the doctor assured her that her father would be alive when she returned. Marjorie sobbed much of the night—partly for herself and partly for her mother. She felt so helpless, separated from her family by the Pacific Ocean, and ached to be home. "I reflected on the news we had received," Gordon recorded afterward, "a birth and a death, as if one had canceled out the other. I spent much time in reflection on life, its purposes, what a fragile thing it is, and the wonder of it all."[55]

The Hinckleys returned immediately to the United States. The chapel was filled to overflowing the day of LeRoy Pay's funeral, and Elder Hinckley eulogized his father-in-law as a gentle man who had gone through life quietly doing good.

Elder Hinckley's next international trip, this one to South America in May 1970, was the setting for an unnerving series of events. After presiding over a stake conference in Lima, he flew on to Santiago. It wasn't until two days later that a cable from President Allen E Litster of the Andes Mission reached him with the news that less than a minute after his plane had left Lima, Peru had been hit with a devastating earthquake, and four missionaries in northern Peru were missing. Elder Hinckley immediately tried to reach President Litster, and when his call finally went through several hours later and he learned that the missionaries had not been located, he promised to return to Peru the next morning. "I knew about an important meeting Elder Hinckley had back in Salt Lake City at week's end," President Litster remembered. "When I asked him about that meeting, he replied, 'I cannot in good conscience go home while there are missionaries missing.'" When President Litster later mentioned his surprise that Elder Hinckley would drop everything to return to Peru, Elder Hinckley responded, "President, every man needs someone with whom to counsel." That night Elder Hinckley had a terrible time getting to sleep. "I had repeated thoughts of our missionaries," he wrote in his journal. "But there came the reassurance that they were not dead but were in difficult circumstances and that we must do something for them as quickly as possible and, furthermore, that they were working very hard to help the wounded and dying."[56]

The next day, after some difficulty, Elder Hinckley found a flight to Lima. He and President Litster had just returned to the mission home when a call came through from the missing missionaries, who had finally managed to find a ham radio operator who could put through a phone patch to Lima. Later President Litster related what had happened as Elder Hinckley spoke with the missionaries: "The small room where the ham radio operator was located was crammed with people waiting for their turn to use the radio, and the missionaries said it was sheer bedlam inside. Each radio conversation was broadcast over a loud-speaker, so everyone in the room could hear what was being said. As Elder Hinckley's voice came over the speaker in that room crammed with people clamoring to get on the radio, an immediate hush fell across the room. Though he was speaking in English, and these people all spoke Spanish, they began to talk among each other in whispers and ask, 'Who is that man?' There was a sense, even amidst chaos, that that voice belonged to no ordinary man."[57] That night Elder Hinckley noted in his journal regarding the missionaries, who were all fine, "This, of course, was an emotional thing to get this news after all of the worry."[58]

For the next three days, Elder Hinckley and President Litster continued to coordinate relief efforts, arranged for distribution of welfare supplies through the Peruvian Red Cross, and drove through the country to inspect damage and comfort members and missionaries. Damage in Lima was less extensive than in northern Peru, where entire villages and cities had been leveled. His reaction upon arriving in Chimbote was typical: "What a sickening sight. Almost every home was seriously damaged and fetid water stood in ponds in all of the low areas. . . . Chimbote is a city of desolation. [It] . . . smells like a fish center, and this, together with the sickening smells incident to the conditions now found here, makes the place repulsive. I felt sorry for our missionaries, and yet they all want to stay and help the Saints rebuild their homes."[59]

When he felt that he had done as much as he could, Elder Hinckley returned home. There would be other trips to South America, many of them more pleasant, but few in which he would be of any greater assistance than he had been in Peru.[60]

Other unexpected events were more welcome. Elder Hinckley was surprised when, in February 1971, the University of Utah honored him with its Distinguished Alumnus Award, the highest honor the Alumni Association conferred on a former student.[61] Despite his intimate involvement now with BYU, he had never lost his allegiance to its in-state rival and was proud that he had graduated from the University of Utah during the "bottom of the Depression." As a man who was pro-education, pro-learning, and pro-university, Gordon found this recognition by his alma mater immensely satisfying. Ironically, three months later, as a member of the executive committee of the BYU board of trustees, he was involved in the selection of Dallin H. Oaks as president of BYU.[62]

Perhaps the biggest surprise of 1971, however, came in May when Elder Hinckley was assigned to supervise the eight missions of the European-Germanic area: Austria, Germany Central, Germany North, Germany South, Germany West, Switzerland, Italy North, and Italy South.[63] After just two years overseeing the work in South America, he was not expecting the change in responsibility. "The area is vast, the problems are so many, and the demands on my time so great that I have not been able to do as much as I should like to have done," he recorded. Nonetheless, he had toured every mission in his area, helped to create stakes in Lima and São Paulo, directed the acquisition of an attractive piece of property in downtown Buenos Aires for a stake center, made progress in resolving a complicated visa situation with the Argentine government, and created new missions in Colombia and Ecuador. Most important, he had grown to love the Saints in South America. "Still, I should have done much more," he wrote. "But now we go to Europe, and I hope with all my heart that I might be able to accomplish good there."[64]

Elder Hinckley lost no time making his first trip to Europe. Assigned by President Joseph Fielding Smith to attend the Church's first-ever area conference, to be held in Manchester, England, in late August, he left a month early to allow time for careful inspection of the missions under his care. Jane, who had just graduated from high school, joined her parents on their tour of Switzerland, Germany, and Italy. The contrast between this and Elder Hinckley's experience in South America and Asia was immediately noticeable. For example, the passport inspection in Zurich was so cursory that they didn't even stamp Jane's passport, which disappointed her. The spirit among the faithful Saints was wonderful, but the missionary harvest, compared to that in South America and even in Asia, was modest.

In Bern the Hinckleys participated in a youth conference. Jane made friends with several English-speaking youth in attendance, though Marjorie wrote home that one of the most humorous moments was watching her dance with a German boy in dead silence. And when their visit to the servicemen's district in Stuttgart coincided with a dance that evening, so many people made a fuss about Jane's being there that, as her mother related, "she is on a stubborn and says she is *not* going to attend."[65]

While in Germany the three Hinckleys visited Dachau, formerly the site of a Nazi concentration camp. "It is sickening," Elder Hinckley commented. "But it is something that perhaps ought to be seen as a stark reminder of man's inhumanity to man when the gospel of Jesus Christ is not in the hearts of the people."[66]

The Hinckleys then traveled to Manchester, England, where they joined President Smith, President Harold B. Lee, Elder Thomas S. Monson, and other General Authorities at King's Hall in the Bell-Vue Centre, which was filled to its 12,000-seat capacity for two days of conference. The sight overwhelmed Elder Hinckley, who couldn't restrain the tears as he walked into the vast arena and found it filled with members from all over the British Isles. When he rose to speak in the Sunday afternoon session, he felt impressed to set aside his prepared address and simply offer his testimony. "I don't know when I have been more deeply touched in my heart than I have here in this conference," he said. "I was born in America, but the power of faith came to me when I was a missionary in England." Continuing, he sounded what for him was a familiar theme: that the strength of the Church lay not in its buildings or programs but in the testimonies of its members.[67]

After the conference, Elder Hinckley invited Elder Spencer W. Kimball and his wife, Camilla, to spend a day in Preston touring the sites where Elder Kimball's grandfather, Elder Heber C. Kimball, had initiated the work in 1837. The Kimballs readily accepted the invitation, and Elder Hinckley escorted them to the home on St. Wilford Street where Heber Kimball and others had had a contest with evil spirits; Vauxhall Chapel, from whose pulpit they had preached; and the River Ribble, where they had performed the first baptisms. It was a "richly rewarding day," as

Elder Hinckley assessed it, and the Kimballs used the photograph Elder Hinckley took of them standing beside the River Ribble on their Christmas card that year.

The Hinckleys hadn't been home from Europe for two months before they were preparing to return, in October 1971. It seemed to Elder Hinckley that, though he was gone for extended periods of time—for a decade now he had routinely spent at least three months a year abroad—the trips were relatively brief in terms of the work to be done. The more he traveled, the more certain he was that, as the Church grew, the Brethren would have to change their mode of operation.

For the time being, however, he and Marjorie were off again to Europe, where they included in their itinerary a servicemen's conference in Berchtesgaden. After Marjorie spoke at a women's session, dozens of sisters stopped Elder Hinckley to tell him she had been the highlight of the conference. He recorded: "She has tremendous rapport with the women and expresses herself marvelously well. I cannot help but reflect on the tremendous growth she has made since she first started touring the missions. In those early days she was frightened. Now she speaks with sureness and conviction."[68]

During this trip they again received unwelcome news from home—Elder Richard L. Evans was gravely ill—and that evening Elder Hinckley was preoccupied with thoughts about his colleagues of the Twelve. LeGrand Richards and Hugh B. Brown were aging, and just a few days earlier Elder Hinckley had helped administer to Delbert Stapley. Spencer Kimball had recently been diagnosed with throat cancer, yet Elder Hinckley noted, "Nothing keeps him down. I have never known a man so zealously at work in furthering the Kingdom of God."[69] A prayer circle had been held for Elder Kimball, and when Elder Hinckley anointed him there was a tremble throughout his "whole body, and it continued and there was a holy refining sweet influence through the whole meeting."[70] Nonetheless, the Quorum would no doubt change dramatically in the next few years. "It is disconcerting," he wrote. "I love these brethren. I feel as one with them."[71] A week later Elder Evans, who at sixty-five years of age was one of the younger members of the Quorum, passed away, and Elder Hinckley was called back to Salt Lake City.

A few days after the funeral, President Lee approached Elder Hinckley about assuming some of Elder Evans's responsibilities. Earlier in the year President Lee had asked him to spearhead an exhaustive study of the temple ordinances and to give direction for temple work. Now he added responsibility for the Tabernacle Choir broadcast.

In addition, for nearly two years, Elder Hinckley had been involved in creating a public relations department for the Church. Under President Lee's direction, a small committee had explored ways to manage the Church's image more professionally. Elder Evans had been a central figure in this planning, and with his death President Lee asked Elder Hinckley to supervise this pioneering effort in public relations. "I am so heavily loaded that I don't know how I can carry it," he admitted in his journal.[72] Ironically, although the pressure and load weighed on him at times, he conceded: "I feel better when I am working according to the usual pattern. A number of meetings and much to do."[73]

In early 1972 Elder Hinckley was released from his longstanding assignment as chairman of the children's age-group Correlation Committee and assigned, with Elders Thomas S. Monson and Boyd K. Packer, as an adviser to the First Presidency on matters of correlation, doctrine, and Church procedure. This trio gave direction for all Church instructional materials, periodicals, translation services, and so forth.[74]

The first two months of 1972 also brought with them two rare opportunities to participate in temple dedications, both of them in Utah. On January 18, President Joseph Fielding Smith read the dedicatory prayer and also spoke in the first session of the Ogden Temple dedication. When the Provo Temple was dedicated the following month, he spoke at both sessions.[75]

Then, less than five months later, on Sunday afternoon, July 2, President Smith quietly passed away. Four days later he was eulogized in an impressive funeral that filled the Tabernacle to capacity, and the next morning, the Quorum of the Twelve Apostles met to effect the reorganization of the First Presidency. Elder Hinckley described this transition: "When President Joseph Fielding Smith passed quietly from life unto death . . . there was no doubt in the minds of the members of the Council of the Twelve who should succeed him as President of the

Church. On Friday morning, July 7, they met together in the sacred precincts of the Salt Lake Temple. In that quiet and holy place, with subdued hearts, they sought the whisperings of the Spirit. All hearts were as one in response to those whisperings. Harold Bingham Lee, . . . refined and polished through thirty-one years of service in the apostleship, was named President of The Church of Jesus Christ of Latter-day Saints and Prophet, Seer, and Revelator."[76] President Lee named N. Eldon Tanner and Marion G. Romney as his first and second counselors.

Over the years the new Church President and Elder Hinckley had developed a warm and collegial relationship. He had served on the Correlation Committee under Elder Lee's direction, and in recent years Elder Lee had often delegated delicate assignments to his junior colleague. In the process, he had won the confidence of President Lee.

Just a few weeks later, President Lee asked Elder Hinckley, who had been assigned to reorganize the London England Stake, if he and Sister Lee might accompany the Hinckleys to Europe. The Hinckleys were both surprised and thrilled at the prospects of traveling with President Lee, who wished also to visit Italy, Greece, and the Holy Land—the first visit of a Church President there in this dispensation. Before their departure President Lee mentioned in a meeting with the General Authorities: "There is no one I would rather travel with than Elder Gordon B. Hinckley. I know the strength of his testimony."[77]

The Hinckleys flew to England in advance of President Lee and were at Heathrow Airport to meet him and Sister Lee when they arrived on September 13, looking weary as they dragged their luggage behind them. Thus began a remarkable experience for Elder and Sister Hinckley as they and the Lees traveled throughout Europe, meeting with groups large and small who were elated to be in the presence of the newly ordained President of the Church.

In London, the two Church leaders were guests of honor at a luncheon hosted by Lord Thomson of Fleet, head of one of the world's largest publishing empires and a friend of the Church.[78] There they also reorganized the London Stake, with Elder Hinckley taking the lead. As the Saturday evening session was beginning, President Lee asked him if he had yet identified the new stake president. "I think so," he responded, "but I am concerned about his age. He is only thirty-one." President Lee said nothing. Later, as the meeting progressed, he passed a handwritten note to Elder Hinckley that said simply, "I was thirty-one when I became a stake president." That settled any remaining question in Elder Hinckley's mind, and he issued the call to the young bishop in question. Before retiring that night he wrote: "These experiences are always interesting. You worry, you interview, you pray, and then in a remarkable but unexplainable way, impressions come as to the right man."[79] Indeed, he had an absolute conviction, gained from firsthand experience, that priesthood leaders were called of God. The process was sometimes quick and clear-cut, and on other occasions agonizing. But in each case the Lord directed this work.

From England the quartet traveled to Athens, where they met with government officials in an attempt to legally establish the identity of the Church as a "house of prayer." Early the next morning, they climbed Mars Hill in time to see the sun rise over the Acropolis. There they listened to President Lee recite Paul's famous sermon on the "Unknown God." Later, at the Church President's invitation, Elder Hinckley offered a prayer in which he asked the Lord to touch the hearts of Greek officials, to stay the hand of the adversary, and to bless the Saints there with faith to go forward. The simple prayer was both eloquent and powerful, so much so that President Lee declared that it would stand as a rededication of the land.[80]

The Lees and Hinckleys then flew on to the Holy Land for three days they would never forget. Between meetings with dignitaries and government officials, including Teddy Kollek, the mayor of Jerusalem, they visited many of the sites central to the Savior's life. From Bethlehem to Capernaum, from the Mount of Temptation to the Mount of Transfiguration, they reviewed the ministry of Jesus Christ. But the capstone of their visit occurred at the Garden Tomb. One evening, as a bright September moon filtered through the olive trees there, President Lee organized the Jerusalem Branch, the first unit of the Church to be organized in the Holy Land in nearly two thousand years. During his remarks he reminisced about an experience he had had when he visited the tomb in 1958. On that occasion he had received the clear impression that this was indeed the place where the body of Jesus Christ had been carried after the Crucifixion and where the Miracle of all miracles had taken place. As President Lee shared his experience and then bore testimony of the risen Lord, Elder Hinckley felt the sweet yet powerful confirmation of the Spirit. "No one present will ever forget this occasion," he recorded that night.[81]

Throughout their trip, President Lee had struggled with exhaustion and overall weariness. That night, as the Hinckleys were preparing to retire, Sister Lee called their room to ask if Elder Hinckley would give President Lee a blessing. He immediately called President Edwin Q. Cannon of the Swiss Mission, who was traveling with them, and the two went to the prophet's room. This was not the first time Elder Hinckley had administered to President Lee, and he knew something of the illnesses with which he had contended through the years. But this night President Lee's appearance startled him. His face was drawn, and he looked almost gray. Elder Hinckley wondered if they shouldn't locate a doctor, but President Lee wanted only the blessing. After President Cannon had anointed the prophet, Elder Hinckley sealed the blessing. "I felt the power of the Spirit of the Lord as I spoke," he recorded. "I felt confident that the Lord would heal His servant."[82]

About two o'clock in the morning, he was awakened by the sound of President Lee in the room next door coughing a deep, rumbling cough that continued for some time until suddenly it stopped. The next morning, when he asked the Church President how he felt, he replied simply, "Better." It wasn't until a day later, by which time his health seemed remarkably improved, that he confided what had happened. During the coughing spell he had expelled two clots of blood. Immediately his shortness of breath had ceased, his back pains had subsided, and his extreme weariness diminished. "We had to come to the land of miracles to witness a miracle within ourselves," he told Elder Hinckley. In his journal President Lee wrote: "I now realize I was skirting on the brink of eternity and a miracle, in this land of even greater miracles, was extended by a merciful God who obviously was prolonging my ministry."[83]

From the land of miracles, the Church leaders and their

wives traveled to Rome, where they arrived late in the evening to find that they had been booked into elaborate hotel suites. The extravagance troubled Elder Hinckley, and early the next morning he went to the front desk to request a standard room. President Lee happened to walk by at that moment, and he asked his colleague what he was doing. "I'm changing my room," Elder Hinckley responded. "The President of the Church deserves a suite, but I don't." President Lee immediately responded, "While you're changing your suite, change mine."

From Italy, the quartet pressed on to Switzerland and then finally to New York City, where President Lee and Elder Hinckley held a press conference in the Waldorf Astoria. More than twenty media representatives, including editors and correspondents from *Time*, UPI and the AP, the *Washington Post*, and the New York Times Religious News Service, attended the event. After Elder Hinckley's introductory comments, in which he explained that the Church had enjoyed a 94 percent increase in membership since 1960, President Lee fielded questions for an hour about the Church's rapid growth, finances, and welfare program.[84] Surprisingly, the only question regarding blacks and the priesthood was asked afterward by a reporter who approached the Church leaders privately. In general, they were pleased with the event and felt it had allowed them to present a positive view of the Church.

As they flew the last leg of their return trip to Salt Lake City, Elder Hinckley recorded his feelings about the unique experience of traveling for two weeks with the President of the Church: "We have witnessed a restoration of the President's health. . . . And for Marge and me it has been an incomparable experience, one we shall never forget. The unfailing kindness of President Lee and his delightful companion made traveling with them a joy and a privilege. . . . We have borne testimony to the Saints in England, Greece, Israel, Italy, and Switzerland. We have walked where Jesus walked and testified of His divinity as the Son of the Living God. . . . We have proclaimed the prophetic calling of Joseph Smith and affirmed the prophetic calling of his successor in office, Harold B. Lee. This has been a journey to remember. This has been an experience to cherish."[85]

The following week, in a meeting of all General Authorities

prior to October general conference, President Lee invited Elder Hinckley to report on their trip. "As I spoke of our visit to the Holy Land, I was overcome by a conviction within me of the divinity of the Lord Jesus Christ who gave his life for the sins of mankind," he recorded afterward. "I had difficulty speaking. President Lee was visibly moved as were others of the Brethren. When I concluded President Lee stood up. He spoke of the miracle that had occurred in him while we were in Jerusalem. He said it was too sacred to discuss even under these circumstances. He was deeply touched and shed tears. . . . He said again that if ever he had any doubt of my calling as an Apostle and of the power of the priesthood manifest through me, that doubt had gone."[86]

CHAPTER SEVENTEEN

THE CONSTANCY OF CHANGE

Elder and Sister Hinckley were finding an old adage to be true—there was nothing so constant as change. Early 1973 brought news of a significant and long-awaited international development: On January 23, U.S. President Richard M. Nixon announced that a cease-fire agreement ending hostilities between the United States and Vietnam had been reached and that U.S. troops would begin to return home. "Surely we have cause to rejoice over this turn of events," Elder Hinckley noted in his journal, at the same time thinking of the thousands of LDS soldiers he had met through the years—those who would be coming home and those whose families would never see them again. He only hoped that the seeds of missionary work planted during the long years of conflict would eventually bear fruit.

Other trends exposed a society whose ethical moorings were shifting. When the Supreme Court ruled liberally in *Roe v. Wade*, allowing for a woman's right to abortion in the first trimester of pregnancy, President Lee called Elders Benson, Hinckley, and Monson to his office to confer with the First Presidency on how or if the Church should respond. After they discussed the possibility of issuing a statement that would in effect take exception with the Court's action, Elder Hinckley suggested an alternative course of action: Rather than appear to censure the judiciary, the Church could simply restate its position. Such action would reaffirm to Church members that doctrine had not changed without reprimanding the nation's highest tribunal. Elder Hinckley feared he had overstepped his bounds by making such a strong appeal to the First Presidency, and he was relieved when President Lee concurred with his recommendation and expressed appreciation for it.[1]

It was not unusual for President Lee to involve Elder

Hinckley in various deliberations. One issue about which they conferred regularly was temple work. Elder Hinckley now served as chairman of the Temple Committee, a time-consuming and taxing responsibility. Even with his previous heavy involvement in this area, he had had "no idea there were so many things requiring attention" in the temples.[2] Among other concerns, he was preoccupied with a worry that had dogged him for years—that thousands of members lived beyond reasonable distance from a temple.

Too many times he had organized stakes in various areas of the world in which few of the brethren interviewed for leadership positions had been to the temple. He found himself wondering if there weren't a way to build smaller, less expensive temples and to build more of them throughout the world. He even discussed his concerns and ideas with President Lee. "Are not the saints in South America . . . as worthy of the blessings of the temple as the people in Washington?" Elder Hinckley mused in one journal entry.[3] He later noted: "The Church could build [many smaller] temples for the cost of the Washington Temple [then under construction]. It would take the temples to the people instead of having the people travel great distances to get to them."[4]

President Lee had assigned Elder Hinckley to attend a youth conference in Johannesburg, South Africa, and he suggested that he return home via São Paulo to scout possible temple sites. Accordingly, in May 1973 the Hinckleys left for South Africa, and they enjoyed their first experience there immensely. Elder Hinckley spoke fourteen times during his three days in South Africa, and after the last meeting concluded he wrote: "We are weary tonight. So tired. The schedule of the day has been hectic but it has been one of the most spiritual days I have experienced, with a tremendous outpouring of the Spirit of the Lord. . . . What a marvelous experience it has been for us to be here in South Africa among the faithful Latter-day Saints. The country is beautiful, but the people are more beautiful. My heart reaches out to them."[5] From Johannesburg the Hinckleys made the long flight across the South Atlantic to São Paulo. After searching for temple sites there, Elder Hinckley returned to Salt Lake City enthusiastic not only about the prospects for building a temple in Brazil but about the pattern such a step could establish throughout the world.

He also greatly enjoyed experiences that reinforced his connection with the Church's heritage. In late May he joined Presidents Kimball and Romney as they dedicated five newly restored buildings in Nauvoo. "As we stand on this ground," he recorded in his journal, "we can almost feel the spirit of Joseph Smith. The beauty of these rolling green hills with the mighty river sweeping past is something of majesty." Throughout the day Elder Hinckley's thoughts returned again and again to the Prophet, to his own grandfather, and to those who had built with such hope on this piece of swampland. There was an unmistakable spirit in Nauvoo, and he felt certain the area would become an attraction for members and nonmembers alike.[6]

There were other glorious moments ahead. A week later Elder Hinckley reorganized the Cumorah Stake in Rochester, New York. Early Saturday morning he and President Bryant Rossiter of the Cumorah Stake, Regional Representative Mark Weed, and President William Siddoway of the Cumorah Mission visited the Sacred Grove, and, as before, he was deeply affected by the experience. "It was a magnificent morning after three weeks of rain," he wrote. "In the grove we were alone. The birds were singing, and the sun was filtering through the trees. It was a tremendously inspirational experience to stand on sacred ground where this dispensation was opened with the visitation of God the Eternal Father and the resurrected Lord, Jesus Christ, to the boy Joseph Smith. We bowed our heads, and I offered prayer in behalf of the group. I think I shall not forget the experience of this morning in this sacred place."[7] Such experiences reinforced within him an "ever-growing compulsion to bear testimony of the divinity of the Lord and of the mission of the Prophet Joseph Smith. I think this world needs this more than any other thing," he reflected.[8]

Ten days later Elder Hinckley returned to the East Coast, this time for satisfying personal reasons. Clark was graduating with his MBA from Harvard, and his father was anxious to attend commencement as well as to be reunited with Marjorie, who had stayed in the East after their return from South Africa to visit Virginia and her family in Connecticut and to spend time with

Clark and his fiancée, Kathleen Hansen, who were planning to marry in October. Elder Hinckley was overjoyed to be with his wife again—three weeks of separation was too much. And he was proud of his son and impressed with graduation rites at the prestigious Ivy League school. The next day, they visited Barnstable, Massachusetts, a sleepy village near where Governor Thomas Hinckley of the Plymouth Colony had established a farm; in the old cemetery there they found numerous headstones bearing the name *Hinckley*. Such experiences always stirred great emotion and gratitude within Elder Hinckley.

But he was equally grateful to return to Salt Lake City with Marjorie. He preferred to have her with him when he was traveling, and he didn't care for being at home alone. On one occasion when she left a day ahead of him for Australia so she could stop in Hawaii to see Kathy, he returned to an empty house and "reflected on how lonesome life would be without a loved companion."[9]

The summer of 1973 brought with it a variety of unique experiences—most of which Marjorie was able to share with him. In late June, Lord Thomson of Fleet and his son, Kenneth Thomson, visited Salt Lake City. Wendell Ashton coordinated Church-related events for the dignitary's visit, and when the British newspaper magnate agreed to attend an LDS service, Brother Ashton arranged for Elder Hinckley to speak there. Elder Hinckley was less willing when President Lee asked him and Marjorie to accompany Lord Thomson's party on an outing to Lake Powell in southern Utah. Elder Hinckley, who had no desire to spend two days cruising around on a boat, accepted the assignment reluctantly. He hadn't been swimming in years, at least partly because of a recurring ear problem that had resulted in dozens of minor surgeries in which his left eardrum was pierced to relieve pressure. While they were enjoying the beauties of Lake Powell, however, Wendell Ashton overheard Lord Thomson telling his son, "Kenneth, this man Hinckley is remarkable. [British Prime Minister] Edward Heath can't even come close to him." Some years later, son Kenneth Thomson remembered the Lake Powell outing and referred to the "magical moments" he had spent with the Hinckleys and Wendell Ashton, "the companionship and personal thoughts, shared among friends in the most peaceful setting imaginable. . . . At such moments a person's character is likely to be more transparent than usual and one is likely to start shuffling one's priorities a little. Gordon Hinckley did not need to be concerned about the transparency of his character or to do any shuffling. He had his priorities exactly right."[10] After the Lake Powell trip Elder Hinckley conceded that the brief respite was more enjoyable than he had expected. He was even coaxed into the water for an afternoon of swimming.

He felt more comfortable, though under a good deal more pressure, participating in an area conference in Munich in August 1973, which was attended by members from as far away as Beirut, Cairo, and Athens. In a BYU devotional address a month later he described how the conference had affected him: "It was a tremendous experience to sit in that great Olympic sports hall and look into the faces of 14,000 Latter-day Saints who had gathered from across Europe. Two days before, I had met with the missionaries of the Germany South Mission and had felt something of their discouragement. . . . Out of all their efforts there have come only a convert here and another there. . . . But when I saw that great body of Saints in Munich I saw the fruits of their faith. . . . I saw a thousand doors knocked on for every man and woman and child present. . . . I heard the prayers, the pleadings of missionaries to be led to someone who would accept the truth. I saw those missionaries going up one street and down another in bitter winter weather and the scorching heat of summer. . . . When I looked over that vast congregation I knew that faith had been rewarded and that . . . a miracle had come to pass."[11]

After the area conference, at President Lee's invitation, the Hinckleys again enjoyed the privilege of accompanying him and Sister Lee—this time to Vienna and London. Elder Hinckley was grateful for the opportunity to travel a second time with President Lee. For as long as he could remember, he had had strong feelings about Joseph Smith and the prophets who succeeded him. At times he still found it hard to believe that it was his privilege to associate with prophets of God.

In his October 1973 conference address, Elder Hinckley bore testimony of the divine callings of both Joseph Smith and

President Lee: "As one who recently walked with him as a junior companion in the missions of Europe and England, I have seen young people eagerly press about him with tears in their eyes and smiles . . . upon their faces. I have seen missionaries sit enraptured as he taught from the scriptures. . . . I have seen few things more touching than a strong young man embracing the President and then later with tear-moistened eyes saying, 'Never have I been so near to heaven.' As one to whom the Spirit has borne witness, I testify of his prophetic calling, and add my voice to the voices of our people over the earth, 'We thank thee, O God, for a prophet to guide us in these latter days.'"[12]

Less than two weeks after the Hinckleys returned from England they were off again, this time to Australia to conduct a seminar for the ten mission presidents serving throughout the South Pacific. This was Elder Hinckley's first flight on a Boeing 747, and he wondered as he stood at the bottom of the steps how such a monstrous aircraft could fly. Their trip was even more enjoyable than usual because Kathy and her eldest daughter, Heather, joined them in Australia. As Elder Hinckley often said, usually with a sigh, "We're a traveling family." Their travel itineraries, however, routed them home on separate flights. During the Hinckleys' layover in Honolulu, they walked to the observation deck for fresh air and while there saw Kathy and Heather arriving on another flight. Kathy didn't hear her parents call to them. Elder Hinckley mused: "It made me think that perhaps this is the way it will be in the life to come—we will be able to look down upon our posterity, but they will not be able to see us. We will share their joys and sorrows. We will try to shout to them and help them and guide them, but they will have to have their own experiences, exercising their free agency, and accepting the penalties or the blessings derived from their actions."[13]

Meanwhile, it was wonderful to have their family reunited whenever possible, and the entire clan gathered in Salt Lake City for Clark and Kathleen's marriage in the Salt Lake Temple, which Elder Hinckley performed the day following the October 1973 general conference. With four of their five children now married, Elder and Sister Hinckley only hoped that Jane, soon to turn twenty, would be equally fortunate in finding a companion. "She is a beautiful and delightful girl," he noted, "and other members of the family say she has her father around her little finger. I think I would not protest that too much."[14] Their family was all but grown; soon Jane too would be gone from home. On another occasion he wrote: "I remember when Jane was born. I figured that when she was twenty years of age, I would be sixty-three. That seemed old at the time, but those years have passed quickly, and while I am now nearly sixty-three, I still feel relatively young in spirits."[15]

Jane spent Christmas that year with Dick's family in southern California, so Gordon and Marjorie celebrated a quiet holiday at home. The serenity of the season was shattered the following evening, however, when at 8:55 P.M. their phone rang. It was Wendell Ashton calling with unbelievable news: President Lee had just died.

The Hinckleys were stunned. President Lee had seemed tired the past few days, but not enough to warrant undue concern. "What a terrible shock this is!" Elder Hinckley wrote. "It is unbelievable. . . . He who we thought would live so long because he seemed so vigorous. He has been president for less than eighteen months, but he has left an indelible mark upon the Church. How we shall miss him, but how evident it is that the Lord took him for a purpose known only to the Lord."[16]

Invited to speak at the funeral, Elder Hinckley pleaded for inspiration to say something worthy of his prophet-leader. His mind raced back nearly thirty years, sorting through the experiences they had shared. President Lee was the General Authority who had set him apart as a stake president and indicated that the Lord had greater opportunities in store for him. They had stood together on Mars Hill and read the words of Paul. And Elder Hinckley had been voice in the life-preserving blessing that unforgettable night in Jerusalem. On Elder Hinckley's wall hung a portrait President Lee had given him the Christmas before, inscribed: "To Gordon B. Hinckley, beloved friend and associate with full assurance of my respect and deep affection for one of God's true noblemen. Affectionately, Harold B. Lee." President Lee was not only Elder Hinckley's leader and mentor, he was his friend.

On Saturday, December 29, a capacity Tabernacle audience witnessed an inspiring service during which Elder Hinckley reminisced about his unique association with President Lee and spoke of the departed leader as a humble, benevolent, and loyal servant of God: "Reporters and others have spoken of his passing as 'untimely.' I believe and know that the death of no man of God is ever untimely. Our Father sets the time. . . . We sorrow, properly, for our loss is great. We weep, for we loved him, but . . . I am as certain that his passing was as much the will of the Lord as was his preservation and preparation through the years for the high and holy calling which he filled so nobly."[17]

The following afternoon, the fourteen apostles came fasting to the Salt Lake Temple. After they partook of the sacrament, each in turn expressed his conviction that the Lord had spoken and Spencer W. Kimball should be ordained President of the Church. President Kimball selected N. Eldon Tanner and Marion G. Romney as his first and second counselors. For the third time in less than four years, Elder Hinckley participated in this solemn occasion, and the simplicity of it all was overwhelming. "It is marvelous the way the Church . . . passes through a transition of this kind with scarcely a ripple," he wrote in his journal that evening. "No other organization on earth can do it. To witness such a change becomes a compelling testimony of the divinity of this work."[18]

For several reasons, December 1973 was a month that neither Elder nor Sister Hinckley would soon forget. The prophet, a dear friend and inspired leader, died without warning, precipitating a reorganization that in time would have tremendous effect on Elder Hinckley personally. And he and Marjorie celebrated their last Christmas in their East Millcreek home.

Since boyhood, Elder Hinckley had been attached to East Millcreek, and he had learned to find respite in the soil. He loved to sink a shovel into the earth, see the water come rushing down a ditch, and take a pair of shears to an unruly bush. He valued land, and through the years he had acquired, subdivided, and sold various plots of ground, including lots where he thought they might enjoy living. But buying property was one thing—actually moving was another.

In late 1972 he and Marjorie purchased a lot in the Ensign Downs subdivision less than a mile from downtown Salt Lake

City. Homes had been built on surrounding lots, and they realized there would soon be pressure to do something with the "weed patch" they owned. "I very much dislike leaving East Millcreek," he lamented in the fall of 1972. "But I am confident there would be wisdom in our building a home and living closer to the office. We would be of greater service to the Lord if we did not spend so much time commuting back and forth and working around the old place. The decision is difficult, but I suppose one of these days we shall have the courage to make it."[19]

Early in 1973 they determined they could no longer postpone a move. They were getting no younger, and if anything Elder Hinckley's load at Church headquarters continued to increase. It made sense to be closer to both the office and the airport. Reluctantly they looked at various lots and even toured condominiums, but dismissed the notion of moving into a "filing cabinet." Finally, though he was discouraged at the prospects of starting over with landscaping, decorating, and handling everything incident to building a home, Elder Hinckley designed a house for the Ensign Downs lot. Even as footings were dug and the first concrete poured in late spring, however, neither he nor Marjorie was sure if they would move there or sell the home when it was completed.

By September they were still vacillating. One Saturday they stopped at the property en route to the airport. "[We still wonder] whether we are crazy to make this move—to leave our trees and lawns and a thousand remembrances of our sweat and tears of thirty-two summers to begin new plantings at our age," he confided in his journal. "Furthermore, we will be leaving our white house. I have lived in a white house all my life, and that in itself could become the subject of an essay." White house aside, it was almost more than he could tolerate to think of living on a lot barren of trees. "I am satisfied that when the place is landscaped it will be attractive, but trees do not grow tall in a day."[20]

After an agonizing period of indecision, they decided there would never be a better time to move, and on New Year's Eve, Elder Hinckley recorded his feelings about the home he had built and remodeled again and again to suit the needs of his growing family:

> How sentimentally sad we are about leaving. We built this home in the days of our poverty. How we labored to make it attractive. The trees and shrubs we planted—more than five hundred, each requiring a hole I dug in rocky soil. The gallons and gallons of white paint we have brushed on during the past thirty-two years. The scores of yards of carpets we have laid and worn out and replaced. . . . Marge and Dick planted the large back lawn one spring when I was away on a Church assignment. . . . Here we played together as our children grew, and here we prayed together. Here we and our children came to know our Heavenly Father, that He lives, and listens, and answers.
>
> I might go on to write a book . . . not for the world, but for those five children, their spouses and posterity. And if I can get into words the story of that home there will be tears and laughter, and a great, quiet, pervading spirit of love that will touch the hearts of those who read, for those who lived and grew there loved one another, they loved their neighbors, they loved their God and the Lord Jesus Christ. . . .
>
> The new place is not finished. But the time is not distant when we must go; and tonight, sitting before a fire of wood of our own planting and cutting, we feel a great sense of melancholy, and love and appreciation for one another.[21]

Early in February 1974 the move began. Marjorie packed box after box, maintaining that she now knew what it was like to prepare for death and then bury yourself. Everything inspired a deluge of memories. There was the old mailbox in which she had received letters from missionary sons and love notes from her grandchildren. There were shuttered windows, louvered doors, and woodwork she had painted and repainted, and the oven in which she had baked pies on the last day of school each year for Clark and his friends. They had called this house *home* most of their married life, and it was next to impossible to imagine living anywhere else. Leaving East Millcreek was made easier, however, when a family friend agreed to rent the house; in time they permanently abandoned thoughts of selling the homestead, which stayed in the family and eventually was remodeled (again) to suit the needs of others.

Though the new house on Capitol Hill was of their own design, it took time before the Hinckleys felt at home there. With boxes still waiting to be unpacked, they left in mid-February for Japan. Elder Hinckley had once again been assigned to supervise the work in the Orient, and this was his first trip back in nearly four years. Both he and Sister Hinckley were eager to greet old friends, and apparently their Japanese hosts felt likewise, for after clearing customs in Tokyo, the visitors were met in the terminal by a large group of Saints holding "Welcome Home, Elder and Sister Hinckley" signs. How therapeutic after their recent upheaval in Salt Lake City to feel so welcome and at home halfway around the world!

The next morning Elder Hinckley described his excitement at being back in the Orient: "Something is tingling in my bones this morning as I sense that I am here in Japan visiting with the Saints and the missionaries. I have been here so many times, in sickness and in health, in sorrow and in rejoicing. And now it seems that the dark days of pioneering are behind us and that the Church is on solid footing."[22] The feeling seemed to be mutual. After one meeting at a Tokyo ward, he noted: "I have never seen such a welcome. . . . At the close of the meeting we were literally besieged. People were pushing so hard to get to us that I was afraid someone was going to get hurt, and it might have been me. When we finally got away, I was so tired and weary I could hardly hold my head up."[23]

Despite his joy in returning to Asia, Elder Hinckley noticed a distressing trend: too many converts were being lost. "Too many are coming in the front door and going out the back," he worried aloud.

One of his most significant objectives on this trip was to identify a temple site in Tokyo. After looking at various properties and considering everything from transportation to lodging for Saints visiting from other parts of Asia, Elder Hinckley returned to Salt Lake City with a recommendation for the First Presidency. As chairman of the Temple Committee he was constantly thinking about ways to make temple ordinances more readily available to Church members worldwide, and the prospect of building a temple in Japan was electrifying.

During the summer he and President Kimball discussed the possibility of building two more temples in the United States—one in the Northwest, probably Seattle, Washington, and another in Atlanta, Georgia. Elder Hinckley was assigned to look for sites in both locations. And as the magnificent new Washington

Temple neared completion, he visited the capital city to review details for the prededication open house and dedicatory services. Situated in wooded Kensington, Maryland, along the Beltway some thirty minutes from downtown, this temple provided a singular opportunity for Church leaders to mingle with the nation's influential, and elaborate plans were drawn for escorting dignitaries through the temple during the open house.

On September 9, President and Sister Kimball, President Romney, and Elder Hinckley arrived in Washington, D.C., to lay the cornerstone and inaugurate the open house. The following evening members of Congress turned out in large numbers to tour the building during an invitation-only opening. And the next morning diplomats began to arrive for personally scheduled tours that allowed President Kimball, President Romney, and Elder Hinckley to spend time with them one-on-one. To almost every foreign dignitary, Elder Hinckley was able to make a personal comment about his or her native country and people. When First Lady Betty Ford paid a visit, President Kimball invited Elder Hinckley to join him in escorting her through the edifice; in one of the sealing rooms he invited Elder Hinckley to explain the concept of eternal marriage.[24] As Elder Hinckley watched Mrs. Ford having her photograph taken with President Kimball, and later listened to Chief Justice Warren Burger speak movingly of the temple as a symbol of Christianity, he thought of earlier days when the Saints had found no recourse in the legal system. How far the Church had come in the respect and confidence of public officials since 1839, when Joseph Smith had been repudiated in Washington! He also found himself thinking about the future. As he rode along the Beltway surrounding the nation's capital and marveled at the dramatic sight of the temple spires rising heavenward from a hill in the adjacent woods, he remembered the words spoken by the Lord: "A city that is set on an hill cannot be hid." (Matthew 5:14.) "Not alone the Washington Temple," he thought, "but this entire people have become as a city upon a hill which cannot be hid."[25]

The next morning Elder Hinckley offered the invocation in the House of Representatives. Prior to entering the House chamber, he was instructed carefully in protocol. There were, as usual, few congressmen present when the prayer was offered, but Elder Hinckley was unperturbed about the sparse attendance and quoted President Kimball, who had offered the prayer in the Senate the day before: "That's all right. I was not going to pray to them anyway." Elder Hinckley did think the small attendance ironic: "I suppose that most of these Congressmen feel that they don't have to be present for a prayer."[26]

By the time the First Presidency and other General Authorities, including Elder Hinckley, returned to Washington, D.C., in November to dedicate the new temple, three quarters of a million visitors had toured the gleaming white structure. The Hinckleys flew to Washington from West Virginia, where he had presided at a stake conference, and that night he awoke with a raging fever. The next day, when the First Presidency arrived, he was flat on his back. When President Kimball heard about his condition, he immediately sent Dr. Russell M. Nelson, who had accompanied the aging Elder Hugh B. Brown to Washington, to examine him. Dr. Nelson suspected an infection and took his patient to the Georgetown Medical Center for tests. So on the first day of dedication, while his Brethren feasted in a rich spiritual outpouring, a weak Elder Hinckley underwent a variety of tests. Though disheartened at missing Tuesday's opening session, Elder Hinckley was philosophical about the turn of events. "This is the first day of the dedication of the Washington Temple," he noted in his journal. "I belong in the temple, and I, instead, am . . . seriously ill. I don't know the meaning of it all, but I feel satisfied there is some meaning."[27]

The tests confirmed Dr. Nelson's diagnosis, and Gordon returned to the hotel to recuperate. After both President Kimball and President Romney stopped by his hotel room to give him blessings, he added, "What a marvelous thing it is to have the confidence of these great brethren. What a truly wonderful thing it is to have the powers of heaven called down in your behalf."[28] After two days of convalescence he felt up to attending a session and was even able to deliver a talk before the dedication concluded.[29]

Marjorie and Jane had planned while in the East to visit Clark and Kathleen, who now lived in New York City, but Marjorie was reluctant to send her husband home while he was still weak. He insisted they not alter their plans, however, and returned to Salt Lake City alone on Marjorie's birthday. With his wife in mind he wrote: "She is sixty-three today, but she has so much of life and love and gladness. Everyone she knows seems to love her because she has a genuine interest in people. She is concerned with their problems and their needs. How fortunate I am to have such a companion."[30]

Marjorie handled well the nontraditional lifestyle her husband's Church assignments imposed upon her. When it came to rearing the family and keeping everyone closely connected despite distance, she carried the lion's share of the load and did so with good cheer. The glare of prominence, long absences, rigorous travel, overlooked birthdays and anniversaries, holidays spent in obscure corners of the world, jet lag layered upon jet lag—she had supported her husband through these and a host of other occupational hazards. She knew what it was to remain at home, particularly when the children were young, while he traveled from country to country for weeks at a time, yet she had also cheerfully endured one exhausting trip after another during which she sometimes saw little more than the insides of chapels and hotels and the route to and from the airport.

Deborah Goodson, whose husband served as president of the Philippines Manila Mission in the mid-1970s, said: "Sister Hinckley was a trooper. It was sticky hot in the Philippines, and none of the buildings were air conditioned. But she went everywhere, did everything, traveled when she was exhausted, and always had a sense of humor about what happened. One day we were trying to cross the street in typhoon-like weather when Sister Hinckley tripped on a curb and went down. Undaunted, she popped back up as though nothing had happened and marched straight on."[31]

Marjorie had learned to be ready at a moment's notice to speak, for her husband rarely gave her advance warning. But she handled even those circumstances with her characteristic light touch. "What would you do if you were married to a man like this?" she would ask an audience after he had given her only seconds to collect her thoughts. "It is clear to me that he hasn't figured out what he wants to talk about yet. That is why he has called on me," she would continue, prompting a ripple of laughter through the audience. For his part, Elder Hinckley seemed to expect the good-natured ribbing, and congregations enjoyed the banter that revealed their warmth and approachability. He also appreciated how effective she was in front of an audience, and he often noted when her remarks had made a noticeable difference. "Marge spoke well," was a common journal entry. "She speaks and bears testimony as a mother and grandmother, and the people love her."

She had also learned to tolerate her husband's personality quirks, one of which was his tendency to make last-minute decisions on things as major as international travel. One incident became family legend. The night before one of his Asian tours he still had not decided if she was going to accompany him. When Marjorie finally asked if she should plan to leave with him the next morning, he responded with a hint of impatience, "Do we have to decide that *right now?*"

Many women would have come unhinged at such indecision and inconvenience, but Marjorie had long since decided to dismiss temporary annoyances as just that: temporary. Indeed, she had found that being the wife of a General Authority required a unique combination of fierce independence and unwavering support. At times she wanted to laugh out loud when she was asked what it was like to be married to a Church leader, as if that made her some sort of celebrity. *If you only knew*, she usually thought, knowing full well that only other women in the same situation could understand the ironies, opportunities, challenges, and blessings inherent in their way of life. All in all, her tendency to see humor in many situations, her ability to find joy in everything from the mundane to the exotic, and her complete faith in the Lord suited her well to their peculiar routine, which she not only accepted but enjoyed immensely.

Despite the demands that sent them globe-trotting on a regular basis, both Elder and Sister Hinckley went to great lengths to stay close to their children and grandchildren scattered around the country. When she traveled with her husband, Marjorie often left early and routed herself through a city where their children lived. He did the same, sometimes taking long detours to spend even a few hours with family (if the rerouting didn't increase the airfare). Marjorie sent hundreds of postcards to grandchildren from every corner of the world and letters by the dozen to family members. She carried a notepad with her on planes, to meetings, and even from room to room when she was home.

After Kathy and her family moved to Hawaii, Marjorie indulged in long-distance telephone calls now and again, as she confessed in one letter: "This direct dialing system they have to Hawaii is likely to ruin my financial budget permanently. It is such a temptation and after rationalizing for two or three days I just dial on impulse. I did come up with a good one, and that is the fact that we, as a two-member family, spend zero on entertainment, so this is my entertainment money. . . . I enjoy every expensive minute of it."[32] And when Elder Hinckley brought home a letter from Kathy, collected during a layover in Hawaii, she wrote back immediately: "I did appreciate the letter you sent with Dad. It saved me hours of fruitless pumping to find out what was really going on out there in the Pacific."[33]

In reality, Elder Hinckley was never happier than when surrounded by family. "It seems almost a dream," he confided in his journal. "Only yesterday, all five [children] were at home, noisy and happy and worried about the future. We were all crowded in the house which is small even today. Then, however, it did not seem small. The boys were digging caves and building tree huts, and the girls were playing with dolls. . . . Let us hope that the quiet . . . will occasionally be broken by lively and happy grandchildren."[34] Indeed, there seemed to be no danger of lasting peace and quiet within the Hinckley family, and he routinely found the humor in dealing with his rambunctious and growing posterity. After a visit from Virginia and her three young children he noted: "They hadn't been in the house five minutes before they were into everything. They tipped bottles upside down, practically ruined my hat, practically ruined the carpet, practically ruined my good disposition. They are to be with us for a week. All medicines have been placed high, and I am even putting the matches out of reach lest they burn the house down."[35] Such diversions, however, provided a welcome respite from his normal routine and helped keep his feet planted firmly on the ground.

The Hinckleys seemed ever aware of the major decisions and challenges each member of the family was facing. Marjorie in particular functioned as the family nerve center. She kept track of everyone's comings and goings—what each grandchild was doing in school, whom they were dating and whether or not she should be worried, who had what ailment or Church calling, who was traveling where, which grandchildren were due for a sleepover, and who was in need of some extra attention. Family and friends alike gravitated to her, as she had a way of helping people feel good about themselves. She was a "world-class" worrier, though, and her children teased her about who was "at the top of mother's worry list." A few months before Clark's marriage, for instance, she had fussed over the fact that Jane (who was still young) was in love, but Clark (who was nearing the end of graduate school without having found a wife) wasn't. Soon after that, Clark fell in love with Kathleen and they were married, and then Jane became engaged to marry Roger Dudley. That development—the forthcoming marriage of their youngest child—signaled a major turning point. As Elder Hinckley noted, "A man can feel old and become reflective with his memories if he thinks very much of the growing up and scattering of his children."[36]

Regardless of age, when family members were together, laughter was inevitable, as were other distinctive traits. Virginia explained one secret to maintaining family unity: "We don't keep score. If we remember a birthday, it's a bonus." And for all of their father's responsibility, none of the Hinckley offspring seemed impressed with their own importance—they spurned invitations to give talks on "what it was like to grow up in a General Authority's home." Kathy had a conversation one day in which friends were naming prominent families in the Church. After several surnames had been identified, one friend looked at her and added, "And the Hinckleys, of course." Kathy at first thought her friend was joking, and was flabbergasted to find that she wasn't.

Later, one of Dick's daughters in junior high was assigned to write about someone who had excelled in some way, and she immediately thought of her maternal grandfather, whose distinguished tennis career had included coaching the Davis Cup team. During her interview with him, he asked why she didn't write about her Grandpa Hinckley. After a pause she asked with some confusion, "What has *he* ever done?" On another occasion, her younger brother, then age five, spent an hour one evening alone with his grandfather, who by that time was serving in the First Presidency. "What do presidents do?" he asked his grandpa. "Make decisions," was his answer. "Hmm," the boy responded, unimpressed. "My other grandpa does magic."[37]

At Church headquarters, there was no question about all that Elder Hinckley had done and was doing as a member of the Quorum of the Twelve. He admired those who did what they said they would do, and he adopted that standard personally. He also tried to operate according to other basic principles: that you do the best you can regardless of circumstances, that you can get a lot done if you don't care who gets the credit, and that it is more important to focus on responsibilities than on privileges. "There is nothing in all the world so satisfying as a task well done," he said on occasion. "There is no reward so pleasing as that which comes with the mastery of a difficult problem."[38] Of tasks to do and problems to master, he had plenty.

He was increasingly concerned that the Church sponsored too many rigid and complex programs that obscured the simple power of the gospel. But he was having some influence administratively. On February 13, 1975, in a meeting of the First Presidency and the Twelve, he was gratified to learn that a proposal Elder Hunter, Elder Monson, and he had made was being implemented. They had proposed that the Quorum of the Twelve be constituted as a committee of the whole, responsible ultimately for the programs of the Church, and that the quorum be divided into committees that would serve as advisers to various programs. In this restructuring, his own committee assignments changed, and he was given responsibility for the Melchizedek Priesthood, Public Communications, and Temple Committees.

For the first time in forty years he had no direct responsibility for missionary work. Though he felt passionately about that area of the work, it was invigorating to switch his focus for a time. Two months later, on April 10, 1975, he was named chairman of the executive committee of the BYU board of trustees. He also continued to serve as president of the Deseret News

Publishing Company. Though circulation of the daily newspaper had decreased, the paper was financially stronger than ever in its history.[39]

There was momentum elsewhere as well. Changes were being implemented Churchwide to accommodate a rapidly growing membership. The year before, President Kimball had delivered a stirring address on missionary work to a gathering of Regional Representatives—"the greatest talk ever given in these seminars. . . . None of us can ever be quite the same after that," Elder Hinckley said afterward.[40] President Kimball asked the assembled leaders to lengthen their stride, and he led out by doing so himself.[41]

In May 1975 the First Presidency announced the creation of the area supervisory program. Six Assistants to the Twelve were assigned to oversee Church activities while living outside the United States and Canada, and the Twelve were named as advisers to the areas. (Elder Hinckley was assigned the Atlantic North Area.) On July 24, President Kimball dedicated the new twenty-eight-story Church Office Building. Elder Hinckley wondered how long it would take to fill what at the time seemed an enormous amount of office space.

But the Church was moving forward as never before. In February 1975, at an area conference in São Paulo, Brazil, President Kimball announced that a temple would be built there, and in April he returned to his native Arizona to rededicate the refurbished Arizona Temple. Elder Hinckley participated in that event as well as the preceding open house, the first day of which was reserved for ministers invited to tour the edifice as guests. President Kimball asked Elder Hinckley to respond to the clergymen's questions, and one query in particular from a Protestant minister gave him opportunity to emphasize the foundation upon which the Church was built: "I have been all through this building, but nowhere have I seen any representation of the cross, the symbol of Christianity. Why is this when you say you believe in Jesus Christ?"

Elder Hinckley paused, phrasing his reply carefully: "I do not wish to give offense to any of my Christian brethren who use the cross on the steeples of their cathedrals and at the altars of their chapels, or who wear it on their vestments. But for us, the cross is the symbol of the dying Christ, while our message is a declaration of the living Christ." The minister followed with a second question: "If you do not use the cross, what is the symbol of your religion?" Again Elder Hinckley's answer was direct: "The lives of our people are the only meaningful expression of our faith and, in fact, the symbol of our worship."[42]

In August 1975, Elder Hinckley accompanied President Kimball and other Church leaders to the Far East for area conferences in Tokyo, Hong Kong, Taipei, Manila, and Seoul. During the Tokyo conference, President Kimball announced that a temple would be built there, the first in the Far East, and the response was overwhelming. Yoshihiko Kikuchi, who was in attendance, said: "The whole congregation clapped their hands with inexpressible joy. It was the Sabbath, so they shouldn't have clapped. But they didn't know how else to express their joy. There was a special feeling in that conference. There were no dry eyes in that congregation."[43] Elder Hinckley was pleased to learn that the temple would be built on the site he had recommended.

For him, the trip was both inspiring and poignant. He marveled that the Church had matured so remarkably throughout the area he had supervised fifteen years earlier. As he entered the Araneta Coliseum in Manila and saw 18,000 members crowded into the largest indoor meeting place in the Philippines, he wept openly. "There was a spirit of euphoria at that conference because it was the first time that many Filipino Saints had been gathered in one place at the same time," said President Ray Goodson of the Philippines Manila Mission. "President Hinckley was as excited as a little boy at Christmas. When he stood to speak he began, 'Is there any doubt now in anyone's mind where the real growth in the Church is?' He was thrilled."[44]

In his remarks, Elder Hinckley offered the Filipino members a glimpse into the future. "It is my firm conviction that what we have seen thus far is but a prologue to what shall take place in this nation," he said. "We have one stake now. There will be many stakes. We have a few buildings. There will be scores of buildings. And it is my conviction that someday there will be a temple of God in this land."[45]

It was also in the Philippines that the trip's most uncomfortable experience occurred. Standing in for President Kimball at a press conference, Elder Hinckley was asked to comment on a recent statement by Betty Ford, the wife of U.S. President Gerald Ford, who had said that she wouldn't be surprised if her teenage daughter were to have an affair. "We very much deplore the deterioration of moral standards throughout the world," he responded. "We advocate strongly and seriously adherence to moral standards. . . . We cannot expect a great and good society unless morality resides in people." The Associated Press and United Press International interpreted his remarks as criticism and sent them out over news wires. His statement was published in newspapers throughout the world. Even *Time* magazine reported the incident.[46]

Elder Hinckley had not meant his response to be an affront to the First Lady but simply a restatement of the Church's position on morality, and he was embarrassed by the attention. Nonetheless, in his October general conference address he continued his censure of declining morals by praising spouses who were faithful to each other and denouncing an inordinate emphasis on sex as the "weakening rot seeping into the very fiber of society." He asserted, however: "I am satisfied that there are millions upon millions of good people in this and in other lands. . . . I am one who believes that the situation is far from hopeless. . . . The tide, high and menacing as it is, can be turned back."[47]

High tides and swelling seas were something Elder and Sister Hinckley became acquainted with in a most uncomfortable way just a couple of months later when they embarked on another international journey, one that demanded faith as well as nerves of steel along the way. After forming a new stake on the island of Vava'u in Tonga, Elder Hinckley learned that their scheduled flight to Nuku'alofa had been canceled and that the only way they could get there was to charter a boat. When it docked at the pier, he was chagrined to find that he and Sister Hinckley were sailing on an old ship used to carry mail and freight. Compounding their discomfort, the water became rough shortly after they put out to sea. The old diesel engine pounded up and down as the boat slowly cut its way through the white-capped ocean waves. Their berth in the cabin below was nothing but a slab of plywood with a thin mattress, and the heat in the hold exaggerated the motion of the ship.

Elder Hinckley described the experience in his journal: "I looked at my watch at 3:30 in the morning. Heavy winds were shaking the boat, and it bounced up and down terribly. . . . The porthole was open, and sea water was coming through. . . . A thousand thoughts passed through my mind as we jostled up and down, becoming bilious from the heat, the fumes, and the motion of the ship. . . . I thought of Paul being shipwrecked. I thought of the terrible hazards of getting in lifeboats out in the Pacific. The sky began to lighten about 5:00, and I . . . went up on deck where I could get fresh air blowing in my face. . . . I must add that I prayed earnestly to the Lord that we would be preserved and protected and reach our destination in safety. . . . We were all dizzy and somewhat sick, a little embarrassed to acknowledge it, but earnestly wishing within ourselves that this journey would soon end."[48] It was twenty hours before they docked at Nuku'alofa. Elder Hinckley couldn't remember when he had been so relieved to set his feet on dry land.

With the growth of the Church exploding worldwide, he knew he could expect to travel to the world's far reaches and to encounter such experiences on occasion. The October 1975 general conference brought further evidence of progress as President Kimball activated the First Quorum of the Seventy; a year later he called all Assistants to the Twelve and members of the First Council of the Seventy to serve in the new quorum.

The Hinckleys also marked significant milestones during 1975. It was both a glorious and a sobering day when Elder Hinckley performed the marriage of his and Marjorie's youngest daughter, Jane, to Roger Dudley. That evening he reflected on the good fortune of having both sons serve missions and all five children marry in the temple. "This remarkable achievement stands as a great tribute to their good mother," he said simply.[49] Marjorie expressed it differently in a letter to Kathy: "I am reminded of what Mother said—that she didn't mind getting old herself, but she couldn't stand to see her children get old."[50]

The second landmark event was laced with irony. In June, Elder Hinckley turned sixty-five, an age that under other circumstances might have signaled retirement but instead brought with it a workload more demanding than ever. For her part, Marjorie was philosophical about their advancing age. After trying to console a younger friend who was traumatized over turning fifty, she remarked: "Fifty was my favorite age. It takes about that long to learn to quit competing and settle down to living. It is the age I would like to be through all eternity."[51]

Though their children were now all married, the Hinckleys discovered that their concerns, conversations, and prayers still revolved largely around their offspring. One morning Elder Hinckley was awakened early with thoughts about Clark. His impressions were strong enough that he noted in his journal: "It is strange that a man my age worries about his children who are mature adults in their own right. I guess I am like other parents. One never gets through worrying about his children and grandchildren even when they are doing well."[52]

As with most mothers and grandmothers trying to keep track of their husbands and growing posterity, there were times when Marjorie wondered if she was doing anything more than sustained wheel-spinning. During a luncheon of General Authority wives, at which the women saw a skit depicting the life of prolific writer and leader Susa Young Gates, she turned to Camilla Kimball and said, "It makes me wonder what I am doing with my life." "You are running to and from," Sister Kimball quipped in return. "She was right," Marjorie concluded. "I am running to and from and shiver to think that someday I will have to account for the time spent."[53]

Time was something there was never enough of, and she had the normal challenge of squeezing family, Church, and everything else into the hours available. When Virginia asked her to help with a Relief Society lesson, she decided to skip her own meeting. But then her Relief Society president called, asking if she would give the opening prayer. "I nearly tripped over my tongue trying to make being too busy sound reasonable," she related afterward.[54] Her general outlook, however, was more practical than self-critical. "I have a new project," she wrote to Kathy, "one chapter a day from each of the standard works. I have been on it for four days and am only 3 days behind. Better to have tried and failed than never to have tried."[55]

Apparently the tendency to shoehorn too much into any twenty-four-hour period was a Hinckley family trait. During one month when Virginia had her hands full with a heavy load of family and Church responsibilities, Marjorie outlined the list of things pressuring her second-oldest daughter and concluded matter-of-factly, "Life gets that way every once in a while when you belong to the true church."[56] After spending a hectic day with Clark's family, who had relocated to Utah, she shook her head at the events that had unfolded: "Clark painted their living room on Saturday. . . . In the middle of it they discovered their bishop had been taken to the hospital with pneumonia, so nothing would do but Kathleen stop to make a chocolate cake and spaghetti with home-cooked sauce and the whole works to take over to the family for dinner. They finished up the painting and pushing the furniture back at 1:30 A.M., then got up early Sunday morning to prepare 2½-minute talks they both had to give. I don't know what it is about this family that they always do things the hard way, but I guess we were not born to be Saturday golfers."[57]

The children came by their tendencies honestly. Jane and Roger had moved into the family home in East Millcreek, and their parents now found that the reasons to run out to the old house seemed to never end. No one better understood the inner workings of the home than its creator, and one repair and project after another begged for his attention. Marjorie described a comical turn of events that transpired during one of their visits: "Saturday we went out to Jane's again to work on the shower. . . . When we got home I had left a pan of spaghetti with hamburger boiling away on the stove. The house was full of thick air and pungent smell. . . . [Then Dad] found that he had pulled the hose inside with the spray sprinkler on and had absent-mindedly turned on the tap. Water was hitting the ceiling and spraying from wall to wall to wall. I simply cracked up. We looked at each other in total disbelief and wondered whatever was going to become of us. Like Pres. [J. Reuben] Clark used to say, 'Old age is a blankety blank blank.' We opened up the windows, swept out the water, and decided to get away from it all by going over to see Clark and Kathleen."[58]

Less than two weeks later, Elder and Sister Hinckley were

preparing to host a dinner for twenty people at their new home during the annual mission presidents' seminar. "I don't understand it," Marjorie wrote. "We got this place all slicked up not too long ago and here we are again in a frantic mess with a party coming up. . . . Brown Floral had a sale and there are about 15 cans of various trees and shrubs waiting to be planted. The driveway is in the process of being formed up for the brick and once again it looks like the Hinckleys just moved in. The neighbors look over here and scratch their heads. I think we are out of our element among these manicured yards with husbands and fathers who watch tennis matches on Saturday."[59] The results, though slow in coming, were nonetheless impressive. One day a new neighbor from out of town rang the Hinckleys' doorbell and asked Marjorie who had done their landscaping. "My husband," she responded. "Could he stop by and give me a bid on my place?" the woman inquired.

There was simply not enough time to do everything, which meant the Hinckleys had to decline many social invitations. Marjorie insisted, however, that they attend Gordon's fifty-year high school class reunion on May 28, 1976, and then described the festivities in a family letter: "What a hoot! [The class] took over the entire hotel. The boys who sat at the head table were announced as they entered the ball room with all spotlights turned on them while they took their places. Dad was right up there with the . . . old student body president. In fact, they invited him to give the opening prayer. Dinner was served to 840 bald-headed men and plump women. . . . It was a gala affair. Ray Bradford and the group played all the 'I'm Forever Blowing Bubbles' songs on the saxophone and trumpet. Dad, who didn't want to go in the first place, had the time of his life. He was the little bashful boy who had made good."[60]

A month later, in July 1976, the Hinckleys attended bicentennial activities in Washington, D.C., including a concert at the Kennedy Center, receptions, and a devotional at which President Kimball addressed more than 23,000 people in the Capitol Centre at Landover, Maryland. In advance of the trip Marjorie detailed the upcoming events, adding: "Dad has five talks to prepare, some of which will go over Washington TV and radio, so he is under a lot of pressure. Where oh where is that peace and rest?

But I suppose when and if it ever comes that will be far worse than the pressure."[61]

Peace and rest didn't appear to be something Elder Hinckley could expect anytime soon. In May 1976 four executive committees were established within the Quorum of the Twelve, and Elder Hinckley was asked to chair the Melchizedek Priesthood Executive Committee, which was responsible for all Melchizedek and Aaronic Priesthood activities and organizational functions, including the auxiliaries, Church magazines, music, graphics and editing, and all activity programs. A month later all stakes and missions throughout the world were placed under the direct supervision of area advisers and area supervisors. Elder Hinckley continued to advise the area composed of Japan, Korea, the Philippines, and Southeast Asia, which now encompassed seventeen missions, seven stakes, and forty-two districts.[62] Marjorie described the effect of these changes: "There was a great reshuffling of assignments last week and we held our breath for fear we would be transferred out of the Orient, but they forgot we were there again, so that should go on for another year now. [Dad] did lose the temple assignment, which was quite sad for him as he has been involved with the temples since 1953. . . . But he will head up the Melchizedek Priesthood Committee which is a big assignment. . . . He is happy for the challenge."[63]

In addition to the administering part of his various stewardships, Elder Hinckley also had many opportunities to engage in a ministry of a more personal kind. He returned home from a round of conferences in Arizona in a "super good mood," as Marjorie described it, after he had engaged in a fruitful gospel discussion with a professor he met on the flight. On one transoceanic flight he found himself seated next to a young man who was reading *Joseph Smith, an American Prophet*, and he couldn't resist initiating a conversation. He learned that his seatmate was intrigued by the notion of modern-day prophets, and before their long discussion ended he bore his testimony of the Prophet Joseph Smith. On another occasion, he sat next to a young executive who admired the Mormons but could not accept Joseph Smith's story. When Elder Hinckley asked where he had obtained his information, the man admitted that it had come from his own church. Elder Hinckley then asked what company he worked for. "IBM," the man responded. "How would you feel if your customers learned about your products from a Xerox representative?" Elder Hinckley inquired. Before they parted, Elder Hinckley pledged to send him some literature and promised him that if he read it prayerfully, he would receive a spiritual witness of the doctrines and of the prophet who had reintroduced them to the world.[64]

Elder Hinckley's attention wasn't confined to nonmembers. President Spencer Palmer of the Korean Mission watched him endure all manner of circumstances to meet with members. "He didn't mind getting out and sloshing around with the people," President Palmer remembered. "I took him to Taegu in the middle of monsoon rains. We couldn't find any transportation, so we had to walk several miles to an out-of-the-way LDS chapel. It was raining, his glasses were streaked with water, and he was muddy up to his shins. I was embarrassed that we hadn't provided better conditions for an apostle. After we had trudged along for a distance, he looked at me, shook his head, and said, 'If only my Brethren could see me now.' Then suddenly, as we walked by a row of shanties with a group of children standing outside, he got tears in his eyes and said, 'Oh, President. Isn't this sad? Our Heavenly Father's children deserve more.' Finally we made it to the chapel and he gave a wonderful talk to the bedraggled, wet people who were waiting for him. They were thrilled when he walked through the door."[65]

During one of the Hinckleys' visits to the Philippines, President Goodson's wife, Deborah, was confined to bed with a difficult pregnancy. In her condition, she worried about having such prestigious guests. "The Hinckleys made themselves at home, and each day found a few minutes to come to my room and visit," she remembered. "One day Elder Hinckley brought an armful of books he thought I might enjoy. It was a little thing, but I knew what kind of schedule he kept and that this was his way of showing his concern."[66]

Elder Hinckley had his own way of connecting with people. Though eloquent in his use of language, he was neither sentimental nor flowery. But when he told a gathering of Saints that he loved them and that they were as fine a group of members as any in the world, they believed him and were determined to prove him right. When he joked with them about their country and customs and found humor in something only an insider would appreciate, they felt that he knew and accepted them. When he poked fun at himself, they enjoyed being welcomed into his circle. And when he bore his testimony, they felt the strength of his convictions and the power of his faith. No branch or ward was too small or too far out of the way to deserve his attention, and his mere presence in outlying areas communicated his devotion to the people as well as to the Lord.

One Sunday the phone rang not long after he arrived at a stake center in California to preside at a stake conference. The call was for him, and after a few moments he excused himself from the first meeting, asked the stake president to carry on in his absence, and went to see a missionary companion who had not been active in the Church for years. Awkward at first, their conversation warmed as they caught up on the four intervening decades. Before leaving, Elder Hinckley asked his old friend if he would consider returning to church, and the man consented to try. Some time later Elder Hinckley received a welcome letter from his friend that began, "I'm back, and how wonderful it feels to be home again."[67]

As far as Elder Hinckley was concerned, no soul was beyond reach, as he explained in a general conference address: "To you . . . who have taken your spiritual inheritance and left, and now find an emptiness in your lives, the way is open for your return. . . . I think I know why some of you left. You were offended by a thoughtless individual who injured you. . . . Or you may have been drawn to other company or habits which you felt were incompatible with association in the Church. Or you may have felt yourself wiser in the wisdom of the world than those of your Church associates. . . . I am not here to dwell on the reasons. I hope you will not. Put the past behind you. . . . This, my beloved friends, is what the gospel is all about—to make bad men good and good men better."[68]

Elder Hinckley was an optimist about the gospel and its power to change lives. Assigned to speak at BYU on the expanding Church, he titled his remarks simply "Things Are Getting Better." The days ahead, he believed, would be the most glorious the Church had ever seen. Although there would be setbacks, he was confident that the gospel would triumph.[69] As evidence for his ever-present good cheer, he pointed to numerous positive indicators. It was remarkable to contemplate what had happened between 1951, when President McKay became President of the Church, and the end of 1976. Church membership had more than tripled (from 1,147,157 to 3,742,749), and the number of stakes had quadrupled (191 to 798). Most telling, whereas only 1,801 missionaries were set apart in 1951, now more than 25,000 were serving.

On occasion Elder Hinckley mentioned, in typically understated fashion, that he was "at least superficially acquainted" with the missionary program of the Church and that in this rapidly shrinking world the field truly was white and ready for harvest. His convictions about missionary work were in harmony with those of President Kimball, who boldly prophesied that congregations would be established in such places as Russia, Mongolia, and Yugoslavia.[70]

From Elder Hinckley's perspective, the future looked bright. Yes, the challenges were great. But, as he often said to colleagues and friends, the only way he knew to get anything done was to get on his knees and plead with the Lord, and then get on his feet and go to work.[71] He knew something of which he spoke, for he had practiced this preachment for decades. What he didn't know was that the hardest work he would ever do still lay ahead.

CHAPTER EIGHTEEN

THE CHURCH MOVES FORWARD

Elder Hinckley couldn't remember a period when there had been more to do and less time in which to do it. The Church was growing, and that growth demanded more of each General Authority, particularly members of the Twelve. After some of their weekly temple meetings, Elder Hinckley noted how weary he felt. "This is a little difficult to understand, since these meetings are inspirational," he wrote on one occasion. "However, they are so very important and the matters considered are of such seriousness that I think we all feel tired when we have been there for anywhere from five to six hours. These are certainly among the most important meetings held in the Church, and I believe in all the world."[1]

In the early spring of 1977 President Tanner called Elder Hinckley into his office and asked if he wasn't loaded too heavily. "You are responsible for many of the programs of the Church, and you cannot keep up with everything," he said. Accordingly, he recommended that, among other things, Elder Hinckley be released as president of the Deseret News Publishing Company. Elder Hinckley agreed that the change would be welcome.

Sister Hinckley described one sequence of events from early 1977: "Somehow Dad made it down to Phoenix last Saturday from where he had to drive 100 miles south to his conference assignment. He left [with] . . . a terrific head cold. But by some small miracle he looked better when he finally got home Sunday night. . . . He still has a big bass voice and is worried about being in condition for two solemn assemblies this weekend. . . . The

President requests that they fast for the two days, eating only one meal at 10 P.M. after the meetings. I don't know how President Kimball keeps it up, as they go almost every other weekend. . . . When one sees the way they work compared to the life of U.S. Presidents described in *Upstairs at the White House*, one wonders what we are trying to prove. Dad could not get over the fact that Eisenhower could spend weekends playing bridge with the entire responsibility of the United States of America on his shoulders. . . . But the wonderful thing was that he said he learned one thing from reading the book and that was that one doesn't have to be a workaholic to be famous. Not that it will make any difference—but it was nice to have him say it."[2]

Elder Hinckley revealed the nature of his schedule at the beginning of one address to religious educators: "It was almost foolish of me to try to be here tonight. I was scolded by the stewardess for trying to get off the plane before it stopped. I have had a long and crowded day. I arose early this morning and dictated these notes. I then hurried to the temple to perform a marriage, rushed to the barber to get my hair clipped, hurried to the airport to fly to Seattle, attended two meetings there, then rushed to the airport, flew back, and I am here. It is too much to put that much into one day, and it is symptomatic of the jostling, busy times in which we live." He wasn't likely to change his pattern, however. In the same message he encouraged his audience to keep growing, regardless of age. "Your industry in so doing will cause the years to pass faster than you might wish, but they will be filled with a sweet and wonderful zest that will add flavor to your life," he said.[3]

Such a schedule made Elder Hinckley wonder if the sheer volume of work was taking him too far away from the people. After he and Marjorie read the biography of President Kimball, in which some of the prophet's early mission tours were described, she wrote her daughter, "I guess those days are gone forever. The brethren are getting farther and farther away from the people. It is a melancholy prospect. As we read of some of his mission tours, Dad longed for the good old days, hard as they were."[4]

He missed the personal contact most, the individual connection with members. The growth of the Church, however, was making it increasingly difficult to maintain those relationships. The Hinckleys did what they could to keep in touch with their friends around the world. Augusto A. Lim, who presided over the first stake in Manila, learned that Elder Hinckley expected a visit from him when he came to Salt Lake City for general conference: "He wanted to be kept abreast of what was happening in the Philippines—not so much with the statistics . . . but more particularly about people. He was concerned with what was happening to his friends in their personal lives."[5] Indeed, conference provided a semiannual opportunity to renew friendships from all over the world. After one conference Sister Hinckley reported to the family: "Most of the conference visitors have gone home. There are still a few around . . . and we will try to have them up for lunch next week. We had a group for lunch on Saturday and another group on Monday. Sunday night was a bash. I think that is the last time we can have the Orientals to an open house unless we hold it in the Salt Palace."[6]

Such relationships, however, were what made the frequent travel bearable. In January 1977 the Hinckleys were off again to Asia. They loved returning to Hong Kong, the site of a mission presidents' seminar for those serving in Asia. After their three days there he wrote, "We felt a tug in our hearts as we left Hong Kong. . . . We have had so much to do with the Church here, that we leave with sadness each time we depart, without any idea as to whether we shall return again."[7] The tedious exit requirements at Hong Kong's Kai Tak Airport prompted another observation: "Someday I would like to write a book on the man with the rubber stamp. Life is a series of rubber stamps with our eternal passports being marked by those who judge us along the way and clear us if all is in order."[8]

There was little time to indulge in much regret or introspection, however, for Hong Kong was only their first stop in a long and ambitious trip. After an overnight stop in Bangkok, they flew on to Kuala Lumpur, the capital of Malaysia—a first for both of them. Some of Elder Hinckley's colleagues had questioned why he had included it on his itinerary. But as he and Marjorie disembarked from the airplane, they saw coming toward them an American member of the Church, who invited the Hinckleys to his home. There they met several other LDS families, some of whom had driven for hours over crude roads carved through the jungle, and held a tender, spiritual meeting. One woman who lived up-country far from any other Latter-day Saints broke into tears upon meeting Elder Hinckley. At day's end he recorded: "I learned tonight why we had come to Kuala Lumpur. At the close of the meeting, the Saints presented us an engraved pewter plate, indicating that I was the first General Authority to ever visit this city."[9]

The next morning they headed for India, and there they met with small groups in several villages. Most of the people were poor and illiterate, though Elder Hinckley felt encouraged when he met two or three men who were well educated and showed leadership promise. "Life here is not like going back 100 years," Marjorie wrote home, "but like going back to Old Testament times. Women are all dressed in saris. White horned cows and donkeys carrying their burdens, women filling their jugs at the well. . . . I think of my elaborate home in America and I wonder what the Lord thinks of our living in such opulence. On the other hand, the Lord has provided the good things of the earth for the benefit of his people—if only the good things could be more evenly distributed."[10]

The plane ride from India to Cairo was tedious—twenty-two hours, including stops in Bangalore, Bombay, and Pakistan—and when they finally arrived in Egypt, the Hinckleys were exhausted and anxious to meet their hosts. The customs officer, however, had something else in mind. "The Bureau of Investigation . . . removed all of Dad's papers including his little black notebook and began to pore over them," Marjorie reported. "Even the laundry marks on his shirts were scrutinized. He had dictated his daily diary on tapes and they took all of those. The entire plane load of people stood in line during all of this for the better part of an hour while we were interrogated."[11] They were finally allowed to enter the country, but only after Elder Hinckley's papers and tapes had been confiscated.

He later uncovered the motivation for such scrutiny. There were strict laws in Egypt against converting Muslims to Christianity. When planning his itinerary, Elder Hinckley had written to the members in Cairo about his planned stop there, but the letter had never reached them. "It is now perfectly evident that the secret police received notice of my arrival and were waiting for me when I reached Cairo," he recorded. "It gave me an uneasy feeling to realize that I was being followed. Now they were having my papers translated in an effort to find something in them to confirm their suspicions. I realized that a false interpretation of some of my notes could have grave consequences, and earnestly prayed that no trouble would result, particularly to hinder the future of the Church in Egypt."[12]

Despite the scare, their visit to Egypt proved fascinating. They climbed inside the massive Cheops Pyramid and visited other ruins. And after gathering with small groups of Saints who were meeting quietly in homes, Elder Hinckley left believing there was hope for working among the nine million Christians living in Egypt. Back at the airport, he retrieved all of his materials except one cassette. All in all, his foray into Egypt ended better than it had begun.

The Hinckleys flew on to London and then headed home after a difficult trip that had taken them around the world in two weeks' time. Though the number of members he had visited was modest, he believed occasional visits in primitive areas were necessary if the Church was to fulfill its destiny. From initial plantings would eventually come a bountiful harvest.

The year 1977 brought a number of other major excursions. In the spring Elder and Sister Hinckley spent almost two weeks touring the missions in Australia, and while there they celebrated their fortieth wedding anniversary. The missionaries of the Australia Perth Mission presented Sister Hinckley with a corsage, something her husband had not had time to arrange for himself. He was nonetheless aware of how much she had come to mean to him. "We could write quite a volume on the past forty years," he reflected. "Our hair is grey and our figures have slipped. We have had our struggles and our problems. But by and large, life has been good. We have been marvelously blessed. At this age, one begins to sense the meaning of eternity and the value of eternal companionship. Had we been at home tonight, we likely would have had some kind of a family dinner. As it is, we are far from home in the service of the Lord, and it is a sweet experience."[13]

Late spring took them again to the Orient. Elder Hinckley

was particularly concerned about two Vietnamese priesthood leaders who had been left behind in the evacuation of Saigon, and his primary objective for stopping in Hong Kong was to see what he could learn about them. He made little headway and found it difficult to leave. "But life for a member of the Council of the Twelve is a series of greetings and farewells," he noted.[14]

During Elder Hinckley's July recess he and Marjorie spent a week in upstate New York. The purpose for their trip east was to attend the Hill Cumorah Pageant, meet with missionaries, and handle other Church business, but through the kindness of Milton H. Barlow, then serving as mission president, the Hinckleys also enjoyed a few days' respite in a condominium near Lake Canandaigua. During their stay Marjorie took the last stitch in an elaborate tablecloth she had been embroidering for twenty-seven months during their travels. Elder Hinckley declared it to be the most widely traveled tablecloth in existence. And as he watched sailors manage their boats on the choppy lake, he marveled at the way they sailed by turning into the wind and then tacking back and forth. "It is so with the life of a man," he philosophized. "By setting his course and knowing the rules of seamanship as they apply to life, he can move forward and upward even in the face of adversity."[15]

It was impossible to be in the Palmyra area without focusing on the life of the Prophet Joseph Smith, and Elder Hinckley was grateful for uninterrupted time to study the Book of Mormon and review some of his notes about the Prophet. One morning he recorded that his heart had been touched by the Spirit as he read, and that he had experienced a reaffirmation of the divinity of the Book of Mormon and the prophetic calling of Joseph Smith.

Indeed, he never tired of studying or speaking about Joseph Smith. In his April 1977 conference address, he bore eloquent witness of the man through whom the gospel of Jesus Christ was restored. Declaring that he did not understand those who expressed admiration for the Church but could not accept Joseph Smith as prophet, he said: "That statement is a contradiction. If you accept the revelation, you must accept the revelator." He then clarified the Prophet's unique role: "We do not worship the Prophet. We worship God our Eternal Father, and the risen Lord

Jesus Christ. But we acknowledge him, we proclaim him, we respect him, we reverence him as an instrument in the hands of the Almighty in restoring to the earth the ancient truths of the divine gospel."[16]

Some years later, in a BYU symposium on Joseph Smith, he would state: "I have walked about the beautiful grounds in Sharon, Windsor County, Vermont, where Joseph was born December 23, 1805. . . . I have walked where he walked through the fields to the Sacred Grove . . . and there came into my heart a conviction that what the Prophet described actually happened in 1820 there amidst the trees. I have climbed the slopes of the Hill Cumorah. I have walked the banks of the Susquehanna River. I have been to Kirtland, to Independence, Liberty, Far West, Adam-ondi-Ahman, Nauvoo, and Carthage. While I have never met Joseph Smith, I think I have come to know him, at least in some small measure. I know that he was foreordained to a mighty work to serve as an instrument of the Almighty in bringing to pass a restoration of the work of God of all previous dispensations of time. . . . I know that in the natural course of events before many years I will step across the threshold to stand before my Maker and my Lord and give an accounting of my life. And I hope that I shall have the opportunity of embracing the Prophet Joseph Smith and of thanking him and of speaking of my love for him."[17]

Central to Elder Hinckley's testimony was a fierce loyalty to the Presidents of the Church. In both prepared addresses and private interchange he represented and defended their divine callings. When an influential man asked him to deliver to President Kimball a packet of materials encouraging the Church to change its policy on a certain issue, Elder Hinckley was not subtle in his response: "I told him there was no future for him in this kind of campaign, that anything he said or did would not affect a decision of this matter, that it has never been the policy of the Church to take a stand simply on the basis of popularity. . . . I gave him my testimony that no one was more anxious to do the will of the Lord than President Spencer W. Kimball, and that he and his counselors and the members of the Council of the Twelve prayed often for the direction of the Lord in all of their undertakings. I told him that we either have a prophet, or we don't have a prophet. If we have a prophet, we have everything. If we do not have a prophet, then we have nothing."[18]

In August 1977, Elder and Sister Hinckley accompanied President and Sister Kimball to Switzerland, where they installed a new temple presidency, and to England, where Elder Hinckley organized the Crawley England Stake. And it was with particular pleasure that they returned to the British Isles in the late spring of 1978 when, with Elder David B. Haight, Elder Hinckley reorganized the stakes in the London area. Their stay was exciting by any standard: when fire broke out in their hotel, they lugged their bags down six flights of steps to escape danger. Despite the inconvenience, Marjorie reported, "Dad's never happier than when he is riding the London underground without a chaperon."[19] Then Sunday morning brought an unforgettable event: Members of the six London-area stakes gathered in Royal Albert Hall just two blocks from the Hyde Park Chapel for the reorganization of those stakes and the creation of three new ones.

Forty-five years earlier, as a missionary, Elder Hinckley had paid a shilling and sixpence to hear Fritz Kreisler play the violin in the magnificent old building with its five tiers of balconies, red velvet drapes, and gold filigree. Now he occupied that same stage as he presided over a meeting of nearly five thousand English Saints. With thoughts of past and present surging through his mind, Elder Hinckley struggled in vain to restrain his emotions. Tears flowed as he expressed his love for the British Saints and promised them that if they were obedient, the gospel would grow in their land. "As I looked up into the balcony where I had once sat as a young missionary and thought of being down in front as an elder of The Church of Jesus Christ of Latter-day Saints, I never dreamed such a thing could happen," he later said. "I have a vision, I think, of the majesty and the strength of this work as it moves over the earth."[20]

Though on occasion it seemed to Elder Hinckley that his life was one long excursion with periodic layovers at home, that really wasn't the case. His time in Salt Lake City flew by, however, for the press of responsibility rarely abated. After he was appointed to the executive committee of Zion's National Bank, Marjorie reported to the family: "He went to their first meeting yesterday and decided that banking is a very complicated business, and he feels very inadequate. But it is nice to have a challenge at an age when most men are retiring. So many of our friends all around us are retiring that we are getting a complex."[21] Certainly the challenges seemed never to end. His responsibilities as chairman of the executive committee of Bonneville's board of directors remained demanding, as the broadcast conglomerate continued to acquire new stations and investigate progressive technologies that could increase the Church's reach across the world. This work, however, was almost fun for Elder Hinckley, who was both fascinated by and concerned about media.

In his keynote address at the twenty-fifth anniversary of BYU's Media Production Studios on September 1, 1978, he sounded a familiar theme, expressing his fascination with technology as well as his horror that it was being used to advance that which was demeaning and degrading. "[We have the] challenge to use these marvelous techniques for that which teaches truth, which builds faith, which motivates improvement in behavior, and which stirs the soul to a sense of the eternal nature of man as a son of God," he said.[22] The topic intrigued and worried Elder Hinckley, and when he came across an article warning that protracted television viewing could seriously damage a child's ability to think, he sent copies to his own children with a scribbled note: "This is a most perceptive article on this subject—one of the best I have seen. It is worth reading and reflecting on—since you have both children and a television set. Love, Dad."[23]

Elder Hinckley continued to sit on numerous Church committees, and in the early spring of 1978 he and Elder Packer were appointed as advisers to the Historical Department—an assignment tailor-made for a Church history aficionado. His love for the past was evident in his remarks at the dedication of the new Temple Square South Visitors Center on June 1, 1978, where he repeated President Brigham Young's prophecy that Salt Lake City would "become the great highway of nations, and that kings and emperors, and the noble and wise of the earth would visit us here. It is of singular importance that the beautiful visitors center to the north of this square . . . has become inadequate to accommodate the crowds of visitors who come every day of the year. They include some of the rulers of the earth, and the learned, the noble and the wise."[24]

As memorable events went, however, few if any rivaled the one that occurred later that same day. After the monthly temple meeting of the General Authorities, President Kimball excused all present except his counselors and the Twelve and then raised a subject that had been discussed repeatedly during preceding months—that of conferring the priesthood on worthy males of all races. After inviting a lengthy discussion of the issue, acknowledging how he had worried over this matter and how vigorously he had pleaded with the Lord for direction, President Kimball led out in prayer. Elder Hinckley recorded his impressions of the experience: "There was a hallowed and sanctified atmosphere in the room. For me, it felt as if a conduit opened between the heavenly throne and the kneeling, pleading prophet of God who was joined by his Brethren. The Spirit of God was there. And by the power of the Holy Ghost there came to that prophet an assurance that the thing for which he prayed was right, that the time had come, and that now the wondrous blessings of the priesthood should be extended to worthy men everywhere regardless of lineage. Every man in that circle, by the power of the Holy Ghost, knew the same thing. . . . No voice audible to our physical ears was heard. But the voice of the Spirit whispered with certainty into our minds and our very souls. . . . Not one of us who was present on that occasion was ever quite the same after that."[25]

Though electrifying and intensely spiritual, the day's events did not come as a great surprise to Elder Hinckley. "Not only had President Kimball agonized over this situation, but President Lee and President McKay had before him," he later explained. "It was, however, a wonderful development. President Kimball was bold in petitioning the Lord for this revelation. He wrestled over it. He worked at it. He went to the Lord again and again. And when the revelation came, there was among the Twelve a tremendous feeling of gratitude for this unspeakable blessing."[26] In a letter dated June 8, the First Presidency announced the stunning news that all worthy males were now eligible to receive the priesthood.

▪ ▪ ▪ ▪ ▪

The Church was progressing in every measurable dimension, and with such growth came the need for near constant reworking of the administrative machinery. The April 1978 general conference marked a significant milestone for Elder Hinckley personally, who twenty years earlier had first spoken from the Tabernacle pulpit as a General Authority. In his remarks he briefly looked at the growth of the Church during the intervening two decades. There were now nearly four million members of the Church, compared with a million and a half in 1958. And there were 937 stakes as compared with 273 the year he was called as an Assistant to the Twelve. It was hard for him to comprehend the growth he had witnessed. If indeed the greatest problem in the Church was the swell in membership, as both President Kimball and President Lee before him had stated, it was a wonderful problem with which to deal.[27]

Even more exciting was a knowledge of how and where that growth was occurring. The first stake outside North America and Hawaii had been established in Auckland, New Zealand, in 1958. But since 1971 more than half of the new stakes had been created outside the United States. On one weekend in September 1976, Elder Howard W. Hunter had organized sixteen stakes in the Mexico City area. And on February 18, 1979, President Ezra Taft Benson created the one thousandth stake of Zion—this one in Nauvoo, Illinois.

It was an era of progress and innovation, and the Church was taking unprecedented steps forward. In the fall of 1978 it was announced that those called to English-speaking missions would receive four weeks of training and those learning languages would receive eight at the new Missionary Training Center in Provo, Utah. At the October 1978 general conference, in an address to Regional Representatives, President Kimball left no doubt about their charge to move the work forward: "We have an obligation, a duty, a divine commission to preach the gospel in every nation and to every creature. . . . It seems as though the Lord is moving upon the affairs of men and nations to hasten their day of readiness when leaders will permit the elect among them to receive the gospel of Jesus Christ. . . . Much of the technology for telling the truths of the gospel seems to be in place, but we seem tardy as a people in availing ourselves of it. Technology and developments in transportation have made the world smaller, but it is still a big world so far as numbers of people are concerned when we think of nations like China, the Soviet Union, India, the whole continent of Africa, and our Arab brothers and sisters—hundreds of millions of our Father's children."[28] Elder Hinckley had been an early convert to the potential of media to spread the gospel, and he constantly urged Bonneville executives to harness evolving technology for the Church's good.

Behind all the statistics and developments, however, lay the most optimistic and hopeful aspect of the work in which they were engaged. Elder Hinckley repeatedly declared that the real strength of the Church was found not in its buildings, corporations, or other tangible assets but in the testimonies of its people.[29] An experience with a young naval officer from Asia who had come to the United States for advanced training illustrated his conviction. The officer had been intrigued about the lifestyle of some of his associates in the U.S. Navy, and he inquired about their beliefs. Though not a Christian, he had been moved when he learned about the Prophet Joseph Smith, and he was subsequently baptized. Before returning to his native land he was introduced to Elder Hinckley, who asked what would happen when he returned home. His face clouded as he replied: "My family will be disappointed. I suppose they will cast me out. They will regard me as dead. As for my future and my career, I assume that all opportunity will be foreclosed against me." "Are you willing to pay so great a price for the gospel?" Elder Hinckley questioned. Tears rose to the young man's eyes as he responded, "It's true, isn't it?" When Elder Hinckley replied, "Yes, it's true," the man concluded, "Then what else matters?"[30] Such commitment stirred Elder Hinckley's soul and spurred him forward when he was tired, frustrated, or wondering if he was doing much good. He must never forget, he often cautioned himself, that behind all the numbers were people—men and women, boys and girls—whose lives had been transformed by the power of the gospel. In such lay the power and strength of the Church.

Such feelings may have prompted him in his April 1979 conference address to appeal to those who had strayed: "If there be any within the sound of my voice today who by word or act have denied the faith . . . there is a way for you to turn about, and add your strength and faith to the strength and faith of others in building the kingdom of God." He then referred to a man sitting in the Tabernacle whose obsession with a career had clouded his faith. But he had retraced his steps and was now serving as both a stake president and a senior officer in one of the nation's premier industrial corporations. "My beloved brethren and sisters who may also have drifted," Elder Hinckley concluded, "the Church needs you, and you need the Church. You will find many ears that will listen with understanding. There will be many hands to help you find your way back."[31]

There seemed never to be a shortage of people listening to Elder Hinckley. When he arrived at Madrid's Barajas International Airport in August 1978, he was met not only by five hundred members of the Church but also by television crews from two Spanish stations that broadcast his remarks to the country's estimated 22.5 million viewers. He also met with Spain's King Juan Carlos I and Jośe Luis Alvarez, the mayor of Madrid. This was not the first time Spanish journalists and dignitaries had demonstrated interest in the Church, but it did seem to signal a dramatic change in attitude in a country that had only recently legalized religious liberty.[32]

The scene in Johannesburg, South Africa, nearly three months later was somewhat different. More than three thousand Church members gathered to hear President Kimball, Elder Hinckley, and three other General Authorities for the first-ever area conference on that continent. From the South African bush and through the guerrilla warfare of Rhodesia the Saints came. Tears flowed freely as members gathered with their leaders in what most assumed would be a once-in-a-lifetime experience.

From South Africa the party flew to South America for more area conferences and the dedication of the São Paulo Temple in Brazil on October 30, 1978. How wonderful it was to see members of all races in the temple's celestial room! Indeed, the dedication of this temple in a land where many Saints were of mixed lineage was poignant evidence of the effect of the recent revelation on priesthood.

President Kimball continued to keep a vigorous pace, and Elder Hinckley participated with him in many events. On March 13, 1979, he joined the President and other General Authorities in rededicating the Logan Temple following an extensive remodeling. In June he accompanied President Kimball to Houston, Texas, where they addressed 17,000 members in the first area conference held in the United States. Speaking about missionary work, President Kimball urged older couples to serve missions. "Many people are—what do you call it?" he asked, turning to Elder Hinckley, who was seated behind him. "Retiring," Elder Hinckley prompted. "Yes," the President continued. "They are retiring too early. They could go on missions."[33]

There had been nothing retiring about President Kimball, and when he began to slow down in the fall of 1979, it was not by choice. On September 7, he underwent surgery to relieve pressure from an accumulation of blood on the brain. To the relief of his Brethren, he recovered sufficiently to speak five times at general conference a month later. In November, however, his condition deteriorated, and he underwent a second surgery around Thanksgiving. This time he did not regain his strength as quickly.

With all the Brethren, Elder Hinckley was concerned about the prophet's health. Apart from his love for President Kimball, a milestone of unusual import—the sesquicentennial anniversary of the organization of the Church—was just a few months away, and he hoped the President would be strong enough to lead out in the commemoration. As chairman of the sesquicentennial executive committee, Elder Hinckley relished the opportunity to focus on the Church's beginnings. He believed events of the past should be celebrated, and this landmark anniversary provided an unparalleled opportunity. Accordingly, in his October 1979 conference address he reminded members that six months hence the Church would participate in a great celebration and challenged them to reread the Book of Mormon before then.[34]

In connection with the sesquicentennial, Elder Hinckley committed to writing some of his feelings about the significance of

Enjoying the 1981 Holiday Bowl in which BYU defeated Washington State 38–36

With Marjorie hosting the Queen of Thailand

Sealing a temple cornerstone in place

PHOTO BY JED CLARK/CHURCH PHOTO SERVICES

An all-too-familiar experience between 1981 and 1985—presiding over general conference alone

PHOTO COURTESY LDS CHURCH ARCHIVES

With President Spencer W. Kimball at general conference

PHOTO BY GERALD W. SILVER/CHURCH NEWS

Dedicating the Apia Samoa Temple with (left to right) Elders H. Burke Peterson, John H. Groberg, L. Tom Perry, Howard W. Hunter, Marvin J. Ashton, and William Grant Bangerter in August 1983

PHOTO BY JOHN L. HART/CHURCH NEWS

At the dedication of the Tahiti Temple in October 1983

Enjoying time with grandchildren

Hosting actor Jimmy Stewart on January 29, 1985

President Hinckley served as President Benson's first counselor for nearly a decade (1985–94)

President Ezra Taft Benson enjoys a light moment with his counselors prior to a session of general conference

With a young Swedish friend at the dedication of the Stockholm Temple in July 1985

Baptizing the first member of the Church in Burma, September 1987

PHOTO BY WELDEN ANDERSEN/CHURCH PHOTO SERVICES

Meeting with Ambassador Piet Koornhof (center) from South Africa and Consul General Victor Zazeraji, February 1989

PHOTO BY GARRY BRYANT/DESERET NEWS

Greeting Yuri Dubinin, Soviet Ambassador to the United States, April 27, 1990

At his eightieth birthday party in June 1990

PHOTO BY BUSATH PHOTOGRAPHY

The Hinckley family, taken during Gordon's eightieth birthday celebration

Hosting the visit of the Honorable S.T.K. Katenta-Apuli, Ambassador from the Republic of Ghana, October 18, 1990

Meeting Father Leonard Boyle, Prefect of the Vatican Library in Rome, March 1992

With Elders M. Russell Ballard (far left), and Spencer J. Condie (second from right), meeting King Juan Carlos I and Queen Sofia at the Royal Palace in Madrid, Spain. The king was recuperating from a skiing injury

OFFICIAL WHITE HOUSE PHOTOGRAPH

With President Thomas S. Monson, greeting President George Bush on July 17, 1992

PHOTO BY DON GRAYSTON/CHURCH NEWS

On June 5, 1994, Howard W. Hunter was ordained President of the Church, with Gordon B. Hinckley and Thomas S. Monson as his counselors

With Staff Sgt. Roy Monroe of the Royal Canadian Mounted Police and Gary Fox at the rededication of the Alberta Temple in June 1991

Enjoying Utah's canyons during the summer of 1994

Inspecting the growth of new trees after a devastating fire in Yellowstone National Park

Sharing his trademark wit from the Tabernacle pulpit

With President Howard W. Hunter, greeting Wallace B. Smith,
president of the Reorganized Church of Jesus Christ of Latter Day Saints

PHOTO BY DON GRAYSTON/CHURCH NEWS

President Hinckley with his counselors, Presidents Thomas S. Monson and James E. Faust

PHOTO BY DON GRAYSTON/CHURCH NEWS

On March 13, 1995, President Hinckley's ordination as the fifteenth President of the Church was announced at a press conference in the Joseph Smith Memorial Building

Being interviewed by Charles Sherrill of KSL-TV after visiting President Clinton at the White House on November 13, 1995

PHOTO BY LOWELL R. HARDY

Showing off a halibut during a brief vacation near Glacier Bay, Alaska, in June 1995

this milestone. His essay on Joseph Smith was entered into the March 27 *Congressional Record,* and the sesquicentennial edition of the *Ensign* published his "150-Year Drama: A Personal View of Our History," in which he rehearsed signal events from the Church's founding era. Though still far from being a perfect society, he wrote, the Church now flourished in a world of secularism, and its work would roll forth to fill the whole world. "What a terrible price has been paid for what we have today," he asserted, adding: "All of the work of the past is but prelude to the work of the future. . . . There must be much more dedication, devotion, consecration. There must be a great expansion and a great acceleration. . . . This is his work. He will overrule for its blessing in the future as he has in the past. His Spirit will brood over the nations according to his will and wisdom."[35] The acceleration of the work was beyond question. On Wednesday, April 2, 1980, in preconference meetings with priesthood leaders, President Kimball announced plans to construct seven new temples—in Sydney, Buenos Aires, Santiago, Apia (Western Samoa), Nuku'alofa (Tonga), Papeete (Tahiti), and Atlanta.

Among his responsibilities for overseeing the master plan for marking the Church's 150th anniversary, Elder Hinckley supervised arrangements for a segment of the April 1980 general conference to originate from the Peter Whitmer farm and newly completed meetinghouse and visitors center in Fayette, New York. For the first time, conference was broadcast from two locations and linked by satellite transmission. Elder Hinckley had encouraged Bonneville's venture into the satellite arena, and he believed that this initial experiment foreshadowed future possibilities for broadcasting conference throughout the world.[36] Beamed to the Salt Lake Tabernacle by satellite and projected on seventeen-foot-high screens next to the organ pipes, the highlight of the Fayette proceedings was the dedication of the Whitmer home and the new meetinghouse by President Kimball.

Saturday morning, as customary, the first general session of conference began with President Kimball presiding at the Tabernacle. But the session on the morning of April 6—Easter Sunday—was anything but traditional. After the first hour the meeting switched to the reconstructed log farmhouse in Fayette, where President Kimball stood behind the wooden box in which

Joseph Smith had placed the gold plates after receiving them from the angel Moroni. Seated behind him were Elder Hinckley and Elder Hugh W. Pinnock, as well as descendants of three of the six original members of the Church, a direct descendant of the Prophet Joseph Smith, and Eldred G. Smith, the Church Patriarch Emeritus.

Following brief introductory remarks from President Kimball, Elder Hinckley read a proclamation from the First Presidency and the Quorum of the Twelve reaffirming that the gospel of Jesus Christ had been restored. Meanwhile, President Kimball and Elder Pinnock walked a hundred yards to the Fayette Branch meetinghouse and were in position there as Elder Hinckley concluded and the telecast switched to the Fayette chapel. From there President Kimball, Elder Hinckley, and Elder Pinnock delivered their conference addresses.

This day fulfilled many dreams for Elder Hinckley, who had played a pivotal role in preparing the Whitmer farm for the sesquicentennial celebration. Several years earlier, during a trip to Fayette, he had learned of plans to build a modest red brick meetinghouse for the branch on a piece of property near the farm. He was disturbed with what he saw, and in a subsequent temple meeting expressed his feelings: "The Whitmer farm is a place of tremendously significant history, and it deserves more than a little building. It will be a sad mistake if we proceed as planned." When President Tanner asked for his recommendation, he suggested that they build a New England-style chapel on the farm and re-create the original Whitmer cabin in which the Church had been organized. "That's a big project," President Tanner responded. "Yes, and it will cost some money," Elder Hinckley replied. "But there is only one place where the Church was organized, and outside of the First Vision, the coming forth of the Book of Mormon, and the restoration of the priesthood, nothing is of greater historical significance."[37] With President Tanner's authorization, Elder Hinckley met with the real estate and building departments and conferred with architects who designed the white chapel with a visitors center at one end. To now be participating in this historic commemoration on a site that bore structures commensurate with its history was for him a deeply emotional and spiritual experience.

As one who both revered the past and championed the advancements of the day, Elder Hinckley found in this celebration a remarkable melding of past, present, and future. "One wonders whether any of [those who helped organize the Church], other than Joseph Smith who saw with prophetic vision, had any idea of the greatness of the thing they were beginning," Elder Hinckley said in his conference address. "Those of us who are here today, reliving the events of history, are filled with emotion as our words and faces are caught by the wondrous technique of television, flung to a satellite high in the heavens, then fed back to an earth station and placed on a screen before those in the great Tabernacle. . . . As we think of this miracle, our minds are drawn by contrast to chapters in that epic and painful movement of the Church from these farmlands of rural New York to the valley of the Great Salt Lake, and thence to the nations of the earth." He concluded with words of testimony: "[The Church's] history has been heroic. It stands today a tower of strength, an anchor of certainty in an unsettled world. Its future is secure as the church and kingdom of God."[38] In a simple prayer President Kimball then dedicated the chapel, farm home, and other buildings on the Whitmer farm.[39]

For Elder Hinckley, whose ongoing study of Church history had filled him with a passion for the people and places of yore, accompanying President Kimball on this historic occasion was an unparalleled privilege. "On the morning of April 6th when we drove to this scene, I had great difficulty restraining tears because of the strong emotions that welled within me," he later recorded. "I felt particularly emotional over standing in the restored Whitmer home under circumstances designed to simulate the meeting which occurred 150 years earlier where the Prophet Joseph Smith and his associates stood. Those of us who were in the little log house on April 6, 1980, were touched by the Spirit of the Lord in a wonderful way, as we were also when we moved over to the chapel. I was moved and impressed to reflect on the wonderful ways of the Almighty and of the terrible price paid by those who have gone before us for what we enjoy today. There came a strong and certain reaffirmation of my conviction that God our Eternal Father lives and that Jesus is the Christ, the Savior and the Redeemer of the world, that the Father and the

Son in very deed appeared to the boy Joseph Smith in the grove. . . . I knew with renewed certitude that the Book of Mormon is exactly what Joseph said it is [and] . . . I felt to rejoice over the opportunity to be a part of this great eternal work restored to the earth."[40]

Elder Hinckley's knowledge of the area did not forestall a few moments of anxiety Sunday evening. After conference the leaders and their wives planned to have dinner together in nearby Rochester, New York, and agreed to meet at a specified time and place. Without Elder Hinckley, Elder Pinnock, or Church Security realizing it, President Kimball accepted a ride back to the city with members and on impulse asked them to stop at the Hill Cumorah so he could greet the missionaries there. When those still at the farm home realized the prophet was missing, a hasty search ensued. "Everyone was worried," said Elder Pinnock. "Security was embarrassed. We searched and searched. When we finally located President Kimball at the Hill Cumorah Visitors Center, Elder Hinckley was enormously relieved and grateful that he hadn't lost the prophet. Several times since then he has said to me, 'Remember when we lost the prophet?' "[41]

The sesquicentennial attracted the local and national press. President Kimball and Elder Hinckley were interviewed by the news media in Fayette, and Monday morning Elder Hinckley and LDS businessman J. Willard Marriott Jr. were interviewed live on *The Today Show,* the nation's top-rated morning news program. After briefly outlining the Church's beginnings and growth, co-host Tom Brokaw asked Elder Hinckley to identify the key to the Church's success. "It meets the spiritual and social needs of members and gives motivation to their lives. It is an anchor of sorts in an uncertain world," he responded.[42] Though he was always anxious about representing the Church before the press, as even the slightest miscue could cause long-term public relations damage, Elder Hinckley was comfortable and able to respond to double-edged questions without becoming flustered or defensive. His public relations instincts had been honed through years of experience on both sides of the interview setting.

On December 5, 1979, Sonia Johnson had been excommunicated from the Church, and her claim that the disciplinary action was a by-product of her support of the Equal Rights Amendment had caught the fancy of the national media. Elder Hinckley acted several times as a Church spokesman on the matter. On other occasions he responded to questions on everything from the Church's position on blacks and the priesthood to abortion and homosexuality.[43] Regardless of the topic, Elder Hinckley was unflappable under fire.

In addition to meeting the press, there were other concerns that demanded his time and attention. As chairman of BYU's executive committee, he was immersed in the affairs of the dynamic university. In 1977 BYU President Dallin Oaks had written the First Presidency suggesting that the six years he had served at BYU might be an ideal tenure for a university president. They had thanked him for his recommendation but taken no action. Then, in a meeting with Church leaders on April 11, 1980, in which he was invited to identify candidates qualified to prepare legal position papers for the Church on sensitive church-state issues, President Oaks again raised the question of his tenure at BYU, admitted that he would welcome the challenge of such scholarly work, and suggested it might be time for someone fresh at BYU.

Three days later, when President Oaks's flight from Chicago to Salt Lake City was delayed by bad weather, he was presented with the opportunity to make his case to Elder Hinckley, who had not been in the April 11 meeting. President Oaks noted: "Just as I was sitting down, Elder and Sister Gordon B. Hinckley rushed on the plane after a breathless dash from a connecting flight to catch this departure rather than their much later and delayed scheduled connecting flight. . . . I had a strong impression that my long delay today was no coincidence but was for the purpose of meeting Elder Hinckley . . . and talking about my release or leave of absence to do the Church legal and public policy study. . . . I told him . . . that a release rather than a leave of absence would be best for the university. . . . He took this soberly and promised to discuss it with his colleagues."[44]

Elder Hinckley was true to his word. Though reluctant to lose an excellent BYU president, as chairman of the Church's Special Affairs Committee he recognized the pressing need for the scholarly research in question and acknowledged there was likely no better candidate than Dallin Oaks. The week of May 6, 1980, President Oaks's release and Jeffrey R. Holland's appointment as BYU president were made public in two surprise and separate announcements. As commissioner of Church Education, Brother Holland had chaired the search committee for a new president—all two days' worth—and he was speechless when summoned to the First Presidency's office and told of his new assignment. "President, you must be kidding," he exclaimed to President Kimball, who issued the call. President Tanner laughed at Brother Holland's response, and President Kimball chuckled before replying, "Brother Holland, in this room we don't kid a lot."[45]

President Holland had just returned to his office when the phone rang. It was Elder Hinckley, who asked just one question: "Have you been with the First Presidency this morning?" "Yes sir, I have," President Holland responded. "Well, I guess that ends the search, doesn't it? Good luck!" Chuckling, he hung up the phone.

President Oaks's release was effective August 1, and in his remaining months as university president he had opportunity to interact with Elder Hinckley in a memorable way. BYU's popular performing group, the Young Ambassadors, had been invited to tour China in the early summer of 1980, and Elder Hinckley was assigned to accompany President and Sister Oaks and the BYU troupe. Although he had traveled extensively throughout Asia, this would be his first trip to mainland China, and during the last two weeks of May he and Sister Hinckley visited the great cities of this vast land. President Oaks recorded his impressions: "Virtually everyone we see in the morning on their way to work here wears a navy blue tunic much like the top of a pair of army fatigues. . . . .[T]he entire picture is one of sameness. . . . Elder Hinckley characterized the hordes of bicycle riders as typical of the attitude in the country. Everyone pedals stolidly without any attempt to pass the person in front of them. All is secure and steady with nothing competitive in evidence."[46]

This trip to Asia was different in other ways from previous visits, as Marjorie explained: "Dad has no responsibilities and goes around in grey slacks, blue shirt and blue blazer. I scarcely know him. We go sightseeing nearly every day. The most impressive was the Great Wall of China. . . . It goes for 3,000 miles thru the mountains. We hiked up the wall . . . to a lookout point which . . . was a monumental effort, one flight of steps after another. Some of our party did not make it all the way, but we had our pride to deal with. It was a warm spring day and about 10,000 Chinese had the same idea."[47]

Throughout their tour the BYU company was hosted by high-ranking officials representing the Communist party. At these receptions President Oaks found himself in an awkward position, for as university president he was singled out for special recognition. Because of Chinese sensitivity to religious matters, the university had of necessity downplayed Elder Hinckley's title and role; yet President Oaks was uneasy that a member of the Twelve was being overlooked. About four days into the tour he hit upon a way to rectify the situation, and at the next opportunity he introduced Elder Hinckley to his Communist hosts as the "Chairman of the Committee of our University." "There were many oohs and aahs at this point," President Oaks recorded. "It had occurred to me that 'chairman' and 'committee' were both words that would translate well in this culture, and they did."[48] When they returned from China, President Oaks enjoyed telling other members of the Twelve that Elder Hinckley was "chairman of BYU's central committee."

Casual opportunities to mingle with the Chinese as well as Communist party representatives occurred daily. One afternoon a crowd of several hundred materialized when the Young Ambassadors spontaneously began to sing on a public street. President Oaks wrote: "Elder Hinckley held what amounted to a street meeting by explaining through an interpreter . . . that we were Americans who had come to express our friendship for them and who were grateful for their hospitality and warmth. He spoke directly with an older man, asking him if he was a grandfather, and the man said yes, he had five grandchildren. Elder Hinckley said he had twenty-one, and the crowd exclaimed in astonishment. He is so skillful at interacting, and remarked later how much he is 'fascinated' by the Asian people."[49]

One Sunday in Shanghai the group attended a large Christian church into which some fifteen hundred people had crowded. Elder Hinckley learned that there was freedom to preach without fear of censorship but that no separate denominations were functioning. When he asked if missionaries from other countries were welcome in China, a Communist party representative immediately interjected, "Don't they have enough to do at home?" President Oaks noted: "Elder Hinckley and I discussed how this meeting had been very heartening in demonstrating how many Christians had retained their faith. . . . At the same time, the outlook was quite discouraging for any formal missionary activities in a church with loyalty to a prophet in America. It will require a miracle to reinstitute the work in China, but I believe that miracle will be forthcoming."[50]

After the group's performance at a teachers college in Nanking, one gathering of Chinese students asked the young Americans why they were so happy. "It is because of our faith in Jesus Christ," they replied. Elder Hinckley reported later, "Here were the youth of America—wholesome, clean, happy—expressing themselves with beauty to the people of China. Political borders evaporated."[51] All in all, the trip was everything Elder Hinckley had hoped it would be. After a fortnight, he and Sister Hinckley took leave of the group and returned home by way of Hong Kong, Japan, and Korea.

Marjorie's frequent postcards to grandchildren provided her family half a world away with glimpses of life on the road. From Korea she wrote: "There are hundreds of people on the beach today, but . . . it is hard to enjoy this alone. As I walked along the beach I pretended one of you was with me."[52] Another card mentioned a friend in Korea: "We are in Pusan today with our friend Rhee Ho Nam. You have met him at our house at conference time. . . . He went down to the beach at 6 A.M. this morning to get fresh shrimp from the first fishing boat that came in. We are eating it at his home tonite. It will be a real treat."[53]

Not every culinary experience was as pleasant, as Marjorie's postcard following a stop at a Hong Kong McDonald's explained: "I told them I wanted a plain bun without sesame seeds. They served me a plain bun with no hamburger also, just a little catsup. Our Chinese and their English is not all that good."[54] A postcard from Kowloon described an afternoon there: "This is a typical street scene in Hong Kong. Grandpa and I had to hold onto each other so we wouldn't get separated and lost.

The noise in the streets is so loud we have to shout to each other to be heard."[55]

Asia remained a favorite destination, and just five months after their excursion to China, Elder and Sister Hinckley joined President and Sister Kimball and other General Authorities for a three-week tour that included area conferences in the Philippines, Hong Kong, Taiwan, Korea, and Japan, as well as a singular event: the dedication of the Tokyo Temple. "Dad has to give 8 talks on this tour and is not prepared with even one. It is driving him up the wall," Marjorie wrote Virginia's family.[56] Pressure notwithstanding, these gatherings in Asia offered welcome reunions with old friends and revealed in dramatic fashion the growth of the Church in those lands. In meeting after meeting he tried without success to contain his emotions as he looked upon those who had pioneered the work in the Orient. In muggy Manila he reminded the audience that only one native Filipino, David Lagman, had been present when missionary work was inaugurated in the spring of 1961. In a tender display of affection and respect, Elder Hinckley called Brother Lagman, who as a counselor in the Philippines Manila Mission presidency was seated on the stand, to the podium, put his arm around him, and thanked him for all he had done to help spread the gospel.

At the Hong Kong conference, Elder Yoshihiko Kikuchi of the Seventy, the first native-born Japanese man called as a General Authority, provoked laughter during the priesthood session when he suggested a program for converting the entire city of 5.2 million: "If each member living in Hong Kong brings just one convert into the Church each year, then the whole city could be baptized in eleven years." Elder Hinckley, who conducted the meeting, prompted more laughter when he said, "You have just listened to Elder Kikuchi, who has been using one of those Japanese calculators."[57]

Weather for the conference in Korea was as cold as it had been hot in the Philippines. Sister Hinckley wrote home: "Had a missionary mtg. with over 400 in the stake house this afternoon. Pres. Kimball called on me to speak. Very frightening. Could not hire out a hall big enough for area conference so they have constructed an amphitheater on Church grounds. It is raining and blowing and freezing cold. All are praying for rain to stop before morning."[58] During the same meeting, Elder Hinckley asked the missionaries to pray that the elements would be tempered. That night it rained hard and snowed intermittently, but the next morning the skies were clear. The temperature, however, plummeted to 28 degrees F., forcing the first session of conference inside the Seoul 4th Ward chapel. Thousands of members who couldn't find seats in the building sat outside and listened to the message over a public address system. The afternoon session was moved outdoors so that those who couldn't squeeze into the building could see President Kimball and the other visiting leaders, all of whom sat huddled on the stand in heavy coats and blankets.

While in Korea, Elder Hinckley presided over the creation of the Kwangju Stake. The previous year, when he and Sister Hinckley had arrived in Pusan to create a stake there, members had greeted them at the airport with flowers and banners proclaiming "The Saints of the Pusan Mission Love Elder Hinckley" and "Did You Bring a Stake?" Elder Hinckley had then organized both the Pusan and Seoul North stakes, the fourth and fifth in the country respectively.

Such assignments were demanding but provided opportunities to be guided by the Spirit. In the creation of one stake in Korea, Elder Hinckley was assisted by Elder Arthur K. Nishimoto, the Regional Representative for Japan and Korea. After a long day of interviewing brethren, they had yet to settle on which of three men should be called as stake patriarch. Elder Hinckley suggested they kneel in prayer and invited his colleague to be voice. "This was a most humbling experience," Elder Nishimoto recalled. "We ended the day without naming a patriarch. The next morning, as we sat on the stand before the meeting, I looked at my watch and realized it was just five minutes before the hour. I knew that a patriarch had not yet been called. No sooner had that thought passed through my mind than Elder Hinckley asked me to call one of the brethren we had been considering. I knew instantly that he had received the answer. What a great lesson. I learned never to act upon any sacred duty until moved by the Spirit."[59]

From Korea the group flew to Japan, where President Kimball dedicated the Tokyo Temple on October 27, 1980, in an intensely spiritual service. For Elder Hinckley, the dedication was an emotional as well as spiritual feast. He thought back to his first trips to Asia twenty years earlier, when small groups of Saints had gathered in dingy, rented buildings, and reflected on the sacrifices so many had made to join the Church and stay active.

At the conclusion of the Asia area conferences, Elder Hinckley remained in Japan to create the first stake in the Japan Sendai Mission. When he and Sister Hinckley arrived in Sendai after an exhausting week, the first thing he asked mission president Kiyoshi Sakai was, "Do I have time to comb my hair?" meaning, "Have you allowed me any time in my personal schedule?" Sunday evening, after the stake had been created, Elder Hinckley invited members of the new stake presidency to the mission home for an orientation meeting. Not feeling well, he went to his room to rest in the late afternoon. Just before the meeting he asked a surprised President Sakai if he had any consecrated oil and then added, "I am so exhausted; would you give me a blessing?" President Sakai remembered, "I was so afraid and felt too weak to bless an Apostle of the Lord. I told him I could not give the blessing in English. Elder Hinckley said Japanese would be fine. So Elder Hitoshi Kashikura, the Regional Representative, and I proceeded." After the blessing had been pronounced, Elder Hinckley said simply, "Thank you, thank you. Now I can go home tomorrow."

The next morning Elder Hinckley looked strong and healthy, and when President Sakai asked how he felt he responded, "*Dai Jobu*, more than fine. I am well." A few days later President Sakai received a letter of thanks from Elder Hinckley, who wrote: "We arrived home on schedule, tired, but happy with the opportunity that had been ours to travel with President Kimball, and as a conclusion to that long journey, to organize the new stake in Sendai. I was sick while I was there, and I so much appreciate the blessing which you gave me. I immediately began to feel better after that. My recovery was quick and total. Sister Hinckley and I are deeply grateful for the privilege of staying in your mission home."[60]

There were times when the press and intensity of work got to him. "This sounds repetitious," Marjorie wrote family members in early 1980, "but I have never known Dad to be so busy. He is trying to keep so many balls in the air he does not do justice to anything and it is frustrating for him. He said last night that he is weary of sitting in meeting after meeting trying to be smarter than he is. At a time when most men retire he seems to be stretching himself further and further. I told him two nights ago that the sink drain is plugged, but he has not even made reference to the problem as yet."[61] And prior to yet another speaking engagement she noted, "Tonight Dad speaks to the Mayflower Society. . . . He spent most of yesterday preparing a talk. He is sick, sick, sick of grinding out words."[62]

Indeed, he appeared to be constantly either behind a pulpit or attending a never-ending sequence of social events connected with his various stewardships. In January 1981 the Hinckleys participated in a BYU-sponsored occasion when the U.S. Ambassador from China culminated his visit to Utah with dinner at the home of President and Sister Holland. Marjorie described the event: "After dinner a handful of the Young Ambassadors with whom we toured China last May entertained with some of the songs from their tour. To see those beautiful kids again and hear those songs . . . was a thrill. Many of the songs they sang were in Mandarin and they also gave their memorized speeches about brotherhood in Mandarin. The ambassador was completely captivated. He could scarcely believe his ears. No place but BYU with its Chinese speaking RMs could this happen."[63]

Meeting with VIPs and dignitaries was all in a day's work for Elder Hinckley. There was nothing routine, however, about accompanying President Kimball to the White House in March 1981 for a meeting with President Ronald Reagan, to whom they presented a book outlining his family history. The newly elected U.S. president expressed sincere pleasure at the gift and declared that this was one volume he would find time to study.

Temple work, which was the capstone of family history research, was moving forward as never before. The following month, at the April 1981 general conference, President Kimball electrified the Tabernacle audience and Church membership worldwide by announcing plans to build nine temples—two in the United States (Chicago and Dallas) and the remaining seven scattered across four continents and one island nation: Frankfurt, Stockholm, Guatemala City, Lima, Johannesburg, Seoul, and Manila. Never before had the Church been engaged in such an ambitious agenda of temple building. Elder Hinckley was overjoyed. He could imagine the jubilation of the Saints in each of these areas, but in particular envisioned those living in Korea and the Philippines. How far the work had come in those corners of the vineyard! At times progress had seemed slow, but the cumulative effect of years of work was reaping an almost unbelievable harvest.

In early May 1981 the Hinckleys again accompanied BYU's Young Ambassadors on tour, this time to Scandinavia, Yugoslavia, Romania, and Russia. From Yugoslavia, Marjorie fired off a postcard to Dick's family that, among other things, revealed her husband's frame of mind: "Dad is very restless. I am loving it. . . . We are well."[64] As much as Elder Hinckley enjoyed the Young Ambassadors, this tour was too much like a vacation, and after a few days he was anxious to get back to work. He returned home by way of Japan, where, with Elder Kikuchi, he organized the Tokyo South and Hiroshima Stakes—the nineteenth and twentieth in that land.

During the conference at which the Tokyo South Stake was organized, Elder Hinckley had just completed conducting the sustaining of the new stake presidency when he abruptly paused for an uncomfortable length of time. Finally he said solemnly, "We have yet one more calling to make, and this one was not part of today's agenda. My old and faithful friend, Brother Kan Watanabe, is attending the meeting today, and the Lord has made it known that he would like to call Brother Watanabe as a patriarch in the [neighboring] Machida Stake." Brother Watanabe said: "All attending that day were very surprised with this sudden announcement, but no one was more surprised than I. Following the meeting I was ordained as a patriarch under the hands of Elder Hinckley. This experience was one of the most clear examples in my life of a prophet, seer, and revelator in action."[65]

Some experiences were, though tender, much more sobering. Only a few weeks later, on July 1, Sister Freda Joan Lee, the widow of President Harold B. Lee, passed away one day short of her eighty-fourth birthday. Elder Hinckley represented the Quorum of the Twelve in eulogizing Sister Lee and related experiences he and Sister Hinckley had had with the Lees in their various travels. President Kimball also spoke, though briefly. His voice was weak, and his words came out in a near whisper.

Life was fragile. Elder Hinckley's colleagues and friends were beginning to pass on, and it was a little unsettling. In particular, he worried about President Kimball, who since the latter part of 1980 had gradually declined in health and energy. There were days at a time when he didn't feel up to coming into the office, and it was beginning to look as though he might never regain his former vitality. Elder Hinckley found it difficult to watch President Kimball suffer the toll of advancing age. He often wished there were more he and his Brethren could do to ease the prophet's load.

CHAPTER NINETEEN

THE FIRST PRESIDENCY

Early the morning of Wednesday, July 15, 1981, President Kimball called his personal secretary, D. Arthur Haycock, into his office and told him that after prayerful consideration he felt impressed to call a third counselor in the First Presidency, and that his choice was Elder Gordon B. Hinckley. Brother Haycock spontaneously lifted both hands high in a show of support and offered: "I can vote for him with both hands. I don't think you could ever make a better selection." President Kimball had already talked with Presidents Tanner and Romney about the proposed change in the First Presidency, and they were supportive.

At President Kimball's request, Brother Haycock phoned Elder Hinckley and invited him to the President's office. Minutes later he was seated across the desk from the prophet. President Kimball got right to the point: He had decided to call another counselor in the First Presidency. What did Elder Hinckley think of that? His first reaction was curiosity. Why, he wondered, was the President of the Church confiding something of this nature in him? He responded that there was precedent for such action and that, in any case, the President of the Church was free to do whatever he wished in such matters. President Kimball smiled, expressed appreciation for Elder Hinckley, and then said simply, "I would like *you* to serve as my counselor."

Elder Hinckley was stunned. President Kimball's words hit him like a tidal wave. After a few moments of silence, he managed to say that he was overwhelmed and that he felt totally inadequate to assume such responsibility. If President Kimball had confidence in him, however, he would do his best to serve, and he would be pleased to lighten the prophet's burden any way he could.

Somewhat shaken and totally preoccupied with what had just occurred, he left President Kimball's office and hurried to a meeting of the Utah Power & Light Company board. But he couldn't keep his mind on the meeting. Later that afternoon he met with President Tanner; though both men knew of the morning's event, neither spoke of it. "This has been a day for sober reflection and prayer," he noted that evening.[1]

Because the General Authorities had scattered during their traditional July recess, the Quorum of the Twelve was not scheduled to meet again until early August. Rather than wait until then, however, President Kimball asked that the Twelve be summoned from their vacations to a special meeting on Thursday morning, July 23. When Elder L. Tom Perry received word of the unscheduled meeting, he had an immediate impression: "Before I even left for Salt Lake City I knew that President Kimball was going to call Elder Hinckley as a counselor, and that he was just what President Kimball needed."[2]

During the days between his call and the meeting of the Twelve, Elder Hinckley was consumed with what President Kimball had told him and distracted by his new circumstances. "I have done much of praying, and much of reflecting," he noted in his journal.[3] He reread his patriarchal blessing, which sixty years earlier had indicated that he would "become a mighty and valiant leader in the middle of Israel." He also struggled with the thought of leaving the Quorum of the Twelve, where he had served for nearly twenty years. "I have felt a sense of sadness and depression the last few days," he admitted privately. "It has almost overwhelmed me."[4]

Clark and his family were visiting Utah that week, and as they prepared to return to their home in Michigan, Elder Hinckley told his younger son that he didn't know when he would see them again, that some changes might be coming in his routine. Smiling, Clark teased, "You mean, you're going emeritus already!" He said nothing further. In fact, he had not yet said anything to Marjorie, although she already seemed to know that something was brewing.

After one of the longest weeks of his life, at 9:00 on the designated morning the First Presidency and the Quorum of the Twelve convened in the Salt Lake Temple. There President

Kimball proposed that Elder Hinckley be made a counselor in the First Presidency. The Twelve sustained the action, and President Kimball set him apart in that office. He then proposed that Neal A. Maxwell be called to fill the resulting vacancy in the Quorum of the Twelve, and he subsequently ordained Elder Maxwell. Each member of the First Presidency and the Twelve had opportunity to express their support. Said President Tanner: "I think this will be a great assistance to the President. He has chosen a man who has been here [at headquarters] longer than anyone. He understands Church procedure, and he has proven himself to be a very faithful, devoted member, and I can sustain him with both hands." Others offered similar expressions.

Finally President Kimball asked President Hinckley to share his feelings. "I feel totally inadequate," he began. "I feel overwhelmed. . . . I think my only qualification, if I have any, is that I love President Kimball and I love his counselors. I love the Lord. I love His work. I know this is His work. I know President Kimball is His prophet; and if there is anything I can do by reason of the meager talents I might have and by the blessings of the Lord, I stand ready to do whatever is necessary. . . . I want to say to you brethren in the Twelve that I have a very sad feeling about leaving this group. I presume this may be only a temporary absence in the natural course of events, but I love the Quorum of the Twelve." Turning then to President Kimball, he concluded: "I pledge to you my loyalty, my love, my consecrated effort, and whatever help I can give. I feel like a pygmy among giants as I think of you and President Tanner and President Romney. . . . I feel like a little boy moving into the big league."[5]

At 10:45 President Kimball held a press conference to announce the appointments of President Hinckley and Elder Maxwell. Just before it began, President Hinckley made a quick phone call home to tell Marjorie what had happened. Kathy and her family were visiting from out of town, and she was with her mother when the phone rang. "Mother took the call from Dad," she remembers, "and when she hung up the phone she had tears in her eyes. Finally she said, 'Dad has just been called as a counselor in the First Presidency.' I was absolutely shocked. I can remember feeling an unbelievable kind of surprise. It never crossed my mind that something like this could happen. As we talked, we were convinced that this would be short term, and that he would go back to the Quorum and life would return to normal."[6]

The phone in President Hinckley's office began to ring immediately after the press conference, followed by countless telegrams, hand-delivered notes of congratulations, and other acknowledgments. Overwhelmed by the events, he returned home feeling an unexpected weight on his shoulders and an uncharacteristic gloom. "I have put on a veneer of smiles," he confided in his journal, "but I feel under a deep cloud of depression. I suppose it is the spirit of the adversary, but it is real indeed."[7] Marjorie, however, was upbeat about her husband's change in assignment. "I was happy that he was going to be able to help President Kimball, because I knew he needed the help," she explained. "I also felt that Gordon would be able to do anything he needed him to do."[8]

For President Hinckley the new calling induced anxiety and apprehension. There was precedent for calling an additional counselor to serve in the First Presidency—at one point President McKay had had five counselors—but though President Kimball's health had been deteriorating, he had two able and experienced counselors who were vigorous and alert. President Hinckley realized that his addition to the Presidency would alter the pattern they had enjoyed for nearly eight years, and he worried that his presence would be intrusive. In addition, he was sensitive to the fact that four men senior to him remained in the Quorum of the Twelve and worried that they might feel slighted by President Kimball's action.

A subsequent *Church News* editorial from one of those four, Elder Mark E. Petersen, was significant: "As a member of the First Presidency, President Hinckley will provide superb assistance. He is truly one of the great men of the Church, and has been for years. . . . His close association with the First Presidency from the days of President David O. McKay and President Stephen L Richards, under whom he worked personally and closely, qualify him most effectively for his new task. But his own great and humble spirit, his intelligent approach to the work, his remarkable consideration for his fellowmen, especially endear him to the people of the Church."[9] Grateful for Elder Petersen's public indication of support, President Hinckley was nonetheless mindful of the Brethren whose tenure exceeded his own.

The circumstances attending President Hinckley's addition to the First Presidency were indeed exceptional. Arthur Haycock recorded his perspective on the unique sequence of events:

> For some time prior to the calls President Kimball extended to President Hinckley and Elder Maxwell, the President had not been at all well. . . . [He] was very noticeably suffering the effects of the oncoming of his last and most serious operation. It seemed difficult for him to concentrate and make decisions and because he was frequently very tired . . . it was necessary for him to take a rest two or three times a day while at the office. Nevertheless, when he called me into his office to advise that he was naming Elder Hinckley as a member of the First Presidency and Elder Maxwell to the Twelve, his mind was clear and his actions as definite and controlled as if it had been 30 or 40 years ago. Immediately following the call of President Hinckley and Elder Maxwell, President Kimball seemed to revert at once to his former condition of . . . general ill health.

Perhaps no one spent more time with President Kimball during his tenure as President of the Church than did Arthur Haycock, who added: "In my 46 years of close association with the last six presidents of the Church, I can say unequivocally that, to me personally, this is the greatest testimony of direct revelation I have ever witnessed. . . . There is no doubt in my mind that the Lord strengthened President Kimball in mind and body and raised him up and inspired him to call [President Hinckley and Elder Maxwell] to their high offices so that His work could continue on."[10]

President Hinckley slept little the night after his setting apart. The overwhelming events of the day jockeyed for position in his mind and rendered sleep impossible. The next morning he made his first public appearance as a member of the First Presidency and with Sister Hinckley rode with President Romney in the Days of '47 Parade in Salt Lake City. Twenty years earlier, leaders in the San Antonio Stake had presented him with a Stetson hat that had sat in a box on his closet shelf ever since. That morning he was happy he had held on to it all those years, though he felt awkward riding along the parade route. "There was much mentioning of our names, and it was all a little embarrassing," he recorded afterward.[11]

During the following weeks, President Hinckley was the object of more attention than he cared for. He took little notice, however, for he was focused on making his transition from the Quorum of the Twelve to the First Presidency as seamless as possible. Presidents Tanner and Romney welcomed him warmly into their circle, but the new circumstances were at first uncomfortable. "I felt like a fifth wheel," he admitted. "These two strong men had been in the Presidency for years. President Tanner had been a counselor to three other Presidents, President Romney to two. They had experience, a great deal of it. But there wasn't any question in my mind that in those circumstances the Lord had acted directly. I didn't know why he chose me, but I did know that I was chosen, so I had no choice but to press forward."[12]

During one of their first meetings together as a newly constituted First Presidency, a discussion ensued about whether President Hinckley should be sustained as a counselor *to* or *in* the First Presidency. He felt it presumptuous to suggest that he was a counselor *to* the Presidency, implying that he had been brought on to counsel all three members, so President Kimball determined that he would be designated as a counselor *in* the First Presidency. And soon thereafter President Hinckley moved into an office in the southeast corner of the main floor so that he could be closer to his colleagues. It was a homecoming of sorts, for he had occupied the same office years earlier when he managed the Missionary Department. "It appears that I have come full circle," he wrote, noting the irony of his long tenure in the Church Administration Building.[13]

Despite the uncomfortable process of integrating himself into the daily routine of the First Presidency, President Hinckley soon saw the wisdom of President Kimball's call of an additional counselor. Just six weeks later the prophet underwent his third and most serious brain operation. His recovery was slow and discouraging, and at times his condition was even desperate. More than once President Hinckley left the hospital feeling depressed about the prophet's health and pessimistic about his recovery.

After two weeks, however, President Kimball's vital signs stabilized and he was moved from intensive care into a private room. At the same time, President Tanner's health began to deteriorate from the long-term effects of Parkinson's disease. These circumstances weighed heavily upon President Hinckley, who was still adjusting to his new role. His visibility had increased exponentially because so many events required the presence of a member of the Presidency, which was already shorthanded.

In August he participated in the cornerstone laying at the Jordan River Temple, presided and spoke at BYU commencement, and dedicated the national headquarters of the Sons of Utah Pioneers.[14] The week before October general conference he greeted visitors at the traditional VIP showing during the prededication open house of the Jordan River Temple and represented the First Presidency at the general Relief Society meeting. In his remarks he praised Sister Kimball while providing a glimpse of President Kimball's condition: "I have seen her frequently as she has stood by the side of her husband day and night during the illness which he has suffered. Her loyalty to him, the evidence of her unflagging love for him, her tender care of him, have become as the threads of a beautiful tapestry. Her prayers in his behalf, her pleadings with the Lord, have been those of a woman of strength."

In striking contrast, he also referred to an increasingly vocal group with which he had become more familiar since his call to the Presidency: "There is rampant among us a spirit of criticism. . . . None of us is perfect; all of us occasionally make mistakes. . . . Men and women who carry heavy responsibility do not need criticism, they need encouragement. One can disagree with the policy without being disagreeable concerning the policymaker." He concluded with a plea: "Restrain your tongues in criticism of others. It is so easy to find fault. It is so much nobler to speak constructively."[15]

With his first general conference as a member of the First Presidency approaching, and President Kimball confined to a hospital bed, President Hinckley realized that members of the Church would be looking to him and the other counselors for direction. In a temple meeting of General Authorities prior to conference, his attention was drawn to the portraits of the former Presidents of the Church that hung there. "I was called on to give my testimony," he noted, "and among other things expressed my view . . . that there are councils in heaven as there are here; and I have the feeling that a council is in session there with all of the prior presidents of the Church who are custodians of the work in this dispensation under the direction of the Lord whose church this is. In our present circumstances, with President Kimball so seriously ill, many questions naturally arise. I am confident that the heavenly council is considering these matters and that they have the power, or have available to them the power, to govern the time frame in the affairs of the Church as well as the course it will take. I therefore have peace in my heart concerning the present and the future." After he sat down, President Hinckley had an interesting impression: "I saw President Lee looking at me from his portrait, smiling as if to indicate that he knew what the future holds."[16]

The immediate future included his being sustained on Saturday morning, October 3, as a counselor in the First Presidency. This conference for him was significant because it marked both a milestone and an anniversary: Exactly twenty years earlier he had been called to the Quorum of the Twelve, and now he was delivering his first address as a counselor in the First Presidency. He spoke of the "worrisome responsibility" and "satisfying experience" that had been his during previous years and thanked members the world over for their kindness, loyalty, and conviction. Then he referred to the announcement that a network of five hundred satellite dishes would be placed in stake centers around the United States and Canada to link members and Church leaders. This development was particularly gratifying as he had, with Bonneville executives, for years investigated various technologies to develop just such a network and had toured a plant in southern California where satellites were being built. Of that experience he said, "As I learned what a satellite and a transponder were, how far above the earth they would orbit, that they worked through the conversion of sunlight to electricity through voltaic cells, and so forth, I got the picture. I could envision the tremendous impact a network of satellites would have on our people. This was the culmination of years of effort in trying to find a way to communicate with our members."[17]

Referring then to his own circumstances, President Hinckley concluded his address: "And now a new assignment has come. . . . This sacred calling has made me aware of my weaknesses. If I have offended at any time, I apologize and hope you will forgive me. Whether this assignment be lengthy or brief, I pledge my best effort, given with love and faith."[18] After conference President Hinckley recorded in his journal: "The absence of President Kimball has been noticed by all, but . . . the Spirit of the Lord has been with us and we have cause to be grateful."[19] Two weeks later President Kimball was released from the hospital, and he and Camilla moved into an apartment in the Hotel Utah.

By November 1981, when the Jordan River Temple was dedicated, President Hinckley was already beginning to feel the burdens of the First Presidency gradually shift to him. Although President Kimball attended one session each of the five days of dedication, he was weak and unable to speak. President Tanner had difficulty speaking clearly, and after the first two sessions he returned to the office. President Romney's eyesight was failing, and he found it difficult to read even large type, but he and President Hinckley alternated conducting sessions and reading the dedicatory prayer. In all his involvement with temple dedications for more than twenty-five years, President Hinckley had never led out in this way. He felt weary after fifteen sessions in five days, but it was a jubilant weariness from which he readily recovered. "There has been an outpouring of the Spirit of the Lord and we have much reason for rejoicing," he summarized. "The only dark cloud has been President Kimball's condition."[20]

The daily affairs of the Church were multifaceted and complex and demanded attention despite the fragile health of the prophet and his first and second counselors. During the first few months of his new assignment, President Hinckley both marveled at and was sobered by the detail and sheer volume of issues that came before the First Presidency, which was the court of last resort on any important decision. In early December 1981, he noted, "I find that there are few days off in this job. Even weekends are consumed by business that must be taken care of."[21]

They considered issues affecting various Church-owned businesses and pondered organizational changes that would make the ecclesiastical hierarchy more efficient; called and set apart temple presidencies and sealers; considered names of men to be called as General Authorities or mission presidents; and handled a plethora of details related to the Church's burgeoning bureaucracy. With President Kimball's authorization they reviewed divorce clearances for those wishing to go to the temple, cancellations of sealings, and restorations of blessings, always causing President Hinckley to anguish over the suffering that attended transgression. "It is almost impossible to believe that some of our people get into the kind of sin they do," he lamented in one journal entry. "One evil thing begets another, until they are entrapped in a terrible web. Excommunication usually follows, and then there are years of regret before there is baptism and eventually a restoration of former blessings. But the wonderful thing is that there is repentance and forgiveness." The process weighed on him. "I do not like to sit in judgment. . . . However, it is a necessary responsibility. I constantly hope and pray that if we err we will err on the side of mercy. The Lord Himself will be their judge."[22] He often cautioned his Brethren that such judgments affected not only the person in question but subsequent generations as well. Indeed, he was finding that most First Presidency decisions had grave consequences.

By late December, President Kimball's condition had improved enough that he went occasionally to the office. After a rare meeting of the full Presidency two days before Christmas, President Hinckley summarized: "[We] advised him that in his absence we . . . have been endeavoring to take care of the ongoing work of the First Presidency, that no changes in personnel, policies, or procedures have been made, and that if and when such changes are proposed, they will be presented to President Kimball for his review and approval. He acknowledged this with appreciation."[23]

Such was the pattern the counselors followed before organizing in March 1982 three new Church executive committees: the Missionary Executive Council, Priesthood Executive Council, and Temple and Genealogy Executive Council. Each would be chaired by a member of the Presidency and would consist also of three members of the Twelve, two presidents of the Seventy, and a member of the Presiding Bishopric. President Hinckley chaired the Missionary Executive Council, which gave him responsibility for an area in which he had been engaged again and again.[24]

President Kimball felt well enough to attend the opening and closing sessions of the April 1982 general conference. Though his address was read for him by Arthur Haycock, on Sunday afternoon he stepped to the Tabernacle pulpit briefly and extended his love and bore testimony.[25] It would be the last time he occupied the pulpit during general conference. President Tanner also spoke briefly during the closing moments.[26]

In his Sunday morning address, President Hinckley referred to the significant benchmark the Church had reached just the week before—membership now stood at five million—but hailed it as a milestone rather than a summit. "This is a time to ask ourselves whether . . . we are any nearer perfection in the virtue of our individual lives," he began. "The milestone of five million members has real significance only to the degree that we as a people bring the gospel into our lives and demonstrate its fruits in our actions." Then, perhaps thinking of antagonists who continued to criticize the Church, he appealed to members: "I urge you to see the big picture and cease worrying about the little blemishes. . . . Of course, there are aberrations in our history. There are blemishes to be found, if searched for, in the lives of all men, including our leaders past and present. But these are only incidental to the magnitude of their service and to the greatness of their contributions. Keep before you the big picture, for this cause is as large as all mankind and as broad as all eternity." Finally, he pleaded with the Saints to emulate the devotion of Joseph Smith and other early leaders, whose faith under the most trying circumstances had been remarkable: "Great sacrifice was made in the past to bring us to this level of growth. Lives were forfeited, and those not a few. We are not asked to give up our lives, and actually very little of our comfort. But we are expected to give of our loyalty, our devotion, our hearts, minds, might, and strength to the on-rolling of this, the Lord's work."[27]

April conference provided the setting for other significant events. On Wednesday of that week, the First Presidency announced that four new temples would be built—in Boise,

Denver, Taipei (Taiwan), and Guayaquil (Ecuador). And in the preconference meeting with Regional Representatives, President Hinckley made two striking announcements. First, after much deliberation, it had been decided that the term of missionary service for single elders would be reduced from twenty-four to eighteen months. Second, when congregations in need of new meetinghouses qualified as tithing-worthy (meaning a specified percentage were full tithe-payers), all costs for building the structures would come from general Church funds.[28] President Hinckley had previously served on the committee that had recommended this change in funding buildings, and he was pleased with the new policy. He noted on one occasion in his journal: "Personally I feel that tithing is the Lord's law of finance for his Church, that we should teach our people to pay an honest tithe, and in large measure rely on that to do the work of the Church."[29]

It was the consecrated offerings of the Saints that allowed the Church to pursue a multitude of projects, including some that reached fruition later that summer. On August 14, President Hinckley dedicated seventeen restored historical sites in Nauvoo, including the Nauvoo Temple block, and spoke of the faith it had taken both to build and later to leave Nauvoo.[30]

Eleven days later he arrived in Manila to break ground for a temple, proclaiming this an event that represented the fruits of modern-day pioneers. His elation over the prospect of inaugurating the construction of a temple in the Philippines was dampened only slightly by the fact that Manila lay in the path of a hurricane. The wind raged all day, remembered Ruben Lacanienta, chairman of the temple fund-raising committee. "Then around 4:00 P.M., nature seemed to calm down and we were able to proceed with the ceremony as planned. A few minutes after the final amen, the wind began blowing hard again. It was something I cannot forget."[31] Despite the severe weather, more than two thousand Filipinos attended the groundbreaking. Two days later President Hinckley broke ground for a temple in Taipei. These two events in the Orient filled him with emotions too tender to articulate. Could it be just twenty years since he had first traveled up and down this part of the world? In some respects, it seemed like yesterday. He could remember hoping for the day when a temple would be located somewhere in Asia. Now the second and third were under way.

President Hinckley returned home to host U.S. President Ronald Reagan, who in early September visited Utah to get a firsthand look at the Church's welfare system. The president seemed impressed with what he saw at a local welfare cannery and remarked that if other groups across the nation had followed suit, the country would not be facing a welfare crisis. President Hinckley enjoyed the experience and noted afterward that he felt the nation's president was a man of integrity.[32]

By mid-1982 the day-to-day responsibilities of the First Presidency had shifted almost entirely to President Hinckley. He found it impossible to take the hiatus from the office that General Authorities enjoy during July and only hoped that with fewer scheduled meetings he could dispose of some of the accumulated items begging for his attention. Most days he carried home a briefcase filled with work. He rarely felt on top of things, though in retrospect he could see that a tremendous amount of business had been transacted. It was fruitless to speculate about how long he would serve in this capacity, and he tried to keep his work up-to-date so he could move back into the Quorum at any time.

In his journal he described something of the worry that enveloped him: "The responsibility I carry frightens me. The president of the Church is unable to handle any detailed matters of business. President N. Eldon Tanner, his first counselor, suffers seriously in his speech and walking. . . . His mind is good, but he has difficulty of expression. President Marion G. Romney . . . has serious problems of recall. . . . I pray each day for strength and wisdom and inspiration. . . . This is the marvelous work and a wonder of which the Lord spoke, and I carry so heavy a responsibility in it. Sometimes I could weep with concern. But there comes the assurance that the Lord put me here for His purpose, and if I will be humble and seek the direction of the Holy Spirit, He will use me according to His will to accomplish His purposes."[33]

If President Hinckley himself missed meetings of the First Presidency, his absence was sorely noted. When in the spring of 1982 he became quite ill and tried unsuccessfully to control an apparently serious infection with antibiotics, he reluctantly agreed to be admitted to LDS Hospital. Though he had been an outpatient before, this was the first time he had endured an overnight stay in a hospital, and the timing couldn't have been worse. With the other members of the First Presidency beset with serious limitations, he did not want his hospitalization made public for fear that it would worry members of the Church. When he returned home four days later, after undergoing a myriad of tests, he was still weak from the effects of the illness and able to do little more than rest in bed. But he had received a clean bill of health.

In late summer, after returning from an overseas trip, President Hinckley felt almost guilty about being gone for so long. "I am here to help the members of the First Presidency, who urgently need help," he wrote. "When I am not here, a heavy burden is placed upon them, and their health is such that they cannot carry it adequately. I really ought to stay home. But I need the stimulation that comes from getting out with the people. To stay here all of the time, and to do little else than attend meetings and make decisions, leads to dullness and a lack of understanding of the problems of people across the world."[34]

Meanwhile, there were challenges right at home. For some time his sister Ruth Willes had been suffering with cancer. After an illness that alternated signs of recovery with periods of decline, her condition worsened quickly and dramatically, and the family was summoned to her bedside in mid-September 1982. At the invitation of Ruth's husband, Gordon offered a prayer in which he pleaded with the Lord to release his sister from the miseries of her physical body. About an hour later, she was gone. "There was a wonderfully sanctifying and sacred feeling about the room," he described. "We all felt it. We had tears in our eyes, but not for regretting her going. We had prayed that she would. It was just such a wonderfully spiritual occasion." He and Marjorie drove home that rainy night feeling that they had just had one of the sacred experiences of their lives.[35]

Each member of the First Presidency attended at least some portion of the October 1982 general conference, though again President Kimball's address was read for him. President Romney was showing the signs of his age, but his sense of humor was as keen as ever. President Hinckley explained during his opening remarks at the priesthood session, "When President Romney learned that President Kimball and President Tanner would not be here, he leaned over to me and said, 'We are getting down to the kids.'" Then later in the session, as President Hinckley began his address, he quipped: "President Romney was to have spoken when I concluded, and he has asked that he be excused from doing so and that I take all the time. They really are turning it over to the kids!"[36]

President Tanner spoke only briefly at conference, bearing his testimony during the Sunday afternoon session. It was to be his last message. On November 23, the Tuesday before Thanksgiving, he attended the First Presidency meeting. Late Friday evening he called President Kimball to inquire about his health. Less than four hours later, he quietly passed away. At 1:20 A.M. Arthur Haycock called President Hinckley with the news, and at daybreak they together informed President Kimball.

In his remarks at the funeral, President Hinckley rejoiced that though President Tanner's body had worn out, his mind had remained alert to the end. "It is a marvelous and wonderful thing when an individual at 84 retains his mental acuity and his capacity to reason and is able to call up the experiences of the past as they pertain to the problems of the present," he said. He then admitted feeling a "terrifying sense of loss and a tremendous loneliness" at President Tanner's passing.[37] "I feel as one who has tremendous responsibility without authority," he confided in his journal.[38]

On December 2, 1982, the First Presidency was reorganized. President Kimball asked President Romney to serve as first counselor and President Hinckley as second.[39] President Romney set President Hinckley apart in a brief blessing that included the promise that he would be able to operate in his holy office under the direction of the Spirit to the "blessing and glorification of the Church" and that he would have health and strength and vigor of mind, body, and spirit. "It was a great honor when I was named a counselor," President Hinckley recorded that evening, "[but] I have always felt that the naming of a counselor when there were already two counselors was something of an aberration of the organization outlined by the Lord. I now feel that in terms of the revelation the First Presidency is properly organized."[40]

Nonetheless, after President Tanner's passing President Hinckley felt frighteningly alone. Three nights after the funeral, he accompanied President Kimball to a Churchwide youth fireside broadcast from the Tabernacle—the largest-ever gathering of youth in the Church and the first use of the satellite network for an event other than general conference. With President Romney at home and a fragile President Kimball on the stand, President Hinckley felt the weight of the Church pressing upon him. His bold warning against pornography, petting, drugs, drinking, and immorality demonstrated, however, that he was not inclined to shrink from tackling even sensitive subjects head-on.

Within a month of President Tanner's death, President Romney's condition deteriorated such that he no longer came into the office or participated in meetings of the Presidency. And by now President Kimball was venturing only infrequently out of his Hotel Utah apartment. He periodically attended meetings, but his vitality was gone. It was painful for President Hinckley to watch this dynamic leader slowly decline.

Barring a miraculous turn of events in which either or both of his colleagues would be restored to health, the burden of the First Presidency's office now fell principally to him. The volume, let alone the complexity and gravity, of matters that came before the Presidency was daunting. But workload was less a concern to President Hinckley than were other questions for which there were no simple answers: Which decisions must be made only by the President of the Church, and which were within his delegated authority to make? How would members react to the feeble condition of the Presidency and to the obvious fact that only he was active and healthy? More important, how could he continue the pace President Kimball had set and advance the work of the Church without getting ahead of the President or stepping out of line? There was no manual, no step-by-step outline on how to proceed under such circumstances. Indeed, the dual mandate seemed almost contradictory. At the very least, his was a delicate balance to strike.

The prospects of what lay ahead might have been paralyzing had it not been for President Hinckley's innate optimism and his unwavering faith that the Lord knew the circumstances and would provide direction. "It was a difficult period," he wrote later.

"But I was careful. I had no question about moving ahead where there was established policy. But with anything that called for new policy or decisions that weren't covered by policy, I went to see President Kimball when he was well rested and explained in great detail the things we wished to do. Arthur Haycock went with me and kept a detailed record of every discussion we had. There were times when I returned to President Kimball several times to make sure he was clear about a decision on a given matter. Only when I was sure that he both comprehended our conversations and agreed with the course of action did we move ahead. I also discussed many issues with the Twelve. Often I told them that I was not disposed to move ahead of the President of the Church, that the Lord was at the helm and knew what was going on. This was His Church, and He could do with His leadership as He pleased. He was and is the master of life and death, and directs things according to His pattern. I was satisfied to be patient and to not move ahead of the President on anything. And we didn't."[41]

"President Hinckley was conscientious in bringing matters to the Twelve," recalled Elder Neal A. Maxwell, "some of which he probably didn't need to. He went the extra mile in sharing things that were well within his prerogative as the surviving counselor to handle on his own. He was also reluctant to move on things that would take us a different direction, even though at times it seemed that the President would wish him to proceed. But he had great faith in the process of revelation and in the belief that things would work out. The things that needed doing got done. He didn't lack for boldness, but he understated his role. Unless he was pressed by the Spirit to take certain action, he waited."[42]

After President Tanner's death his responsibilities—many of which concerned Church financial management—shifted to President Hinckley, and gradually President Romney's decreased capacity led to other administrative adjustments. Worried that two of the three major executive councils no longer had functioning chairmen, President Hinckley asked the vice chairmen of those committees, in each case a senior member of the Twelve, to conduct the meetings, and he rotated among them. This approach became the pattern.[43]

Despite the pressure and workload, President Hinckley

adjusted to demands that kept him at his desk long hours during the week, drew him to the office on weekends, and rarely abated in intensity. Dick watched his father deal with the circumstances at hand. "In many respects, the situation with President Kimball, as difficult as it was, was tailor-made for Dad," he said. "It never occurs to him that something is too difficult to manage. Leisure for him is planting trees or pounding nails. He's never as happy as when he's working."[44]

At times, though, the strain made him irritable. On Thursday, December 23, 1982, he was annoyed to find that most of the Church employees had left for home by early afternoon. He complained in his journal: "I do not know why people feel justified in leaving early when they are given a holiday tomorrow and again on Monday. As a matter of fact, I do not know why the Church offices should be closed on Monday. This is an international organization now, and a tremendous operation where business must be handled every day except Saturday and Sunday." In a postscript, he tempered his comments: "Well, it's Christmas, and I had better feel happy and generous than grumble. I suppose it is the tremendous pressures that weigh on me that develop in me something of a critical spirit on occasions."[45]

He spent half of Christmas Eve day at the office and felt better for having caught up with several nagging tasks that had been hanging over his head. Early Christmas morning he and Marjorie drove to the MTC in Provo to speak to the missionaries. He had determined the time of their visit, hoping they could cheer those who might be homesick on their first Christmas away from home. They spent the rest of the day with family, and at day's end he summarized: "We have so much to be thankful for. I feel a profound sense of gratitude. Marjorie and I are feeling something of the effects of growing old. But we have good health for which I feel so thankful. I am able to carry on a rigorous schedule of work in the greatest cause on earth. . . . We have the confidence and the love and respect of wonderful people. We have a great family. All of our children are active in the Church. They appear to be happily married in every case. They have beautiful children of their own, and we have the love of our grandchildren. We live in comfort but without ostentation. . . . We love each other. And above all, we have faith in God our

Eternal Father and in the Lord Jesus Christ whose birth we commemorate this day."[46]

Neither President Kimball nor President Romney was able to attend the April 1983 general conference, the first at which President Hinckley alone represented the First Presidency. Members who now heard him speak more frequently were becoming familiar with his unique phraseology, almost formal in construction, that mirrored patterns found in the classics and the scriptures. They were also coming to expect discreet flashes of his sense of humor, a candid discussion of sensitive topics when called for, and his testimony and reassurance that the Lord was in charge and all was well.

In his remarks, President Hinckley attempted to dispel rumors about the prophet's health and to assure members that the Church was moving forward. Explaining that President Kimball had not spent several months in a hospital or been in a coma, as some had publicized, he acknowledged that the prophet was weak and his body was tired. Those facts, however, changed neither the scope and extent of his past service nor the fact that he continued to preside over the Church. Said President Hinckley: "What a magnificent example he has been for all of us. He has given impetus to this work in a remarkable way. The whole Church has quickened its pace and lengthened its stride in response to his clarion call. He has been a prophet to us, a prophet whose vision and revelation have reached out to the people of the entire earth."[47]

By the summer of 1983, when President Romney was hospitalized with pneumonia and heart problems, the First Presidency was essentially a one-man operation. President Hinckley noted in his journal: "If anyone should read this in the future, he probably will weary of the procession of meetings. I weary of them also. But they are the stuff of which my life is made. They consume my time. They tax my intellect and cause me to plead with the Lord for inspiration. I chair most of them. . . . This has been going on now for a good while. I have no idea how long it will last. For as long as I am called upon to do so, I shall give my best effort and hope and pray that the decisions reached will be the right decisions."[48] Another day he recorded only, "After the First Presidency meeting, I spent the day dealing with correspondence and other matters which come in as a constant, unyielding stream."[49]

He was ever aware of the need to balance the pressures of the office with his desire to spend as much time among the people as possible. During the summer he dedicated the renovated Assembly Hall on Temple Square and the new N. Eldon Tanner Building at BYU, dedicated four temples, and broke ground for another. When he spoke to the BYU student body on September 20, 1983, he had just returned on an all-night flight from dedicating the temple in Santiago, Chile, and he offered a glimpse of his routine: "Prior to that were similar experiences in Atlanta, Samoa, Tonga, and other parts of the world. I think I have spoken to fifteen different congregations in the last ten days, scattered from California to Santiago, Chile, to Detroit, Michigan. Just ahead is the general conference, for which much preparation is needed. I do not have a speech writer. I have only the opportunity to pray and work. When I have concluded today, you may conclude that I should have prayed more and written less."[50]

His wit surfaced often as he handled the circumstances he had inherited. When neither President Kimball nor President Romney was able to attend the mission presidents' seminar in July, President Hinckley cited health concerns as the reason for their absence and then drew a hearty round of laughter when he added: "I know how they feel. I had a birthday myself yesterday."[51]

As upon President Hinckley fell the weight of directing the affairs of the First Presidency, the Quorum of the Twelve, under President Ezra Taft Benson's leadership, helped pick up the slack. Said Elder Boyd K. Packer: "No one sustained President Hinckley more vocally and fully than did President Benson. When matters came to the Twelve from the First Presidency, he would say, 'Brethren, we must be about this *now*.'"[52] President Hinckley greatly appreciated President Benson's support: "President Benson was my senior by eleven years in age and eighteen years in the apostleship. But without reservation and without hesitancy he sustained me in my office in the Presidency. I took many matters to the Twelve for discussion and consideration and he, as the leader of the quorum, was unfailingly loyal to the office of the First Presidency. It was a great lesson to me. I hope it was to the entire Church."[53]

President Hinckley in turn was faithful to the scope and limits of his stewardship, forwarding many matters to the Twelve, for he was unwilling to move ahead on decisions of any magnitude without the full support of his Brethren. Nonetheless, at times the load he carried seemed overwhelming. One day, when faced with an unusually difficult situation for which there appeared to be no resolution, he dropped to his knees to petition the Lord's help. He later related what took place: "There came into my mind the words, 'Be still and know that I am God.' I knew again that this was His work, that He would not let it fail, that all I had to do was work at it and do my best, and that the work would move forward."[54]

Elder Thomas S. Monson reflected on President Hinckley's role during this unique period in the Church's history: "President Hinckley found himself in a most challenging situation, because President Kimball was still the prophet. Even though a man may be impaired physically, he might not be impaired mentally or spiritually. President Hinckley had the unenviable task of not going too far too fast, but of going far enough. He always had the rounded ability and common sense to do what a counselor should do—that of never intruding on what belonged solely to the President. He was the only member of the First Presidency in attendance many times in our meetings of the Presidency and the Twelve. We made certain we were in total agreement on any issue before we moved forward. We had worked many years with President Kimball, and we knew how President Kimball felt about many matters and what his decisions would most likely be. When President Kimball was unable to make some of the decisions that otherwise would have been his, President Hinckley knew what the prophet would want him to do. Short of assuming that prophetic mantle, he moved as far as he could."[55]

Working in concert with the Twelve, President Hinckley kept the work of the Church moving forward. Between October 1983 and April 1984 he held a regional conference in London; dedicated temples in Tahiti and Mexico City, as well as the new Museum of Church History and Art in Salt Lake City; and honored innumerable speaking assignments. At the April 1984 general conference, he announced the first calls of men to the First Quorum of the Seventy who would serve three- to five-year terms. These Brethren were later sustained to the Second Quorum of the Seventy, created in 1989, with a term of service standardized at five years.

One visible reminder of President Kimball's condition was the continuation of vacancies in the Quorum of the Twelve. In January 1983 Elder LeGrand Richards had passed away. At the April 1983 general conference, Church members anticipated the call of a new apostle, but the vacancy was not filled. When October conference passed without a new member of the Twelve having been called, some members were just disappointed; others more critical began to speculate about the delay and even to second-guess the system that allowed an aging prophet to stay in office. Matters were complicated further by Elder Mark E. Petersen's death a year to the day after Elder Richards's. With President Hinckley short-handed in the First Presidency, it was imperative that the Quorum be fully organized. But the nomination and call of apostles was the prerogative of the President of the Church, and though President Hinckley was concerned about the vacancies, he was unwilling to move ahead without President Kimball. Anticipation mounted as the April 1984 general conference approached.

Dr. Russell M. Nelson, a noted heart surgeon in Salt Lake City, was one of several doctors who were caring for President Kimball. Aware of the prophet's condition, he assumed there was no way two new apostles would be called. He was particularly surprised, therefore, to be summoned to a meeting with President Hinckley the afternoon of Friday, April 6. When he responded affirmatively to a question about whether his life was in order, President Hinckley said, "Good, because tomorrow we're presenting your name to be sustained as one of the Twelve Apostles." Dallin H. Oaks, former president of BYU and then a Utah Supreme Court justice, was similarly called.

After the two new apostles had been presented for a sustaining vote, President Hinckley assured the Saints that these calls had been issued only with the sanction of President Kimball and under the direction of the Lord. "I want to give you my testimony that they were chosen and called by the spirit of prophecy and revelation," he stated. "While President Kimball is unable to stand at this pulpit and speak to us, we are on occasion able to converse with him, and he has given his authorization to that which has been done. We would not have proceeded without him."[56]

He also sought to allay any concern about the state of the Church. In the priesthood session President Hinckley delivered by his own definition an "annual report to the shareholders," assuring those present that, despite an "insidious effort going on to try to undermine the Church and destroy its credibility, even among its own members," the Church was healthy, its finances in sound condition, and its membership of 5.4 million thriving. "Some of our critics and enemies challenge us to give the number of those who have left the Church during the year," he said. "I assure you that they are relatively few in number. Each time I see such a request I feel sorry for the individual." He then referred to the hundreds of church buildings under construction and the five new temples (Bogota, Toronto, Portland, San Diego, and Las Vegas) announced that morning, and added: "How wonderful it is to be a part of a growing, advancing organization. . . . The Church has never taken a backward step since it was organized in 1830—and it never will. It is the cause of the Master. It is the church of God."[57]

The next day, speaking to the general membership, he declared: "It is now almost three years since I was called by President Kimball to serve as a counselor in the First Presidency. . . . During a substantial part of that period I have humbly tried to carry a great and awesome responsibility. I have known something of loneliness and worry and deep concern. I have prayed earnestly for direction and strength and guidance. . . . I am somewhat familiar with the history of this Church, and I do not hesitate to say that there has never been greater unity in its leading councils and the relationships of those councils one to another, than there is today. I love my brethren. To a man they are loyal. . . . Without hesitation they respond to every call regardless of personal convenience. They are true disciples of the Lord Jesus Christ. . . . The work goes on in majesty and power. The kingdom grows, solidly and consistently. . . . God be thanked for the wonder of his work and for the mysterious and certain way in which it moves forward."[58]

CHAPTER TWENTY

FORWARD WITH NEVER A BACKWARD STEP

Unity among the leading councils of the Church, particularly in light of President Kimball's feeble condition, was vital, for the Church was attracting increased attention from a host of critics, some of whom distributed their message through the media. Films such as *The God Makers*, which attacked the Church and belittled sacred gospel ordinances, had received much attention. When the Arizona Chapter of the National Conference of Christians and Jews proclaimed the film "essentially unfair" and an inaccurate portrayal of "the Mormon faith, Mormon church history or anything else about the spirit of the Mormon faith," President Hinckley met personally with the chapter's representatives and thanked them for challenging the allegations.[1]

Criticism sprang from other sources as well. In April 1980 President Hinckley had written: "Let us hope and pray that the days of burnings, drivings, and murders are forever behind us. But there will likely continue to be criticism and attacks of many kinds on the Church and its people. It will be of a more sophisticated nature than it has been in the past; and in the future, as before, we may expect much of it to come from those within the ranks of the Church—members of record while apostate in spirit."[2] His words were proving prophetic, for some of the most vitriolic of critics were coming from inside the Church.

Certain LDS scholars, feminists, historians, and other detractors were becoming increasingly vocal with their claims that Church leaders had not been forthcoming about some of the difficulties in both the Church's past and its present.[3] President

Hinckley was evidently aware of the critics and annoyed by their tactics; at the BYU–Hawaii commencement in the summer of 1983, he spoke openly about cynics who appeared intent on undermining the Church: "These people who are our critics have overlooked the glory and wonder of this work. In their cultivated faultfinding, they see not the majesty of the great onrolling of this cause. They have lost sight of the spark that was kindled in Palmyra that is now lighting fires of faith across the earth. . . . We have those critics who appear to wish to cull out of a vast panorama of information those items that demean and belittle some of the men and women of the past who worked so hard in laying the foundation of this great cause."

He continued, elaborating on a theme about which he felt passionately: "We are not trapped by our history. That history contains the foundation of this work. It sets forth in some detail the circumstances and the events connected with the Restoration of the gospel. . . . If the picture is not always complete, or if there are various versions differing somewhat concerning certain events, intellectual honesty would dictate that there is nothing new in this. . . . The New Testament includes four gospels. The tone of each is the same, but the various writers made particular choices of what they wished to emphasize, and only by reading them all and harmonizing them do we get the fullest possible picture of the Son of God." He concluded by admonishing his audience to stop seeking out the storms and to enjoy the sunlight and accentuate the positive.[4]

A few months later, at the 1983 October general conference, he pursued the same theme: "We recognize that our forebears were human. They doubtless made mistakes. . . . But the mistakes were minor, when compared with the marvelous work which they accomplished. To highlight the mistakes and gloss over the greater good is to draw a caricature. Caricatures are amusing, but they are often ugly and dishonest."[5]

Certain complaints seemed to surface again and again, including those from women who claimed that the Church's patriarchal organization undervalued the contributions of women, and President Hinckley repeatedly sought to defuse their rhetoric. At a general women's meeting he addressed those who asked why they were not entitled to hold the priesthood:

"To that I can say only the Lord, through revelation, could alter that situation. He has not done so, so it is profitless for us to speculate and worry about it. May I suggest, rather, that you dwell on the remarkable blessings that are yours, the great positive privileges of your lives as women of the Church . . . and the transcendent spiritual gifts that may be yours." He then identified ten blessings and privileges of LDS women, among them the spirit of prophecy, the opportunity to preside, and the privilege of motherhood.[6]

During 1984 President Hinckley conducted a series of solemn assemblies in the Salt Lake Temple and elsewhere in which local priesthood officers assembled to partake of the sacrament and receive instruction from their leaders. The purpose of these meetings, he recorded in his journal, was to "speak to the brethren to strengthen them spiritually and to assist them in meeting those who are striving with great diligence to undermine the faith of the Saints and who are trying to destroy the Church. There are many and they are effective, and we cannot simply close our eyes."[7] In countless settings he encouraged men and women, regardless of their circumstances, to look for the positive.

It was an approach that he not only preached but practiced. In President Hinckley's view, one needed only to look honestly at the Church to see that it was a dynamic entity moving ahead in a manner unparalleled by any other contemporary religious organization. He was confident that, despite its challenges, it would continue to move forward with never a backward step—and there were many indications that such was the case.

When Church financial officers presented a study projecting that, even with its aggressive building program, the Church's income would exceed expenditures through the turn of the century, President Hinckley noted: "This is reassuring. However, anyone with faith in this work would know that the Lord will take care of His church and its growth. The faith of the people will assure that."[8]

By the end of 1984 President Hinckley had dedicated temples in Sydney, Manila, Dallas, Taipei, and Guatemala City; hosted an ongoing stream of dignitaries; and spoken to groups large and small, including 7,000 members of the American Legion and their families in the Tabernacle. During his stirring address there, he spoke of having stood at the Tomb of the Unknown Soldier in Arlington Cemetery, the cenotaph in London's White Hall, the Arc de Triomphe in Paris, the Punch Bowl in Hawaii, and Fort Bonafacio on the outskirts of Manila, and then proclaimed: "The roots of this nation were planted in the great fundamentals of the Judeo-Christian doctrine. From this source came the concept of the dignity of the individual, and the recognition of the worth of the soul. These are the very foundation of our liberty. It seems that among us so many have almost lost sight of that truth. It is our great inheritance. It came from God. Without it, America has little virtue to guide its future. With it, we are unassailable. As was declared of old, 'Blessed is the nation whose God is the Lord.' . . . I feel to say that [military preparedness] will not save us if we as a people and a nation lack the heart and the will to cultivate within ourselves moral strength and a recognition of God as our unfailing guide and helper."[9] The former national commander of the American Legion, J. Milton Patrick, wrote afterward, "President Hinckley's patriotic message to us, along with the Tabernacle Choir, was one of the most remarkable events of my lifetime."[10]

A visit that same month from President Ronald Reagan was particularly memorable. Joking that it was hard to know what to get the man who had everything, President Hinckley presented the commander-in-chief with a copy of the scriptures, quoted several verses pertaining to America, told him that the leaders of the Church remembered him in their prayers, and asked if it would be permissible to offer a benediction on his visit. When President Reagan agreed, President Hinckley invited Elder Oaks to offer a prayer, and he later recorded: "Brother Oaks gave a beautiful prayer. I felt that the president was deeply touched in his heart. He was most appreciative as he left us, and I felt that the Lord had answered our prayers, that we had been involved in a most significant occasion when a member of the First Presidency, representing the President of the Church, had read to the president of the United States . . . the word of the Lord concerning this nation and the Constitution which was framed by men whom the God of heaven had raised up unto this very purpose."[11]

The year also saw important developments in Church

organization. In November the First Presidency announced that, beginning January 1, 1985, the term of full-time missionary service for single elders would revert to twenty-four months. But the year's most far-reaching innovation was introduced in June when President Hinckley announced that Area Presidencies would now oversee the work in thirteen geographic areas of the world. In something of an experiment, three of the Area Presidencies would reside overseas. President Hinckley explained that the Church's dynamic growth demanded flexibility in administration and that the organization must somehow reconsider the tendency for rigid rule making, bureaucratic procedure, and policy development. "We can't lick every postage stamp in Salt Lake City. We have to do something about decentralizing authority," he told a group of new mission presidents the following month. He later elaborated on the significance of this administrative innovation: "It became evident that we had to make some decentralization. I brought that up a number of times, with the Twelve and in other discussions. Out of all this discussion came the concept of Area Presidencies . . . accountable through the Quorum of the Twelve and on up to the First Presidency."[12] On subsequent occasions President Hinckley pleaded with department heads at the Church Office Building to embrace simplicity. As thrilling as growth was, he abhorred bureaucracy and at times felt himself swimming helplessly against a mounting tide.

Nonetheless, he was profoundly grateful for the growing body of faithful Church members, and he often said so. In the priesthood session at the October 1984 general conference, for example, he laid aside his prepared remarks and spoke extemporaneously: "I thank you from the bottom of my heart for the goodness of your lives. I thank you for your examples before your families and before the world. You bring honor to this church. . . . You indulge your generous instincts in giving to the poor, in befriending the lonely, in standing up for the very best in our society. You are the sweet fruits of this beautiful gospel." He acknowledged that such support sustained him during otherwise bleak moments: "Your sustaining vote in this conference means more than I can express. Sometimes when I think the load is heavy and the burdens are many, I think of you who not only raise your hands in affirmation, but also give of your hearts, time, and substance in loyal support."[13]

The next morning he reminded the vast congregation linked by satellite transmission that the work of the Church was moving forward and that he had no misconception about his own role. "It is a great honor to stand before you and speak to Latter-day Saints across the world," he said. "I am not here as a substitute for the President of the Church. I am speaking as his second counselor, a responsibility I did not seek but one which I have accepted as a sacred call, in the fulfillment of which I have tried to lift some of the heavy burdens of office from the shoulders of our beloved President and move forward the work of the Lord with diligence. President Kimball is the prophet of the Lord. None other can or will take his place for so long as he lives."[14]

Following the adjournment of the Sunday afternoon session of conference that fall day in 1984, President Hinckley took Marjorie to LDS Hospital for surgery to correct an intestinal problem that had caused her extreme discomfort during the preceding months. She recovered from the surgery quickly and within a few weeks had regained her vitality. It was a good thing, for Marjorie provided her husband with a much-needed sense of balance. When the weight of the world was pressing in on him, she seemed to know how to lighten his mood. The humor that had always characterized their relationship was ever present. When she returned home one afternoon to find him working at his desk, having been evicted from his office while minor repairs were made, she laughed and asked if it was really necessary for him to wear his tie at home. He replied that he didn't have to, but that his speech into the dictating machine was more dignified when he did.

Marjorie's effect upon her husband was obvious to those who traveled with them. When illness forced her to miss the dedication of the Sydney Temple, President Hinckley was restless. Phone calls home helped, but he did not enjoy traveling alone. During one quick trip to South America when Marjorie stayed home, he lamented in his journal: "I miss having Marjorie with me on this journey. I feel that I am only half here when she is not with me."[15]

Furthermore, wherever they went, the Saints responded to Sister Hinckley's simple and sincere testimony, her warmth and unpretentious manner, and her spirit of good cheer. Said Elder L. Tom Perry, who with his wife traveled with the Hinckleys on occasion: "Marjorie Hinckley is the perfect balance for President Hinckley. She is full of life and full of enthusiasm. When you travel with President Hinckley, you had better have your track shoes on, because he fills in every minute. He keeps himself highly programmed so that he can meet with as many people as possible; but she is the balance. She makes certain that he spends time greeting people before rushing off to another meeting. Everyone feels comfortable around her."[16]

Kathy, their eldest, explained: "We have always seen what Dad was doing as part of his work ethic: you do the job you're asked to do, and when that job is over, you do the next job. I can't remember ever connecting what he was doing with power or position. Part of that has to do with Mother. Her expectations for life were so simple that she has never seen herself as anyone special."[17]

President and Sister Hinckley's children were now rearing children of their own, and some traits seemed to pass automatically from one generation to the next. Anytime two or more Hinckleys were together, their trademark family humor surfaced. His children knew his quirks and teased him mercilessly about them. When his daughters joined him downtown one day for lunch in the Church Administration Building, he warned them: "There will be no laughing in the dining room."

Nonetheless, they were a great source of support for each other. Kathy's eldest daughter, Heather, and her husband, Tom Blair, moved into the Hinckleys' basement apartment. It so happened that their stay fell in an era when some of President Hinckley's critics had threatened him, and Church Security insisted on increasing protective measures. An elaborate security system, so sensitive that it set off an alarm if anything heavy was dropped to the floor, was installed. Late one night Tom received a phone call from a worried security officer who indicated that the garage and kitchen doors were open and asked him to check upstairs immediately. The only "weapon" Tom could find was a broom, so upstairs he crept with it in hand. The doors were indeed open. "I wondered if I should run back to Grandma and Grandpa's room, but then I heard footsteps from that direction. I started walking faster with my broom, and suddenly I turned the corner and there was a man who was as big as I was. We both gasped. Just as I was getting ready to swing I realized it was Grandpa, who had heard something and gotten up to investigate. We sat down on the floor and laughed until we were sick."[18]

Tom and Heather assisted with a number of chores around their grandparents' home. "I hope we helped in some way," Tom said. "But the real reason Grandpa and Grandma invited us to live with them was that they saw an opportunity to help us get through school and to spend some time with us as well. You would think the last thing they needed, when Grandpa had the weight of the Church on his shoulders, was grandchildren living in their basement. But what they did for us is indicative of their generosity towards and concern for their family."[19]

When it was possible for family members to share unobtrusively in the experiences President Hinckley was having, they did so. Occasionally when he traveled to a temple dedication or regional conference he invited children or grandchildren along, always at personal expense. Though he never called attention to his family and preferred that no one knew they were there, he liked having them in the congregation. When the Chicago Temple was dedicated, for example, both Kathy's and Clark's families joined their parents in the Windy City. By day they enjoyed the dedicatory services together and in the evenings gathered in President and Sister Hinckley's hotel room for a family reunion in miniature.

"I don't know that we ever saw Dad as a man destined for greatness," Clark conceded. "To us, he was just Dad. He treated us the same when he was a member of the First Presidency as he did when he was a Church employee. What did occur to me as I grew older was that if Dad had had a career outside the Church, he would probably have been enormously successful at it."[20]

December 1984 and the new year following brought events both sobering and sublime. Though President Hinckley had never been much of a sports fan, even he enjoyed festivities surrounding the Holiday Bowl between BYU and Michigan at San

Diego's Jack Murphy stadium. Anticipation before the game was enormous, with BYU entering the contest as the only undefeated team in the nation. When asked in a pregame press conference how he felt BYU would do, President Hinckley responded: "I'm a perennial optimist. . . . But pride goeth before the fall. I don't want to predict too much before the game."[21]

When BYU triumphed in a hard-fought game over the Big Ten squad and was named the nation's number-one football team, President Hinckley joined in the euphoria. At a rally held nearly a month later in the Marriott Center, he inspired a spontaneous roar when he stepped to the microphone and began: "It has been a great evening. I don't like to confess this, but I haven't applauded this vigorously since Washington beat Oklahoma [knocking the latter out of the national championship race]." He continued: "Not only has BYU become famous . . . but the sponsoring institution has become honored and respected and widely known as an institution that expects much from its people and gets much from its people." Earlier in the evening BYU coach LaVell Edwards credited President Hinckley with a role in the Cougars' grid success: "He was with us long before we became famous," LaVell said. "Through him, we received approval to expand the stadium, without which this never would have happened tonight."[22]

December and January were not as kind in other settings, however. Six days before Christmas, a fire broke out in the Wilberg Mine overlooking Castle Dale, Utah, some 150 miles southeast of Salt Lake City. Twenty-seven miners trapped beneath the surface died, and the grief-stricken mining community was thrust into mourning. The day after Christmas, President Hinckley spoke at an emotional memorial service. When the mother of one of the victims concluded her remarks, she turned toward him on the stand, and he instinctively stood and embraced her in an expression of sympathy. No one could explain why such disasters occurred, President Hinckley said. But he assured those gathered that God, who was aware of the sparrow's fall, was also aware of their loss, and then promised, "He will be there to comfort and sustain you; and, as the years pass, the sharpness of today's pain will soften and a divine balm will heal your broken hearts."[23]

Just two weeks later there was additional sobering news, this of a more personal nature. On Thursday, January 10, Elder G. Homer Durham suffered a cardiac arrest, and by evening he was gone. Friends since boyhood, President Hinckley and Elder Durham had enjoyed an enduring relationship filled with respect, common interests, and concern for each other. The two had shared a love of literature and learning, had preached in Hyde Park together as missionaries, and had explored Europe before returning home. They had even collaborated on the hymn "My Redeemer Lives"—Elder Durham composing the music, President Hinckley penning the lyrics—a poignant rendition of which was performed at the funeral. In a voice ranging from powerful to trembling with emotion, President Hinckley eulogized his friend of more than sixty years as a man of faith who had walked with presidents and kings but never lost the common touch. Elder Durham was the sixth of President Hinckley's missionary associates to pass away. On days such as this one, he felt very alone.

He often felt very much alone in the First Presidency as well. In nearly every meeting he attended, the two chairs next to his remained empty. What he had initially assumed would be a short-term assignment as a counselor to President Kimball had now stretched to nearly four years—and for more than half of that time he had been the sole visible member of the Presidency. It had been almost three years since President Kimball had last stepped to the Tabernacle pulpit during general conference, and his absence was glaring.

Despite his tendency to see the positive, there were times when President Hinckley felt the sting of isolation. "At times I feel very lonely as I am faced with the responsibility of making difficult decisions that concern the Church, the lives of people, and other organizations as well," he recorded in early January 1985.[24] On one occasion after the First Presidency and Quorum of the Twelve had wrestled with a difficult challenge, he leaned back in his chair and said, "Brethren, sometimes I get weary of being a judge." There were days when he felt like the Church ombudsman, the court of last resort for anyone who was disgruntled with a Church department or organization, and he found it impossible to shake loose from the constant stream of appointments. "People need a listening ear and they are not [always] getting it," he noted. "People are more important than programs and efficiency."[25]

At the same time, he missed the regular association of his Brethren in the Twelve and looked forward to the day when he would return to full-time service in the Quorum. Although he took as many matters to them as he could, there were some decisions that he alone could make, and others that for the time being had to be set aside. Occasionally he thought of President J. Reuben Clark Jr., who had also served as a counselor to a prophet in feeble health and had once remarked privately that having responsibility without commensurate authority was the personification of misery. With firsthand experience acquired in the crucible of the Church's governing council, President Hinckley now understood what this counselor to three Church Presidents had meant.

Among his General Authority colleagues and others with whom he had worked through the years, President Hinckley's talents as a leader and administrator were well documented. But now these strengths were even more in evidence. His Brethren found that he had a sixth sense when it came to handling issues laced with religious, social, or political complexities; his instincts were remarkable. "President Hinckley has a rare combination of expression and judgment," Elder Neal A. Maxwell explained. "He gets to the bottom of complex issues quickly. I remember a time when I was asked to look into an incident involving a General Authority. When I asked President Hinckley how to proceed, he said simply, 'He'll tell you what happened. You can trust his judgment.' That was that. There was no long oration. He has an enviable capacity for summation. There are fifteen men in the First Presidency and the Twelve, none of whom is a shrinking violet. When we become absorbed in big issues, it is wonderful to have someone speak in a summational way. Otherwise, we could burn up a lot of time getting to the heart of the matter."[26]

Rodney H. Brady, who was named president and chief executive officer of Bonneville International in May 1985, observed

President Hinckley's approach to management: "If a decision requires information from others not in a meeting, he calls those individuals on the phone, asks the questions, and makes decisions on the spot rather than delaying the decision by calling another meeting. When his colleagues want to revisit issues after decisions and commitments have been made, he typically responds, 'We have already covered that ground and given our word to others, now let us move forward to other issues.' And when we have been faced with particularly important decisions, he has often turned to the scriptures on the credenza behind his desk and located a passage that clarified the direction we should take."[27]

While President Hinckley's associates admired his efficiency and impressive leadership skills, they also appreciated his sense of humor, which broke the ice on many occasions and offered respite from otherwise ponderous meetings. "If a little humor crept in to provide some relief from the weighty decisions that had to be made, he employed that talent effectively," said Elder Russell M. Nelson. "As an example, when he was essentially alone in the First Presidency, he would consult with the Twelve about individuals who desired baptism but whose past life was checkered. I remember the case of a man requesting baptism who had killed someone and subsequently been released from jail. President Hinckley said something like, 'It's amazing. The police can't find these people, but our missionaries can.' The weight of responsibility was so heavy that he rescued himself by allowing humor to carry him through."[28]

Derek Metcalfe, the managing director of the Temple Department, recounted the events in a meeting chaired by President Hinckley in which they discussed the situation of an elderly gentleman whose mental capacity had dimmed and who didn't understand that some of his property had been sold to the Church. When he found that a chapel was going up on what he thought was his land, he showed up at the building site waving a shotgun and making ominous threats. "President Hinckley listened as we related the story," said Derek, "and then said, 'I sympathize with him. That's how I feel when you bring in some of the plans you have for temples!' When meetings get tense, President Hinckley has a way of lightening them, which is wonderful because that sort of thing has to come from the presiding officer. He has the ability to do that."[29]

In one meeting held early in the afternoon, Church Educational System administrators presented their budget for the coming year. Feelings became intense, and at one point another board member turned to President Hinckley and asked, "What do *you* think?" President Hinckley, who had been listening with his chin resting on the palms of his hands, replied: "I think I am never again going to have stuffed pork chops for lunch." Everyone laughed and the tension was defused.

When inspecting building projects, he often referred to "Hinckley's Law": "It will cost more and take longer than they said it would." About such matters, he knew whereof he spoke, for under his care fell the weighty responsibility of overseeing disbursement of Church funds. He chaired the Budget and Appropriations Committee, an executive committee of the Council on the Disposition of the Tithes that met weekly to consider all major Church expenditures. A typical agenda might include discussion of a score or more chapels to be built, temples under construction, buildings in need of renovation, and special projects calling for large sums of money.

President Hinckley was financially conservative, and during discussions regarding major expenses he often took from his desk a small coin given to him years earlier in Jerusalem representing the widow's mite. He kept the artifact in his office as a constant reminder of the "fearsome responsibility of spending that which comes of the consecrations of the members of the Church."[30] He frequently explained that most of the Church's assets were not revenue-producing; disbursement of Church resources, therefore, demanded utmost care. But he also seemed to realize when large expenditures were both appropriate and necessary. "President Hinckley has a fiduciary sense about money," said Elder Maxwell. "He realizes that we really do exist on the tithes of Church members. I went to him with brochures of two or three hotels we might stay at during a trip to Sweden. He looked them over, selected the least expensive one, and said: 'This one looks nice enough. We'll take it.' On the other hand, he is indignant about foolish conservatism and has often referred to his experience of having to beg for an entire ream of paper when he first started to work for the Church. He has remarkable balance when it comes to money."[31]

When, for example, President Hinckley first reviewed drawings of the temple proposed for Freiberg in the German Democratic Republic, he felt the building needed major revisions to give it greater dignity. Though his requested modifications would add substantially to the cost, he responded that ten years from now Church leaders wouldn't miss the money but would be perpetually critical of the structure if it wasn't designed properly from the outset. By contrast, however, when feted at an elaborate and expensive banquet by Church leaders in one Far Eastern country, he was embarrassed. "I wish they would not do things of this kind for us," he noted. "Money spent for this lunch would have kept a missionary in the field for a month."[32]

President Hinckley was a driving force behind the invitation to members to participate in a special day of fasting on January 27, 1985, and to contribute to a relief fund for victims of famine in Africa and other third-world nations. The response was overwhelming. At the April 1985 general conference he revealed that over six million dollars had been donated, two-thirds of which had already been placed with four reputable international relief organizations for disbursement. "Thank you for what you have done," he told the Saints. "Many contributed far more than the value of two meals. You have cast bread upon the waters, and it will return to you as you experience the peace of generous hearts."[33]

That conference served as a backdrop for a significant missionary-related milestone when, for the first time in twenty-four years, every mission president in the Church gathered in Salt Lake City to receive instruction from the General Authorities. Noting that he had been associated with missionary work for fifty-two years, President Hinckley expressed his hope that out of this gathering would come a new vitality for the work. And he promised that those who lost themselves in the service of God would find that the process would save them: "This is one of the great miracles of our time—the transformation that comes into the lives of [those] who go out to teach the gospel. . . . They subject themselves to the discipline of the mission field. That becomes a remarkable blessing. They establish habits of work. They discover the values in life that are most important. They develop in their hearts a fervent testimony. . . . The future of the Church will be so much the stronger by reason of missionary service."[34]

During the six months between the April and October conferences of 1985, President Hinckley's activities included events both joyous and sobering. Less than two weeks after April conference, Elder Bruce R. McConkie passed away following a long bout with cancer. President Hinckley and Elder McConkie had served together for years on the Missionary Executive Committee, and his passing revived pangs of loneliness in President Hinckley, who was the concluding speaker at the funeral. "Three great trees have fallen in the forest in the last months," he said, referring to Elders LeGrand Richards, Mark E. Petersen, and now Bruce R. McConkie. "I felt like a little puppy trying to keep up with [Elder McConkie] as he took his long measured steps," he continued. "So it has been with most of us in keeping up with the stride of his mind in scholarship in the gospel."[35]

By contrast, the most glorious of occasions for President Hinckley were temple dedications, and this was proving to be an unprecedented era of temple building. Between the spring of 1982 and the fall of 1985, he broke ground for temples in Manila, Taipei, Dallas, Chicago, Denver, and Frankfurt; presided at temple dedications in Atlanta, Western Samoa, Tonga, Santiago, Tahiti, Mexico City, Boise, Sydney, Manila, Dallas, Taipei, Guatemala City, Freiberg, Stockholm, Chicago, and Johannesburg; and rededicated the refurbished Manti Temple. With the dedication of the temple in South Africa there were now houses of the Lord on every continent except Antarctica. President Hinckley not only dedicated in three years as many temples as had been built in all the previous history of the Church, but he took keen personal interest in each temple's design and construction. If a temple didn't have a celestial reach in its design, the architects heard about it. If an interior didn't create the desired atmosphere, workers were invited to start over. And he often scouted for property personally, climbing to the tops of hills and walking across sites himself before finalizing a location.[36]

Since the early 1950s one of President Hinckley's primary areas of focus had been temple work, and he often reflected on the urgency he had felt years earlier to build a larger number of smaller temples in an effort to take them to the people. Now he found himself participating in the fulfillment of the mandate to take the blessings of the temple to worthy men and women everywhere.

In many respects, he was ideally suited for these assignments, and those who accompanied him marveled at his capacity. Though he typically conducted and spoke in every dedicatory session—of which there were sometimes more than twenty—he did so without notes, rarely if ever repeated himself, and suited a message to each audience. After the dedication of the Chicago Temple in August 1985, he noted that he had spoken in 185 dedicatory sessions during the previous twenty-eight months and had presided over and conducted sixteen cornerstone ceremonies.

Each dedication reflected the unique customs and circumstances of the land or area, but the Spirit was always the same—profound and penetrating. And for various reasons, each dedication was memorable. In Guatemala City in December 1984, three-fourths of those present were descendants of Father Lehi, and President Hinckley felt as though he could almost see generations of their forebears. Between sessions, when he walked out a rear exit to get some fresh air, he found a group of native Saints, some of them barefoot, who had traveled hundreds of miles to attend. He could not hold back the tears as he contemplated their circumstances and the phenomenal effort they had made to come to Guatemala City.[37]

The Freiberg Temple's seven dedicatory sessions were a pentecost. President Monson's influence in the Communist-controlled German Democratic Republic had been instrumental in opening the way for the construction of this edifice. Recalling his own visit to Dresden, Meissen, and Leipzig fifty years earlier en route home from his mission, President Hinckley said he had never dreamed that such a structure would one day stand here, and that completion of this temple was evidence of the Lord's hand in softening the hearts of government officials who permitted it to be built. "We shed many tears; we wept with them;

we prayed with them; we sorrowed with them; we rejoiced with them," he said of that experience. "It touched me to the depths of my soul when I saw the faith, the love of the Lord, the loyalty to the gospel in the hearts of Saints in the German Democratic Republic."[38]

During the dedication of the Papeete Tahiti Temple, President Hinckley had an emotional reunion with the nurse who had assisted him twenty years earlier in the aftermath of the tragic boat accident off Maupiti Island and who had since joined the Church. In his remarks at several sessions he referred to the women who had died that fateful day: "I hope with all my heart [their] husbands are worthy to come to this house and have their beautiful wives sealed to them."[39]

His experience at the Johannesburg Temple dedication was likewise poignant. To see black and white Saints gathered in a service of eternal import in a country where racial tension had spawned hate and oppression stirred President Hinckley's soul. In his remarks he referred to the strife of that nation and prophesied: "Newspapers and television across the world present a dramatic picture of the flames of South Africa. But I am confident things will work out for your blessing. Things may get worse before they get better, but I am confident they will get better."[40]

Each temple dedication in Asia was a highlight for President Hinckley, whose tender feelings for the Oriental Saints were enduring. During dedicatory services for the Manila Philippines Temple he said, "Never has there been a time that I have felt such a surge of emotion and been touched by the Spirit more than I feel now." He struggled to rein in his emotions as he added: "I don't know of any place in the world where the harvest has been so great in such a short period of time. The Lord has touched this land in a miraculous and marvelous way."[41]

While touring the refurbished Manti Temple the night before the dedicatory services, President Hinckley again had difficulty holding back tears. "Something happens to me when I go into these temples," he explained the next day about the four built during the pioneer era. "I see the magnificence of the workmanship wrought with rudimentary tools. I have been in most of the great buildings of the world—palaces of kings and houses of parliaments—and in none of those places have I had the kind of feeling I get in coming to these early pioneer houses of God."[42] During one session he called upon Sister Hinckley to bear her testimony and tell the story of her grandfather, who had died from injuries sustained while hanging the building's heavy east doors. "I think it was the highlight of all the talks given," he noted proudly afterward.[43]

In each dedication President Hinckley wove into his sermons the stories of faithful Saints who had pioneered the work in their area, thereby calling attention to service that might otherwise have gone unnoticed. And regardless of country, continent, or languages spoken, he counseled temple-goers to find in the house of the Lord a place of sanctuary where they could retreat from the cares of the world and feast upon the blessings of eternity. "We never have a temple dedication when we do not have two audiences: those who sit here and those on the other side who are with us," he often explained. He invited Saints old and young to prepare for the dedications by cleansing their lives of anything displeasing to the Lord. "The temple experience is a sanctifying experience," he repeatedly taught, adding the promise, "There is no better way to cultivate a spirit of unselfishness among our people, to encourage fidelity between husbands and wives, to draw nearer to the Lord than to go to his holy house."[44]

The magnificent spiritual outpouring of a temple dedication stood in stark contrast to other matters that came regularly to President Hinckley's attention. Letters poured in to the First Presidency from heartbroken men and women whose lives had been shattered by the misdeeds of others. "Many of these letters are fraught with sadness," he said during one general priesthood meeting.[45] "They tell of personal tragedies, of families in distress, of broken homes and broken hearts. In reading them, I am at times almost overwhelmed by the great burdens that many people carry." As the one robust member of the Presidency, it was left to him to address difficult moral and social issues that were wreaking increasing havoc in society. Pornography, child and spouse abuse, drugs, adultery and fornication, homosexuality—his denunciation of each was unmistakable. Men who abused their children or wives were unworthy to hold the priesthood and would answer to God: "If there be any within the sound of my voice who are guilty of such practices, let them repent forthwith, make amends where possible, develop within themselves that discipline which can curb such evil practices, plead with the Lord for forgiveness, and resolve within their hearts henceforth to walk with clean hands."[46]

President Hinckley's counsel was direct and typically exposed the ironies associated with inappropriate behavior. On the issue of illicit drugs, he said: "Some have even used as an alibi the fact that drugs are not mentioned in the Word of Wisdom. What a miserable excuse. There is likewise no mention of the hazards of diving into an empty swimming pool or of jumping from an overpass onto the freeway. . . . To you who may be partaking, I repeat, stop immediately. To you who at any time in the future may be tempted, I urge you to stand your ground."[47]

President Hinckley frequently counseled members to strengthen and sustain one another. "Ours is the task of raising the sights of those of our people who fail to realize the great potential that lies within them."[48] He often cited Brigham Young's plea, made when he learned that two handcart companies were in jeopardy, to "go and bring in those people now on the plains." Such a pronouncement squared with his commitment to those languishing on the plains of discouragement, despair, and sin. As he said on one occasion, representative of many others: "I know that all about us there are many who are in need of help and who are deserving of rescue. Our mission in life, as followers of the Lord Jesus Christ, must be a mission of saving. . . . We can do more to help those who live on the edge of survival."[49] And he always identified the ultimate Source of comfort and peace: "Ours is a ministry of healing, with a duty to bind the wounds and ease the pain of those who suffer. Upon a world afflicted with greed and contention, upon families distressed by argument and selfishness, upon individuals burdened with sin and troubles and sorrows, I invoke the healing power of Christ, giving my witness of its efficacy and wonder."[50]

His empathy for those who suffered may have been developed partly in the crucible of his own experience. He himself was forced to suffer—almost always in silence—over vicious attacks from enemies determined to humiliate and disgrace him. As the only visible member of the First Presidency, he was an easy target, a lightning rod of sorts. There were those who apparently believed that if they could discredit President Hinckley, they would also undermine and threaten the stability of the Church hierarchy. Consequently, over time he was accused of everything from dishonesty and political maneuvering to repulsive moral transgression.

His prominence left him open to bizarre attacks. Ironically, the most vocal critics came from within the Church—liberal scholars, historians, feminists, and others who felt they or their causes weren't being treated fairly or who took issue with the direction or statements of Church leaders. After a visit from one such individual, President Hinckley reflected: "Our problems do not arise from people outside the Church, but from those within who speak of their faith and their love for the work. They do not seem to realize how critics of the Church feast on such materials. . . . I am sorry [they] do not seem to realize the damage [they] can do."[51]

Even when the criticism became front-page news, President Hinckley was typically optimistic about the future. "When challenges arose that seemed to distract our focus," Elder James E. Faust explained, "President Hinckley often reminded us, 'Brethren, things have never been better in the Church than they are now. The Lord is watching over the kingdom, and we will work through our challenges and our problems.' Such an attitude goes back to the wellspring of his faith and the commitment to the Church that he has developed so richly during his life."[52] Indeed, if President Hinckley had a personal motto it was, in his own words: "Things will work out. If you keep trying and praying and working, things will work out. They always do. If you want to die at an early age, dwell on the negative. Accentuate the positive, and you'll be around for a while."[53]

Blessed with an overarching view of the Church in this dispensation, President Hinckley saw past the temporary annoyances. "Critics may wear out their lives in trying to deny or demean or cast doubt," he said in general conference, "but . . . this mission . . . is larger than any race or nation or generation. . . . It is a cause without parallel. . . . You and I may fail as individuals and miss the blessing. But his work cannot fail. There will always be those he will raise up to accomplish it."[54]

With such a philosophy embedded deep within, President Hinckley pressed forward through the constant pressure and occasional loneliness. His approach was practical; his pace, unrelenting. In September 1985 he told the BYU student body: "It has now been more than four years since I was called into the Presidency. For two and a half of those years, not of my own wish, I have had thrust upon me the burden of the day-to-day work of the office of the Presidency. Please do not misunderstand me. I am not complaining. I have been blessed by the Lord in a marvelous and wonderful way."[55]

In general, President Hinckley continued in the simple and pragmatic pattern he had established years before. As he noted one Sunday, after agonizing over a talk he was to give the following week in a Churchwide fireside for husbands and wives, "I pray to the Lord earnestly for help, and then go to work."[56] At times things fell nicely into place; on other occasions they didn't. As he prepared for the October 1985 general conference, for example, the Sunday before conference his talks were still not prepared. "After pleading with the Lord for help, I . . . dictated the talk to be given Sunday morning. . . . I was also inspired with what I might try to do for the General Priesthood meeting. It is remarkable how things begin to fall into place when the Lord takes hold after we try and become frustrated in the process."[57]

Despite the challenges, his motivations were unencumbered and straightforward. "I am driven by two resolutions," he stated during that same conference. "The first is to serve the Lord to the very best of my ability. I think I understand, in some small measure at least, what that means. The second is to serve His chosen prophet, President Spencer W. Kimball, and lift from his shoulders every burden that I legitimately can. I consider these to be sacred and binding obligations and more important than all other considerations."[58]

He acknowledged in the priesthood session that President Kimball was "not very strong" and was suffering "from the infirmities of age," but he again assured members that the work was moving forward and doing so under divinely established procedure, with no action of consequence taken without unanimity of feeling in the highest councils of the Church.[59] At that conference Elder M. Russell Ballard was called to the Quorum of the Twelve, filling the vacancy created by the death of Elder McConkie. President Kimball participated in the ordination—the last it would be his privilege to be involved in, for although President Hinckley didn't know it at the time, the October 1985 conference was the last one he would preside over alone. Before the Presidency changed, however, he became the focal point of another controversy involving the Church.

During the previous three years President Hinckley had on occasion met with Mark Hofmann, a Salt Lake City rare-documents dealer who had come forward with several troublesome historical documents that challenged Joseph Smith's account of the Restoration. Then-Elder Hinckley had been among the first General Authorities to meet Hofmann when, on April 22, 1980, Elder G. Homer Durham, then serving as managing director of the Historical Department, had called to tell him about this university student who was in possession of an old Bible that contained an interesting document. Elder Durham asked Elder Hinckley and Elder Packer, both of whom were serving as advisers to the Historical Department, if they would meet with Hofmann. They agreed, and later were present when Elder Durham introduced Hofmann to the First Presidency and showed them what was later referred to as the Anthon transcript—or, as President Tanner noted in his journal, what "appeared to be the original paper copied by Joseph Smith from the [gold] plates and given to Martin Harris to take to New York City for examination by Professor [Charles] Anthon."[60] Though not entirely forthcoming about the provenance of the document, Hofmann indicated he had discovered the manuscript in the Bible, which he said he had purchased from a Salt Lake City man who had obtained it in the 1950s from a granddaughter of Joseph Smith's sister Katharine in Carthage, Illinois.

Another Hofmann discovery subsequently aroused widespread attention from Church members, detractors, and officials of the Reorganized Church of Jesus Christ of Latter Day Saints—the record of a father's blessing Joseph Smith purportedly gave his son Joseph Smith III in which he blessed the eleven-year-old boy to be his "successor to the Presidency of the High

Priesthood," or, as some interpreted it, President of the Church.[61] Hofmann claimed to have located the blessing in a collection of writings of Thomas Bullock, who had served as a clerk to the Prophet Joseph Smith.

Elder Hinckley first saw the Joseph Smith III blessing on February 27, 1981, and though neither he nor his colleagues of the Twelve were concerned that the letter undermined the doctrine of prophetic succession, he recognized that one interpretation of the document could provide critics with fodder for their dissection of the long-established practice. With this in mind, he devoted his April 1981 conference address to the blessing, explaining that Church leaders had publicized the discovery despite the realization that critics might seize the opportunity to suggest a flaw in the Church's line of authority. In a gesture of goodwill, he reported, the First Presidency and the Quorum of the Twelve had given the document to the Reorganized Church, whose presidents had been lineal descendants of Joseph Smith.

He concluded his address with a ringing endorsement of the Lord's pattern of succession: "That same authority which Joseph held, those same keys and powers which were the very essence of his divinely given right to preside, were by him conferred upon the Twelve Apostles with Brigham Young at their head. Every president of the Church since then has come to that most high and sacred office out of the Council of the Twelve. Each of these men has been blessed with the spirit and power of revelation from on high. There has been an unbroken chain from Joseph Smith, Jr., to Spencer W. Kimball."[62]

Critics debated the ramifications of the Joseph Smith III blessing, as well as other Hofmann documents that contained unflattering innuendos about early Church leaders or events associated with the Restoration. Then, on January 3, 1984, an acquaintance of Hofmann's, Lyn Jacobs, showed President Hinckley a letter from Martin Harris to W. W. Phelps in which an account of Joseph Smith's discovery of the gold plates contained noticeable differences from the official version. Reference to a spirit that "transfigured" himself from a "white salamander" ignited a fury of controversy among critics, scholars, and lay members of the Church. Describing as it did the early origins of the Church in spiritualistic terms, the "Salamander Letter" appeared to confirm other documents regarding the purported treasure-hunting activities of Joseph Smith. Jacobs said he had obtained the letter from an eastern collector whose name he had received from Hofmann.

The Twelve subsequently asked that research be conducted to place the document in historical context and to verify its authenticity. In the meantime, other memorabilia surfaced that questioned the veracity of the Church's beginnings. The majority of these documents were brought to President Hinckley's attention, and he took them to the Twelve for discussion and ultimately made most of them a matter of public record. Of the Salamander Letter he noted: "We have nothing to hide. Our enemies will try to make much of this letter, but any fair-minded individual who will read it in terms of the time it was written and the language of the day will not see it as detrimental to the history of those events connected with the restoration of the gospel."[63]

Controversy over the Salamander Letter reached a zenith on Saturday, August 25, 1984, when *Los Angeles Times* religion writer John Dart published a lengthy article in which he asserted that the letter threatened to "alter the idealized portrait of church founder Joseph Smith." Among conservative Protestant critics of the LDS church, Dart maintained, the Salamander Letter was now regarded as "one of the greatest evidences against the divine origin of the Book of Mormon."[64] Elder Thomas S. Monson, on assignment in Frankfurt, was surprised to see the *International Herald Tribune*'s headline, "The Mormons and the White Salamander: 1830 Letter, If Authenticated, Would Prove Founder's Interest in the Occult."

Though the unfolding controversy weighed on him, President Hinckley was coolheaded in both his reactions and his response. These events weighed on his mind, however. At the October 1984 general conference he spoke of the Church's four cornerstones, among them the First Vision and the Book of Mormon: "For more than a century and a half, enemies, critics, and some would-be scholars have worn out their lives trying to disprove the validity of [the First Vision]. Of course they cannot understand it. The things of God are understood by the Spirit of God."[65]

In April 1985, Salt Lake area businessman Steven F. Christensen, who as a collector of historical memorabilia had purchased the Salamander Letter from Hofmann, presented the document to President Hinckley, who accepted it on behalf of the Church. Later that month the *Church News* carried the complete text of the letter. The First Presidency statement accompanying the article quoted President Hinckley: "No one, of course, can be certain that Martin Harris wrote the document. However, at this point we accept the judgment of the examiner that there is no indication that it is a forgery. This does not preclude the possibility that it may have been forged at a time when the Church had many enemies. It is, however, an interesting document of the times." He concluded with the assurance that the letter had nothing to do with the divine underpinnings of the Restoration. "The real test of the faith which both Martin Harris and W. W. Phelps had in Joseph Smith and his work is found in their lives, in the sacrifices they made for their membership in the Church, and in the testimonies they bore to the end of their lives."[66]

President Hinckley carried the burden of responding to the questions, attacks, and insults that followed. Not long thereafter he noted in his journal: "The media, feasting on anything they can dig up that might prove embarrassing to the Church, are having a field day. It will not adversely hurt the work in the long term, but it does produce some wounds among the weak and those of little faith."[67] He felt confident, however, that the Church would emerge from the controversy unscathed. "I do not fear truth. I welcome it!" he said many times. "But I wish all of my facts in their proper context, with emphasis on those elements which explain the great growth and power of this organization."[68]

Over the years he frequently encouraged the Saints to see critics for who they were. To a Churchwide young adult audience, for example, he referred to the controversial letters and then prophesied: "[The Church] will weather every storm that beats against it. It will outlast every critic who rises to mock it. It carries the name of Him whose it is, even the Lord Jesus Christ."[69] It was hard for him to understand the critics' point of view, for after years of his own ongoing study of Church history, he not only had a personal witness of Joseph Smith's divine calling but found in him an exquisite model of optimism and faith.

It was as though he couldn't study, teach, or testify enough about this prophet of God. On one occasion a few priesthood leaders in Salt Lake City and their families were invited to attend a family home evening with President Hinckley. During his informal remarks, he asked all the children age eighteen and under to stand. "I *love* the Prophet Joseph Smith," he said with feeling, asking them to repeat the phrase with him. After they had done so, President Hinckley concluded: "Please write in your journal that I stood and bore my testimony of the Prophet Joseph Smith, and that I love him."

It was almost impossible for President Hinckley to understand or have much patience with those who tried repeatedly to undermine the Prophet during the various phases of the document scandal. Unfortunately, the Hofmann-promoted memorabilia proved to be not only spiritually but physically lethal. On the morning of October 15, 1985, tragic news riveted the residents of Salt Lake City and the Intermountain West: Two members of the Church, Steven F. Christensen and Kathy Sheets, had been killed within ninety minutes of each other by bombs concealed in packages. The community was shocked and bewildered. Initially, some believed the murders to be connected to a troubled business venture spearheaded by Christensen and Gary Sheets, the other victim's husband. Others speculated that the tragedies were linked to the Salamander Letter. Church Security immediately increased its protection of President Hinckley, who couldn't imagine that the horrifying events held any relationship to him.

The next day a third explosion ripped through a car parked just a block north of Church headquarters. Within minutes two Church Security officers arrived breathless at President Hinckley's office; the remainder of the afternoon they shuttled in and out with updates. Mark Hofmann had been seriously injured in the blast. With Hofmann's involvement, the documents connection seemed more likely. President Hinckley conferred much of the afternoon with Elders Dallin H. Oaks and Hugh W. Pinnock, who had met with Hofmann regarding what the documents dealer referred to as the McLellin Collection, papers from William E. McLellin, a former member of the Twelve who had wavered between devotion and dissidence throughout his life. They agreed that Elder Oaks should immediately tell the police what he knew about Christensen and Hofmann's connection with the McLellin transaction.

Over the next few days the Church in general and President Hinckley in particular took a beating in the press. Some reporters accused him of acting unilaterally in obtaining documents and speculated about how a Church leader could have become involved in what was beginning to look like documents fraud. Some even implied a sinister element in his association with Hofmann. After reading one such article President Hinckley noted: "I was disgusted. They are not interested in finding a solution to the murders. They are interested only in trying to make the Church look suspect."[70] The following day he added: "I have never seen such a barrage of press innuendo, much of it downright false. The Church, as might be expected, is the target, and my name is used prominently . . . because Mark Hofmann met with me on several occasions concerning the Church acquiring various historical documents."[71]

The morning of October 23, the Church held a press conference to clarify its relationship with Hofmann, Christensen, and others involved in what was now a murder investigation. Representatives of CBS, the BBC, the major wire services, and other international and national news agencies were among the large contingent of reporters who filed into the auditorium of the Church Office Building. Flanked by Elders Oaks and Pinnock, President Hinckley expressed sympathy to the families of the bombing victims, explained that the Church had cooperated fully with law-enforcement officials, reviewed his and the Church's association with Mark Hofmann, elaborated on his personal interest in Church history, and explained what little he knew about the McLellin Collection. In response to a question about the Church's proclivity for collecting historical materials, he stated that from the beginning leaders had been admonished to keep records.

"If this goes on," he quipped, "we will have to find a lot more room to house all the newspaper clippings." Returning to a serious tone, he added: "But we have a mandate. We would suppose the institution for which you work keeps a history, a corporate history. We have an obligation to keep a history of the

Church and we regard that very seriously. We are going over to dedicate the new genealogical building . . . [which is] essentially a historical library. It has cost a very handsome sum and it's a beautiful archive. The finest in the world and the purpose of it is historical—historical research."[72]

The news conference quelled some of the rumors that had flown about Salt Lake City, and, as promised, later that morning President Hinckley dedicated the Church Genealogical Library, calling it the jewel in the genealogical research crown and adding that this was a "day of rejoicing beyond the veil."[73] It was ironic that with his lifelong interest in Church history and temple work, which relied so heavily on family history research, President Hinckley found himself in the middle of an ugly ordeal involving controversial historical documents.

Before going to the auditorium for the press conference, he had reread section 10 of the Doctrine and Covenants, which dealt with the lost 116 pages of the Book of Mormon manuscript. In this revelation, given through the Prophet Joseph Smith, the Lord declared, "I will not suffer that they shall destroy my work; yea, I will show unto them that my wisdom is greater than the cunning of the devil" (D&C 10:43). Feeling that he and the other Brethren had been blessed in their statements, he reflected that night: "We are witnessing that. The Church will triumph. We have done nothing wrong."[74]

His impression proved prophetic. In February 1986 the documents dealer was charged with twenty-eight criminal charges, among them two capital counts of murder and thirteen counts of theft by deception.[75] Eleven months later, on January 23, 1987, Mark Hofmann pleaded guilty to second-degree murder in the deaths of Steven Christensen and Kathy Sheets. Later, during interviews with prosecuting attorneys, he boasted about fooling the Church's highest leaders and confessed to having forged, among other documents, the Salamander Letter, the Joseph Smith III blessing, and the Anthon transcript.[76]

Although Hofmann's admission of guilt removed any lingering questions the documents had raised about the veracity of Joseph Smith's account of the Restoration, President Hinckley continued to field criticism over his perceived connection to Hofmann. One question recurred in numerous letters and phone calls to the office of the First Presidency: "How could a member of the First Presidency be duped and unable to discern the evil intentions of a man like Mark Hofmann?" The criticism hurt President Hinckley, whose few meetings with Hofmann had been prompted by what he thought were legitimate reasons to pursue historical materials.

The evening before the transcript of Hofmann's confession was made public, President Hinckley noted: "I was advised that Hofmann mentions my name a number of times in these confessions. I suppose that is to be expected. I accepted him to come into my office on a basis of trust. . . . During [those] years I was . . . heavily burdened with Church administration and met hundreds of people in my office to discuss scores of matters. The visits of Hofmann were of minor importance to me in terms of the many other larger matters with which I had to deal. They came of my desire to conduct an open door policy while serving as the functioning member of the First Presidency."[77]

President Hinckley later summarized the Hofmann affair: "I frankly admit that Hofmann tricked us. He also tricked experts from New York to Utah, however. We bought those documents only after the assurance that they were genuine. And when we released documents to the press, we stated that we had no way of knowing for sure if they were authentic. I am not ashamed to admit that we were victimized. It is not the first time the Church has found itself in such a position. Joseph Smith was victimized again and again. The Savior was victimized. I am sorry to say that sometimes it happens."[78]

The worst of the negative publicity regarding the Hofmann bombings could not have come at a more inopportune time. The evening of the press conference at which President Hinckley explained the Church's connection with Hofmann, he noted: "I am weary to the bone with problems. I need to get out in the sun and the air and relax a little, but I see no prospect. President Kimball is not well. The nurses think that he may be failing. All of this has added to my concern and has become the burden of my prayers."[79] The following day when President Kimball joined the Twelve in the temple, he was lethargic and his face was flushed. After only a few minutes, he returned to his apartment.

President Hinckley admitted, "I have felt today as if the world were caving in around me."[80]

On November 4, 1985, President Hinckley and Arthur Haycock visited President Kimball in his apartment and gave him a blessing. As distinct from previous blessings, President Hinckley could not find the words to promise him a renewal of strength. Rather, he felt impressed to say that he would have peace of mind and body and relief from pain. The following evening, he and Sister Hinckley toured the Ramses II exhibit on display at BYU. As they returned to Salt Lake City, their driver called ahead for information on President Kimball's condition, and he was instructed to take President Hinckley directly to the prophet's apartment. When President Hinckley arrived at 10:25 P.M., Arthur Haycock met him at the door. The president had passed away a few minutes earlier.

Though the news was not unexpected, emotion welled up within President Hinckley. He talked quietly with Sister Kimball and called President Ezra Taft Benson and the secretary to the First Presidency. With little else to do until morning, he returned home, but before retiring he recorded: "President Spencer Woolley Kimball belongs to the ages. He was a great and remarkable man. . . . I have served as his counselor since July 23, 1981. Since the death of President Tanner and the disability of President Romney, I have been alone in carrying the weight of the Presidency, except for the Lord, who has blessed and magnified me. The First Presidency is now dissolved. I take my place in the Council of the Twelve. . . . Tonight I am weary and spent. The pressures and stresses of the past seem to have caught up with me. This has been a unique time in the history of the Church. There has never been another time like it. I suppose there will never again be one. I thank the Lord from the bottom of my heart for His blessings and mourn the loss of His beloved prophet."[81]

Four days later, on Saturday, November 9, Elder Hinckley, at President Benson's request, conducted the funeral services that eulogized the beloved President of the Church. Leaving his prepared remarks unread, he reminded mourners of something President Kimball had once said to him when he had tried to encourage the prophet to slow down: "My life is like my shoes, to be worn out in service." President Hinckley concluded, simply, "He so lived and so died."[82] That night Elder Hinckley wrote: "It has been a bleak day. I feel a certain deep loneliness. I have carried the burden of the Presidency for the past three years. I am tired. I do not know what will happen in the reorganization of the Presidency. I do know that things will never be the same. I am grateful to the Lord for the opportunity He has given me, although it has been difficult at times. No one will ever know quite what I have been through."[83]

The following morning, the members of the Quorum of the Twelve went fasting to the temple. There, in a process in which Elder Hinckley was now participating for the fourth time, a new President of the Church was ordained. President Ezra Taft Benson then indicated that he wished Gordon B. Hinckley to serve as first counselor and Thomas S. Monson to serve as second. Marion G. Romney was named President of the Twelve, with Howard W. Hunter as Acting President.

"I am honored and grateful," President Hinckley recorded that night. Though he was somewhat surprised at President Benson's request that he continue on in the First Presidency, he added, "I will do all I can to help President Benson as I have tried to help President Kimball."[84]

CHAPTER TWENTY-ONE

FIRST COUNSELOR

When President Kimball died, more than 40 percent of the members of the Church had never known any other prophet. Membership had nearly doubled—from 3.3 to 5.9 million—during his twelve-year presidency. Where there had been fifteen temples in operation in 1973, there were now thirty-six, with eleven more planned or under construction. The number of missions had increased from 108 to 188, and missionaries in the field from approximately eighteen to nearly thirty thousand.[1]

President Benson and President Hinckley enjoyed a warm relationship, with President Hinckley supportive of the prophet and President Benson openly grateful for the testimony, talents, and strength of his first counselor. Though his service in a fully functioning First Presidency differed from his role in President Kimball's administration, President Hinckley welcomed the adjustment. "From the moment President Benson asked me to accept the call as his counselor, I determined that I would serve as faithfully and loyally as I was capable of doing," he observed later. "The past was behind us, and it was not my place to bring up the decisions of the past Presidency as we had made them unless he made reference to them. Of course he was different from President Kimball, but he was nevertheless a strong, able leader, and I had great respect for him. It wasn't difficult making the shift. Every time there's a change in administration, a shift has to be made, and that will always be the case. No two of us are cut from the same bolt of cloth, and thank heavens that is the case."[2] He also looked forward to associating more closely with President Thomas S. Monson, with whom he had worked in various capacities for a number of years. He valued his colleague's numerous talents and good judgment and was grateful for their friendship.

After their second meeting as a newly constituted First Presidency, President Hinckley noted, "It is wonderful to have others to share the burden of decision."[3] And less than a week later, after they determined to try to get along without a meeting on Mondays, he added, "I still have more work to do than I can get done, notwithstanding the fact that the Presidency is organized. However, the big shift in the load is in not having to make the decisions alone."[4]

Away from the Church Administration Building there were other changes for both President and Sister Hinckley. For at least a couple of years, they had agonized over the increasing difficulty of maintaining their home on Capitol Hill, where they had now lived for more than a decade. Upkeep on the yard, snow removal, and their heavy travel schedules finally brought them to the reluctant conclusion that it was time to try condominium living, and they purchased a unit in Governor's Plaza in downtown Salt Lake City. Shortly before they moved he lamented: "When we built this home . . . eleven-and-a-half years ago, I planted trees. They have now grown large. . . . We have many quaking aspens, we have shrubs of various varieties, we have three peach trees that bear fruit, four apple trees, three plums, three cherries. When we move into the apartment we will have none of these, and we will miss them. But we will not miss the hundreds of thousands of leaves that fall from them in the autumn. Still, as I walked about the place today . . . thoughts came into my mind concerning whether we are doing the right thing. . . . Only my age prompts me in this direction."[5]

The day before Thanksgiving they closed on both the sale of their home and the purchase of the condominium. The next day they moved from old residence to new. There were adjustments: They had lived there but a few weeks when President Hinckley noted, after repeated trips to the car via a long elevator ride to haul groceries and other packages, "I feel more like a dray horse than anything else."[6] But one of the nicest things about living in "a filing cabinet," as he insisted on calling their abode, was that preparation for a major trip required little more than turning off the lights and locking the door—which they did as they left for a week in Korea and the dedication of the temple in Seoul.

This dedication, which commenced on December 14, 1985,

had been scheduled long before President Benson became President of the Church, and he chose not to interrupt the plan already in place for President Hinckley to preside at the event. This was a trip President and Sister Hinckley had eagerly anticipated, and once they arrived in Korea both were enveloped in the warmth of treasured memories as they renewed friendships with the Korean Saints, many of whom they had known for twenty-five years. "We have many wonderful friends here, and they are easy to love," President Hinckley recorded in his journal.

As he walked about the newly finished edifice on a slight rise in metropolitan Seoul, President Hinckley found himself reflecting about the way the property for the temple had been acquired almost twenty years earlier. President Spencer Palmer of the Korean Mission had purchased the hillside lot when it suddenly became available, in the process incurring the displeasure of the Church's real estate office. But Elder Hinckley had intervened, and on a subsequent trip to Korea with President Hugh B. Brown he had inspected the property. President Brown had suggested that it would be a wonderful place to build a temple, and now, nineteen years later, his prophecy was being fulfilled.[7]

The day of the dedication dawned clear and cold in Seoul as a frigid Siberian wind blew across the country. Nonetheless, when the Hinckleys arrived at the temple around 8:30 A.M., long lines had already formed. "It is a beautiful building," President Hinckley wrote in his journal. "The workmanship appears to be excellent. I am impressed with the furniture, which is first-grade Korean. I insisted on this."[8]

It was not surprising that he had difficulty containing his emotions throughout the dedication of this first temple on mainland Asia. During various sessions he spoke of his early visits to Korea and of all he had seen since: "I have grown old coming to Korea. I have had so many experiences here; some have been painful, many have been beautiful. I recall when there were so very few and the work was so very weak. . . . I remember my first winter visit. Snow was flying through the sky. . . . I walked the streets of this city and saw many people without housing, living in boxes trying to keep warm."[9] He declared that he had shed more tears for Korea than any other place in the world and then spoke of President Kimball's promise, given at an area conference five years earlier, that if the Saints would be faithful they would eat better, be better clothed, and live better. "We have witnessed the fulfillment of that promise among the faithful," he proclaimed.[10]

Six dedicatory sessions and two days later, President Hinckley was bone weary but satisfied that the Lord had accepted the new temple. "We have experienced a great outpouring of the Spirit of the Lord," he reflected. "There will never be another occasion like this in the history of the Church in Korea."[11]

Half the fun for Sister Hinckley was finding ways to share their unique experiences with the family. "None of the travel was ever lost on Mother," Kathy explained. "She absorbed everything she saw and heard, and then wrote spellbinding letters and made a full report when she got home. Sights, sounds, memories—everything. It was a production! She loved the people she met, and as we learned of them from her, we loved them too. When Mother described the dedication of the temple in Seoul, she went into great detail about the Korean women in their beautiful native dresses who lined the sidewalks as they came out of the dedication. She relived all of it—and helped us live it. Right in the middle of her description, which had us mesmerized, my father looked up and said, 'Dresses? What dresses?' "[12]

The building of temples and the resultant ordinance work showed no sign of slowing under the new First Presidency. While serving as President Benson's first counselor, President Hinckley would participate in the dedication of temples in Denver and Las Vegas and preside at dedicatory sessions in Lima, Portland, Toronto, and San Diego and at the rededication of the refurbished Alberta, London, Swiss, and Chicago Temples. He joined in the groundbreaking ceremony for the Bountiful Temple and presided at the groundbreaking for the Mt. Timpanogos Temple in American Fork, Utah. At times he marveled at what was happening around the world. Brigham Young had lived to see the completion of just one of the four temples for which he had selected sites in Utah. By the conclusion of President Benson's term as President of the Church, there would be forty-five temples in operation.[13]

In the solemn assembly convened during the Sunday afternoon session of the April 1986 general conference, members of the Church had the opportunity to sustain President Benson and his counselors. Earlier that morning President Hinckley spoke of the process, "beautiful in its simplicity" and absent of electioneering or campaigning, that led to the selection of a prophet of God. "I give you my testimony that it is the Lord who selected Ezra Taft Benson to become a member of the Council of the Twelve almost forty-three years ago," he testified. "It is the Lord who over these years has tested and disciplined him, schooled and prepared him. . . . As one who knows him and who stands at his side, I bear witness that he is a man of faith, of tested leadership, of profound love for the Lord and His work, of love for the sons and daughters of God everywhere."

President Hinckley concluded with prophetic words: "Under President Benson's leadership, the work of the Lord will continue to move forward. No power under the heavens can deflect it from its course. We may expect that there will be some who will try. Their efforts will be like chipping away at a granite block with a chisel of wood. The stone will not be damaged, but the chisel will be broken."[14]

Indeed, the Church was growing dramatically. The month before the April 1986 general conference the number of missionaries in the field passed the 30,000 mark, yet during the general priesthood meeting President Hinckley issued an impassioned plea: "The Church needs you. The Lord needs you. The world needs you—yes, ten thousand more of you."[15] In April 1987 the First Presidency announced the creation of four new areas, and in September they discontinued the International Mission, directing responsibility for its territory to the respective Area Presidencies. In May 1988 Elder Neal A. Maxwell organized the Aba Nigeria Stake, the first in West Africa; the following month the Church was granted legal recognition in Hungary; and in October 1988 Elder David B. Haight created the 1700th stake, in Manaus, Brazil, a city of 1.5 million people in the heart of the Amazon jungle. The following year, at the April 1989 general conference, the Second Quorum of the Seventy was created. The gospel was spreading into the world's far reaches.

The First Presidency not only directed the explosive growth

but eagerly addressed the range of other issues that came before them on a daily basis. From issuing statements on gambling and AIDS to dealing with repercussions when missionaries were expelled from Ghana and local congregations were ordered to disband, they handled the multifarious matters that came to their attention, most of them sensitive and complicated.

As the Church increased in size, complexity, and scope, President Hinckley never lacked for things to do, and Sister Hinckley occasionally smiled as she reflected on her initial reaction that her husband's call to the First Presidency would be only of a short duration. That looked to be less likely all the time. In the meantime, her challenge was to somehow keep up with him, though at times he seemed almost ageless. Still, aches and pains reminded them both that they weren't getting any younger, and there were other events that signaled the calendar's relentless progression. In November 1986 Marjorie's children hosted a gala surprise party to celebrate her seventy-fifth birthday. Old friends from the First Ward, where she and Gordon had lived as children, as well as from East Millcreek and Capitol Hill, turned the celebration into a reunion of her closest and dearest friends. Marjorie recalled her seventieth birthday, when she had repeated to herself all day something she had heard Stephen L Richards's wife say when she was in her nineties: "Oh, to be seventy again! You can do anything when you are seventy!" Now she bragged about being the same age as President Ronald Reagan and said optimistically: "These *are* golden years. We no longer have to compete with anyone. We don't have to prove anything—we just have to enjoy it all."[16]

At the evening's conclusion, President Hinckley paid tribute to his wife of nearly fifty years. "When a seventy-five-year-old woman is married to a seventy-six-year-old man," he said, "they know that this season is more like autumn than it is spring. Their prayer is for a mild and pleasant winter." Afterward he reflected privately: "[Ours] has been a happy and wonderful and rewarding marriage. We have known lean times and fat times, bad times and good times. We have loved and respected one another. There is cause for much of gratitude and gladness."[17]

For all his optimism, even President Hinckley realized that

his "winter" would not consist solely of pleasant experiences. Though it was a relief to sit as a member of a fully functioning First Presidency, President Hinckley still carried the major responsibility for certain vexatious dilemmas that came before that council. One such decision was determining the fate of the Hotel Utah, which for seventy-six years had served Salt Lake City as a premier hostelry but by now had become outdated and worn out. For two years he, Presiding Bishop Robert D. Hales, and others had painstakingly studied the situation. The building was a signal landmark in the city's downtown, and almost everyone—residents, city and county officials, prominent businessmen, restorationists, other General Authorities and Church leaders—had an opinion about what should be done with it.

To tear down the grand old hotel would invite a maelstrom, yet it was difficult for the Church to rationalize commitment to the hotel business when a number of national hotel chains had constructed newer, more efficient hotels in the Salt Lake City area. During the previous five years the hotel had lost several million dollars, and studies indicated it would require an investment of at least forty million dollars to renovate the building. Further, the hotel business itself was fraught with challenges for the Church—among them, the issue of whether to serve alcohol. After lengthy discussions the First Presidency and Quorum of the Twelve were in full accord: The Church must stanch the flow of red ink and get out of the hotel business.

The question remained of what to do with the building. After months of intense evaluation and deliberation, the First Presidency, with President Hinckley taking the lead, determined to renovate the structure for Church purposes. By doing so they could preserve the hotel's exquisite architecture, including its beautiful lobby. Accordingly, on March 12, 1987, they released a statement indicating that the Hotel Utah would close on August 31, and that specific details about the renovation would be announced later. "No one feels sadder about the closing of the Hotel than I do," President Hinckley reflected privately. "It is a landmark in the community, and a testimony of the Church's leadership in the community. However, it has been woefully unprofitable for years. We simply cannot go on making up its deficits. . . . I am confident that in the long run the wisdom of this decision will be made evident. In the meantime we will take a good deal of flak. We should be accustomed to this by now . . . although I would prefer that we not have to take it." He continued, acknowledging the pressure he felt over this issue: "By assignment I have carried the brunt of the responsibility of this decision. It has been difficult and worrisome. It has not been hastily made. . . . It has been an agonizing period in my life. I have worried and prayed about it. [But] every facet of the problem has been presented to the full Presidency and the Council of the Twelve, and there is unity among us. And when there is perfect unity in our meetings, after fervent prayer, we know the course is right."[18]

Reaction was swift, sharp, and in some cases mean-spirited and personal. President Hinckley was targeted as the villain in the drama, and letters from irate businessmen and even longtime friends and associates protested the decision, claiming that closure of the hotel would permanently undermine tourism and the economy of downtown Salt Lake City. He and the Church were criticized for not consulting with the public before making an announcement of such consequence. How could the Church seriously consider reducing the city's signature hotel to an office building? One *Salt Lake Tribune* columnist wrote: "Most people I know greeted the surprising news of Hotel Utah's closure with disbelief. A mixture of sadness, frustration and anger followed closely the initial shock. . . . The church has placed its own, narrower interests ahead of those of the community. . . . Though the church argues it has taken the long view, it really has lapsed into parochialism. Over time, the church's decision will hurt the community, both spiritually and economically, and as a result it will damage the church as well."[19] Salt Lake City Mayor Palmer DePaulis was quoted in the *New York Times* as stating, "I feel terrible. Not only are we losing our flagship hotel; we are losing our prestige as a community."[20] The Utah Heritage Foundation fought the decision from the outset, and a full-page ad in the *Tribune* carried a petition of nearly one thousand names, including those of two former Utah governors, urging the Church to reconsider.

The criticism was painful. Though President Hinckley realized that even the insults directed toward him reflected frustration with the Church, it was difficult to maintain a calm exterior. But he methodically answered one complaint after another, promising the public that the Church would protect the integrity of the building and that the public would not be disappointed with the finished product. "This will be a beautiful facility. Please trust us," he said again and again, including on the eve of the closure when he delivered a statement from the hotel's Empire Room: "Following completion of the work, this will not be a dark spot in the heart of the city. You will be warmly welcomed. We ask only one thing. That is that you have confidence in us, who, with you, love this community, and who have done very much to make of the core area of the city a place of unmatched beauty. . . . That beauty will not be diminished in the actions to be taken with this treasured and gracious gathering place long known for its warmth and hospitality."[21]

The hotel became President Hinckley's personal project, and he closely supervised every phase of its renovation. He envisioned a variety of uses for the building and was tireless in communicating a vision of what the Hotel Utah could ultimately become. By the time the building was gutted, he and Sister Hinckley had moved to a condominium in the Gateway Apartments just east of the block that housed the Church Administration Building and Hotel Utah, and he monitored progress on the project almost daily with binoculars from his balcony. One ballroom was converted to a chapel, and other areas became small meeting rooms. Ballrooms and dining rooms were beautifully renovated for receptions and formal gatherings, and the popular Roof Restaurant was restored on the top floor. Above all else, President Hinckley was adamant that the Church keep faith with the community and preserve the lobby and mezzanine for use by the public.

He hoped also to find a way to encourage Temple Square visitors to walk across the street and visit the new building. After considering dozens of options, he hit upon the idea of remodeling the grand ballroom as a theater where large audiences could view an epic film portraying the heritage of the Latter-day Saints. Initially the idea of an IMAX theater was explored, but it became apparent that constructing such a screen in the existing space would be unwieldy. President Hinckley did, however, contact Academy Award–winning director Kieth

Merrill, who had extensive experience with IMAX as well as other large-format films, and invited him to produce the movie he had in mind.

Elder L. Tom Perry, who served on the committee that oversaw the hotel's renovation, said: "I sat one day with President Hinckley and Kieth Merrill as we discussed the direction this film might take. Kieth sat at one end of the desk, and I was at the other. I watched President Hinckley almost dictate a script while Kieth typed furiously on his laptop computer. Kieth actually wrote the script, but the ideas were President Hinckley's. He had the vision. He knew exactly what effect he wished the production to have on those who would see it."[22] On that score, President Hinckley was clear: "I want people to leave with a feeling for the tremendous sacrifice that is part of this work. I want them to leave the theater crying."[23] He reviewed each draft of the script and made numerous suggestions until it finally met with his approval. Indeed, no detail on the movie or on the entire renovation escaped his attention.[24]

There were no easy decisions as far as the massive hotel renovation was concerned. But then, problems that reached the First Presidency were almost always serious in scope and far-reaching in implication. "The easy issues are resolved before they ever get to the First Presidency," said Presiding Bishop Robert D. Hales, who worked closely with President Hinckley on many projects relative to the Church's temporal affairs. "The ones that remain are Solomon-like. I met with President Hinckley on questions so difficult, and about which he had such concern, that he would suggest that we kneel together in prayer. He is a bright man with extraordinary judgment, but when he comes up against an insoluble problem, he goes to his knees. When he says, 'We'll take it under consideration,' it means he'll wait until he has the feeling that a certain course of action is right. He cannot be pushed or pressured into a decision. He measures before he cuts."[25]

There was never an end to problems that required a combination of good judgment, patience, and inspiration. In the late 1980s certain self-proclaimed enemies of the Church revived their efforts to embarrass the Church by discrediting President

Hinckley, and they attempted to do so by accusing him of unspeakable moral transgressions. "We want Gordon Hinckley to know that he cannot hide his sins from God and the Mormon people," a public statement from one group threatened. The accusations intensified in October 1988 when members of this group staged a demonstration in front of the Church Administration Building to accuse him of the unseemly behavior. The following Monday, they repeated their allegations at a press conference in the offices of the *Salt Lake Tribune*.[26]

President Hinckley, who had been in Colombia inspecting a proposed temple site the day of the protest, was embarrassed and hurt by the ugly accusations and the distasteful public display; with the attacks made public, he wrote President Benson formally requesting him to authorize an official investigation. "These scurrilous attacks are . . . obviously intended to injure not only me, but also the Church," President Hinckley's letter explained. "I feel the time has come when a thorough, independent examination of these allegations should be made. . . . It will be for the good of the Church to get all matters pertinent to this in the record."[27] He recorded privately: "It is bad enough to have these enemies of the Church putting forth their scurrilous statements. I want my Brethren to know for sure that there is absolutely no substance to them."[28] He also wanted a record verifying the facts for future generations. President Benson responded by appointing a committee composed of President Howard W. Hunter and Elders James E. Faust and Dallin H. Oaks, all experienced lawyers, to oversee the investigation, and they retained the services of a highly respected non-Mormon attorney to conduct an exhaustive independent investigation of the claims.

Other developments fueled the fire. The anti-Mormon film *God Makers II* and a video entitled *The True Story of President Gordon B. Hinckley* were released, both of which perpetuated the offensive allegations. After viewing the video, President Hinckley read a statement in a meeting of the First Presidency and the Quorum of the Twelve in which he "categorically and unequivocally" denied every accusation and declared: "Has this been painful? Of course. To have one's name dragged through the slime is indeed painful. . . . If those who have fabricated these accusations have derived happiness from my pain, let that be their bitter satisfaction."[29]

After an extensive probe, the lead attorney and his investigators rejected every accusation and concluded that the allegations against President Hinckley were pure fabrication. Some of those who had "testified" against him retracted their statements, and some admitted that they had been paid to lie. Further, the Anti-Defamation League blasted *God Makers II* as a "blasphemous attempt" to discredit the Church and a threat to "religious liberty," and the president of the National Conference of Christians and Jews condemned the film as "religious bigotry."[30] President Hinckley was relieved when the matter was put to rest and the facts verifying his integrity entered as part of the official record of the Church.

For their part, President Hunter, Elder Faust, and Elder Oaks had wrestled with the age-old dilemma that confronts public figures accused of personal misconduct. The First Amendment provides sweeping protection for those who make allegations against public figures, and they are subject to legal consequence only if their statements can be proved to be malicious—which necessitates bringing the case to trial. The Brethren feared that even though the Church would prevail in a lawsuit, President Hinckley's name and reputation would be sullied by a trial that would attract widespread attention. They also felt it unwise for President Hinckley to issue a statement denying the allegations, which were so preposterous that no responsible media in Salt Lake City even picked them up; a public response almost certainly would have elevated the story to front-page news. Such a statement would also have provided a platform from which the charges could be trumpeted for months before they were ultimately exposed as false. In addition, their exposure as false would come in a single report that would fail to reach many who had heard the repetitious coverage of the charges. The only prudent recourse, the Brethren determined, was to set the facts straight for the records of the Church and hope that honorable men and women would see through the scurrilous claims.

During a meeting of the Public Affairs Committee held during this period, one individual suggested ways President Hinckley might respond and perhaps even retaliate. President

Hinckley's reaction was immediate: "I won't do anything. You can't spread garbage without getting some of it on yourself."

President Faust said of the situation: "We knew from the outset that there wasn't the slightest element of truth to the accusations, but it hurt us to see how deeply President Hinckley was hurt. What is significant, however, is how he responded to the attacks. Despite his own suffering, he showed tremendous restraint, all of which demonstrated the bigness of his soul and the greatness of his character."[31]

The ordeal was, nonetheless, painful for President Hinckley. "My natural inclination was to fight back," he acknowledged later. "But I was an apostle of the Lord Jesus Christ, and I knew I must turn the other cheek, go forward, and not let this derail me."[32]

Throughout the episode, President Hinckley was sustained by his General Authority colleagues and others who supported and stood by him. Some years later he considered these attacks from a different vantage point when he recalled something President Lee had once told him—that every man who became President of the Church had first been tested in the crucible of affliction. "I guess these episodes were my crucible. They were vicious," he concluded.[33]

During difficult times President Hinckley occasionally reflected on a talk he had given nearly twenty years earlier at BYU, "The Loneliness of Leadership," and thought that, ironically, he hadn't known the half of it. "The price of leadership is loneliness," he had stated. "The price of adherence to conscience is loneliness. The price of adherence to principle is loneliness." He had concluded with a pronouncement that was prophetic: "A man has to live with his principles. A man has to live with his convictions. A man has to live with his testimony. Unless he does so, he is miserable—dreadfully miserable. And while there may be thorns, while there may be disappointment, while there may be trouble and travail, heartache and heartbreak, and desperate loneliness, there will be peace and comfort and strength."[34]

As before, his enduring sense of optimism helped him survive the criticism and the burdens he shouldered—an optimism rooted in his unwavering faith that the Lord was in charge and that He would overrule for good. Nothing dulled a personality quite like a negative outlook, President Hinckley often said, and he believed what he preached. A man of vision who could see beyond the here and now, he had a natural propensity for fixing his attention on where the Church was going rather than becoming bogged down by the disappointments that occurred in its everyday management. On one occasion he told the BYU student body how he viewed his lot in life: "I still feel young, with a love for life, its challenges, and its pleasures. . . . My life has been rich with challenges and associations. I have wrestled with problems large and small. I have known something of discouragement and on a few occasions have felt the exhilaration of achievement. I feel a deep sense of gratitude for the marvelous and generous blessings of the Lord. Among these is the opportunity to be associated with His great cause and kingdom."[35]

He enjoyed quoting an article he had clipped years earlier: "Most putts don't drop. Most beef is tough. Most children grow up to be just people. Most successful marriages require a high degree of mutual toleration. Most jobs are more often dull than otherwise. Life is like an old-time rail journey—delays, sidetracks, smoke, dust, cinders, and jolts, interspersed only occasionally by beautiful vistas and thrilling bursts of speed. The trick is to thank the Lord for letting you have the ride."[36]

When a distinguished Protestant minister called on the First Presidency and asked how they felt about the condition of the world and its people, President Hinckley responded: "I feel very optimistic. . . . I feel the spirit of Christ is brooding over the nations of the earth. Of course there are problems, many and serious. . . . [But] there are men and women by the tens of thousands who are reaching out . . . to help those in distress. . . . I feel optimistic—guardedly so, yes, because of the extent of evil in the world. But . . . goodness is gaining, and the work of the Lord is growing in strength and power."[37]

President Hinckley's passion for living was irresistible to members of the Church; they enjoyed a presiding official who was approachable and who had his own unique way of establishing rapport. After accompanying him to a regional conference in the Midwest, Elder Russell M. Nelson reported: "When it was President Hinckley's turn to speak he stood and said, 'It's good to be in Indiana. I don't know why, but it's good to be here,' and everyone roared. If I had said that, it wouldn't have been funny. But he has an uncanny way of making an audience feel as though he is one of them."[38] In countries outside the United States, he greeted the Saints in their own language, even if all he knew was just a phrase. Whether "*Mabuhay!*" in the Philippines, "*Guten Tag*" in Germany, or "*Buenos Dias*" in South and Central America, his welcome was always enthusiastic.

After attending seven regional conferences in seven states with President Hinckley, Elder Nelson learned what others who traveled with him also observed. Regardless of the destination, he knew something about the history of the area and its people. In the pear-growing area of Medford, Oregon, for example, President Hinckley started a priesthood leadership meeting with a dissertation on fruit trees and how important it was to prune trees in February so that there would be fruit in September. "President Hinckley doesn't expect to be bowed to and prefers to be treated as though he is an ordinary worker," said Elder Nelson. "But he isn't ordinary in any respect. He is a multifaceted genius. He understands anatomy and physiology better than any non-physician I have worked with. He talks with builders about finials and mullions and speaks the language unique to their profession. When questions arise that have legal ramifications, he typically says, 'I'm no lawyer, but it seems to me that . . . ' and then renders an opinion that my lawyer colleagues insist would be a credit to any lawyer. Whether it is medicine or law, education or plumbing, it doesn't seem to matter. He grasps things quickly, has an amazing breadth of knowledge, and can apply what he knows."[39]

A man with an insatiable appetite for learning, President Hinckley not only read widely but found other ways to increase his knowledge and understanding of specialized areas of expertise. After observing him at another regional conference, Elder Nelson reported: "One of the security officers assigned to us worked for the local police department. We had time between sessions, and President Hinckley grilled that officer for an hour about their procedures, techniques, and even the equipment they used. I marveled that he knew which questions to ask, each of which was law-enforcement specific."[40] Bishop Robert D. Hales added: "I have never met an individual who can become so well informed through reading and through contact with people. When he spends an evening at dinner with someone, he leaves knowing something about that individual's expertise."[41]

As son Clark progressed in his own career, he came to appreciate his father's unusual strengths. "Dad has incredible common sense and seems to instinctively know the best way to proceed with something," he said. "He is a good judge of people, and he is bright. He also has a phenomenal memory, particularly for names and faces. He consumes the *Wall Street Journal*, and those who worked with him on the Zion's Bank board were amazed that he not only read it but could apply what he gleaned to the discussions at the bank."[42]

The members of the Twelve had frequent opportunity to observe similar phenomena. "What makes President Hinckley unique," Elder Neal A. Maxwell explained, "is that he remembers what he has read and distills that which he wishes to retain. His is an integrated intellect. He can draw upon what he knows to make prudent decisions."[43] Elder M. Russell Ballard concurred: "When you combine President Hinckley's good judgment with his wealth of experience—years of supervising the construction of buildings and temples, acquisition of property, and so forth—he knows what to watch for and what questions to ask. He doesn't need to be told something twice. Once he focuses on a problem, he can hit the bull's-eye as fast as anybody I've known."[44]

President Hinckley's reservoir of knowledge was augmented by several decades of heavy travel and study that had given him an enviable familiarity with the world and its peoples as well as a tremendous respect for its history. He enthusiastically supported opportunities to spotlight achievements from days of yore. "I am one who believes in celebrations," he explained. "I am one who believes in commemorating great events of the past. When we do so, we bring to life . . . men and women of history who did significant things of which we need reminding."[45]

Few celebrations stirred him as did the one marking the sesquicentennial of the inauguration of missionary work in the British Isles, which commemoration was engineered by Wendell J. Ashton, then serving as a mission president in London. The evening of Friday, July 24, 1987, the Hinckleys accompanied President and Sister Benson to London's elegant Savoy Hotel for the gala anniversary banquet. Former British Prime Minister Edward Heath and Sir Rhodes Boyson, a member of Parliament and former member of Prime Minister Margaret Thatcher's cabinet, attended the elegant affair, as did a host of other dignitaries, including several members of British nobility and many government and business leaders. As the guests were ushered into the banquet hall, the Trumpeters of the Lifeguards played a few measures of "Come, Come Ye Saints." After dinner, President Benson gave a brief introduction, and President Ronald Reagan sent a message via video. Kenneth Thomson, Lord Thomson of Fleet, had traveled from Canada for the express purpose of introducing President Hinckley. In an effusive tribute he related key events in President Hinckley's life and then declared: "That, very briefly, is the background of President Hinckley. But of course it fails woefully to do justice to the man's great character, his deep moral and religious integrity, his outstanding administrative ability, and his almost boundless energy and drive."[46] President Hinckley then delivered the keynote address, "Truth Shall Prevail." Afterward Lord Thomson wrote him, "Your speech was outstanding, Gordon. The message and the way you conveyed it were simply superb. Your quiet inner confidence and faith make you a very special person. . . . Thank you for providing me with one of the greatest honours in my life."[47]

Early the next morning President and Sister Hinckley boarded the train for Preston. As they traveled through the English countryside, he reflected on the train ride he had made fifty-four years earlier when he had first set foot in Lancashire. Later that day, as he dedicated a marker in Avenham Park on the bank of the River Ribble, where the first LDS converts were baptized on July 30, 1837, he was overwhelmed by his emotions. After he had taken care of his obligations, he went by his old missionary address at 15 Wadham Road. To his surprise, the lady of the house was home and assented to their coming inside. When he asked if he might take a look at the upstairs bedroom where he had lived, she replied, "Yes, but don't get in the bed." That evening he recorded: "Marjorie and I went up into the bedroom where Brother Bramwell and I had lived and where I made an important decision in my life to think less of myself and work with greater devotion as a missionary. This was a great experience for me to come back to this place."[48]

The following morning, 12,000 Latter-day Saints filled Birmingham's National Exhibition Centre for one of six regional conferences held in Britain that day. In his address President Hinckley admitted that he had never dreamed he would return to participate in such a historic celebration.[49] He and Sister Hinckley returned home exuberant over their experience in a land so tender to their hearts.

Other festivities demanded Gordon and Marjorie's attention as well. As their fiftieth wedding anniversary approached, President Hinckley asked his wife how she would like to celebrate the milestone. "I want to walk the streets of Hong Kong with my children," she responded quickly, echoing a wish she had repeated countless times through the years. She knew her dream was just that—a fantasy—but when her children realized that nothing would please their parents more, they decided to gather in Hong Kong at their own expense during President Hinckley's next assignment in the Orient. It was a mountain-moving kind of project to get all five children and their spouses to Hong Kong at the right time and place. But on the evening of Sunday, September 6, 1987, all ten of them converged on the Shangri La Hotel in Kowloon for the family reunion of a lifetime.

The next three days, while their children traveled into mainland China, President and Sister Hinckley handled an assignment in Burma with the Area President, Elder Jacob de Jager. Lines from Kipling ran through President Hinckley's mind as he and Marjorie sweltered in a taxi in the congested Rangoon traffic: "Only mad dogs and Englishmen stay out in the noonday sun." Conditions in their hotel were primitive, with lizards crawling over the ceiling and walls of their room and two inches of stagnant water puddled on the bathroom floor. But any concern resulting from such inconveniences dissipated when, on the shore of Inya Lake on the morning of September 8, 1987, President Hinckley dedicated Burma for the teaching of the gospel. The following morning he and Elder de Jager baptized the first members of the Church there.

Late that night they returned to Hong Kong, and the next day Sister Hinckley's dream of three and a half decades materialized when she and her husband joined their children in touring the local sights, dickering with vendors in side-street shops, sampling the cuisine, and enjoying the noise, congestion, and spicy smells of the unique Asian metropolis. "I had heard Mother describe Hong Kong in such detail," said Kathy, "that I felt as though I had come home. To finally be in Hong Kong with my parents was like stepping into Mother's and Dad's other world." In addition to the usual tourist attractions, everyone wanted to see the places they had heard their father describe for years. Particularly emotional was their visit to Kam Tong Hall, the dark building that Elder Hinckley had thought looked like a "haunted house" when he first saw it but that had subsequently been transformed into a beautiful structure overlooking the magnificent harbor. "We had heard about this building from the day Dad saw it," Clark explained. "To us, it was a legendary landmark. He had come home scared to death after recommending that the Church purchase an expensive piece of property that needed so much work. But that property became a gathering place for the Church in the Orient. To stand there together as a family was a remarkable experience. It was as though we now shared in all the trips he had taken for years."[50]

From Hong Kong, the family flew to Seoul for a regional conference and there witnessed firsthand the obvious affection between their parents and the Korean Saints. "Watching Mother and Dad in that setting was unlike anything I had ever seen," Virginia said. "We had always known they had a tender place in their hearts for the Oriental Saints, but we had no idea of the depth of emotion until we saw them engulfed by crowds of people who wished to shake their hands or embrace them. We thought of the days Dad had traveled the length of Korea to meet with just a few members here and there, and then looked at the thousands who came to these meetings. It was as though we were seeing the fruits of his labors."[51] Clark summarized: "Dad knew everybody—their names, their history, when they were baptized, what positions they had held, who they had married, and what their children's names were. The Orient has been such a big part of his life, and of ours vicariously. So much of what we grew up with around the dinner table focused on Asia. To meet the people and see the sites he had talked about for decades was the experience of a lifetime."[52]

Among other things, his children saw firsthand what anyone who traveled with President Hinckley knew—that he moved at a frenetic pace, packed his schedule as tightly as possible, and was simply indefatigable. It was not unusual for those traveling with him to get early-morning calls explaining that he had been up part of the night and had some items to discuss before they began the day's activities. If there was ever a block of unscheduled time, he squeezed in another meeting with missionaries or paid a courtesy call on local dignitaries or clergy. And even when he returned from a long trip, he allowed himself little time to recoup and readjust. After touching down on the East Coast following a trip to Tel Aviv, he headed directly for a regional conference in West Virginia, noting at day's end, "We are suffering from jet lag, but there are things to do and we keep going."[53] The morning after he returned to Salt Lake City he was at the office early to set apart three mission presidents and to examine what had piled up during his absence. "I went through the accumulated mail and discovered, as usual, that there are plenty of problems that are constantly recurring," he noted on that occasion.[54]

In September 1988 President and Sister Hinckley joined Elder and Sister Oaks and the Asia Area Presidency in the Philippines to conduct the first area priesthood training meeting outside the United States. Stake and district presidents, Regional Representatives, mission presidents, the MTC president, and the temple president attended the meetings, which were designed to test the merits of training priesthood leaders in the field rather than having them travel to Salt Lake City at conference time. By the afternoon session of the all-day affair, Elder Oaks was feeling the effects of jet lag. But, he noted, "President Hinckley spoke during the 11th hour of continuous meetings. . . . I couldn't see that his performance was impaired at all. He is really remarkable."[55]

The strain of nine days in the Philippines, during which they spoke to more than 1400 missionaries and 28,000 members, did begin to wear on President Hinckley, however, as he recorded in his journal: "I was sick and wobbly and weak this morning. But there is no time to slow down. This schedule is of my own making. I have only myself to blame. But I did not come to the Philippines for a vacation, but rather to do such good as I can. This means travel and meetings."[56] While on such trips he typically announced that he would never set such a demanding schedule again, but then he proceeded to plan his next itinerary the same way.

As tiring as was the travel, meeting with the Saints rejuvenated him. Few things thrilled or motivated him more than seeing the Church grow and mature around the world. After meeting with priesthood leaders in Quito, Ecuador, on one occasion he noted: "One stake . . . is comprised entirely of Otovalo Indians. . . . These brethren sat together on my left as I spoke to them. Their dark hair was combed straight back and braided. They have strong, serene faces. They were dressed in white trousers and warm woolen serapes. They had light slippers on their feet. I suppose they work in their fields barefooted, and wear these slippers only for formal gatherings. They were tremendously impressive. They are the descendants of Father Lehi and Mother Sariah. It is wonderful to see such in the Church and to see them growing in capacity to handle responsibility." He added the following day: "I have not been to Quito in some years, and what a pleasure to come back and find this kind of strength in the Church. The work will continue to grow here in a marvelous and remarkable way."[57]

Such experiences made the pace he kept worth the effort, and accordingly President Hinckley remained involved in as many issues as time and energy allowed and as President Benson, who was beginning to slow down, wished him to be. Indeed, there were some organizations and matters about which President Hinckley felt so deeply that even as a member of the First Presidency he chose to remain personally involved. Such was the case with Bonneville International and with BYU, where he chaired the board's executive committee.

Though the university at times faced thorny issues, many of which were complicated by the school's connection to the Church, President Hinckley was upbeat and enthusiastic about the world's largest church-owned institution of higher learning. Throughout Jeffrey R. Holland's nine-year term as president of BYU (1980–89), he worked closely with President Hinckley. He said later: "President Hinckley was wonderfully suited to his role at BYU because he loves education, he studies, he reads. This is a man who read the *Iliad* and the *Odyssey* in the original Greek. He was always pro-university, pro-education, pro-learning, and pro-growth. He was comfortable in his role and comfortable on campus. Faculty and students alike loved having him come. Even when difficult problems arose and disturbing things happened, he would say, 'Things will work out.'"[58] Such was his approach to dealing with the fierce opposition that arose from Orthodox Jews during construction of BYU's Jerusalem Center, with the mounting challenge of funding the university, and with increasing controversy over the intense competition for admission.

President Hinckley spoke frequently at BYU devotionals and firesides and often conducted the university's convocation and graduation ceremonies. It was he who, dressed in the robes of academia, conducted the convocation in October 1989 installing Rex E. Lee as BYU's new president after President Holland was called to serve in the First Quorum of the Seventy.[59]

He enjoyed his association with the academic world and was complimented when his modest achievements, as he referred to them, were singled out for attention. President Hinckley was awarded an honorary doctoral degree from Westminster College, an honorary doctor of humanities degree from Utah State University, an honorary doctor of human letters degree from the University of Utah, and honorary doctorates from Southern Utah University in Cedar City and from BYU. He appreciated these recognitions, for he was devoted to the learning process, as he explained to one group of religious educators: "None of us . . . knows enough. The learning process is an endless process. We must read, we must observe, we must assimilate, and we must ponder that to which we expose our minds. I believe . . . in the evolution of the mind, the heart, and the soul of man. I believe in improvement. I believe in growth."[60] He often quoted German philosopher Georg Hegel, who stated that those who don't read history will most likely repeat it. In a message to the

BYU student body, he added: "I deplore the terrible waste of the intellectual resources of so many people . . . who devote countless hours watching mindless drivel. . . . This old world needs straightening up. It needs leadership."[61]

Regardless of the setting, President Hinckley was not one to mince words when the situation called for straight talk—though his remarks were frequently flavored with both humor and compassion. His comments at one general priesthood meeting were vintage Hinckley: "Altogether too many men, leaving their wives at home in the morning and going to work, where they find attractively dressed . . . young women, regard themselves as . . . an irresistible catch. They complain that their wives do not look the same as they did twenty years ago when they married them. To which I say, Who would, after living with you for twenty years?"[62]

When critics accused him of delivering a "secret message" at a Regional Representatives seminar, he addressed the issue openly at a subsequent general women's meeting: "Recently I heard that someone had secured a copy of my talk, looking upon that as a singular accomplishment, as if it had been given in a secret and sinister manner, designed to keep it from the world. This is nonsense. I am therefore on this occasion going to take the liberty of rereading that portion of the talk which pertains to a matter over which some women of the Church appear to be greatly exercised. I give it to all . . . because of the activities of a few who evidently are seeking to lead others in the paths which they are following. I speak of those who advocate the offering of prayers to our Mother in Heaven." After quoting at length from the earlier address, he concluded: "Search as I have, I find nowhere in the standard works an account where Jesus prayed other than to His Father in Heaven or where He instructed the people to pray other than to His Father in Heaven. I have looked in vain for any instance where any President of the Church . . . has offered a prayer to 'our Mother in Heaven.' I suppose those . . . who use this expression and who try to further its use are well-meaning, but they are misguided."[63]

At a conference on working women sponsored by the University of Utah, he encouraged women to educate themselves and take advantage of the fact that the entire field of human endeavor was open to women. But he also made it clear that a woman's first allegiance was to her children.[64]

At least partially out of impatience over criticism of the Church's influence in Utah state affairs, he told the Governor's Conference on Utah's Future that he knew of no other community or state where a church contributed so much to the economy, that Church members had the right and responsibility to involve themselves in civic affairs, and that nothing good would come of criticizing the Church's influence in the state. He concluded by extending the olive branch: "If there be wounds over such matters, I want to heal them. There is no need for them. We are all essentially people of good will and generous hearts who must work together to strengthen not only the economy but every other important facet of the environment in which we live."[65]

Despite his frank approach to difficult topics, President Hinckley delivered such counsel within a framework of charity. "What I have spoken, I have said with a desire to be helpful and, in some cases, in the spirit of a rebuke followed by an increase of love toward those whom I may have rebuked," he said in one instance typical of countless others.[66] If anything, he erred on the side of compassion when it came to matters of Church discipline. He often said to his Brethren, "We've got to think of the family. Remember those cases in pioneer days when someone was excommunicated and we lost a whole family or a family for generations as a result." Said Elder Oaks, "He has a broad vision when it comes to consequences, and he has often counseled us to look beyond the immediate when making decisions that would affect a person's future."[67]

Likewise, he mourned with those who mourned. Having buried his mother at an early age, lost his father, and watched siblings in their prime pass on, he knew something of the grief caused by the separation of death. When President Romney died in May 1988, he reminisced about their service together and paid tribute to him as a friend, leader, and ardent defender of the Book of Mormon.[68] When friends and relatives passed away, he attended the services if at all possible. The family of Raymond Holbrook, a distant cousin, was startled when President

Hinckley arrived for the noon funeral of their father. A son of the deceased said: "To my knowledge, no one from the immediate family notified President Hinckley of the funeral. Nevertheless, despite a hectic schedule, he [came] and spoke of my father's abilities and service. His brief comments were powerful and greatly appreciated by all of us."[69]

Few memorial services were more poignant than one in late May 1989 for Elder Todd Wilson, who with his companion had been shot and killed in the streets of La Paz, Bolivia. "Missionaries are so dear to the entire church that when one is lost through death the entire church grieves," President Hinckley began his remarks. Though many have died for the gospel, he said, "only a few have been gunned down by hateful men. . . . The [name] of Todd Wilson . . . will be engraved forever in the history of this church as [one of] those who lived as faithful servants of God and died as martyrs to his eternal work." Before returning home, President Hinckley visited with Todd's younger brother, who the night before the murder had been interviewed for his mission. "He will go," President Hinckley said simply.[70] Unfortunately, this would not be the last such funeral President Hinckley would attend as a representative of the First Presidency.

Thankfully, most of his assignments were not as sobering—many were occasions for celebration and reflection. In June 1989, he joined President Benson in dedicating the renovated Carthage Jail complex—an event made more meaningful when he was reminded of his father's efforts five decades earlier to refurbish the jail while he was serving as president of the Northern States Mission. "Few could foresee the future stature of the man whose blood stained the floor of this jail," President Hinckley said in his address. With the wife of the governor of Illinois present, he concluded: "Ours is the duty to forgive and put behind us the troubles of the past. Ours is the obligation to rise above old animosities. Ours is the privilege to build well on that foundation laid long ago." The event attracted widespread interest, including that of the *Washington Post*, which published a report of the proceedings.[71]

The magnitude of what had transpired in Nauvoo and at

Carthage was seared into his soul. "I am always deeply affected when I walk where Joseph walked and when I stand where he was shot and killed," he explained on many occasions. "Let it be remembered . . . by every one of us . . . that we would not be here . . . were it not for the divine mission of the Prophet Joseph Smith and the testimony of the reality and divinity of his calling that burned in the hearts of his contemporaries and followers who laid the foundation of this great work that so richly blesses our lives."[72]

In September 1989 President Hinckley addressed a BYU symposium commemorating the sesquicentennial anniversary of the founding of Nauvoo. His poetic description revealed the intensity of his feelings about the "City of Joseph": "Nauvoo didn't grow in ragtail fashion as so many cities in early America did. It rose like the sunrise, planned from the beginning. It faded like the sunset after a short day. . . . This place fairly rang with the cutting and shaping of lumber, with the chiseling of stone, with the hammering of hot iron on the anvil, with the surveying and building of streets, the plowing of farmland, the planting and tilling of the soil, the gathering of the harvest." Such a description led to a tribute to the people who lived there: "I am not saying that the Saints enjoyed it. It was terrible. But there was something magnificent about the way they held up their heads and kept on going notwithstanding the travail through which they passed."[73]

It was not surprising that President Hinckley admired the virtue of persistence, for he, too, kept on going. His only respite from the pace and pressure was a small country cottage that he and Sister Hinckley built. When his schedule permitted, they stayed overnight on Friday and spent Saturday there so he could work outside, dig and plant, irrigate and prune, and eat fruit from his own trees. As he puttered outside his small home, he relished his deliverance from the confines of downtown.

One sequence of events demonstrated the property's therapeutic value. In July 1989, he decided to take a few days of vacation. "I am burned out," he acknowledged. "I have no desire to go anywhere and play. I simply would like to get out and work, and I have a big project to do." Unusually heavy winter snow had crushed the roof of a storage shed on his property, and he was determined to replace it. Day after day he worked in the hot sun until he was exhausted. One evening he recorded, "My energy for the day is spent, but it has been a happy spending."[74] He dedicated July 4 to measuring, sawing, and hammering. "I worked the way I did when I was 50. I did not think I could do it, but I have done it," he noted. At the end of that week, with his project nearing completion, he exulted that he had been able to largely forget the office. President Monson had called to say that President Benson was not feeling well. "Except for matters of this kind I have kept my mind on other things," he wrote.[75] His children often saw their father when he stole away to the cottage. "He goes to the basement for hours, working with his tools," Jane explained. "Some people play golf. Dad putters around in his basement."[76]

The combination of heavy responsibility—and its attendant pressure—with relief now and again to dig in the soil suited President Hinckley well. Two months after the week off he reflected on the richness of his life. "It has been a wonderful summer," he told the BYU student body. "I have not traveled as a tourist. I have not been to the beach and walked in the sand. I have not been to resorts or places of fun. . . . With the exception of a half dozen days, I have been in my office up against the stresses that are felt there. . . . There are decisions to be made every day, and some of these are difficult. The guidance of the Lord is sought in all of these deliberations. The work is demanding, but there is something wonderfully stimulating in the very challenge of it. It is a marvelous thing to sit where one can see, at least in some measure, the whole broad encompassing picture of this great throbbing, viable, growing phenomenon the Lord has called The Church of Jesus Christ of Latter-day Saints. This summer I took a few days away from the office. . . . I spent a few days . . . perspiring in the sun, stirring the earth, and witnessing the miracles of nature. How wonderful a thing it is to stand on the soft earth after the sun has set and darkness comes. . . . I look up to the stars and sense in some small degree the majesty and wonder and magnitude of the universe, the awesome greatness of its Creator and Governor, and the implications of my own place as a child of God."[77]

CHAPTER TWENTY-TWO

THE OPENING OF NEW DOORS

One of the most dramatic events of the twentieth century began without fanfare or warning. At the stroke of midnight on November 9, 1989—at which time, the East German government had announced, all border restrictions on crossing into West Germany would be lifted—tens of thousands of Berliners on both sides of the wall surged through the newly opened checkpoints. Horns honked and bells rang, and men and women sang, shouted, and wiped tears from their eyes as sledgehammers began physically dismantling the twenty-eight-mile barrier that since 1961 had stood as the ultimate symbol of oppression and isolation.

The subsequent transformation of Eastern Europe was even more incredible, for a great tide of freedom swept from country to country. A bloodless revolution toppled the government in Czechoslovakia; Romania's brutal regime came to an abrupt and inglorious end; Poland became the first Iron Curtain country to form a non-Communist, multiparty parliament; Hungary opened its borders; and by the end of 1990 all fifteen Soviet republics had declared some form of autonomy.[1] These astounding developments were hailed around the world, but perhaps nowhere were they greeted with more gratitude than at Church headquarters, where leaders recognized them as the fulfillment of prophecy and a dramatic answer to prayer.

For years the Church had made repeated efforts to gain entrance to Eastern Bloc countries. Under assignment from the First Presidency, President Thomas S. Monson had had major responsibilities in East Germany for more than two decades, and his influence had opened many doors. Perhaps the most conspicuous evidence of progress had been the dedication in June 1985 of the Freiberg Temple in the German Democratic Republic.

And in late 1988, following President Monson's negotiations with GDR officials, missionaries had been allowed to enter the country and members living there had received permission to leave and serve missions elsewhere in the world. Though there was no doubt in President Hinckley's mind that the Eastern Bloc would one day open to the Church, the speed with which the Berlin Wall came down amazed him. "It was a miracle," he recalled. "The Lord moved to shake off the bonds under which those people had lived for so long. The time had come when in His wisdom there should be an opportunity to teach the gospel in that part of the world."[2]

Less than a month later, at the First Presidency Christmas devotional, President Hinckley hailed the recent events as a "Christmas present of gigantic proportions to millions who have been under a yoke of bondage" and declared that the Spirit of Christ was "brooding over much of the earth." Not for many years had there been a Christmas like this. "We have witnessed in the past few weeks, and particularly in recent days, miracles undreamed of only a short time ago," he continued. "The shackles of enslavement are falling. The ruthless atheism that in some areas has hung as a cloud of darkness for decades is now being dissipated."[3]

When asked about the Church's policy toward expansion, President Hinckley had typically responded, "We go where we're invited to go, when we're invited to go there." Spurred on by the revolutionary developments in Eastern Europe, the Church moved quickly to establish new missions. Even still, some events in April 1990 surprised him. That month, the Soviet Union's ambassador to the United States, Yuri V. Dubinin, and his wife, Liana, visited Salt Lake City at the invitation of the American-Armenian Bridge of Friendship, a project sponsored by industrialist Jon Huntsman to fund construction in Armenia, where 450,000 people had been left homeless by a massive earthquake. During an interview with the ambassador outside the Huntsman home, a reporter asked Dubinin if the Soviet Union would allow the Church to enter his country. Without hesitating, he responded that the Mormon church had "absolute freedom" to come to the Soviet Union. The reporter turned to a startled President Hinckley for comment, and he replied that the Church had an obligation to carry the gospel to the world, and though they had enjoyed conversations with Soviet officials, no decisions had yet been made.[4]

Later that evening, the ambassador told President Hinckley: "Our friendship with your church is not so long, but it began in a very important moment for us and for the Armenian victims of the earthquake. It was a wonderful and very touching manifestation that all of us are human beings." The ambassador ended his visit by speaking at the invitation of President Jon Huntsman to a session of conference in the Salt Lake Monument Park Stake. There he said, "I would like to take this opportunity to thank the American people and your church, which was one of the first to come to our aid."[5]

By July 1990, largely due to the diligent and inspired efforts of Elder Russell M. Nelson and Elder Hans B. Ringger, president of the Europe Area, missions had opened in Prague, Warsaw, and Budapest, and the Finland Helsinki East Mission was organized with the intent of concentrating on missionary work in the former Soviet Union. In early fall President and Sister Hinckley traveled to Eastern Europe for a firsthand look at conditions there. They were honored when Poland's minister of religion met them upon their arrival in Warsaw, and when they were permitted an audience with the chief of ministers of the Polish government. Before leaving the country they also met with Church members and inspected a new chapel under construction in Warsaw. In Czechoslovakia and Budapest, they met with small groups of members and missionaries. "We have had a remarkable experience in these new countries which have just shaken off the yoke of Communism," President Hinckley noted as they prepared to return home. "This is a season of miracles in Eastern Europe. Two years ago people would have thought it impossible that such things could happen. However the new governments are unstable and the economy in each nation is in bad condition. I fear this will be a very difficult winter with food shortages and unemployment."[6] Just three days after they arrived back in Salt Lake City, registration of the Leningrad Branch of the Church was formally approved. And the following year, on June 24, 1991, the Russian Republic granted formal recognition to the Church.

▪ ▪ ▪ ▪ ▪

As stunning as these events were, there were revolutionary developments in nonpolitical arenas as well. On November 25, 1989, the First Presidency announced a major change in policy for financing local Church units in the United States and Canada. All funds required to operate local units, including those needed to construct buildings, would come from the tithes and offerings of the Church, and members would no longer have budget assessments. For years leaders had looked to this day. During his eight years in the First Presidency, President Hinckley had encouraged financial policies that would put the Church in the economic position to allow this step.

"This idea wasn't new. It had been discussed for years," President Hinckley explained. "But it was a bold step, because the amount of money involved was staggering. To lift all local contributions beyond tithes and offerings from the people and have the Church assume the cost of acquiring real estate, building and maintaining buildings, and running programs required a tremendous act of faith. We talked about this for a long time in the First Presidency and Quorum of the Twelve, and it received very serious consideration. The decision to move ahead was tremendously significant."[7]

On February 18, 1990, President Hinckley presided at a Churchwide fireside in which he, President Monson, and Elder Boyd K. Packer explained the principles underlying this significant operational change. Reflecting on his experience as a stake president who had been charged with raising funds to build chapels and carry on a full program of activity, he said: "In those days we would have thought the Millennium had come if we had received word that the Church would bear all of the costs of providing land, all of the costs incident to building construction, operation, and maintenance, let alone an activity and administration budget. . . . It is not the Millennium, but this long-hoped-for and prayed-for day has come. Though I have been a party to its inauguration, I still stand in awe at what has happened. . . . I have been a personal witness to this whole unfolding miracle."

His message revealed the intensity of his feelings about the Church's finances: "The Church is not so wealthy that it can indiscriminately scatter its resources. We must be extremely careful and wise, and I believe inspired, if this program, which involves many millions of dollars, is to function."[8]

President Hinckley frequently marveled at the simplicity of the Lord's law of finance. After a meeting with President Monson and the Presiding Bishopric in which they reviewed a quarterly financial report, he noted: "Because of the faith of the people the Church is in good financial condition. We who are officers of the Church have a very special and sacred trust concerning the funds of the Church. It is a matter of deep and anxious concern to me. I wish to be prudent, and above all things inspired."[9] Just a few weeks later, he implored the Church's department heads to exercise prudence and economy as they prepared the next year's budget: "Never has the Church been in a better position financially than it is today, but prosperity can be a fragile thing."[10]

There was further financial history making when the First Presidency announced that, effective January 1, 1991, the contributions required to maintain full-time missionaries from the U.S. and Canada would be equalized. This possibility had likewise been considered for decades and in recent months had been discussed again and again—after which deliberations President Hinckley always noted, "This is a matter that weighs very heavily upon me."[11] After the meeting of the First Presidency and Quorum of the Twelve in which the decision was reached, President Hinckley recorded his feelings: "We made the very historic decision to average all missionary costs. This is a matter that has been discussed over a period of many, many years. It means that regardless of where a missionary goes, the cost will be the same. It means that half of the missionary families will be subsidizing the costs of the other half. But there is a definite element of equity in it. . . . This is a matter over which I feel great and serious concern. . . . We have set aside the tradition of more than a century."[12]

Since the death of President Tanner in 1982, no man had borne more responsibility for, or had more influence on, the financial well-being of the Church than had President Hinckley. Bishop Robert D. Hales said: "President Hinckley's understanding of banking and economics is incredible, particularly in view of the fact that his career has been based largely at Church headquarters. Yet his influence on the investment strategy of the Church and upon the way we handle our physical facilities and assets has been nothing short of remarkable. He has a long-term view. He seems to know when it is necessary to spend money, and when resources must be conserved."[13] President Hinckley was meticulous and demanding, for example, about the care given each phase and detail of temple construction. "We have been criticized for the cost of [temples], a cost which results from the exceptional quality of the workmanship and the materials that go into them," he acknowledged in a general conference address. "Those who criticize do not understand that these houses are dedicated as the abode of Deity and, as Brigham Young stated, are to stand through the Millennium."[14]

Aside from those unprecedented political and financial reformations, the year 1990 ushered in several noteworthy events in the Hinckley family, one of which occurred on April 15, when Richard Hinckley was called to serve as president of the Salt Lake Emigration Stake. "His being called as a stake president creates a remarkable thing," President Hinckley reflected, "four generations of stake presidents. It is a great tribute to him and a great opportunity. We are proud of him."[15] Clark was serving in a stake presidency in Arizona, and President Hinckley was grateful that his sons were willing and able to handle such assignments.

When President Hinckley set apart the new President Hinckley, it was not the first such privilege he had enjoyed with his children. The year before he had set apart Virginia as a member of the Primary General Board, and two years later had a similar experience when she was named first counselor to Janette C. Hales in the general presidency of the Young Women. He felt some concern that charges of nepotism might be leveled about her appointment and initially discouraged her call when Sister Hales made the recommendation, but he was pleased that she was worthy and capable.

President Hinckley had been surrounded by strong women his entire life. His mother had been an accomplished professional prior to her marriage and a devoted mother thereafter, and Marjorie had been a wonderful mother and a tremendous support to him—all while maintaining her own voice and independence. Now his daughters were carrying on in the same manner, each of them articulate, talented, and spirited. He teased them about their strong wills but was privately delighted that they were, each of them, independent thinkers who were faithful and orthodox without being necessarily wedded to convention. He both recognized and valued the influence women had, not only on the home and society but within the gospel kingdom, and he championed their cause at every opportunity.

Admittedly, he was chagrined by the dissenting voices of some women who felt they should be able to hold the priesthood, concerned about the number of young women who were inactive, and disheartened about the suffering of some at the hands of abusive or unfaithful husbands. But he also recognized that within women lay tremendous power and responsibility for molding society and making a vital contribution to the Church. "The Church has been in the forefront in training the daughters of Zion and in giving them responsibility," he said. "We believe and have taught consistently from the earliest days of the Church that a woman's greatest mission in life is an honorable and happy marriage with the rearing of an honorable and happy family. . . . But this is not inconsistent with other activities. There are tremendous responsibilities for women in the Church as well as in the community consistent with and in total harmony with marriage, motherhood, and the rearing of good and able children."[16]

Speaking in a general women's meeting, he challenged women to "rise to the stature of the divine" within them. "I see my own companion. . . . Is her contribution less acceptable before the Lord than is mine? I am satisfied it is not. She has walked quietly at my side, sustained me in my responsibilities, reared and blessed our children, served in many capacities in the Church, and spread an unmitigated measure of cheer and goodness wherever she has gone."[17] Beginning with his wife, the women of his own family were carrying their share of the load.

The year 1990 also marked a significant personal milestone for President Hinckley. Though it was almost impossible to believe, it had been eighty years since his parents had welcomed him into their home. In the intervening years he had logged millions of miles in the air, had seen the world's far reaches and rubbed shoulders with the world's prominent and influential, and had given more than a half century's service to the Lord's kingdom.

On the eve of President Hinckley's eightieth birthday, his family hosted a dinner in his honor for the General Authorities and their wives on the twenty-sixth floor of the Church Office Building. Each of his children and their spouses participated in a "Life with Father" presentation that reviewed highlights of his eight decades while pointing out his idiosyncrasies and personality quirks in humorous detail. President Monson paid him a warm tribute, and the evening concluded with a few remarks from the guest of honor himself, who conceded that both he and Marjorie were getting along in years and that the "rivets are getting a little loose and the solder is getting a little soft." Nevertheless, he couldn't help but reflect on the unique privileges that had been his: "I have been around the Church Office Building longer than any other man except Joseph Anderson, who is in his 101st year. I have had many, many friends . . . good and wonderful people who have blessed my life and from whom I've learned a great deal. I've known disappointment at times. But by and large it really has been a great and good life."[18]

The climax of his birthday celebration occurred the next morning, when he and Marjorie attended a session at the Salt Lake Temple with their children and adult grandchildren—nineteen in all. It was a wonderful morning, made all the better by the realization that all of their children and spouses, along with grandchildren old enough, were worthy to participate. Before retiring he wrote: "This is my 80th birthday. It does not seem possible. I cannot believe it. I do not feel old. I get out of breath rather easily, and get tired, but I still feel alert and that I can carry my load." After a few other observations, he concluded: "I feel a spirit of great gratitude and deep reverence for my beloved mother who died at the age of 50 and my wonderful father. No one could have had better parents. . . . I hope I have brought some measure of honor to their names."[19] With these celebrations past, he hoped there would be an end to the fuss. When he went to church the next morning, however, many friends, having read notice of his birthday in the *Church News*, commented on the occasion. "I would feel much better if it were not so well known," he wrote. "I do not wish to be tagged as an old man."[20]

President Hinckley may have felt physically capable of carrying his load in the First Presidency, but little by little he was forced to reduce his commitments elsewhere. He had resigned in 1985 from the Utah Power and Light board of directors, and in June 1990 he reluctantly retired from the Zion's National Bank board of directors after twenty-four years of service. He had enjoyed those associations, but the press of other responsibilities made it necessary to lighten his load.

Only occasionally did he spend a day home sick, and even then he usually attributed the ailment to stress. In August 1990 he had a small skin cancer removed, but that procedure did little more than force him to take it easy that day. And in November 1992 he submitted to arthroscopic surgery on his knee, made necessary after he injured it climbing Rocky Ridge in Wyoming. That minor operation kept him away from the office only a couple of days.

In a letter to a missionary grandson, Sister Hinckley provided a glimpse of the schedule she and her husband were keeping: "A week ago we went to Hawaii, but not to relax. On Sunday we held 3 regional conferences on 3 different islands. A brutal schedule, but very rewarding. The last one was on Molokai. They seldom have visitors and have never had a member of the First Presidency. They were so excited—they piled leis on us up to our ears. We got home 9 P.M. on Tues. and Gramps was at the office at 7 A.M. the next morning. His secretary put on his desk a list of assignments for the next 60 days. Enough to give a younger man a faint heart. There is no let-up and Gramps is suffering from severe burn-out, but somehow with the help of the Lord he will make it. . . . Sometimes when the pressures mount I have to remember that Joseph Smith *did have a vision* and though we give our whole souls to the work we are still unprofitable servants."[21]

In one address to the BYU student body President Hinckley revealed something of the strain under which he routinely operated: "I cannot understand how I agreed to come here today," he began. "We have just concluded a general conference of the Church and a number of associated meetings. I am hoarse from speaking and feel drained of things to speak about. . . . The day after tomorrow I leave for London for a regional conference to be followed by the rededication of the London Temple and then the rededication of the Swiss Temple. There will be dedicatory prayers and many talks to be given. . . . How did I ever agree to come here today? I ask myself. Do you have the same problem? . . . Someone asks you to do something far in advance, and you agree without really thinking of what that will entail. Then, when the day is upon you, you doubt your capacity, you worry, you ask why you ever agreed, and you pray for inspiration and enlightenment to fulfill your commitment."[22]

When he arrived home from that trip to Europe—which proved glorious because of the rededications themselves but also because he rekindled friendships formed during the original dedications—President Hinckley felt unusually weary. "On this plane ride home I have let down. I feel extremely tired. Since we left here a week ago Friday, I have given some 22 talks, each one different. At the age of 82 I am trying to work the way I did at 52."[23] In another letter to a grandson, Sister Hinckley acknowledged: "Grandpa wrestles with tremendous problems and decisions every day. I am not sure whether that is what keeps him young or whether it is what makes his hair whiter and whiter. But when he sees some of his peers he is grateful for the challenge. The worst possible situation is to have nothing to do."[24] One of President Hinckley's frequent journal entries after a heavy day was simply, "I retired weary but happy."

Physical labor provided the best relief to his busy calendar. "I work in my office all day long and then go to my home in the Gateway condominiums without going outside. I do not know whether it is summer, autumn, winter, or spring," he complained. "This may be an exaggeration, but it is not very much of an exaggeration."[25] Not only did he thrive on the sun and fresh air, but he prided himself on being able to tolerate rigorous work. When the roof of his toolshed in East Millcreek sprang a leak, he insisted on repairing it himself. "Marjorie scolded me for even thinking of getting on the roof at the age of 83," he noted. "As is the case with most men of my age I paid little attention to her scolding, climbed the ladder, and worked on the roof. Foolish? Yes. But the roof will no longer leak."[26]

It was fortunate that both President Hinckley and President Monson could tolerate a vigorous pace, because President Benson was declining in health. At eighty-six, he had been the second oldest man ordained President of the Church, and through the first two years of his presidency he kept a full schedule and traveled regularly. In October 1987 he suffered a mild heart attack, but the incident caused him only temporary difficulty. During 1988, however, his energy began to decrease, and he missed an increasing number of meetings. In October 1988, President Hinckley stepped in when President Benson didn't feel up to speaking at BYU: "He is now in his ninetieth year and does not have as much energy as he once had," President Hinckley began. "Neither will you when you reach that age—if you ever reach it. I bring you his love and blessing. He asked me to fill his assignment this morning, and that is what counselors are for."[27]

By the summer of 1989, when President Hinckley conducted President Benson's ninetieth birthday celebration at the Tabernacle, the prophet was frail. He attended but did not speak at the April 1990 general conference. From that time forward his general health deteriorated, and only occasionally did he meet with the Brethren. After he attended one meeting in the temple in the spring of 1991, President Hinckley noted: "It was very good to have him there. He said nothing, but his countenance was radiant."[28]

At first it was a little unnerving for President Hinckley to watch the prophet's health fail, for once again he found himself serving as counselor to an aging Church President whose physical strength and mental acuity were gradually slipping and unlikely to improve. There was at least one major difference this time, however, for he was joined in the First Presidency by an able, vital second counselor who shared the workload and with whom he could confer over difficult matters that demanded resolution.

He was enormously grateful for President Monson, and as the burden of leading the Church fell increasingly to the two of them, he often remarked, "We have been here before." One notation in his journal is representative: "The pressures of my work at the office are tremendous. . . . I have to make decisions. I am serving as the first counselor to the President of the Church, who is unable in his present circumstances to handle any of the business of the Church."[29]

President Hinckley planned to accompany the Tabernacle Choir on its historic tour to the Holy Land during December 1992 but at the last minute decided to stay home because President Benson was not well and Howard W. Hunter, President of the Twelve, lay seriously ill in the hospital. "It is a great opportunity that I miss, but I feel my duty is here," he recorded.[30] By the following spring, President Benson was generally lethargic. And after President Hunter underwent gallbladder surgery in May 1993, his condition deteriorated. President Hinckley was in London when he received word from President Monson that both men were in serious condition and that he might have to return to Salt Lake City on a moment's notice.

As had been the case during President Kimball's declining years, President Hinckley and, this time, President Monson were faced with achieving the delicate balance of moving the work forward while not overstepping their boundaries as counselors. Several times President Hinckley openly addressed the sensitive issue of the prophet's failing health and what that meant to the Church as a whole. "Brother Monson and I . . . do as has been done before, and that is to move forward the work of the Church, while being very careful not to get ahead of the President nor to undertake any departure of any kind from long-established policy without his knowledge and full approval," he explained in a general priesthood meeting. "We postpone action when we are not fully certain of our course and do not move forward until we have the blessing of our President and that assurance which comes from the Spirit of the Lord. We pray for our President. We pray often and with great earnestness. We love him and know our proper relationship to him. . . . Do not fear, . . . there is a Presidency over this Church. I hope it will not sound egotistical when I say that it has been put in place by the Lord. . . . We have no other desire than the desire to do His will concerning His kingdom and His people."[31]

Those who interacted with President Hinckley on day-to-day

matters found that he practiced what he preached. Ted Simmons, managing director of physical facilities for the Church, regularly brought matters for consideration before the Appropriations Committee. "Throughout President Benson's illness President Hinckley made it clear that he was not the prophet and that he in no way presumed to operate in that role," he said. "He constantly deferred to what the President of the Church would want done. It wasn't so much what he said but how he conducted himself. There are no top-level executives I know of in the business world who could have subordinated themselves quite as he did, and for so long."[32]

There were times, many of them, when Presidents Hinckley and Monson refused to move forward on an issue until they were sure they had received assent from an alert President Benson. Elder Oaks witnessed one such instance that occurred while the Twelve were enjoying a social function in President Benson's apartment. "I knew that President Hinckley was going to clear a particular matter with President Benson," he recalled. "At one point President Hinckley motioned for me to join the two of them in one corner of the room so that I could witness the conversation. I saw that the prophet was tracking the discussion entirely, and with that the First Presidency was able to move forward on that issue. If President Hinckley felt something was a decision for the President and not something within the delegated authority of counselors, he would not move ahead. His integrity on that process was 100 percent."[33]

President Benson's fragile condition did not impede the work. On September 1, 1991, Church membership reached eight million. The kingdom was growing in other ways as well, as evidenced by the increasing size of and diversity within the First and Second Quorums of the Seventy. Among many others, in the early nineties President Hinckley set apart as General Authorities Elders Han In Sang from Korea, Kwok Yuen Tai from Hong Kong, and Augusto A. Lim from the Philippines, each of whom he had known during his extensive travels throughout Asia.

The Church was also making progress on other fronts, including its relationship with leaders of the Reorganized Church of Jesus Christ of Latter Day Saints. Largely through the efforts of Allen C. Rozsa, director of the visitors center in

Independence, Missouri, the Tabernacle Choir was invited to perform in the Reorganized Church's Auditorium at the conclusion of its 1992 tour to Canada and the Midwest. The invitation was tendered on the condition that President Hinckley attend the performance and address the congregation. Accordingly, on July 31 he and Sister Hinckley spent the day in Independence, Missouri, as guests of Reorganized Church President Wallace B. Smith. Among other things, President Smith showed President Hinckley the printer's manuscript of the Book of Mormon. "It was tremendously fascinating to me to see with my own eyes and touch with my own hands this very precious document," President Hinckley wrote. "It was worth the trip here to see this precious treasure." There was a good spirit between the leaders, and after their time together President Hinckley concluded, "No one could have been treated more graciously than we were treated by these good people."[34]

The concert that evening was magnificent. Both President Smith and President Hinckley offered brief remarks to the sell-out audience of 5200 prior to the performance, and there was generous and sustained applause as they concluded. "Outside of the Salt Lake Tabernacle, I have never heard the choir sing more beautifully or more powerfully," noted President Hinckley afterward. When the choir followed their traditional encore number, "The Battle Hymn of the Republic," with "God Be with You Till We Meet Again," there were few dry eyes in the Auditorium.[35]

President Hinckley savored these experiences away from headquarters, out among the people. Such exposure was one of the best antidotes he knew for the insularity of the Church Administration Building, which could distort a General Authority's judgment if he weren't careful. For President Hinckley, his family provided another reality check; they weren't at all in awe of their father and didn't hesitate to speak their minds about almost any topic.

On occasion, the Hinckleys invited their children and grandchildren to travel with them, though President Hinckley was always uneasy lest anyone assume—always incorrectly—that the Church was footing the bill. For example, two teenage granddaughters, Jessica Dudley and Amy Pearce, joined them at their own expense on a trip to France. While there President Hinckley took them and his wife to the American Military Cemetery where Stanford was buried and told them the story of his older brother's passing. Before leaving France, he bought a bouquet of flowers, returned to the cemetery, and placed it on the grave. "I then offered a prayer standing on this hallowed ground," he recorded. "We lingered for a short time and then left. I may never get back there again. I am grateful for the opportunity to have been there."[36]

Both granddaughters were amazed at this rare glimpse of their grandfather's sentimentality. "You will never believe this, but Grandpa actually bought fresh flowers," Jessica exclaimed to her parents upon her return, marveling over his extravagance. The girls also enjoyed their grandparents' undivided attention and couldn't stop talking about the history and poetry Grandpa Hinckley recited as they drove around Paris, made a quick trip to the Louvre, and saw the Eiffel Tower. The experience was rejuvenating for President Hinckley as well, who noted upon its conclusion: "Our granddaughters will never forget this. . . . They have had a wonderful time together talking constantly. And they have seen things which have stirred within them emotions that they will remember. I am so glad that we have brought them. . . . It has been one of the best trips in my life. Having these granddaughters with us has added to that happiness. They have seen their old grandfather in a new light as he has spoken to large congregations in the various meetings that have been held."[37]

All of the grandchildren adored their grandparents. Marjorie was known throughout the family as the "groovy grandma," a reputation earned after countless shopping trips, sleepovers, and grandchildren's parties. Even in her eighties she planned Christmas celebrations complete with activities for all ages. "Everyone loves to be around Mother and Dad," Jane said. "They are so enthusiastic about life. They expect each day to bring a new adventure. None of us can resist their optimism and enthusiasm."[38]

Grandson Michael Hinckley could never understand it when friends made comments suggesting that he must not get much time with his grandfather. "It seems as though I see him all the time," he explained. "Even though I know he comes home from work with a million things he would like to do, sometimes I stop by just to talk. He never seems to mind. He's always there for family events—priesthood ordinations, baptisms, courts of honor, farewells, and parties. I've never felt cheated."[39]

Families—his own and those of the world at large—were frequently on President Hinckley's mind. He often said that "you need heaven's help in rearing heaven's child." In a January 1994 satellite broadcast sponsored by the Primary, titled "Behold Your Little Ones," he lamented that millions of children were abused and neglected and suffering at the hand of evil and selfish people.[40] Speaking at the annual convention of American Mothers in May 1994 he repeated a common theme: "I am more concerned about the moral deficit than I am about the budget deficit. The strength of a nation lies in the homes of its people." He then decried the "filth, the rot, the violence and profanity" spewing into the home via television. "If we could follow a slogan that says, 'Turn off the TV and open a good book,' we would do something of substance in strengthening another generation," he insisted.[41]

That same month he told members of the Washington, D.C., chapter of the BYU Management Society that the country was "experiencing a moral and ethical disaster": "We have lost a tremendous reservoir of values. . . . There has been more of scientific discovery during my lifetime than during all of the centuries of time that preceded it. But in some things we are slipping back into the jungle in terms of real civilization." Then, describing the quality of life his parents had created in his boyhood home, he declared: "Every child is the product of a home. We have a terrible youth problem, but I am convinced we have a greater parent problem. . . . I submit that there is nothing any of us can do that will have greater long-term benefit than to rekindle wherever possible the spirit of the homes in which we grew up."[42]

Threats to the sanctity and success of family life were increasing and insidious. In February 1994 the First Presidency issued a statement opposing the legalization of same-sex marriages, and President Hinckley frequently took aim at pornography and the sleaze that could be found in nearly every sector of professional entertainment. When Salt Lake City's Pioneer Memorial Theater allowed increasing profanity and vulgarity in its productions, he registered a formal objection and withdrew the annual grant from the Church's foundation.[43]

President Hinckley's concern for the present was linked to his reverence for the past. Few men had spoken more often or more eloquently about the Saints' pioneer heritage and its importance to the modern Church. And perhaps no one had participated in as many dedications and commemorations.

One series of dedications that held particular meaning for both President and Sister Hinckley took place on August 15, 1992, on the high plains of Wyoming. There they hiked to Independence Rock, Devil's Gate, Martin's Cove, the Willie Rescue Site, Rocky Ridge, and Rock Creek Hollow, all of which were significant to the Willie and Martin handcart companies and the Hunt and Hodgett wagon trains. Many had died—including James Goble, the brother of Sister Hinckley's grandmother—in this desolate area before rescue parties dispatched by Brigham Young reached them, and President Hinckley had taken an active interest in acquiring these sites. Members of the Riverton Wyoming Stake insisted you couldn't say the word *handcart* without uttering *Hinckley* in the same breath.

For President and Sister Hinckley, these hallowed places were sobering but inspirational reminders of men and women who had perished for their convictions. In his journal he noted: "As I dictate this I am looking at Independence Rock. . . . It is quite an experience to walk where our pioneer forefathers struggled so hard on this journey they made to the west in search of peace and the opportunity to worship according to their conscience. . . . A few miles west of Independence Rock is Devil's Gate. . . . The Martin and Willie Companies both experienced difficulties here. . . . It was bitter cold, snowing and the land was covered with snow. The temperature dropped one night to 11 degrees below zero. . . . Here they unloaded all the gear they could get rid of so that they could ride in the rescue wagons and get to the Salt Lake Valley as quickly as possible. . . . We are traveling today in luxury. . . . We have had good food this morning. . . . We are just a group of 1992 dudes."[44] President Hinckley struggled to maintain his composure as he dedicated monuments at Martin's Cove, the Willie Rescue Site, and then Rocky Ridge, all of which had been erected by members of the Riverton Wyoming Stake under the direction of President R. Scott Lorimer.[45]

He found great pleasure also in leading out in the commemoration of the centennial of the Salt Lake Temple dedication, and devoted his address in the Sunday morning session of the April 1993 general conference to the anniversary. After recounting the miraculous events associated with building the temple, he reported on the progress of current temple projects and then concluded by announcing that he had invited the Tabernacle Choir to sing the "Hosanna Anthem," with the congregation joining in singing "The Spirit of God Like a Fire Is Burning." "I hope that as we do so, there will be stirred within each of us a flaming testimony of the divinity of this work," he explained. He was not disappointed with the results. The congregation rose spontaneously as they began to sing, and the effect was electric. "It was a great and moving and wonderful experience," he recorded later. "It was such an experience as I have never quite felt in a conference before."[46]

President Hinckley continued to be personally involved with every phase of temple work and temple building. No inconvenience was too great if it made a temple more accessible to more people. When heavy rains kept a group of Irish Saints from arriving at the London Temple in time for their scheduled session during the rededication, President Hinckley offered to either delay the session or add another one just for them. During the dedication of the Lima Peru Temple, a group of Bolivians en route there called several times with news that their bus kept breaking down. When President Hinckley was informed that the bus had broken down yet again and it looked as though they would miss even the last session, he replied, "The next time they call, let them know that whenever they arrive there will be a session for them, even if it's 2:00 in the morning."[47]

When the First Presidency determined that two new temple films should be produced, President Benson assigned President Hinckley to supervise their production. He labored over the script and the overall project, which consumed him for months. Among other refinements, he authorized the production of a musical soundtrack to add another dimension to the finished product. When he was told, upon completion of the filming, that recording the ceremony in the required languages could take as long as two years, his response was predictable. "He listened to us carefully and was very gracious," said Derek Metcalfe, managing director of the Temple Department. "But when we were through he said, 'I can see your problem. I really can. But we have just four months to complete this project. There must be another way to accomplish this.' We went to work, and through a miraculous series of events located an engineer abroad who had just developed a process that allowed us to complete the work in the allotted time."[48]

Whenever possible, President Hinckley continued to select locations for temples himself. "President Hinckley has tromped around countless hills looking for temple sites," said Elder Neal A. Maxwell. "It is not his way to sit back and have the temple committee say, 'We think a temple is needed here and we have found a location.' He wants to walk to the top of the hill himself and feel what there is to be felt there. It is almost as though he has always felt a responsibility to President McKay for temples and temple work."[49] In a journal entry President Hinckley revealed the source of his motivation: "Every temple the Church has built has been a beautiful structure. We have never sold a temple or torn one down. Enemies of the Church dispossessed us of the Kirtland and Nauvoo temples. But of 45 temples since built, all have been kept in beautiful operating condition. It is imperative that a temple be in a stable area. I look at its life in terms of at least a century and longer."[50]

Philippe Kradolfer was serving as director of temporal affairs for the South America North Area when he was assigned to look for a temple site in Guayaquil, Ecuador. After an intense search, he located six sites for President Hinckley's inspection on a one-day stop in that city. Philippe took him to the first site, and though that property was attractive, he seemed more curious about what lay beyond a group of nearby trees. Philippe told him that it was swampland. That and other factors discouraged President Hinckley about the location, and they subsequently visited the five other sites. Finding nothing that interested him, he asked Philippe to take him back to the first location, and again he asked what lay beyond a group of trees that bordered the property. This time the party set off to explore the area with President Hinckley giving directions as they drove, suggesting which way to turn and when. Suddenly they spotted an unpaved road. "At that moment President Hinckley said, 'This is precisely where we are going,'" Philippe remembered. "The little road led to a gorgeous piece of property that oversees the whole of Guayaquil. None of us said a word as President Hinckley got out of the car and walked to the edge of the property. As he stood alone looking down upon the city, tears filled my eyes because I knew that a prophet had found the site for the temple."[51]

President Hinckley felt strongly that temple building must move forward in an unprecedented way. At one meeting of the Temple Sites and Construction Committee, which he chaired, he expressed frustration at delays in obtaining architectural renderings for approved temples: "I told them that we must build more temples and we must build them more quickly. This is the season to build temples. They are needed, and we have the means to do so. The Lord will hold us accountable if we do not work with greater accomplishment than we are now doing."[52]

He was particularly anxious to select a site in Hong Kong and had on several occasions scouted locations. In July 1992 he made a quick trip there with Ted Simmons for the purpose of looking at and, he hoped, selecting property for a temple. As they toured various sites, he continued to feel unsettled about what they saw, and the decision weighed on him. Then, early one morning, he had an unusual experience. "Something very interesting came into my mind," he recorded. "I did not hear a voice with my natural ears. But into my mind there came the voice of the Spirit. It said, 'Why are you worried about this? You have a wonderful piece of property where the mission home and the small chapel stand. They are in the very heart of Kowloon, in the location with the best transportation. . . . Build a building of [several] stories. It can include a chapel and classrooms on the first two floors and a temple on the top two or three floors.' . . . I relaxed and went back to sleep."[53]

Apparently he didn't sleep long, for at 5:15 A.M. the telephone rang in Ted Simmons's room. "President Hinckley couldn't wait any longer to call and share with me the impression he had had that we could raze the mission home on the Kowloon property and build in its place a multistory building that would double as office building and temple," Ted remembered. "After all his worry about a temple site in Hong Kong, he had received the direction he sought. He couldn't have been more excited than he was that morning about finally resolving a dilemma that had burdened him for so long."[54]

The ultimate experience associated with a temple was its dedication, and as he prepared to dedicate the San Diego Temple in April 1993, President Hinckley calculated that of the forty-five temples then in operation, he had participated in the dedication or rededication of all but five. "I came fasting," he wrote of his preparation for this dedication. "I always feel the weight of responsibility when we dedicate a temple."[55] Twenty-three sessions later, he noted, "We are weary tonight. But it is weariness mixed with happiness."[56] Elder L. Tom Perry accompanied President Hinckley to the Manila Temple dedication, and what he observed there was not unusual: "President Hinckley spoke at every session, and each talk was unique. He seemed to sense the needs of each group and impart a message suited for them. His spiritual instincts were remarkable. The feeling there was so tender that when the choir came in for the last number of the last session and lined up behind us, we could feel their tears drop on our coats."[57]

President Hinckley's instincts had likewise proven on target with the massive restoration project drawing to a close on the northeast corner of Main Street and South Temple in downtown Salt Lake City. Renovation of the Hotel Utah demanded a combination of good judgment about physical facilities and meticulous attention to detail. In the spring of 1993, while final touches were being made on the building's interior, President Hinckley and the other Brethren reviewed the final version of *Legacy*, the movie produced exclusively for the new large-screen theater, and pronounced it magnificent. It appeared that everything would be ready for the dedication in late June. Even a name for the historic building had been selected and announced: the Utah Building. Though he had been the one to suggest the name, President

Hinckley felt unsettled as the date of dedication neared. It bothered him that the new designation had no connection to the Church. To complicate matters, a building under construction just two blocks away had been named the Utah One Building.

On the evening of Wednesday, May 5, President Hinckley retired feeling worried about obstacles that had arisen over permits for the temple in Hong Kong. But it was concern about the name of the former Hotel Utah that awakened him in the middle of the night. After trying unsuccessfully to go back to sleep, he finally got up and stared out the window at the historic block that housed the old hotel, the Church Administration and Office Buildings, and the Lion and Beehive Houses. For a few moments his mind raced back and forth between past and present. He had spent a lot of his life on that block—beginning at the Deseret Gym as a boy and continuing as a teenager at LDS High School, where the campus had included both a Young Building and a Smith Building—one named for Brigham Young, the other for Joseph F. Smith.

Then he had a powerful and clear impression: There were many monuments to Brigham Young in downtown Salt Lake City, but none to the Prophet Joseph Smith except a statue within the walls of Temple Square. The Hotel Utah, which had been exquisitely restored and would not only serve various Church functions but provide the public with many reasons to visit its precincts, should be named the Joseph Smith Memorial Building. There was already a building carrying that name at BYU: the home of BYU's Department of Religious Education, which he had dedicated eighteen months earlier. But he was unconcerned about the duplication. "I wish there were a Joseph Smith Memorial Building in every large city in the world," he noted.[58]

The next morning, he described his middle-of-the-night experience and recommended the name change first to President Monson and then to the Twelve in their temple meeting. Their reaction was unanimous: the restored hotel would be the Joseph Smith Memorial Building. President Hinckley then decided that they needed a piece of art commemorating the Prophet to place in the elegant but massive lobby. He considered the painting of Joseph Smith that hung in the Church Administration Building, but felt it would be dwarfed by the huge hall. Then Bishop David Burton, first counselor in the Presiding Bishopric, informed him that a statue of the Prophet had been shipped to Salt Lake City after having been removed during remodeling from the visitors center in Independence. President Hinckley and President Monson went to the warehouse to view the crated statue, which even lying unclean on its back was magnificent. Nine feet tall, cut from Carrara marble, the heroic-sized piece of art promised to add the finishing touch to the grand building. A few days later President Hinckley spent part of the afternoon in the lobby trying to determine the statue's placement. With help from a tall worker, who stood on a chair to approximate the size of the statue, he experimented with various locations until he decided that the statue would stand on the west side of the lobby in front of a reception room that would be named, appropriately, the Nauvoo Room.

On June 27, 1993, the 149th anniversary of the martyrdom of the Prophet Joseph Smith, President Hinckley dedicated the Joseph Smith Memorial Building. "This is a wonderful day—the completion of a tremendous project, which I am confident was inspired by the Lord," he told the assembled audience. He acknowledged that the effort had proved expensive. "Some people may feel in their hearts that we have been extravagant. We hope there won't be any feelings of that kind. . . . Nothing is too good to remember the Prophet Joseph Smith." Referring to the name of the renovated hotel, President Hinckley declared simply, "I think the Lord wanted this building named the Joseph Smith Memorial Building." He concluded his remarks with an emphatic declaration: "I love the Prophet Joseph Smith. I love the Prophet Joseph Smith!"[59]

Response to the building was overwhelming. After the dedication and extended open house, during which more than 70,000 people toured the structure, President Hinckley received hundreds of letters congratulating him and the Church on what was universally regarded as a magnificent restoration. Many individuals offered apologies for their earlier expressions of resentment. The Utah Heritage Foundation conceded: "The Joseph Smith Memorial Building is an outstanding restoration/ renovation project. The vision and skill that have gone into this project have produced a first-class building. The grand architecture, the beautiful spaces and the distinguished history of the former Hotel Utah have not been vanquished. Exceptional craftsmanship with great attention to detail and design is evident throughout the building. . . . The Church of Jesus Christ of Latter-day Saints is to be complimented and praised."[60]

President Hinckley was pleased when, several months later, he learned that as early as 1902 the YMMIA General Board had recommended to the First Presidency and the Twelve that the Church construct a building honoring Joseph Smith on the corner where the Hotel Utah was later built.[61] Apparently the Smith family knew of the discussions, for in 1909 Joseph Fielding Smith expressed disappointment when the decision was made to build a hotel there. "The Utah hotel is being erected on the old Deseret News corner, where we had for so long been given to expect that a Memorial building to the Prophet and grandfather Hyrum Smith was to be built," he wrote to his brother. "I cannot help but feel that the erection of this building on that corner is going to be a great big mistake—with a capital *M*."[62] After learning about the earlier discussions, President Hinckley wrote, "I think it was inspiration, and I believe revelation, that came to me when I could not sleep one night, that the building should carry the name of the Joseph Smith Memorial Building."[63]

Elder Richard G. Scott summarized: "The Joseph Smith Memorial Building is an example of the breadth of President Hinckley's strengths. He is a man of vision who sees beyond the here and now. He is unusually adept at temporal affairs and can speak the language of builders and artisans. He has great faith in the Lord, and knows how to receive revelation. It is unusual to find someone who is so skilled with the pragmatic and yet gifted in communicating and receiving spiritual truth. His range of capability is remarkable."[64]

President Hinckley's breadth of experience and understanding also made him comfortable hosting the world's prominent. He often encouraged youth to develop a "social ease, the capacity to mix and mingle with people wherever you meet them," and he knew whereof he spoke.[65] "President Hinckley can converse intelligently about anything with anyone," said President

Thomas S. Monson. "He knows how to ask the right questions and how to make our guests feel that he is sincerely interested in them. He is perfectly at home with high and low, and can converse with ease about everything from satellite technology to pruning trees."[66]

When the Lord Mayor of London and his wife, the Lady Mayoress, visited Salt Lake City, the First Presidency hosted a dinner in their honor with President Hinckley serving as master of ceremonies. Wendell Ashton, who attended the elegant event, noted: "They were dumbfounded at the way President Hinckley talked about the streets and bridges in London, mimicked an English dialect, and spoke of plum pudding and other British conventions. After returning home the Lord Mayor told the Consul General to the United States that of all his visits in Canada and the United States, the best one of all was the evening he spent with the Mormon church's First Presidency."[67]

When President Hinckley hosted a luncheon honoring Philip Caldwell, chairman of the board and chief executive officer of Ford Motor Company, he welcomed him with, "Your advertisements used to say, 'There's a Ford in your future,' but I'd like you to know there is a Ford in my past—the first auto the Hinckley family ever owned." He then produced the radiator cap from his father's 1916 Model T Ford and reminisced about driving and repairing the vehicle as a boy.[68]

During a trip to Spain in the spring of 1992, he met with King Juan Carlos I and Queen Sofia and presented the Spanish monarch with a leatherbound copy of the Book of Mormon. Elder M. Russell Ballard accompanied President Hinckley on the visit. "It was remarkable to watch President Hinckley in action," he reported. "He recalled meeting the King several years earlier in Santiago de Compostela, and mentioned that his son Clark had been one of the Church's first missionaries to Spain in 1969. After putting everyone at ease and engaging the royal couple in conversation, he spoke to them about the Book of Mormon with the same fervor he had had with missionaries the day before. He was comfortable in the presence of royalty, and he made his hosts feel at ease with him."[69] During the same trip, on a stopover in Rome, he and Elder Spencer Condie visited Father Leonard Boyle, prefect of the Vatican Library. "The two men greeted each other like longtime friends," Elder Condie said. "Father Boyle was amazed with President Hinckley's knowledge of books and the techniques used to prevent their aging. As the visit drew to a close, the prefect observed in his thick Irish brogue, 'President Hinckley is truly a very remarkable man.'"[70]

Indeed, the dignitaries who visited the First Presidency in Salt Lake City formed an impressive roster of the world's influential. President Hinckley appreciated several memorable visits with President George Bush, including one in July 1992, about which he noted afterward: "We talked about our missionary work in various parts of the world. He asked how we go about opening a new country. He seemed sincerely curious. We told him the procedures we follow. We talked about our program to strengthen families. He was deeply interested. We were free to ask anything and he did not hesitate to respond. He talked openly and freely and in a very friendly way." After their meeting, he and President Monson escorted the president into the foyer where a large number of reporters had gathered. When one media representative asked him a political question, President Bush responded, "I am not here to discuss politics. It would be inappropriate for me to discuss these things in these sacred precincts." President Hinckley's reaction was one of admiration: "I felt it was a classic answer, and the expression of a gentleman who carries respect for that which is good and sacred."[71] After his visit, President Bush wrote President Hinckley: "The fact that your church has an active mission program around the world is a wonderful thing. Not only does the program project commitment by the individual missionaries, but it also shows the church's concern for this wonderful but troubled world in which we live. You do care and that comes through loud and clear.[72]

Those who worked closely with President Hinckley marveled not only at his social ease but at the range of his administrative skills. After observing him in countless settings, Lowell R. Hardy, his personal secretary, stated simply that he was the most effective leader he had ever met.[73] BYU President Rex Lee put President Hinckley's strengths in context: "I've had direct contact with two U.S. Presidents, three attorneys general, and lots of Cabinet officers. But I have never known anyone who has a greater capacity to see the forest and the trees, the big picture and the very small details at the same time and [to] keep both in perspective like President Hinckley does."[74]

Ted Simmons, who met frequently with President Hinckley over matters related to the construction of buildings and other facilities, explained: "President Hinckley is a good student. There's not a business theory or practice he hasn't been exposed to, but he's also very savvy. He understands the pressure points in business, and he has phenomenal recall. I dare not quote him a figure unless I am absolutely certain it is correct, because he will remember it precisely. I have to obtain permission from the Appropriations Committee for every building project we undertake over a certain dollar amount, and it is amazing how often, when I take in a proposal to remodel a building, he says, 'Didn't we spend *x* amount on that building just six years ago?' More often than not his memory is precisely correct, and we've got thousands of buildings throughout the world. He has the capacity for infinite detail but at the same time the breadth of vision to see how it all fits together."[75]

President Monson, who had participated with him in countless meetings and other events, said: "President Hinckley can juggle a lot of balls in the air at the same time. He can go from a meeting where the item is welfare to another where the topic is auditing and then to another where proselyting is being discussed, and be able to instantly switch gears and give undivided attention to that subject."[76]

Nonetheless, President Hinckley couldn't be pushed to premature decisions. To the consternation of his Brethren, some proposals ended up in his left bottom drawer, or "pending" file, and he refused to force a decision that didn't feel right. Elder Henry B. Eyring, who as a member of the Presiding Bishopric for seven years met with him at least weekly, said, "He has a great sense of timing and of proportion. He knows which things matter, and he knows when it's better to wait."[77]

There were those who described President Hinckley as a workaholic, though he didn't see himself that way. He did, however, admire a work ethic. One weekend with the luxury of no official assignment, he and Sister Hinckley attended a stake conference in a rural area of southeastern Utah. He found in that area a congregation of farmers whose livelihood depended on the law of the harvest. "They know that you do not reap wheat after sowing oats," he said later of the experience. "They know that you do not get a racehorse from a scrub mare. They know that if you are to build another great generation, you must work with vision and faith." After two days in the area among these principled and unpretentious people, Sister Hinckley told her husband, "These are the kind who constitute the glue that holds the Church together." He elaborated, with admiration: "I do not wish to imply that I could not find such [people] in cities and towns all over the world . . . , but somehow there seemed so much larger a percentage of them among the folks whom we visited. Their feet were planted on the solid earth. They knew the meaning of work without respect to hours or season."[78]

President Hinckley's own zeal for the work was no respecter of clock or calendar. When Marjorie asked one day if he really needed to push himself so hard, he responded, "Dear, don't you understand? I *love* what I do!" Through more than five decades of service, he had acquired an expansive view of the Church and its future, and he had spent much of his life trying to lift others to see the same. He believed the Lord held the destiny of the Church in His hands, and that confidence gave him the courage to press forward during difficult times. "Survey large fields and cultivate small ones," he often admonished the Saints, quoting President Harold B. Lee. "We ought to recognize something of the breadth and depth and height—grand and wonderful, large and all-encompassing—of the program of the Lord, and then work with diligence to meet our responsibility for our assigned portion of that program," he explained in one general conference message. "Each of us has a small field to cultivate. While so doing, we must never lose sight of the greater picture, the large composite of the divine destiny of this work."[79]

He elaborated on that theme in another general conference: "I invite you to look beyond the narrow boundaries of your own wards and rise to the larger vision of this, the work of God. We have a challenge to meet, a work to do beyond the comprehension of any of us—that is, to assist our Heavenly Father to save His sons and daughters of all generations. . . . No body of people on the face of the earth has received a stronger mandate from the God of heaven than have we of this Church."[80]

In view of the vision he had of the Church's future, it is not surprising that President Hinckley grew impatient with critics who continued to take jabs at the organization. After a group of self-described unbelievers published a Church "history" in which they concluded that its future looked dim, he responded: "Without wishing to seem impertinent, I should like to ask what the authors know about that future. They know nothing of the prophetic mission of the Church! The future must have looked extremely dim in the 1830s. It must have looked impossible back in those Ohio-Missouri days. But notwithstanding poverty, notwithstanding robbing, notwithstanding murders, notwithstanding confiscation and drivings and disenfranchisement forced upon the Saints in the ensuing years, the work moved steadily on. It has continued to go forward. Never before has it been so strong. Never before has it been so widespread. Never before have there been so many in whose hearts has burned an unquenchable knowledge of the truth."[81]

He continued with his perspective and testimony: "It is the work of the Almighty. It is the work of his Beloved Son, the Lord Jesus Christ. It is the gospel of salvation. Men and women may oppose now, just as others opposed in those days. But the work goes on because it is true and it is divine. These are the best of times in the history of this work."[82]

One point of contention that appeared unlikely to be resolved any time soon, however, was that fueled by antagonists who, as time passed and it became clear that President Benson would not regain his strength, pressed for a "contemporary" policy of succession that would honorably "release" a feeble President. Consequently, President Hinckley repeatedly addressed the issue. In the October 1992 general conference he told of a recent flight he had taken in which the passengers had been prepared for an emergency landing after the hydraulic system malfunctioned. An off-duty, non-LDS pilot on the flight moved among passengers, trying to reassure them. To one nearly hysterical woman he said, pointing to President Hinckley, "Do you know who that is?" When she shook her head, he replied,

"That is President Hinckley of the Mormon church, and he has a lot more work to do. Don't worry. This plane will be all right."

President Hinckley spoke about the redundancy system engineered into the plane that allowed the experienced crew, who had been trained for such an emergency, to land the aircraft safely. He then drew an analogy to the Lord's system of government: "We love and respect and honor and look to the prophet of this day, President Ezra Taft Benson. . . . But he has reached an age where he cannot do many of the things he once did. . . . Some people, evidently not knowing the system, worry that because of the President's age, the Church faces a crisis. They seem not to realize that there is a backup system. In the very nature of this system, there is always on board a trained crew. . . . They have been thoroughly schooled in Church procedures. More importantly, they also hold the keys of the eternal priesthood of God." President Hinckley concluded with his testimony: "For eleven-plus years, I have served as a Counselor in the First Presidency. I know how the system works. I know that it is divine in its plan and in its authority."[83]

During the fall of 1993, certain critics took up another banner when extensive publicity was given to disciplinary councils held in Utah on six members who had spoken out against the Church or its leaders. While Church leaders, both general and local, remained silent, the dissidents took their complaints to the press. During this period President Hinckley noted, "We have received many sad and disappointing letters from people who have accepted the one-sided newspaper reports concerning a handful who have been excommunicated. I am distressed by all of this. I could brush it off, I suppose, but it hurts me to see people who, not knowing all of the facts, jump to conclusions and become bitterly critical of the Church. I am in a very difficult situation. I am one of the . . . senior active officers of the Church. But I am not the President. I do my best, and pray that the Lord will inspire and direct me to the blessing of His work and to His glory and the glory of His Beloved Son."[84]

On October 17, the First Presidency issued a statement reviewing the Church's policy on discipline in which they acknowledged "deep regret" over anyone's loss of Church membership and explained that considerations of confidentiality prohibited public comment by Church leaders in such matters. They reaffirmed that they had the responsibility to preserve the Church's doctrinal purity and allowed that faithful members could distinguish between mere differences of opinion and those activities formally defined as apostasy.[85]

In spite of the media attention accorded the critics, they were a relative few when compared to the thousands, even millions, who marveled at the manner in which President Hinckley, President Monson, and other Church officials carried on under the circumstances. At the end of 1993, with President Benson confined to his home and showing no improvement, and President Hunter in poor health, President Hinckley reflected, "I am grateful that I feel as well as I do. I am 83 years of age, and carry a full schedule of work. I try to get some exercise and try to be wise in my diet, although this is not easy. . . . I am able to handle almost anything that I should do. For this measure of strength and health I am deeply grateful to the Lord."[86]

During the first few months of 1994 President Benson's condition remained about the same, but President Hunter was admitted to the hospital with another serious condition. Then, early on Friday, February 25, President Hinckley received word that his friend of more than fifty years and personal secretary to five Presidents of the Church, D. Arthur Haycock, had suddenly passed away. And if that weren't enough, later the same day Elder Marvin J. Ashton of the Quorum of the Twelve died. "This has been a hard day," he noted simply.[87]

Nevertheless, President Hinckley pressed on. In the April 1994 conference he once again addressed the subject of President Benson's health and affirmed the divinely mandated law of succession and Church government: "Let it be understood by all that Jesus Christ stands at the head of this church which bears His sacred name. He is watching over it. He is guiding it. . . . I do not worry about the circumstances in which we find ourselves. I accept these circumstances as an expression of His will. I likewise accept the responsibility, acting with my Brethren, to do all we can to move forward this holy work."[88] At the same conference, Presiding Bishop Robert D. Hales was called to the Quorum of the Twelve, filling the vacancy occasioned by Elder

Ashton's death, and Elder Merrill J. Bateman was sustained as Presiding Bishop.

Two weeks later, President Hinckley made a five-day trip to Scandinavia to preside at regional conferences in Sweden and Finland. After a productive weekend filled with wonderful meetings and association with "strong and able men and women" who impressed him greatly, he noted: "This has been a highly successful trip. We have held three regional conferences in three days. This has required some unusual scheduling and flying from city to city. But it has worked out smoothly and well. . . . We have accomplished in one weekend what would normally require two weekends to take care of. My brethren have been somewhat critical of me for doing this. . . . However, I am grateful that I have done it. . . . I have left my testimony and my blessings with members of the Church in two nations. . . . I hope that we may have done some good."[89] He was grateful to return to Salt Lake City, however. "It is wonderful to be with my dear wife again after a separation of only a few days," he recorded. "The older we grow, the more we become a part of one another's lives."[90]

During the spring President Hinckley was inducted into the Sons of the American Revolution and presented with its Distinguished Citizenship medal.[91] The recognition was meaningful in that it highlighted his heritage, which he prized. In terms of personal historical connections, however, there were few places as meaningful as Cove Fort. In 1988 President Hinckley had acted as both giver and receiver when the descendants of Ira Hinckley had given the deed to the pioneer fort to the Church. After an extensive restoration project, the fort was now ready to be dedicated, and on May 21, 1994, President and Sister Hinckley, members of their extended family, and two thousand others gathered in Millard County, Utah, for the ceremony. President Hinckley was equally anxious to inspect a small log house—the cabin in which his father had been born in Coalville, Utah—that had been moved and restored just east of the fort. This was a personal project, and, as he might have expected, the small cabin fell victim to Hinckley's Law. Nevertheless, it was wonderful to see such tangible evidences of both his father's and grandfather's lives, and as he walked about the grounds, he was stirred by the feeling that his forebears were present.

President Hinckley was in good spirits as he convened the dedicatory service that hot summer day. After several other speakers—including Colleen Maxwell, Elder Maxwell's wife and a great-granddaughter of Ira Hinckley, and President Hunter, whose health had improved markedly during preceding weeks—President Hinckley finally stood to speak. "I know it's hot out here and it's miserable, but you came expecting this," he began. "And moreover, the whole theme of this structure is endurance, so do the best you can." He laughed at his own humor, and the audience joined in. Then he continued: "I am grateful to be here. This is an emotional experience for me. . . . When I see what has been accomplished here, I am deeply moved. It took Grandfather and his associates seven months without any resources except their bare hands to build what was built here. It has taken the Church with all of its resources nearly seven years to restore it." He acknowledged that if his grandfather were looking down on the scene he might wonder, "Why all the fuss?" and then smile at the staff of professionals involved in recreating the barn that had been built as a matter of course in his day. "He had no architect. He had no surveyor. He had no engineer. He had no committee to whom he could appeal to settle his problems. And that was probably a blessing," President Hinckley joked.

Several times during his address, he paused to allow his emotions to subside. His feelings seemed most tender as he spoke of the women who had lived at the fort and there given birth and nurtured all who walked and lived within its precincts.[92]

That evening he recorded a sentiment he had expressed on other occasions when the Church devoted funds to the preservation of its history: "The restoration has been expensive, but as the years pass these costs will all be forgotten, and this outpost in the wilderness . . . will afford countless opportunities for telling the story of the past and building faith in the lives of those present. . . . I consider it a miracle that all of this happened. I know the hand of the Lord was in it."[93]

PHOTO BY GERALD W. SILVER/DESERET NEWS

On President Hinckley's eighty-fifth birthday, his nephew Mark Willes, then president of General Mills, wrote on the back of this unique memento: "As my last official act as an officer and director of General Mills, I am sending you this Wheaties box. Some of the greatest champions of all times have had their pictures on the front of these boxes. It seemed only right that you and Aunt Marge should be so honored."

Surrounded by family at his eighty-fifth birthday party on June 23, 1995

PHOTO BY MIKE CANNON/CHURCH NEWS

Walking along Albert Dock in Liverpool, England, August 31, 1995, the point from which thousands of early Latter-day Saints embarked for the United States

With Salt Lake Mayor Deedee Corradini at the dedication of the Brigham Young Historic Park, October 2, 1995

PHOTO BY LOWELL R. HARDY

Surprising the members of the Promontory (Utah) Branch on Sunday, October 15, 1995

PHOTO COURTESY ASSOCIATED PRESS/WHITE HOUSE

With Elder Neal A. Maxwell (far left) and James A. Harmon of New York City, meeting with President Bill Clinton and Vice President Al Gore in the White House in November 1995

PHOTO BY LOWELL R. HARDY

Greeting Randee Wootton, age five, in Denver, Colorado, April 14, 1996

Responding during a media luncheon at New York City's Harvard Club in November 1995. Mike Wallace and Robert Anderson from CBS's *60 Minutes* were among the attendees

PHOTO BY DON GRAYSTON/CHURCH NEWS

PHOTO BY DON GRAYSTON/CHURCH NEWS

Showing Mike Wallace around Temple Square during his visit to Salt Lake City in December 1995

Former Prime Minister Margaret Thatcher accepts an honorary doctorate from BYU on March 5, 1996

Enjoying a few moments before the convocation ceremony with BYU President Merrill J. Bateman and Lady Thatcher (reflected in the mirror are Elder Jeffrey R. Holland and Sir Denis Thatcher)

PHOTO BY MARK A. PHILBRICK/BYU

Presiding at the inauguration of Merrill J. Bateman on April 25, 1996, as president of Brigham Young University

PHOTO COURTESY ASSOCIATED PRESS/STEVE C. WILSON

With Utah industrialist Jon M. Huntsman on October 2, 1995, at the Utah Health Sciences Center, where Huntsman established an institute for the study of cancer

PHOTO BY LOWELL R. HARDY

Greeting Robert E. Hunter, the U.S. Ambassador-at-Large to NATO, and (right) Alan John Blinken, U.S. Ambassador to Belgium, during his visit to Brussels in June 1996

PHOTO BY GERRY AVANT/CHURCH NEWS

PHOTO BY GERRY AVANT/CHURCH NEWS

Being feted with a colorful welcome on May 27, 1996, at the Overseas Chinese Town of Shenzhen Special Economic Zone in Shenzhen, China

PHOTO BY LOWELL R. HARDY

Walking among the white crosses at the American Military Cemetery in Manila during his May 1996 visit to the Philippines

PHOTO BY LOWELL R. HARDY

Enjoying a few moments with Marjorie in Manila, Philippines, May 30, 1996

PHOTO BY LOWELL R. HARDY

With Elder and Sister Joseph B. Wirthlin and Elder and Sister John H. Groberg, meeting on May 29, 1996, with a small group of Saints in Ho Chi Minh City, Vietnam

Entering Manila's Araneta Coliseum on May 30, 1996, to find a crowd of more than 35,000—the largest indoor audience to ever hear a President of the Church

After the Araneta Coliseum fireside, bidding the Filipino people farewell

PHOTO BY LOWELL R. HARDY

With the Wirthlins, Grobergs, and missionaries on the grounds of the Cambodiana Hotel in Phnom Penh, Cambodia, where he dedicated the country May 29, 1996

PHOTO BY LOWELL R. HARDY

With their children: (back row) Virginia and Jim Pearce, Jane and Richard Hinckley, Jane and Roger Dudley; (front row) Clark and Kathleen Hinckley, Alan and Kathleen Barnes in front of the Garden Tomb in Jerusalem in June 1996

PHOTO BY RAVELL CALL/CHURCH NEWS

Leading the Utah Centennial wagon train into Cove Fort, Utah, June 24, 1996

PHOTO BY JOHN HART/CHURCH NEWS

Visiting Jerusalem in June 1996

Reading from the Book of Luke on Shepherd's Field in the Holy Land, June 19, 1996

At the groundbreaking of the St. Louis Missouri Temple

PHOTO BY LOWELL R. HARDY

Relaxing at the Polynesian Cultural Center, February 19, 1996

With his counselors and
members of the Quorum of the Twelve
in the summer of 1995:
(back row) President Boyd K. Packer,
Elders L. Tom Perry, David B. Haight,
Neal A. Maxwell, Russell M. Nelson,
Dallin H. Oaks, M. Russell Ballard,
Joseph B. Wirthlin, Richard G. Scott,
Robert D. Hales, Jeffrey R. Holland,
Henry B. Eyring;
(front row) Presidents Thomas S. Monson
and James E. Faust

PHOTOGRAPH BY ACEY HARPER ©1996

President Hinckley knew also that President Benson's health was in the hands of the Lord, and throughout May 1994 the prophet's condition deteriorated further. On Saturday, May 28, President Hinckley returned from a quick trip to Nashville (which he had undertaken because he was to receive the Silver Buffalo, the Boy Scouts' highest national award) to learn that President Benson had slipped into a coma. He went directly to the prophet's apartment, and as he stood at President Benson's side, he felt a surge of gratitude for the prophet's life and service. Before leaving, President Hinckley laid his hands on President Benson's head one last time and pronounced a blessing that promised him peace and joy. At that moment he knew that the President would not live much longer.[94]

Two days later, on Memorial Day, at 2:40 P.M., President Hinckley received the news: President Benson had died. He immediately called President Hunter and President Monson and began the process of notifying the Twelve. It was hard for him to concentrate, however. For though he had expected the news, he was flooded with emotions as he thought about his relationship with the man he had served as a counselor for just under a decade. The following morning at 9:00, when the Twelve assembled to initiate preparations for the funeral and burial of the President of the Church, President Hunter presided, and President Hinckley and President Monson resumed their places in the Quorum.

President Benson's passing prompted expressions of condolence from dignitaries around the world who were respectful not only of his ecclesiastical service but of his distinguished career as a former U.S. Cabinet officer. On Saturday, June 4, a solemn but stirring funeral service marked the passing of the thirteenth President of the Church. At President Hunter's request President Hinckley conducted and spoke at the services. "For more than thirty-two years I sat in councils with him," he reminisced. "I have been the beneficiary of his kindness and deferential manner. I have been blessed by his wisdom. I have seen the spirit of prophecy rest upon him. I have knelt with him and heard him pray." He then concluded with a passage from the Book of Mormon: "Had he been speaking during those last hours, I think he might have spoken these final words of Enos. . . . 'And I soon go to the place of my rest, which is with my Redeemer; for I know that in him I shall rest. And I rejoice in the day when my mortal shall put on immortality, and shall stand before him; then shall I see his face with pleasure, and he will say unto me: 'Come unto me, ye blessed, there is a place prepared for you in the mansions of my Father.' . . . From all of us across this broad world who have been the beneficiaries of his kindness, his service, and his life, we say thank you and good-bye, dear friend."[95]

The next morning, Sunday, June 5, the members of the Twelve gathered in the Salt Lake Temple to reorganize the First Presidency. During the meeting each apostle had opportunity to express himself, with Elder Hinckley leading out. "I indicated that I felt it was essential that the First Presidency be reorganized immediately," he recorded of his comments. "It is necessary to carry on the business of the Church. The people wish to hear the voice of a living prophet. I expressed my love for President Hunter and assured him of my willingness to do anything to help him."[96] After all had spoken, and it was clear that there was total unity among the fourteen men who had gathered for this sacred occasion, President Hinckley was voice in setting apart Howard W. Hunter as President of the Church. President Hunter then set President Hinckley apart as his first counselor and as President of the Quorum of the Twelve, President Monson as second counselor, and President Boyd K. Packer as Acting President of the Twelve. Without fanfare, but with an overpowering witness of the Spirit that all was in accordance with the Lord's will, the Church moved onward in an effortless manner.

CHAPTER TWENTY-THREE

FIRST COUNSELOR A SECOND TIME

President Hinckley hadn't necessarily expected the new Church President to ask him to remain in the First Presidency. But now that he had been called to continue in the role he had filled for nearly thirteen years, President Hinckley pledged to serve President Hunter with the same fidelity and energy he had afforded Presidents Kimball and Benson.

For twenty years he had sat next to President Hunter in the Quorum of the Twelve, and the soft-spoken, unassuming lawyer from California had long since won his esteem and affection. "He was a gracious man," President Hinckley said later. "He seldom got upset, and yet he had a lot of steel in him. He could take a stand and be firm about it, but his demeanor was one of kindness and consideration at all times. He was a man of great wisdom who thought clearly and could express himself succinctly. He quietly did his business without a lot of fuss and fanfare. I appreciated Howard Hunter so very much."[1]

President Hinckley had watched as President Hunter cared for his wife, Claire, during her extended illness, and he greatly admired this man whose patience seemed inexhaustible. "His tenderness concerning his wife, his absolute dedication to her and her comfort, was a remarkable and beautiful thing," President Hinckley commented. "He didn't talk about it. He had to be prodded even to speak about what he was experiencing. But once in a while, in a quiet way, he would express his feelings. His devotion to his wife in her frail condition was indicative of the man."[2] Claire Hunter passed away in 1983. When President

Hunter decided to remarry nearly seven years later, he honored President Hinckley with the request that he perform his sealing to Inis Egan Stanton in the Salt Lake Temple.

He expressed at the first opportunity his feelings about the privilege of working closely with President Hunter. On Monday morning, June 6, the First Presidency and Quorum of the Twelve gathered in the Church Administration Building to announce the reorganization of the First Presidency.[3]

In a brief statement, President Hunter caught the attention of Church members around the world with his gentle and compassionate manner and his invitation to live with "ever more attention to the life and example of Jesus Christ" and to "establish the temple of the Lord as the great symbol of membership." It was, he continued, the deepest desire of his heart to have every member of the Church temple worthy.[4]

Members of the Church responded enthusiastically to their new President. Nearly four years had passed since they had heard from the prophet, and listening to President Hunter speak was both reassuring and invigorating. His health had been frail in recent years, but for the time being he was strong and vibrant. As a columnist for the *Salt Lake Tribune* wrote: "The focus on his frailty seems to miss an important aspect of a religious leader, the power of his spirit. And [President] Hunter's soars."[5]

Indeed, the new Church President's gentle and kindly manner, accentuated perhaps by his reliance on a wheelchair or walker, endeared him to his vast flock, who immediately began to focus intently on the two invitations President Hunter had identified: to emulate the Master and to become a temple-attending people.

President Hinckley could readily endorse both subjects. Just four days after the press conference he flew to England to break ground for a second temple in the British Isles, this one to be located just a few miles outside of Preston in nearby Chorley, where he had first served as a missionary. He had been thrilled at the prospects of this second temple in Britain, and his emotions were tender as he arrived at the temple site on the overcast but otherwise glorious Sunday of June 12, having presided at two regional conferences over the weekend. When he saw that a crowd of more than ten thousand had assembled, he was overwhelmed with the realization of how the Church had matured in northern England. And when he learned that a man from Nelson with whom he had proselytized as a young missionary, Robert Pickles, was in the audience, he immediately set off through the crowd, searching for the familiar face. He finally spotted his longtime friend, and tears flowed as he embraced his missionary colleague.

Beginning with that unexpected reunion, the day was filled with moments that moved and overwhelmed President Hinckley, who confessed during his remarks at the groundbreaking that he would never have dreamed that a temple would be built there.[6] He returned home emotionally and spiritually drained, but grateful for having had the experience.[7]

There were other important days straight ahead. In late June, President Hunter called Elder Jeffrey R. Holland to serve as a member of the Quorum of the Twelve, filling the vacancy created by President Benson's death. The morning of his call, Elder Holland was invited to join the Twelve during their temple meeting, which was in progress when he arrived. "President Hinckley came out into the hall to get me, and I will never forget what he said and did," Elder Holland remembered. "He could see how shaken I was by the call that had come. He put his arm around me and said, simply, 'Welcome, dear friend.' When he walked me through the door, everyone in the room stood up. I was already emotional, but I was unprepared for the emotion that rose within me upon entering that room and seeing the Brethren stand. I am sure President Hinckley understood what I was feeling, because he stood right by me, held my arm, and gave me time to regain my composure. It was an overwhelming experience, but of all the things he could have said to me, the phrase he chose was so brotherly, so collegial. Here was a man I had reported to for most of the past fifteen years, putting his arm around me as if I were a colleague. I will never forget the sweetness of those three words, 'Welcome, dear friend.'"[8]

Just two days later President and Sister Hinckley accompanied President and Sister Hunter and Elder and Sister M. Russell Ballard to Nauvoo, Illinois, to participate in commemorating the sesquicentennial anniversary of the martyrdom of Joseph and

Hyrum Smith. Sunday, June 26, dawned hot and humid, but President Hinckley's spirits were high during meetings at the Nauvoo stake center, the Nauvoo Temple block, and the Carthage Jail. At the commemoration Sunday afternoon at the temple block, he referred to the tragic tale of a temple left behind as the Saints moved west across the Iowa prairie; then he unveiled a sunstone, on permanent loan from the state of Illinois, to be housed in a secure and permanent shelter there.[9]

At each event President Hunter bore strong testimony of the brothers whose sacrifice had been so significant to the Restoration. Elder Ballard's comments on the life and mission of Hyrum Smith were likewise powerful. President Hinckley bore testimony of the Prophet who had ushered in the dispensation of the fulness of times. "The glorious work, begun by him who was killed at Carthage, has grown in a miraculous and wonderful way," he said. "We pause in reverence here this evening. We reflect on the miracle of the life begun in the green hills of Vermont and ended here in the jail of Carthage. That life was not long, less than thirty-nine years. But the fruits of that life have been something almost beyond comprehension. This great cause of The Church of Jesus Christ has been more precious than life itself to thousands upon thousands who have died in its service. Witnesses have gone into the world by the hundreds of thousands to bear testimony of Joseph Smith's calling as a Prophet of God. . . . God bless the memory of Joseph Smith."[10]

Preceding the satellite fireside, President Hinckley and Elder Ballard held a press conference at the Carthage Visitors Center. Asked to contrast the conditions the Church faced in June 1844 with those of 1994, President Hinckley responded: "Their problem 150 years ago was a mob with painted faces. Our problem is accommodating growth. That's a fact as we move over the earth with tremendous responsibilities to provide meetinghouses for our people and train leadership wherever we go." He added, "But what a wonderful problem it is."[11]

Indeed, it was impossible now, with the Church enjoying tremendous strength around the world, for President Hinckley to imagine how the small band of Saints in June 1844 had felt when they heard the devastating news that their prophet-leader was gone. Each time he walked into the upper room in the

Carthage Jail where the evil deed was perpetrated, he was overwhelmed by the pathos of it. How far the Church had come since those days of heartache and travail! Just a few weeks later the Missionary Department announced that missionaries had now visited one-third of the U.S. population. The Church was beginning to come out of obscurity.

After the stirring events in Nauvoo, President Hinckley was grateful to return home to a few days of vacation during early July, which he and Sister Hinckley spent at their country home. "I find that I get weary by the end of the week," he conceded. "My health is remarkably good, but at eighty-four the spring unwinds rather quickly. Getting out in the country helps to rewind it."[12]

He and Sister Hinckley were also rejuvenated by a drive through Yellowstone Park en route home from a five-stake fireside at Ricks College. It had been years since they had enjoyed the beauties of the country's oldest national park, and President Hinckley was horrified by the millions of dead trees that remained from the devastating fire of 1988. But he was also fascinated by the renewal of nature in progress as thousands of tiny new trees blanketed the forest floor. "The forest is being renewed," he recorded. "Another generation is taking the place of the old and the dead. These are the remarkable processes of life and its generations."[13]

Just a month later, members of the Church witnessed a renewal of their own. At the solemn assembly session that opened the 164th semiannual general conference, President Howard W. Hunter was sustained as the fourteenth President of the Church. Having a prophet who was able to preside and speak to the conference audience not only thrilled the Saints but seemed to revitalize President Hinckley, who in conducting the solemn assembly was obviously pleased at leading out in this expression of support for President Hunter.

During his opening address, President Hunter reemphasized the two areas of focus he had identified during his June press conference statement. With his plea that the Saints establish the temple as the symbol of their membership, it seemed fitting that he had the opportunity to preside at the dedication of the

Orlando Florida Temple a week after general conference. It was the first time a prophet had attended a temple dedication since President Benson had presided over the dedication of the Las Vegas Temple in 1989.

Within the following three months the First Presidency announced plans to build another temple in the Southeast, this one in Nashville, Tennessee, and two more temples in South America: one in Cochabamba, Bolivia, and the other in the northern Brazilian city of Recife.

As 1994 drew to a close, there were signs that President Hunter's strength and health were beginning to wane. He spoke at the First Presidency Christmas Devotional on December 4, and the second week of December he created the Church's two thousandth stake, this one in Mexico City. But by the time of the dedication of the Bountiful Temple in January 1995, he seemed unusually frail and weak. He was, however, able to read the dedicatory prayer and speak in the first session. President Hinckley noted afterward: "The prayer was rather lengthy and he spoke rather lengthily. It was too much. He had difficulty. It is hard for him to stand. I am deeply grateful that President Hunter was able to dedicate this temple. Unless a miracle occurs, he likely will not have opportunity to dedicate another. He is now 87. He suffers from a number of serious afflictions. It is wonderful that he has been able to do this."[14]

President Hunter attended and presided over five more of the twenty-eight sessions, but two days before the dedication concluded he was admitted to LDS Hospital for exhaustion. The hospital stay proved to be a critical turning point, for after a thorough examination, President Hunter received the disheartening news that his former prostate cancer had not only returned but spread to the bone. The day after the temple dedication concluded, President Hinckley paid President Hunter a visit, and afterward he noted the gravity of the situation: "I asked him plainly, 'Howard, do you have pain?' He replied . . . 'No, Gordon, I do not have any pain.' That, I feel, is most significant. Nevertheless, I came away with a feeling of serious apprehension. He is in the hands of the Lord. He could live for a good while or he could go any day. There came into my mind, 'Be still, and know that I am God.'"[15]

For some time it had been hard for President Hinckley to avoid comments from individuals, even colleagues, who spoke openly about what they considered to be inevitable—that it was only a matter of time until he became President of the Church. President Hinckley was impatient with (and sometimes upset about) such comments and innuendos, and he routinely cut short any conversation headed that direction. When Elders Faust and Ballard approached him in late February 1995 about the script for a video about his life that the Church wished to produce, President Hinckley was uncooperative. "I told them that I would not go along with any such thing at this time," he recorded. "It would be totally unfitting, inappropriate, and counter to my feelings to make it appear as if I were standing in the wings waiting to take over the leadership of the Church."[16]

Naturally, President Hinckley knew he was next in seniority after President Hunter, but he tried desperately to avoid thinking about becoming President of the Church. Nothing good, he believed, would come of such activity. "What I did say to myself," he later admitted, "was, 'The Lord is at the head of this Church, and you don't need to worry about it. Just do what you are supposed to do. You are an old man, and anything can happen. The Lord can move you out of the way in an instant.' That is as far as my thinking went."[17]

The weeks following President Hunter's diagnosis were filled with uncertainty. Though his condition steadily declined, there were days when he rebounded sufficiently to make it appear that he might yet live for a time. After one several-day period in which there was substantial improvement in the prophet's condition, President Hinckley noted optimistically: "One of his doctors called me this evening to say that to him it was a most remarkable thing and that he had no medical explanation for the extent of the change. It is an answer to many prayers."[18] Two days later he wrote: "We received good reports on President Hunter again today. None of us knows what all of this means. It may be another surge before a sudden decline. It may be a gradual return to some degree of strength and duty. He is in the hands of the Lord, whose work this is."[19]

Indeed, other than days in which his condition had worsened significantly, President Hunter continued to work with the assistance of his personal secretary, Lowell R. Hardy, who took work to the prophet's apartment almost daily. "President Hunter was bound and determined to do his part," Lowell said, "and we worked together until two days before his death. Toward the end he was in pain, but he could endure pain like no man I've ever known."[20]

President Hunter did not feel up to attending the annual award dinner of the National Conference of Christians and Jews (NCCJ), held February 21, at which President Hinckley was honored for his contributions as a world religious leader. The evening was filled with accolades and tributes, including one from Lord Thomson of Fleet, which read in part: "President Gordon B. Hinckley has for many years set the highest example of dedication to God and his fellow man. Indefatigable in the pursuit of his religious and personal beliefs, he has been the personification of total professional and personal integrity."[21]

After hearing a string of commendations and receiving the gift of an olive-wood statuette of Moses crafted expressly for the occasion by George Lama of Bethlehem, President Hinckley stepped to the microphone and said to the large audience assembled in the Salt Lake City Marriott's Grand Ballroom: "Maybe with Moses I can lead you out of this wilderness! I've been to these dinners before, and I know how long they can go on." After the laughter died down, he admitted that it was "almost embarrassing" to receive such an honor, adding, "I've tried to do only that which every man ought to do without any thought of recognition."[22]

During the week following the NCCJ banquet, President Hunter's health declined steadily. President Hinckley realized that the prophet would likely not recover, though he continued to hope and pray for a miracle. Numerous times he expressed the sentiment: "I will not count President Hunter out. I have seen the Hunter miracle before. He could rally again."[23] Nonetheless, it became almost impossible for President Hinckley to avoid thinking about the ramifications for him personally. It seemed inconceivable to him that one such as he should be next in line to become President of the Church. The very thought overwhelmed and terrified him, and he and Sister Hinckley pleaded with the Lord to extend President Hunter's life. On Monday, February 27, President Hinckley went to President Hunter's apartment immediately after returning from weekend assignments in California and, at President Hunter's request, gave the prophet a blessing. Lowell Hardy, who was present and also participated in the ordinance, said: "President Hinckley pleaded with the Lord for President Hunter's life, but he also clearly stated that President Hunter was in the Lord's hands. It was a very moving experience. Afterward they held hands and reminisced about their thirty-five years together as General Authorities. After a time I excused myself because I felt as though something important was taking place between those two men. It was as though the mantle was being prepared to pass."[24]

After President Hinckley returned home that night, he recorded: "President Hunter seemed extremely feeble to me. I came away with the feeling that he cannot last long. He is suffering much of pain. My heart reaches out to him."[25]

On the first day of March, President Hinckley took note of the changing seasons and recorded: "March is a month of intermittent storm and sunshine. It is almost life-like in the rhythm of its moods. We know that there will be storms, but that the snow which falls will not linger. We know also that spring will soon be here in all of its glory."[26]

His words were both poetic and prophetic, for two days later, on the morning of Friday, March 3, 1995, President Hinckley received the phone call he had hoped would never come. President Hunter had passed away. Accompanied by President Monson, he went immediately to the prophet's apartment. After trying to comfort Sister Hunter, President Hinckley called his wife and said simply, "He's gone." Sister Hinckley began to cry. "I can't describe the void and the loneliness I felt," she reflected later. "President Hunter had gone, and we were left to carry on. I felt so sad, so alone. Gordon did, too. He was numb. And he felt very, very lonely. There was no one left who could understand what he was going through."[27]

As soon as Marjorie's sister Evelyn heard the news, she called her older sibling. "Marge, how are you feeling?" she asked. In a feeble attempt to interject some humor into her otherwise somber mood, Sister Hinckley responded, "I have just been sitting here wondering how a nice girl like me got into a mess like this."

Though President Hinckley would not be ordained President of the Church for nine days, the mantle had shifted instantly and without ceremony to him. "I had sat next to President Hunter for twenty years before being called into the First Presidency," President Hinckley remembered. "How I loved him! How I mourned his passing! I was possessed with a terrible feeling of inadequacy. Though I had served in the First Presidency for fourteen years, and knew something about the office of the President of the Church, I had no idea how overwhelming it would feel."[28]

President Hinckley set arrangements in motion for President Hunter's funeral, but the next few hours went by in a blur. To compound matters, his and Sister Hinckley's longtime friend Eudora Durham, the widow of G. Homer Durham, was gravely ill; that Friday afternoon they went to the hospital for what would be their last visit with her. He then spent the rest of the day at the office, going through the motions, but he had difficulty concentrating. That night he noted simply: "A tremendous responsibility has fallen on my shoulders. It seems impossible to believe that the Lord has thrust upon me this most sacred office and calling. I can only pray and plead for help."[29]

For President Hinckley, some things changed without delay. The Brethren immediately looked to him as the presiding authority, and there were other adjustments as well. "Church Security has now surrounded me like a flock of eagles," he wrote the day following President Hunter's death. "They have taken from me all liberty to come and go. I have had freedom to drive as I pleased and go where I wished. Now I suppose all of that is gone. This morning I wanted to go out to my little place in the country. Day before yesterday I would have been perfectly free to do so. Now one man must drive us out, and a follow-up car is behind."[30] Nonetheless, he went out to the cottage for a few hours and planted some peony roots. He spent that afternoon working at his desk at home and looking ahead to a week he knew would be busy and emotional.

On Tuesday, March 7, President Hunter's body lay in state in the rotunda of the Church Administration Building as more than 25,000 people filed silently past to pay their last respects to the fourteenth President of the Church. The following morning, March 8, the capacity audience in the Tabernacle arose as President and Sister Hinckley and President and Sister Monson entered the building ahead of the casket and funeral party. President Hunter's two counselors took their places on both sides of the empty red chair that until days before had been occupied by their leader. President Hinckley was subdued as he conducted and spoke at the service. "His chair is vacant this day, and I feel that vacancy," he acknowledged. "From our point of view, it is tragic that he has served so briefly as President and prophet, seer and revelator of the Church. . . . But during this brief period he touched the hearts of countless thousands at home and abroad."[31]

The funeral and graveside services were beautiful, but by day's end, President Hinckley felt as though all of the emotion had been drained out of him. That night he noted: "President Hunter . . . is gone. His memorial services are completed. The burdens of leadership of the Church rest on my narrow shoulders. It is an awesome responsibility and even a terrifying thought to think of it. However, it is the Lord's Church. My responsibility will be to stand strong and listen for the quiet voice of the Spirit."[32]

The weighty events of the previous week had been spiritually and emotionally overwhelming, and heavy decisions rested upon President Hinckley. Early Thursday morning, he arranged to spend time alone on the fourth floor of the Salt Lake Temple. With a Church Security officer positioned near the elevator to secure the floor, President Hinckley went into the meeting room of the First Presidency and Quorum of the Twelve and locked the doors:

> I removed my street shoes and put on my temple moccasins. . . . It was a wonderful experience. I read from the scriptures, from the Old Testament, the New Testament, the Book of Mormon, and the Pearl of Great Price. On the west wall are three paintings of the Savior—one depicts the calling of the Twelve, two depicts the Crucifixion, three depicts the Resurrection. . . . I took the time to study them. I was particularly impressed with the painting of the Crucifixion. There by myself, as I reflected, I thought much of the

> price my Savior paid for my redemption. I thought of the overwhelming responsibility of standing as His prophet in the earth. I was subdued and wept over my feelings of inadequacy.
>
> On the north wall is a portrait of the Prophet Joseph Smith, on the south wall is a portrait of his brother, Hyrum. Between these and reaching around along the east wall are portraits of all of the Presidents of the Church from Brigham Young to Howard W. Hunter. I walked around in front of these portraits and looked into the eyes of the men there represented. I felt almost as if I could speak with them. I felt almost as if they were speaking to me and giving me reassurance. . . . I sat down in the chair which I have occupied as first counselor to the President. I spent a good deal of time looking at those portraits. Every one seemed almost to come alive. Their eyes seemed to be upon me. I felt that they were encouraging me and pledging their support. They seemed to say to me that they had spoken in my behalf in a council held in the heavens, that I had no need to fear, that I would be blessed and sustained in my ministry.
>
> I got on my knees and pleaded with the Lord. I spoke with Him at length in prayer. . . . I am confident that by the power of the Spirit, I heard the word of the Lord, not vocally, but as a warmth that was felt within my heart concerning the questions I had raised in prayer.[33]

After his time in the temple, President Hinckley felt a measure of peace about what lay ahead. "I feel better, and I have a much firmer assurance in my heart that the Lord is working His will with reference to His cause and kingdom, that I will be sustained as President of the Church and prophet, seer, and revelator, and so serve for such time as the Lord wills," he wrote afterward. "With the confirmation of the Spirit in my heart, I am now ready to go forward to do the very best work I know how to do. It is difficult for me to believe that the Lord is placing me in this most high and sacred responsibility. . . . I hope that the Lord has trained me to do what He expects of me. I will give Him total loyalty, and I will certainly seek His direction."[34]

On Sunday morning, March 12, the fourteen apostles came fasting to the Salt Lake Temple. Five times previously President Hinckley had participated in the sacred experience of ordaining a new President of the Church. Never, not even nine months earlier when a frail Howard Hunter had been so ordained, had he imagined that he would be the focus of attention in such a setting. But he also knew, as did the members of the Quorum of the Twelve, that the Lord had spoken. In countless settings, he had taught and defended the doctrine of prophetic succession. Most notably, during nearly fourteen years in the First Presidency he had unfailingly preserved the integrity of that office. Though it was still impossible for him to imagine, he was to be the fifteenth President of The Church of Jesus Christ of Latter-day Saints.

After each of the Brethren had opportunity to express his feelings about reorganizing the First Presidency, President Hinckley indicated that he wished for Elders Thomas S. Monson and James E. Faust to serve as his first and second counselor, respectively. President Monson was then voice in setting apart the new President of the Church.

That night President Hinckley wrote: "It was all over. So smooth is the transition of administration under the plan of the Lord. There is nothing of the noise and campaigning of politics, or the processes found in business leadership. . . . One must assume that he who becomes the President of the Church has been selected by the Lord, who has power over life and death, and who preserves and trains a man through long years of service. I returned home, greatly sobered, almost overwhelmed. No one who has not occupied this chair can fully appreciate the impact one experiences. Although I have served as counselor to three Presidents of the Church, the feeling I now experience is totally different."[35]

CHAPTER TWENTY-FOUR

PRESIDENT OF THE CHURCH

"It was a startling tableau—a healthy president of The Church of Jesus Christ of Latter-day Saints standing before a flock of surprised reporters and asking if they had any questions," wrote a *Deseret News* reporter about the press conference announcing President Hinckley's ordination. "Few in the ornate lobby of the Joseph Smith Memorial Building knew it had been fully 21 years since any man who served as the faith's 'prophet, seer, and revelator' had held a news conference. But they realized what they were seeing was rare and that a statement was being made. . . . His robust performance had a galvanizing effect on church employees. There were smiles everywhere, and the switchboard lit up with calls of support from rank-and-file members."[1]

President Hinckley recorded afterward: "Words of appreciation came from many quarters. I watched the evening news, and this was the lead story. The reporters were most positive and almost enthusiastic. They made note of the fact that this is the first time that a newly sustained President of the Church had conducted a question-and-answer session in over twenty years. I did not realize this, but I suppose that is right. I am glad that is behind me, and I am grateful to the Lord for His blessing."[2]

The reaction from friends, colleagues, members around the world, and dignitaries with whom President Hinckley had associated was swift and supportive, as telegrams, cards, and letters of congratulations poured into his office. From former U.S. President George Bush came a simple but sincere greeting: "As you assume your important responsibilities, I just want to check in to wish you well and to pay my respects. I have great admiration for the work of the Church. I know your challenge will be great; but I also know you, and I am sure things will go well."[3]

President James E. Faust voiced a sentiment shared by many

General Authorities: "I don't know of any man who has come to the Presidency of this Church who has been so well prepared for the responsibility. President Hinckley has known and worked with every Church President from Heber J. Grant to Howard W. Hunter, and has been tutored by all of the great leaders of our time one-on-one in a very personal way."[4] President Boyd K. Packer's assessment was unequivocal: "No man in the history of the Church has traveled so far to so many places in the world with the purpose of preaching the gospel, blessing the Saints, and fostering the redemption of the dead. He made all of those trips to Asia when traveling there was tiring and difficult. He has been the length of South America again and again. He was in the Pacific when we lost those Saints to that horrible shipwreck, in Peru when a devastating earthquake hit, and in Korea during a coup d'état. He has seen it all, and has been everywhere and done almost everything as it relates to Church administration."[5]

The morning after the press conference, the new First Presidency met together in the Presidency's council room for the first time, and the experience aroused a variety of tender emotions within President Hinckley. Afterward he reflected: "It will be sixty years ago in July that I first came into this room as a newly returned missionary to meet with the First Presidency at the request of my mission president, Elder Joseph F. Merrill of the Council of the Twelve. It is difficult to realize what has happened since then. To think that I now sit where President Heber J. Grant sat at that time. He was a giant of a man whom I loved."[6]

For all of the meetings he had attended in that room, many of which he had conducted and presided over, things were different now. "I had previously been in a situation of having responsibility without authority," he explained. "Suddenly I had responsibility and authority, and that in and of itself posed new challenges and great concerns, even worrisome concerns at times. There is a vast difference between being a counselor and a president. It was so when I was a counselor in a stake presidency and was subsequently named the stake president. And it is so now. There's an emphasis on the article *the*—*the* President of the Church, *the* prophet, seer, and revelator—that is both different and frightening. As close as I had been to the President of the Church, I had no idea how different things would be as President of the Church."[7]

One immediate difference was the reaction his presence elicited from members of the Church. He had been presiding at meetings for decades and during that time had met with thousands of congregations, but now whenever he entered a room, a chapel, an arena, or a meeting place of any kind, everyone stood. He couldn't even attend his home ward without being the center of conspicuous attention. Almost always the audience sang "We Thank Thee, O God, for a Prophet," and though he always trained his thoughts on the Prophet Joseph Smith during that hymn, it was hard not to feel self-conscious. After several months, President Hinckley admitted: "The people are so expressive in their feelings that it makes me ask myself if I could possibly be worthy of the love and confidence of all these people. It is hard not to wonder if I'm measuring up to what the Lord expects of me, and if I'm capable of doing what needs to be done. I feel the responsibility very keenly."[8]

Nothing from his previous experience compared with the attention he generated wherever he went. Though he was grateful for the overwhelming kindness and expressions of support, he was uncomfortable with unfettered emotion that bordered at times on adoration. In numerous settings he repeated his warning that "adulation is poison" and that the twin traps of praise and prominence had ambushed countless men and women. "Few people can bear the burden of notoriety," President Hinckley said simply, and he was determined to keep things in their proper perspective. It was his office people were honoring, not him personally, he constantly reminded himself.[9] He had often given similar counsel to others. When one of his missionary grandsons was named an assistant to the mission president, he wrote: "We congratulate you most warmly on this recognition of your faithfulness and your ability. All who have met you speak most highly of you. That is a wonderful thing. I know you are the kind who will not let this sort of praise go to your head."[10] To a group of young adults he pleaded: "Be humble. Don't be arrogant. . . . The world is full of arrogant people. How obnoxious is an arrogant man!"[11]

His preachments were consistent with the way he had

handled his visibility for years. The profound changes in his own life notwithstanding, his sense of humor was still intact. After he and Sister Hinckley had moved into the official residence of the President of the Church, his grandson Michael teased them that they were now so insulated they no longer had even a mailbox to call their own. "You're not even people anymore. You're nameless." "Well, we're the hardest working nobodies you'll ever know," his grandfather shot back.[12]

Because of the timing of his ordination, President Hinckley did not have even the luxury of a few weeks to adapt to his new circumstances. With less than three weeks before general conference to prepare for a solemn assembly and his first remarks to the Church as its President, he approached those assignments solemnly. "I hope that what I say at general conference will be inspired words that will represent the voice of the Lord to the people and will come by way of inspiration through me," he confided in his journal. "This is an almost terrifying responsibility."[13]

The April general conference was not the first opportunity he had as President to address a Tabernacle and worldwide audience, however. The Saturday before conference—not quite two weeks since his ordination—he spoke at the general Young Women meeting. Though perhaps few recognized the relationship, the first time President Hinckley was introduced at the Tabernacle pulpit as President of the Church, the honor was performed by his daughter Virginia, who conducted the Young Women meeting and whose voice caught slightly when she said, "It will now be our privilege to hear from President Gordon B. Hinckley, President and prophet of The Church of Jesus Christ of Latter-day Saints." "It hadn't even occurred to me until we got to the Tabernacle that night that I would be introducing Dad in that setting," she said later. "But it was a poetic moment. You find yourself at these little intersections of life that don't have any real meaning in a global sense, but that are satisfying and meaningful personally. It was wonderful to share that moment with him."[14]

One week later, on Saturday morning, April 1, the Tabernacle was again filled to capacity, and thousands who hadn't been able to find seats inside spilled onto the grounds of Temple Square as the solemn-assembly session of the 165th semiannual general conference was convened. President Hinckley conducted but turned the process of sustaining the new First Presidency and other General Authorities and auxiliary officers over to President Monson. He seemed subdued as he participated in the proceedings during which the First Presidency, followed in turn by the Quorum of the Twelve, both quorums of the Seventy and the Presiding Bishopric, the Melchizedek Priesthood, and the Aaronic Priesthood sustained him as President of the Church. In a departure from tradition, the women of the Relief Society (eighteen years of age and older) were invited to stand and offer their sustaining vote, followed by young women twelve to eighteen. Finally the membership at large stood. Sustained also was Elder Henry B. Eyring as the newest member of the Twelve.

The afternoon before general conference began, President Hinckley had invited Elder Eyring to his office, and there for the first time as President of the Church extended an apostolic call. "President Hinckley was very gentle, very kind, even quiet," Elder Eyring said. "The very language he used, the way he talked with me, led me to believe that he knew more than he was telling me and left me to know from whence the call had come. He has a wonderful way of stepping aside and letting the Lord do His work. I don't think I have ever walked away from an encounter with President Hinckley where I've not known that I was in the presence of a man whom God directed."[15]

President Hinckley knew something of the feelings that attended a call to such high and holy office. After the first day of general conference he recorded: "For me personally it was an extremely solemn assembly in which my feelings were subdued and my heart filled with gratitude. . . . How thankful I feel to the Lord for His great blessings upon me and to the people who have raised their hands in sustaining me. It is difficult to believe that I hold the office to which I have been called. I pray for strength, for guidance, for revelation, for faith, and for life in which to accomplish what the Lord would have done. One has to know that all of this is His doing. That knowledge has a tremendously sobering effect upon me. . . . It has been a wonderful day. There will never be another quite like it in my life. I am almost overcome by a sense of responsibility to my Father in Heaven, to my Lord and Savior, to the membership of the Church, and to all the world."[16]

Many conference addresses were filled with expressions of support for President Hinckley and his counselors, among them remarks by Elder David B. Haight: "No man better understands the Church, nor is better known to the members of the Church, than President Gordon B. Hinckley. . . . I testify that [he] has been carefully prepared for this divine calling from before the foundations of the earth in heavenly councils. . . . President Hinckley is not only a man for all seasons—but for all the world! . . . In the prescribed manner, we have accepted and sustained him. Through him—as has been done through prophets of old—revelation will be made available to us to meet the challenges of a modern society and advance the mission of the Church throughout the world."[17]

In his first general conference address to the Saints, President Hinckley referred to his new assignment and the emotions it had aroused: "Mine has been the special privilege to serve as a counselor to three great Presidents. I think I know something of the meaning of heavy responsibility. But with all of that, I have, during these past few days, been overwhelmed with feelings of inadequacy and total dependency upon the Lord, who is my head and whose church this is. . . . Years ago I gave a talk on the loneliness of leadership. Now for the first time I realize the full import of that loneliness. I do not know why this mantle has fallen upon my shoulders. I suppose some of you may also wonder. But we are here."

He concluded with a call to action that revealed his zeal for the work and sounded a theme he had taught many times before: "This church does not belong to its President. Its head is the Lord Jesus Christ, whose name each of us has taken upon ourselves. We are all in this great endeavor together. . . . Your obligation is as serious in your sphere of responsibility as is my obligation in my sphere. . . . The time has come for us to stand a little taller, to lift our eyes and stretch our minds to a greater comprehension and understanding of the grand millennial mission of this The Church of Jesus Christ of Latter-day Saints. This is a season to be strong. It is a time to move forward without hesitation, knowing well the meaning, the breadth, and the importance of our mission. It is a time to do what is right regardless of the consequences that might follow. . . . We have nothing to fear. God is at the helm. He will overrule for the good of this work."[18]

Weary but exuberant at the close of conference, President Hinckley noted in his journal: "It has been a glorious general conference. We have been blessed of the Lord. . . . The Brethren have all spoken very well. The music has been superb. I think we are off to a good start, because the Lord has been so kind and generous toward us. To the Father and to the Son go all honor and praise and glory. How thankful I am to be a part of this work."[19]

As President Hinckley had said countless times, the work would continue to move forward with no backward step. He had assumed leadership of a Church that now had a membership in excess of nine million, had 47,000 missionaries serving in 303 missions, and was organized in 156 nations and territories. To keep pace with the staggering growth, he announced during conference the honorable release of all Regional Representatives and then indicated that Area Authorities would be called to work under the direction of Area Presidencies, thus helping decentralize administrative authority and keep General Authorities closer to the people.[20]

He too intended to stay close to the people. For the better part of fifteen years the President of the Church had been unable to travel and move comfortably among the Saints, and from the outset President Hinckley desired to get out among the members, thank them for their faith and faithfulness, express his love, and bear testimony of the divinity of the work. Accordingly, he adopted an ambitious schedule. When later in April he was introduced in an interview for an East Coast radio station as the first "sitting President of the Church to visit New England since President Joseph F. Smith," he responded with characteristic wit but also a foreshadowing of the pace he intended to keep, "I am not a sitting President, I am a running President." Indeed, those who worked closely with him quickly found that it would be a challenge to keep up with their eighty-four-year-old leader.

It seemed he couldn't squeeze enough into the days, which though laden with pressure and heavy responsibility were also rich in diversity. President Hinckley's enthusiasm for the work and excitement over all that was happening were, if anything, greater than ever. From time to time he remarked that his only regret was that he was as old as he was, and that there was so much ahead that he would never see. Sister Hinckley shared much of the same enthusiasm. "I just can't believe what is happening in the Church. It *never* gets old," she exclaimed on one occasion. "Every day is so exciting. When you see what is happening throughout the world it is thrilling just to get up every morning and anticipate what is going to happen that day."[21]

Many days President Hinckley arrived early at the office and stayed late, and most weekends found him meeting with large groups of Saints. During the first eighteen months of his presidency he presided at regional conferences or spoke to large audiences (from seven to thirty thousand) in St. Louis; Pocatello; Sacramento; Boston; Tacoma, Washington; Veracruz, Mexico; Honolulu; Corpus Christi, Texas; Charlotte, North Carolina; Heber City and Springville, Utah; Anchorage and Juneau; Rexburg, Idaho; Ft. Worth; Denver; Pittsburgh; Tulsa; and Kansas City, among many others. In February 1996 he addressed what was believed to be the largest gathering of young LDS married couples ever assembled in BYU's Marriott Center.

Wherever he traveled he looked for opportunities to touch as many as possible—usually in large congregations, but when possible one-on-one. And he nearly always met with the missionaries, greeting so many of them personally that his arthritic right hand went numb. His approach with the missionaries was often disarming and a little unexpected. "You're not much to look at, but you're all the Lord has," he would tease. "You young women look beautiful, attractive, well dressed. And you elders—well, I can tell how long you've been out by looking at your collars." He would then share some of his own experiences as a missionary, speak of those who had died while laying the foundation of the modern gospel kingdom, teach from the scriptures, and conclude with a fervent testimony: "I love you. I know missionary work isn't easy. I know something of your problems, your worries, your challenges, and your hopes. Be the kind of missionary your mother thinks you are. When missionaries come into the field, they not only save others, but they save themselves and sometimes their families. Never forget that I told you that the gospel of Jesus Christ is true. Don't ever forget it."[22]

The reaction to President Hinckley among missionaries and members alike was overwhelming. It was reassuring, even exhilarating, to have as President of the Church a man who was physically and mentally vigorous. Many members, in fact, had never experienced such a phenomenon. One institute instructor explained that her students "were on fire about President Hinckley," adding that none of them could remember hearing a President of the Church speak.[23]

Among other things, the Saints were energized by a leader who framed everything he said and did with optimism and a sense of vision. To congregations large and small, and even in press briefings with journalists from around the world, President Hinckley delivered a message of hope, declared that there had never been a better time in the history of the world to be alive, and encouraged all to catch the grand millennial vision of the gospel kingdom and to go forward with faith.

When, for example, a reporter from the *New York Times* asked him if it wasn't time to slow the growth of the Church in order to make it more manageable, he responded: "Oh, no! Growth is wonderful. It involves great challenges and brings serious problems, but what a wonderful thing to be growing and alive and viable and vital in this world. It's a tremendous thing. I think it's just wonderful to see this great pulsating [organization]. [I wish you could] go across the world as I have opportunity to do and meet with our people and see what's happening—it is a most encouraging, wonderful thing."

During the same interview, President Hinckley made opportunity to enumerate some of the ambitious projects with which the Church was involved. "Our Article of Faith says 'if there is anything virtuous, lovely, or of good report or praiseworthy, we seek after these things,'" he began. "What do you think of what this little church is trying to do, with its emphasis on education? BYU is the largest private university in America. Go down on that campus and look at those students—tremendous! They are clean-cut, decent-looking kids, great men and women. The seminary and institute program involves two or three hundred thousand across the world who come of their own volition to study religion. We maintain the largest family history resource in the world open to the public. We have some 47,000 missionaries out in the world at their own expense. We're building between three and four hundred new buildings a year to accommodate the needs of our people across the world. This isn't any peanut organization. It is a world church with a world vision centered on the welfare of the individual."[24]

While purveyors of gloom and doom bemoaned the fate of the younger generation, President Hinckley repeatedly proclaimed that today's youth represented the finest generation in the world's history. It quickly became a signature of his ministry to hold youth firesides whenever possible as he traveled. In a scene replayed dozens of times in other areas of the country, more than ten thousand youth lined up hours in advance for a fireside in St. George, Utah. The Spirit was powerful during President Hinckley's hour-long message, which he began by recalling an experience he had had while working for the railroad. A baggage car destined for Newark, New Jersey, ended up in New Orleans when a careless operator in the St. Louis railroad yard inaccurately moved a switch a few inches, sending the lost car off in the wrong direction. "It began with a little thing, the moving of a switchpoint," the prophet taught. "That's the way our lives are. The penitentiary is full of people who moved a switchpoint in their lives just a little." Choose the right, he admonished the audience. "Your opportunities are so tremendous, so wonderful. You've come on the scene of the world in the greatest age in the history of mankind. Nobody else who ever lived on this earth has had quite the advantages that you have." True to his pattern, he didn't conclude before expressing his confidence: "Don't you ever forget, my dear young friends . . . that each of you is a child of God and that your Father in heaven expects great things of you. . . . I hope you will remember this, that Brother Hinckley told you that you can do it."[25]

His message to an audience of institute students in the Salt Lake Tabernacle carried much the same theme. He pleaded with them to shun pornography, premarital sex, and vulgarity in its various forms, comparing such vices to corrosive salt that eats through a person's protective armor. "The makers and marketers of this slimy stuff grow wealthy while the character of their customers decays," he told the capacity audience. After counseling them to marry appropriately and to get a good education, he said: "The picture never looked brighter. The opportunities were never greater. . . . I have now worked a full twenty years beyond what has been considered the normal retirement age. But I do not feel old! I feel enthusiastic about this great cause of which we are part. Why? Because I know it is the work of the Almighty, and that it transcends every other work under the heavens."[26]

President Hinckley rarely spoke without sharing his vision, almost as a rallying cry, of the future of the work. In doing so he often exposed a unique amalgam of strengths—reverence for past prophets and leaders combined with an eagerness to explore new territory. Indeed, he seemed to straddle the centuries. He was a unique blend of pioneer heritage and twenty-first-century vision—all of which he seasoned with boundless optimism.

In the October 1995 general conference he referred to his recent experience of standing on Albert Dock in Liverpool and trying to visualize the faith and fortitude of those who had risked life and limb to follow their convictions to the new world. He then paid tribute to their pioneer leader: "I can scarcely comprehend the magnitude of Brigham Young's faith in leading thousands of people into the wilderness. He had never seen this country, except as he had seen it in vision. It was an act of boldness almost beyond comprehension."

President Hinckley continued, exulting over what he saw as the future of the gospel kingdom: "How glorious is the past of this great cause. It is filled with heroism, courage, boldness, and faith. How wondrous is the present as we move forward to bless the lives of people wherever they will hearken to the message of the servants of the Lord. . . . Back in the days of the great Depression, an old sign dangled by one staple from a piece of rusting barbed wire. The owner of the farm had written: 'Burned out by drought,/Drowned out by flud waters,/Et out by jackrabbits,/Sold out by sheriff,/Still here!' So it is with us. There have been makers of threats, naysayers, and criers of doom. They have tried in every conceivable way to injure and destroy this church. But we are still here, stronger and more determined to move it forward. To me it is exciting. It is wonderful. . . . I invite every one of you, wherever you may be as members of this church, to stand on your feet and with a song in your heart move forward. . . . Together we shall stay the course and keep the faith, the Almighty being our strength."[27]

With his regard for generations past, it seemed fitting that President Hinckley presided over the Church during a period of significant historical commemorations. On January 4, 1996, he addressed a capacity audience in the Tabernacle at a celebration marking the centennial anniversary of Utah's statehood.[28] On June 29 of that year, he rededicated the refurbished and restored "This Is the Place" Monument at the mouth of Emigration Canyon, and in early July he made quick visits to Nauvoo, Palmyra, and Council Bluffs, where he participated in a celebration commemorating the Mormon Trail, dedicated the reconstructed Kanesville Tabernacle where Brigham Young was ordained President of the Church, and delivered a fireside address to an audience of ten thousand near where the Mormon Trail Center, announced a year earlier by the First Presidency, was under construction in the area known historically as Winter Quarters.[29]

He seemed to be the dignitary of choice for dedications and groundbreakings of all kinds. He presided at the groundbreaking of the Howard W. Hunter Law Library on the BYU campus on May 1, 1995, and the following month joined President Monson in breaking ground for the Brigham Young Historic Park, located on an acre in downtown Salt Lake City that had once been part of Brigham Young's farm. Other names had been suggested for the park, but President Hinckley would have nothing of them, as he noted in his journal: "This was part of his farm. He is buried nearby. He constructed the Eagle Gate originally. He constructed the Beehive House and the Lion House and lived in the latter. This is his neighborhood and I felt it should be so designated."[30] Less than four months later he dedicated the park as well as the new state-of-the-art Ezra Taft Benson Science Building on the campus of Brigham Young University. In April 1996 he dedicated the David O. McKay Events Center on the campus of Utah Valley State College in Orem, Utah. And in July he dedicated the new Ensign Peak Nature Park in Salt Lake City.

These dedications and other commemorations were more than mere ritual to President Hinckley; during his years in the First Presidency he had been unflagging in his efforts to maintain an appealing, attractive ambience in downtown Salt Lake City, where Temple Square and the Church administration block were located. As chairman of the board of Zions Securities Corporation, the Church's property-management arm, he had strongly encouraged the construction of office buildings, condominiums, and other structures—among them the Eagle Gate apartment building and Eagle Gate Plaza, the Deseret Apartments on South Temple at the head of Second East, a multistory office building on the southwest corner of Main and South Temple streets and another on Social Hall Avenue—to help keep the city center viable and active. A letter from a prominent Salt Lake City attorney reflects others that came from those in the community who recognized and appreciated President Hinckley's commitment to Utah's capital city. "I know that you, in your Presidency of the Church, have dedicated more temples around the world than any of your predecessors. This accomplishment is certainly noteworthy. However, in my judgment, often the greatest satisfaction comes from what is being done 'at home.' Your work in creating the Brigham Young Park, the City Creek Canyon Park, and now the Ensign Peak Nature Park will mean beautiful oases for many, many generations to come. . . . Thank you from one who, with his family, shares these beautiful places."[31]

Salt Lake City Mayor Deedee Corradini met frequently with the First Presidency on issues related to the city's welfare and future. "We have a wonderful relationship with the LDS Church, and have enjoyed very meaningful partnerships in recent years. The City Creek and Brigham Young parks, for example, are both just glorious. What were two ugly parking lots are now two of our most beautiful parks. President Hinckley has vision for the city. He cares deeply about downtown and its people, and is eager to discuss the most difficult issues that confront us. He and his counselors always want to know who needs help. I can't think of a time we have approached them about assisting us that they have not responded in some measure."[32]

His varied and numerous contributions notwithstanding, it was impossible for President Hinckley to accommodate more than a small portion of the requests that came to his office. But those who worked closely with him, and even those who came into contact for brief periods of time, marvelled at his energy, stamina, and drive. At times, however, his crowded calendar got to him. After one weekend trip to a regional conference on the East Coast, he returned home exhausted. "I felt terribly weary," he wrote in his journal, "so tired I could hardly get in the shower. It has been a very busy four days, and I am weary. But that is what I am here for, to get tired in the service of the Lord."[33]

Occasionally he took time to relax, and his favorite diversion remained his small home in the country. "We spent most of the day at our cottage," he wrote after an afternoon there. "I love this place. Living in a multistory building downtown, it is wonderful to plant my feet on the sod. I love the grass, the trees, the shrubs, the birds. I worked physically and became bone tired. I thought that I might spend a little time preparing for [general] conference, but I did not. I got my mind on other things and rested."[34]

There were some unique opportunities to relieve the pressure that never left him now. For as President of the Church, it was more than pressure—it was the unrelenting burden of the prophetic mantle, which was at once glorious and terrible. After presiding in June 1995 at a regional conference in Anchorage, Alaska, and speaking to members in outlying areas (some traveled ten hours by ferry to attend), he and Sister Hinckley accepted an invitation to spend three days cruising the waterways of Glacier Bay National Park. The experience was rejuvenating.

"We dressed in casual clothes, which was a great relief," President Hinckley recorded. "We had come to rest, to take time to reflect beneath the stars, to fish, and to see the marvelous handiwork of the Creator." As they moved through the park, they saw humpback whales and bald eagles, caught halibut, and enjoyed the pristine splendor of Alaska. President Hinckley recorded in his journal: "I arose early this morning and went out on the deck. It was difficult to kneel down in the little cabin room, and so I went out on the foredeck and there stood and offered my morning prayer. I felt inspired by the beauty of the scenery—the surrounding mountains thickly covered with timber that is virgin, never having seen the woodsman's saw or axe. I reflected on the wonders of nature, these great glacial waters, icy cold, and brilliant in the sunlight." That day he was the first to catch a fish, and he noted: "Several cameras were trained on me. I appreciated this, because I want to take some photographs to show President Monson, who does a lot of fishing, that I too can catch a fish."[35] Before leaving he reflected, "Being out like this is medicine for the soul."[36]

Ironically, though the mantle he bore as President of the Church was heavy, certain pressures from earlier days were now gone. "I cannot imagine," explained Elder Russell M. Nelson, "how challenging it was for President Hinckley during times past to know that if the work was going to move forward, he essentially had to move it in that direction. But at the same time he had to be careful to defer to the prophet. During all of those years, he never gave any indication that he was impatient or burdened. His first allegiance was *always* to the President of the Church. I suppose, though, that none of us will ever know how much of his time and energy were devoted to being deferential to the President and to carrying out assignments in a way that he knew conformed to the President's wishes. I feel a great sense of relief for him now, that he can move things forward without waiting for anyone else."[37]

His colleagues of the General Authorities and other key administrators at Church headquarters immediately noticed an increased tempo in almost every area of administration. "President Hinckley is an incrementalist," said Elder Maxwell. "He will not always go for bold, sweeping moves. But on a decision-by-decision basis, a pattern emerges that is bold. Take missionary work, for example. If we watch his influence on just that one area, I believe we will see him make a series of decisions that will result in more effective missionary work that gives us greater retention of new converts. I won't be surprised if he builds in half a dozen procedural changes that significantly improve missionary work."[38]

President Hinckley was not necessarily bound by convention. Just because something had always been done a certain way did not argue for its continuance. "President Hinckley has been working here at headquarters for over sixty years," President Packer explained, "and he has been tutored by some of the great men of this dispensation. It is what I call the 'unwritten order of things' that is conveyed from one generation of leaders to the next. From his experience here, he understands where the built-in liberties of the President of the Church are, and he also knows where the built-in limits are."[39]

He surprised the BYU community in November 1995 by naming a General Authority, Presiding Bishop Merrill J. Bateman, to succeed Rex Lee as president of BYU. And he whetted the audience's appetite at the outset of the April 1996 general conference with hints of plans to build a large assembly hall with seating four or five times that of the Tabernacle.

When the First Presidency and Quorum of the Twelve issued a Proclamation on the Family—the first official proclamation since April 6, 1980—he chose to introduce it at the general Relief Society meeting held on September 23, 1995, rather than wait for a more predictable unveiling the following week at general conference. He announced the significant document by stating that it had been prepared as a message "to the Church and to the world as a declaration and reaffirmation of standards, doctrines, and practices relative to the family which the prophets, seers, and revelators of this church have repeatedly stated throughout its history." He then read the proclamation, which reaffirmed the sanctity of marriage, the significance of family, and the importance of chastity, concluding: "We warn that individuals who violate covenants of chastity, who abuse spouse or offspring, or who fail to fulfill family responsibilities will one day stand accountable before God. Further, we warn that the disintegration of the family will bring upon individuals, communities, and nations the calamities foretold by ancient and modern prophets. We call upon responsible citizens and officers of government everywhere to promote those measures designed to maintain and strengthen the family as the fundamental unit of society."[40]

About that meeting Elaine L. Jack, general president of the Relief Society, said: "President Hinckley honored the women of the Church when he read the proclamation in the general women's meeting, because women have long been considered the keepers of the home. I don't believe he was singling out mothers as more significant than fathers in the family structure, but simply acknowledging the value he places on their vital role. It was a wonderful statement for the entire Church, as well as an indication of his respect for women."[41]

There were other ways he demonstrated his regard for women. He had lived nearly sixty years with a woman who didn't hesitate to speak her mind, and their daughters were each of them faithful but forthright. "I reared them that way," he said proudly. When speaking at priesthood leadership sessions, he almost always counseled leaders to cherish their wives and to be good to their children, and during general meetings he often emphasized the influence of mothers: "In this age when more and more women are turning to daily work, how tremendous it is once in a while to stop and recognize that the greatest job any woman ever does is in nurturing and teaching and lifting and encouraging and rearing her children in righteousness and truth. . . . I hope the women of the Church will not slight this greatest responsibility in favor of a lesser responsibility. . . . How grateful I am for mothers. Mothers have been the great carriers and purveyors of faith throughout the history of this Church."[42]

His comments to an audience of young adults at a morningside in Colorado Springs, Colorado, were revealing: "I know that I am a child of God, part of His plan of creation, and that Adam is my father. . . . [But] there was one after that, and that was Eve. She was the crowning creation. Don't you young men ever think that you're so smart in comparison with young women. The Lord created you . . . and then, as His prime creation, He created woman—Eve, she was the sublime, ultimate in all of His creations. Don't any of you young men develop any kind of a superiority complex. It isn't scriptural."[43]

To a gathering of three thousand young married couples assembled at BYU in the Marriott Center, he shared something of his and Sister Hinckley's experience together: "We were still in the bottom of the Depression when we were married. I had a little job with a salary of $165 per month, and we had no savings. I do not know how we had the nerve to get married. I guess we just got married because we loved one another, and we closed our eyes and jumped. But I think we did so with faith. We were seated in our home the other evening. The lights were low and I looked over at my wife. I looked at her hands. . . . We are getting old. We don't stand as tall as we once did. Our hands are wrinkled and the veins show and there is a little arthritis. . . . Tears came into my eyes as I thought of our lives together, of the sorrows we have known, of the defeats we have known, of the struggles we have had, of the triumphs we have enjoyed, the glad times, the sad times, the good times, the bad times."[44] He couldn't have been more pleased when BYU presented Sister Hinckley with its Exemplary Womanhood Award in February 1996, and three months later he attended an evening fireside featuring his wife and daughters at the annual women's conference at BYU. The audience of nearly 12,000 enjoyed the rare opportunity to witness an intimate conversation with Sister Hinckley. Virginia, in her brief introduction, gave a foretaste of the easy-going, often humorous commentary the congregation could expect: "Our father is here, probably out of self-protection. We realize he can always jump up and bring the meeting to a close if we get out of control." In prerecorded video segments that outlined his wife's life, President Hinckley called her the lodestar of their family who had gently guided their lives. Referring to their fifty-ninth wedding anniversary, which they had celebrated the week before, Sister Hinckley said, "It's been fifty-nine years of heaven on earth."[45]

It was the subject of and the proclamation on the family that framed the conversation President Hinckley and Elder Neal A. Maxwell had in early November 1995 with U.S. President Bill Clinton during a visit to the White House. "It is our feeling that if you're going to fix the nation, you need to start by fixing families. That's the place to begin," President Hinckley told the chief executive before presenting him with a copy of the proclamation and with two large volumes containing six generations of his and the First Lady's family history. President Clinton immediately pulled a coffee table into position so that he and President

Hinckley could look through the books together, and twice expressed his gratitude for the unusual gift.

After a pleasant and cordial meeting that centered largely on family-related issues, and as the men rose to say their good-byes, one of President Clinton's senior aides suggested it might be appropriate to invite President Hinckley to offer a word of prayer. The president agreed, and all present gathered in a loose circle. "I had my arm around the back of the President and his arm was around my back, and I offered prayer," President Hinckley recorded of the experience. "I thought it was a rather wonderful thing, to pray for the President of the United States in his office. When we left he expressed his gratitude for our coming. I thought he was sincere."[46]

There were other opportunities for President Hinckley to interact with dignitaries of international repute. When Margaret, Lady Thatcher, visited Utah in March 1996, he hosted the former British prime minister at a luncheon and participated in a special convocation at BYU, where she was awarded an honorary doctorate. After a stirring address in which she declared that no country could survive without dedication to its moral foundation, President Hinckley said, "As we've listened to you, we know why you were called the Iron Lady."[47] And he made his first-ever visit to Salt Lake City's Jewish synagogue, the Congregation of Kol Ami, when he and his counselors attended a memorial service following the assassination of Israeli Prime Minister Yitzhak Rabin. Out of respect the First Presidency donned black yarmulkes, head coverings traditionally worn by men at Jewish gatherings, as they entered the synagogue's sanctuary, and President Hinckley offered brief remarks during the service.[48]

Such high-profile engagements and other obligations now occupied enough of President Hinckley's time that, though a hands-on administrator by nature, he was forced to delegate to others some things he had done for years. For example, in January 1996 the First Presidency announced that, in order for General Authorities to more fully focus on their ministry, they would no longer be authorized to sit on boards of directors of companies, including those owned by the Church—which would involve his stepping down as chairman of the board of

Bonneville International.[49] He also yielded his seat on various Church committees that he had long directed.

There were certain responsibilities, however, that he was unwilling to relinquish—among them the selection of temple sites and other matters related to the temple. President Hinckley made it clear to all who had responsibility for these massive projects that they must find ways to do more, and to do it more quickly. After one meeting in which he urged that more architectural help be solicited to expedite the design and construction of new temples, he recorded in his journal: "I have very strong feelings about this. This is the season in which to do this work. We have the resources with which to do it. The need exists. I think the Lord will hold us accountable if we do not pursue these matters with all diligence."[50] In one setting Ted Simmons, the Church's managing director of physical facilities, joked that he was an inch shorter because President Hinckley had been "pounding" him so hard about accelerating the work of temple building. President Hinckley quickly interjected, "Yes, and you'll be another inch shorter if you don't get with it."[51]

In May 1995 President Hinckley and President Faust presided at the "groundbreaking" of the temple in Vernal, Utah, which signaled the beginning of an innovative project to renovate and expand the Uintah Stake Tabernacle, marking the first time a temple would be constructed from an existing building. President Hinckley testified that this decision had been reached after much deliberation and under the inspiration of the Lord, and he called upon members to prepare spiritually for the temple: "Let's clean up our lives. Let's reach heavenward a little more. Let's be more faithful Latter-day Saints. Let us choose the right more frequently in all of our decisions. Let us walk more worthily before the Lord as His sons and daughters in anticipation of the day when we can gather together and worship in this completed house."[52]

It was not uncommon for President Hinckley to make overnight trips to cities in the United States and even to other countries to inspect potential temple sites. For some time he and others had searched for a location in the Hartford, Connecticut, area, and though a site had been identified, he felt uneasy about it. He had pleaded with the Lord for direction in the matter, and as he left for a regional conference on the East Coast in April 1995 he was determined to return with a firm decision about the placement of this temple.

After a day of looking at property in New York and Connecticut, he was still unsettled. The next day, in a luncheon meeting with stake presidents in the Boston area, President Hinckley spoke candidly with them concerning the challenge of determining a location for a temple in the East. "Brethren, I am frustrated," he admitted. "We have looked high and low around the Hartford, Connecticut, area for property, and nothing has developed. Do any of you have any suggestions?" President Kenneth G. Hutchins of the Boston Stake volunteered that he believed the Church owned a prime piece of property on a hill overlooking Boston that had never been developed. At that, President Hinckley turned the meeting over to Elder Neal A. Maxwell, who was traveling with him, and immediately left to inspect the site. Later that evening President Hinckley recorded what happened when he walked about the property: "As I stood there I had an electric feeling that this is the place, that the Lord inspired its acquisition and its retention. Very few seemed to know anything about it. . . . I think I know why I have had such a very difficult time determining the situation concerning Hartford. I have prayed about it. I have come here three or four times. I have studied maps and tables of membership. With all of this I have not had a strong confirmation. I felt a confirmation as I stood in Belmont on this property this afternoon. This is the place for a House of the Lord in the New England area."[53] During the priesthood session of the October general conference President Hinckley apologized to the Connecticut Saints, explaining that the temple previously slated for their area would not be built, and then announced that temples would be constructed in both Boston and White Plains, New York. By 1996 the First Presidency also announced plans to build temples in Monterrey, Mexico, and Billings, Montana.

The anxiety President Hinckley felt over the location of a temple on the East Coast was representative of the weighty matters that fell on his and his counselors' shoulders. Other issues weren't as readily resolved. "One thing about which I feel deep concern is the members of the Church who fall away," he explained a year after becoming President of the Church. "I have tremendous appreciation and a deep love for members who are faithful, but I worry greatly about those who drift away—what we can do to bring them back, and how we can prevent that drift in the first place."[54]

He was concerned also about the growing size of the Church's organization and the attendant bureaucracy, and early in his presidency he asked the Presiding Bishopric to commission a study to evaluate the overall effectiveness of Church administration. "I worry about whether or not everything we're doing needs to be done in terms of the great mission of the Church," he said. "Are we as efficient as we ought to be? What can we do to get the best return for tithing dollars spent?"[55]

He often tried to get both general and local leaders to see the Church's burgeoning bureaucracy in perspective and to find ways to avoid relegating the Church's spiritual growth to a position beneath its administrative function. Though he felt that some progress had been made in decentralizing Church government, there was much left to do. As he said on one occasion: "We must never become so engrossed with numbers and the masses that we lose sight of the fact that it is the individual who counts—his problems, his dreams, his aspirations, his desires, his heart."[56]

"We have been through a building era in which the process of administering a worldwide Church has been established," President Packer explained, "and President Hinckley has had a vital part in all of that. But now he is expressing a clear vision of where we are to go. He has sent the signal that the spiritual ministry and the message of the redemption and the Atonement and the ministry of Jesus Christ must be emphasized in a Church that is well organized, and that the imprint of that message is more important than remodeling the system. He has called upon us of the Twelve to find the way to get the apostolic witness borne to all the nations of the world."[57] In December 1995 the First Presidency and Quorum of the Twelve unveiled a new Church logo, which featured more prominently the words *Jesus Christ*.

President Hinckley also worried about the level of spirituality among faithful members of the Church. To one audience after another, he bore witness of the Savior as the only solution to the world's ills. In his first Christmas message as President of the Church, he spoke tenderly of the Savior's condescension and marveled at His willingness to set aside every privilege of his Divine Sonship and come to earth under humble circumstances: "The story of Christmas is so much larger than the story of His birth in Bethlehem. It is the very core of the entire plan drawn and adopted for the salvation of the sons and daughters of God of all generations. His birth cannot be separated from His earthly ministry. Neither can it be detached from His divine sacrifice. . . . I feel so profoundly grateful for that birth. But that birth would not be remembered but for the gift He made to all of us through His mortal ministry, followed by the terrible pain and suffering of His death, to rise glorious and triumphant as the Redeemer of the world."[58]

At the April 1996 general conference, which fell on Easter Sunday, President Hinckley bore powerful testimony of the glory of the Risen Lord: "Through the centuries untold numbers have paid with the sacrifice of their comforts, their fortunes, their very lives for the convictions they carried in their hearts of the reality of the risen, living Lord. And then comes the ringing testimony of the Prophet of this dispensation that in a wondrous theophany he saw and was spoken to by the Almighty Father and the Risen Son. That vision, glorious beyond description, became the wellspring of this The Church of Jesus Christ of Latter-day Saints. . . . Towering above all mankind stands Jesus the Christ, the King of glory, the unblemished Messiah, the Lord Emmanuel. . . . He lives! He lives, resplendent and wonderful, the living Son of the living God."[59]

In his Easter Sunday message President Hinckley also testified that only through the Atonement of Jesus Christ could the pain of death be replaced by the peace of eternal life. "Whenever the cold hand of death strikes, there shines through the gloom and the darkness of that hour the triumphant figure of the Lord Jesus Christ. . . . He is our comfort, our only true comfort, when the dark shroud of earthly night closes about us as the spirit departs the human form."[60] He bore that same testimony whenever he spoke at the funerals of family members and friends, several of whom passed away during the first eighteen months of his presidency.

He was in England in August 1995 when he learned of the passing of his half-sister, Carol Cannon, and his longtime friend and former missionary companion, Wendell J. Ashton. Seven months later, in March 1996, former BYU President Rex E. Lee died after a courageous battle with cancer. In October 1995 President Hinckley had spoken to a record-setting audience of 25,875 at BYU's Marriott Center and during his address praised President Lee, whose resignation had been announced effective January 1, 1996. "He has led this institution with a growing commitment to excellence," he said. "He has even brought a smile to the rock-jawed visage of LaVell Edwards, a great accomplishment in and of itself."[61] At President Lee's funeral, President Hinckley admitted that he had felt a foreboding when he spoke at the BYU devotional that it would be his last opportunity to speak about President Lee where he could hear him.

Indeed, President Hinckley tried never to let an opportunity pass to express gratitude for the service, faith, and faithfulness of members of the Church, whether individually or to a congregation at large. "Thank you, my brothers and sisters, for the goodness of your lives," he said again and again. "Thank you for your efforts in trying to measure up to the very high standards of this the Lord's Church. Thank you for your faith. Thank you for your sustaining hands and hearts. Thank you for your prayers."[62]

He had always been tenderhearted about members of the Church, but now he seemed even more so. Tears flowed easily. Perhaps no one noticed the transformation more than Sister Hinckley, who frequently referred to her husband when he called on her to speak. "I have known this man since we were in high school, and I have never known him to say anything or do anything that would not be appropriate for an apostle," she said on one occasion, mirroring many others. "But he is a different man now than he was before he was ordained President of the Church. I know this embarrasses him, and I will probably get scolded when I get home, but I know he is a prophet of God. I have seen the power of the Lord magnify him. I have seen him solve problems that seemed to be almost unsolvable because the

Lord has given him the inspiration and the answers he needed to move the work along. I remember that he's almost, but not quite, perfect—but that more importantly, he bears the mantle of prophet."[63]

President Hinckley's colleagues in the First Presidency and Quorum of the Twelve, and indeed millions of members throughout the world, had also gained a testimony of his divinely appointed calling. "He makes you better," Elder Eyring explained. "When I'm with him, I'm wiser. It is because he brings down the power of heaven into my life. He never says, 'Hal, I think you'll be inspired,' he just acts as though I will be. I have had several experiences with him when I have thought, 'That's an idea I've never had before. Why did I have it while I was with him? Why was I able to express something to him that I had never understood before?' One great gift of a prophet is that he brings revelation to other people. I have had the experience of walking away from a meeting with him, knowing that I was given more than I had when I walked in, because I was in his presence. It is a wonderful gift. He doesn't just bring out the best in me, he helps heaven bring out the best in me. I don't know how he does it, but he has that gift. And I believe it will be transferred across the Church, such that all those who really want to help this prophet will find themselves more able to help than they've ever been before."[64]

Elder David B. Haight, who had worked many years with President Hinckley as a member of Bonneville International's board of directors, summarized his feelings: "The world is prepared for us to move forward, and we are entering a period of tremendous growth and opportunity. Barriers are coming down, and President Hinckley has the vision, the experience, and the inspired direction to move us forward."[65]

CHAPTER TWENTY-FIVE

OUT OF OBSCURITY

As President Hinckley traveled throughout the Church, meeting with the Saints in congregations large and small, his remarks and testimony followed a characteristic theme: that the faith and faithfulness of each member was vital, that the Church was not "an American church" but one that was growing in vibrant fashion wherever it was organized, and that the future of this organization was bright. "We've only begun," he told a fireside audience in Crawley, England. "We have scarcely scratched the surface in the matter of carrying forward this work to the world. But we're moving out boldly. I think of those marvelous words spoken by the Lord to the Prophet Joseph Smith in the misery and loneliness of Liberty Jail when, after months of being in that cold, foul, dungeon-like place, he cried out in discouragement, 'O God, where art thou?' And among those words which came in response were these: 'The ends of the earth shall inquire after thy name, and fools shall have thee in derision, and hell shall rage against thee; while the pure in heart . . . shall seek counsel, and authority, and blessings constantly from under thy hand.' [D&C 121:1; 122:1–2.] I am a witness to the fulfillment of that prophecy. Each of you is a witness. This is the great day of prophecy fulfilled, and what a great thing it is to be a part of it!"[1]

As he brought the April 1996 general conference to a close, he referred to the oft-quoted prophecy included in the dedicatory prayer of the Kirtland Temple—that the kingdom would "become a great mountain and fill the whole earth" and that the Church would "come forth out of the wilderness of darkness"—and then concluded, "We are witnessing the answer to that remarkable pleading. Increasingly the Church is being recognized at home and abroad for what it truly is."[2]

Many of his General Authority colleagues believed that he

himself was integral to the fulfillment of that prophecy. "President Hinckley is helping to lead the Church out of obscurity," Elder Neal A. Maxwell stated. "The Church can't move forward as it needs to if we are hidden under a bushel. Someone has to step out, and President Hinckley is willing to do so. He is a man of history and modernity at the same time, and he has marvelous gifts of expression that enable him to present our message in a way that appeals to people everywhere."[3]

Indeed, through the years President Hinckley had learned to talk comfortably about the gospel with rich and poor, high and low, and he had a way of doing so without being patronizing or presumptuous. After accompanying him for nearly three weeks in Asia, Elder Joseph B. Wirthlin said: "President Hinckley is lifting the Church to a new height of admiration in the world. He knows how to present our message to people not of our faith. His instincts tell him what to say, how to say it, and when to speak up."[4] He had often counseled members to cultivate a spirit of tolerance for those of varying religious and philosophical persuasions, and he insisted that it was possible to disagree without being disagreeable. "We must cultivate a spirit of affirmative gratitude for those who do not see things quite as we see them," he told one congregation. "We do not in any way have to compromise our theology, our convictions, our knowledge of eternal truth as it has been revealed by the God of Heaven. We can offer our own witness of the truth, quietly, sincerely, honestly, but never in a manner that will give offense to others."[5]

He also believed the Church could better capitalize on its use of media in spreading the gospel message, and during the first year of his administration he explored ways that communications technology could be utilized to teach the gospel more effectively to more people. "I constantly ask myself what I can do to help the 50,000 missionaries who are laboring so diligently in the mission field," he explained. "If we could find ways to cause people to bump into the gospel in the normal course of their lives, rather than waiting for missionaries to knock on their doors, it would be one of the greatest things we could do."[6]

As eager as President Hinckley was to step up the Church's media efforts, perhaps even he had no idea how personally involved he would become in breaking new public relations ground. In November 1995 he and Elder Maxwell flew to New York City to attend a luncheon arranged by Edelman Public Relations Worldwide, an international public relations firm contracted by the Church to help improve its image and increase its visibility. In that setting President Hinckley was to meet with some of the nation's most influential media and business executives. "An assignment such as that worries me terribly," he acknowledged openly. "I had prayed about it very earnestly. I realized, of course, that I was representing the Church and that the slightest error or slip could cause a great deal of harm and undo countless good done by so many over the years. It was a worrisome responsibility."[7]

President Hinckley arrived at the prestigious Harvard Club in midtown Manhattan to find assembled an impressive roster of guests, among them *Newsweek* editor-in-chief Richard Smith; John Mack Carter, president of Hearst Magazine Enterprises; Andrew Heyward, vice president and executive producer of the *CBS Evening News;* Associated Press religion editor David Briggs; and Mike Wallace, the senior reporter from CBS's *60 Minutes.*

The thirty or so opinion leaders were seated in such a way that all had easy access to each other. After lunch, Elder Maxwell introduced President Hinckley, referring in so doing to his experience as a young missionary preaching to hecklers in London's Hyde Park. President Hinckley played off the introduction as he began, remarking, "After an experience like that, even Mike Wallace doesn't look too formidable." At that, the tone was set for a congenial and sometimes humorous interchange. President Hinckley continued with an overview of the international scope of the Church, commented on its missionary, humanitarian, and educational pursuits, and then offered to answer questions.

Some of the inquiries that followed were predictable. One question centered on the issue of women and the priesthood, another on excommunication and dissent within the Church. Another comment dealt with the Church's emphasis on family history research, and one media executive asked President Hinckley to elaborate on misconceptions that surrounded the Church and its members. He answered each question candidly and without hesitation or any hint of awkwardness. Toward the end of the discussion one guest offered: "President Hinckley, you are obviously not afraid to answer the tough questions. It has been my perception in the past that there were certain secretisms to the workings of the Church. By your very presence, you indicate to me an openness. Is this a new openness, and is the Church concentrating on opening up some of its formerly less known facets to the public?" President Hinckley responded: "There is only one situation that we don't talk about, and that is the sacred work that takes place in our temples. . . . We enter into covenants and ordinances there that are sacred and of a character that we don't talk about in public. . . . But the door is wide open on everything else."

In one memorable interchange, Mike Wallace acknowledged that he had accepted the invitation to the luncheon reluctantly, assuming the Mormon Church President would be an elderly gentleman out of touch with the times. When, during his comment, he mentioned that President Hinckley was a mere eight years older than he was, President Hinckley interrupted him, "And here I thought we were the same age, Mike." At that, the room erupted in laughter and scattered applause. Wallace continued by admitting that he had therefore been surprised to hear President Hinckley refer to San Francisco 49er quarterback Steve Young and had found it interesting that he would be familiar with a popular sports figure. "I would like to do a profile of you, of the President of the Mormon Church," Wallace invited. After pausing for a few moments, President Hinckley responded, "Thank you. I'll take a chance."[8]

At the luncheon's conclusion, one guest after another shook President Hinckley's hand and thanked him for the unprecedented interchange. One distinguished media executive said, "Mr. Hinckley, I am not a member of your church, but I can understand why people would join." A woman who described herself as liberal in her political and social orientation volunteered that despite their ideological differences she saw in President Hinckley a man she could respect. He was relieved and grateful at the outcome, as he reflected later: "It was quite an experience. Here was this crowd of hard-bitten executives, journalists, and star-studded media and business people, who were willing to listen to an eighty-five-year-old man from Salt

Lake City. The Lord blessed us, and that's all there is to it."[9] He recorded afterward: "I felt a deep sense of appreciation to the Lord, who blessed me. I know He magnified me. I know that He put words in my mouth. . . . I had almost dreaded coming back here and facing these people. All of the credit belongs to the Lord. I freely and gladly acknowledge it."[10]

Mike Wallace later admitted that President Hinckley's "very presence at the Harvard Club" both surprised and impressed him. "I wondered why he was there," he conceded, "and frankly I was intrigued. The Mormons had always been a fascinating subject, not just because of their religion but also because of their lifestyle and the secretive attitude they had maintained." Wallace subsequently extended President Hinckley a more formal invitation to sit for the *60 Minutes* interview.[11]

By the time he returned to Salt Lake City, however, President Hinckley was having second thoughts about his positive response to Wallace's offer. The reporters of *60 Minutes* were known for their investigative journalism, and he realized there was some risk in proceeding. "There were certainly some naysayers back at Church headquarters who were concerned about President Hinckley going ahead with the interview," explained Bruce Olsen, managing director of Church Public Affairs, who had attended the Harvard Club luncheon. "President Hinckley knew the negatives as well as anyone. He asked me to talk with industry professionals and get their advice, and he listened carefully to his counselors and others whom he trusted. After doing his homework, he prayed earnestly about the matter and decided to proceed. Even then, he was worried. But it was fascinating to watch the prophet of the Lord follow the pattern he would advocate for members of the Church: He did all he could to be prepared personally, and then he turned it over to the Lord."[12] As part of his preparation, he spent several evenings identifying questions Wallace might ask him and writing out the answers in detail.

On December 4 President Hinckley spent the day with an advance team from *60 Minutes*, and two weeks later, on December 18, Wallace engaged him in several hours of "eyeball-to-eyeball interview," as President Hinckley later described it. Wallace began by asking President Hinckley why he had agreed to the "rare" interview. "Because I felt it was an opportunity to tell the people of America something about this great cause in which I have such a keen interest," President Hinckley responded. "But that is not traditional with Mormons," Wallace insisted. "Can you tell me the last President of the Mormon Church who went on nationwide television to do an interview with no questions ahead of time so that you know what is coming?" When President Hinckley conceded that he couldn't, Wallace stated, "So, Gordon Hinckley decided, apparently, that there is a message that the Mormon Church has for America and, for that matter, the world." "Yes, indeed," President Hinckley replied. "And that message is?" Wallace probed. "That there is a way to greater peace. There is a way to greater harmony in our living. There is a way to revive the values that have made America strong. There is a way to improve things," President Hinckley said.

The two men enjoyed rapport from the outset. When Wallace asked if the Church's aggressive proselytizing was to show "the rest of us heathens what we are missing," President Hinckley responded, "It is to tell the rest of you what you are missing, yes." But such banter provided opportunity to elaborate. "And what is it that we are missing?" Wallace pursued. "You are missing the lift that comes of living close to the Lord and of knowing that life is really purposeful, that it is a mission rather than just a career. There is something wonderful about having some concept of who you are as a son of God with a divine destiny, and that you can make more of your life than you may have been making of it."

When Wallace asked President Hinckley if God talked to him as a prophet, he responded by referring to Elijah's experience in hearing the still small voice. "That's the voice of the Spirit, and I want to give you my testimony that it is real." Asked how he accounted for the rapid growth of a church that was so demanding of its people, President Hinckley responded in a tone typical of his answers throughout the grueling experience: "We have great expectations concerning our people. We have standards that we expect them to live by and to uphold. It is demanding. And that is one of the things that attracts people to this Church. It stands as an anchor in a world of shifting values. They feel they have something solid that they are standing on while the ground is moving beneath them. People are looking for something of substance and strength, based on eternal truth and eternal values."

After Wallace compared the beginnings of the Church to some cultish movements, President Hinckley responded: "Look at the fruits. That's the test. Look at this Church. From its organization in 1830 it has gone steadily forward. It has never taken a backward step. Its history is heroic. The coming of our people to these valleys of the mountains is one of the great epics of America. They gave their lives for this cause because they loved it, because they knew of its truth. They were hard-working people. They tamed this desert. They made it blossom as the rose. This isn't the work of charlatans. This isn't the work of idle dreamers."

When asked if he believed in an afterlife, President Hinckley answered, "I certainly do. I think life after this life is as certain as life here. I believe we lived before we came here, that we live here for a purpose . . ."

"Wait, wait," Wallace interrupted. "You believe we lived before we came here?"

"Oh, absolutely, as intelligences, as spirits," President Hinckley replied.

"There was a spirit of Gordon Hinckley?" Wallace asked.

"Absolutely, and of Mike Wallace."

"I hope not," Wallace joked.

"Life is an eternal thing, Mike," President Hinckley continued. "It is part of an eternal plan, our Father's plan for His sons and daughters, whom He loves. His work and His glory is to bring about the immortality and eternal life of His sons and daughters. It has purpose. It is meaningful."[13]

Though their encounter was mentally demanding and stressful in view of the potential ramifications, President Hinckley found Wallace to be professional, well prepared, and respectful. In turn, Wallace described President Hinckley in complimentary terms. "Generally speaking, he's first rate," he said afterward, "but compared with other eighty-five-year-olds, he is incredibly responsive. There was no question that he found difficult or unpleasant. He came to talk." Wallace added that he expected the

60 Minutes segment to tell a story about the Church that had never been told by the Church's President on prime-time television.[14]

Prior to airing the *60 Minutes* segment featuring President Hinckley, Wallace and his crew returned to Salt Lake City for a second interview. This time Wallace probed on such subjects as abortion, child abuse, and political expediency. "Some skeptics say that major changes in Church policy have come from political pressure rather than as revelations from God," Wallace challenged. "For example, the business of ending polygamy wasn't a revelation but came because Utah wanted to become a state." President Hinckley replied: "One of the purposes of a prophet is to seek the wisdom and the will of the Lord. It was the case with Moses when he led the children of Israel out of Egypt. It was the case for the Old Testament prophets when people were faced with oppression. That is the purpose of a prophet, to give answers to people with regard to the dilemmas in which they find themselves. Is it a matter of political expediency? No. Inspired guidance? Yes."[15]

Despite his positive experience with Wallace, as the time between the initial interviews and the program's airing stretched, President Hinckley became increasingly worried. In his concluding remarks at the Sunday afternoon session of the April 1996 general conference, he referred to his experience with the "tough" senior reporter from *60 Minutes* and acknowledged something of his concern about the program scheduled to air that evening. He explained that he had consented to the interview because he felt it presented an opportunity to communicate "some affirmative aspects of our culture and message" to millions. "I concluded that it was better to lean into the stiff wind of opportunity than to simply hunker down and do nothing," he said, garnering a tremendous response in the Tabernacle from an audience delighted at the prophet's candor. "We have no idea what the outcome will be. . . . If it turns out to be favorable, I will be grateful. Otherwise, I pledge I'll never get my foot in that kind of trap again."[16]

Later that evening, when President Hinckley finally saw his interview with Mike Wallace as edited for the *60 Minutes* broadcast, he was enormously relieved to find that the program was evenhanded and respectful, that controversial topics were discussed without distortion, and that his comments had for the most part been used in context. Wallace had been, he felt, "very decent" to him and the Church.

"Frankly, nearly everything about this assignment surprised me," Wallace admitted afterward. "I was surprised by Gordon Hinckley's humor and his candor, neither of which I expected. We raised the issues that were on the minds of the skeptics, he was willing to answer every question, and his answers were reasonable. I was impressed with his staff. They were cooperative and accommodating, did not appear to be suspicious of our motives, and treated us with respect. The people around Mr. Hinckley obviously have confidence in him, but I didn't sense the 'fear of the CEO syndrome' that you find in many large organizations. We have done stories on many organizations, including churches, but I can honestly say we have never had an experience quite like that one."[17]

Many Church members responded enthusiastically to the program, invigorated by a President who made no apology for the organization he led, who revealed a light but effective touch in presenting the merits of the gospel to a nonmember audience, and who deftly handled the glare of the national spotlight. The *Salt Lake Tribune* reported, "Veteran TV interviewer Mike Wallace looked like he was tossing softballs to Mormon Church President Gordon B. Hinckley during the *60 Minutes* segment on the LDS faith that aired Sunday on CBS, but it may have been a case of the media-savvy Hinckley deflecting hardballs."[18] One professional LDS woman said: "President Hinckley carries an almost palpable feeling of hope and optimism that is infectious. He entreats, he enthuses, he lifts. One of my nonmember colleagues from the Midwest called after watching the program. I thought he had a cold until he admitted that tears were running down his cheeks. 'That Hinckley is really something,' he said. 'He really touched me. I'm sixty years old. If I were twenty years old, you'd have me.'"[19]

Letters poured into the offices of the First Presidency and CBS. "I think Gordon Hinckley wanted to get his Mormon gospel in front of a lot of people, and it worked," Wallace indicated several weeks after the program aired. "Response to the piece has been extraordinary. Usually mail comes for a week or two, and then drops off precipitously. But we were still getting letters a month after the program. An unusual number of letters indicated that we were balanced and fair, and of course some wrote asking why we hadn't probed more deeply into one thing or another, but that comes with the territory."[20]

Though the extent of the program's impact was impossible to measure, mission presidents and missionaries reported instances in which it seemed to have influenced or motivated investigators. Members wrote President Hinckley to report a variety of reactions and results. Some told of family members who after years of antagonism had softened toward the Church; others mentioned professional colleagues whose interest had been stimulated by the program; one even wrote about fielding referrals over the Internet.

One nonmember viewer wrote Mike Wallace: "I enjoyed your Mormon segment Easter Sunday. Apparently their growth is threatening to some, but if we judge any group by their fruits, these people do provide an anchor in a sea of ever-changing values. Fifty thousand chaste missionaries in 150 countries probably do more good for society than all the government social programs put together."[21]

President Boyd K. Packer evaluated the program's effect. "President Hinckley was greatly worried about the outcome. We all felt and told him that things would work out fine. But it proved to be even better than we thought it would be. He was ideally suited to the challenge, which provided a public visiting of the President as he has always been—pleasant, forthright, unapologetic about the gospel, and unintimidated by anyone."[22] Said Bruce Olsen, who handled all arrangements with CBS and coordinated the interview through Edelman: "What we had was a journalist talking to a journalist. President Hinckley's early training added to his ability to communicate articulately but with humor and to be a little self-deprecating, which worked magically in that setting. I don't know if anyone else could have done it quite like he did, because he has such a unique combination of strengths."[23]

Indeed, President Hinckley seemed to exhibit unusual dexterity when it came to dealing with the press. The *60 Minutes* interview, which reached at least forty million people and attracted immediate and global attention, was only one of many interchanges he allowed with both national and international journalists. During the first eighteen months of his presidency, he held major news conferences in New York City, Japan, Korea, Mexico, England, Germany, and Council Bluffs, Iowa, and was interviewed by reporters from the *New York Times, Wall Street Journal*, BBC, London News Radio, ABS-CBN TV in the Philippines, and numerous other news organizations. In one interview after another, he answered questions about whether Mormons were Christians, explained the Church's rapid growth in a day when established religions were declining in membership, and elaborated on everything from women and politics to abortion, homosexuality, and family values. He spoke with ease and without fear or apology. He had a way of boldly articulating the Church's virtues without being overbearing, of explaining the benefits of living the gospel without slighting other religions or special-interest groups.

Always he painted a hopeful picture about not only the Church but the world in general. To a reporter from the *New York Times* he said: "I see so much good in people everywhere. Wonderful things are happening around the world. This is a great age in the history of the earth." Later in the interview he added: "Ours is a multicultural organization with a common purpose, and that is to offer the individual an opportunity for growth, for happiness, and to give an encouraging upward reach to people wherever we find them. . . . We believe in being happy. The gospel is the message of good news, and it's a way of happiness, the Lord's way of happiness. Now, you might find somebody who's sour here and there, but don't think he represents the entire Church."[24]

He returned often to the theme of "shifting values," refusing to apologize for the Church's strict codes of conduct. In an interview with a correspondent from the London News Service he stated: "I noticed in the *London Times* yesterday that one Church had set up 'ten commandments' on the behavior of priests. That's an interesting thing to me. Any church ought to expect of its priesthood the observance of the very highest ideals of moral behavior. We stand for those things. Shifting values soon lose interest for anyone. It's constancy that people want when the world is changing around them, and we believe that we are providing that. Our doctrine, our teaching, our basic theological foundation is found in some premises that are constant and unchangeable, the first of which is that God is our Eternal Father, and we as His children are accountable to Him for our behavior. The second is that Jesus is the Redeemer of the world, the Living Son of the Living God, the Resurrection and the Life, He who set the pattern for our lives, and we ought to be trying to the degree that we can to be living those principles."[25]

He began every press conference with a brief statement about the Church, during which he established a rapport with that particular press corps. Sometimes he used humor; often he displayed an impressive familiarity with the area or the people he was visiting, thereby creating the feeling that he was "one of them." At a formal luncheon for representatives of thirteen of the largest newspapers and magazines in Seoul, Korea, for example, he began by stating that he had been coming to Korea for thirty-six years, that he loved the Korean people and was impressed with their industry, their focus on family values, and their interest in education. And he also teased them a little. "We have a strict code of health," he explained. "We abstain from alcohol, tobacco, coffee, and tea. As has been said, I am eighty-five years of age. I enjoy good health—and that isn't because I eat *kimchee*." He added that the Church had invested millions of dollars in Korea in houses of worship but had not taken any money out of the country, and that in Korea local Church units were led by Koreans. Before he finished, he bore his testimony that Jesus Christ is the Son of God, that Joseph Smith is a prophet, and that the Book of Mormon is the word of God.

"President Hinckley respects the media, but he is not afraid of them," explained Elder Maxwell, who witnessed his performance in similar settings. "And he has such a solid grasp of both Church history and facts about the Church today that he is not likely to be thrown by a question that he hasn't already thought about or processed in his own mind. He is able to give answers of sound-bite length that are important. He is quick mentally and equal to the engagements that come up. And he doesn't feel compelled to gloss over any of our shortcomings as a people. He doesn't put forward any gilding or veneer. As a result, reporters respond to his genuineness. He has the capacity to connect with people from all stations and in that respect is eminently prepared to tell our story to the world."[26]

President Hinckley was also anxious to get out personally into the world, and he quickly distinguished himself as a traveling President. He explained his motivation during the April 1996 general conference: "I am determined that while I have strength I will get out among the people at home and abroad to express my appreciation, to give encouragement, to build faith, to teach, to add my testimony to theirs and at the same time to draw strength from them. . . . I intend to keep moving with energy for as long as I can. I wish to mingle with the people I love."[27]

"President Hinckley is tireless," President Packer acknowledged. "He's got all of us running to keep up with him."[28] Elder Maxwell told a group of missionaries in the Far East: "President Hinckley has unusual ability and mobility that are allowing him to cover the planet in an unusual way. You are the first generation to see the globalization of the Church. No one has played a greater role in that effort than President Hinckley."[29]

It perhaps came as no surprise that President Hinckley chose to make his first international trip as President of the Church to Great Britain, a place for which he had long had an abiding affection. "Something happened inside of me in England that was so significant and deep-rooted that I have never gotten over it," he said in an attempt to explain his feelings for the British Isles. "It is the same thing I have seen happen to thousands of other young men and women who commit themselves to the Lord, and their faith in Him becomes their anchor. Everything good that has happened to me is a result of what happened while I lived in that land."[30]

He admitted early in the trip that he was so anxious to meet with the Saints that his zeal may have outpaced his wisdom in planning his schedule. Almost every day he and Sister Hinckley traveled by car to a new city, often more than a hundred miles away, and met with missionaries, inspected property, gave media interviews, and held special firesides for the members. In all he delivered fourteen addresses to nearly eight thousand Saints during the whirlwind trip, which revealed just how much stamina the eighty-five-year-old Church President had. "He is only happy when he is getting things done," Sister Hinckley said afterward. "I just try to keep up with him, and that isn't easy. He is a very young eighty-five."[31]

With the looming presence of the famous cathedral just a few kilometers down the road, President Hinckley presided over the creation of a stake in Canterbury, the seat of the Church of England and the site to which Christian pilgrims had journeyed since the Middle Ages. From there he slowly worked his way north to London and then on up to Liverpool. In one meeting after another with missionaries and members who drove long distances and arrived hours in advance to get a seat, President Hinckley's emotions rose to the surface. During the rededication of the storied Hyde Park Chapel on London's famous Exhibition Road, he began with the familiar claim, "This is my town. This place carries for me a particular charm, a reminder of great and marvelous experiences with wonderful people."

The next day he returned to the chapel to speak with missionaries from the London Mission. "You have talking to you today one old, worn out, beaten down British missionary," he began before sharing some of his own experiences in England and then admonishing the young men and women not to be discouraged. "I know about knocking on doors and fighting off dogs and having doors slammed in your face. I know it's hard. But so what? What a power you are! What capacity you have to change lives! Perhaps not many. But one here and another there listens to you. And in time, an entire ward of people have accepted the gospel. You can never foretell the consequences of that which you do when you teach the gospel of Jesus Christ. The Church was small and weak when I served here. Now we have 160,000 members in these islands."[32]

Sister Hinckley complemented her husband with her warm manner, sense of humor, and sincere expression of testimony. Without exception the Saints enjoyed the exchanges between the two. In one meeting President Hinckley introduced her by saying, "I am going to exercise my prerogative and call on Sister Hinckley to speak. This is something for which I will pay a dear price, but so be it." Sister Hinckley countered with: "What would you do if you were married to a man like that? There used to be two important men in my life—my husband and the President of the Church. Now, all of a sudden, there's only one." Typically her friendly manner and wit were but a prelude to the bearing of sincere testimony. "Every day of my life I know with more certainty that this is the gospel of our Savior," she said. "I just have to pinch myself to believe that I have witnessed what is going on across this wonderful Church. I can't tell you how much it means to us that you would be here. You strengthen *our* testimonies just by being here."[33]

Their love for the Saints was everywhere evident. In Liverpool, President Hinckley went down into the audience after the closing song to shake hands with members who had traveled from the Isle of Man to attend the meeting. President Ray Turner of the Liverpool Stake explained the significance of this action: "With overnight stays the Isle of Man is a two- or three-day journey. It is expensive and time-consuming. Because we only heard three weeks in advance that the prophet was coming, some members had already booked holidays abroad. But they canceled their holidays, many of them losing money to do so, in order to listen to the prophet. For many Saints here this was a once-in-a-lifetime experience."[34]

President Hinckley's final stop before returning home was Dublin, where he became the first Church President to visit the Emerald Isle in forty-two years. Area President Graham W. Doxey summarized his week with the prophet in the British Isles: "It has been marvelous to see the faces of the people who come with great expectation and feast on everything President Hinckley says. They love his humor and the fact that he is down to earth. He understands their problems. He bears testimony and encourages them to move forward. Seeing the response of the people to a prophet of God has been a joy."[35]

A month after his return from Britain, at the October 1995 general conference, President Hinckley announced that if current trends continued, the Church would celebrate a meaningful milestone sometime in February 1996, when there would be more members of the Church living outside the United States than in. On February 26, 1996, a *Deseret News* front-page story indicated that the mark had in fact been reached, and that the Church was currently welcoming an average of 950 new members a day.[36] "The crossover of that line is a wonderfully significant thing," President Hinckley explained. "It represents the fruit of a tremendous outreach. The God of Heaven, whose servants we are, never intended that this should be a narrow, parochial work."[37]

It seemed appropriate that such a milestone was reached early in President Hinckley's administration, for he had covered the world in a remarkable way throughout his lifetime and was determined to continue the practice. In May 1996 he turned his trip to Asia to dedicate the Hong Kong Temple into a whirlwind eighteen-day canvassing of the Orient, with visits to multiple cities in Japan, Korea, and the Philippines, as well as stops in Taiwan, Okinawa, Cambodia, Vietnam, and mainland China. Elder and Sister Joseph B. Wirthlin accompanied the Hinckleys throughout their journey.

Like his earlier trip to Great Britain, President Hinckley's return to the Orient was a tender homecoming. Everywhere he went, huge crowds gathered to greet and hear from him. They were responding to the visit not only of the President of the Church but of a man who had spent a tremendous amount of time among them during preceding decades. In that process he had established a distinctive rapport with the Saints in each country. Nearly everywhere he went the people confessed that they secretly felt President Hinckley had special affection for them. Said President Pak Byung Kyu, president of the MTC in Seoul, "We Koreans feel that President Hinckley loves us and our country in a special way. President Hinckley is *our* President." The president of the Hong Kong Temple, President Ng Kat Hing, said, "President Hinckley has been coming to Hong Kong for many years, and he has told us many times that this is one of his favorite places to visit. He loves the Chinese people in a way different from others."[38] Similar sentiments were expressed in each country.

President Hinckley's emotions were visible for all to see as he repeatedly struggled for words to express the depth of his feelings for the Oriental Saints, protesting often that "tears come easily to an old man." But in truth his age had nothing to do with the fact that in one meeting after another, from country to country, he wept as he looked upon huge congregations of Asian Saints.

President Hinckley's first meeting in Hong Kong was with the missionaries, and he was filled with enthusiasm as he stepped to the pulpit and proclaimed: "How marvelous it is to be here with you! I feel as if I have come home. Coming to this city, to dedicate a temple, represents the fulfillment of one of the greatest dreams of my life."[39] He enjoyed teasing the missionaries about the hazards of local drinking water. "Bottled or boiled or be dead, that's my motto in some of the remote areas of the world," he joked, then continued in a more serious vein: "It is a tremendous opportunity to work among the Chinese, who are hard to reach at times. But when the gospel touches lives, they turn around. These people are as entitled to the gospel as any on this earth. Every time you bring a convert into this church you bless a life and the generations yet to come. So make hay while you're under the Union Jack."[40]

His comment referred to the impending change of Hong Kong, in July 1997, from British rule to governance from Beijing. In that meeting and elsewhere he spoke of the upcoming sequence of events: "No one knows what will happen in 1997. But we have faith that everything will work out and go forward. I have that faith. I feel optimistic about it. I think we will go forward without hindrance. I don't know how or when we will enter China. I leave that in the hands of the Lord. So even though this is a time of uncertainty in Hong Kong, we will face it with faith."[41]

There was no uncertainty about what he had come to Hong Kong to do, and on May 26 and 27, accompanied by President Monson, Elder Maxwell, Elder Wirthlin, and the Asia Area Presidency—Elders Kwok Yuen Tai, John H. Groberg, and Rulon G. Craven—President Hinckley presided over and participated in each of the seven dedicatory sessions of the Hong Kong Temple. He was delighted to find that the temple's workmanship was excellent and the architecture and decor were uniquely and beautifully Chinese.

Indeed, the dedication of the temple, to which Saints from as far away as Beijing and Singapore traveled, was a watershed event for President Hinckley. In his brief remarks during the cornerstone-laying ceremony, President Monson explained that no temple had ever received such close scrutiny from President Hinckley as had this one. "When we see him wipe his eyes throughout the next two days," President Monson said, "the tears won't be from hay fever but from the heart and soul of our President."[42] In the first session President Hinckley admitted, "This is a very emotional time for me. This temple represents the fulfillment of a dream and an answer to many prayers. I first came here thirty-six years ago, when we had tiny branches that met in rented rooms. I remember trying to explain how the Church operated, diagramming it out on a chalkboard to a handful of leaders. In those difficult days I scarcely dreamed we would have what we have here today. But with this temple the Church has now reached maturity in Hong Kong. If ever I felt the inspiration of the Lord at any time in my life, it was in connection with this building."[43]

Immediately upon conclusion of the seventh dedicatory session, President and Sister Hinckley traveled by bus for an overnight trip to Shenzhen, China, where they received a red-carpet welcome from dignitaries representing the Overseas Chinese Town of Shenzhen Special Economic Zone and the Chinese Folk Villages—sister communities with the Polynesian Cultural Center in Hawaii. President Hinckley's visit marked the first of a President of the Church to mainland China. It is possible that he was also the first to be feted in such an extravagant manner. More than five hundred dancers and performers in brightly colored costumes lined the walkways to greet President and Sister Hinckley as they arrived at the folk villages, and glittering confetti shot from small cannons added sparkle to the reception he received at each location. Though slightly embarrassed at the overwhelming welcome, he was impressed with the Chinese attractions and grateful for the hospitality of his hosts. As he left Shenzhen, President Hinckley knew he would not soon forget these experiences in Hong Kong and on mainland China.[44]

From China President Hinckley traveled to Cambodia and then to Vietnam. He dedicated Cambodia for the preaching of the gospel, and while in Hanoi he felt impressed to offer what he described as an "addendum" to the original dedicatory prayer and dedicated the entire land of Vietnam. He also met with several small groups in both countries, gatherings that unleashed a flood of memories from days when he had held similar meetings throughout Asia.

These forays into the world's remote areas allowed him to bolster the spirits of those laying the foundations upon which future generations would build. Over and over, in areas where convert baptisms came slowly, he told the people there was no cause for discouragement, that the Church would grow. This was more than rhetoric. He gave the same advice to his own grandson serving a mission in the former Eastern Bloc: "Your parents have told me that the area where you are now laboring is much more difficult than where you previously served. It is difficult and sometimes discouraging to open a new area. It is the history of this work that pioneering is always difficult. However, once a foundation is securely laid, then tremendous results follow afterward."[45]

Indeed, he had seen that pattern emerge again and again. Perhaps nowhere in the world were the fruits of pioneering more dramatic than in the Philippines, where he flew from Hanoi. President Hinckley felt an unusual affinity for the warm, gregarious Filipinos, as well as a personal interest in the explosive growth of the Church—there were now more than 375,000 members—that he referred to as the "Miracle of Manila." Many Filipino Saints not only revered him as the prophet but shared a feeling of kinship as well, and they demonstrated their devotion in dramatic fashion. By midafternoon on May 29, 1996, the Araneta Coliseum, where an evening fireside was to be held, was filled beyond capacity. Lines had begun to form at 7:00 A.M. for a meeting that wasn't scheduled to begin for twelve hours. The official count later indicated that some 35,000 members had crowded into the coliseum's 25,000 seats as well as the aisles and concourses. Many Saints had traveled twenty hours by boat and bus to reach Manila. For some, the cost of the journey equalled several months' salary. One woman from the Lingayen Philippines Stake said of her motivation to make the trip: "We have come from a far place to see President Hinckley. He is a living prophet." She wept as she continued, "I am so glad to be here because now I can hear with my own ears a voice coming from the Lord, just like the Book of Mormon people did."[46]

When word reached President Hinckley that the coliseum

was full and that the building manager wondered if there was any way they could begin the meeting early, he immediately said, "Let's go." He and Sister Hinckley entered the vast arena to find it packed with what was believed to be the largest audience in an indoor facility ever to hear a President of the Church in person. As if on cue, the congregation spontaneously rose to their feet, applauded, and then began singing an emotional rendition of "We Thank Thee, O God, for a Prophet."

The Spirit was powerful as President Hinckley addressed the massive audience. Toward the end of his message, he gave voice to something that had perhaps been on his mind throughout this Asian trip: "I don't know whether I'll ever come here again. It's a big world, and I am trying to get around among our people. I just want to take this occasion to speak to you in a very personal way. I have in my heart a special feeling for the people of this nation. You have suffered so much in times past." He concluded by pronouncing a blessing upon all assembled: "In the authority of the apostolic office, in the authority of the keys of the Presidency of this Church, I bless you that if you will walk in faith, you will have food on your tables and clothing on your backs and shelter over your heads, and will constantly rejoice. Please accept of my love, my great feeling of love for you."[47]

As he was preparing to return to the United States, President Hinckley learned that his plane would land briefly for refueling on the island of Saipan in the Central Pacific. He immediately asked Elder Ben B. Banks, president of the Philippines Area, if there were missionaries or members on Saipan and, learning that there were both, asked him to invite the Saints to the airport. When they landed there late that night, President and Sister Hinckley were welcomed enthusiastically by several dozen members and missionaries offering leis and warm greetings.

President Hinckley returned from Asia having addressed nearly 60,000 members of the Church in firesides and special conferences; presided over seven dedicatory sessions at the Hong Kong Temple, plus the cornerstone-laying ceremony; and visited eight countries plus Hong Kong and Saipan. When asked how he maintained such a pace, he joked, "I go to bed every night and make sure I get up the next morning. I just keep going." Then he admitted, "The climate in this part of the world is enervating. But you get your lift from the people. They give me the energy to keep going. I love being among the Saints."[48]

"The last couple of weeks have been similar to running a marathon," Elder Wirthlin acknowledged at the journey's end. "But it has been an unusual privilege to recognize in President Hinckley something special, something unusual. He is superb in every way—spiritually, intellectually, and physically. He is a polished stone who has been groomed through his years as a General Authority." From his vantage point, Elder Wirthlin witnessed the obvious affection that existed between the prophet and the Oriental Saints. "President Hinckley has the enthusiasm and optimism so necessary in countries where the people have suffered so much. He loves the people of Asia, but of course he loves them everywhere. That's why he keeps such a busy schedule and extends himself as much as he can for the best good of the members of the Church. To him, poor and rich look the same. I have known President Hinckley since boyhood, and I always knew he was remarkable, but I never knew how remarkable until I spent eighteen days at his side in the Orient. I returned home a better man."[49]

President Hinckley had only a week at home before leaving on another ambitious journey, this one a two-week trip to Europe and the Holy Land. Again, the impetus for the trip was temple related, as he broke ground for a temple in Madrid. But he also visited the Saints in Brussels, The Hague, Copenhagen, Berlin, and the Holy Land.

Wherever he went, his presence aroused attention from dignitaries and the press. In Madrid, two prominent government officials attended the groundbreaking, where President Hinckley focused his remarks on the Church's desire to be a good citizen of Spain: "I hope we will be good neighbors to those who live around here. I promise you and the officials of Madrid that what is built here will be beautiful. We will build a temple, a stake center, a missionary training center, and some other facilities to accommodate the needs of our people. The structure will be beautiful and the grounds will be beautiful. This will be a hallowed and sacred place."[50] After President Hinckley and other officials turned over the first shovelfuls of soil, a young boy and girl were invited to come forward and take a turn with the shovels. As the youth dug into the dusty soil, a cheer rose from the crowd and a seasoned photographer from the city's press corps shouted, "Bravo!"

In Brussels, President Hinckley was welcomed by Ambassador Robert E. Hunter, the U.S. permanent representative to NATO, and Alan John Blinken, U.S. Ambassador to Belgium. Four days later, in interviews with two of Berlin's largest newspapers, *Berliner Zeitung* and *Die Welt*, the reporter from the latter began by stating that his paper was circulated in some 130 countries. "We have you beat. We're in 155," President Hinckley joked in response. The resulting article described Gordon B. Hinckley as "a charming man one would gladly have as a neighbor," adding that "the head and prophet of The Church of Jesus Christ of Latter-day Saints . . . makes a warmhearted, gracious impression." The article continued with a report of the Berlin regional conference, attended by more than 3700 members: "One saw many happy families clothed in white, girls in bright ankle-length dresses, and young men with black bow ties flock to the meeting. They often call the Mormon Church the 'Happy Church,' which can't be far wrong. Naturally, Mr. Hinckley had a message for us all: We must come back to God. He gives us light and understanding in a time in which all old standards are breaking down. The intact family that lives in love and shared understanding and in which there is prayer is the true source of strength of a nation."[51]

From Berlin, President and Sister Hinckley flew to the Holy Land, where they again visited sites central to the Savior's life and ministry. At the conclusion of their stay, he spoke to members of the Israel District in the auditorium of the BYU Jerusalem Center, rehearsing his visits to Bethlehem, the Sea of Galilee, the Mount of Beatitudes, Masada, Megiddo, Nazareth, the Upper Room, Gethsemane, and the Garden Tomb. "When we were at Gethsemane today," he shared with the congregation, "we went across the street into that grotto, sat in the shade, and read the scriptures. I think that His plea to His Father, when He sweat drops of blood in His agony, was to spare Him that great pain and suffering and anguish if that were possible. But He said His Father's will be done, not His. I think it was more than the certainty of the Crucifixion that weighed upon Him. It was His place in the whole eternal plan of the creation of the earth, of the peopling of the earth, of the divine plan under which men might be redeemed and move on to eternal life if they are willing to accept His commandments and live by them. His great message was a twofold message of love and peace in an atmosphere of hatred and conflict. . . . Of course there were other great teachers. There were others who taught the Golden Rule. There were others who taught great concepts of love and peace. But here is one who taught with great power and then sealed that teaching with His very life in an offering beyond comprehension."[52]

President Hinckley returned home on a Saturday evening to a schedule that showed no respect for jet lag or his age. Sunday at 8:00 A.M. he addressed the annual mission presidents' seminar at the MTC in Provo; then he returned to Salt Lake City and spoke to a capacity audience of Kiwanis International members in the Tabernacle. The following day he and Sister Hinckley drove to Cove Fort, Utah, where his brother Sherman was serving as director of the visitors center, to participate in the arrival there of the Utah Centennial wagon train, and he spoke to an audience of nearly twenty thousand gathered for "family home evening with the prophet." During his remarks he contrasted his travels of the past five weeks, during which he had visited seventeen countries, with the challenges faced by those who had colonized the West and laid the foundations of the restored gospel: "As we flew over this trail of our people [en route home from Jerusalem], when we could see between the clouds, the picture that kept going through my mind was of plodding wagons going fifteen miles a day in the heat and dust, with buffalo and rattlesnakes by the thousands to contend with. I don't know of anything else that compares with the coming of our people to the valleys of the mountains. What a price has been paid for that which we enjoy. We flew over that trail at 524 miles an hour." And he then returned to a familiar theme: "We have become a well-known people. The Church is coming out of darkness and obscurity across the world in a remarkable and wonderful way, in fulfillment of the plea made in the dedicatory prayer of the Kirtland Temple when the Prophet pleaded that it would come out of obscurity and darkness and stand fair as the moon and clear as the sun and terrible as an army with banners."[53]

It was almost impossible for President Hinckley to visit Cove Fort without thinking of his forebears, particularly his grandfather and father, who had left a legacy of faith and devotion that he had spent a lifetime trying to emulate. His grandfather had helped pioneer the West, and perhaps from that example he had acquired an abiding respect for those who blazed trails into the unknown. And it had been his father who, years earlier, had admonished him to forget himself and go to work. Through good times and bad, during joyous moments and experiences laden with frustration and heartache, while enduring layovers in smoke-filled airports and long, turbulent flights from one continent to another, he had taken his father's counsel to heart: Indeed, he had long since ceased to be concerned principally about his own needs and comfort and had forgotten himself and gone to work. Consequently, his was a ministry that had spanned more than half the twentieth century, had covered the globe, and had required him again and again to do some modern-day pioneering of his own. There were few corners of the world in which he hadn't walked, talked, listened, taught, and testified, and there were literally no peoples for whom he did not feel great affection and esteem.

In his concluding remarks at the April 1996 general conference, President Hinckley once again shared his enthusiasm for the work in which he had been engaged his entire life: "There are still those, not a few, who criticize and rebel, who apostatize and lift their voices against this work. We have always had them. They speak their piece as they walk across the stage of life, and then they are soon forgotten. . . . [But] we go forward, marching as with an army with banners emblazoned with the everlasting truth. We are a cause that is militant for truth and goodness. We are a body of Christian soldiers 'marching as to war, with the cross of Jesus going on before.' . . . Everywhere we go we see great vitality in this work. There is enthusiasm wherever it is organized. It is the work of the Redeemer. It is the gospel of good news. It is something to be happy and excited about."[54]

He didn't reserve such zeal and vision for the Tabernacle

pulpit. Indeed, everywhere he traveled, as he raised his voice in congregations large and small, in secular as well as religious settings, his prescience and optimism about what lay ahead, his energy, and his testimony of the Risen Lord and the Church that bore His name were infectious. During the rededication of London's Hyde Park Chapel, he told the overflow multicultural audience: "I've seen it all, from very small beginnings when we had only rented halls to tonight with this large congregation. You are a fulfillment tonight of the great words of Jeremiah, who said, speaking in the name of the Lord, 'I will take you one of a city, and two of a family, and I will bring you to Zion: and I will give you pastures according to mine heart.' (Jeremiah 3:14–15.) You are the fulfillment of that. This is Zion for you, and you are being fed by the message of the Lord."

His interest, as he explained, was never in the number of converts but in the power of the message to change people's lives: "What a glorious work this is! How thankful I am, how grateful I am, for the gospel of Jesus Christ. . . . I have seen the miracles of the gospel in this land. I have seen men who were dissolute in their lives, but who were touched by the power of this gospel and became giants. I have seen women who were chore women who have become queens in this work. That's the whole purpose of it . . . to lead the way, to lift us up, to point the path that we can walk to eternal glory."[55]

In some respects, he *had* seen it all—everything from a staff at Church headquarters whose numbers could be counted on two hands to a sprawling organization that spanned the globe with thousands of employees and further thousands of dedicated volunteers; from intimate gatherings of fledgling members in the Orient to overflowing audiences of capable and dedicated Saints in massive halls there; from a missionary program crippled by the side effects of war to a force of over fifty thousand; from the dedication of the first temple outside North America to the construction and dedication of dozens of temples on foreign soil; from a Church that essentially employed no media to one that could communicate instantly and globally with its millions of members via a sophisticated satellite network and other advanced technologies.

"I marvel at what is happening in this Church," he told a

fireside audience in Crawley, England, representative of numerous other settings. "But I am not surprised, because I know its mission. I know its destiny. I know what the Lord has said concerning it, that it should roll forth and fill the whole earth. . . . There is nothing like this work anywhere else on earth, my brothers and sisters. I know people in many churches, and I have friends in various churches, and I appreciate them. But I know that this is the only true and living church upon the face of the whole earth. The Lord Himself has declared it to be so, and I make no apology for it. It may sound egotistical, it may sound arrogant, but I wasn't the author of that statement. The Lord Himself is the author, and I believe it with all my heart."

He went on to bear powerful testimony: "God lives. He is our Eternal Father, the Creator and Governor of the Universe, the Almighty who is above all. He who is above all deigned to talk with a boy in a grove of trees in upstate New York. He who is above all will hear your prayer and hear mine. He lives. Jesus is the Christ, the foreordained Son of God who condescended to come to earth, who was born in a manger, in a conquered nation among a vassal people, the Son of God, the Only Begotten of the Father in the flesh, the Firstborn of the Father and the Author of our salvation. He is our Redeemer, our Savior, through whose Atonement eternal life is made possible for all who will walk in obedience to His teachings. May testimony grow in our hearts that this is in reality the church of the living God and that it will continue to gain momentum and move forward to fulfill its divine destiny."[56]

Since 1933, when he had accepted a call to serve in the European Mission, Gordon B. Hinckley had devoted essentially his entire life to the onward march of the gospel kingdom. All he had learned, everything he had witnessed had filled him with an impenetrable testimony of the work of God. Now, as President of the Church, he would continue to press forward, admonishing all within his reach and influence to follow what he had found to be the only straight and secure course, the scriptural words given to him by his father when he left for his mission: "Be not afraid, only believe."

I know that my Redeemer lives,
Triumphant Savior, Son of God,
Victorious over pain and death,
My King, my Leader, and my Lord.

He lives, my one sure rock of faith,
The one bright hope of men on earth,
The beacon to a better way,
The light beyond the veil of death.

Oh, give me thy sweet Spirit still,
The peace that comes alone from thee,
The faith to walk the lonely road
That leads to thine eternity.

Gordon B. Hinckley
Hymns, no. 135

APPENDIX A

TIME LINE

1 July 1843	Ira Nathaniel Hinckley baptized in Nauvoo, Illinois
9 July 1867	Bryant S. Hinckley (father of GBH) born in Coalville, Summit County, Utah, to Ira Nathaniel and Angeline W. Hinckley
1867	Ira Nathaniel Hinckley called by Brigham Young to build fort at Cove Creek, Utah
23 June 1910	GBH born in Salt Lake City to Bryant S. and Ada Bitner Hinckley
23 November 1911	Marjorie Pay born in Nephi, Utah, to LeRoy and Georgetta Pay
1917	GBH entered school at the Hamilton School
1918	Older brother Stanford died of pneumonia in France during World War I
28 April 1919	Baptized by his father
June 1928	Graduated from LDS High School
24 October 1929	Wall Street crash plunged country into the Great Depression
9 November 1930	Ada Bitner Hinckley died
June 1932	Graduated from University of Utah
1933–35	Served as missionary in European Mission, headquartered in London, England
August 1935	Became executive secretary of Church Radio, Publicity, and Mission Literature Committee
1936–37	Served as Sunday School superintendent of Liberty Stake
29 April 1937	Married Marjorie Pay
1937–46	Served on Sunday School General Board
1939	Supervised production of Church exhibit at San Francisco World's Fair on Treasure Island
31 March 1939	Kathleen Hinckley born
November 1940–May 1941	Built home in East Millcreek
2 May 1941	Richard Gordon Hinckley born
7 December 1941	Japan bombed Pearl Harbor, inciting United States entry into World War II
1943	Accepted position as assistant superintendent of Salt Lake City Union Depot and Railroad Company
Summer 1944	Promoted to assistant manager of mail, baggage, and express at Denver and Rio Grande Railroad headquarters in Denver, Colorado
January 1945	Family moved to Denver
8 February 1945	Virginia Hinckley born
7 May 1945	Germany surrendered
14 May 1945	President Heber J. Grant died

21 May 1945	George Albert Smith ordained as eighth President of the Church
7 September 1945	Japanese surrendered, bringing World War II to a close
Fall 1945	Family returned to Salt Lake City
20 April 1946	Called as second counselor to President Lamont B. Gundersen, Salt Lake East Millcreek Stake presidency
30 October 1947	Clark Bryant Hinckley born
24 January 1948	Supervised reconstruction of Henry Bigler cabin commemorating centennial of discovery of gold in Coloma, California
14 November 1948	Called as first counselor in East Millcreek Stake presidency
October 1949	General conference first broadcast over KSL Television
25 June 1950	North Korea invaded South Korea
4 April 1951	President George Albert Smith died
9 April 1951	David O. McKay sustained as ninth President of the Church
1951	Called by President Stephen L Richards to serve as executive secretary of the General Missionary Committee
27 July 1953	Accord ending Korean War signed at Panmunjom
5 August 1953	David O. McKay broke ground for temple in Zollikofen, Switzerland
1953	Asked by President McKay to help with preparation of temple instruction to be presented in different languages in Swiss Temple
27 February 1954	Jane Hinckley born
11–15 September 1955	Attended dedication of Swiss Temple
11–14 March 1956	Attended dedication of Los Angeles Temple
28 October 1956	Called as president of Salt Lake East Millcreek Stake by Elders Harold B. Lee and George Q. Morris
6 April 1958	Called as Assistant to the Quorum of the Twelve; Church membership just over 1.5 million in 273 stakes, 2500 wards and branches
20 April 1958	Attended dedication of New Zealand Temple
17 August 1958	Released as president of East Millcreek Stake
7–9 September 1958	Attended dedication of London Temple
17 May 1959	Dedicated East Millcreek Stake Center and Second Ward chapel
19 May 1959	President Stephen L Richards died
13 November 1959	Performed marriage of Kathleen to Alan Barnes in Salt Lake Temple
Early 1960	Given responsibility by President Henry D. Moyle to supervise the Southern Far East and Northern Far East Missions
March 1960	First Presidency asked General Priesthood Committee, chaired by Harold B. Lee, to study Church programs and curriculum with object of providing for better "correlation"
29 April–18 June 1960	Made first trip to Asia (Japan, Korea, Okinawa, Taiwan, Philippines, Hong Kong)
28 April 1961	Initiated missionary work in Philippines during sunrise service at American Battle Memorial Cemetery in Manila; one native Filipino member in attendance
16 May 1961	Was in Seoul, Korea, during coup d'état
5 June 1961	Bryant S. Hinckley died
30 September 1961	Sustained a member of the Quorum of the Twelve; Church had 1.8 million members in 345 stakes
February–March 1962	GBH took Marjorie with him for first time to Asia

March 1962	Age at which young men were called on missions lowered from twenty to nineteen
Summer 1962	Accompanied President Henry D. Moyle on tour of twenty-one missions in Great Britain and Europe
31 January 1963	David O. McKay reorganized Missionary Executive Committee with Joseph Fielding Smith as chairman, Marion G. Romney, Gordon B. Hinckley, and Boyd K. Packer as members
22 May 1963	Dedicated Haapu Branch in Tahiti; boatload of Church members returning to Maupiti Island killed in shipwreck
July 1963	Richard returned from mission in Germany
18 September 1963	President Henry D. Moyle died
4 October 1963	First Presidency reorganized with Hugh B. Brown as first counselor and N. Eldon Tanner as second; Thomas S. Monson, age thirty-six, called to Quorum of the Twelve
6 October 1963	Spoke on CBS "Church of the Air" program
20 October 1963	Dedicated Pearl Harbor Stake Center
22 November 1963	President John F. Kennedy assassinated
September 1964	Public announcement of creation of Bonneville International, with GBH as a vice president and signatory
17 November 1964	Participated in Oakland Temple dedication, at which President David O. McKay presided
November–December 1964	Traveled around the world with Marjorie, stopping in Asia, India, the Holy Land, Greece, Germany, Belgium, and England
10 September 1965	Performed marriage of Virginia to James Pearce in Salt Lake Temple
22 September 1965	Due to Vietnam War, missionary quota of two per ward established within U.S. to comply with Selective Service
28 October 1965	Joseph Fielding Smith and Thorpe B. Isaacson appointed as counselors in First Presidency
29 January 1966	Presented first copy of Chinese translation of the Book of Mormon to President David O. McKay
1 May 1966	First stake in South America created at São Paulo, Brazil
Summer 1966	Hinckley family visited New York City for World's Fair
30 September 1966	Was one of three incorporators of Deseret Management Corporation
9–23 October 1966	Dedicated chapels in Seoul, Korea; Naha, Okinawa; Taipei, Taiwan; and Makati, Philippines
29 October 1966	Visited Saigon with Elder Marion D. Hanks and Keith E. Garner
30 October 1966	Atop Caravelle Hotel in Saigon, dedicated South Vietnam for preaching of gospel
2 November 1966	With Elder Marion D. Hanks, dedicated Thailand for preaching of gospel in Bangkok's Lumpini Park
Early 1967	Korean edition of the Book of Mormon published
March 1967	Clark entered LTM en route to North Argentine Mission
11–27 April 1967	Accompanied President Hugh B. Brown on first visit to Orient by member of First Presidency
11–19 May 1967	Made first trip to South America
28 July 1967	Performed marriage of Richard to Jane Everett Freed in Salt Lake Temple
29 September 1967	Sixty-nine men called as Regional Representatives

30 October–2 November 1967	Attended servicemen's conference in Berchtesgaden, Germany
12 May–5 November 1968	Involved in helping defeat liquor-by-the-drink referendum in Utah
1 June 1968	Released as area supervisor in Asia; given responsibility for work in South America
22 November–3 December 1968	Made first trip to South America as area supervisor
June 1969	First missionaries sent to Spain, Clark Hinckley among them
1 November 1969	Southeast Asia Mission, headquartered in Singapore, formally opened
18 January 1970	President David O. McKay died at age ninety-six
23 January 1970	Joseph Fielding Smith ordained tenth President of the Church; Harold B. Lee and N. Eldon Tanner named as counselors
2 February 1970	Youngest sister, Sylvia, passed away after bout with cancer
22 February 1970	Organized Lima Peru Stake
13 March 1970	With Elders Ezra Taft Benson and Hugh B. Brown, dedicated Mormon Pavilion at Expo '70 World's Fair in Osaka, Japan
15 March 1970	With Elder Ezra Taft Benson, created the first stake in Asia in Tokyo, Japan
16 March 1970	With Elder Ezra Taft Benson, created Japan East Mission
April 1970	Appointed as adviser to Primary and Sunday School; also chaired Children's Correlation Committee
5 April 1970	Boyd K. Packer called to Quorum of the Twelve
31 May 1970	Devastating earthquake hit Peru seconds after GBH's plane departed from Lima; he returned on 4 June to assist Saints there
24 July 1970	President Richard M. Nixon visited Salt Lake City
25 February 1971	Received Distinguished Service Award from University of Utah Alumni Association
18 May 1971	Assigned to direct European-Germanic Area
29 June 1971	Named president and chairman of executive committee, Deseret News Publishing Company
30 July 1971	Made first trip to Germany and Switzerland as area supervisor
27–29 August 1971	Attended first area conference of Church in Manchester, England
19 October 1971	With Elders Thomas S. Monson and Boyd K. Packer, helped organize Genesis Group for black Saints
12 November 1971	Attended inauguration of Dallin H. Oaks as president of BYU
18 January 1972	President Joseph Fielding Smith dedicated Ogden Temple
5 February 1972	Released as chairman of the Children's Correlation Committee; assigned as one of three advisers to First Presidency on matters of correlation, doctrine, and Church procedure
9 February 1972	President Joseph Fielding Smith dedicated Provo Temple
18 February 1972	Named to Utah Power and Light board of directors
2 July 1972	President Joseph Fielding Smith died at age ninety-five
7 July 1972	Harold B. Lee ordained eleventh President of the Church; N. Eldon Tanner and Marion G. Romney named as counselors
September 1972	Traveled to Holy Land with President Harold B. Lee

19 September 1972	Visited Mars Hill in Greece and offered prayer there that President Lee said would stand as rededication of land of Greece
28 September 1972	Attended press conference at Waldorf Astoria in New York City with President Harold B. Lee upon return from Europe and Holy Land
25 May 1973	With President Spencer W. Kimball, spoke at dedication of Brigham Young home plus four other restored buildings in Nauvoo
25 August 1973	Attended Munich Area Conference
27 August 1973	Traveled through Britain with President and Sister Lee
8 October 1973	Performed marriage of Clark to Kathleen Hansen in Salt Lake Temple
26 December 1973	President Harold B. Lee died at age seventy-four
29 December 1973	Spoke at President Lee's funeral
30 December 1973	Spencer W. Kimball ordained twelfth President of the Church; N. Eldon Tanner and Marion G. Romney named as counselors
April 1974	At general conference, President Kimball delivered landmark talk about missionary work to Regional Representatives—according to GBH, the "greatest ever given in these seminars"
26 June 1974	Met with Jerusalem mayor Teddy Kollek regarding Orson Hyde Memorial Garden
September 1974	Hosted special guests at Washington Temple open house, including First Lady Betty Ford
9 September 1974	Attended and offered benediction at cornerstone-laying ceremony for Washington Temple
12 September 1974	Offered invocation in Congress
19 November 1974	Participated in dedication of Washington Temple, at which President Kimball presided
13 February 1975	Received new assignments, removing him from the missionary committee for the first time in forty years
17–18 March 1975	Hosted VIP tours for ministers at Arizona Temple prior to rededication
10 April 1975	Named chairman of executive committee, BYU board of trustees
15–16 April 1975	President Kimball rededicated Arizona Temple after remodeling; GBH attended and spoke
3 May 1975	First Presidency announced creation of area supervisory program; GBH assigned as adviser to Atlantic North Area
10 June 1975	Performed marriage of Jane to Roger Dudley in Salt Lal Temple
27 June 1975	End of auxiliary conferences announced during opening session of 1975 June Conference
24 July 1975	President Kimball dedicated 28-story Church Office Building
August 1975	Attended area conferences in Asia, including meetings in Tokyo, Hong Kong, Taipei, Manila, Seoul; Tokyo Temple announced
3 October 1975	President Kimball announced new organization of First Quorum of the Seventy
10 October 1975	Met Japanese emperor in San Francisco

3 April 1976	Members attending general conference accepted Joseph Smith's Vision of the Celestial Kingdom and Joseph F. Smith's Vision of the Redemption of the Dead for addition to Pearl of Great Price (these scriptures became part of D&C on 6 June 1979)
June 1976	All stakes and missions in world placed under direct supervision of area advisers and supervisors; GBH assigned Japan, Korea, Southeast Asia, and Philippines
5 June 1976	Four executive committees established within Quorum of the Twelve; GBH assigned to chair Melchizedek Priesthood Executive Committee
15–24 December 1977	Traveled to Japan with BYU football team
8 February 1978	Named to executive committee, Zion's National Bank board
31 March 1978	President Kimball announced in Regional Representatives' seminar that stake conferences would be held semiannually rather than quarterly
Spring 1978	Appointed with Elder Boyd K. Packer as adviser to Historical Department
28 May 1978	With Elder David B. Haight, presided over creation of three stakes in Royal Albert Hall in London
1 June 1978	Spoke at dedicatory service for South Visitors Center on Temple Square
9 June 1978	In letter dated 8 June, First Presidency announced revelation that all worthy males were now eligible to receive priesthood. On 30 September Saints accepted this revelation by sustaining vote at general conference
August 1978	Met King Juan Carlos I of Spain and José Luis Alvarez, mayor of Madrid
9 September 1978	New missionary training program announced: Missionaries assigned to English-speaking missions to receive four weeks of training; those learning languages to receive eight weeks of training at Missionary Training Center
30 September 1978	James E. Faust called to Quorum of the Twelve; new emeritus status for General Authorities announced in general conference
24 October 1978	Attended South Africa Area Conference
30 October 1978	Attended dedication of São Paulo Temple, presided over by President Kimball
18 February 1979	Church's 1,000th stake created at Nauvoo, Illinois
13 March 1979	Attended rededication of Logan Temple
20 April 1979	Received honorary Doctor of Humanities degree at BYU
23–24 June 1979	Attended Houston Area Conference, first in continental U.S.
7 September 1979	President Kimball had first brain surgery for subdural hematoma
26 October 1979	Received title to Newel K. Whitney Store in behalf of the Church
November 1979	President Kimball had second brain surgery
27 March 1980	GBH essay on Joseph Smith included in *Congressional Record*
6 April 1980	Joined President Kimball and Elder Hugh W. Pinnock in Peter Whitmer's farm home in Fayette, New York, for sesquicentennial satellite broadcast; read proclamation from First Presidency and Quorum of the Twelve
7 April 1980	With J. Willard Marriott Jr., was interviewed by Tom Brokaw on *Today* show

9 May 1980	Announcement of Jeffrey R. Holland as new BYU president
13–27 May 1980	Accompanied BYU Young Ambassadors to China
18 October–1 November 1980	Attended area conferences in Philippines, Hong Kong, Taiwan, and Japan
27 October 1980	Attended dedication of Tokyo Temple, at which President Kimball presided
17 November 1980	Attended dedication of Seattle Temple, at which President Kimball presided
27 February 1981	First saw "Joseph Smith III" document
13 March 1981	Accompanied President Kimball to meet President Ronald Reagan
April 1981	President Kimball announced plans to build temples in Chicago, Dallas, Guatemala City, Lima, Frankfurt, Stockholm, Seoul, Manila, and Johannesburg
May 1981	Accompanied BYU performing groups to Yugoslavia, Romania, and Russia
30–31 May 1981	On way home from Russia, stopped in Japan to organize Tokyo South Stake and Hiroshima Stake
15 July 1981	Called by President Kimball to serve as counselor in the First Presidency
23 July 1981	Set apart as counselor to President Spencer W. Kimball
15 August 1981	Participated in cornerstone laying at Jordan River Temple
23 August 1981	Dedicated national headquarters of Sons of Utah Pioneers
5 September 1981	President Kimball had third and most serious brain surgery
3 October 1981	Network of five hundred satellite dishes announced for stake centers outside Utah
16 November 1981	Participated in Jordan River Temple dedication, at which President Marion G. Romney presided
18 March 1982	Three Church executive committees announced: Missionary Executive Committee, Priesthood Executive Committee, Temple and Genealogy Executive Committee (later the Temple and Family History Executive Council)
April 1982	Announced that temples would be built in Boise, Denver, Guayaquil, and Taipei
1 April 1982	Announced that Church membership had reached five million
2 April 1982	At general conference, changes in financing Church meetinghouses were announced, shifting construction costs to general Church funds and utility costs to local units
2 April 1982	Announced that missionaries would serve eighteen rather than twenty-four months
6 May 1982	Admitted to LDS Hospital for first-ever overnight hospital stay
30 June 1982	Equal Rights Amendment defeated after ten-year struggle
14 August 1982	Dedicated seventeen historical sites in Nauvoo
25, 27 August 1982	Presided at groundbreaking for Manila and Taipei Temples
10 September 1982	Hosted President Ronald Reagan in tour of Church cannery to see Church welfare program in operation
13 September 1982	Ruth Hinckley Willes, sister of GBH, died of cancer
3 October 1982	First Presidency announced addition of subtitle to the Book of Mormon: "Another Testament of Jesus Christ"
27 November 1982	President N. Eldon Tanner died
2 December 1982	First Presidency reorganized; GBH called as second counselor to President Kimball

5 December 1982	Conducted and spoke at Churchwide youth fireside on morality in first use of the satellite network beyond general conference
22 January 1983	Presided at groundbreaking for Dallas Temple
4 March 1983	First Presidency authorized purchase of document purported to be original agreement between Joseph Smith and E. B. Grandin for publication of Book of Mormon
3 April 1983	Rededicated renovated Assembly Hall on Temple Square
1–4 June 1983	Dedicated Atlanta Temple
5–7 August 1983	Dedicated temple in Apia, Western Samoa
9 August 1983	Dedicated temple in Tonga
13 August 1983	Presided at groundbreaking of Chicago Temple
15–17 September 1983	Dedicated temple in Santiago, Chile
27–29 October 1983	Dedicated temple in Papeete, Tahiti
2–4 December 1983	Dedicated Mexico City Temple
4 April 1984	Dedicated Museum of Church History and Art in Salt Lake City
7 April 1984	First temporary members of First Quorum of Seventy called for three- to five-year terms
7 April 1984	First Presidency announced plans to build temples in Las Vegas, Portland, San Diego, Toronto, and Bogota
19 May 1984	Presided at groundbreaking of Denver Temple
25–30 May 1984	Dedicated Boise Idaho Temple
June 1984	First Presidency announced call of Area Presidencies from members of First Quorum of Seventy to direct thirteen geographical areas around the world
20–23 September 1984	Dedicated Sydney Australia Temple
25–27 September 1984	Dedicated Manila Philippines Temple
19 October 1984	Dedicated Dallas Texas Temple
28 October 1984	Church's 1500th stake—Ciudad Obregon Mexico Yaqui Stake—created 150 years after first stake was organized in Kirtland, Ohio
17–18 November 1984	Dedicated Taipei Taiwan Temple
26 November 1984	First Presidency announced that, beginning 1 January, term of full-time missionary service for single elders would return to twenty-four months
14–16 December 1984	Dedicated Guatemala City Temple
January 1985	Latter-day Saints in U.S. participated in special fast to benefit victims of famine in Africa and other parts of the world. Fast raised more than $6 million
10 March 1985	Spoke at Churchwide fireside on using new LDS editions of scriptures
3 April 1985	Spoke at historic gathering of all mission presidents from around the world
29–30 June 1985	Dedicated Freiberg Temple in German Democratic Republic
1 July 1985	Presided at groundbreaking for Frankfurt Temple
2–4 July 1985	Dedicated Stockholm Temple
28 July 1985	Spoke at commemoration ceremony of fiftieth anniversary of Angel Moroni Monument at Hill Cumorah
9–13 August 1985	Dedicated Chicago Temple
24–25 August 1985	Dedicated Johannesburg South Africa Temple
15 October 1985	Steven F. Christensen and Kathy Sheets killed by bombs
16 October 1985	Mark Hofmann injured by bomb

23 October 1985	With Elders Dallin H. Oaks and Hugh W. Pinnock, held press conference regarding Mark Hoffman documents and related murders
23 October 1985	Dedicated Church Genealogical Library (renamed Family History Library in 1987)
5 November 1985	President Spencer W. Kimball died at age ninety
9 November 1985	Spoke at President Kimball's funeral
10 November 1985	Ezra Taft Benson ordained thirteenth President of the Church; Gordon B. Hinckley and Thomas S. Monson named as counselors
30 November 1985	Presided at groundbreaking of Las Vegas Temple
14 December 1985	Dedicated Seoul Korea Temple
10 January 1986	Dedicated Lima Peru Temple
20 February 1986	Received Silver Beaver Award from Great Salt Lake Council of Boy Scouts of America
March 1986	Church's missionary force surpassed 30,000
6 April 1986	Solemn assembly for President Ezra Taft Benson; GBH sustained as first counselor, Thomas S. Monson as second counselor
19–20 April 1986	Presided at regional conference in Buenos Aires
30 April 1986	Church membership reached an estimated six million
31 May 1986	Received honorary doctorate from Westminster College
7 June 1986	Received honorary doctor of humanities degree from Utah State University
20 September 1986	Presided at groundbreaking of Portland Temple
4 October 1986	Seventies quorums in stakes throughout Church discontinued; responsibility for teaching gospel assigned to all priesthood holders
5 October 1986	First Presidency issued statement opposing legalization of gambling and government sponsorship of lotteries
24 October 1986	Participated in dedication of Denver Colorado Temple, at which President Benson presided
23 January 1987	Documents dealer Mark Hofmann imprisoned after a plea-bargain arrangement in which he admitted responsibility for bombing deaths; he also confessed he had forged the "Salamander Letter" and other documents relating to Church
27 January 1987	Soviet Union leader Mikhail Gorbachev proposed economic and social reforms that signaled era of "glasnost" or openness in Communist countries
12 March 1987	Announced that Hotel Utah, a landmark in downtown Salt Lake City for seventy-six years, would close as hotel and be renovated as meetinghouse and office building
24–26 July 1987	Attended commemoration in London, England, of Church's 150th anniversary of first missionary work in Great Britain
3–14 September 1987	Traveled to Hong Kong with children for fiftieth wedding anniversary
15 October 1987	President Benson suffered a mild heart attack
20 May 1988	President Marion G. Romney died
1 June 1988	Church was granted legal recognition in Hungary
2 July 1988	Met with President José Sarney of Brazil and presented Book of Mormon to him
24–28 October 1988	President Monson led delegation of Church leaders to meet with German Democratic Republic's top government officials

12 November 1988	President Monson announced that Church had been granted rights to send missionaries to GDR and for LDS youth from GDR to serve as missionaries in other countries
1 April 1989	Second Quorum of Seventy created; all General Authorities serving five-year terms sustained as members
16 May 1989	President Howard W. Hunter dedicated the BYU Jerusalem Center
15 June 1989	Ground broken for first LDS meetinghouse in Poland
27 June 1989	Dedicated renovated Carthage Jail complex with President Benson; highlighted commemoration of 150th anniversary of Mormon settlement of Nauvoo
19 August 1989	Dedicated Portland Oregon Temple
7 October 1989	Dedicated four final restoration projects in Nauvoo as part of sesquicentennial celebration
8 October 1989	Dedicated addition to Chicago Temple
27 October 1989	Presided at and conducted convocation to install Rex Lee as BYU's tenth president
8 November 1989	Honored by Utah Chapter of Freedoms Foundation at Valley Forge for cultivating patriotism
9 November 1989	Berlin Wall came down
25 November 1989	Budget allowance program for financing local Church units in U.S. and Canada announced by First Presidency
16 December 1989	Dedicated Las Vegas Nevada Temple
27–29 April 1990	Soviet Union's ambassador to U.S., Yuri V. Dubinin, made historic visit to Utah and announced that LDS missionaries were welcome in Russia
4 May 1990	Received Distinguished Citizenship award from Sons of American Revolution
July 1990	New missions in Czechoslovakia, Hungary, and Poland highlighted record of twenty-nine missions created in 1990
25 August 1990	Dedicated Toronto Ontario Temple
13 September 1990	Registration of Leningrad Branch of Church approved by Council of Religious Affairs in the Soviet Union
19, 23 September 1990	President Benson underwent surgeries to remove subdural hematomas
November 1990	First Presidency announced new policy for U.S. and Canada, effective 1 January 1991, to equalize contributions required to maintain full-time missionaries
1 May 1991	500,000th full-time missionary in this dispensation called
22–24 June 1991	Rededicated Alberta Temple
24 June 1991	Russian Republic, largest in former Soviet Union, granted formal recognition to Church
1 September 1991	Church membership reached eight million
9 March 1992	Presented Book of Mormon to King Juan Carlos I of Spain
4 April 1992	Virginia Hinckley Pearce sustained as first counselor in Young Women General Presidency
12 June 1992	Received honorary doctorate from University of Utah
17 July 1992	President George Bush visited First Presidency
15 August 1992	Commemorated "Second Rescue" of ill-fated Willie and Martin handcart companies; dedicated three monuments near South Pass, Wyoming
18 October 1992	During rededication of London Temple, announced that land had been acquired in Preston for second temple in British Isles

23–25 October 1992	Rededicated Swiss Temple
25 April 1993	Dedicated San Diego Temple
27 June 1993	Dedicated renovated Hotel Utah, now renamed Joseph Smith Memorial Building
9 October 1993	Presided at groundbreaking for Mt. Timpanogos Temple in American Fork, Utah
30 October 1993	Presided at groundbreaking of St. Louis Temple
4 December 1993	Announced temple for Santo Domingo, Dominican Republic
13 February 1994	First Presidency announced that Uintah Tabernacle in Vernal, Utah, would be converted into a temple
19 February 1994	First Presidency issued statement opposing efforts to legalize same-gender marriages
6 March 1994	Announced that government of Cambodia had officially recognized Church; missionary couples would be sent to Cambodia to perform humanitarian services
10 March 1994	Dedicated three new buildings at Missionary Training Center
21 May 1994	Dedicated restored fort at Cove Fort, Utah
27 May 1994	Received Silver Buffalo Award at national Boy Scouts of America annual meeting
30 May 1994	President Ezra Taft Benson died at age ninety-four
3 June 1994	Received honorary doctor of humanities degree from Southern Utah University, Cedar City, Utah
5 June 1994	President Howard W. Hunter ordained fourteenth President of the Church; President Hinckley set apart as first counselor and President of Quorum of the Twelve, President Monson as second counselor
12 June 1994	Presided at groundbreaking for Preston England Temple
26 June 1994	With President Hunter and Elder Ballard, spoke at three events in Nauvoo and Carthage commemorating 150th anniversary of Martyrdom
29 June 1994	Received Minuteman Award from Utah National Guard
23 July 1994	Dedicated monument and burial site of fifteen handcart pioneers of Willie company on high plains of Wyoming
6 August 1994	Missionary Department announced that one-third of U.S. population had been visited by Church representatives and that 36 percent had friends or relatives who were LDS
8–16 August 1994	President Hunter took first trip out of United States since becoming President of Church; met with temple workers at Swiss Temple and addressed Lausanne Ward members
1 October 1994	Howard W. Hunter sustained as President of the Church in solemn assembly; President Hinckley sustained as first counselor and President of Twelve, President Monson as second counselor
9–11 October 1994	Participated in dedication of Orlando Florida Temple, at which President Hunter presided
November 1994	First Presidency announced plans to build temple in Nashville, Tennessee
11 December 1994	President Hunter created 2,000th stake of Church in Mexico City
8–14 January 1995	Participated in dedication of Bountiful Utah Temple, at which President Hunter presided

12 January 1995	President Hunter hospitalized for four days for treatment of prostate cancer
21 January 1995	First Presidency announced temples for Cochabamba, Bolivia, and Recife, Brazil
21 February 1995	Honored by Utah Region of National Conference of Christians and Jews
3 March 1995	President Howard W. Hunter died at age eighty-seven
12 March 1995	Ordained fifteenth President of the Church by President Thomas S. Monson; President Monson set apart as first counselor, President James E. Faust as second counselor
1 April 1995	Sustained as President of the Church at a solemn assembly; Henry B. Eyring called to Quorum of the Twelve; all Regional Representatives released and Area Authority position announced
April–August 1995	Presided at regional conferences in St. Louis, Missouri; Boston, Massachusetts; Springville and Heber City, Utah; Santa Rosa and Vacaville, California; Pocatello, Idaho; Anchorage, Alaska; and Tacoma, Washington
13 May 1995	Presided at groundbreaking for Vernal Tabernacle to be transformed into a temple
24 August–2 September 1995	Presided at creation of Canterbury England Stake, rededicated Hyde Park Chapel in London, and met with Saints in England and Ireland
23 September 1995	Addressed general Relief Society meeting—read Proclamation on the Family from First Presidency and Quorum of the Twelve
30 September 1995	Announced temples in White Plains, New York, and Boston, Massachusetts
29 October 1995	Presided at regional conference in Rexburg, Idaho
2 November 1995	Named Presiding Bishop Merrill J. Bateman president of BYU and member of First Quorum of Seventy
6 November 1995	Spoke at service in Salt Lake City memorializing assassination of Israeli Prime Minister Yitzhak Rabin
13 November 1995	Met with President Bill Clinton and Vice President Al Gore at White House
13 November 1995	Spoke at luncheon in New York City's Harvard Club
18 December 1995	Interviewed by Mike Wallace from CBS's *60 Minutes*
23 December 1995	First Presidency and Quorum of the Twelve released new Church logo featuring more prominently the words *Jesus Christ*
27 December 1995	First Presidency announced temple in Monterrey, Mexico
4 January 1996	Spoke at Utah centennial celebration in Tabernacle
7 January 1996	Presided at regional conference in Corpus Christi, Texas
18 January 1996	Announced publicly that General Authorities would no longer sit on boards of directors so that they could more fully dedicate themselves to their ministry
January–April 1996	Presided at regional conferences in Veracruz, Mexico; Oahu, Hawaii; Charlotte, North Carolina; Fort Worth, Texas; the BYU married students; Smithfield and Logan, Utah; and Pittsburgh, Pennsylvania
26 February 1996	*Deseret News* announced that Latter-day Saints living outside U.S. now outnumbered members living in the country
28 February 1996	Sister Hinckley received BYU's Exemplary Womanhood Award

5 March 1996	Conferred honorary doctorates on Lady Margaret Thatcher and Rex E. Lee at Brigham Young University special service
10 March 1996	Interviewed second time by Mike Wallace
15 March 1996	Spoke at funeral of Rex E. Lee, former president of BYU
7 April 1996	Profile of President Hinckley and the Church aired on *60 Minutes*
25 April 1996	Presided at inauguration of BYU President Merrill J. Bateman
30 March 1996	Spoke at General Young Women Meeting
26 April 1996	Spoke to 18,000 full-time missionaries serving in the United States and Canada via satellite
16 May–2 June 1996	Traveled to Asia for meetings in Tokyo, Osaka, and Fukuoka, Japan; Naha, Okinawa; Pusan and Seoul, Korea; Taipei, Taiwan; Hong Kong; Phnom Penh, Cambodia; Ho Chi Minh City and Hanoi, Vietnam; Manila and Cebu City, Philippines
26–27 May 1996	Dedicated Hong Kong Temple
27–28 May 1996	Traveled into mainland China, with an overnight stay in Shenzhen
29 May 1996	Dedicated Cambodia for preaching of gospel; in Hanoi, offered "addendum" to original dedicatory prayer to include the entire country of Vietnam
30 May 1996	Addressed 35,000 Filipino Saints at Araneta Coliseum in Manila
11 June 1996	Presided at groundbreaking of Madrid Temple in Spain
12–14 June 1996	Spoke to missionaries and members in Brussels, The Hague, and Copenhagen
15–16 June 1996	Presided at regional conference in Berlin, Germany
17–22 June 1996	Visited Holy Land
23 June 1996	Addressed mission presidents' seminar at the MTC, and spoke to Kiwanis International convention at the Tabernacle
24 June 1996	Spoke to crowd of more than 10,000 at "family home evening" at Cove Fort, Utah
29 June 1996	Rededicated This Is the Place Monument in Salt Lake City and spoke to crowd of some 10,000
29 June 1996	Received Golden Plate Award from American Academy of Achievement in Sun Valley, Idaho
11–14 July 1996	Visited Nauvoo, Palmyra, the Hill Cumorah Pageant, the Sacred Grove, Council Bluffs (including dedication of the Kanesville Tabernacle), Tulsa, Oklahoma, and Kansas City, Missouri
4 August 1996	Spoke at Provo Centennial Fireside at Marriott Center
30 August 1996	Announced Billings Montana Temple
1 September 1996	Spoke to American Legion convention in Tabernacle
2 September 1996	Honored by American Legion with "Good Guy Award"
14–15 September 1996	Presided at Eugene Oregon regional conference
17 September 1996	Spoke to more than 23,000 BYU students at Marriott Center

APPENDIX B

PRESS INTERVIEWS

Appendix B contains excerpts from major interviews and press conferences in which President Hinckley participated during his first eighteen months as President of the Church. Excerpts are arranged according to interview.

INTERVIEW BY PHIL RIESEN, KUTV TELEVISION, SALT LAKE CITY, 12 MAY 1995

Q. For many churches in America, declining membership is the crisis to be reckoned with. It's just the opposite, it seems, for the Mormon church. There is explosive growth within the Church. Is that one of the main things you have to deal with now, managing that growth?

A. Growth is a serious problem for us, of course. But it is a wonderful problem. What a wonderful thing, to be growing, to be vital and alive and moving forward. And that's what is happening now. That entails many problems—acquisition of land, building of chapels, building of temples, all of these things. But it is a wonderful problem to face, really, when all is said and done.

Q. For a long while nonmembers, and perhaps even some members in good standing, of the Church sort of looked at the Church as "them against us." It was the "Mormons" and the "non-Mormons." That had a tendency to drive a wedge in communities and neighborhoods. Are you concerned that that perception is still there? And if you are concerned about it, are you working hard to erase, to eradicate that sort of thing?

A. I am concerned about any vestige of that kind that may be left. We want to be good neighbors; we want to be good friends. We feel we can differ theologically with people without being disagreeable in any sense. We hope they feel the same way toward us. We have many friends and many associations with people who are not of our faith, with whom we deal constantly, and we have a wonderful relationship. It disturbs me when I hear about any antagonisms of the kind that you've mentioned. I don't think they are necessary. I hope that we can overcome them.

Q. What would you do, what would you say to members of the Church and nonmembers of the Church that would help alleviate that beyond what you have just said to me?

A. Be friendly. Be understanding. Be tolerant. Be considerate. Be respectful of the opinions and feelings of other people. Recognize their virtues; don't look for their faults. Look for their strengths and their virtues, and you will find strength and virtues that will be helpful in your own life.

Q. The Church has a way of dealing with dissident members that to even the nonmembers of the Church seems at times a bit harsh. I know the reasons must go much deeper than what appears on the surface, but the message that is portrayed, it seems, when a member is disfellowshipped or excommunicated is "Stray from the central belief and you're out. Don't question or you're out." Does that perceived rigidity lead to miscommunication and problems?

A. I think the problem is not understood. In the first place, the Church does not talk about what takes place in disciplinary councils where such matters are considered. Those who are dealt with there are the ones who speak; the Church doesn't respond generally to that kind of thing. It would be inappropriate for me to discuss, for instance, any particular case because the First Presidency becomes the court of appeal in these matters and I am not familiar with the details. When they come to us in the proper form, we will give careful consideration to them and make a judgment at that time. But really, this is a minor thing—a little handful who, over a period of some years now, have been excommunicated—in comparison with the tremendous growth that is going on. We are talking of five, six, seven, eight cases in a church of nine million people. Really, it is minuscule. For those people who are dealt with it is a major thing, of course, and I don't want to minimize it. We regard it with seriousness, great seriousness. We value every member of this church, active or inactive. We want to help lift them. We want them to be happy. We want to encourage them. We want them to grow in faith and faithfulness. That is our aim and objective. When cases come along they are handled on a local basis in all instances.

Q. And you in your conference talks have almost extended an olive branch to the people who have left the Church.

A. I have. I have. They are always welcome to come back. They will find many to welcome them with great warmth and love and affection. We are anxious to help them all. We have no antagonism against people. We are trying to be as Christlike as we can be.

Q. How does the Church feel about bringing the Olympics to Utah? I know there has been no official stand taken.

A. Institutionally we have remained neutral because we know that it's a two-sided question and that we have members on both sides of that question. If Salt Lake gets the bid and becomes the city for the 2002 Winter Olympics, we will be cooperative, we will be helpful, we will do what we can to take advantage of the opportunity that will be afforded through the visits of people from all over the world who will gather here. We hope that it will be a productive time.

Q. Are you troubled by what you see going on in the world today? I mean, when you stop and think about the insanity of Oklahoma City, the diseases running rampant in our culture and our society because of all kinds of different things, the wars and the rumors of war. Are you troubled by what you see in the world?

A. I am deeply troubled, seriously troubled. I can't understand why there is so much of hatred in the world, why there needs to be hatred of any kind. We ought to live together as sons and daughters of God. We have a common Father. That means that we are brothers and sisters and we ought to live together in that way. The deplorable conditions that we see of civil war and conflict and all of the problems of hunger and strife and poverty across the world, yes, and right at home—the disintegration of the family that we see so broadly across this nation, yes, I feel a very deep concern. Suffering troubles me. I just do not like to see people suffer. And in so many cases it would be avoidable if they would live the simple law of the golden rule: Doing unto others as they would be done by would so change this troubled world. And that is our message, a message of peace and of mutual respect of one to another. That is the burden of what we have to teach.

Q. It is probably nearly impossible to explain the reverence Church members feel for you and your position. And it's probably almost equally impossible to explain to nonmembers of the Church who you are and what you stand for. I think we have gotten some degree of understanding about that in this interview. But could you say a few words to each side of that equation that I just gave you, something that might lead both sides to a deeper understanding of who Gordon B. Hinckley is?

A. In the first place, of course, this is a tremendous and sacred trust which is imposed upon me. I do not take it lightly. It is a very serious responsibility and one which I regard most seriously. I have only one desire, and that is to bring about an increased measure of happiness in the lives of people. We have a scripture which says that "wickedness never was happiness." People are happy when they are living right, when they are doing the right things. That is my desire, to increase that through the teachings of the gospel of Jesus Christ, who is our Master and our Lord and whose name is carried in the name of this church. And in that spirit we want to reach out to our own people and those not of our own faith. I think we have done a great deal of reaching out in the Church in recent times. We have extended our humanitarian aid across the world. We've given millions of dollars, really, to the aid of the suffering in many nations. We've sent tons and tons of clothing, of medical supplies, of all kinds of things to help people who are not of our faith. We've worked with the organizations of other churches in accomplishing that. We feel an obligation to all humanity, and I hope that we are doing what we can to fill that obligation. And we want to exercise that same spirit of charity and love and mutual respect in our own neighborhoods, our own communities, in the city, in the state in which we live, and help those not only of our own faith but of other faiths. And we say to those of other faiths, look at us, investigate us, study us. If we have anything of good report to offer to you, accept it—and we look for the good in you and recognize much of it and hope that you will see some of the good in us.

Q. Your legacy as President of the Church undoubtedly will be your decades of service to the Church and the community. Beyond your position as President, what would you want your grandchildren and your great-grandchildren to remember Grandpa Hinckley for?

A. I would hope that I might be held in remembrance as a man who tried to do some good in the world, to make the world a better place, to improve it. And as a man who walked with integrity with his associates, both those in the Church and out of the Church, with love and appreciation for the goodness that he saw in people wherever he went.

INTERVIEW BY GUSTAV NIEBUHR, *THE NEW YORK TIMES*, 17 JULY 1995

Q. Have you made any provisions should you become incapacitated?

A. It's all built into the system. I have two counselors—able, experienced, remarkably fine men. If anything happens to me that I am unable to function, they carry on. I had that experience myself. There was a time during President Kimball's tenure that I was the only counselor able to function and I had that experience. And I had that experience likewise with President Monson during the tenure of President Benson. The work goes on. It didn't slacken at all. It went forward on its course. And that's another thing that's interesting—the man who succeeds to the presidency of the Church comes out of a long experience. He's come from the newest man in the Council of the Twelve to the senior man in the Council of the Twelve. During that time of service, he's traveled widely across the world; he develops a world perspective. He knows the program of the Church intimately. He's trained, he's educated, he's winnowed and refined and the chaff is blown off during years of service before he becomes the President of the Church.

Q. So revelation may be received through the First Presidency?

A. Oh, yes, it has to be. This is a vital organization. Things are happening all across the world every day. . . . We have strong local leaders in whom we have confidence. This church operates on the basis of trust, so to speak. It begins at the top and works down. Now, once in a while there's a glitch. Once in a while there's a failure. Once in a while there's some freakish thing that might happen, but that's seldom, and it's really an aberration.

Q. I would like to get your broad views of the Church and American society.

A. Let me say first as a basic premise that no nation can afford to shut religion out of its public life. I think that the history of Communism provides a credible background for that statement. But our Founding Fathers certainly did not have in mind any system under which religion would be foreclosed as a part of the lives of the people of this nation, nor that there should be a prohibition against a public expression of humility for the Almighty and the seeking of His blessings upon the people of the land. Let me say further that we, institutionally as a church, have upheld the principle of the separation of church and state. The Founding Fathers had come out of a background where there was a state church, and they wanted no more of it. And we believe that they were inspired by the Almighty in the writing of the Constitution and the Bill of Rights, the first amendment to that Constitution, which provided for freedom of worship. Hopefully, there will never be a time in our national life when there will be any kind of legal attempt to foreclose that practice. Now, anything that can be done to encourage the spirituality of the people, and acknowledgment of the Almighty on their part, and the humility and strength that will come therefrom, ought to receive encouragement so long as its aim is not to foster any particular religion or theology.

Q. As President of a church that endured real persecution in the nineteenth century, do you think there has been discrimination in the last fifteen or twenty years in our society?

A. Certainly there have been instances of it. I think there's no question about it. Unfortunately, people can't seem to be tolerant and respectful of the views of others in so many cases. We must cultivate in this land an attitude of tolerance and respect for the beliefs and rights of others. We must cultivate an increased spirit of civility among people in their expressions one to another, and toward the beliefs and practices of others. We can disagree with people without being disagreeable. We can disagree without raising our voices and becoming angry and vindictive in our ways. We must learn to do so. We must practice a greater spirit of Christ in our lives, we as a Christian community, of love one for another, and extend that to all people regardless of whom they worship or how they worship, so long as they do not infringe upon the rights of others.

Q. There are probably few places in the world as well equipped as Salt Lake City is to handle the diversity of languages that will present themselves when the Olympics come to Utah.

A. Yes, we can talk to the people in their own tongues. I tell you, this missionary program is a miracle. You take a nineteen-year-old boy and call him to serve as a missionary of this church, and you put on his narrow shoulders the responsibility of representing this church before the world; you put your trust and confidence in him and ordain him to the priesthood to serve in that capacity. And he goes out and he mingles with the rich and the poor in lands across the world, whether it be walking up and down the steep roads of Victoria Island in Hong Kong, or in the dark of night in the winters of Norway, Sweden, and Finland, or wherever. They learn to appreciate people, not as tourists but sitting with them at their firesides in their homes, discussing this great church and what it can mean to them and what effect it will have in their lives. And things happen. People listen to them and they join the Church. They're baptized and they become leaders. It is wonderful! Really, it is a miracle! And they learn languages and speak them like natives. I was told once that the American ambassador to Finland said, "There are only two groups of people who learn Finnish—babies and Mormon missionaries."

INTERVIEW WITH LAWRENCE SPICER, LONDON NEWS SERVICE, LONDON, ENGLAND, 28 AUGUST 1995

Q. You are the fastest-growing Christian denomination in this country. What do you reckon accounts for that success?

A. We think that people have in their hearts a desire to improve their lives and develop their spirituality. There is within each of us something that longs for a kinship with the Almighty, and we feel that there is a response to that as we teach concerning that. We feel we are meeting the needs of people. We have a great program for the development of spirituality and for learning and for sociality and all of the things that satisfy the needs of people.

Q. What is it that The Church of Jesus Christ of Latter-day Saints has, in your view, that makes it more attractive to some people than the established churches?

A. The Church is a constant in a world of change. It is an anchor in a world of shifting values. It emphasizes the importance of family, and all of us have to know that family life is unraveling across the world. We are holding onto the family. We are trying to strengthen the family. We teach family ideals. We have a great program for the development of family solidarity, and we think that's satisfying a human need and offers hope to many, many people who are desperately looking for something as fathers and mothers. Divorce is rampant across the world, and growing. There is a need for stability. The family is the basic organization of society. A nation can be no stronger than the strength of its families.

Q. Your detractors refer to you as a very "right-wing" church, and very recently in this country we've seen television programs that comment on the Mormons as such. Do you think this is because you are unchanging?

A. I'd rather be "right-wing" than "wrong-wing," and I think that we have perhaps been on the conservative side of things. We are not among those who are out experimenting with everything all the time. The doctrine remains unchangeable. We modify the program from time to time to accommodate certain needs and certain situations, but the doctrine remains constant, and it's that constancy that provides this foundation which becomes a straight and narrow path, if you please, on which to walk.

Q. You are accused of being a "white" church.

A. We are not a "white church," for goodness sakes. I was here at a meeting in Wandsworth where I suppose 50 percent of those in that congregation were of African descent. One of the men who was installed as a member of the stake presidency, as we call it—the head of a diocese—is a black man from Accra, Ghana. We are reaching out across the world. I was with a little group of missionaries today who were in training. One was from St. Petersburg, one from Moscow, one from Budapest, one from Paris, one from Spain—and that's indicative of what's happening. This is a great cosmopolitan body. It is marvelous what is happening. I was here as a missionary sixty-two years ago, and to note the contrast between our congregations then and our congregations now has been wonderful. We might have been considered a white church then. They were all white Englishmen. But today it is a cosmopolitan group, just as cosmopolitan as London itself. The languages in which we are dealing are wide and varied and, really, it's a miraculous thing.

Q. How far do you see your church entering into the ecumenical movement, which is strong in this country?

A. We like to be able to get along with all people. We recognize the good in all churches. We recognize the value of religion generally. We say to everyone, we tell you to live the teachings which you have received from your church. We invite you to come and learn from us, to see if we can add to those teachings and enhance your life and your understanding of things sacred and divine. We work with people on common causes, many of them, all across the world. We recognize theological differences. We believe that we can disagree theologically without being disagreeable, and we hope to do so. We have been rather careful about surrendering in any way our doctrinal standards or anything of that kind as part of an ecumenical effort, but we certainly have worked with people, and do work with people, and want to work with other groups in tackling common social problems.

PRESS CONFERENCE AT THE HARVARD CLUB, NEW YORK CITY, NEW YORK, 13 NOVEMBER 1995

Opening Statement by President Hinckley:

Ladies and Gentlemen, thank you very much for being here. It has been suggested that we come and talk about the Church just a little. I would like to point out two or three things that I hope might be of interest to you concerning what we are trying to do and perhaps what we are accomplishing. We are no longer a Utah church. We once were regarded as a Utah church. Fifty years ago, 55 percent of the membership of the Church resided in the state of Utah. Seventeen percent of the membership of the Church now resides in the state of Utah. We are now working in some 155 nations and territories. We have 22,000 congregations who meet each Sunday and speak a great variety of languages, from pole to pole almost, as it were. There is a tremendous vigor and vitality about this work, about this program, and we hope that it is touching for good the lives of people in the many lands in which we operate.

We have a core of missionaries. Our missionary system is different. We invite our young men, call them when they are nineteen years of age, to give two years of their lives to go out. And you will find them everywhere from Thailand to Argentina. Next February our statistical people tell us that for the first time in our history we will have more members of the Church outside the United States than we have in the United States. I think that is a significant thing. We now have more than nine million members, and we are growing at the rate of about a million each three to three and a half years. It took the Church a hundred years to reach its first million, and, as I say, we are now growing at the rate of about a million each three and a half years. And that impetus will increase as the years pass.

We have this great body of young men and some young women. It is a great thing. It is a remarkable program. It is a program under which, at a time when a young man is most prone to think of himself, he is sent where he can forget himself in the service of others. It has tremendous consequences.

We are carrying on a great welfare and humanitarian service. Our welfare program, as we know it today, was begun during the Great Depression and puts tremendous emphasis on self-reliance. We try to teach our people to be self-reliant and, when they can't take care of their own needs, to enlist the help of their families. And when those needs cannot be met by the families, then the Church moves in to help them. We have a great program that involves farm properties, ranching properties, field properties where people can work and grow that which they eat. We have flour mills, we have grain storage, we have meat-processing plants, we have all of these things. We operate 99 storehouses, more than 100 employment centers, 46 thrift stores. In 1994, members donated the equivalent of over 150,000 days of labor in such facilities to help those who are in distress and in need. During the past ten years the Church has provided disaster relief and self-reliance development in 109 countries. The value has exceeded $30 million per year in humanitarian gifts to those not of our faith in many parts of the world. There are, on an average, 400 humanitarian projects each year. We have, for instance, underwritten in large measure an orphanage in India and a boarding school for the blind in Kenya in which 300 blind children in a school operated by the Salvation Army are supplied with mattresses and blankets for their beds, storage boxes for personal items, pajamas, towels and soap, educational supplies, and things such as that. In Albania full-time Church service volunteers have been providing training through attendance in a hospital for severely malnourished infants and at a pediatrics and family practice department of the medical school in the struggling country of Albania. More than $1.3 million in food, soap, clothing assistance have been provided to tens of thousands of refugees in Rwanda and Burundi. And so it goes. We have assisted with flood conditions in China, in Korea, many places.

We think that we have added to the health of the nation. We try to live by a code of health which we feel is divinely inspired. You would be interested to know that Utah has the lowest number of reported deaths from cancer—124 per 100,000. Active Church members are about one-third as likely to contract cancer as is the general population according to a study made by a professor at the University of California.

We put great emphasis on education. The high school graduation rate in Utah is 85.1 percent, as compared to a national average of 75.2 percent. We teach as a principle of our doctrine that the glory of God is intelligence, and that is reflected in our membership. Incidentally, a study recently made indicates that the higher the education level of those who are members of the Church, the more active, the more faithful, the more diligent they are in their work. I think that is a unique thing. The activity rate is higher among Ph.D.s than it is among high school graduates, which says something of tremendous significance.

We advocate strong family relationships. We have problems, of course we do. But with all of these in Utah, where 70 percent of the population is LDS, we have the fewest births to unmarried women per capita in the United States—135 per one thousand live births—whereas the national average is 300 per one thousand live births.

We have a tremendous program for religious education for our young people. Not in the public schools, but in harmony, if I can say, with the public schools. We conduct seminaries on private properties adjacent to public schools wherever we can do so. That program reaches out to over 600,000 youth across the world.

As we grow we have to build buildings. We have about 375 buildings under construction at all times, which means about 375 new buildings a year. That is a tremendous undertaking. I do not know of any other organization that is building 375 new houses of worship a year across the world. I think it is all indicative of the vitality and the strength and the outreach of this great organization. People are coming into the Church—solid, wonderful people.

Again, thank you very much for being here. If you have questions, comments, suggestions, we would be happy to talk with you.

Q. When any organization and especially when a church decides to hire a public relations firm, a spinmeister, what is it they are trying to spin? Are you concerned about misconceptions about the Mormon Church?

A. There are still many ideas that persist concerning us. We are not well-known, our people. We have grown up in the West. The Church originated in Palmyra, New York. You have all heard of the Mormon migration to the West and the establishment of modern irrigation practice by Mormon people in the West, where we established some three or four hundred different communities. Utah is now being discovered, but it wasn't for a long, long time. We would like to clear up that misconception and let people come to know us for what we are and what we are trying to accomplish.

Q. Are there any conflicts between your convictions about families and women's roles within the family and the aspirations of some women to occupy leadership positions in your church?

A. We have a few, yes. We have a few women who feel that women should hold the priesthood. We have a great women's organization. I believe it is the largest women's organization in the world—our women's Relief Society. They have their own officers who preside over their own organization. They carry forward a tremendous program of education among women. I think they are happy. They are doing a great work. Now, of course we have a few who say, "I should do this, and I should have this, and so forth," and they talk of women's rights. We believe in women's rights. We try to foster them. I think you will discover that the women of this church are happy. There may be a few who are unhappy. But you would find that in any society.

INTERVIEW WITH MIKE WALLACE, SALT LAKE CITY, UTAH, 18 DECEMBER 1995

Q. Since World War II, we seem to be splintering; we seem to be becoming more selfish, more self-absorbed, less community-minded. Families don't seem to mean so much, and morality has gone to hell in a handbasket. Why?

A. The basic failure is in our homes. Parents haven't measured up to their responsibilities. It is evident. A nation will rise no higher than the strength of its homes. If you want to reform a nation, you begin with families, with parents who teach their children principles and values that are positive and affirmative and will lead them to worthwhile endeavors. That is the basic failure that has taken place in America. And we are making a tremendous effort to bring about greater solidarity in families. Parents have no greater responsibility in this world than the bringing up of their children in the right way, and they will have no greater satisfaction as the years pass than to see those children grow in integrity and honesty and make something of their lives, adding to society because they are a part of it.

Q. Your church has a very strict health code. Why is that a part of religion?

A. The body is the temple of the spirit. The body is sacred. It was created in the image of God. It is something to be cared for and used for good purposes. It ought to be taken care of, and this thing which we call the Word of Wisdom, which is a code of health, is most helpful in doing that.

Q. For some, particularly those who are not Mormons, your teachings demand conformity, rigidity. Those are the complaints one hears.

A. Oh, yes, you may hear those complaints. I don't think it is so. I don't think there is substance to it. Our people have tremendous liberty. They are free to live their lives as they please.

Q. Are they?

A. Oh, absolutely. Surely. They have to make choices. It is the old eternal battle that has been going on since the war in heaven, spoken of in the book of Revelation. The forces of evil against the forces of good. We all exercise agency in the choices we make.

Q. You also have a moral code.

A. We believe in chastity before marriage and total fidelity after marriage. That sums it up. That is the way to happiness in living. That is the way to satisfaction. It brings peace in the heart and peace in the home.

Q. Some of the students we've talked to say that the health code is easy compared to no premarital sex. And that does not mean necessarily intercourse. They say that not smoking or not drinking is a clear line, but that the sexual line is somewhere way before intercourse and they are confused, some of them anyway, about where that line is.

A. Oh, I think they know. Any young man or woman who has grown up in this church knows where that line is. When you see yourself slipping, begin to exercise some self-discipline. And if it is a serious problem, take it to the Lord. Talk with God about it. Share your burden with Him. He will give you strength. He will help you. They know that. I am confident they know that.

Q. Why must only men run the Church?

A. "Only men" do not run the Church. Men have their place in the Church. Men hold the priesthood offices of the Church. But women have a tremendous place in this church. They have their own organization. It was started in 1842 by the Prophet Joseph Smith, called the Relief Society, because its initial purpose was to administer help to those in need. It has grown to be, I think, the largest women's organization in the world with a membership of more than three million. They have their own offices, their own presidency, their own board. That reaches down to the smallest unit of the Church everywhere in the world.

Q. But they don't have the power.

A. They have office. They have responsibility. They have control of their organization.

Q. But you run it. The men run it. Look, I'm not being . . .
A. The men hold the priesthood, yes. But my wife is my companion. In this Church the man neither walks ahead of his wife nor behind his wife but at her side. They are co-equals in this life in a great enterprise.

Q. There are those who say that Mormonism began as a cult. You don't like to hear that.
A. I don't know what that means, really. But if it has negative connotations, I don't accept it as applying to this church. People may have applied it, they may have applied it in the early days. But look, here is this great church now. There are only six churches in America with more members than this church. We are the second church in membership in the state of California. We are reaching out across the world. We are in more than 150 nations. This is a great, strong, viable organization with a tremendous outreach across the world. . . . You will find our people in business institutions, high in educational circles, in politics, in government, in whatever. We are ordinary people trying to do an extraordinary work.

Q. It's expensive to be a Mormon.
A. Oh, it isn't expensive. You are living by the law of the Lord—tithing.
Q. But ten percent of your gross goes to the Church and you have nothing to do with the way the money is spent. An average Mormon, that is.
A. The average Mormon has a good deal to do with it. He is a member of the Church. That money is spent in his local unit.
Q. But he has nothing to do with how it is going to be spent.
A. If he is a bishop, he has the expenditures of his ward. A lot of that money comes back to the local units. What is that money used for? It is used for Church purposes.
Q. What are Church purposes exactly?
A. Building chapels. About 375 a year. Think about that. New buildings each year to accommodate the needs of the growing membership. It is used for education. We maintain the largest private, Church-sponsored university in the world, Brigham Young University, with its 27,000 students on that campus, as well as other campuses. We maintain a tremendous institute of religion program, where we have off-campus connection with the major universities of America. You will find institutes at UCLA, USC, Harvard, Yale, Princeton, the University of New York, the University of Massachusetts, the Massachusetts Institute of Technology, and so forth.

When it comes to the financial circumstances of the Church, we have all funds carefully audited. We have a corps of auditors who are qualified CPAs, who are independent from all other agencies of the Church and who report only to the First Presidency of the Church. We try to be very careful. I keep on the credenza behind my desk a widow's mite that was given me in Jerusalem many years ago as a reminder, a constant reminder, of the sanctity of the funds which we have to deal with. They come from the widow, they are her offering as well as the tithe of the rich man, and they are to be used with care and discretion for the purposes of the Lord. We treat them carefully and safeguard them and try in every way that we can to see that they are used as we feel the Lord would have them used for the upbuilding of His work and the betterment of people.

Q. Young men and women give two years of their lives to serve as missionaries?
A. Young women serve eighteen months. The work is strenuous, it is difficult. It isn't easy to go to New York, or London, or Tokyo and knock on doors and face people you have never met before. But it does something for you. It does two or three things. It creates in the first place a feeling of reliance upon the Lord. It isn't easy for a young man to do that. It builds within him something of strength and capacity. If he goes to a foreign land, he develops expertise in the language; he learns to speak the language of the people. Wherever he goes he comes to know the people among whom he serves and brings back with him something of their culture, their way of doing things, with appreciation and respect for them and their conditions and

circumstances. There is nothing like it. When you think that we have nearly 50,000 out right now, and that number is constantly rotating so that it touches the lives of hundreds of thousands of these people. . . . I can walk down the streets of Salt Lake City with you and meet people who speak fluently in Japanese and Chinese and Swedish and Norwegian and Finnish and Spanish and Portuguese, and who have love in their hearts for the people among whom they served.

Q. Why are members of the Church expected to keep a year's supply of food, clothing, and fuel?

A. We teach self-reliance as a principle of life, that we ought to provide for ourselves and take care of our own needs. And so we encourage our people to have something, to plan ahead, keep a little food on hand, to establish a savings account, if possible, against a rainy day. Catastrophes come to people sometimes when least expected—unemployment, sickness, things of the kind. The individual, as we teach, ought to do for himself all that he can. When he has exhausted his resources, he ought to turn to his family to assist him. When the family can't do it, the Church takes over. And when the Church takes over, our great desire is to first take care of his immediate needs and then to help him for so long as he needs to be helped, but in that process to assist him in training, in securing employment, in finding some way of getting on his feet again. That's the whole objective of this great welfare program.

Q. Mr. President, the Church actively campaigned against the Equal Rights Amendment.

A. Yes, indeed. And I think the wisdom of that has been shown in what has happened. We weren't alone in that. We did take an active part in that and have had no regrets concerning it. We think the outcome was what it should have been.

Q. Why are you against equal rights for women?

A. We give women things that I think no other organization in the world gives. Opportunity for education. We stress it. Opportunity for growth. Opportunity to pray in public meetings. Opportunity to speak in public meetings. Opportunity to reach out and serve. They serve on the board of trustees of our university, where their voices are heard. They are heard in many of our councils.

Q. Why is Salt Lake City so clean?

A. Well, we hope it is a reflection of the people who live here.

Q. It is astonishing to walk down the streets of Salt Lake City.

A. We hope it will stay that way. I hope that it reflects, in some measure at least, some of the teachings of this church. Look at the beauties of Temple Square right there in the heart of the city, the very core of the city. Look at that magnificent temple and that great tabernacle. They were built with vision, by people with culture, with refinement, with artistry. They're not the work of charlatans. They are the work of people who had a great vision to do beautiful things.

Q. The Mormons, Mr. President, call you a "living Moses," a prophet who literally communicates with Jesus. How do you do that?

A. I do it in prayer. Let me say first that there is a tremendous history behind this church, a history of prophecy, a history of revelation, and a backlog of decisions which set the pattern of the Church so that there aren't constant recurring problems that require any special dispensation. But there are occasionally things that arise where the will of the Lord is sought, and in those circumstances I think the best way I could describe the process is to liken it to the experience of Elijah as set forth in First Kings. Elijah spoke to the Lord and there was a wind, a great wind, and the Lord was not in the wind. And there was a tempest, or an earthquake, and the Lord was not in the earthquake. And there was a fire, and the Lord was not in the fire. And after the fire a still, small voice, which I describe as the whisperings of the Spirit. Now, let me just say, categorically, that the things of God are understood by the Spirit of God, and one must have and seek and cultivate that Spirit, and there comes understanding and it is real. I can give testimony of that.

Q. Why is your church so aggressive about spreading the word, having missionaries knock on doors where they may not be welcome and where they're obviously not invited?

A. We believe that the Lord meant what He said when He said, "Go ye into all the world and preach the gospel to every creature." We believe in that mandate. We think it rests upon us to try to fulfill it. We are doing that with all of the energy and resources that we have.

Q. How do you view non-Mormons?

A. With love and respect. I have many non-Mormon friends. I respect them. I have the greatest of admiration for them.

Q. Despite the fact that they haven't really seen the light yet?

A. Yes. To anybody who is not of this church, I say we recognize all of the virtues and the good that you have. Bring it with you and see if we might add to it.

Q. Tell me about Brigham Young.

A. Brigham Young had a prophetic vision. Can anyone doubt it who looks around here today? No. And that's the way it is with this church. It has been led by revelation. We believe all that God has revealed, all that He does now reveal, and that He will yet reveal many great and important things pertaining to the kingdom of God for the blessing of His sons and daughters wherever they may be found.

SECOND INTERVIEW WITH MIKE WALLACE, SALT LAKE CITY, UTAH, 10 MARCH 1996

Q. As you know, some skeptics say that major changes in Church policy have come from political pressures, not necessarily as revelations from God. For example, the business of ending polygamy, say the skeptics, wasn't because it was revelation but because Utah wanted to become a state.

A. One of the purposes of a prophet is to seek the wisdom and the will of the Lord and to teach his people accordingly. It was the case with Moses when he led the children of Israel out of Egypt. It was the case for the Old Testament prophets when people were faced with oppression and trouble and difficulty. That is the purpose of a prophet, to give answers to people for the dilemmas in which they find themselves. That is what happens. That is what we see happen. Is it a matter of expediency, political expediency? No. Inspired guidance? Yes.

Q. How big a problem, Mr. President, is child abuse in the Mormon church?

A. I hope it isn't a big problem. We have had some problems. This is a serious phenomenon that is finding expression all over the world. It is a terrible thing. It is a wicked thing. It is a reprehensible thing. It is a thing of which I have spoken about time and again.

Q. What are you doing to reduce it?

A. We are doing everything we know how to reduce it. We are teaching our people. We are talking about it. We have set up a course of instruction for our bishops all across the nation. All last year we carried on an educational program. We have set up a hotline for them where they can get professional counseling and help with these problems. We have issued a journal dealing with child abuse, spouse abuse, abuse of the elderly, the whole problem of abuse. We are concerned about it. I am deeply concerned about the victims. My heart reaches out to them. I want to do everything we can to ease the pain, to preclude the happening of this evil and wicked thing. . . . I know of no other organization in this world that has taken more extensive measures, tried harder, done more to tackle this problem, to work with it, to do something to make a change. We recognize the terrible nature of it and we want to help our people, reach out to them, assist them.

Q. One sociologist tells us that the root of the problem is the fact that men, in effect, in your church have authority over women so that your clergymen tend to sympathize with the men being abusers instead of with the abused.

A. That is one person's opinion. I don't think there is any substance to it. I think that the men of this church, the bishops of this church, the officers of this church are as concerned with the welfare of the women of the Church as they are with the men of the Church and with the children of the Church. I wouldn't hesitate to say that for one minute. I am confident of that. I have been around a long time. I have known this church from the ground up, inside and out, over a very, very long period of time. I am eighty-five years of age now and I've lived with it all my life and I think I know how it functions. I think I know the attitude of our people. Now, there will be a blip here, a blip there, a mistake here, a mistake there. But by and large the work is wonderful, and vast good is being accomplished, and the welfare of women and children is as seriously considered as is the welfare of the men in this church, if not more so.

MEDIA LUNCHEON AND PRESS CONFERENCE, TOKYO MIYAKO HOTEL, 18 MAY 1996

Opening Statement by President Hinckley:

I am here in the interests of The Church of Jesus Christ of Latter-day Saints, the church of which I am pleased to be a part—an organization which we feel is doing vast good throughout the world. We're expanding and growing consistently and rapidly. We are now in 155 nations and territories. Our worldwide membership is now about nine and a half million people, and we are growing at a rate of about a million every three years. I am grateful for our membership in Japan. We have something over 100,000 members here. We have about 300 congregations. We have constructed about 180 buildings, and we have strong and stable members in Japan. All of our local leaders are native Japanese. They preside over our local congregations. They do it on a volunteer basis. . . . As a church we place great emphasis on the family. We believe that the family is the basic unit of society. No nation will be stronger than the strength of its families. If you want to reform any society, you begin by reforming the family, so we put great emphasis on strengthening family life. We believe in education. We foster education. We operate the largest private, religion-owned university in the world—Brigham Young University at Provo, Utah—and many young Japanese students have attended Brigham Young University and have graduated from that university. We deplore terrorism. We think it is a terrible evil wherever it manifests itself. We read with great sorrow the news report of the poison gas attacks that were carried on in Tokyo. Twelve of our employees were victims of those attacks, and many of our people suffered. We believe in the rule of law. If we have a grievance, we have to settle it in a lawful way and not with terroristic activity of any kind. Our entire aim is to teach the gospel of Jesus Christ, which is the gospel of peace among people. Our voice is a voice of peace to the entire world. We speak the words of Jesus Christ, who said, "Peace I give unto you."

Q. There are some historians who say that when they try to conduct historical research about the Church, they are not able to gain access to historical documents and materials, and that when they publish something that may not be exactly in accordance with the Church's views, they may even be excommunicated or leave the Church.

A. This church came about as a result of intellectual curiosity. We believe in education, as I have said. We spend a substantial part of our budget on education of our young people. We expect them to think. We expect them to investigate. We expect them to use their minds and dig deeply for knowledge in all fields. If we have a motto, it is this: "The glory of God is intelligence." Now, we have been investigated ever since the Church was organized. Scores and scores of people have investigated and written about us. Some of them have worn out their lives doing so. But some of the things in our libraries are of a confidential nature. We have a trust concerning the confidentiality of some of those matters, such as private diaries, but there has been very little of our story that has not been plowed over and plowed over. Scores of books have been written and the Church just goes on and on, and grows and grows. I don't think we have anything to be ashamed of there in any sense. I think we have so much to be proud of. . . . We have only one request, that you judge us by our fruits. Judge us by what the Church is doing, what it is accomplishing across the world. It is a marvelous thing that is happening. It is so positive in its message and so positive in its growth. Of course, we have critics. Of course, we make a mistake now and again. Of course, we fail in some things once in a while. That is to be expected. But overall, the picture is one of growth, of stability, of strength, of improvement, and of accomplishment.

Q. A certain number of scholars say that the Mormon church is not sensitive to the rights of women. There are no women in the General Authority leadership positions.

A. We have probably the largest women's organization in the world—over three million members—with their own leadership, with their own program, with their own courses of study, their own officers. I don't know of any other religious organization in the world that gives women as great an opportunity as they have in The Church of Jesus Christ of Latter-day Saints. I believe that my wife is just as important as I am in the plan of the Lord. In the Mormon way, the wife walks neither behind nor ahead of her husband, but at his side as his companion, his equal. I have three daughters and two sons. I love my daughters as much as I love my sons—maybe a little more so, they are so kind to me. But, I think our Father in Heaven regards His daughters the same way. I don't apologize for one minute for the Church's program for women. We have women sitting on the board of trustees of Brigham Young University; women spoke in the last general conference of the Church; they speak in our worship services, they offer prayers, they have all the advantages that the Church has to offer.

Q. We understand that the Church has proclaimed that it is against racial discrimination, but in the early days of the Church there was racial discrimination.

A. Let me say that we are just as vigorous in carrying forward our missionary program in Ghana, West Africa, as we are in Japan. I was in Ghana a while ago, and I looked into the faces of a great congregation that filled a big theater, all wonderful members of this church, all black—marvelous people, happy people, doing a great work. I have in my own heart, I can honestly say, a love for the sons and daughters of God everywhere. For thirty-six years I have worked with the Japanese and the Koreans and the Chinese, the Filipinos, the Vietnamese, the Indians, the Malaysians; they are my brothers and sisters, they are my friends and associates in this work. I have never felt any racial prejudice of any kind, and I have worked with the people in Africa. No, we cannot be accused, I think, of racial prejudice. The fact is, we are reaching out, we are going into these countries, reaching out, spending hundreds of millions of yen, as it were, reaching out across the world to embrace people everywhere in a great brotherhood and sisterhood united in the gospel of Jesus Christ.

Q. You speak of the entire human family as one large family. Does that include the Islamics and the Buddhists? Do you recognize at all that they should be members of the family as Buddhists or Islamics, or is it your mission to convert all of them into Christianity?

A. We recognize all people as sons and daughters of God. If God is our Father, then all of us are brothers and sisters, and we so recognize people. Now, we have Muslim people living in the United States. We recently made the facilities of our cannery available to them without any cost to them so that they might can food for their people in Bosnia. We are not actively proselyting in the Muslim nations, but we respect them and honor them in their religion and thank them for all the good they accomplish.

PRESS CONFERENCE IN SEOUL, KOREA, 22 MAY 1996

Opening Statement by President Hinckley:

Thank you for being here today. You do us a great honor by your presence. I had an appointment to go to Hong Kong and I said, "If I'm going to Hong Kong, I'll go to Japan and Korea on the way." I am not a stranger to this part of the world. I have been coming here since 1960. I think I have been here at least fifteen times. I was here in 1961 when the coup occurred. I was a witness to what took place on that occasion. I had something to do with a newspaper in the United States, and I sent a story on that coup long before the Associated Press knew what was going on. I very much enjoy this land. I like to come here. I like the people. I have many friends here.

I represent The Church of Jesus Christ of Latter-day Saints, which is growing rapidly across the world. We are now in 155 different nations and territories. We have a membership of about nine and a half million people. More of our people live outside of the United States than live in the United States, and so we have become a great worldwide church. This is the seventh largest church in the United States. It is the second largest church in the state of California, and wherever we go we are growing.

When I first came to Korea in 1960, we had a little handful of people. Today, we have almost 70,000 members of the Church in Korea. We have constructed eighty-eight buildings in this land, houses of worship. We have spent millions of dollars in building these facilities in Korea. We have never taken any money out of this land, but we have brought a great deal of money into this land to bless the people. We now have about 22,000 congregations across the world, with about 128 congregations who gather in worship services every Sunday in South Korea. Ours is a very demanding religion. We try to follow a strict code of health. We abstain from the use of alcohol and tobacco, and even from coffee and tea. We feel that all of this leads to good health. I am eighty-five years of age. I will be eighty-six next month, and I feel great. I am thankful to say I enjoy good health. Now, that isn't because I eat *kimchee*. Some *kimchee* I like, some *kimchee* I don't like.

I have had many wonderful experiences here over the years, and I am glad to be back. I am glad to see the Church growing here. We do not get involved in politics. We believe in the separation of church and state. We place great emphasis on good, wholesome family life. We believe that the family is the basic unit of society. If you want to build a strong nation, you cultivate strong families, and we have a program for this. Every Monday night, all across the world, our people observe what we call family home evening, where father and mother sit down with their children and read the scriptures together, discuss family problems, and try to resolve those problems in a spirit of love and harmony. We are a church which emphasizes the need for education. We maintain the largest private religious university in the world—Brigham Young University. I am chairman of the board of trustees of that university. I have always admired the great emphasis which the Koreans place on education and I am grateful for the emphasis which we, as a church, place on education.

Now, as I come here today, I can't help noticing the differences between what I find today and what I found the first time I came. Back then, in 1960, there was very much of poverty in this land, much of hunger. People were homeless; there were many orphans. I'm glad to see the prosperity of Korea. My dear friends, thank you for being with us. If you have a few questions, I would be happy to try to answer them.

Q. My understanding is that the Mormon church is not Protestant and also not Catholic. What is the basic characteristic of your church?

A. We believe in Jesus Christ as the Son of God. The official name of the Church is The Church of Jesus Christ of Latter-day Saints, and He is the central figure in all of our worship. We do not have a paid ministry. All of the local congregations of the Church, more than 22,000 of them, are presided over by local men who volunteer their time and their services in standing as the local leaders. All of the men work at their regular vocations and then serve as local leaders. They can do it because they have many others to assist them. Every adult member of the Church ought to have some responsibility in the Church, and that is the program which we follow and a very important differentiation.

Q. Your church originated 166 years ago by Joseph Smith?

A. Yes.

Q. You have the Book of Mormon in addition to the Bible? What does it contain?

A. The Book of Mormon is a translation of an ancient record that speaks of Jesus Christ. It becomes another witness, along with the Bible, of the divine mission of Jesus Christ. The Lord said, in the mouth of two or more witnesses shall all things be established. The Book of Mormon becomes that second witness. Do we believe in the Bible? Yes. Do we accept the Bible as the word of God? Yes. And the Book of Mormon becomes a companion with the Bible, the two standing hand in hand as witnesses of the divinity of Jesus Christ.

Now, there is another difference. Every man in this church who lives a clean life may hold the priesthood, may serve in that priesthood, may exercise that priesthood.

And there are other differences as well. We have a great volunteer missionary force. We have 50,000 missionaries. We have in Korea about 400 missionaries. About 20 percent of those are native Korean young men and young women. The young women serve for a period of eighteen months. The young men serve for a period of twenty-four months—two years. They go at their own expense and at the expense of their families. The Church does not compensate them. And they do a remarkable work wherever they go. It is a remarkable program.

Also, we are now building about 375 new buildings each year across the world. People ask how we can do it. We can do it because we do not have a paid ministry. The money of the Church which comes from the volunteer contributions of the people is spent to build facilities for the people rather than for any other purpose.

Q. In most religions the one who established the Church becomes a very important figure. What is your position on Joseph Smith?

A. Thank you for your question. It is a good question. Joseph Smith was the instrument through which this church was organized. In answer to his humble prayer, there appeared to him God the Eternal Father and the Lord Jesus Christ, and he restored the church which was upon the earth when Jesus was upon the earth. And, as the first President of the Church and the first prophet of the Church, he is held in very high esteem by us as a people. There have been fifteen Presidents of the Church, fourteen in succession from the time of Joseph Smith, and I have the high honor of serving as the fifteenth President of the Church.

Q. In the world there are many churches, like Catholics and Protestants and so forth. Many of them have hundreds if not thousands of years of history. Why do we need another church like the Mormon church?

A. Let me say first that we respect all other churches. We do not stand out in opposition to other churches. We respect all men for all the good that they do and we say to those of all churches, we honor the good that you do and we invite you to come and see what further good we can do for you. We think that we have some significant things to offer which are not found in other churches. But, I repeat, we respect all men. We believe in worshipping God according to the dictates of our own conscience and allow all men the same privilege, let them worship how, where, or what they may.

Q. We understand that you do not drink even coffee and tea. This is very restricted compared to other Christian churches. We have heard that the reason is for health purposes, but is there any religious reason behind this practice?

A. Yes. We believe that we are sons and daughters of God. He is our Eternal Father in Heaven. The body which we have is the temple of the spirit, and the body is sacred, and the body should not be abused. The body should be cared for. Health is a very precious thing. Anyone who is sick knows that. Because of the divine nature of man as a son of God, and our belief that the body is the temple that houses the spirit, we should take care of it. So yes, there is a religious purpose in this.

Q. What type of services for the community do you perform? Some churches send out doctors and are social-service providers. It looks as though you are purely preaching the gospel.

A. We carry on a great humanitarian work throughout the world. We send hundreds of thousands of dollars of clothing, food, medicine, educational materials, as well as money to help those in distress and need across the world. We have a great program to help those in need among ourselves. This is a unique feature. One Sunday a month, all members of the Church are expected to fast—to go without two meals—and contribute the value of those meals to help the poor and the needy and those in distress. We have a great welfare program under which all work together to help those in need. It is a marvelous humanitarian program.

PRESS CONFERENCE IN CONJUNCTION WITH GRAND ENCAMPMENT CELEBRATION, COUNCIL BLUFFS, IOWA, 13 JULY 1996

Opening Statement by President Hinckley:

I am delighted to be here in this beautiful state of Iowa. As we flew in a little while ago, I just could not help marveling at the magnificent beauty of the farms of Iowa. There is no greater farmland or better farms anywhere in the world than right here. If wherever agriculture is practiced it could be practiced as it is practiced in Iowa, there would be far less hunger in the world, I am confident of that. This is such a beautiful state. I wonder why our people did not stop here and stay here. But they said they wanted to go to a place "where the devil cannot come and dig us out." That is where they went, leaving this magnificent area in 1847.

We flew on Thursday morning to Nauvoo. We traveled 1,088 miles in two hours and eight minutes from Salt Lake City to Burlington, Iowa. I contrasted that with the fact that when the pioneer company crossed Iowa, they averaged two and a quarter miles a day, if the information I have is correct.

I want to thank the people of Iowa for the tremendous interest they have had in the 150th anniversary of the exodus of our people, which is a most singular thing. Ninety percent of the participants in these celebrations are not members of the Church but are people with a respect for our people and a love for the history of this area. What has happened has really been noteworthy in every respect. We could not have asked for anything more. Today we will dedicate the re-creation of the old log tabernacle at Miller's Hollow, as it was known in the days when the original was built, where Brigham Young was sustained as President of the Church on December 27, 1847, he having gone west to the valley of the Great Salt Lake and then having come back here. That proved the strength and the mettle of the man. I do not know how they stood that long, long ride, most of them in springless wagons jolting over the roughest kind of roads that were really no more than trails in Iowa, hub deep in the mud part of the way. Wherever they went, traveling was done with great difficulty and very slowly. They really blazed a trail from the Mississippi to the valley of the Great Salt Lake.

Well, my very deep appreciation to all who have participated and are participating to make of this a great celebration of a very significant part of American history.

Q. What do you see as the three greatest challenges facing the Church as you enter the twenty-first century?

A. Well, one word sums it up, and that is growth. Now the three great challenges are to increase the momentum of our work, which I think we can do, I am confident we can do. Secondly, to accommodate the growth with new buildings, which are required wherever we go. And the training of local leadership. All of our local congregations are presided over by volunteer workers not compensated financially in any way. As we grow it becomes necessary to train leaders, and that is a challenge. That is the same challenge that Brigham Young faced. We have faced it all through the years and will continue to face it as the Church grows across the world. But thus far we have met that challenge and, I think, handled it very, very well. We are building buildings in many countries, at the rate of about 375 new buildings a year across the world, which is really phenomenal. We have a tremendous program for training local leadership. Those are the challenges as I see them.

Q. Since many members of the Church are outside the United States, why should they care about this kind of historical reenactment [as was taking place in Council Bluffs, Iowa, on this occasion]? What does the Mormon Battalion mean, for example, to somebody in the Philippines?

A. I have just been among those people. They are proud of their church and they are proud of the roots of that church. They are proud of the foundation on which it is established. They want to know about it. They do come to know about it. They study about it, and it gives them the strength that comes of knowing that what they have has a tremendous background of courage and fortitude and sacrifice and faith. That to me is of tremendous significance to our people all across the world.

Q. The Mormon migration was one of the greatest movements of people in American history. How has that carried over into today's Church?

A. We are still pioneering. We have never ceased pioneering from the time that we did pioneer, that our people left Nauvoo and came here and then moved from here up the Elkhorn and the Platte and the Sweetwater, over the highlands of Wyoming, and down eventually into the valley of the Great Salt Lake. There was adventure in that. But the purpose of it was to find a place where they could establish themselves and worship God according to the dictates of conscience and afford that same privilege to others whom they invited among their midst. Now, we are still reaching out across the world into places that scarcely seemed possible to access a few years ago. Wherever we go, we go in the front door. We establish our credentials with government officials and move in in an open way, nothing secret or clandestine about the way it is done. It is all done open and above board with full knowledge of public officials. I have witnessed personally the growth of the Church in the Philippines. It was my privilege to open the missionary work there in 1961, when we were able to find one native Filipino member of the Church in a meeting which we held in May of 1961. The other day we were in Manila and had a congregation, so we were told by the manager of the facility, of some 35,000 in that great Araneta Coliseum in Manila. To me it is a miracle having been there, so to speak, on the ground floor when we opened the work in that great land of the Philippines. We are reaching out everywhere, and that takes pioneering. Our missionaries do not live under the best of circumstances when they go to some of these areas, but they go forward and do their work, and it bears fruit. Before long we have a handful of members, then a hundred members, and then five hundred members, and then a thousand members, and so on.

NOTES AND SOURCES

Limitations of space make it impossible to indicate every source examined in the preparation of this biography. The published articles about, public papers of, and addresses, articles, and books by Gordon B. Hinckley are voluminous, and a complete listing of them would require a book-sized presentation. I have therefore included only those materials I consulted directly in the writing of this biography.

Though President Hinckley's journal is somewhat inconsistent (his entries for some years are extensive, for others, sporadic), it nevertheless provided a wealth of information, both factual and contextual. I have also drawn heavily from nearly thirty personal interviews with President Hinckley, as well as in-depth interviews with Sister Hinckley, each of their children, and other family members, including his brother Sherman Hinckley, his sister Ramona Sullivan, and several grandchildren. Presidents Thomas S. Monson and James E. Faust, each member of the Quorum of the Twelve Apostles, and numerous other General Authorities and other Church leaders, as well as associates with whom he has worked through the years, also granted interviews. Unless specified otherwise, all interviews cited in the notes were conducted by me. Literally thousands of magazine and newspaper articles by and about President Hinckley exist, and those, along with the transcripts and published accounts of hundreds of his addresses and articles, were critical to the text.

President Hinckley's father, Bryant S. Hinckley, was a prolific writer, and some of his materials were most useful in providing background and context, including: *What of the Mormons? A Brief Study of The Church of Jesus Christ of Latter-day Saints* (Salt Lake City: Corporation of the President, 1947); *Some Distinctive Features of Mormonism* (Salt Lake City: Deseret Book, 1951); and *The Faith of Our Pioneer Fathers* (Salt Lake City: Deseret Book, 1956). In addition, many of his articles were published in various Church periodicals. Genealogical records and other sources provided important family history information, including "Bryant S. Hinckley," an unpublished address delivered before the Ira Nathaniel Hinckley family, 4 April 1955; "Ira Nathaniel Hinckley Biography and Family History," 1957, Harold B. Lee Library at Brigham Young University; Larry C. Porter, "A Historical Analysis of Cove Fort, Utah," master's thesis, BYU, May 1966; Parnell Hinckley, ed., "Ira Nathaniel Hinckley: Some Events of His Life," Harold B. Lee Library, BYU; "The Name and Family of Hinckley or Hinkley," compiled by the Media Research Bureau, Washington, D.C.; "Ira Nathaniel Hinckley Diary, 1857–1858," J. Reuben Clark Library, BYU; "Autobiography of Bryant Stringham Hinckley," arr. Ruth Hinckley Willes, unpublished manuscript; "The Story of Ada Bitner Hinckley," as told by Ruth Hinckley Willes, comp. Joseph Simmons Willes, unpublished manuscript, 1980; Ruth Hinckley Willes, "Reminiscences," unpublished manuscript, December 1972; "Philip LeRoy Pay," unpublished family history; "Georgetta Paxman Pay," unpublished family history; *One Hundred Years of History of Millard County,* comp. Stella H. Day and Sebrina C. Ekins (Salt Lake City: Daughters of Utah Pioneers, 1951); and *Governors of New Plymouth and Massachusetts Bay Colonies,* published circa 1851, copy available in the Harvard University Library.

The following biographical overviews of President Hinckley's life were informational: LaMar S. Williams, "Gordon B. Hinckley: Assistant to the Twelve," *Improvement Era,* June 1958, p. 396; Wendell J. Ashton, "Gordon B. Hinckley of the Quorum of the Twelve," *Improvement Era,* December 1961, pp. 906–7; Neal A. Maxwell, "President Gordon B. Hinckley: The Spiritual Sculpturing of a Righteous Soul," *Ensign,* January 1982, pp. 7–13; Boyd K. Packer, "President Gordon B. Hinckley: First Counselor," *Ensign,* February 1986, pp. 3–9; M. Russell Ballard, "President Gordon B. Hinckley: An Anchor of Faith," *Ensign,* September 1994, pp. 6–11; Jeffrey R. Holland, "President Gordon B. Hinckley: Stalwart and Brave He Stands," *Ensign,* June 1995, pp. 2–13; "Life with Father," unpublished manuscript by the children of Gordon B. Hinckley, July 1980; and "Gordon B. Hinckley: Man of Integrity, 15th President of the Church," video, Corporation of the President, 1995.

The oral histories of Dwayne N. Andersen, Paul C. Andrus, Elder Yoshihiko Kikuchi, and Elder Adney Y. Komatsu, conducted as part of the James Moyle Oral History Program and housed in the Archives, Historical Department of The Church of Jesus Christ of Latter-day Saints (hereinafter LDS Church Archives), were helpful, as was the interview of President Hinckley conducted by Robert W. Collins as part of the General Authorities Video Biographies Project on 18 April 1990.

General reference texts that provided important back-ground information on a variety of subjects include: *Our Glorious Century* (Pleasantville, New York: Reader's Digest Association, Inc., 1994); *Who Built America? Working People & the Nation's Economy, Politics, Culture & Society* (New York: Pantheon Books, 1992); David Halberstam, *The Fifties* (New York: Villard Books, 1993); "British Mission History," LDS Church Archives; James B. Allen and Glen Leonard, *The Story of the Latter-day Saints,* 2d ed. (Salt Lake City: Deseret Book, 1992); John Henry Evans, "Historical Sketches of the Latter-day Saints' University," unpublished paper, Salt Lake City, Utah, 1913; William E. Felt, "The Inception and Growth of the LDS Business College," unpublished paper, 1 February 1982; Conrad H. Thorne, "Research Study in Public Relations of the Mormon Church," unpublished research paper, 18 April 1966; *Millennial Star,* volumes 95–97, 1934–35; Heber Grant Wolsey, "The History of Radio Station KSL from 1922 to Television," Ph.D. dissertation, Michigan State University, 1967; W. Dee Halverson, "Bonneville International Corporation Historical Record 1922–1992," unpublished internal corporate document, 1992; Robert G. Athearn, *Rebel of the Rockies: A History of the Denver and Rio Grande Western Railroad* (New Haven and London: Yale University Press, 1962); and the Journal History of The Church of Jesus Christ of Latter-day Saints, LDS Church Archives.

Chapter One
CARRY ON!

1. For this and all subsequent quotations from the press conference, see "First Presidency Reorganization Announcement: Gordon B. Hinckley Press Conference," unpublished transcript, LDS Church Public Communications, 13 March 1995.
2. See *Deseret News,* 18 March 1995.
3. *Hymns of The Church of Jesus Christ of Latter-day Saints* (Salt Lake City: The Church of Jesus Christ of Latter-day Saints, 1985), no. 255.
4. See David L. George, ed., *The Family Book of Best Loved Poems* (Garden City, N.Y.: Hanover House, 1952), p. 90.
5. Gordon B. Hinckley, "Let Love Be the Lodestar of Your Life," *Ensign,* May 1989, p. 66.
6. In *Conference Report,* October 1981, pp. 5-6.
7. Gordon B. Hinckley, "Go Forward with Faith," *Ensign,* August 1986, p. 5.
8. In *Conference Report,* April 1958, pp. 123, 125.

Chapter Two
OF PILGRIMS AND PIONEERS

1. See *Governors of New Plymouth and Massachusetts Bay Colony,* circa 1851, pp. 201–2; copy at Harvard University Library.
2. *Governors of New Plymouth,* p. 202.
3. *Governors of New Plymouth,* p. 208.
4. "The Name and Family of Hinckley or Hinkley," comp. the Media Research Bureau, Washington, D.C.; see also "Ira Nathaniel Hinckley: Some Events of His Life," unpublished manuscript in possession of family, pp. 1–2.
5. See Bryant S. Hinckley, address delivered to Ira Nathaniel Hinckley family, 4 April 1955; reprinted in "Hinckley Family Memo," undated.
6. See Larry C. Porter, "Beginnings of the Restoration: Canada, an 'Effectual Door' to the British Isles," in *Truth Will Prevail,* ed. V. Ben Bloxham, James R. Moss, and Larry C. Porter (Salt Lake City: Deseret Book, 1987), pp. 17–18.
7. See Gordon B. Hinckley, "Nauvoo Temple Site Address," 26 June 1994; also "Address at Cove Fort Dedication," 21 May 1994, both transcripts of unpublished addresses.
8. See "Church Emigration of 1850," Journal History of the Church, Archives, Historical Department of The Church of Jesus Christ of Latter-day Saints (hereinafter LDS Church Archives).
9. See Orson F. Whitney, *History of Utah,* 4 vols. (Salt Lake City: George Q. Cannon & Sons, 1904), 4:211–12.
10. Whitney, *History of Utah,* 4:211–12.
11. Brigham Young to Ira Hinckley, 12 April 1867, LDS Church Archives.
12. "Ira Nathaniel Hinckley: Some Events," p. 10.
13. See "Ira Nathaniel Hinckley: Some Events," p. 10; also Ira Nathaniel Hinckley to G. A. Smith, undated letter; *Church News,* 30 April 1994, p. 7.
14. See *Cove Creek Gazette,* vol. 1, no. 1 (Spring 1975), p. 3.
15. "Ira Nathaniel Hinckley: Some Events," p. 16.
16. "Ira Nathaniel Hinckley: Some Events," pp. 14–15.
17. "Ira Nathaniel Hinckley: Some Events," p. 10.
18. See Andrew Jenson, *Encyclopedic History of The Church of Jesus Christ of Latter-day Saints* (Salt Lake City: Deseret News Publishing, 1941), pp. 161–62; also Allan Kent

Powell, *Utah History Encyclopedia* (Salt Lake City: University of Utah Press, 1994), pp. 119–20; *Cove Creek Gazette*, vol. 1, no. 1 (Spring 1975), p. 3; Stella H. Day and Sebrina C. Ekins, *One Hundred Years of History of Millard County* (Salt Lake City: Daughters of Utah Pioneers, 1951).

19. Elizabeth Wood Kane, *Twelve Mormon Homes* (Salt Lake City: Tanner Trust Fund, University of Utah Library, 1974), pp. 74–76.
20. See "Ira Nathaniel Hinckley: Some Events," p. 49.
21. Journal History, 23 April 1869.
22. "Ira Nathaniel Hinckley: Some Events," p. 23.
23. "Ira Nathaniel Hinckley: Some Events," p. 47; also Cove Fort Dedication brochure, 9 May 1992, LDS Church Archives.
24. "Ira Nathaniel Hinckley: Some Events," p. 12; see also Jenson, *Encyclopedic History*, pp. 504–5; Andrew Jenson, comp., *Church Chronology* (Salt Lake City: Deseret News, 1899), 22 July 1877.
25. "Ira Nathaniel Hinckley: Some Events," p. 25.
26. "Ira Nathaniel Hinckley: Some Events," p. 17; see also Frank Esshom, *Pioneers and Prominent Men of Utah* (Salt Lake City: Utah Pioneers Book Publishing, 1913), p. 936.
27. See Gordon B. Hinckley, "Pioneer Era Influences Leader's Life," *Church News*, 11 July 1948.
28. See "The Autobiography of Bryant Stringham Hinckley," comp. Ruth Hinckley Willes, unpublished manuscript in possession of family, p. 27.
29. "Autobiography of Bryant Stringham Hinckley," p. 30.
30. *Church News*, 20 June 1948.
31. See Boyd K. Packer, "President Gordon B. Hinckley: First Counselor," *Ensign*, February 1986, p. 5.
32. See "The Story of Ada Bitner Hinckley," as told by Ruth Hinckley Willes, comp. Joseph Simmons Willes, 1980, unpublished manuscript in possession of family.
33. "Story of Ada Bitner Hinckley," pp. 48–49.
34. Patriarchal blessing given by John Smith to Ada Bitner, February 1901, reproduced in "Story of Ada Bitner Hinckley," pp. 47–48.
35. Patriarchal blessing given by Jno Ashman to Bryant S. Hinckley, 8 August 1895, LDS Church Archives.

Chapter Three
BIRTH AND BOYHOOD

1. *Salt Lake Tribune*, 10 June 1910, p. 6.
2. *Salt Lake Tribune*, 23 June 1910, p. 1.
3. See *Salt Lake Herald-Republic*, 10 June 1910, p. 1.
4. See Gordon B. Hinckley, "Memories of My Mother: Ada Bitner Hinckley," circa 1980, unpublished manuscript in possession of family.
5. See Dell Van Orden, "Pres. Hinckley Stood Tall Even As Youngster," *Deseret News*, 23 June 1995.
6. Gordon B. Hinckley, "Some Lessons I Learned As a Boy," *Ensign*, May 1993, p. 54.
7. "Mutual Work," *Improvement Era*, June 1910, p. 761.
8. See Gordon B. Hinckley, "Tithing: An Opportunity to Prove Our Faithfulness," *Ensign*, May 1982, p. 40.
9. Gordon B. Hinckley, "'Behold Your Little Ones,'" *Ensign*, November 1978, p. 18.

10. Interview with Gordon B. Hinckley (hereinafter referred to as GBH in interviews, letters, and journal entries), 19 October 1994.
11. See "Some Lessons I Learned As a Boy," p. 53; also Interview with GBH, 19 October 1994.
12. See Gordon B. Hinckley, "Take Not the Name of God in Vain," *Ensign,* November 1987, p. 46.
13. See Gordon B. Hinckley, "To the Bishops of the Church," *Ensign,* November 1988, pp. 49, 51.
14. See "Tithing: An Opportunity to Prove Our Faithfulness," p. 40.
15. Bryant S. Hinckley to Ada Bitner Hinckley, 9 February 1915; see also "Story of Ada Bitner Hinckley," p. 63.
16. Interview with GBH, 19 October 1994.
17. Interview with GBH, 7 December 1994.
18. See Gordon B. Hinckley, "A Principle with Promise," *Improvement Era,* April 1965, p. 520.
19. See Gordon B. Hinckley, "'If Ye Be Willing and Obedient,'" *Ensign,* December 1971, p. 123.
20. *Hymns,* no. 27.
21. See Gordon B. Hinckley, "Praise to the Man," *Ensign,* August 1983, p. 2; also Gordon B. Hinckley, "Joseph the Seer," *Ensign,* May 1977, p. 66; Gordon B. Hinckley, "As One Who Loves the Prophet," address delivered at BYU Symposium on the Life and Ministry of the Prophet Joseph Smith, 22 February 1992.
22. See "Hinckley Family Herald," 25 December 1939, p. 1.
23. "Some Lessons I Learned As a Boy," pp. 54, 59.
24. Bryant S. Hinckley to Ada Bitner Hinckley, 9 February 1915; see also "Story of Ada Bitner Hinckley," p. 68.
25. See address delivered to Ira Nathaniel Hinckley family, 4 April 1955.
26. *Deseret News,* 10 October 1918.
27. See *Deseret News,* 28 January 1996.
28. Interview with Sherman Hinckley, 12 November 1994.

Chapter Four
A BOY BECOMES A YOUNG MAN

1. Interview with Ramona Hinckley Sullivan, 5 June 1989.
2. *Salt Lake Tribune,* 27 June 1923, p. 1.
3. See *Deseret News,* 21 May 1927; also *Salt Lake Tribune,* 21 May 1927.
4. See Andrew Jenson, *Encyclopedic History,* pp. 432–33. Bryant S. Hinckley was set apart as president of the Liberty Stake by President Rudger Clawson of the Quorum of the Twelve on Thursday, May 18, 1925.
5. Alonzo A. Hinckley to Bryant S. Hinckley, 27 December 1932.
6. Bryant S. Hinckley, "The Essentials of a Sound Religion," *Liahona: The Elders' Journal,* vol. 34, no. 3 (14 July 1936), p. 1055.
7. "Hinckley Family Herald," 25 December 1939, p. 1, privately published and issued newspaper.
8. *Who Built America? Working People & the Nation's Economy, Politics, Culture & Society* (New York: Pantheon Books, 1992), p. 317.
9. See *Who Built America?* p. 319.

10. Interview with GBH, 16 November 1994.
11. "Autobiography of Bryant Stringham Hinckley," p. 35.
12. See *Catalogue of the University of Utah* (Salt Lake City: University of Utah, 1928), p. 44.
13. "Gordon B. Hinckley: Man of Integrity, 15th President of the Church," transcript of video production, 1995.
14. Interview with GBH, 16 November 1994.
15. Interview with GBH, 16 November 1994.
16. Adapted from "'God Hath Not Given Us the Spirit of Fear,'" *Ensign*, October 1984, pp. 4–5; originally delivered 5 November 1983 at University of Utah Institute.
17. Wendell J. Ashton, "Gordon B. Hinckley of the Quorum of the Twelve," *Improvement Era*, December 1961, pp. 980–82.
18. See Ada B. Hinckley, "The Gold Star Pilgrimage," *Improvement Era*, December 1930, pp. 73–75.
19. Ada B. Hinckley to Bryant S. Hinckley, 19 July 1930.
20. Ada Bitner Hinckley Journal, 12 August 1930.
21. Ada B. Hinckley to Bryant S. Hinckley, 1 August 1930.
22. Ada B. Hinckley to Bryant S. Hinckley, 4 August 1930.
23. "Remembrances of Ruth Hinckley Willes," unpublished notes in possession of family, 1940.
24. Bryant S. Hinckley to Children, 4 November 1930.
25. "Story of Ada Bitner Hinckley," p. 75.
26. "Some Lessons I Learned As a Boy," p. 54.
27. Gordon B. Hinckley, *The Wondrous Power of a Mother* (Salt Lake City: Deseret Book, 1989), p. 1.
28. GBH to Bryant S. Hinckley, 25 December 1933.
29. "Remembrances of Ruth Hinckley Willes."
30. Gordon B. Hinckley, address to Belle Spafford Conference on Women, 23 February 1990.
31. Interview with Ramona Hinckley Sullivan, 5 June 1989.
32. Interview with Ramona Hinckley Sullivan, 5 June 1989.
33. Transcript of LaRene Gaunt Interview with GBH, 13 October 1993.
34. LaRene Gaunt Interview with GBH, 13 October 1993.
35. Gordon B. Hinckley, "Four B's for Boys," *Ensign*, November 1981, p. 40.
36. Gordon B. Hinckley, "Blessed Are the Merciful," *Ensign*, May 1990, p. 70.
37. Address delivered to Ira Nathaniel Hinckley family, 4 April 1955.
38. "Some Lessons I Learned As a Boy," p. 59.

Chapter Five
A MISSION AND BEYOND

1. See Ashton, "Gordon B. Hinckley of the Quorum of the Twelve," p. 906.
2. Interview with Marjorie P. Hinckley (hereinafter referred to as MPH in interviews and letters), 20 October 1994.
3. Quoted in Packer, "President Gordon B. Hinckley: First Counselor," p. 7.
4. See *Latter-day Saints' Millennial Star*, 13 July 1933.
5. See "Record of Missionary," Gordon B. Hinckley, LDS Church Archives.

6. Interview with GBH, 16 November 1994.
7. See James B. Allen, Ronald K. Esplin, and David J. Whittaker, *Men with a Mission: The Quorum of the Twelve Apostles in the British Isles* (Salt Lake City: Deseret Book, 1992), pp. 28–36.
8. See Gordon B. Hinckley, "Taking the Gospel to Britain: A Declaration of Vision, Faith, Courage, and Truth," *Ensign*, July 1987, p. 7; also "A Declaration to the World," *BYU Studies*, Winter 1987, pp. 9–10; "Gordon B. Hinckley: Man of Integrity," video.
9. See *Millennial Star*, 26 October 1933.
10. GBH to Marjorie Pay, 30 January 1934.
11. Gordon B. Hinckley, "A Missionary Holiday," *Millennial Star*, 27 July 1933.
12. Gordon B. Hinckley, "Discover Yourself," *Millennial Star*, 14 September 1933.
13. GBH to Marjorie Pay, undated.
14. See "Elders' Labor Record of Liverpool Conference of the British Mission of The Church of Jesus Christ of Latter-day Saints," Gordon B. Hinckley, LDS Church Archives.
15. Thomas Gray, "Elegy Written in a Country Churchyard."
16. Interview with Robert Pickles, 28 January 1995.
17. Interview with Robert Pickles, 28 January 1995.
18. GBH to Marjorie Pay, 1 February 1934.
19. *Millennial Star*, 8 March 1934.
20. See "Elders' Labor Record of Liverpool Conference."
21. See GBH to Arthur C. Porter, 24 March 1938.
22. See Jeffrey R. Holland, "Stalwart and Brave He Stands," *Ensign*, June 1995, p. 8.
23. Interview with GBH, 7 December 1994.
24. British Mission History, May 1935, LDS Church Archives; also *Millennial Star*, 28 February 1935; 7 April 1935.
25. *Millennial Star*, 21 December 1933.
26. From "Andrea del Sarto"; as quoted in Gordon B. Hinckley, "The Sunday School as a Missionary," *Ensign*, August 1971, p. 30.
27. "Gordon B. Hinckley: Man of Integrity," video; see also "'If Ye Be Willing and Obedient,'" p. 125; Interview with GBH, 7 December 1994.
28. See Gordon B. Hinckley, "Reverence and Morality," *Ensign*, May 1987, p. 45.
29. See *The Wondrous Power of a Mother*, pp. 1–2.
30. GBH to Ruth Hinckley, 3 February 1934.
31. GBH to Ruth Hinckley, 9 November 1934.
32. See Gordon B. Hinckley, "Live the Gospel," *Ensign*, November 1984, p. 86.
33. Gordon B. Hinckley, "'Whosoever Will Save His Life,'" *Ensign*, August 1982, p. 5.
34. GBH to Bryant S. Hinckley, 25 December 1933.
35. GBH to Ruth Hinckley, 9 November 1934.
36. *Millennial Star*, 27 June 1935.
37. G. Homer Durham, address to Windsor Club, 27 December 1984.
38. Gordon B. Hinckley, "The Question of a Mission," *Ensign*, May 1986, p. 40.
39. "Taking the Gospel to Britain," p. 7.
40. Wendell J. Ashton Journal, 20 June 1935.
41. Interview with GBH, 7 December 1994.
42. G. Homer Durham Journal, 21 June 1935.
43. G. Homer Durham Journal, 23 June 1935.

44. Interview with GBH, 7 December 1994.
45. *The Wondrous Power of a Mother,* p. 8.
46. Interview with GBH, 7 December 1994.
47. G. Homer Durham Journal, 2 July 1935.
48. See "Utah Mormons Dedicate Shaft in New York," *Carthage Republican,* 31 July 1935.
49. "Pioneer Frontiers," *Deseret News,* 25 July 1936.
50. Interview with GBH, 7 December 1994.
51. Heber J. Grant Journal, 20 August 1935.
52. Heber J. Grant to Sister Rees, 21 August 1935

Chapter Six

GETTING STARTED: THE CHALLENGES BEGIN

1. GBH to Joseph F. Merrill, 29 November 1935.
2. GBH to Joseph F. Merrill, 20 November 1935.
3. GBH to Joseph F. Merrill, 11 December 1935.
4. Gordon B. Hinckley, "Financial and Work Report for Stephen L Richards, 1 January 1936 to 1 July 1936," Radio, Publicity, and Mission Literature Committee Executive Secretary Files, LDS Church Archives.
5. See GBH to Joseph F. Merrill, 20 May 1936.
6. *Church News,* 24 January 1942.
7. *Church News,* 24 January 1942.
8. GBH to Mr. Price, 6 August 1941.
9. GBH to J. F. Merrill, 31 March 1936.
10. LeGrand Richards to Radio, Publicity, and Mission Literature Committee, 5 August 1936.
11. GBH to LeGrand Richards, 11 August 1936.
12. See Gordon B. Hinckley, "Comments from Missionaries Who Are Using Our 15 Minute Programs in New England," unpublished document, circa 1939, M259, R129c, LDS Church Archives.
13. "Financial and Work Report."
14. J. F. Merrill to GBH, 8 May 1936.
15. See "Financial and Work Report."
16. See Heber Grant Wolsey, "The History of Radio Station KSL from 1922 to Television," Ph.D. dissertation, Michigan State University, 1967, p. 175.
17. *Deseret News,* 25 July 1936.
18. *Deseret News,* 13 November 1937.
19. See Gordon B. Hinckley, "A Story," unpublished manuscript, 3 January 1938, LDS Church Archives.
20. See Gordon B. Hinckley, "Twenty-Five Years of Radio Ministry," *Church News,* 26 April 1947, p. 5.
21. See G. William Richards, "Report on Golden Gate International Exposition"; "Calamis Article for September," 1 September 1940; Elder G. William Richards to GBH, 19 June 1940; 12 August 1940; 26 August 1940; Radio, Publicity, and Mission Literature Committee Executive Secretary Files.
22. G. William Richards to First Presidency, 27 September 1940.
23. B. H. Roberts, *A Comprehensive History of The Church of Jesus Christ of Latter-day Saints,* 6 vols. (Provo, Utah: Brigham Young University Press, 1965), vol. 3, plate following p. 362.

24. GBH to G. L. Price, 20 May 1940.
25. Interview with GBH, 4 January 1995.
26. Mr. Price to GBH, 26 October 1939.
27. GBH to Mr. Price, 27 March 1941.
28. Mr. Price to GBH, 11 July 1941.
29. Mr. Price to GBH, 19 December 1941.
30. GBH to Mr. Price, 4 October 1941.
31. GBH to G. L. Price, 26 April 1939.
32. GBH to G. L. Price, 30 March 1940.
33. GBH to Joel Ricks, 24 June 1937.
34. GBH to Mr. Price, 5 June 1942.
35. Interview with Ramona Hinckley Sullivan, 5 June 1989.
36. Gordon B. Hinckley, "The Faith of the Pioneers," *Ensign,* July 1984, p. 3.
37. Gordon B. Hinckley, "A City Set Upon a Hill," *Ensign,* November 1974, p. 99.
38. Interview with MPH, 20 October 1994.
39. GBH to G. Homer Durham, 27 March 1939.
40. GBH to G. Homer Durham, 27 March 1939.
41. Interview with GBH, 4 January 1995.
42. GBH to Frank Harris, 23 January 1936.
43. Interview with MPH, 20 October 1994.
44. Interview with GBH, 4 January 1995.

Chapter Seven
MARJORIE AND THE ART OF HOME BUILDING

1. Interview with MPH, 20 October 1994.
2. See "Mary Goble Pay: Death Strikes the Handcart Company," in *A Believing People: Literature of the Latter-day Saints* (Salt Lake City: Bookcraft, 1979), p. 111.
3. *A Believing People,* p. 106; also "Life of Mary Goble Pay: June 2, 1843–September 25, 1913," from "A Pioneer Story," 1856, p. 3, LDS Church Archives.
4. *Journal of Discourses,* 26 vols. (London: Latter-day Saints' Book Depot, 1856–86), 4:113.
5. *A Believing People,* p. 107.
6. See "Georgetta Paxman Pay Life Story," unpublished manuscript in possession of family, p. 12.
7. "Georgetta Paxman Pay Life Story," p. 22.
8. Interview with MPH, 20 October 1994.
9. Interview with MPH, 20 October 1994.
10. Interview with MPH, 20 October 1994.
11. Interview with MPH, 20 October 1994.
12. "Phillip LeRoy Pay Life Story," unpublished manuscript in possession of family, p. 36.
13. "An Evening with Marjorie P. Hinckley and Her Daughters," 1996 Women's Conference at BYU, fireside, 2 May 1996.
14. Interview with MPH, 20 October 1994.
15. Interview with MPH, 20 October 1994.
16. Interview with MPH, 20 October 1994.
17. Interview with MPH, 20 October 1994.

18. Interview with MPH, 20 October 1994.
19. Interview with MPH, 20 October 1994.
20. Interview with MPH, 20 October 1994.
21. In *The Wondrous Power of a Mother,* p. 15.
22. Interview with MPH, 20 October 1994.
23. Gordon B. Hinckley, "This I Believe," BYU Devotional Address, 1 March 1992; see also Interview with GBH, 4 January 1995.
24. See *Salt Lake Tribune,* 17 November 1937.
25. See *Instructor,* June 1943, contents page.
26. Interview with GBH, 1 February 1995.
27. Interview with MPH, 20 October 1994.
28. GBH to G. Homer Durham, 27 March 1939.
29. Interview with GBH, 1 February 1995.
30. Interview with MPH, 20 October 1994.
31. "Hinckley Family Herald," 25 December 1939.
32. Interview with MPH, 16 March 1995.
33. Interview with MPH, 16 March 1995.
34. "English-Born Leader Guides Destiny of 102,000 Children," *Church News,* 4 April 1964.
35. Interview with MPH, 20 October 1994.
36. GBH to Mr. Price, 20 August 1941.
37. GBH to Mr. Price, 22 September 1941.

Chapter Eight
WORLD WAR II AND ITS AFTERMATH

1. GBH to G. L. Price, 31 December 1941.
2. Interview with GBH, 4 January 1995.
3. GBH to G. L. Price, 21 May 1942.
4. GBH to G. L. Price, 25 June 1942.
5. See Stephen E. Ambrose, "World War II Remembered," *The World Almanac and Book of Facts 1995* (Mahwah, N.J.: Funk and Wagnalls, 1994), p. 37.
6. See Henry Swan, "What Business Must Do Now," address delivered to Utah Manufacturer's Association, Salt Lake City, 5 February 1943.
7. "Take Not the Name of God in Vain," p. 46.
8. See LaRene Gaunt Interview with GBH, 13 October 1993.
9. See Robert G. Athearn, "Railroad Renaissance in the Rockies," *Utah Historical Quarterly,* January 1957, pp. 18–19.
10. Interview with GBH, 4 January 1995.
11. MPH to GBH, undated.
12. MPH to Family, 26 January 1945.
13. MPH to Mama and Papa and All My Little Sisters, 7 February 1945.
14. See MPH to Family, 19 January 1945.
15. Interview with GBH, 4 January 1995.
16. Interview with GBH, 4 January 1995.
17. MPH to Family, 29 May 1945.
18. See MPH to GBH, 26 August 1945.

19. See MPH to Family, undated.
20. MPH to GBH, Sunday evening, undated.
21. See Interview with GBH, 4 January 1995.
22. As cited in L. Brent Goates to GBH, 17 November 1982.
23. See Ashton, "Gordon B. Hinckley of the Quorum of the Twelve," p. 978.
24. Gordon B. Hinckley, *What of the Mormons?* (Salt Lake City: The Church of Jesus Christ of Latter-day Saints, 1947), p. 1.
25. See, for example, 1947 *Church News* articles under dates October 18, 25; November 1, 8, 15, 22, 29; December 6, 13, 20, 27.
26. *Look,* 19 June 1951, pp. 5–6.
27. See, for example, "Twenty-Five Years of Radio Ministry," pp. 4–5.
28. Interview with MPH, 16 March 1995.

Chapter Nine
ON THE FIRING LINE

1. See *Conference Report,* April 1951, pp. 150–51.
2. See James B. Allen and Glen M. Leonard, *The Story of the Latter-day Saints,* 2d ed. (Salt Lake City: Deseret Book, 1992), pp. 567–68.
3. Gordon B. Hinckley, "The Healing Power of Christ," *Ensign,* November 1988, p. 54.
4. See "Mission Literature Survey of Foreign Missions and Languages, 1946–1956," LDS Church Archives.
5. Joseph C. Goulden, *Korea: The Untold Story* (New York: Times Books, 1982), p. 3.
6. See Stephen L Richards and Robert W. Barker, "General Memorandum Regarding Missionary System, The Church of Jesus Christ of Latter-day Saints and Selective Service," LDS Church Archives.
7. See W. Glenn Harmon to Stephen L Richards, 10 May 1951.
8. GBH memo, undated (circa 1951), Executive Secretary General Files, 1940–1962, LDS Church Archives.
9. See Interview with GBH, 4 January 1995.
10. See GBH memo regarding Preston, Idaho, draft board situation, undated.
11. See, for example, Gordon B. Hinckley, "Memorandum of Meeting Between President Stephen L Richards and General J. Wallace West and Colonel Oscar Gray, December 20, 1951," LDS Church Archives; also Arthur V. Watkins to Stephen L Richards, 2 April 1951.
12. See GBH memo, "Number of Missionaries in the Field as of December 31," undated; also *1993–94 Church Almanac* (Salt Lake City: Deseret News, 1992), p. 400.
13. See First Presidency to Presidents of Stakes and Bishops of Wards, 10 July 1953; also *Salt Lake Tribune,* 15 July 1953, p. 15.
14. See Report of President Stephen L Richards, Conference with General James A. May, Selective Service Agent of State of Nevada, 25 September 1953; Missionary Department Executive Secretary Files, LDS Church Archives.
15. Ned L. Mangelson memorandum, 27 April 1995.
16. Interview with GBH, 4 January 1995; see also Interview with MPH, 16 March 1995.
17. See *Congressional Record,* House of Representatives, 28 June 1955.
18. See First Presidency to Presidents of Stakes and Bishops of Wards, 1 September 1955; also *Church News,* 17 September 1955, p. 13.

19. Interview with GBH, 4 January 1995; see also Gordon B. Hinckley, "President Stephen L Richards: 1879–1959," *Improvement Era,* June 1959, p. 488.
20. See Interview with GBH, 4 January 1995.
21. Stephen L Richards to GBH, 22 December 1953.
22. See Allen and Leonard, *Story of the Latter-day Saints,* pp. 567–68; also *1993–94 Church Almanac,* p. 400.
23. See *Our Glorious Century* (Pleasantville, N.Y.: Reader's Digest Association, 1994), p. 266.
24. See "President Stephen L Richards: 1879–1959," pp. 488–89; also *1995–96 Church Almanac* (Salt Lake City: Deseret News, 1994), pp. 383, 418–20.
25. Interview with GBH, 4 January 1995.
26. See S. Dilworth Young, "Gordon B. Hinckley—An Impression," *Relief Society Magazine,* vol. 45 (1958), pp. 358–59.
27. Introduction by William E. Berrett to Gordon B. Hinckley, "Building an Eternal Home," address delivered at BYU, 4 November 1959.
28. See GBH to Stephen L Richards, 25 June 1951.
29. See Gordon B. Hinckley, "Committee Decisions," memo to Stephen L Richards, 21 February 1951, Missionary Department Executive Secretary General Files.
30. GBH to Stephen L Richards, 28 September 1951.
31. Interview with Thomas S. Monson, 28 April 1995.
32. Interview with GBH, 4 January 1995.
33. Gordon B. Hinckley, "Ready to Harvest," *Improvement Era,* July 1961, p. 508.
34. Gordon B. Hinckley, "We Have a Work to Do," *Ensign,* February 1988, pp. 2, 6.
35. See Gordon B. Hinckley, "The Widow's Mite," BYU Devotional Address, 17 September 1985.

Chapter Ten
LIFE WITH FATHER

1. Interview with Virginia Hinckley Pearce, 12 October 1994.
2. Interview with Kathleen Hinckley Barnes, 17 October 1994.
3. Interview with GBH, 1 February 1995.
4. Interview with Clark Bryant Hinckley, 17 November 1994.
5. Interview with Richard Gordon Hinckley, 21 October 1994.
6. Interview with Richard Gordon Hinckley, 21 October 1994.
7. Interview with Kathleen Hinckley Barnes, 17 October 1994.
8. GBH to David J. Gourley, 31 July 1952.
9. Interview with Jane Hinckley Dudley, 9 November 1994.
10. Interview with Clark Bryant Hinckley, 11 April 1996.
11. Gordon B. Hinckley, "Cornerstones of a Happy Home," transcript of satellite fireside address, 29 January 1984, p. 5.
12. Interview with Clark Bryant Hinckley, 11 April 1996.
13. Interview with Virginia Hinckley Pearce, 12 October 1994.
14. Interview with Richard Gordon Hinckley, 21 October 1994.
15. Interview with Kathleen Hinckley Barnes, 17 October 1994.
16. See "'Behold Your Little Ones,'" p. 19.
17. Interview with Virginia Hinckley Pearce, 12 October 1994.

18. Interview with Richard Gordon Hinckley, 21 October 1994.
19. Interview with Virginia Hinckley Pearce, 12 October 1994.
20. Gordon B. Hinckley, address delivered at Churchwide youth fireside, 5 December 1982.
21. Interview with Richard Gordon Hinckley, 21 October 1994.
22. Interview with MPH, 20 October 1994.
23. Gordon B. Hinckley, "Except the Lord Build the House . . . ," *Ensign,* June 1971, p. 72.
24. Interview with Virginia Hinckley Pearce, 12 October 1994.
25. Interview with Clark Bryant Hinckley, 17 November 1994.
26. Interview with Virginia Hinckley Pearce, 12 October 1994.
27. Interview with Kathleen Hinckley Barnes, 17 October 1994.
28. Interview with Jane Hinckley Dudley, 9 November 1994.
29. Interview with MPH, 20 October 1994.
30. Interview with MPH, 20 October 1994.
31. Interview with Kathleen Hinckley Barnes, 17 October 1994.
32. Interview with Kathleen Hinckley Barnes, 17 October 1994.
33. Interview with Jane Hinckley Dudley, 9 November 1994.
34. "An Evening with Marjorie Hinckley."
35. See "'Behold Your Little Ones,'" p. 18.

Chapter Eleven
TEMPLES TO DOT THE EARTH

1. See Ashton, "Gordon B. Hinckley of the Quorum of the Twelve," p. 978.
2. See Dale Z. Kirby, "The History of the Swiss Temple," July 1969, LDS Church Archives.
3. Interview with GBH, 1 February 1995.
4. MPH to Kathie, Dick, Gin, Clark, and Jane, 2 September 1955.
5. Interview with MPH, 16 March 1995.
6. Interview with GBH, 1 February 1995.
7. Interview with MPH, 16 March 1995.
8. *Improvement Era,* December 1955, p. 911.
9. Gordon B. Hinckley, Address to Norwegian and Danish Session, Dedication of Swiss Temple, 14 September 1955, LDS Church Archives.
10. In *Conference Report,* 6 April 1958, pp. 123–24.
11. GBH to Stephen L Richards, 17 September 1955.
12. See "David O. McKay," *Improvement Era,* December 1955, p. 911; also Kirby, "History of the Swiss Temple."
13. "Life with Father," compiled July 1980, unpublished manuscript in possession of family.
14. GBH to Stephen L Richards, 17 September 1955.
15. Interview with MPH, 16 March 1995.
16. In *Conference Report,* 6 April 1958, p. 124.
17. Report from GBH to President McKay, 29 November 1956, Executive Secretary General Files.
18. See Vincent dePaul Lupiano and Ken W. Sayers, *It Was a Very Good Year: A Cultural History of the United States* (Holbrook, Mass.: Adams Publishing, 1994), p. 377.

19. Gordon B. Hinckley, "The Wonder of Jesus," *Improvement Era,* June 1969, p. 74.
20. See Journal History, 28 October 1956.
21. Quoted at Alaska Anchorage missionary meeting, 18 June 1996.
22. See *Conference Report,* 6 April 1958, p. 124.
23. Interview with Clark Bryant Hinckley, 17 November 1994.
24. Gordon B. Hinckley, "Rise to a Larger Vision of the Work," *Ensign,* May 1990, p. 95.
25. "Tithing: An Opportunity to Prove Our Faithfulness," p. 41.
26. GBH to William Granger, Buy-Ryte Food Stores, 28 February 1958.
27. Interview with Clark Bryant Hinckley, 17 November 1994.
28. Interview with MPH, 16 March 1995.
29. "Gordon B. Hinckley: Man of Integrity," video.
30. Address delivered to Ira Nathaniel Hinckley family, 4 April 1955.

Chapter Twelve
ASSISTANT TO THE TWELVE

1. Interview with GBH, 7 March 1995.
2. In *Conference Report,* 6 April 1958, pp. 124–25.
3. *Deseret News,* 7 April 1958.
4. GBH Journal, 10 April 1958.
5. Interview with Kathleen Hinckley Barnes, 17 October 1995.
6. Interview with Virginia Hinckley Pearce, 11 April 1996.
7. See LaMar S. Williams, "Gordon B. Hinckley: Assistant to the Twelve," *Improvement Era,* June 1958, p. 472.
8. Richard Gordon Hinckley, unpublished address, 11 May 1991.
9. See Delbert L. Stapley, in *Conference Report,* October 1958, p. 16.
10. Interview with MPH, 16 March 1995.
11. See Gordon B. Hinckley, "Building an Eternal Home," *BYU Speeches of the Year 1959–1960,* 4 November 1959; also Gordon B. Hinckley, "The Marriage That Endures," *Ensign,* May 1974, p. 24.
12. See *Church News,* 14 June 1958.
13. Harold B. Lee Journal, 17 August 1958, as recorded in L. Brent Goates to GBH, 17 November 1982; see also Journal History, 17 August 1958.
14. See "London's Mormon Temple," *Time,* 15 September 1958, p. 53.
15. See "Building an Eternal Home."
16. MPH to Kathleen Hinckley, 6 September 1958.
17. Gordon B. Hinckley, "The Consequences of Conversion," *BYU Speeches of the Year, 1958–59,* address given 28 January 1959.
18. Interview with GBH, 18 April 1995; also GBH Journal, 16 September 1958.
19. In *Conference Report,* October 1958, p. 14.
20. Interview with GBH, 1 February 1995.
21. Interview with Virginia Hinckley Pearce, 12 October 1994.
22. Interview with GBH, 1 February 1995.
23. "Building an Eternal Home."
24. Interview with Clark Bryant Hinckley, 17 November 1994.
25. "President Stephen L Richards: 1879–1959," p. 489.
26. Interview with GBH, 1 February 1995.

27. Interview with GBH, 18 April 1995.
28. Interview with MPH, 16 March 1995.
29. See "Officials Hail Work of Missionaries," *Deseret News-Telegram*, 5 April 1960.
30. "The Consequences of Conversion."

Chapter Thirteen
WEST MEETS EAST

1. See *The World Book* (Chicago: Field Enterprises Educational Corporation, 1966), 1:735.
2. See "Elder Hinckley to Visit East Missions," *Church News*, 23 April 1960; also GBH Journal, 24–30 April 1960.
3. GBH Journal, 6 May 1960.
4. GBH to Henry D. Moyle, 6 May 1960.
5. GBH Journal, 13 May 1960.
6. GBH Journal, 14 May 1960.
7. GBH Journal, 15 May 1960.
8. See GBH Journal, 16 May 1960.
9. GBH Journal, 19 May 1960.
10. GBH Journal, 21 May 1960.
11. GBH Journal, 21 May 1960.
12. GBH Journal, 21 May 1960.
13. GBH Journal, 23 May 1960.
14. GBH Journal, 21 May 1960.
15. GBH Journal, 19 May 1960.
16. GBH Journal, 18 May 1960.
17. GBH Journal, 20 May 1960.
18. GBH Journal, 26 May 1960.
19. GBH Journal, 27 May 1960.
20. Interview with GBH, 11 July 1995.
21. Interview with GBH, 11 July 1995.
22. GBH Journal, 3 June 1960.
23. Interview with GBH, 18 April 1995.
24. Memo from Kenji Tanaka, 27 April 1995.
25. GBH Journal, 2 June 1960.
26. See memo from Yasuhiro Matsushita, 27 April 1995.
27. See "Ready to Harvest," p. 509.
28. See Interview with Spencer J. Palmer, 13 July 1995.
29. GBH Journal, 4 June 1960.
30. Interview with Han In Sang, 31 March 1995.
31. See Interview with GBH, 18 April 1995.
32. Interview with Han In Sang, 31 March 1995.
33. Interview with Rhee Ho Nam, 13 August 1996.
34. Meeting with missionaries of Seoul and Seoul West Missions, 22 May 1996, YongDong Stake Center, Seoul, Korea.
35. See Misao Toma memo, 11 May 1995.

36. Kensei Nagamine memo, 27 April 1995.
37. GBH Journal, 16 June 1960.
38. GBH Journal, 18 June 1960.
39. GBH Journal, 10 January 1961.
40. GBH Journal, 24 April 1961.
41. GBH Journal, 28 April 1961.
42. Doctrine and Covenants 42:45–46; see also "The Wonder of Jesus," p. 74.
43. GBH Journal, 28 April 1961. Elder Hinckley's prayer read, in part, as follows: "Our Father, and our God, with bowed heads and contrite hearts we approach thee at this time in this sacred place, hallowed by the sacrifices of those who gave their lives for the cherished freedoms of mankind. . . . We invoke thy blessings upon the people of this land, that they shall be friendly and hospitable and kind and gracious to those who shall come here, and that many, yea, Lord, we pray that there shall be many, many thousands who shall receive this message and be blessed thereby. Wilt thou bless them with receptive minds and understanding hearts, and with faith to receive, and with courage to live the principles of the gospel. . . . And we pray that there shall be many men, faithful, good, virtuous, true men, who shall join the Church and receive the blessings of the holy priesthood and who shall grow in leadership that thy work here shall be handled by local brethren under the direction of those who hold the keys of this day and time." (See Official Report of the Philippine Islands Area Conference, 11–12 August 1975, p. 20.)
44. GBH Journal, 28 April 1961.
45. GBH Journal, 12 May 1961.
46. GBH Journal, 10 May 1961.
47. Interview with Han In Sang, 31 March 1995.
48. Interview with GBH, 18 April 1995.
49. GBH Journal, 16 May 1961.
50. GBH Journal, 21 May 1961.
51. See "Ready to Harvest," p. 509.
52. GBH Journal, 26 December 1991.
53. Gordon B. Hinckley, "The Cornerstone," *Improvement Era,* June 1960, pp. 425–26.
54. Interview with Jeffrey R. Holland, 26 May 1995.
55. Interview with Virginia Hinckley Pearce, 12 October 1994.
56. *Deseret News,* 6 June 1961; see also *Salt Lake Tribune,* 5 June 1961; *Deseret News-Telegram,* 5 June 1961.
57. Interview with GBH, 24 May 1995.

Chapter Fourteen
QUORUM OF THE TWELVE

1. In *Conference Report,* 1 October 1961, pp. 115–16.
2. Interview with GBH, 18 April 1995.
3. Interview with Richard Gordon Hinckley, 24 June 1995.
4. Ashton, "Gordon B. Hinckley of the Quorum of the Twelve," p. 983.
5. See Francis M. Gibbons, *David O. McKay: Apostle to the World, Prophet of God* (Salt Lake City: Deseret Book, 1986), p. 406.
6. Interview with MPH, 16 March 1995.

7. Marjorie P. Hinckley, address at Araneta Coliseum, Manila, Philippines, 30 May 1996.
8. See Gordon B. Hinckley, address to BYU student body, 17 October 1962, p. 4.
9. Interview with GBH, 18 April 1995.
10. MPH to Kathy, Alan, and Heather Barnes, 1 March 1962.
11. MPH to Kathy, Alan, and Heather Barnes, 1 March 1962.
12. MPH to Kathy, Alan, Heather, and Dick, 20 March 1962.
13. See "Gordon B. Hinckley: Man of Integrity," video.
14. Interview with Rhee Ho Nam, 13 August 1996.
15. See Excerpt from Minutes of Council of Twelve Meeting, GBH Journal, undated.
16. MPH to Barnes, 1 March 1962.
17. MPH to Kathy, Alan, and Heather Barnes, 21 February 1962.
18. MPH to Barnes, 1 March 1962.
19. MPH to Kathy, Alan, and Heather Barnes, 21 February 1962.
20. MPH to Kathy, Alan, and Heather Barnes, 21 February 1962.
21. MPH to Barnes, 1 March 1962.
22. MPH to Kathy, Alan, and Heather Barnes, 21 February 1962.
23. "An Evening with Marjorie Hinckley."
24. See "Elder Hinckley Reports Tour of Three Missions," *Church News,* 24 March 1962, p. 6.
25. MPH to Kathy, Alan, Heather, and Dick, 20 March 1962.
26. MPH to Kathy, Alan, Heather, and Dick, 20 March 1962.
27. MPH to Kathy, Alan, Heather, and Dick, 20 March 1962.
28. Gordon B. Hinckley, "The Church in the Far East," *Improvement Era,* June 1962, pp. 440–43.
29. See Gordon B. Hinckley, "Magnify Your Calling," *Ensign,* May 1989, pp. 46–47.
30. Gordon B. Hinckley, "President Henry Dinwoodey Moyle: 1889–1963," *Improvement Era,* October 1963, pp. 840, 889.
31. Theodore M. Burton, in *Conference Report,* October 1962, p. 65.
32. N. Eldon Tanner, in *Conference Report,* October 1962, pp. 68–69.
33. Interview with Boyd K. Packer, 10 April 1995.
34. See Gordon B. Hinckley, "Report from the Correlation Committee," *Improvement Era,* December 1962, p. 937.
35. Address to BYU student body, 17 October 1962.
36. Interview with Ray Goodson, 15 June 1995.
37. Gordon B. Hinckley, "The Heavens Are Not Stayed," *Improvement Era,* June 1964, p. 477.
38. Seiji Katanuma to Sheri L. Dew, 27 April 1995.
39. Peggy H. Andersen to Sheri L. Dew, 30 June 1995.
40. Dorothy O. Rea, "Marjorie Pay Hinckley," *Church News,* 23 May 1964.
41. Interview with Augusto A. Lim, 31 March 1995.
42. Interview with Han In Sang, 31 March 1995.
43. Interview with Han In Sang, 31 March 1995.
44. GBH Journal, 1 December 1962.
45. GBH Journal, 2 December 1962.
46. Yoshihiko Kikuchi to Sheri L. Dew, 27 April 1995.

47. Yoshihiko Kikuchi to Sheri L. Dew, 27 April 1995.
48. GBH Journal, 26 November 1962.
49. Interview with GBH, 24 May 1995.
50. See R. Lanier Britsch, *Unto the Islands of the Sea: A History of the Latter-day Saints in the Pacific* (Salt Lake City: Deseret Book, 1986), pp. 78–80.
51. See *Deseret News,* 21 September 1963; also "President Henry Dinwoodey Moyle," pp. 840, 891.
52. See Gordon B. Hinckley, "Except the Lord Build the House," *Improvement Era,* January 1964, pp. 32–33; also *Salt Lake Tribune,* 7 October 1963; *Church News,* 12 October 1963.
53. GBH Journal, 19 October 1963.
54. GBH Journal, 23 October 1963.
55. Mary Ellen Edmunds to Sheri L. Dew, 22 June 1995.
56. Mary Ellen Edmunds to Sheri L. Dew, 22 June 1995.
57. GBH Journal, 27 October 1963.
58. Jane Hinckley Dudley to M. Russell Ballard, 28 June 1994.
59. Gordon B. Hinckley, "The Church in the Orient," *Improvement Era,* March 1964, pp. 166–90.
60. See *Conference Report,* April 1962, pp. 3, 76.
61. See *Deseret News-Telegram,* 28 January 1964.
62. See W. Dee Halverson, "Bonneville International Corporation Historical Record 1922–1992," unpublished corporate document, 1992, pp. 12, 18, 21–25.
63. Dwayne N. Andersen to Sheri L. Dew, April 1995; see also R. Lanier Britsch Interview with Dwayne N. Andersen, James Moyle Oral History Program, LDS Church Archives.
64. Peggy Andersen to Sheri L. Dew, 30 June 1995.
65. GBH Journal, 9 December 1964.
66. GBH Journal, 10 December 1964.
67. GBH Journal, 12 December 1964.
68. GBH Journal, 12 December 1964.
69. GBH Journal, 14 December 1964.
70. GBH Journal, 17 December 1964.
71. GBH Journal, 18 December 1964.
72. GBH Journal, 19 December 1964.
73. GBH Journal, 19 December 1964.
74. Marjorie Hinckley to Flora Benson, 29 January 1965.
75. GBH Journal, 22 December 1964.

Chapter Fifteen
GROWING IN ASIA

1. See "160 Japanese Saints Make Historic Hawaii Temple Trip," *Church News,* 31 July 1965, pp. 3, 6.
2. See GBH Journal, 16 December 1965.
3. See GBH Journal, 25 May 1971; also *1993–94 Church Almanac,* p. 400; *1995–96 Church Almanac,* pp. 418–20.
4. GBH Journal, 17 December 1966.

5. Gordon B. Hinckley, "Mission Calls and Selective Service," *Improvement Era,* December 1965, p. 1145.
6. GBH Journal, 5 August 1966.
7. GBH Journal, 23 June 1966.
8. GBH Journal, 25 December 1965.
9. See Spencer J. Palmer, *The Church in Asia* (Salt Lake City: Deseret Book, 1970), pp. 182–83.
10. GBH Journal, 28 December 1965; also *Improvement Era,* March 1966, p. 170.
11. In *Conference Report,* April 1966, pp. 85–87.
12. "The Wonder of Jesus," pp. 74–75.
13. GBH Journal, 5 April 1969.
14. See GBH Journal, 27–28 July 1966.
15. GBH Journal, 6 October 1966.
16. See, for example, Gordon B. Hinckley, "The Loneliness of Leadership," address delivered 4 November 1969 at BYU.
17. MPH to Kathy, Jane, & Heather, 11 October 1966.
18. Kensei Nagamine to Sheri L. Dew, 27 April 1995.
19. See "Philippines Chapel Dedicated," *Church News,* 10 December 1966.
20. MPH to Kathy Barnes, 24 October 1966.
21. MPH to Kathy Barnes, 24 October 1966.
22. GBH Journal, 28 October 1966.
23. Interview with Allen C. Rozsa, 28 June 1995.
24. Gordon B. Hinckley, "Asian Diary," address delivered 10 January 1967 at BYU; also Allen C. Rozsa to Sheri L. Dew, 20 December 1995.
25. GBH Journal, 29 October 1966.
26. Interview with Allen C. Rozsa, 28 June 1995.
27. GBH Journal, 29 October 1966.
28. See R. Lanier Britsch and Richard C. Holloman Jr., "The Church's Years in Vietnam," *Ensign,* August 1980, pp. 25–30; also Gordon B. Hinckley, "A Silver Thread in the Dark Tapestry of War," *Improvement Era,* June 1968, p. 49.
29. Interview with Allen C. Rozsa, 28 June 1995; see also "Asian Diary"; Allen C. Rozsa to Sheri L. Dew, 20 December 1995; "Church Men Meet on Battlefield," *Deseret News,* 3 October 1966.
30. "A Silver Thread in the Dark Tapestry of War," pp. 49–50.
31. See *The Korean Saints: Personal Stories of Trial and Triumph,* comp. Spencer J. Palmer and Shirley H. Palmer (Provo, Utah: BYU Religious Education, 1995), p. 188.
32. See "Asian Diary."
33. GBH Journal, 1 January 1967.
34. See Interview with Jane Freed Hinckley, 16 April 1996.
35. Interview with Richard Gordon Hinckley, 21 October 1994.
36. GBH Journal, 11 April 1967.
37. GBH Journal, 14 April 1967.
38. GBH Journal, 21 April 1967.
39. GBH Journal, 27 April 1967.
40. GBH Journal, 29 April 1967.
41. GBH Journal, 14 March 1973.
42. GBH Journal, 29 September 1967.

43. GBH Journal, 15 October 1967.
44. See GBH Journal, 25 October 1967.
45. GBH Journal, 26 October 1967.
46. See Gordon B. Hinckley, "Feed the Spirit—Nourish the Soul," *Improvement Era,* December 1967, p. 87.
47. GBH Journal, 1 November 1967; see also "Joseph the Seer," *BYU Speeches of the Year,* 5 December 1967.
48. Gordon B. Hinckley, "Lest We Forget," *BYU Speeches of the Year,* 10 November 1970.
49. Gordon B. Hinckley, *Sharing the Gospel in Military Service* (Salt Lake City: The Church of Jesus Christ of Latter-day Saints, 1970).
50. Interview with Han In Sang, 31 March 1995.
51. GBH to Spencer J. Palmer, 1 August 1966.
52. Interview with Spencer J. Palmer, 13 July 1995.
53. R. Lanier Britsch Interview with Adney Y. Komatsu, James Moyle Oral History Program, 1974; LDS Church Archives.
54. Ray C. Hillam to GBH, 5 March 1996.
55. "Asian Diary."
56. See Gordon B. Hinckley, "A Challenge from Vietnam," *Improvement Era,* June 1967, p. 54.
57. "A Silver Thread in the Dark Tapestry of War," p. 48.
58. See GBH Journal, 20–21 November 1967.
59. GBH Journal, 21 November 1967.
60. GBH Journal, 23 December 1967.
61. GBH Journal, 31 December 1967.

Chapter Sixteen
NEW CONTINENTS, NEW CHALLENGES

1. See Gordon B. Hinckley, Notes from Special Meeting, 12 May 1968.
2. Notes from Special Meeting, 12 May 1968.
3. GBH Journal, 15 May 1968.
4. See *Church News,* 29 June 1968; also "Liquor by the Drink," *Improvement Era,* October 1968, pp. 4–7.
5. *Deseret News,* 4 November 1968.
6. GBH Journal, 4 November 1968.
7. Interview with Thomas S. Monson, 28 April 1995.
8. Interview with Neal A. Maxwell, 30 June 1995.
9. *Sports Illustrated,* 14 December 1970.
10. "Policy Statement of Presidency," *Church News,* 10 January 1970.
11. GBH Journal, 25 November 1973.
12. GBH Journal, 11 November 1968.
13. See *1995–96 Church Almanac,* p. 327.
14. At the end of 1967, 66,729 members lived in South America. Eight years later, by 31 December 1975, membership had more than doubled, to 159,038. (*1977 Church Almanac,* p. 212; *1982 Church Almanac,* p. 222.)
15. GBH Journal, 23 November 1968.
16. GBH Journal, 24 November 1968.

17. See GBH Journal, 24 November 1968.
18. GBH Journal, 27 November 1968.
19. GBH Journal, 28 November 1968.
20. Interview with Clark Bryant Hinckley, 5 July 1995.
21. Interview with Clark Bryant Hinckley, 5 July 1995.
22. Interview with Richard G. Scott, 4 August 1996.
23. GBH Journal, 2 December 1968.
24. GBH Journal, 3 December 1968.
25. In *Conference Report,* October 1969, pp. 113–14.
26. See *Conference Report,* October 1969, pp. 113–14.
27. GBH Journal, 26 September 1968.
28. Interview with GBH, 24 May 1995.
29. GBH Journal, 14 November 1971.
30. Interview with GBH, 24 May 1995.
31. GBH Journal, 11 December 1967.
32. "Feed the Spirit—Nourish the Soul," pp. 85–86.
33. See *Church News,* 2 November 1963.
34. GBH Journal, 9 January 1973.
35. GBH Journal, 15 December 1967.
36. See *Improvement Era,* April 1970, p. 67.
37. Gordon B. Hinckley, "A Friend for Every Child," *Improvement Era,* December 1970, pp. 97–98.
38. GBH Journal, 21 February 1968.
39. Gordon B. Hinckley,"Contend Not with Others, But Pursue a Steady Course," *Improvement Era,* June 1970, p. 39.
40. See GBH Journal, 11 April 1969.
41. Gordon B. Hinckley, "Rise, and Stand Upon Thy Feet," *Improvement Era,* December 1968, p. 69.
42. See GBH Journal, 18 April 1969.
43. GBH Journal, 17 April 1969.
44. GBH Journal, 18 April 1969.
45. GBH Journal, 30 April 1969.
46. GBH Journal, 4 September 1969.
47. GBH Journal, 6 September 1969.
48. GBH Journal, 18 January 1970.
49. Interview with GBH, 11 July 1995.
50. GBH Journal, 6 February 1970.
51. GBH Journal, 25 February 1970.
52. See Interview with Allen E Litster, 24 June 1996.
53. GBH Journal, 7 November 1972.
54. GBH Journal, 12 March 1970.
55. GBH Journal, 17 March 1970.
56. GBH Journal, 3 June 1970; also Interview with Allen E Litster, 24 June 1996.
57. Interview with Allen E Litster, 24 June 1996.
58. GBH Journal, 4 June 1970.
59. GBH Journal, 6 June 1970.

60. See "Elder Hinckley Reports Missionaries Safe in Peru," *Church News,* 13 June 1970, p. 10.
61. See *Deseret News,* 25 February 1971; also *Daily Utah Chronicle,* 26 February 1971.
62. See *Daily Universe,* 5 May 1971; also *Deseret News,* 6 May 1971.
63. See *Church News,* 29 May 1971.
64. GBH Journal, 18 May 1971.
65. MPH to Kathy, Ginny, August 1971.
66. GBH Journal, 11 August 1971.
67. See *Deseret News,* 29 and 30 August, 1971; also *Church News,* 4 September 1971.
68. GBH Journal, 29 October 1971.
69. GBH Journal, 9 November 1971.
70. Edward L. Kimball and Andrew E. Kimball Jr., *Spencer W. Kimball* (Salt Lake City: Bookcraft, 1977), p. 389.
71. GBH Journal, 24 October 1971.
72. GBH Journal, 11 November 1971.
73. GBH Journal, 3 January 1972.
74. See *Church News,* 5 February 1972.
75. See Francis M. Gibbons, *Joseph Fielding Smith: Gospel Scholar, Prophet of God* (Salt Lake City: Deseret Book, 1992), p. 489.
76. Gordon B. Hinckley, "President Harold B. Lee: An Appreciation," *Ensign,* November 1972, p. 11.
77. GBH Journal, 7 September 1972.
78. See GBH Journal, 14–15 September 1972; also *Church News,* 27 September 1972.
79. GBH Journal, 16 September 1972.
80. See GBH Journal, 19 September 1972; also L. Brent Goates, *Harold B. Lee: Prophet and Seer* (Salt Lake City: Bookcraft, 1985), pp. 483–84.
81. See GBH Journal, 20 September 1972; also Gordon B. Hinckley, "Harold Bingham Lee: Humility, Benevolence, Loyalty," *Ensign,* February 1974, p. 89; "Holy Land Tour Thrills Pres. Lee, Elder Hinckley," *Church News,* 16 December 1972, pp. 6, 12.
82. GBH Journal, 20 September 1972.
83. As quoted in Goates, *Harold B. Lee,* p. 486.
84. See Wendell J. Ashton to General Authorities, "Transcript of Answers and Questions at Press Conference with President Harold B. Lee," 10 October 1972; also *Church News,* 30 September 1972.
85. GBH Journal, 18 September 1972.
86. GBH Journal, 4 October 1972.

Chapter Seventeen
THE CONSTANCY OF CHANGE

1. GBH Journal, 24 January 1973.
2. See GBH Journal, 19 December 1972.
3. GBH Journal, 11 January 1973.
4. GBH Journal, 19 April 1973.
5. GBH Journal, 13 May 1973.
6. GBH Journal, 26 May 1973; see also "Church Officials Dedicate 5 Restored Nauvoo Buildings," *Deseret News,* 26 May 1973.

7. GBH Journal, 2 June 1973.
8. GBH Journal, 23 December 1973.
9. GBH Journal, 20 April 1977.
10. Interview with Wendell J. Ashton, 3 February 1995; see also Lord Kenneth Thomson, "Tribute to Gordon B. Hinckley," unpublished address delivered 24 July 1987, London, England.
11. Gordon B. Hinckley, "God Shall Give unto You Knowledge by His Holy Spirit," *Speeches of the Year: BYU Devotional and Ten-Stake Fireside Addresses* (Provo, Utah: BYU Press, 1973), p. 107; also "Here We Build Our Zion: Elder Gordon B. Hinckley Talks about the Church in Europe Today," *Ensign,* August 1973, pp. 5–9.
12. Gordon B. Hinckley, "We Thank Thee, O God, for a Prophet," *Ensign,* January 1974, p. 125.
13. GBH Journal, 23 September 1973.
14. GBH Journal, 8 October 1973.
15. GBH Journal, 21 April 1973.
16. GBH Journal, 26 December 1973.
17. "Harold Bingham Lee: Humility, Benevolence, Loyalty," p. 90; also *Deseret News,* 29 December 1973.
18. GBH Journal, 31 December 1973.
19. GBH Journal, 30 September 1972.
20. GBH Journal, 15 September 1973.
21. GBH Journal, 31 December 1973.
22. GBH Journal, 16 February 1974.
23. GBH Journal, 21 February 1974.
24. See GBH Journal, 11 September 1974.
25. See "A City Set upon a Hill," pp. 98–100.
26. GBH Journal, 12 September 1974; see also *Congressional Record,* 12 September 1974, vol. 120, no. 137, p. H9187. For more on Washington Temple proceedings, see *Newsweek,* 9 September 1974, p. 72; "Washington Temple Formally Completed," *Deseret News,* 9 September 1974; "Mormon Avoids Question on Blacks," *New York Times,* 10 September 1974; "Mormon Temple Completed with Time Capsule Sealing," *Washington Post,* 10 September 1974; "Majestic Temple Completed," *Church News,* 14 September 1974.
27. GBH Journal, 19 November 1974.
28. GBH Journal, 20 November 1974.
29. See GBH Journal, 22 November 1974.
30. GBH Journal, 23 November 1974.
31. Interview with Deborah Goodson, 15 June 1995.
32. MPH to Kathy Barnes, 21 November 1976.
33. MPH to Kathy Barnes, 20 January 1976.
34. GBH Journal, 22 October 1971.
35. GBH Journal, 8 January 1972.
36. GBH Journal, 21 April 1973.
37. Interview with Jane Freed Hinckley, 11 April 1996.
38. Gordon B. Hinckley, "If I Were You, What Would I Do," *BYU 1983–84 Fireside and Devotional Speeches,* 20 September 1983.
39. See "Press Role Emphasized at DesNews Party," *Deseret News,* 12 June 1975.
40. *Spencer W. Kimball,* p. 416.

41. See Spencer W. Kimball, "When the World Will Be Converted," *Ensign,* October 1974, pp. 3–14.
42. See Gordon B. Hinckley, "The Symbol of Christ," *Ensign,* May 1975, p. 94; also "Officials Tour Arizona Temple," *Church News,* 22 March 1975.
43. Gordon Irving Interview with Yoshihiko Kikuchi, James Moyle Oral History Program, 1983; LDS Church Archives.
44. Interview with Ray Goodson, 15 June 1995.
45. Official Report of the Philippines Area Conference, p. 20; LDS Church Archives.
46. See "On Being Normal," *Time,* 25 August 1975; "Was Betty Ford Too Candid?" *Detroit Free Press,* 12 August 1975; "Betty Ford Gains Criticism, Praise for Frank Remarks," *Salt Lake Tribune,* 12 August 1975; "Betty's Remarks Draw Criticism," *Deseret News,* 11 August 1975.
47. Gordon B. Hinckley, "Opposing Evil," *Ensign,* November 1975, p. 38.
48. GBH Journal, 5 December 1975.
49. GBH Journal, 10 June 1975.
50. MPH to Kathy Barnes, undated.
51. MPH to Kathy Barnes, 16 March 1976.
52. GBH Journal, 9 September 1975.
53. See MPH to Kathy Barnes, 9 March 1978.
54. MPH to Kathy Barnes, 1 May 1976.
55. MPH to Kathy Barnes, 11 October 1976.
56. MPH to Kathy Barnes, 16 May 1977.
57. MPH to Kathy Barnes, 20 September 1976.
58. MPH to Kathy Barnes, 8 June 1976.
59. MPH to Kathy Barnes, 20 June 1976.
60. MPH to Kathy Barnes, 3 June 1976.
61. MPH to Kathy Barnes, 29 June 1976.
62. See "4 New Committees Formed," *Church News,* 5 June 1976; also "Area Supervision Worldwide," *Church News,* 26 June 1976.
63. MPH to Kathy Barnes, 27 May 1976.
64. See Gordon B. Hinckley, "Joseph the Seer," *Ensign,* May 1977, pp. 64–65.
65. Interview with Spencer J. Palmer, 13 July 1995.
66. Interview with Deborah Goodson, 15 June 1995.
67. See Gordon B. Hinckley, "Everything to Gain—Nothing to Lose," *Ensign,* November 1976, p. 97.
68. "Everything to Gain—Nothing to Lose," pp. 95–96.
69. See Gordon B. Hinckley, "Be Not Afraid, Only Believe," *Improvement Era,* December 1969, pp. 97–98.
70. See Spencer W. Kimball, "When the World Will Be Converted," *Ensign,* October 1974, pp. 3–14.
71. See, for example, "God Shall Give unto You Knowledge by His Holy Spirit," p. 109.

Chapter Eighteen
THE CHURCH MOVES FORWARD

1. GBH Journal, 13 October 1977.
2. MPH to Kathy Barnes, 2 February 1977.

3. Gordon B. Hinckley, "Four Imperatives for Religious Educators" (Church Educational System, 1978), pp. 1–2.
4. MPH to Kathy Barnes, 2 November 1977.
5. Interview with Augusto A. Lim, 31 March 1995.
6. MPH to Kathy Barnes, 8 April 1977.
7. GBH Journal, 20 January 1977.
8. GBH Journal, 20 January 1977.
9. GBH Journal, 21 January 1977.
10. MPH to Family, 23 January 1977.
11. MPH to Family, 28 January 1977.
12. GBH Journal, 25 January 1977.
13. GBH Journal, 29 April 1977.
14. GBH Journal, 27 May 1977.
15. GBH Journal, 29 July 1977.
16. Gordon B. Hinckley, "Joseph the Seer," *Ensign*, May 1977, pp. 64–65.
17. "As One Who Loves the Prophet."
18. Memorandum, as recorded in GBH Journal, 3 October 1977.
19. MPH to the Barnes, 24 May 1978.
20. Gordon B. Hinckley, Address at Rededication of Hyde Park Chapel, 27 August 1995.
21. MPH to Family, 8 February 1978.
22. "Filmmakers Challenged to Build Faith," *Deseret News*, 2 September 1978.
23. See "TV's 'Disastrous' Impact on Children," *U.S. News & World Report*, 19 January 1981, pp. 43–45.
24. *Church News*, 10 June 1978, p. 3.
25. Gordon B. Hinckley, "Priesthood Restoration," *Ensign*, October 1988, p. 70.
26. Interview with GBH, 9 August 1995.
27. Gordon B. Hinckley, "Be Not Faithless," *Ensign*, May 1978, p. 58; see also Spencer J. Palmer, *The Expanding Church* (Salt Lake City: Deseret Book, 1978), pp. 5–7.
28. Palmer, *The Expanding Church*, p. 7.
29. See Gordon B. Hinckley, "The True Strength of the Church," *Ensign*, July 1973, p. 48.
30. See "The True Strength of the Church," p. 48.
31. Gordon B. Hinckley, "And Peter Went Out and Wept Bitterly," *Ensign*, May 1979, p. 67.
32. See "'Small Means,' Thousands of Miles Away, Help the Church in Spain," *Ensign*, February 1979, p. 76.
33. See Janet Brigham, "Houston Area Conference Report," *Ensign*, August 1979, p. 72.
34. See *Conference Report*, October 1979, pp. 8–11.
35. Gordon B. Hinckley, "150-Year Drama: A Personal View of Our History," *Ensign*, April 1980, pp. 10–14.
36. See "Satellite to Beam Cabin Rites," *Church News*, 5 April 1980.
37. Interview with GBH, 18 October 1995.
38. In *Conference Report*, April 1980, pp. 80–81.
39. See "Whitmer Structures Dedicated to the Lord," *Church News*, 12 April 1980; also "Fayette Links LDS Past, Present," *Deseret News*, 7 April 1980; "Fayette Links Past, Present of Church," *Church News*, 12 April 1980; "Proclamation," *Church News*, 12 April 1980; "Pres. Kimball Leads N.Y. Rites on 150th Anniversary of Church," *Deseret News*, 7 April 1980; G. Homer Durham, "The Sesquicentennial General

Conference Sessions of The Church of Jesus Christ of Latter-day Saints," unpublished memorandum, LDS Church Archives.

40. Gordon B. Hinckley, "Thoughts and Feelings of Gordon B. Hinckley on the Occasion of the General Conference of the Church, Part of Which Originated in Fayette, New York, 6 April 1980," unpublished memorandum, LDS Church Archives.
41. Interview with Hugh W. Pinnock, 14 April 1995.
42. See *Deseret News*, 7 April 1980; *Church News*, 19 April 1980; also "Mormons: Grappling with Growth Pains," *U.S. News & World Report*, 7 April 1980; Joel Kotkin, "Mormon Church at 150: Flourishing, Chafing," *Washington Post*, 6 April 1980.
43. See, for example, *PSA Magazine*, June 1980, pp. 2–6.
44. Dallin H. Oaks Journal, 14 April 1980.
45. Interview with Jeffrey R. Holland, 26 May 1995; see also "New BYU President Appointed," *Deseret News*, 9 May 1980.
46. Dallin H. Oaks Journal, 19 May 1980.
47. MPH to Family, 21 May 1980.
48. Dallin H. Oaks Journal, 20 May 1980.
49. Dallin H. Oaks Journal, 20 May 1980.
50. Dallin H. Oaks Journal, 25 May 1980.
51. *Church News*, 23 August 1980.
52. MPH to Emily Pearce, 31 May 1980.
53. MPH to Laura Pearce, 31 May 1980.
54. MPH to Rosemary Pearce, 15 May 1980.
55. MPH to Emily Pearce, 15 May 1980.
56. MPH to James R. Pearce Family, 16 October 1980.
57. Dell Van Orden, "Saints Throng to Area Meetings in the Far East," *Church News*, 1 November 1980.
58. MPH to the Pearces, 25 October 1980.
59. Arthur K. Nishimoto, "My Experiences with President Gordon B. Hinckley," memo to Sheri L. Dew, 24 May 1995.
60. Related in Kiyoshi Sakai memo to Sheri L. Dew, 27 April 1995.
61. MPH to Barnes, 22 March 1980.
62. MPH to Barnes, 8 November 1980.
63. MPH to Kathy Barnes, 12 January 1981.
64. MPH to Mr. and Mrs. Richard G. Hinckley, 14 May 1981.
65. Kan Watanabe to Sheri L. Dew, 11 May 1995.

Chapter Nineteen
THE FIRST PRESIDENCY

1. GBH Journal, 15 July 1981.
2. Interview with L. Tom Perry, 31 May 1995.
3. GBH Journal, 22 July 1981.
4. GBH Journal, 22 July 1981.
5. Minutes of the Council of the Twelve, 23 July 1981, as recorded in GBH Journal, 23 July 1981.
6. Interview with Kathleen Hinckley Barnes, 17 October 1995.

7. GBH Journal, 23 July 1981.
8. Interview with MPH, 20 October 1994.
9. *Church News,* 1 August 1981.
10. D. Arthur Haycock to GBH, memorandum, 8 June 1984.
11. GBH Journal, 24 July 1981.
12. Interview with GBH, 9 August 1995.
13. GBH Journal, 1 August 1981.
14. See "Cornerstone Put into Place in Jordan River Temple Rites," *Deseret News,* 15 August 1981.
15. Gordon B. Hinckley, "Charity Never Faileth," *Ensign,* November 1981, p. 98; see also *Deseret News,* 28 September 1981.
16. GBH Journal, 1 October 1981.
17. Interview with GBH, 18 October 1995.
18. In *Conference Report,* October 1981, p. 5.
19. GBH Journal, 4 October 1981.
20. GBH Journal, 20 November 1981.
21. GBH Journal, 5 December 1981.
22. GBH Journal, 1 February 1982.
23. GBH Journal, 23 December 1981.
24. See First Presidency Memorandum to All General Authorities and Managing Directors, 18 March 1982.
25. See *Conference Report,* April 1982, p. 108.
26. See "President Kimball Closes Session with 'All Is Well,'" *Deseret News,* 4 April 1982.
27. Gordon B. Hinckley, "Five Million Members—A Milestone and Not a Summit," *Ensign,* May 1982, pp. 44–46.
28. See Gordon B. Hinckley, "A Sacred Trust," Remarks at Meeting of Regional Representatives and Stake Presidents, 2 April 1982.
29. GBH Journal, 30 November 1981.
30. "Pres. Hinckley Dedicates 16 Sites in Nauvoo," *Deseret News,* 14 August 1982.
31. Interview with Ruben Lacanienta, 14 June 1995.
32. See GBH Journal, 10 September 1982.
33. GBH Journal, 2 June 1982.
34. GBH Journal, 31 August 1982.
35. GBH Journal, 13 September 1982.
36. In *Conference Report,* October 1982, pp. 47, 62.
37. "Remarks by President Gordon B. Hinckley, Counselor in the First Presidency," *Ensign,* January 1983, p. 13.
38. GBH Journal, 28 November 1982.
39. See D. Arthur Haycock to GBH memorandum; also "First Presidency Reorganized," *Ensign,* January 1983, p. 14.
40. GBH Journal, 2 December 1982.
41. Interview with GBH, 9 August 1995.
42. Interview with Neal A. Maxwell, 30 June 1995.
43. See GBH Journal, 15 December 1982.
44. Interview with Richard Gordon Hinckley, 21 October 1994.
45. GBH Journal, 23 December 1982.

46. GBH Journal, 25 December 1982.
47. Gordon B. Hinckley, "He Slumbers Not, Nor Sleeps," *Ensign,* May 1983, pp. 5–6; see also "LDS Leader, First Counselor Weak, Tired from Illnesses, Advanced Age," *Salt Lake Tribune,* 17 November 1983.
48. GBH Journal, 13 March 1984.
49. GBH Journal, 30 April 1984.
50. "If I Were You, What Would I Do," p. 8.
51. "Mission Goal: Saving Souls Across World," *Church News,* 3 July 1983.
52. Interview with Boyd K. Packer, 1986.
53. Gordon B. Hinckley, remarks at President Benson's ninetieth birthday commemoration, 30 July 1989.
54. See Holland, "Stalwart and Brave He Stands," p. 12.
55. Interview with Thomas S. Monson, 28 April 1995.
56. Gordon B. Hinckley, "Small Acts Lead to Great Consequences," *Ensign,* May 1984, p. 81; also "Pres. Hinckley Says Lord, Not Men, Called Pair," *Deseret News,* 9 April 1984.
57. Gordon B. Hinckley, "The Miracle Made Possible by Faith," *Ensign,* May 1984, pp. 46–48.
58. Gordon B. Hinckley, "Special Witnesses to Christ," *Ensign,* May 1984, p. 51.

Chapter Twenty
FORWARD WITH NEVER A BACKWARD STEP

1. See "Religious Freedom Is Their Key Aim," *Church News,* 16 September 1984.
2. "150-Year Drama: A Personal View of Our History," pp. 10–14.
3. See "Mormon Infighting Intensifies as Theologians Vie for Power," *Daily Californian* (Berkeley, California), 6 April 1982, p. 20.
4. "Stop Looking for Storms and Enjoy the Sunlight," *Church News,* 3 July 1983.
5. Gordon B. Hinckley, "Be Not Deceived," *Ensign,* November 1983, p. 46.
6. See Gordon B. Hinckley, "Emphasize Positive, Subdue the Negative," *Church News,* 6 October 1985.
7. GBH Journal, 22 April 1984.
8. GBH Journal, 10 February 1984.
9. "Homage Is Paid to Those Who Preserved Freedom," *Church News,* 9 September 1984.
10. *Deseret News,* 27 September 1984.
11. GBH Journal, 4 September 1984.
12. Robert W. Collins Interview with Gordon B. Hinckley, 18 April 1990, General Authorities Video Biographies Project; see also "Church Modifies Area Administration," press release, 24 June 1984; "New Presidencies Announced for 13 Geographic Areas," *Church News,* 24 June 1984; G. Homer Durham, "For the Journal History of the Church," 4 October 1984; "Sweetest, Richest, Most Rewarding Experience," *Church News,* 1 July 1984.
13. Gordon B. Hinckley, "The Good and Faithful Servants," *Ensign,* November 1984, p. 49.
14. Gordon B. Hinckley, "The Cornerstones of Our Faith," *Ensign,* November 1984, p. 50.
15. GBH Journal, 16 October 1988.

16. Interview with L. Tom Perry, 31 May 1995; see also L. Tom Perry, "An Elect Lady," *Ensign,* May 1991, pp. 72–74.
17. Interview with Kathleen Hinckley Barnes, 17 October 1995.
18. Interview with Tom Blair, 16 April 1995.
19. Interview with Tom Blair, 16 April 1995.
20. Interview with Clark Bryant Hinckley, 17 November 1994.
21. See "Top Team: 'No Doubt About it,'" *Church News,* 30 December 1984.
22. See "A Year to Remember, a Team to Remember," *Church News,* 27 January 1985.
23. "Words of Solace and Comfort," *Church News,* 30 December 1984; see also "1700 Gather to Say Their Farewells to Dead Miners," *Deseret News,* 26 December 1984.
24. GBH Journal, 2 January 1985.
25. GBH Journal, 9 January 1985.
26. Interview with Neal A. Maxwell, 30 June 1995.
27. "President Gordon B. Hinckley: As Seen Through the Eyes of Rodney H. Brady," memo to Sheri L. Dew, 1995, pp. 6–7.
28. Interview with Russell M. Nelson, 17 May 1995.
29. Interview with Derek Metcalfe, 8 June 1995.
30. "The Widow's Mite."
31. Interview with Neal A. Maxwell, 30 June 1995.
32. GBH Journal, 21 December 1977.
33. Gordon B. Hinckley, "The Victory Over Death," *Ensign,* May 1985, p. 59; see also "LDS Special Fast Nets Millions for Africans," *Salt Lake Tribune,* 8 April 1985; "LDS Donations to Aid the Hungry Exceed $6 Million," *Deseret News,* 8 April 1985.
34. "Milestone Challenge to Leaders," *Church News,* 14 April 1985; "LDS Mission Presidents Gather for Instruction," *Deseret News,* 4 April 1985.
35. "Elder McConkie Eulogized as 'A Man with a Giant Stride,'" *Deseret News,* 23 April 1985; "Testimony Lingers After Apostle's Death," *Church News,* 28 April 1985.
36. See "5 New Temples Add 'Great Momentum,'" *Church News,* 15 April 1985.
37. Gordon B. Hinckley, "Giving Ourselves to the Service of the Lord," *Ensign,* March 1987, p. 2.
38. "A Pentecost of Feeling," *Church News,* 30 June 1985.
39. "Polynesia's Fifth Temple Dedicated," *Church News,* 6 November 1983.
40. "New Temple Is South Africa's Brightest Jewel," *Church News,* 1 September 1985.
41. "Emotional Rites Note 'Miracle of Philippines,'" *Church News,* 7 October 1984; see also "First Temple in Chinese Realm," *Church News,* 25 November 1984.
42. "Glistening 'New' at 97, Manti Temple Rededicated," *Church News,* 23 June 1985.
43. GBH Journal, 16 June 1985.
44. See "President Hinckley Cites Bond Between Leaders," *Church News,* 4 April 1984.
45. "Questions and Answers," *Ensign,* November 1985, p. 49.
46. Gordon B. Hinckley, "To Please Our Heavenly Father," *Ensign,* May 1985, p. 50.
47. Gordon B. Hinckley, "The Scourge of Illicit Drugs," *Ensign,* November 1989, pp. 49–50.
48. Gordon B. Hinckley, "What This Work Is All About," *Ensign,* November 1982, p. 7.
49. Gordon B. Hinckley, "Our Mission of Saving," *Ensign,* November 1991, p. 59.
50. "The Healing Power of Christ," p. 59.
51. GBH Journal, 15 November 1981.
52. Interview with James E. Faust, 12 April 1995.

53. Interview with GBH, 7 February 1996.
54. "He Slumbers Not, Nor Sleeps," pp. 7–8.
55. "The Widow's Mite."
56. GBH Journal, 22 January 1984.
57. GBH Journal, 29 September 1985.
58. Gordon B. Hinckley, "Rejoice in This Great Era of Temple Building," *Ensign*, November 1985, p. 53.
59. See "Rejoice in This Great Era," p. 53.
60. N. Eldon Tanner Journal, 22 April 1980, as quoted in Richard E. Turley Jr., *Victims: The LDS Church and the Mark Hofmann Case* (Urbana: University of Illinois Press, 1992), p. 32.
61. See Turley, *Victims*, p. 40.
62. In *Conference Report*, April 1981, pp. 27–28.
63. GBH Journal, 10 February 1984.
64. "Mormons Ponder 1830 Letter Altering Idealized Image of Joseph Smith," *Los Angeles Times*, 25 August 1984; see also Turley, *Victims*, pp. 91–92.
65. "Cornerstones of Our Faith," p. 52.
66. *Church News*, 28 April 1985; also Turley, *Victims*, p. 100.
67. GBH Journal, 17 May 1985.
68. "Be Not Deceived," p. 46.
69. "Wealth of Spirit Results from Keeping the Faith," *Church News*, 30 June 1985.
70. GBH, memorandum, 21 October 1985.
71. GBH Journal, 22 October 1985.
72. Transcript of press conference held 23 October 1985; see also Turley, *Victims*, pp. 187–204; "LDS Church Officials Say They Had No Inkling of Document Problems," *Deseret News*, 23 October 1985; "Church Leaders Clarify Role in Documents Transactions," *Church News*, 27 October 1985; "Hofmann Frequently Met LDS Official," *Salt Lake Tribune*, 20 October 1985; "Debts May Have Pressed Hofmann to Make a Sale," *Deseret News*, 23 October 1985.
73. "Pres. Hinckley Dedicates Genealogy 'Crown Jewel,'" *Church News*, 3 November 1985.
74. GBH Journal, 23 October 1985.
75. See Turley, *Victims*, p. 240; also "Documents Have Been Hofmann's Life Since 1980—And They Provide Both Motive and Charges in Murder Case," *Deseret News*, 4 February 1986.
76. See "2 Witnesses Trace Labyrinth of Hofmann's Deals," *Salt Lake Tribune*, 22 April 1986; "Dealer Says Hofmann Documents Were Forged," *Deseret News*, 22 April 1986; "Evidence Alludes to 'Oath' Forgery," *Salt Lake Tribune*, 6 May 1986; "Detective Discusses the Motives for Slayings," *Deseret News*, 14 May 1986; "Hofmann Told Others He Was Shown Secret LDS History," *Salt Lake Tribune*, 17 October 1986; "Mormons Deny Papers Exist That Contradict Origins," *Los Angeles Times*, 17 October 1986; "LDS Church Feels Vindicated by Hofmann," *Salt Lake Tribune*, 1 August 1987; "Transcript Provides More Information on Murders," *Salt Lake Tribune*, 1 August 1987; "Transcripts Unveil True Hofmann—Devoid of Human Conscience," *Deseret News*, 1 August 1987.
77. GBH Journal, 30 July 1987.
78. Interview with GBH, 18 October 1995.
79. GBH Journal, 23 October 1985.
80. GBH Journal, 24 October 1985.

81. GBH Journal, 5 November 1985.
82. See "President Kimball Eulogized As a Man Who 'Knew the Lord,'" *Church News,* 17 November 1985; "President Kimball Eulogized as 'Noble Great One,'" *Deseret News,* 10 November 1985; "Thousands Mourn Leader of Mormons," *Washington Post,* 9 November 1985.
83. GBH Journal, 9 November 1985.
84. GBH Journal, 10 November 1985.

Chapter Twenty-One
FIRST COUNSELOR

1. See "Unprecedented Church Growth Distinguishes Kimball Years," *Church News,* 10 November 1985.
2. Interview with GBH, 18 October 1995.
3. GBH Journal, 12 November 1985.
4. GBH Journal, 18 November 1985.
5. GBH Journal, 7 September 1985.
6. GBH Journal, 24 December 1985.
7. See Interview with Spencer J. Palmer, 13 July 1995.
8. GBH Journal, 14 December 1985.
9. "'Land of Morning Calm' Brightened by Korea Temple," *Church News,* 22 December 1985.
10. GBH Journal, 14 December 1985.
11. GBH Journal, 15 December 1985.
12. Interview with Kathleen Hinckley Barnes, 17 October 1994; see also M. Russell Ballard, "President Gordon B. Hinckley: An Anchor of Faith," *Ensign,* September 1994, pp. 6–11.
13. See *1995–96 Church Almanac,* pp. 329–30.
14. Gordon B. Hinckley, "Come and Partake," *Ensign,* May 1986, p. 47.
15. In *Conference Report,* April 1986, p. 52.
16. Marjorie P. Hinckley, "Building the Kingdom from a Firm Foundation," in *As Women of Faith: Talks Selected from the BYU Women's Conference* (Salt Lake City: Deseret Book, 1989), p. 10.
17. GBH Journal, 22 November 1986.
18. GBH Journal, 12 March 1987.
19. "Church Is Shortsighted in Closing Hotel Utah," *Salt Lake Tribune,* 19 March 1987; see also "Save Hotel Utah! Speak Out," *Salt Lake Tribune,* 19 July 1978, p. 18A.
20. "Plan to Close Hotel Sets Off Classic Utah Struggle," *New York Times,* 3 June 1987, p. 10.
21. "Nostalgia and Poignancy Abound As a Grand Lady Becomes History," *Deseret News,* 1 September 1987; "At Stroke of Midnight 'The Lady' Bows Out Gracefully," *Deseret News,* 31 August 1987; "Church Says Public Will Be Pleased As Hotel Plans Unfold," *Deseret News,* 21 May 1987.
22. Interview with L. Tom Perry, 31 May 1995.
23. Interview with GBH, 22 November 1995.
24. See, for example, Lowell R. Hardy to Kieth Merrill, 10 May 1988.
25. Interview with Robert D. Hales, 26 May 1995.

26. See Interview with James E. Faust, 10 November 1995; also Press Release and Public Statement, Citizens for Morality in Church Government, 1988, LDS Church Archives.
27. GBH to President Ezra Taft Benson, President Thomas S. Monson, Members of the Council of the Twelve, 18 October 1988.
28. GBH Journal, 18 October 1988.
29. "A Statement from President Gordon B. Hinckley," read at the 6 May 1993 meeting of the First Presidency and the Quorum of the Twelve.
30. See "Group Criticizes Anti-Mormon Film," *Deseret News,* 24 December 1992; also "A Statement from President Gordon B. Hinckley"; "Film 'Godmakers II' Condemned by Several Organizations," *Salt Lake Tribune,* 12 December 1992.
31. Interview with James E. Faust, 12 December 1995.
32. Interview with GBH, 18 October 1995.
33. GBH Journal, 18 October 1995.
34. "The Loneliness of Leadership."
35. "If I Were You, What Would I Do," p. 8.
36. Jenkins Lloyd Jones, *Deseret News,* 12 June 1973; as quoted in "Four Imperatives for Religious Educators," p. 4.
37. "Let Love Be the Lodestar of Your Life," p. 65.
38. Interview with Russell M. Nelson, 17 May 1995.
39. Interview with Russell M. Nelson, 17 May 1995.
40. Interview with Russell M. Nelson, 17 May 1995.
41. Interview with Robert D. Hales, 26 May 1995.
42. Interview with Clark Bryant Hinckley, 17 November 1994.
43. Interview with Neal A. Maxwell, 30 June 1995.
44. Interview with M. Russell Ballard, 18 June 1995.
45. "Taking the Gospel to Britain," pp. 2–7.
46. Lord Thomson, "Tribute to Gordon B. Hinckley"; see also GBH Journal, 24 July 1987.
47. Lord Kenneth R. Thomson to GBH, 28 July 1987.
48. GBH Journal, 25 July 1987.
49. "British Strength Lauded in Birmingham," *Church News,* 1 August 1987; see also "Major Events Fill LDS British Calendar," "Markers Tell Where History Was Made," "Liberty Sparked First in Britain," "Church Celebrates Its British History," and "Saga of Church in British Isles Lauded at Anniversary Dinner," *Church News,* 1 August 1987; "LDS Mark 150 Years in the British Isles," *Deseret News,* 25 July 1987.
50. Interview with Clark Bryant Hinckley, 18 November 1994.
51. Interview with Virginia Hinckley Pearce, 12 October 1994.
52. Interview with Clark Bryant Hinckley, 17 November 1994.
53. GBH Journal, 19 June 1988.
54. GBH Journal, 20 June 1988.
55. Dallin H. Oaks Journal, 10 September 1988.
56. GBH Journal, 15 September 1995.
57. GBH Journal, 15–16 November 1986.
58. Interview with Jeffrey R. Holland, 26 May 1995.
59. See "BYU Chief Gets a Big Send-Off at Ceremony," *Deseret News,* 29 April 1989; also "BYU Leader Begins 'Lord's Errand,' *Church News,* 4 November 1989; "Lee

Inaugurated as 10th BYU President," *Deseret News,* 28 October 1989; "BYU Inaugurates Rex Lee as Its 10th President," *Salt Lake Tribune,* 28 October 1989.

60. "Four Imperatives for Religious Educators."
61. Gordon B. Hinckley, "Out of Your Experience Here," *BYU 1990–1991 Devotional and Fireside Speeches,* p. 28.
62. Gordon B. Hinckley, "Our Solemn Responsibilities," *Ensign,* November 1991, p. 51.
63. Gordon B. Hinckley, "Daughters of God," *Ensign,* November 1991, p. 100.
64. See "Ellerbee, Hinckley Differ on Working Women," *Salt Lake Tribune,* 24 February 1990.
65. "Attitude Can Make a 'Great Difference,'" *Church News,* 17 September 1988; "LDS Church Official Says Attacking Church Won't Help Utah," *Salt Lake Tribune,* 8 September 1988; "LDS Church Plays a Substantial Role in Utah Economy, Officials Explain," *Salt Lake Tribune,* 25 December 1989.
66. "Our Solemn Responsibilities," p. 52.
67. Interview with Dallin H. Oaks, 28 June 1995.
68. See "Honoring a 47-Year Ministry," *Church News,* 28 May 1988.
69. John Holbrook to Yoshihiko Kikuchi, 3 April 1995.
70. GBH Journal, 30 May 1989.
71. See "Shrine Honors Founder of Mormons," *Washington Post,* 1 July 1989; also Gordon B. Hinckley, "Carthage Dedication," unpublished address, 27 June 1989; "LDS Church Dedicates the Carthage Jail Complex," *Deseret News,* 27 June 1989; "Hallowed, Sacred Site Made Beautiful Out of Respect, Love," *Church News,* 8 July 1989; "Mormons Dedicate Sacred Jail," *Quad-City Times,* 28 June 1989; "Renovated Carthage Jail Dedicated," *Ensign,* September 1989, p. 74.
72. Gordon B. Hinckley, "A Wonderful Summer," *BYU 1989–1990 Devotional and Fireside Speeches,* pp. 14–15.
73. "Nauvoo's Day of Glory Is Likened to Sunrise, Sunset on Mississippi," *Church News,* 29 September 1989.
74. GBH Journal, 3 July 1989.
75. GBH Journal, 8 July 1989.
76. Interview with Jane Hinckley Dudley, 9 November 1994.
77. "A Wonderful Summer," pp. 11–12.

Chapter Twenty-Two
THE OPENING OF NEW DOORS

1. See "And the Walls Came Tumbling Down," *Our Glorious Century* (Pleasantville, N.Y.: Reader's Digest, 1994), pp. 420–23.
2. Interview with GBH, 22 November 1995.
3. See "European Reform Called Gift to World," *Deseret News,* 4 December 1989; "A Season of Love That Is Felt Anew," *Church News,* 9 December 1989.
4. See "LDS Church Welcome to Come to Soviet Union, Says Envoy," *Salt Lake Tribune,* 28 April 1990; also "Reliving 'LDS Question,'" *Salt Lake Tribune,* 15 October 1995.
5. Gerry Avant, "Soviet Envoy's Utah Visit Is Historic," *Church News,* 5 May 1990; also "Superpowers Beginning Era of Friendship, Soviet Says," *Deseret News,* 28 April 1990.
6. GBH Journal, 7 September 1990.
7. Interview with GBH, 22 November 1995.

8. "Rise to a Larger Vision of the Work," pp. 95–97; see also Boyd K. Packer, "Teach Them Correct Principles," *Ensign,* May 1990, pp. 89–91; Thomas S. Monson, "The Lord's Way," *Ensign,* May 1990, pp. 92–94.
9. GBH Journal, 22 June 1990.
10. GBH Journal, 11 July 1990.
11. See, for example, GBH Journal, 6 June 1990.
12. GBH Journal, 7 June 1990.
13. Interview with Robert D. Hales, 26 May 1995.
14. Gordon B. Hinckley, "This Peaceful House of God," *Ensign,* May 1993, p. 74.
15. GBH Journal, 15 April 1990.
16. Gordon B. Hinckley, "Youth Is the Season," *New Era,* September 1988, p. 47.
17. Gordon B. Hinckley, "Rise to the Stature of the Divine Within You," *Ensign,* November 1989, pp. 95, 97.
18. See GBH Journal, 22 June 1990.
19. GBH Journal, 23 June 1990.
20. GBH Journal, 24 June 1990.
21. MPH to Michael Hinckley, 1 March 1993.
22. Gordon B. Hinckley, "Trust and Accountability," BYU Devotional Address, 13 October 1992.
23. GBH Journal, 25 October 1992.
24. MPH to Michael Hinckley, 24 January 1993.
25. GBH Journal, 1 July 1993.
26. GBH Journal, 21 July 1993.
27. Gordon B. Hinckley, "A Unique and Wonderful University," BYU Devotional Address, 1 October 1988.
28. GBH Journal, 2 May 1991.
29. GBH Journal, 6 February 1993.
30. GBH Journal, 7 December 1992.
31. Gordon B. Hinckley, "'In . . . Counsellors There Is Safety,'" *Ensign,* November 1990, pp. 50–51.
32. Interview with Ted Simmons, 23 January 1996.
33. Interview with Dallin H. Oaks, 28 June 1995.
34. GBH Journal, 31 July 1992.
35. See Interview with Allen C. Rozsa, 28 June 1995.
36. GBH Journal, 13 September 1993.
37. GBH Journal, 13 September 1993; also Interview with Jane Hinckley Dudley, 9 November 1994.
38. Interview with Jane Hinckley Dudley, 9 November 1994.
39. Interview with Michael Richard Hinckley, 23 June 1996.
40. See "Children: The Essence of Love, Hope," *Church News,* 29 January 1994.
41. "Mothers Urged to Back Positive Entertainment," *Deseret News,* 3 May 1994; "Mothers Face Compelling Challenges, Opportunities," *Church News,* 7 May 1994.
42. "Saving the Nation by Changing Our Homes," address to BYU Management Society, 5 March 1994.
43. "Pioneer Memorial Takes Flak for Profanity, May Lose Financial Support of LDS Source," *Salt Lake Tribune,* 11 February 1994.
44. GBH Journal, 15 August 1992.

45. See "Address and Dedication of Willie Rescue Site Monument," 15 August 1992; also GBH Journal, 15 August 1992.
46. GBH Journal, 4 April 1993; also "This Peaceful House of God," p. 75.
47. See Interview with Derek Metcalfe, 8 June 1995.
48. Interview with Derek Metcalfe, 8 June 1995.
49. Interview with Neal A. Maxwell, 30 June 1995.
50. GBH Journal, 19 May 1993.
51. Interview with Philippe Kradolfer, 16 April 1996.
52. GBH Journal, 11 June 1992.
53. GBH Journal, 26 July 1992.
54. Interview with Ted Simmons, 23 January 1996.
55. GBH Journal, 25 April 1993.
56. GBH Journal, 27 April 1993.
57. Interview with L. Tom Perry, 31 May 1995.
58. GBH Journal, 6 May 1993.
59. "A Tour of the Joseph Smith Memorial Building," *Ensign,* September 1993, pp. 32–34; see also "A Heroic Figure," *Ensign,* September 1993, p. 38.
60. "Pleasing Restoration," *Salt Lake Tribune,* 18 August 1993.
61. See Stan Larson, ed., *A Ministry of Meetings: The Apostolic Diaries of Rudger Clawson* (Salt Lake City: Signature Books, 1993), pp. 373–75, 421, 542, 725.
62. Joseph F. Smith Jr. to Elder E. Wesley Smith, 18 August 1909.
63. GBH to Calvin P. Rudd, 9 December 1993.
64. Interview with Richard G. Scott, 4 August 1996.
65. See "Out of Your Experience Here," p. 29.
66. Interview with Thomas S. Monson, 28 April 1995.
67. Interview with Wendell J. Ashton, 3 February 1995.
68. See "Everyone Has Something to Contribute, Says Ford Chairman," *Church News,* 27 November 1983.
69. Interview with M. Russell Ballard, 18 June 1995.
70. Spencer J. Condie to M. Russell Ballard, 9 June 1994.
71. GBH Journal, 17 July 1992.
72. George Bush to GBH, 21 July 1992.
73. Interview with Lowell R. Hardy, 11 May 1995.
74. "A New Church Order," *Salt Lake Tribune,* 14 March 1995.
75. Interview with Ted Simmons, 23 January 1996.
76. Interview with Thomas S. Monson, 28 April 1995.
77. Interview with Henry B. Eyring, 9 August 1995.
78. "Rise to the Stature of the Divine Within You," pp. 94–95.
79. Gordon B. Hinckley, "An Ensign to the Nations," *Ensign,* November 1989, p. 53.
80. "Rise to a Larger Vision of the Work," p. 97.
81. "Go Forward with Faith," p. 5.
82. "Go Forward with Faith," p. 5.
83. Gordon B. Hinckley, "The Church Is On Course," *Ensign,* November 1992, pp. 53–54.
84. GBH Journal, 11 October 1993.
85. See "Statement Released by First Presidency and Quorum of the Twelve," *Ensign,* January 1994, p. 75.

86. GBH Journal, 31 December 1993.
87. See "Elder Ashton a 'Champion of Love,' *Church News,* 5 March 1994, p. 3.
88. Gordon B. Hinckley, "God Is at the Helm," *Ensign,* May 1994, p. 59.
89. GBH Journal, 17 April 1994.
90. GBH Journal, 19 April 1994.
91. See "President Hinckley Honored for Example as 'a Good Citizen,'" *Church News,* 12 May 1990.
92. See "Cove Fort Dedication Video"; also "Fort a Monument to Faith, Fortitude," *Church News,* 28 May 1994; "Pres. Hinckley Hails Cove Fort's Original Builders," *Deseret News,* 22 May 1994.
93. GBH Journal, 21 May 1994.
94. See Gordon B. Hinckley, "Farewell to a Prophet," *Ensign,* July 1994, pp. 37–40.
95. "Farewell to a Prophet," p. 40.
96. GBH Journal, 5 June 1994.

Chapter Twenty-Three
FIRST COUNSELOR A SECOND TIME

1. Interview with GBH, 22 November 1995.
2. Interview with GBH, 22 November 1995.
3. "Pres. Hunter Is Ordained Prophet," *Church News,* 11 June 1994.
4. See "Pres. Hunter Takes Helm of LDS Church," *Deseret News,* 6 June 1994; "Howard W. Hunter Ordained President of the Church," *Tambuli,* August 1994, p. 1; "Mormons Pick Lawyer, 86, as Leader," *New York Times,* 7 June 1994.
5. "First Impressions: Power of Hunter's Spirit Soars," *Salt Lake Tribune,* 7 June 1994.
6. "Ground Broken for Preston Temple," *Church News,* 18 June 1994; "Ground Broken for Preston England Temple," *Ensign,* September 1994, p. 77.
7. See GBH Journal, 12 June 1994.
8. Interview with Jeffrey R. Holland, 26 May 1995.
9. See Gordon B. Hinckley, "Nauvoo Temple Site Sunstone Commemoration Address," 26 June 1994, unpublished manuscript.
10. Gordon B. Hinckley, "Carthage Satellite Broadcast Address," 26 June 1994, unpublished manuscript.
11. "A Time to Remember, Honor, Respect," *Church News,* 2 July 1994, pp. 3, 6–10.
12. GBH Journal, 1 July 1994.
13. GBH Journal, 29 August 1994.
14. GBH Journal, 8 January 1995.
15. GBH Journal, 15 January 1995.
16. GBH Journal, 28 February 1995.
17. Interview with GBH, 22 November 1995.
18. GBH Journal, 29 January 1995.
19. GBH Journal, 31 January 1995.
20. Interview with Lowell R. Hardy, 9 April 1996.
21. Tribute to Gordon B. Hinckley from the Right Honorable Lord Thomson of Fleet.
22. "Christians, Jews Honor LDS Leader," *Church News,* 25 February 1995, p. 3.
23. See, for example, GBH Journal, 1 February 1995.

24. Interview with Lowell R. Hardy, 13 August 1996.
25. GBH Journal, 27 February 1995.
26. GBH Journal, 1 March 1995.
27. Interview with MPH, 16 March 1995.
28. Interview with GBH, 22 November 1995.
29. GBH Journal, 3 March 1995.
30. GBH Journal, 4 March 1995.
31. "Pres. Hinckley: Prophet Taught Under the Plan of the Almighty," *Church News,* 11 March 1995, p. 4.
32. GBH Journal, 8 March 1995.
33. GBH Journal, 9 March 1995.
34. GBH Journal, 9 March 1995.
35. GBH Journal, 12 March 1995.

Chapter Twenty-Four
PRESIDENT OF THE CHURCH

1. "Pres. Hinckley's 'Debut' Impressive," *Deseret News,* 18 March 1995.
2. GBH Journal, 13 March 1995.
3. George Bush to Gordon B. Hinckley, 13 March 1995.
4. Interview with James E. Faust, 12 April 1995.
5. Interview with Boyd K. Packer, 19 April 1995.
6. GBH Journal, 14 March 1995.
7. Interviews with GBH, 18 April 1995 and 22 November 1995.
8. Interview with GBH, 7 February 1996.
9. See Interview with GBH, 9 July 1996.
10. GBH to Michael Richard Hinckley, 17 March 1993.
11. See Gordon B. Hinckley, "True to the Faith," Salt Lake Valley-Wide Institute Fireside, 21 January 1996.
12. Interview with Michael Richard Hinckley, 23 June 1996.
13. GBH Journal, 27 March 1995.
14. Interview with Virginia Hinckley Pearce, 29 March 1996.
15. Interview with Henry B. Eyring, 9 August 1995.
16. GBH Journal, 1 April 1995.
17. David B. Haight, "Sustaining a New Prophet," *Ensign,* May 1995, pp. 36–37.
18. Gordon B. Hinckley, "This Is the Work of the Master," *Ensign,* May 1995, pp. 69, 71.
19. GBH Journal, 2 April 1995.
20. Statistics cited as of December 31, 1994. See "LDS Leaders Sustained in Solemn Assembly" and "Focus Is Unchanging, Pres. Hinckley Says," *Deseret News,* 2 April 1995; "Pres. Hinckley Sustained As Prophet," *Church News,* 8 April 1995; "Hands Go Up and Hearts Go Out to New Prophet," *Salt Lake Tribune,* 2 April 1995.
21. Interview with MPH, 20 October 1994.
22. Address at St. Louis Regional Conference, 16 April 1995.
23. Interview with Carolyn J. Rasmus, 10 April 1996.
24. Transcript of Gustav Niebuhr Interview with GBH, *The New York Times,* 17 July 1995.

25. Address at St. George Youth Fireside, 14 January 1996, Burns Center, Dixie College; see also "Pres. Hinckley Urges Youth to Choose Right," *Church News,* 20 January 1996.
26. Gordon B. Hinckley, "True to the Faith," unpublished address, 21 January 1996; see also "Walk Path of Faith, Young Adults Told," *Church News,* 27 January 1996; "Live True to Faith, Pres. Hinckley Says," *Deseret News,* 22 January 1996.
27. Gordon B. Hinckley, "Stay the Course—Keep the Faith," *Ensign,* November 1995, p. 72.
28. See "Voices of Past, Present, Future Sing Odes to Utah," *Deseret News,* 5 January 1996; "Utahns Remember 1896 and Celebrate Statehood," *Church News,* 13 January 1996.
29. See "This Is the Place," *Deseret News,* 30 June 1996; also "Pres. Hinckley Dedicates Iowa Tabernacle Replica," *Deseret News,* 14 July 1996.
30. GBH Journal, 12 June 1995.
31. Pat Shea to GBH, 9 August 1996.
32. Interview with Deedee Corradini, 13 September 1996.
33. GBH Journal, 23 April 1995.
34. GBH Journal, 16 September 1995.
35. GBH Journal, 20 June 1995.
36. GBH Journal, 22 June 1995.
37. Interview with Russell M. Nelson, 17 May 1995.
38. Interview with Neal A. Maxwell, 30 June 1995.
39. Interview with Boyd K. Packer, 19 April 1996.
40. Gordon B. Hinckley, "Stand Strong Against the Wiles of the World," *Ensign,* November 1995, pp. 100–101.
41. Interview with Elaine L. Jack, 24 April 1996.
42. Address at Heber City and Springville Regional Conference, 14 May 1995.
43. Address at Colorado Springs Young Adult Morningside, 14 April 1996.
44. "Cornerstones for Building Homes," *Church News,* 17 February 1996.
45. "An Evening with Marjorie P. Hinckley."
46. GBH Journal, 13 November 1995.
47. See "Thatcher Focuses on Faith, Families," *Deseret News,* 5 March 1996; also "Lady Thatcher Sees LDS British Influence," *Church News,* 9 March 1996.
48. "First Presidency Attends Jewish Service in Honor of Israel's Slain Leader," *Church News,* 11 November 1995.
49. See *Deseret News,* 18 January 1996.
50. GBH Journal, 18 August 1995.
51. Interview with Ted Simmons, 23 January 1996.
52. "Transformation Begins for Temple," *Church News,* 20 May 1995; "LDS Break Ground for Vernal Temple," *Deseret News,* 14 May 1995.
53. GBH Journal, 22 April 1995.
54. Interview with GBH, 7 February 1996.
55. Interview with GBH, 7 February 1996.
56. Duane Cardall Interview with GBH, "A Trip to England," aired 1 October 1995 on KSL TV.
57. Interview with Boyd K. Packer, 19 April 1996.
58. "Warm Messages, Festive Setting," *Church News,* 9 December 1995.

59. Gordon B. Hinckley, "This Glorious Easter Morn," *Ensign,* May 1996, p. 67.
60. "This Glorious Easter Morn," p. 67.
61. "Prophet Honors Outgoing BYU President," *Church News,* 21 October 1995; "26,000 Hear LDS Prophet Honor Lee," *Deseret News,* 18 October 1995.
62. See, for example, "This Glorious Easter Morn," p. 66.
63. See Marjorie P. Hinckley, remarks at San Diego California East Stake Youth Fireside, 23 March 1996; also Marjorie P. Hinckley, remarks at Plano Texas Regional Conference, 17 March 1996.
64. Interview with Henry B. Eyring, 9 August 1995.
65. Interview with David B. Haight, 18 May 1995.

Chapter Twenty-Five
OUT OF OBSCURITY

1. Address at Crawley, England, Fireside, 26 August 1995.
2. Gordon B. Hinckley, "Remember . . . Thy Church, O Lord," *Ensign,* May 1996, p. 83.
3. Neal A. Maxwell, remarks at meeting with missionaries of Hong Kong Mission, 25 May 1996; see also Interviews with Neal A. Maxwell, 30 June and 9 July 1995.
4. Interview with Joseph B. Wirthlin, 30 May 1996.
5. "Out of Your Experience Here," pp. 29–30.
6. Interview with GBH, 7 February 1996.
7. Interview with GBH, 22 November 1995.
8. For all excerpts from the luncheon press conference, see "Edelman Luncheon Transcript," 13 November 1995, pp. 1–10.
9. Interview with GBH, 7 February 1996.
10. GBH Journal, 13 November 1996.
11. See Sheri Dew Interview with Mike Wallace, 29 April 1996.
12. Interview with Bruce Olsen, 23 April 1996.
13. Transcript of Mike Wallace Interview with Gordon B. Hinckley, 18 December 1995.
14. See "Prophet Interviewed by *60 Minutes,*" *Church News,* 23 December 1995.
15. Transcript of Mike Wallace Interview with Gordon B. Hinckley, 10 March 1996.
16. "Remember . . . Thy Church, O Lord," p. 83.
17. Sheri Dew Interview with Mike Wallace, 29 April 1996.
18. "Hinckley Takes LDS Case to the Nation," *Salt Lake Tribune,* 8 April 1996.
19. Interview with Anne Osborn Poelman, 18 April 1996.
20. Sheri Dew Interview with Mike Wallace, 29 April 1996.
21. Tom Thorkelson to *60 Minutes,* 8 April 1996.
22. Interview with Boyd K. Packer, 19 April 1996.
23. Interview with Bruce Olsen, 23 April 1996.
24. Transcript of Gustav Niebuhr Interview with Gordon B. Hinckley, *The New York Times,* 17 July 1995.
25. Transcript of Lawrence Spicer Interview with Gordon B. Hinckley, London News Service, 28 August 1995.
26. Interview with Neal A. Maxwell, 9 July 1996.
27. Gordon B. Hinckley, "This Glorious Easter Morn," *Ensign,* May 1996, pp. 65–66.
28. Interview with Boyd K. Packer, 19 April 1996.
29. Maxwell, remarks at meeting with missionaries of Hong Kong Mission.

30. Interview with GBH, 18 October 1995.
31. Cardall, "Trip to England."
32. Remarks at meeting with London Mission, 28 August 1995; see also remarks at meeting with London South Mission, 26 August 1995.
33. Marjorie P. Hinckley, remarks at meeting with London Mission, 28 August 1995.
34. *Church News,* 9 September 1995, p. 8.
35. Interview with Graham W. Doxey, 28 March 1995.
36. See "Members Living Abroad Outnumber LDS in U.S.," *Deseret News,* 26 February 1996; also "Over Half LDS Now Outside U.S.," *Church News,* 2 March 1996.
37. "Stay the Course—Keep the Faith," pp. 70–71.
38. Interviews with Pak Byung Kyu, 22 May 1996; and Ng Kat Hing, 25 May 1996.
39. Remarks at meeting with missionaries of Hong Kong Mission, 25 May 1996.
40. Remarks at meeting with missionaries of Hong Kong Mission.
41. Transcript of Duane Cardall Interview with Gordon B. Hinckley, Ho Man Tin chapel, Kowloon, 25 May 1996.
42. Thomas S. Monson, remarks at cornerstone-laying ceremony, Hong Kong Temple, 26 May 1996.
43. Gordon B. Hinckley, Address at Hong Kong Temple Dedication, first session, 26 May 1996.
44. See "President Hinckley Visits China," *Church News,* 1 June 1996, p. 3.
45. GBH to Elder Michael Hinckley, 1 July 1992.
46. Gerry Avant, "Tears Flow, Faith Grows as Filipinos Greet Prophet," *Church News,* 8 June 1996, p. 4.
47. Address at the Araneta Coliseum, Manila, Philippines, 30 May 1996.
48. Transcript of Duane Cardall, Gerry Avant, Sheri Dew Interview with GBH, 30 May 1996.
49. Interview with Joseph B. Wirthlin, 30 May 1996.
50. "Ground Broken for Temple in Madrid," *Church News,* 22 June 1996.
51. *Die Welt,* 17 June 1996.
52. Address at Israel District Fireside, 21 June 1996, BYU Jerusalem Center.
53. Address at Cove Fort, 24 June 1996.
54. "Remember . . . Thy Church, O Lord," p. 83.
55. Address at rededication of Hyde Park Chapel, 27 August 1996, London, England.
56. Address at Crawley, England, Fireside, 26 August 1995.

INDEX